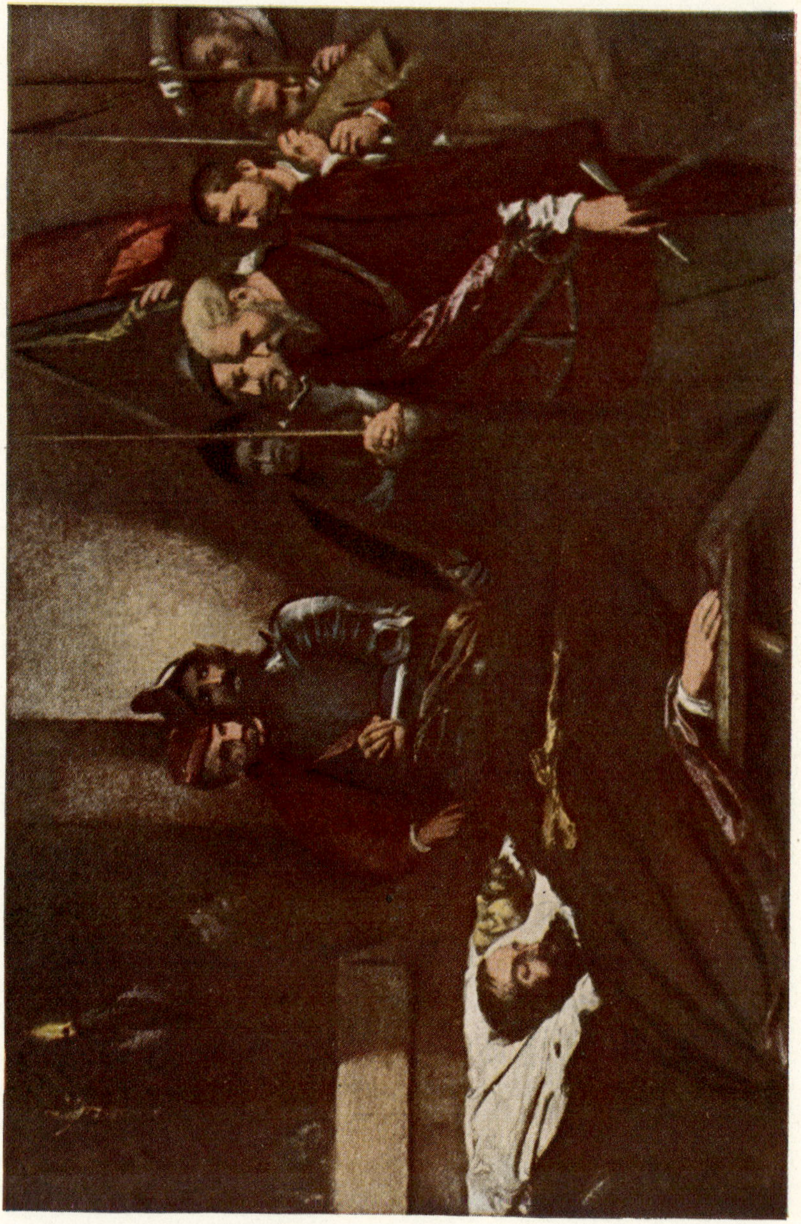

The History *of* Nations

HOLLAND
BELGIUM
SWITZERLAND

MEMORIAL
EDITION

THE HISTORY OF NATIONS
HENRY CABOT LODGE, Ph. D., LL. D. · EDITOR-IN-CHIEF

HOLLAND AND BELGIUM
EDITED BY
W. HAROLD CLAFLIN, M. A.
DEPARTMENT OF HISTORY
HARVARD UNIVERSITY

SWITZERLAND
BY CHARLES DANDLIKER, LL. D.
REVISED AND EDITED BY
ELBERT JAY BENTON, Ph. D.
DEPARTMENT OF HISTORY
WESTERN RESERVE UNIVERSITY

VOLUME XIII

ILLUSTRATED

P · F · COLLIER & SON CORPORATION
PUBLISHERS ∴ NEW YORK

Copyright, 1907, by
JOHN D. MORRIS & COMPANY

Copyright, 1910, by
THE H. W. SNOW & SON COMPANY

Copyright, 1913, by
P. F. COLLIER & SON

Copyright, 1916, by
P. F. COLLIER & SON

Copyright, 1920, by
P. F. COLLIER & SON COMPANY

Copyright, 1928, by
P. F. COLLIER & SON COMPANY

Copyright, 1932, by
P. F. COLLIER & SON COMPANY

Copyright, 1934, by
P. F. COLLIER & SON COMPANY

Copyright, 1936, by
P. F. COLLIER & SON CORPORATION

MANUFACTURED IN U. S. A.

THE HISTORY OF NATIONS

EDITOR-IN-CHIEF

HENRY CABOT LODGE, Ph. D., LL.D.

Associate Editors and Authors

ARCHIBALD HENRY SAYCE, LL.D.,
Professor of Assyriology, Oxford University

CHRISTOPHER JOHNSTON, M.D., Ph.D.,
Associate Professor of Oriental History and Archaeology, Johns Hopkins University; Assistant Professor of Medicine, Duke University Medical School

C. W. C. OMAN,
Professor of History, Oxford University

THEODORE MOMMSEN,
Professor of Ancient History, University of Berlin

ARTHUR C. HOWLAND, Ph.D.,
Henry Chase Lea Professor of European History, University of Pennsylvania

CHARLES MERIVALE, LL.D.,
Dean of Ely; Lecturer in History, Cambridge University

J. HIGGINSON CABOT, Ph.D.,
Department of History, Wellesley College

SIR WILLIAM W. HUNTER, F.R.S.,
Director-General of Statistics in India

GEORGE M. DUTCHER, Ph.D.,
Professor of History, Wesleyan University

SIR ROBERT K. DOUGLAS,
Professor of Chinese, King's College, London

JEREMIAH WHIPPLE JENKS, Ph.D., LL.D.,
Professor of Political Economy and Politics, Cornell University

KWAN-ICHI ASAKAWA, Ph.D.,
Associate Professor of History, Yale University

WILFRED HAROLD MUNRO, L.H.D.,
Emeritus Professor of European History, Brown University

G. MERCER ADAM,
Historian and Editor

FRED MORROW FLING, Ph.D.,
Professor of European History, University of Nebraska

FRANÇOIS AUGUSTE MARIE MIGNET,
Member of the French Academy

JAMES WESTFALL THOMPSON, Ph.D.,
Professor of European History, University of California

SAMUEL RAWSON GARDINER, LL.D.,
Professor of Modern History, King's College, London

P. W. JOYCE, LL.D.,
Commissioner for the Publication of the Ancient Laws of Ireland

ASSOCIATE EDITORS AND AUTHORS—Continued

JUSTIN McCARTHY, LL.D.,
Author and Historian

AUGUSTUS HUNT SHEARER, Litt.D., Ph.D.,
Lecturer in History, University of Buffalo

W. HAROLD CLAFLIN, B.A.,
Department of History, Harvard University

CHARLES DANDLIKER, LL.D.,
President of Zurich University

ELBERT JAY BENTON, Ph.D.,
Dean of Graduate School, Western Reserve University

SIR EDWARD S. CREASY,
Professor of History, University College, London

ARCHIBALD CARY COOLIDGE, Ph.D.,
Professor of History, Harvard University

WILLIAM RICHARD MORFILL, M.A.,
Professor of Russian and Other Slavonic Languages, Oxford University

CHARLES EDMUND FRYER, Ph.D.,
Professor of History, McGill University

E. C. OTTE,
Specialist on Scandinavian History

EDWARD S. CORWIN, Ph.D.,
McCormick Professor of Jurisprudence, Princeton University

PAUL LOUIS LEGER,
Professor of Slav Languages, College de France

WILLIAM E. LINGELBACH, Ph.D.,
Professor of Modern European History, University of Pennsylvania

BAYARD TAYLOR,
Former United States Minister to Germany

SIDNEY B. FAY. Ph.D.,
Professor of History, Harvard University

J. SCOTT KELTIE, LL.D.,
President Royal Geographical Society

ALBERT GALLOWAY KELLER, Ph.D.,
Professor of the Science of Society, Yale University

EDWARD JAMES PAYNE, M.A.,
Fellow of University College, Oxford

PHILIP PATTERSON WELLS, Ph.D.,
Lecturer in History and Librarian of the Law School, Yale University

FREDERICK ALBION OBER,
Historian, Author and Traveler

JAMES WILFORD GARNER, Ph.D.,
Professor of Political Science, University of Illinois

JOHN BACH McMASTER, Litt.D., LL.D.,
Professor of History, University of Pennsylvania

GEORGE THOMAS SURFACE, M.Sc.
Professor of Geography, Emory and Henry College

JAMES LAMONT PERKINS, Managing Editor

The editors and publishers desire to express their appreciation for valuable advice and suggestions received from the following: Hon. Andrew D. White, LL.D., Alfred Thayer Mahan, D.C.L., LL.D., Hon Charles Emory Smith, LL.D., Professor Edward Gaylord Bourne, Ph.D., Charles F. Thwing, LL.D., Dr. Emil Reich, William Elliot Griffis, LL.D., Professor John Martin Vincent, Ph.D., LL.D., Melvil Dewey, LL.D., Alston Ellis, LL.D., Professor Charles H. McCarthy, Ph.D., Professor Herman V. Ames, Ph.D., Professor Walter L. Fleming, Ph.D., Professor David Y. Thomas, Ph.D., Mr. Otto Reich and Mr. Francis J. Reynolds.

NOTE

The editors of "The History of Nations" concluded their work with the chronicling of events to October, 1905, and all additions thereafter, bringing the histories to date, have been supplied by the publishers.

CONTENTS

HISTORY OF HOLLAND AND BELGIUM

PART I

THE RISE OF THE NETHERLANDS. 50 B. C.-1555 A. D.

CHAPTER	PAGE
I. Before Invasion of the Franks. 50 B. C.-250 A. D.	3
II. Struggle of Franks and Saxons. 250-800 A. D.	11
III. Rise of the Counts. 800-1018	16
IV. Decline of Feudalism and Growth of the Towns 1018-1384	24
V. Power of the House of Burgundy. 1384-1506	36
VI. Margaret of Austria and Charles V of Spain 1506-1555	53

PART II

THE STRUGGLE FOR LIBERTY. 1555-1648

VII. Condition of the Netherlands under Philip II of Spain. 1555-1566	67
VIII. Commencement of the Revolution. 1566	85
IX. Surrender of Valenciennes and Tyranny of Alva. 1566-1573	98
X. Appointment of Requesens and Pacification of Ghent. 1573-1576	116
XI. Revolt from Sovereignty and Declaration of Independence. 1576-1580	125
XII. Edict of Philip and Murder of Prince of Orange 1580-1584	135
XIII. Alexander, Duke of Parma. 1584-1592	145
XIV. Successes of Prince Maurice and Death of Philip II. 1592-1599	160
XV. Prince Maurice and Spinola. 1599-1605	170
XVI. Dutch Disasters and the Twelve Years' Peace 1606-1619	182

CONTENTS

CHAPTER		PAGE
XVII.	Renewal of War with Spain and the Despotism of Prince Maurice. 1619-1625	201
XVIII.	Frederick Henry and the Peace of Westphalia 1625-1648	208

PART III

THE DUTCH REPUBLIC. 1648-1813

XIX.	War with England. 1648-1678	225
XX.	William III. and Louis XIV. 1678-1713	242
XXI.	Decline of the Republic. 1713-1794	253
XXII.	The French Invasion. 1794-1813	265

PART IV

THE KINGDOMS OF HOLLAND AND BELGIUM. 1814-1935

XXIII.	William I. as Prince and Sovereign of the Netherlands. 1814-1815	279
XXIV.	The Belgian Revolution. 1815-1832	291
XXV.	Belgium as an Independent Kingdom. 1830-1914	304
XXVI.	The German Invasion of Belgium. 1914	312e
XXVII.	Belgium under the Germans. 1914-1918	312p
XXVIII.	Peace and Reconstruction in Belgium. 1919-1935	312y
XXIX.	The Kingdom of the Netherlands. 1840-1935	313

HISTORY OF SWITZERLAND

PART I

EARLY SWITZERLAND AND THE RISE OF THE CONFEDERATION. ——1516 A.D.

I.	The Ancient Races and Their Civilization. 1000 B.C.-750 A.D.	327
II.	Union under Carlovingian and German Rule 750-1057	340
III.	Territorial Divisions. 1057-1218	347
IV.	Formation of the Leagues. 1218-1315	357
V.	Growth of the Confederation. 1315-1400	372
VI.	Switzerland at the Height of Her Power. 1400-1516	389

CONTENTS

CHAPTER	PAGE
VII. The Era of the Reformation. 1516-1600	431
VIII. Religious Wars and the Aristocratic Constitution. 1600-1712	461

PART II

MODERN SWITZERLAND. 1712-1935

IX. Political Disunion of the Eighteenth Century 1712-1798	487
X. Revolution and Attempts at Reorganization 1798-1830	503
XI. Internal Reorganization. 1830-1848	533
XII. The Consolidation of the Federal States. 1848-1874	556
XIII. Centralization and Socialism 1874-1914	569
XIV. Switzerland a Neutral Nation—Home of the League of Nations. 1914-1935	595
Bibliography	605

LIST OF ILLUSTRATIONS

THE CIVIC GUARDS OF BRUSSELS PAYING THEIR LAST HOMAGE TO THE DECAPITATED BODIES OF COUNTS EGMONT AND HORN . *Frontispiece*

	FACING PAGE
BALDWIN VI. GRANTS FLANDRIAN CONSTITUTION	38
THE ATTEMPT OF THE CHURCH TO RESTORE REASON TO JOANNA OF SPAIN	54
THE SPANISH FURY	134
PRAYER OF THE SWISS BEFORE THE BATTLE OF SEMPACH	368
THE FLIGHT OF CHARLES THE BOLD	416

TEXT MAPS

	PAGE
THE NETHERLANDS, SHOWING HEIGHT OF LAND	8
BURGUNDY DOMINIONS UNDER CHARLES THE RASH	49
COMMERCIAL TOWNS OF THE MIDDLE AGES	60
THE NETHERLANDS. 1579	132
THE UNITED PROVINCES AND THE AUSTRIAN NETHERLANDS. 1609	190
WESTERN EUROPE AFTER THE PEACE OF WESTPHALIA	218
HOLLAND AND BELGIUM	302
CENTRAL EUROPE. TENTH AND TWELFTH CENTURIES	348
THE SWISS CONFEDERATION	383
SWITZERLAND AFTER THE CONGRESS OF VIENNA. 1815	526

PART I

THE RISE OF THE NETHERLANDS
50 B. C.-1555 A. D.

HISTORY OF HOLLAND AND BELGIUM

Chapter I

BEFORE INVASION OF THE FRANKS
50 B.C.-250 A.D.

THE little kingdoms of Holland and Belgium are situated in that low and humid plain which, stretching along the ocean over against the southeastern coast of England from the frontiers of France to those of Germany, has borne for ages the fit name of the Netherlands—the Low Countries. This plain, 220 miles in length from north to south and 140 miles in its greatest breadth, is irrigated by the sluggish waters of the Rhine, the Meuse, and the Scheldt.

Two distinct races have in historical times inhabited the plain. The one, occupying the valleys of the Meuse and the Scheldt and the high grounds bordering on France, speak a dialect of the French language and evidently belong to the Gallic race. They are called Walloons and form to-day nearly one-half the population of Belgium. The great mining and manufacturing industries of Belgium are largely in their hands. A large portion of the Belgian people and the great mass of the inhabitants of Holland speak the Low German dialect in its modifications of Flemish and Dutch; and they offer the distinctive characteristics of the Germanic race—being slow, phlegmatic, and persevering, rather than vivacious, with talents for agricultural pursuits, navigation, and commerce. And though closer akin to their Dutch neighbors than to their Walloon compatriots, political differences have tended to separate them; the Flemish language is on the decline and the prevailing speech in Belgium to-day is the French. The history of the last named portion of the people of the Netherlands is completely linked to that of the soil which they occupy. In remote times, when the inhabitants of this plain were few and uncivilized, the country formed but one immense morass, of which the chief part was incessantly inundated and made sterile by the waters of the sea. Pliny the naturalist, who visited the northern coasts, has left us a picture of their state in his days. "There," says he, "the ocean pours in its flood twice every day, and produces a perpetual uncertainty whether the country may be considered as a part of the continent or of the sea. The wretched inhabitants take refuge on the sand-hills, or in little huts, which they construct on the summits of lofty stakes, whose elevation is conformable to that of the highest tides. When the sea rises they appear like navigators; when it retires they seem as though they had been shipwrecked. They subsist on the fish left by the refluent waters, and which they catch in nets formed of rushes or seaweed. Neither tree nor shrub is visible on these shores. The drink of the people is rain water, which they preserve with great care; their fuel, a sort of turf, which they gather and form with the hand. And yet these unfortunate beings dare to complain against their fate when they fall under the power and are incorporated with the empire of Rome!"[1]

The picture of poverty and suffering which this passage presents is heightened when joined to a description of the country. The coasts consisted only of sandbanks or slime, alternately overflowed or left imperfectly dry. A little farther inland trees were to be found, but on a soil so marshy that an inundation or a tempest threw down whole forests, such as are still at times discovered at eight or ten feet depth below the surface. The sea had no limits, the rivers no beds nor banks, the earth no solidity,—for, according to an author of the third century of our era, there was not in the whole of the immense plain a spot of ground that did not yield under the footsteps of man.

It was not the same in the southern parts, which form at present the Walloon country. These high grounds suffered much less from the ravages of the waters. The ancient forest of the Ardennes, extending from the Rhine to the Scheldt, sheltered a numerous though savage population, which in all things resembled the Germans, from whom they derived their descent. The chase and the occupations of rude agriculture sufficed for the wants of a race less poor and less patient, but more unsteady and ambitious, than the fishermen of the lowlands. Thus it is that history presents us with a tribe of warriors and conquerors on the southern frontier of the country, while the scattered inhabitants of the remaining parts seemed to have fixed there without a contest, and to

[1] Pliny, "*Historia Naturalis.*"

have traced out for themselves, by necessity and habit, an existence which any other people must have considered insupportable.

In order to form an idea of the solitude and desolation which once reigned where we now see the most richly cultivated fields, the most thriving villages, and the wealthiest towns of the Continent, the imagination must go back to times which have not left one monument of antiquity and scarcely a vestige of fact for posterity.

The history of the Netherlands is, then, essentially that of a patient and industrious population struggling against every obstacle which nature could oppose to its well-being; and in this contest man triumphed most completely over the elements in those places where they offered the greatest resistance. This extraordinary result was due to the hardy stamp of character imprinted by suffering and danger on those who had the ocean for their foe; to the nature of their country, which presented no lure for conquest; and, finally, to the toleration, the justice, and the liberty nourished among men left to themselves, and who found resources in their social state which rendered change an object neither of their wants nor wishes.

About half a century before the Christian era the obscurity which enveloped the north of Europe began to disperse; and the expedition of Julius Cæsar gave to the civilized world the first notions of the Netherlands, Germany, and England. Cæsar, after having subjugated the chief part of Gaul, turned his arms against the warlike tribes of the Ardennes, who refused to accept his alliance or implore his protection. They were called Belgæ by the Romans, and at once pronounced the least civilized and the bravest of the Gauls. Cæsar there found several ignorant and poor but intrepid clans of warriors, who marched fiercely to encounter him; and, notwithstanding their inferiority in numbers, in weapons, and in tactics, they nearly destroyed the disciplined armies of Rome. They were, however, defeated, and their country ravaged by the invaders, who found less success when they attacked the natives of the low grounds. The Menapians, a people who occupied the present provinces of Flanders and Antwerp, though less numerous than those whom the Romans had last vanquished, arrested their progress both by open fight and by that petty and harassing contest,—that warfare of the people rather than of the soldiery,—so well adapted to the nature of the country. The Roman legions retreated for the first time, and were contented to occupy the higher parts, which now form the Walloon provinces.

But the policy of Cæsar made greater progress than his arms. He had defeated rather than subdued those who had dared the contest. He consolidated his victories without new battles; he offered peace to his enemies, in proposing to them alliance; and he required their aid, as friends, to carry on new wars in other lands. He thus attracted toward him, and ranged under his banners, not only those people situated to the west of the Rhine and the Meuse, but several other nations more to the north, whose territory he had never seen; and particularly the Batavians—a valiant tribe, stated by various ancient authors, and particularly by Tacitus, as a fraction of the Catti, who occupied the space comprised between these rivers. The young men of these warlike people, dazzled by the splendor of the Roman armies, felt proud and happy in being allowed to identify themselves with them. Cæsar encouraged this disposition, and even went so far on some occasions as to deprive the Roman cavalry of their horses, on which he mounted these new allies, who managed them better than the Italian riders.

These auxiliaries were chiefly drawn from Hainault, Luxemburg, and the country of the Batavians, and they formed the best cavalry of the Roman armies, as well as their choicest light infantry force. The Batavians also signalized themselves on many occasions by the skill with which they swam across several great rivers without breaking their squadrons' ranks. They were amply rewarded for their military services and hazardous exploits, and were treated like stanch and valuable allies. But this unequal connection of a mighty empire with a few petty states must have been fatal to the liberty of the weaker party. Its first effect was to destroy all feeling of nationality in a great portion of the population. The young adventurer of this part of the Low Countries, after twenty years of service under the imperial eagles, returned to his native wilds a Roman. The generals of the empire pierced the forests of the Ardennes with causeways, and founded towns in the heart of the country. The result of such innovations was a total amalgamation of the Romans and their new allies, and little by little the national character of the latter became entirely obliterated.

But it must be remarked that this metamorphosis affected only the inhabitants of the high grounds and the Batavians (who were

Hist. Nat. XIII-1

in their origin Germans) properly so called. The scanty population of the rest of the country, endowed with that fidelity to their ancient customs which characterizes the Saxon race, showed no tendency to mix with foreigners, rarely figured in their ranks, and seemed to revolt from the southern refinement which was so little in harmony with their manners and ways of life. It is astonishing, at the first view, that those beings, whose whole existence was a contest against famine or the waves, should show less repugnance than their happier neghbors to receive from Rome an abundant recompense for their services. This race of patriots was divided into two separate peoples. Those to the north of the Rhine were the Frisons; those to the west of the Meuse, the Menapians, already mentioned.

The Frisons differed little from those early inhabitants of the coast, who, perched on their high-built huts, fed on fish and drank the water of the clouds. Slow and successive improvements taught them to cultivate the beans which grew wild among the marshes, and to tend and feed a small and degenerate breed of horned cattle. But if these first steps toward civilization were slow, they were also sure; and they were made by a race of men who could never retrograde in a career once begun.

The Menapians, equally repugnant to foreign impressions, made on their parts a more rapid progress. They were already a maritime people, and carried on a considerable commerce with England. It appears that they exported thither salt, the art of manufacturing which was well known to them; and they brought back in return marl, a most important commodity for the improvement of their land. They also understood the preparation of salting meat, with a perfection that made it in high repute even in Italy; and, finally, we are told by Ptolemy that they had established a colony on the eastern coast of Ireland, not far from Dublin.

The two classes of what forms at present the population of the Netherlands thus followed careers widely different during the long period of the Roman power in these parts of Europe. While those of the highlands and the Batavians distinguished themselves by a long-continued course of military service or servitude, those of the plains improved by degrees their social condition and fitted themselves for a place in civilized Europe. The former received from Rome great marks of favor in exchange for their freedom. The latter, rejecting the honors and distinctions lavished on their neighbors, secured their national independence by trusting to their industry alone for all the advantages they gradually acquired.

Were the means of protecting themselves and their country from the inundations of the sea known and practiced by these ancient inhabitants of the coast, or did they occupy only those elevated points of land which stood out like islands in the middle of the floods? These questions are among the most important

THE NETHERLANDS
SHOWING HEIGHT OF LAND

NORTH SEA

ZUIDER ZEE

GERMANY

FROM SEA LEVEL TO 20 FEET BELOW
FROM SEA LEVEL TO 35 FEET ABOVE
35 TO 80 FEET
ABOVE 80 FEET

BELGIUM

presented by their history, since it was the victorious struggle of man against the ocean that fixed the extent and form of the country. It appears almost certain that dikes were unknown in the time of Cæsar. But as early as 12 B.C. Drusus, the son of the Emperor Augustus, began the construction of dikes and canals north of the Rhine; and ruins of ancient towns of Roman construction have more than once been discovered in places later overflowed by the sea. It is, then, certain that they had learned to imitate those who ruled in the neighboring countries: a result by no means surprising, for even England, the mart of their commerce and the nation with which they had the most constant intercourse, was at that period occupied by the Romans. But the nature of their country repulsed so effectually every attempt at foreign domination that the conquerors of the world left them unmolested and established arsenals and formed communications with Great Britain only at Boulogne and in the island of the Batavians near Leyden.

This isolation formed in itself a powerful and perfect barrier between the inhabitants of the plain and those of the high grounds. The first held firm to their primitive customs and their ancient language; the second finished by speaking Latin and borrowing all the manners and usages of Italy. The moral effect of this contrast was that the people once so famous for their bravery lost, with their liberty, their energy and their courage. One of the Batavian chieftains, named Civilis, formed an exception to this degeneracy, and about the year 70 of our era bravely took up arms for the expulsion of the Romans. He effected prodigies of valor and perseverance, and boldly met and defeated the enemy both by land and sea. Reverses followed his first success, and he finally concluded an honorable treaty, by which his countrymen once more became the allies of Rome. But after this expiring effort of valor the Batavians, even though chosen from all nations for the bodyguards of the Roman emperors, became rapidly degenerate; and when Tacitus wrote, ninety years after Christ, they were already looked on as less brave than the Frisons and the other people beyond the Rhine.

Reduced to a Roman province, the southern portion of the Netherlands was at this period called Belgic Gaul; and the name of Belgium, preserved to our days, has always been applied to distinguish that country situated to the south of the Rhine and the Meuse, an independent kingdom since 1831.

During the establishment of the Roman power in the north of Europe observation was not much excited toward the rapid effects of this degeneracy, compared with the fast-growing vigor of the people of the lowlands. The fact of the Frisons having on one occasion near the year 47 of our era beaten a whole army of Romans, had confirmed their character for intrepidity. But the long stagnation produced in these remote countries by the colossal weight of the empire was broken about the year 250 by an irruption of Germans or Salian Franks, who, passing the Rhine and the Meuse, established themselves in the vicinity of the Menapians, near Antwerp, Breda, and Bois-le-duc. All the nations that had been subjugated by the Roman power appear to have taken arms on this occasion and opposed the intruders. But the Menapians united themselves with these newcomers, and aided them to meet the shock of the imperial armies. Carausius, originally a Menapian pilot, but promoted to the command of a Roman fleet, made common cause with his fellow-citizens, and proclaimed himself emperor of Great Britain, where the naval superiority of the Menapians left him no fear of a competitor. In recompense of the assistance given him by the Franks, he crossed the sea again from his new empire, to aid them in their war with the Batavians, the allies of Rome; and having seized on their island, and massacred nearly the whole of its inhabitants, he there established his faithful friends the Salians. Constantius and his son Constantine the Great vainly strove, even after the death of the brave Carausius, to regain possession of the country, but they were forced to leave the new inhabitants in quiet possession of their conquest.

CHAPTER II

STRUGGLE OF FRANKS AND SAXONS. 250-800 A.D.

FROM this epoch we must trace the progress of a totally new and distinct population in the Netherlands. The Batavians being annihilated, almost without resistance, the Low Countries contained only the free people of the German race. But these people did not agree entirely with each other so as to form one consolidated nation. The Salians and the other petty tribes of Franks, their allies, were essentially warlike, and appeared precisely the same as the original inhabitants of the high grounds. The Menapians and the Frisons, on the contrary, lost nothing of their spirit of commerce and industry. The result of this diversity was a separation between the Franks and the Menapians. While the latter, under the name of Armoricans, joined themselves more closely with the people who bordered the Channel, the Frisons associated themselves with the tribes settled on the limits of the German Ocean and formed with them a connection celebrated under the title of the Saxon League. Thus was formed on all points a union between the maritime races against the inland inhabitants, and their mutual antipathy became more and more developed as the decline of the Roman Empire ended the former struggle between liberty and conquest.

The Netherlands now became the earliest theater of an entirely new movement, the consequences of which were destined to affect the whole world. This country was occupied toward the sea by a people wholly maritime, excepting the narrow space between the Rhine and the Waal, of which the Salian Franks had become possessed. The nature of this marshy soil, in comparison with the sands of Westphalia, Guelders, and North Brabant, was not more strikingly contrasted than was the character of their population. The Franks, who had been for a while under the Roman sway, showed a compound of the violence of savage life and the corruption of civilized society. They were covetous and treacherous, but made excellent soldiers; and at this epoch, which intervened between the power of imperial Rome and that of Germany, the Frank might be morally considered as a borderer on the frontiers of the Middle Ages. The Saxon (and this name comprehends all the tribes of the coast from the Rhine as far north as Denmark), uniting in himself the distinctive qualities of German and navigator, was moderate and sincere, but implacable in his rage. Neither of these two races of men were excelled in point of courage, but the number of Franks who still entered into the service of the Empire diminished the real force of this nation, and naturally tended to disunite it. Therefore, in the subsequent shock of people against people, the Saxons invariably gained the final advantage.

They had no doubt often measured their strength in the most remote times, since the Franks were but the descendants of the ancient tribes of Sicambri and others against whom the Batavians had offered their assistance to Cæsar. Under Augustus the inhabitants of the coast had in the same way joined themselves with Drusus, to oppose these their old enemies. It was also after having been expelled by the Frisons from Guelders that the Salians had passed the Rhine and the Meuse, but in the fourth century the two people recovering their strength, the struggle recommenced, never to terminate—at least between the direct descendants of each. It is believed that it was the Chamari, a race of Saxons nearly connected with those of England, who on this occasion struck the decisive blow on the side of the Saxons. Embarking on board a numerous fleet, they made a descent in the ancient isle of the Batavians, at that time inhabited by the Salians, whom they completely destroyed. Julian the Apostate, the last of the pagan emperors, who was then with a numerous army pursuing his career of early glory in these countries, interfered for the purpose of preventing the expulsion, or at least the utter destruction, of the vanquished, but his efforts were unavailing. The Salians appear to have figured no more in this part of the Low Countries.

The defeat of the Franks was fatal to the peoples of Gaul who had become incorporated with the Romans, for it was from them that the exiled wanderers, still fierce in their ruin, and with arms in their hands, demanded lands and herds—all, in short, which they themselves had lost. From the middle of the fourth century to the end of the fifth there was a succession of invasions in this spirit, which always ended by the subjugation of a part of the country; and which was completed about the year 490, by Clovis making himself master of almost the whole of Gaul. Under this new empire not a vestige of the ancient nations of the Ardennes was left. The civilized population either perished or was reduced to slavery, and all the high grounds were added to the previous conquests of the Salians.

But the maritime population, when once possessed of the whole coast, did not seek to make the slightest progress toward the interior. The element of their enterprise and the object of their ambition was the ocean; and when this hardy and intrepid race became too numerous for their narrow limits, expeditions and colonies beyond the sea carried off their redundant population. The Saxon warriors established themselves near the mouths of the Loire, others settled in Great Britain. It will always remain problematical from what point of the coast these adventurers departed; but many circumstances tend to give weight to the opinion which pronounces those old Saxons to have started from the Netherlands.

Paganism not being yet banished from these countries, the obscurity which would have enveloped them is in some degree dispelled by the recitals of the monks who went among them to preach Christianity. We see in those records, and by the text of some of their early laws, that this maritime people were more industrious, prosperous, and happy than those of France. The men were handsome and richly clothed, and the land well cultivated, and abounding in fruits, milk, and honey. The Saxon merchants carried their trade far into the southern countries. In the meantime the parts of the Netherlands which belonged to France resembled a desert. The monasteries which were there founded were established, according to the words of their charters, amid immense solitudes, and the Frankish nobles only came into Brabant for the sport of bear-hunting in its interminable forests. Thus while the inhabitants of the lowlands as far back as the light of history penetrates appear in a continual state of improvement, those of the high grounds, after frequent vicissitudes, seem to sink into utter degeneracy and subjugation. The latter wished to denationalize themselves and become as though they were foreigners even on their native soil; the former remained firm and faithful to their country and to each other.

But the growth of Frankish power menaced utter ruin to this interesting race. Clovis had succeeded, about the year 485 of our era, in destroying the last remnants of Roman domination in

Gaul. His successors soon extended their empire from the Pyrenees to the Rhine. They had continual contests with the free population of the Low Countries and their nearest neighbors. In the commencement of the seventh century the French king, Clothaire II., exterminated the chief part of the Saxons of Hanover and Westphalia; and the historians of those barbarous times unanimously relate that he caused to be beheaded every inhabitant of the vanquished tribes who exceeded the height of his sword. The Saxon name was thus nearly extinguished in those countries, and the remnant of these various people adopted that of Frisons (*Friesen*), either because they became really incorporated with that nation or merely that they recognized it for the most powerful of their tribes. Friesland, to speak in the language of that age, extended then from the Scheldt to the Weser, and formed a considerable state. But the ascendancy of the Franks was every year becoming more marked, and King Dagobert extended the limits of their power even as far as Utrecht. The descendants of the Menapians, known at that epoch by the different names of Menapians, Flemings, and Toxandrians, fell one after another directly or indirectly under the empire of the Merovingian princes; and the noblest family which existed among the French—that which subsequently took the name of Carolingians—comprised in its dominions nearly the whole of the southern and western parts of the Netherlands.

Between this family, whose chief was called Duke of the Frontier Marshes (*Dux Brabantiæ*), and the free tribes, united under the common name of Frisons, the same struggle was maintained as that which formerly existed between the Salians and the Saxons. Toward the year 700 the French monarchy was torn by anarchy, and under "the lazy kings" lost much of its concentrated power; but every dukedom formed an independent sovereignty, and of all these that of Brabant was the most redoubtable. Nevertheless the Frisons, under their king, Radbod, assumed for a moment the superiority; and Utrecht, where the French had established Christianity, fell again into the power of the pagans. Charles Martel at that time young and but commencing his splendid career, was defeated by the hostile king in the forest of the Ardennes, and though in subsequent conquests he took an ample revenge, Radbod still remained a powerful opponent. It is related of this fierce monarch that he was converted by a Christian missionary, but at the moment in which he put his foot in the water for the ceremony of baptism he suddenly asked the priest where all his old Frison companions in arms had gone after their death? "To hell," replied the priest. "Well, then," said Radbod, drawing back his foot from the water, "I would rather go to hell with them, than to paradise with you and your fellow foreigners!" and he refused to receive the rites of baptism, and remained a pagan.[1]

After the death of Radbod in 179 A.D. Charles Martel, now duke of the Franks, mayor of the palace (or by whatever other of his several titles he may be distinguished), finally triumphed over the long-resisting Frisons. He labored to establish Christianity among them, but they did not understand the Frankish language, and the lot of converting them was consequently reserved for the English. St. Willebrod was the first missionary who met with any success, about the latter end of the seventh century; but it was not till toward the year 750 that this great mission was finally accomplished by St. Boniface, Archbishop of Mainz and the apostle of Germany. Yet the progress of Christianity and the establishment of a foreign sway still met the partial resistance which a conquered but not enervated people are always capable of opposing to their masters. St. Boniface fell a victim to this stubborn spirit. He perished a martyr to his zeal, but perhaps a victim as well to the violent measures of his colleagues, in Friesland, the very province which to this day preserves the name.

The last avenger of Friesland liberty and of the national idols was the illustrious Witikind, to whom the chronicles of his country give the title of first azing, or judge. This intrepid chieftain is considered as a compatriot, not only by the historians of Friesland, but by those of Saxony; both, it would appear, having equal claims to the honor, for the union between the two people was constantly strengthened by intermarriages between the noblest families of each. As long as Witikind remained a pagan and a freeman some doubt existed as to the final fate of Friesland; but when by his conversion he became only a noble of the court of Charlemagne, the slavery of his country was consummated.

[1] This story is also told of other pagan warriors.

CHAPTER III

RISE OF THE COUNTS. 800-1018

EVEN at this advanced epoch of foreign domination there remained as great a difference as ever between the people of the high grounds and the inhabitants of the plain. The latter were, like the rest, incorporated with the great monarchy, but they preserved the remembrance of former independence, and even retained their ancient names. In Flanders Menapians and Flemings were still found, and in the country of Antwerp the Toxandrians were not extinct. All the rest of the coast was still called Friesland. But in the high grounds the names of the old inhabitants were lost. Nations were designated by the names of their rivers, forests, or towns. They were classified as accessories to inanimate things; and having no monuments which reminded them of their origin, they became, as it were, without recollections or associations, and degenerated, almost it may be said, into a people without ancestry.

The physical state of the country had greatly changed from the times of Cæsar to those of Charlemagne. Many parts of the forest of the Ardennes had been cut down or cleared away. Civilization had only appeared for awhile among these woods, to perish like a delicate plant in an ungenial clime; but it seemed to have sucked the very sap from the soil and to have left the people no remains of the vigor of man in his savage state nor of the desperate courage of the warriors of Germany. A race of serfs now cultivated the domains of haughty lords and imperious priests. The clergy had immense possessions in this country—an act of the following century recognizes fourteen thousand families of vassals as belonging to the single abbey of Nivelle. Tournay and Tongres, both episcopal cities, were for that reason somewhat less oppressed than the other ancient towns founded by the Romans, but they appear to have possessed but a poor and degraded population.

The lowlands, on the other hand, announced a striking commencement of improvement and prosperity. The marshes and fens which had arrested and repulsed the progress of imperial Rome had disappeared in every part of the interior. The Meuse and the Scheldt no longer joined at their outlets to desolate the neighboring lands, whether this change was produced by the labors of man or merely by the accumulation of sand deposited by either stream and forming barriers to both. The towns of Courtrai, Bruges, Ghent, Antwerp, Berg-op-Zoom, and Thiel had already a flourishing trade. The last-mentioned town contained in the following century fifty-five churches, a fact from which, in the absence of other evidence, the extent of the population may be conjectured. The formation of dikes for the protection of lands formerly submerged was already well understood and regulated by uniform custom. The plains thus reconquered from the waters were distributed in portions, according to their labor, by those who reclaimed them, except the parts reserved for the chieftain, the church, and the poor. This vital necessity for the construction of dikes had given to the Frison and Flemish population a particular habit of union, good-will, and reciprocal justice, because it was necessary to make common cause in this great work for their mutual preservation. In all other points the detail of the laws and manners of this united people presents a picture similar to that of the Saxons of England, with the sole exception that the people of the Netherlands were milder than the Saxon race properly so called—their long habit of laborious industry exercising its happy influence on the martial spirit original to both. The manufacturing arts were also somewhat more advanced in this part of the Continent than in Great Britain. The Frisons, for example, were the only people who could succeed in making the costly mantles in use among the wealthy Franks.

The government of Charlemagne admitted but one form, borrowed from that of the empire in the period of its decline—a mixture of the spiritual and temporal powers, exercised in the first place by the emperor, and at second hand by the counts and bishops. The counts in those times were not the heads of noble families, as they afterward became, but officers of the government, removable at will, and possessing no hereditary rights. Their incomes did not arise from salaries paid in money, but consisted of lands, of which they had the revenues during the continuance of their authority. These lands being situated in the limits of their administration, each regarded them as his property only for the time being, and considered himself as a tenant at will. How unfavorable such a system was to culture and improvement may be well imagined. The force of possession was, however, frequently opposed to the seignorial rights of the crown; and thus, though all civil dignity and the revenues attached to it were but personal and reclaimable at will, still many dignitaries, taking advantage of the barbarous state of the country in which their isolated cantons were placed, sought by every possible means to render their power and prerogative unalienable and real. The force of the monarchical government, which consists mainly in its centralization, was necessarily weakened by the intervention of local obstacles, before it could pass from the heart of the empire to its limits. Thus it was only by perpetually interposing his personal efforts and flying, as it were, from one end to the other of his dominions that Charlemagne succeeded in preserving his authority. As for the people, without any sort of guarantee against the despotism of the government, they were utterly at the mercy of the nobles or of the sovereign. But this state of servitude was quite incompatible with the union of social powers necessary to a population that had to struggle against the tyranny of the ocean. To repulse its attacks with successful vigor a spirit of complete concert was absolutely required; and the nation being thus united, and consequently strong, the efforts of foreign tyrants were shattered by its resistance, as the waves of the sea that broke against the dikes by which it was defied.

From the time of Charlemagne the people of the ancient Menapia, now become a prosperous commonwealth, formed political associations to raise a barrier against the despotic violence of the Franks. These associations were called Gilden, and in the Latin of the times Gildonia. They comprised, besides their covenants for mutual protection, an obligation which bound every member to give succor to any other, in cases of illness, conflagration, or shipwreck. But the growing force of these social compacts alarmed the quick-sighted despotism of Charlemagne, and they were consequently prohibited both by him and his successors. This popular organization took, however, another form in the northern parts of the country, which still bore the common name of Friesland; for there it was not merely local, but national. The Frisons succeeded in obtaining the sanction of the monarch to concentrate, as it were, those rights which were established under the ancient forms of government.

These rights, which the Frisons secured, according to their own statements, from Charlemagne, but most undoubtedly from some one or other of the earliest emperors, consisted, first, in the freedom of every order of citizens; secondly, in the right of property,—a right which admitted no authority of the sovereign to violate by confiscation, except in cases of downright treason; thirdly, in the privilege of trial by none but native judges, and according to their national usages; fourthly, in a very narrow limitation of the military services which they owed to the king; fifthly, in the hereditary title to feudal property, in direct line, on payment of certain dues or rents. These five principal articles sufficed to render Friesland in its political aspect totally different from the other portions of the monarchy. Their privileges secured, their property inviolable, their duties limited, the Frisons were altogether free from the servitude which weighed down France. It will soon be seen that these special advantages produced a government nearly analogous to that which Magna Charta was the means of founding at a later period in England.

The successors of Charlemagne chiefly signalized their authority by lavishing donations of all kinds on the church. By such means the ecclesiastical power became greater and greater, and in those countries under the sway of France was quite as arbitrary and enormous as that of the nobility. The bishops of Utrecht, Liege, and Tournay became in the course of time the chief personages on that line of the frontier. They had the great advantage over the counts of not being subjected to capricious or tyrannical removals. They therefore, even in civil affairs, played a more considerable part than the latter; and began to render themselves more and more independent in their episcopal cities, which were soon to become so many principalities. The counts, on their parts, used their best exertions to wear out, if they had not the strength to break, the chains which bound them to the footstool of the monarch. They were not all now dependent on the same sovereign, for the empire of Charlemagne was divided among his successors. France, properly so called, was bounded by the Scheldt; the country to the eastward of that river, that is to say, nearly the whole of the Netherlands, belonged first to Lorraine, then to the German kingdom.

In this state of things it happened that in the year 864 Judith, daughter of Charles the Bald, King of France, having survived her husband Ethelwolf, King of England, became attached to a powerful Flemish chieftain called Baldwin. It is not quite certain whether he was count, forester, marquis, or protector of the frontiers, but he certainly enjoyed, no matter under what title, considerable authority in the country, since the Pope on one occasion wrote to Charles the Bald to beware of offending him, lest he should join the Normans and open to them an entrance into France. He carried off Judith to his possessions in Flanders. The king her father, after many ineffectual threats, was forced to consent to their union, and confirmed to Baldwin, with the title of count, the hereditary government of all the country between the Scheldt and the Somme, a river of Picardy. This was the commencement of the celebrated country of Flanders; and this Baldwin is designated in history by the surname of *Bras-de-fer* (Iron-handed), to which his courage had justly entitled him.

The Belgian historians are also desirous of placing about this epoch the first counts of Hainault, and even of Holland. But though it may be true that the chief families of each canton sought then, as at all times, to shake off the yoke, the epoch of their independence can only be fixed at the later period at which they obtained or enforced the privilege of not being deprived of their titles and their feudal estates. The counts of the high grounds and those of Friesland enjoyed at the utmost but a fortuitous privilege of continuance in their rank. Several foreigners had gained a footing and an authority in the country, among others Wickmand, from whom descended the chatelains of Ghent, and the counts of Holland, and Heriold, a Norman prince who had been banished from his own country. This name of Normans, hardly known before the time of Charlemagne, soon became too celebrated. It designated the pagan inhabitants of Denmark, Norway, and Sweden, who, driven by rapacity and want, infested the neighboring seas. The asylum allowed in the dominions of the emperors to some of those exiled outlaws, and the imprudent provocations given by these latter to their adventurous countrymen, attracted various bands of Norman pirates to the shores of Guelders; and from desultory descents upon the coast they soon came to inundate the interior of the country. Flanders alone successfully resisted them during the life of Baldwin Bras-de-fer, but after the death of this brave chieftain there was not a province of the whole country that was not ravaged by these invaders. Their multiplied expeditions threw back the Netherlands at least two centuries, if, indeed, any calculation of the kind may be fairly formed respecting the relative state of population and improvement on the imperfect data that are left us. Several cantons became deserted. The chief cities were reduced to heaps of ruins. The German emperors vainly interposed for the relief of their unfortunate vassals. Finally, an agreement was entered into, in the year 882, with Godfrey, the king or leader of the Normans, by which a peace was purchased on condition of paying him a large subsidy and ceding to him the government of Friesland. But in about two years from this period the fierce barbarian began to complain that the country he had thus gained did not produce grapes, and the immediate inspiration of his rapacity seemed to be the blooming vineyards of France. The emperor, Charles the Fat, anticipating the consequences of a rupture with Godfrey, enticed him to an interview, in which he caused him to be assassinated. His followers, attacked on all points by the people of Friesland, perished almost to a man; and their destruction was completed in 891 by the German king, Arnulf. From that period the scourge of Norman depredation became gradually less felt. They now made but short and desultory attempts on the coast, and their last expedition appears to have taken place about the year 1000, when they threatened, but did not succeed in seizing on, the city of Utrecht.

It is remarkable that although for the space of 150 years the Netherlands were continually the scene of invasion and devastation by these northern barbarians, the political state of the country underwent no important changes. The emperors of Germany were sovereigns of the whole country, with the exception of Flanders. These portions of the empire were still called Lorraine, as well as all which they possessed of what is now called France, and which was that part forming the appanage of Lothaire, the grandson of Charlemagne, and of the Lotheringian kings. The great difficulty of maintaining subordination among the numerous chieftains of this country caused it, in 958, to be divided into two governments, which were called Higher and Lower Lorraine. The latter portion comprised nearly the whole of the Netherlands, which thus became governed by a lieutenant of the emperors. Godfrey, Count of Ardenne, was the first who filled this place; and he soon felt all the perils of the situation, for the other counts saw, with a jealous eye, their equal now promoted into a superior.

The emperor, Otho II., who upheld the authority of his lieutenant, Godfrey, became convinced that the imperial power was too weak to resist singly the opposition of the nobles of the country. He had therefore transferred, about the year 980, the title of duke to a young prince of the royal house of France; and we thus see the duchy of Lower Lorraine governed, in the name of the emperor, by the last two shoots of the branch of Charlemagne, the Dukes Charles and Otho of France, son and grandson of Louis d'Outremer. The first was a gallant prince, and he may be looked on as the founder of the greatness of Brussels, where he fixed his residence. After the death of his brother, Lothaire, the last Carlovingian king of France, Charles struggled in vain against the rising power of Hugh Capet. After some successes he was at length treacherously surprised, and died in prison. Otho, his son, did not signalize his name nor justify his descent by any memorable action, and in him ingloriously perished the name of the Carlovingians.

The death of Otho set the emperor and the great vassals once more in opposition. The German monarch insisted on naming some creature of his own to the dignity of duke; but Lambert II., Count of Louvain, and Robert, Count of Namur, having married the sisters of Otho, respectively claimed the right of inheritance to his title. Baldwin of the Comely Beard, Count of Flanders, joined himself to their league, hoping to extend his power to the eastward of the Scheldt. And in fact the emperor, as the only means of disuniting his too powerful vassals, felt himself obliged to cede Valenciennes and the islands of Zealand to Baldwin. The imperial power thus lost ground at every struggle.

Amid the confusion of these events a power well calculated to rival or even supplant that of the fierce counts was growing up. Many circumstances were combined to extend and consolidate the episcopal sway. It is true that the bishops of Tournay had no temporal authority since the period of their city's being ruined by the Normans. But those of Liege and Utrecht, and more particularly the latter, had accumulated immense possessions; and their power being inalienable, they had nothing to fear from the caprices of sovereign favor, which so often ruined the families of the aristocracy. Those bishops, who were warriors and huntsmen rather than ecclesiastics, possessed, however, in addition to the lance and the sword, the terrible artillery of excommunication and anathema, which they thundered forth without mercy against every laical opponent. And, at the same time, when they succeeded in acquiring new dominions and additional store of wealth, they could not portion it among their children, like the nobles, but it devolved to their successors, who thus became more and more powerful, and gained by degrees an authority almost royal, like that of the ecclesiastical elector of Germany.

Whenever the emperor warred against his lay vassals he was sure of assistance from the bishops, because they were at all times jealous of the power of the counts, and had much less to gain from an alliance with them than with the imperial despots on whose donations they throve, and who repaid their efforts by new privileges and extended possessions. So that when the monarch at length lost the superiority in his contests with the counts, little was wanting to merge his authority altogether in the power of the churchmen. Nevertheless, a first effort of the Bishop of Liege to seize on the rights of the Count of Louvain, in 1013, met with a signal defeat, in a battle which took place at the little village of Stongarde. And five years later the count of the Friesland marshes gave a still more severe lesson to the Bishop of Utrecht. This last merits a more particular mention, from the nature of the quarrel and the importance of its results.

Chapter IV

DECLINE OF FEUDALISM AND GROWTH OF THE TOWNS. 1018-1384

THE district in which Dordrecht is situated, and the grounds in its environs which are at present submerged, formed in those times an island just raised above the waters, and which was called Holland or Holtland (which means *wooded* land, or, according to some, *hollow* land). The formation of this island, or rather its recovery from the waters, being only of recent date, the right to its possession was more disputable than that of long-established countries. All the bishops and abbots whose states bordered the Rhine and the Meuse had, being equally covetous and grasping and mutually resolved to pounce on the prey, made it their common property. A certain Count Dirk, descended from the counts of Ghent, governed about this period the western extremity of Friesland—the country which now forms the province of Holland, and with much difficulty maintained his power against the Frisons, by whom his right was not acknowledged. Beaten out of his own territories by these refractory insurgents, he sought refuge in the ecclesiastical island, where he intrenched himself and founded a town which is believed to have been the origin of Dordrecht, now reputed to be the oldest town in the Netherlands.

This Count Dirk, like all the feudal lords, took advantage of his position to establish and levy certain duties on all the vessels which sailed past his territory, dispossessing in the meantime some vassals of the church, and beating, as we have stated, the Bishop of Utrecht himself. Complaints and appeals without number were laid at the foot of the imperial throne. Godfrey of Eenham, whom the emperor had created Duke of Lower Lorraine, was commanded to call the whole country to arms. The Bishop of Liege, though actually dying, put himself at the head of the expedition, to revenge his brother prelate and punish the audacious spoiler of the church property. But Dirk and his fierce Frisons took Godfrey prisoner and cut his army in pieces. The victor had the good sense and moderation to spare his prisoners, and set them free without ransom. He received in return an imperial amnesty; and from that period the Count of Holland and his posterity formed a barrier against which the ecclesiastical power and the remains of the imperial supremacy continually struggled, only to be shattered in each new assault.[1]

Amid such scenes of feudal anarchy the Duchy of Lorraine was crumbling away on every side. At the same time Flanders under its able counts grew more and more powerful and extensive. In the year 1066 this state, even then flourishing and powerful, furnished assistance both in men and ships to William the Bastard, of Normandy, for the conquest of England. William was son-in-law to Count Baldwin, and recompensed the assistance of his wife's father by an annual payment of three hundred silver marks. It was Mathilda, the Flemish princess and wife of the conqueror, who worked with her own hands the celebrated tapestry of Bayeux, on which is embroidered the whole history of the Conquest, and which is the most curious monument of the state of the arts in that age.

Flanders acquired a positive and considerable superiority over all the other parts of the Netherlands from the first establishment of its counts or earls. The descendants of Baldwin Bras-de-fer, after having valiantly repulsed the Normans toward the end of the ninth century, showed themselves worthy of ruling over an industrious and energetic people. They had built towns, cut down and cleared away forests, and reclaimed inundated lands; above all things they had understood and guarded against the danger of parceling out their states at every succeeding generation, and the county of Flanders passed entire into the hands of the first-born of the family. The stability produced by this state of things had allowed the people to prosper. The Normans now visited the coasts, not as enemies, but as merchants; and Bruges became the mart of the booty acquired by these bold pirates in England and on the high seas. The fisheries had begun to acquire an importance sufficient to establish the herring as one of the chief aliments of the population. Maritime commerce had made such strides that Spain and Portugal were well known to both sailors and traders, and the voyage from Flanders to Lisbon was estimated at fifteen days' sail. Woolen stuffs formed the principal wealth of the country,

[1] John Egmont, an old chronicler, says that the counts of Holland were "a sword in the flanks of the bishops of Utrecht."

but salt, corn, and jewelry were also important branches of traffic; while the youth of Flanders were so famous for their excellence in all martial pursuits, that foreign sovereigns were at all times desirous of obtaining bodies of troops from this nation.

The greatest part of Flanders was attached, as has been seen, to the King of France, and not to Lorraine; but the dependence was little more than nominal. In 1071 the King of France attempted to exercise his authority over the country by naming to the government the Countess Richilde, who had received Hainault and Namur for her dower, and who was left a widow, with sons still in their minority. The people assembled in the principal towns and protested against this intervention of the French monarch. But we must remark that it was only the population of the lowlands (whose sturdy ancestors had ever resisted foreign domination) that now took part in this opposition. The vassals which the Counts of Flanders possessed in the Gallic provinces (the high grounds), and in general all the nobility, pronounced strongly for submission to France, for the principles of political freedom had not yet been fixed in the minds of the inhabitants of those parts of the country. But the lowlanders joined together under Robert surnamed the Frisian, brother of the deceased count, and they so completely defeated the French, the nobles and their unworthy associates of the high ground that they despoiled the usurping Countess Richilde of even her hereditary possessions. In this war perished the celebrated Norman, William Fitz-Osborn, who had flown to the succor of the defeated countess, of whom he was enamored.

Robert the Frisian, not satisfied with having beaten the King of France and the Bishop of Liege, restored in 1076 the grandson of Count Dirk of Holland in the possessions which had been forced from him by the Duke of Lower Lorraine, in the name of the emperor and the Bishop of Utrecht: so that it was this valiant chieftain who, above all others, is entitled to the praise of having successfully opposed the system of foreign domination on all the principal points of the country. Four years later Otho of Nassau was the first to unite in one county the various cantons of Guelders. Finally, in 1086, Henry of Louvain joined to his title that of Count of Brabant, and from this period the country was partitioned pretty nearly as it was destined to remain for several centuries.

In the midst of this gradual organization of the various counties, history for some time loses sight of those Frisons, the maritime people of the north, who took little part in the civil wars of two centuries. But still there was no portion of Europe which at that time offered a finer picture of social improvement than these damp and unhealthful coasts. The name of Frisons extended from the Weser to the westward of the Zuyder Zee, but not quite to the Rhine; and it became usual to consider no longer as Frisons the subjects of the counts of Holland, whom we may now begin to distinguish as Hollanders or Dutch. The Frison race alone refused to recognize the sovereign counts. They boasted of being self-governed, owning no allegiance but to the emperor, and regarding the counts of his nomination as so many officers charged to require obedience to the laws of the country, but themselves obliged in all things to respect them. But the counts of Holland, the bishops of Utrecht, and several German lords, dignified from time to time with the title of counts of Friesland, insisted that it carried with it a personal authority superior to that of the sovereign they represented. The descendants of Count Dirk, a race of men remarkably warlike, were the most violent in this assumption of power. Defeat after defeat, however, punished their obstinacy, and numbers of those princes met death on the pikes of their Frison opponents. The latter had no regular leaders, but at the approach of the enemy the inhabitants of each canton flew to arms, like the members of a single family; and all the feudal forces brought against them failed to subdue this popular militia.

The frequent result of these collisions was the refusal of the Frisons to recognize any authority whatever but that of the national judges. Each canton was governed according to its own laws. If a difficulty arose, the deputies of the nation met together on the borders of the Ems, in a place called " the Trees of Upstal " (*Upstall-boomen*), where three old oaks stood in the middle of an immense plain. In this primitive council place chieftains were chosen, who, on swearing to maintain the laws and oppose the common enemy, were invested with a limited and temporary authority.

It does not appear that Friesland possessed any large towns, with the exception of Staveren. In this respect the Frisons resembled those ancient Germans who had a horror of shutting themselves up within walls. They lived in a way completely patriarchal, dwelling in isolated cabins and with habits of the utmost frugality.

We read in one of their old histories that a whole convent of Benedictines was terrified at the voracity of a German sculptor who was repairing their chapel. They implored him to look elsewhere for his food, because he and his sons consumed enough to exhaust the whole stock of the monastery.

In no part of Europe was the mass of the people so vigorously opposed to the interests of Catholicism in those days. The Frisons successfully resisted the payment of tithes, and as a punishment (according to the monkish chronicles) the sea inflicted upon them repeated inundations. They forced their priests to marry. They acknowledged no ecclesiastical decree, if secular judges, double the number of the priests, did not bear a part in it, and in such fashion interpreted a spirit of liberty which actuated them in calling themselves *Vry-Vriesen,* Free-Frisons.

The eleventh century had been for the Netherlands (with the exception of Friesland and Flanders) an epoch of organization, and had nearly fixed the political existence of the provinces, which were so long confounded in the vast possessions of the empire. It is therefore important to ascertain under what influence and on what basis these provinces became consolidated at that period. Holland and Zealand, animated by the spirit which we may fairly distinguish under the mingled title of Saxon and maritime, countries scarcely accessible and with a vigorous population, possessed, in the descendants of Dirk I., a race of national chieftains who did not attempt despotic rule over so unconquerable a people. In Brabant the maritime towns of Berg-op-Zoom and Antwerp formed, in the Flemish style, so many republics, small but not insignificant; while the southern parts of the province were under the sway of a nobility who crushed, trampled on, or sold their vassals at their pleasure or caprice. The bishopric of Liege offered also the same contrast; the domains of the nobility being governed with the utmost harshness, while those prince-prelates lavished on their plebeian vassals privileges which might have been supposed the fruits of generosity were it not clear that the object was to create an opposition in the lower orders against the turbulent aristocracy, whom they found it impossible to manage single-handed. The wars of these bishops against the petty nobles, who made their castles so many depositories of robbers and plunder, were thus the foundation of public liberty. But in all the rest of the Netherlands, excepting the provinces already mentioned, no form of government existed but that fierce feudality which reduced the people to serfs and turned the social state of man into a cheerless waste of bondage.

It was then that the crusades, with wild and stirring fanaticism, agitated, in the common impulse given to all Europe, even those little states which seemed to slumber in their isolated independence. Nowhere did the voice of Peter the Hermit find a more sympathetic echo than in these lands, still desolated by so many intestine struggles. Godfrey of Bouillon, Duke of Lower Lorraine, took the lead in this chivalric and religious frenzy. With him set out the Counts of Hainault and Flanders, the latter of whom received from the English crusaders the honorable appellation of Fitz St. George. But although the valor of all these princes was conspicuous from the foundation of the kingdom of Jerusalem by Godfrey of Bouillon in 1098 until that of the Latin empire of Constantinople by Baldwin of Flanders in 1204, still the simple gentlemen and peasants of Friesland distinguished themselves no less. They were on all occasions the first to mount the breach or lead the charge; and the Pope's nuncio found himself forced to prohibit the very women of Friesland from embarking for the Holy Land—so anxious were they to share the perils and glory of their husbands and brothers in combating the Saracens.

The outlet given by the crusades to the overboiling ardor of these warlike countries was a source of infinite advantage to their internal economy. Under the rapid progress of civilization the population increased and the fields were cultivated. The nobility, reduced to moderation by the enfeebling consequences of extensive foreign wars, became comparatively impotent in their attempted efforts against domestic freedom. Those of Flanders and Brabant also were almost decimated in the terrible battle of Bouvines, fought between the Emperor Otho and Philip Augustus, King of France. On no occasion, however, had this reduced but not degenerate nobility shown more heroic valor. The Flemish knights, disdaining to mount their horses or form their ranks for the repulse of the French cavalry, composed of common persons, contemptuously received their shock on foot and in the disorder of individual resistance. The brave Buridan of Ypres led his comrades to the fight with the chivalric war-cry, "Let each now think of her he loves!" But the issue of this battle was ruinous to the Belgians, in consequence of the bad generalship of the emperor, who had divided his army into small portions, which were defeated in detail.

While the nobility thus declined the towns began rapidly to develop the elements of popular force. In 1120 a Flemish knight who might descend so far as to marry a woman of the plebeian ranks incurred the penalty of degradation and servitude. In 1220 scarcely a serf was to be found in all Flanders. In 1300 the chiefs of the *gilden,* or trades, were more powerful than the nobles. These dates and these facts must suffice to mark the epoch at which the great mass of the nation arose from the wretchedness in which it was plunged by the Norman invasion and acquired sufficient strength and freedom to form a real political force. But it is remarkable that the same results took place in all the counties or dukedoms of the Lowlands precisely at the same period. In fact, if we start from the year 1200 on this interesting inquiry we shall see the commons attacking, in the first place the petty feudal lords and next the counts and the dukes themselves, as often as justice was denied them. In 1257 the peasants of Holland and the burghers of Utrecht proclaimed freedom and equality, drove out the bishop and the nobles and began a memorable struggle which lasted full two hundred years. In 1260 the townspeople of Flanders appealed to the King of France against the decrees of their count, who ended the quarrel by the loss of his county. In 1303 Mechlin and Louvain, the chief towns of Brabant, expelled the patrician families. A coincidence like this cannot be attributed to trifling or partial causes, such as the misconduct of a single count or other local evil, but to a great general movement in the popular mind, the progress of agriculture and industry in the whole country, superinducing an increase of wealth and intelligence, which, when unrestrained by the influence of a corrupt government, must naturally lead to the liberty and the happiness of a people.

The weaving of woolen and linen cloths was one of the chief sources of this growing prosperity. A prodigious quantity of cloth and linen was manufactured in all parts of the Netherlands. The maritime prosperity acquired an equal increase by the carrying trade, both in imports and exports. Whole fleets of Dutch and Flemish merchant ships repaired regularly to the coasts of Spain and Languedoc. Flanders was already become the great market for England and all the north of Europe.

Legislation naturally followed the movements of those positive and material interests. The earliest of the towns after the invasion of the Normans were in some degree but places of refuge. It was soon, however, established that the regular inhabitants of these bulwarks of the country should not be subjected to any servitude beyond their care and defense, but the citizen who might absent himself for a longer period than forty days was considered a deserter and deprived of his rights. It was about the year 1100 that the commons began to possess the privilege of regulating their internal affairs. They appointed their judges and magistrates and attached to their authority the old custom of ordering all the citizens to assemble or march when the summons of the feudal lord sounded the signal for their assemblage or service. By this means each municipal magistracy had the disposal of a force far superior to those of the nobles, for the population of the towns exceeded both in number and discipline the vassals of the seignorial lands. And these trained bands of the towns made war in a way very different from that hitherto practiced, for the chivalry of the country, making the trade of arms a profession for life, the feuds of the chieftains produced hereditary struggles, almost always slow and mutually disastrous. But the townsmen, forced to tear themselves from every association of home and its manifold endearments, advanced boldly to the object of the contest, never shrinking from the dangers of war from fear of that still greater danger to be found in a prolonged struggle.

Evidence was soon given of the importance of this new nation when it became forced to take up arms against enemies still more redoubtable than the counts. In 1301 the Flemings, who had abandoned their own sovereign to attach themselves to Philip the Fair, King of France, began to repent of their newly formed allegiance and to be weary of the master they had chosen. Two citizens of Bruges, Peter de Koning, a draper, and John Breydel, a butcher, put themselves at the head of their fellow-townsmen and completely dislodged the French troops who garrisoned it. The following year the militia of Bruges and the immediate neighborhood sustained alone, at the battle of Courtrai, the shock of one of the finest armies that France ever sent into the field. Victory soon declared for the gallant men of Bruges; upwards of 3000 of the French chivalry, besides common soldiers, were left dead on the field. In 1304, after a long contested battle, the Flemings forced the King of France to release their count, whom he had held prisoner. "I believe it rains Flemings!" said Philip, astonished to see them crowd on him from all sides of the field. But this multitude of warriors, always ready to meet the foe, were provided for the most part by the towns. In the seignorial system a village hardly furnished more than four or five men, and these only on important occasions; but in that of the towns every citizen was enrolled a soldier to defend the country at all times.

The same system established in Brabant forced the duke of that province to sanction and guarantee the popular privileges and the superiority of the people over the nobility. Such was the result of the famous contract concluded in 1312 at Cortenbergh, by which the duke created a legislative and judicial assembly to meet every twenty-one days for the provincial business, and to consist of fourteen deputies, of whom only four were to be nobles and ten were chosen from the people. The duke was bound by this act to hold himself in obedience to the legislative decisions of the council, and renounced all right of levying arbitrary taxes or duties on the state. Thus were the local privileges of the people by degrees secured and ratified; but the various towns making common cause for general liberty became strictly united together and progressively extended their influence and power. The confederation between Flanders and Brabant was soon consolidated. The burghers of Bruges, who had taken the lead in the grand national union and had been the foremost to expel the foreign force, took umbrage in 1323 at an arbitrary measure of their count, Louis (called of Cressy by posthumous nomination, from his having been killed at that celebrated fight), by which he ceded to the Count of Namur, his great uncle, the port of Ecluse and authorized him to levy duties there in the style of the feudal lords of the high country. It was but the affair of a day to the intrepid citizens to attack the fortress of Ecluse, carry it by assault and take prisoner the old Count of Namur. They destroyed in a short time almost all the strong castles of the nobles throughout the province, and having been joined by all the towns of western Flanders, they finally made prisoners Count Louis himself, with almost the whole of the nobility who had taken refuge with him in the town of Courtrai. But Ghent, actuated by the jealousy which at all times existed between it and Bruges, stood aloof at this crisis. The latter town was obliged to come to a compromise with the count, who soon afterward, on a new quarrel breaking out and supported by the King of France, almost annihilated his sturdy opponents at the battle of Cassel, where the Flemish infantry, commanded by Nicholas Zannekin and others, were literally cut to pieces by the French knights and men-at-arms.

This check proved the absolute necessity of union among the rival cities. Ten years after the battle of Cassel, Ghent set the example of general opposition; this example was promptly followed and the chief towns flew to arms. The celebrated Jacob van Artavelde, commonly called the Brewer of Ghent, put himself at the head of this formidable insurrection. He was a man of distinguished family, who had himself enrolled among the guild of brewers to entitle him to occupy a place in the corporation of Ghent, which he soon succeeded in managing and leading at his pleasure. The tyranny of the count and the French party which supported him became so intolerable to Artavelde that he resolved to assail them at all hazards, unappalled by the fate of his father-in-law, Sohier de Courtrai, who lost his head for a similar attempt, and notwithstanding the hitherto devoted fidelity of his native city to the count. One object only seemed insurmountable. The Flemings had sworn allegiance to the Crown of France, and they revolted at the idea of perjury, even from an extorted oath. But to overcome their scruples Artavelde proposed to acknowledge the claim of Edward III. of England to the French crown. The Flemings readily acceded to this arrangement, quickly overwhelmed Count Louis of Cressy and his French partisans, and then joined, with an army of 60,000 men, the English monarch, who had landed at Antwerp. These numerous auxiliaries rendered Edward's army irresistible, and soon afterward the French and English fleets, both of formidable power, but the latter of inferior force, met near Sluys and engaged in a battle meant to be decisive of the war. Victory remained doubtful during an entire day of fighting, until a Flemish squadron, hastening to the aid of the English, fixed the fate of the combat by the utter defeat of the enemy.

A truce between the two kings did not deprive Artavelde of his well-earned authority. He was invested with the title of ruward, or conservator of the peace, of Flanders, and governed the whole province with almost sovereign sway. It was said that King Edward used familiarly to call him "his dear gossip," and it is certain that there was not a feudal lord of the time whose power was not eclipsed by this leader of the people. One of the principal motives which cemented the attachment of the Flemings to Artavelde was the advantage obtained through his influence with Edward for facilitating the trade with England, whence they procured the chief supply of wool for their manufactories. Edward promised them 70,000 sacks as the reward of their alliance. Artavelde perished in 1345 in a struggle with the weavers of his own city. But the Flemings held firm, nevertheless, in their alliance with England, only regulating the connection by a steady principle of national independence.

Edward knew well how to conciliate and manage these faithful and important auxiliaries during all his continental wars. A Flemish army covered the siege of Calais in 1348, and, under the command of Giles de Rypergherste, a mere weaver of Ghent, they beat the dauphin of France in a pitched battle. But Calais once taken and a truce concluded, the English king abandoned his allies. These, left wholly to their own resources, forced the French and the heir of their count, young Louis de Male, to recognize their right to self-government according to their ancient privileges, and of not being forced to give aid to France in any war against England. Flanders may therefore be pronounced as forming at this epoch, both in right and fact, a truly independent principality.

But such struggles as these left a deep and immovable sentiment of hatred in the minds of the vanquished. Louis de Male longed for the reëstablishment and extension of his authority, and had the art to gain over to his views not only all the nobles, but many of the most influential guilds or trades. Ghent, which long resisted his attempts, was at length reduced by famine, and the count projected the ruin, or at least the total subjection, of this turbulent town. Philip Van Artavelde, a son of Jacob, started forth at this juncture, when the popular cause seemed lost, and joining with his fellow-citizens, John Lyons and Peter du Bois, he led 7000 resolute burghers against 40,000 feudal vassals. He completely defeated the count and took the town of Bruges, where Louis de Male only obtained safety by hiding himself under the bed of an old woman who gave him shelter. Thus once more feudality was defeated in a fresh struggle with civic freedom.

The consequences of this event were immense. They reached to the very heart of France, where the people bore in great discontent the feudal yoke; and Froissart declares that the success of the people of Ghent had nearly overthrown the superiority of the nobility over the people in France. But the king, Charles VI., excited by his uncle, Philip the Bold, Duke of Burgundy, took arms in support of the defeated count and marched with a powerful army against the rebellious burghers. Though defeated in four successive combats, in the last of which, at Roosbeke, in 1382, Artavelde was killed, the Flemings would not submit to their imperious count, who used every persuasion with Charles to continue his assistance for the punishment of these refractory subjects. But the Duke of Burgundy was aware that a too great perseverance would end either in driving the people to despair and the possible defeat of the French or the entire conquest of the country and its junction to the crown of France. He, being son-in-law to Louis de Male and consequently aspiring to the inheritance of Flanders, saw with a keen glance the advantage of a present compromise. On the death, in 1384, of Louis, who is stated to have been murdered by Philip's brother, the Duke of Berri, he concluded a peace with the rebel burghers and entered at once upon the sovereignty of the country.

Chapter V

POWER OF THE HOUSE OF BURGUNDY. 1384-1506

THUS the house of Burgundy, which soon after became so formidable and celebrated, obtained this vast accession to its power. The various changes which had taken place in the neighboring provinces during the continuance of these civil wars had altered the state of Flanders altogether. John d'Avesnes, Count of Hainault, having also succeeded in 1299 to the county of Holland, the two provinces, although separated by Flanders and Brabant, remained from that time under the government of the same chief, who soon became more powerful than the bishops of Utrecht, or even than their formidable rivals, the Frisians.

During the wars which desolated these opposing territories in consequence of the perpetual conflicts for superiority, the power of the various towns insensibly became at least as great as that of the nobles to whom they were constantly opposed. The commercial interests of Holland also were considerably advanced by the influx of Flemish merchants forced to seek refuge there from the convulsions which agitated their province. Every day confirmed and increased the privileges of the people of Brabant, while at Liege the inhabitants gradually began to gain the upper hand and to shake off the former subjection to their sovereign bishops.

Although Philip of Burgundy became Count of Flanders by the death of his father-in-law, in the year 1384, it was not till the following year that he concluded a peace with the people of Ghent and entered into quiet possession of the province. In the same year the Duchess of Brabant, the last descendant of the duke of that province, died, leaving no nearer relative than the Duchess of Burgundy, so that Philip obtained in right of his wife this new and important accession to his dominions. But the consequent increase of the sovereign's power was not, as is often the case, injurious to the liberties or happiness of the people. Philip continued to govern in the interest of the country, which he had the good sense to consider as identified with his own. He augmented the privileges of the towns and negotiated for the return into Flanders of those merchants who had emigrated to Germany and Holland during the continuance of the civil wars. He thus by degrees accustomed his new subjects, so proud of their rights, to submit to his authority; and his peaceable reign was only disturbed by the fatal issue of the expedition of his son, John the Fearless, Count of Nevers, against the Turks. This young prince, filled with ambition and temerity, was offered the command of the force sent by Charles III. of France to the assistance of Sigismund of Hungary in his war against Bayazid. Followed by a numerous body of nobles, he entered on the contest and was defeated and taken prisoner by the Turks at the battle of Nicopolis. His army was totally destroyed and himself only restored to liberty on the payment of an immense ransom.

John the Fearless succeeded in 1404 to the inheritance of all his father's dominions, with the exception of Brabant, of which his younger brother, Anthony of Burgundy, became duke. John, whose ambitious and ferocious character became every day more strongly developed, now aspired to the government of France during the insanity of his cousin, Charles VI. He occupied himself little with the affairs of the Netherlands, from which he only desired to draw supplies of men. But the Flemings, taking no interest in his personal views or private projects, and equally indifferent to the rivalry of England and France, which now began so fearfully to afflict the latter kingdom, forced their ambitious count to declare their province a neutral country; so that the English merchants were admitted as usual to trade in all the ports of Flanders and the Flemings equally well received in England, while the duke made open war against Great Britain in his quality of a prince of France and sovereign of Burgundy. This is probably the earliest well-established instance of such a distinction between the prince and the people.

The spirit of constitutional liberty and legal equality which now animated the various provinces is strongly marked in the history of the time by two striking and characteristic incidents. At the death of Philip the Bold his widow deposited on his tomb her purse and the keys which she carried at her girdle in token of marriage; and by this humiliating ceremony she renounced her rights to a succession overloaded with her husband's debts. In the same year (1404) the widow of Albert, Count of Holland and Hainault, finding herself in similar circumstances, required of the bailiff of Holland and the judges of his court permission to make a like renunciation. The claim was granted, and to fulfill the requisite ceremony she walked at the head of the funeral procession, carrying in her hand a blade of straw, which she placed on the coffin. We thus find that in such cases the reigning families were held liable to follow the common usages of the country. From such instances there required but little progress in the principle of equality to reach the republican contempt for rank, which made the citizens of Bruges in the following century arrest their count for his private debts.

The spirit of independence had reached the same point at Liege. The families of the counts of Holland and Hainault, which were at this time distinguished by the name of Bavarian, because they were only descended from the ancient counts of Netherland extraction in the female line, had sufficient influence to obtain the nomination to the bishopric for a prince who was at the period in his infancy. John of Bavaria—for so he was called, and to his name was afterwards added the epithet of "the Pitiless"—on reaching his majority did not think it necessary to cause himself to be consecrated a priest, but governed as a lay sovereign. The indignant citizens of Liege expelled him and chose another bishop. But the houses of Burgundy and Bavaria, closely allied by intermarriages, made common cause in his quarrel, and John the Fearless, Duke of Burgundy, and William IV., Count of Holland and Hainault, brother of the bishop, replaced by force this cruel and unworthy prelate.

This union of the government over all the provinces in two families so closely connected rendered the preponderance of the rulers too strong for that balance hitherto kept steady by the popular force. The former could on each new quarrel join together and employ against any particular town their whole united resources, whereas the latter could only act by isolated efforts for the maintenance of their separate rights. Such was the cause of a considerable decline in public liberty during the fifteenth century. It is true that John the Fearless gave almost his whole attention to his French political intrigues and to the fierce quarrels which he maintained with the house of Orleans. But his nephew, John, Duke of Brabant, having married, in 1416, his cousin Jacqueline, daughter and heiress of William IV., Count of Holland and Hainault, this branch of the house of Burgundy seemed to get the start of the elder in its progressive influence over the provinces of the Netherlands. The dukes of Guelders, who had changed their title of counts for one of superior rank, acquired no accession of power proportioned to their

BALDWIN VI GRANTS THE FIRST FLANDRIAN CONSTITUTION
Painting by A. Hennebicq

—page 25

new dignity. The bishops of Utrecht became by degrees weaker, private dissensions enfeebled Friesland, Luxemburg was a poor, unimportant dukedom, but Holland, Hainault, and Brabant formed the very heart of the Netherlands, while the elder branch of the same family, under whom they united, possessed Flanders, Artois, and the two Burgundies. To complete the prosperity and power of this latter branch it was soon destined to inherit the entire dominions of the other.

A fact the consequences of which were so important for the whole of Europe merits considerable attention, but it is most difficult to explain at once concisely and clearly the series of accidents, maneuvers, tricks and crimes by which it was accomplished. It must first be remarked that this John of Brabant, now the husband of his cousin Jacqueline, Countess of Holland and Hainault, possessed neither the moral nor physical qualities suited to mate with the most lovely, intrepid and talented woman of her times; nor the vigor and firmness required for the maintenance of an increased, and for those days a considerable, dominion. Jacqueline thoroughly despised her insignificant husband, first in secret and subsequently by those open avowals forced from her by his revolting combination of weakness, cowardice, and tyranny. He tamely allowed the province of Holland to be invaded by the same ungrateful Bishop of Liege, John the Pitiless, whom his wife's father and his own uncle had reëstablished in his justly forfeited authority. But John of Brabant revenged himself for his wife's contempt by a series of domestic persecutions so odious that the states of Brabant interfered for her protection. Finding it, however, impossible to remain in a perpetual contest with a husband whom she hated and despised, she fled from Brussels, where he held his ducal court, and took refuge in England, under the protection of Henry V., at that time in the plenitude of his fame and power.

England at this epoch enjoyed the proudest station in European affairs. John the Fearless, after having caused the murder of his rival, the Duke of Orleans, was himself assassinated on the bridge of Montereau by the followers of the dauphin of France, and in his presence. Philip, Duke of Burgundy, the son and successor of John, had formed a close alliance with Henry V., to revenge his father's murder. After the death of the king he married the latter's sister, and thus united himself still more nearly to the celebrated John, Duke of Bedford, brother of Henry, and regent of France, in

Hist. Nat. xiii-4

the name of his infant nephew, Henry VI. But besides the share on which he reckoned in the spoils of France, Philip also looked with a covetous eye on the inheritance of Jacqueline, his cousin. As soon as he had learned that this princess, so well received in England, was taking measures for having her marriage annulled, to enable her to espouse the Duke of Gloucester, also the brother of Henry V., and subsequently known by the appellation of " the Good Duke Humphrey," he was tormented by a double anxiety. He in the first place dreaded that Jacqueline might have children by her marriage with Gloucester, and thus deprive him of his right of succession to her states; and in the next he was jealous of the possible domination of England in the Netherlands as well as in France. He therefore soon became self-absolved from all his vows of revenge in the cause of his murdered father and labored solely for the object of his personal aggrandizement. To break his connection with Bedford, to treat secretly with the dauphin, his father's assassin, or at least the witness and warrant for his assassination, and to shuffle from party to party as occasion required were movements of no difficulty to Philip, surnamed " the Good." He openly espoused the cause of his infamous relative, John of Brabant, sent a powerful army into Hainault, which Gloucester vainly strove to defend in right of Jacqueline, and next seized on Holland and Zealand, where he met with a long but ineffectual resistance on the part of the courageous woman he so mercilessly oppressed. Jacqueline, deprived of the assistance of her stanch but ruined friends,[1] and abandoned by Gloucester (who, on the refusal of Pope Martin V. to sanction her divorce, had married another woman, and but feebly aided the efforts of the former to maintain her rights), was now left a widow by the death of John of Brabant. But Philip, without a shadow of justice, pursued his designs against her dominions and finally despoiled her of her last possessions, and even of the title of

[1] We must not omit to notice the existence of two factions which for nearly two centuries divided and agitated the whole population of Holland and Zealand. One bore the title of *Hoeks* (fishing-hooks); the other was called *Kaabeljauws* (cod-fish). The origin of these burlesque denominations was a dispute between two parties at a feast, as to whether the cod-fish took the hook, or the hook the cod-fish. This apparently frivolous dispute was made the pretext for a serious quarrel, and the partisans of the nobles and those of the towns ranged themselves at either side, and assumed different badges of distinction. The *Hoeks*, partisans of the towns, wore red caps; the *Kaabeljauws* wore gray ones. In Jacqueline's quarrel with Philip of Burgundy she was supported by the former; and it was not till long after that the extinction of that popular and turbulent faction struck a final blow to the dissensions of both.

countess, which she forfeited by her marriage with Vrank Van Borselen, a gentleman of Zealand, contrary to a compact to which Philip's tyranny had forced her to consent. After a career, one of the most checkered and romantic which is recorded in history, the beautiful and hitherto unfortunate Jacqueline found repose and happiness in the tranquillity of private life; and her death in 1436, at the age of thirty-six, removed all restraint from Philip's thirst for aggrandizement. As if fortune had conspired for the rapid consolidation of his greatness, the death of Philip, Count of St. Pol, who had succeeded his brother John in the dukedom of Brabant, gave him the sovereignty of that extensive province, and his dominions soon extended to the very limits of Picardy, by the Peace of Arras, concluded with the dauphin, now become Charles VII., and by his finally contracting a strict alliance with France.

Philip of Burgundy, thus become sovereign of dominions at once so extensive and compact, had the precaution and address to obtain from the emperor a formal renunciation of his existing, though almost nominal, rights as lord paramount. He next purchased the title of the Duchess of Luxemburg, and thus the states of the house of Burgundy gained an extent about equal to that of the existing kingdoms of the Netherlands and of Belgium. For although on the north and east they did not include Friesland, the bishopric of Utrecht, Guelders, or the province of Liege, still on the south and west they comprised French Flanders, the Boulonnais, Artois, and a part of Picardy, besides Burgundy. But it has been already seen how limited an authority was possessed by the rulers of the maritime provinces. Flanders in particular, the most populous and wealthy, strictly preserved its republican institutions. Ghent and Bruges were the two great towns of the province, and each maintained its individual authority over its respective territory with great indifference to the will or the wishes of the sovereign duke. Philip, however, had the policy to divide most effectually these rival towns. After having fallen into the hands of the people of Bruges, whom he made a vain attempt to surprise, and who massacred numbers of his followers before his eyes, he forced them to submission by the assistance of the citizens of Ghent, who sanctioned the banishment of the chief men of the vanquished town. But some years later Ghent was in its turn oppressed and punished for having resisted the payment of some new tax. It found no support from the rest of Flanders. Nevertheless this powerful city singly maintained the war for the space of two years, but the intrepid burghers finally yielded to the veterans of the duke, formed to victory in the French wars. The principal privileges of Ghent were on this occasion revoked and annulled.

During these transactions the province of Holland, which enjoyed a degree of liberty almost equal with Flanders, had declared war against the Hanseatic towns on its own proper authority. Supported by Zealand, which formed a distinct country, but was strictly united to it by a common interest, Holland equipped a fleet against the pirates which infested their coasts and assailed their commerce and soon forced them to submission. Philip in the meantime contrived to manage the conflicting elements of his power with great subtlety. Notwithstanding his ambitious and despotic character, he conducted himself so cautiously that his people by common consent confirmed his title of "the Good," which was somewhat inappropriately given to him at the earlier epoch.

Philip had an only son, born and reared in the midst of that ostentatious greatness which he looked on as his own by divine right; whereas his father remembered that it had chiefly become his by fortuitous acquirement and much of it by means not likely to look well in the sight of Heaven. This son was Charles, Count of Charolais, afterward celebrated under the name of Charles the Rash. He gave, even in the lifetime of his father, a striking specimen of despotism to the people of Holland. Appointed stadtholder [1] of that province in 1457, he appropriated to himself several important successions, forced the inhabitants to labor in the formation of dikes for the security of the property thus acquired, and, in a word, conducted himself as an absolute master. Soon afterwards he broke out into open opposition to his father, who had complained of this undutiful and impetuous son to the states of the provinces, venting his grief in lamentations instead of punishing his people's wrongs. In fact, Philip was declining daily. Yet even when dying he preserved his natural haughtiness and energy, and, being provoked by the insubordination of the people of Liege, he had himself carried to the scene of their punishment. The refractory town of Dinant, on the Meuse, was utterly destroyed by the two counts and 600 of the citizens were drowned in the river in cold blood.

---

[1] Stadtholder is the more usual spelling, but stadholder would be more correct, meaning, literally, steadholder, and not stadt (*i. e.*, city) holder, as the common form suggests.

The following year Philip expired, leaving to Charles his long wished-for inheritance.

The reign of Philip had produced a revolution in Belgian manners, for his example and the great increase of wealth had introduced habits of luxury hitherto quite unknown. He had also brought into fashion romantic notions of military honor, love, and chivalry, which, while they certainly softened the character of the nobility, contained nevertheless a certain mixture of frivolity and extravagance. The celebrated Order of the Golden Fleece, which was introduced by Philip, was less an institution based on grounds of rational magnificence than a puerile emblem of his passion for Isabella of Portugal, his third wife. The verses of a contemporary poet induced him to make a vow for the conquest of Constantinople from the Turks. He certainly never attempted to execute this senseless crusade, but he did not omit so fair an opportunity for levying new taxes on his people.

In some respects, at least, a totally different government was looked for on the part of his son and successor, who was by nature and habit a mere soldier. Charles began his career by seizing on all the money and jewels left by his father; he next dismissed the crowd of useless functionaries who, under the pretense of managing, had fed upon the treasures of the state. But this salutary and sweeping reform was only effected to enable the sovereign to pursue uncontrolled the most fatal of all passions, that of war. Nothing can better paint the true character of this haughty and impetuous prince than his crest (a branch of holly) and his motto, "Who touches it, pricks himself." Charles had conceived a furious and not ill-founded hatred for his base yet formidable neighbor and rival, Louis XI. of France. The latter had succeeded in obtaining from Philip the restitution of some towns in Picardy—cause sufficient to excite the resentment of his inflammable successor, who during his father's lifetime took open part with some of the vassals of France in a temporary struggle against the throne. Louis, who had been worsted in a combat where both he and Charles bore a part, was not behindhand in his hatred. But inasmuch as one was haughty, audacious, and intemperate, the other was cunning, cool, and treacherous. Charles was the proudest, most daring, and most unmanageable prince that ever made the sword the type and the guarantee of greatness; Louis the most subtle, dissimulating and treacherous king that ever wove in his closet a tissue of hollow diplomacy and bad faith in government. The struggle between these sovereigns was unequal only in respect to this difference of character, for France, subdivided as it still was, and exhausted by the wars with England, was not comparable, either as regarded men, money, or the other resources of the state, to the compact and prosperous dominions of Burgundy.

Charles showed some symptoms of good sense and greatness of mind soon after his accession to power that encouraged illusory hopes as to his future career. Scarcely was he proclaimed Count of Flanders at Ghent when the populace, surrounding his hotel, absolutely insisted on and extorted his consent to the restitution of their ancient privileges. Furious as Charles was at this bold proof of insubordination, he did not revenge it; and he treated with equal indulgence the city of Mechlin, which had expelled its governor and rased the citadel. The people of Liege, having revolted against their bishop, Louis of Bourbon, who was closely connected with the house of Burgundy, were defeated by the duke in 1467, but he treated them with clemency; and immediately after this event, in February, 1468, he concluded with Edward IV. of England an alliance, offensive and defensive, against France.

The real motive of this alliance was rivalry and hatred of Louis. The ostensible pretext was this monarch's having made war against the Duke of Brittany, Charles's old ally in the short contest in which he, while yet but count, had measured his strength with his rival after he became king. The present union between England and Burgundy was too powerful not to alarm Louis; he demanded an explanatory conference with Charles, and the town of Peronne in Picardy was fixed on for the meeting. Louis, willing to imitate the boldness of his rival, who had formerly come to meet him in the very midst of his army, now came to the rendezvous almost alone. But he was severely mortified, and near paying a greater penalty than fright, for this hazardous conduct. The duke, having received intelligence of a new revolt at Liege excited by some of the agents of France, instantly made Louis prisoner. The excess of his rage and hatred might have carried him to a more disgraceful extremity had not Louis by force of bribery gained over some of the duke's most influential counselors, who succeeded in appeasing his rage. He contented himself with humiliating, when he was disposed to punish. He forced his captive to accompany him to Liege and witness the ruin of this unfortunate town, which he delivered over to plunder; and having given this lesson to Louis he set him at liberty.

From this time on the character of Charles exhibited more and more those dangerous traits which finally brought him to ruin. A tireless worker, his ambition presented to him so many fields of endeavor that he attempted all things at once, and so failed in most. A naturally rash and excitable nature, complicated by attacks of brain fever, led him often to excesses and obscured the better traits of his character. In his court he had no friends and few faithful servants, for he seemed to delight in humiliating those around him. For his subjects he cared little or nothing. He founded his power on force and terror. "I would far rather be hated than despised," he cried one day to the people of Ghent. Indeed, he regarded the people of the Netherlands as mere instruments of his ambition, from whom he could wring the supplies to pay the bands of mercenary soldiers whom he employed in preference to the old feudal levies. When the taxes necessary for the support and pay of these bands of mercenaries caused the people to murmur, Charles laughed at their complaints and severely punished some of the most refractory of them.

In 1472, in alliance with the King of England, Edward IV., he entered France at the head of his army, to assist the Duke of Brittany; but at the moment when nothing seemed to oppose the most extensive views of his ambition he lost by his hot-brained caprice every advantage within his easy reach. He chose to sit down before Beauvais, and thus made of this town, which lay in his road, a complete stumbling-block on his path of conquest. The time he lost before its walls caused the defeat and ruin of his unsupported, or as might be said his abandoned, ally, who made the best terms he could with Louis; and thus Charles's presumption and obstinacy paralyzed all the efforts of his courage and power. But he soon afterward acquired the duchy of Guelders from the old Duke Arnoul, who had been temporarily despoiled of it by his son, Adolphus. It was almost a hereditary consequence in this family that the children should revolt and rebel against their parents. Adolphus had the effrontery to found his justification on the argument that his father having reigned forty-four years he was fully entitled to his share—a fine practical authority for greedy and expectant heirs. The old father replied to this reasoning by offering to meet his son in single combat. Charles cut short the affair by making Adolphus prisoner and seizing on the disputed territory, for which he, however, paid Arnoul the sum of 220,000 florins.

After this acquisition Charles conceived and had much at heart the design of becoming king, the first time that the Netherlands were considered sufficiently important and consolidated to entitle their possessor to that title. To lead to this object he offered to the Emperor of Germany the hand of his daughter Mary for his son Maximilian. The emperor acceded to the proposition and repaired to the city of Treves to meet Charles and countenance his coronation. But the insolence and selfishness of the latter put an end to the project. He humiliated the emperor, who was of a niggardly and mean-spirited disposition, by appearing with a train so numerous and sumptuous as totally to eclipse the imperial retinue, and deeply offended him by wishing to postpone the marriage, from his jealousy of creating for himself a rival in a son-in-law who might embitter his old age as he had that of his own father. The mortified emperor quitted the place in high dudgeon, and the projected kingdom was doomed to a delay of some centuries.

Charles, urged on by the double motive of thirst for aggrandizement and vexation at his late failure, attempted, under pretext of some internal dissensions, to gain possession of Cologne and its territory, which belonged to the empire; and at the same time planned the invasion of France, in concert with his brother-in-law, Edward IV., who had recovered possession of England. But the town of Neuss, in the archbishopric of Cologne, occupied him a full year before its walls. The emperor, who came to its succor, actually besieged the besiegers in their camp, and the dispute was terminated by leaving it to the arbitration of the Pope's legate and placing the contested town in his keeping. This half triumph gained by Charles saved Louis wholly from destruction. Edward, who had landed in France with a numerous force, seeing no appearance of his Burgundian allies, made peace with Louis; and Charles, who arrived in all haste, but not till after the treaty was signed, upbraided and abused the English king, and turned a warm friend into an inveterate enemy.

Louis, whose crooked policy had so far succeeded on all occasions, now seemed to favor Charles's plans of aggrandizement, and to recognize his pretended right to Lorraine, which legitimately belonged to the empire, and the invasion of which by Charles would be sure to set him at variance with the whole of Germany.

The infatuated duke, blind to the ruin to which he was thus hurrying, abandoned to Louis, in return for this insidious support, the constable of St. Pol, a nobleman who had long maintained his independence in Picardy, where he had large possessions, and who was fitted to be a valuable friend or formidable enemy to either. Charles now marched against, and soon overcame, Lorraine. Thence he turned his army against the Swiss, who were allies to the conquered province, but who sent the most submissive dissuasions to the invader. They begged for peace, assuring Charles that their romantic but sterile mountains were not altogether worth the bridles of his splendidly equipped cavalry. But the more they humbled themselves, the higher was his haughtiness raised. It appeared that he had at this period conceived the project of uniting in one common conquest the ancient dominions of Lothaire I., who had possessed the whole of the countries traversed by the Rhine, the Rhone, and the Po; and he even spoke of passing the Alps, like Hannibal, for the invasion of Italy.

Switzerland was, by moral analogy as well as physical fact, the rock against which these extravagant projects were shattered. The troops with which Charles engaged the hardy mountaineers in the gorges of the Alps near the town of Granson were literally crushed to atoms by the stones and fragments of granite detached from the heights and hurled down upon their heads. Charles, after this defeat, returned to the charge six weeks later, having rallied his army and drawn reinforcements from Burgundy. But Louis had dispatched a body of cavalry to the Swiss, a force in which they were before deficient, and thus augmented, their army amounted to 25,000 men. They took up a position, skillfully chosen, on the borders of the Lake of Morat, where they were attacked by Charles at the head of 30,000 soldiers of all ranks. The result was the total defeat of the latter, with the loss of 10,000 killed, whose bones, gathered into an immense heap, and bleaching in the winds, remained for above three centuries a terrible monument of rashness and injustice, as well as of patriotism and valor.

Charles was now plunged into a state of profound melancholy, but he soon burst from this gloomy mood into one of renewed fierceness and fatal desperation. Nine months after the battle of Morat he reëntered Lorraine at the head of an army not composed of his faithful militia of the Netherlands, but of those mercenaries in whom it was madness to place trust. The reinforcements meant to be dispatched to him by those provinces were kept back by the artifices of the Count of Campo Basso, an Italian who commanded his cavalry, and who only gained his confidence basely to betray it. René, Duke of Lorraine, at the head of the confederate forces, offered battle to Charles under the walls of Nancy, and the night before the combat Campo Basso went over to the enemy with the troops under his command. Still Charles had the way open for retreat. Fresh troops from Burgundy and Flanders were on their march to join him, but he would not be dissuaded from his resolution to fight, and he resolved to try his fortune once more with his dispirited and shattered army. On this occasion the fate of Charles was decided, and the fortune of Louis triumphant. The rash and ill-fated duke lost both the battle and his life. His body, mutilated with wounds, was found the next day, and buried with great pomp in the town of Nancy, by the orders of the generous victor, the Duke of Lorraine.

With Charles fell the power of the house of Burgundy. The great Burgundian state lacking in coherence and national unity, was soon ground to pieces between France and Germany. Charles left to his only daughter, then eighteen years of age, the inheritance of his extensive dominions, and with them that of the hatred and jealousy which he had so largely excited. External spoliation immediately commenced, and internal disunion quickly followed. Louis XI. seized on Burgundy and a part of Artois as fiefs devolving to the crown in default of male issue. Several of the provinces refused to pay the new subsidies commanded in the name of Mary, Flanders alone showing a disposition to uphold the rights of the young princess. The states were assembled at Ghent and ambassadors sent to the King of France, in the hopes of obtaining peace on reasonable terms. Louis, true to his system of subtle perfidy, placed before one of those ambassadors, the burgomaster of Ghent, a letter from the inexperienced princess, which proved her intention to govern by the counsel of her father's ancient ministers, rather than by that of the deputies of the nation. This was enough to decide the indignant Flemings to render themselves at once masters of the government and get rid of the ministers whom they hated. Two Burgundian nobles, Hugonet and Imbercourt, were arrested, accused of treason, and beheaded under the very eyes of their agonized and outraged mistress, who threw herself before the frenzied multitude, vainly imploring mercy for these

1477

innocent men. The people having thus completely gained the upper hand over the Burgundian influence, Mary was sovereign of the Netherlands but in name.

It would have now been easy for Louis XI. to have obtained for the dauphin, his son, the hand of this hitherto unfortunate but interesting princess, but he thought himself sufficiently strong and cunning to gain possession of her states without such an alliance.

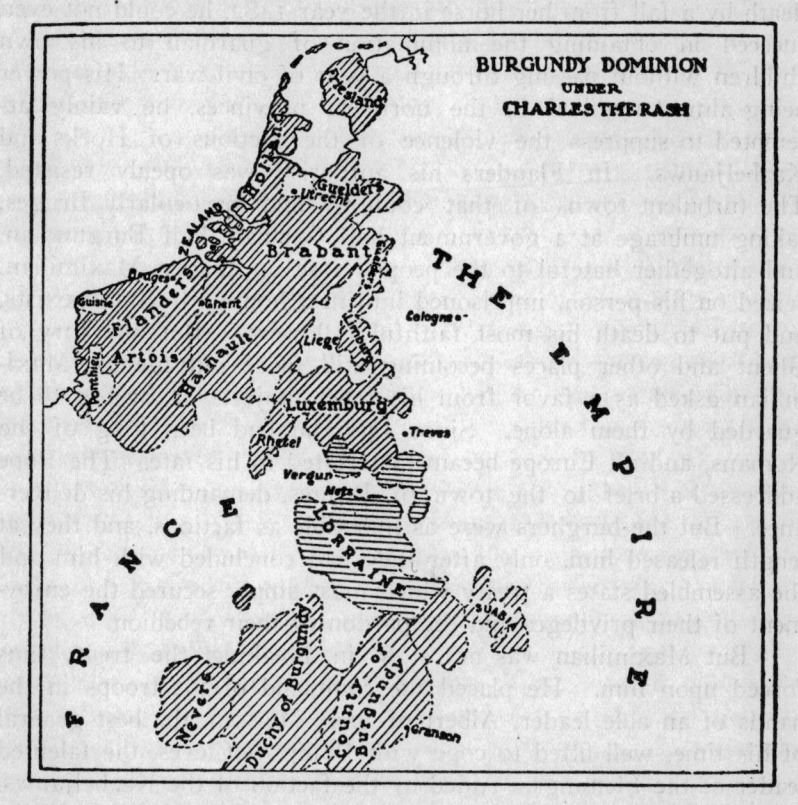

BURGUNDY DOMINION UNDER CHARLES THE RASH

Mary, however, thus in some measure disdained if not actually rejected by Louis, soon after married her first-intended husband, Maximilian of Austria, son of the Emperor Frederick III., a prince so absolutely destitute, in consequence of his father's parsimony, that she was obliged to borrow money from the towns of Flanders to defray the expenses of his suite. Nevertheless he seemed equally acceptable to his bride and to his new subjects. They not only supplied all his wants, but enabled him to maintain the war against Louis XI., whom they defeated at the battle of Guinegate in Picardy, and forced to make peace on more favorable terms than they had hoped for. But these wealthy provinces were not more zealous for the national defense than bent on the maintenance of their local privileges, which Maximilian little understood, and sympathized with less. He was bred in the school of absolute despotism, and his duchess having met with an early death by a fall from her horse in the year 1482, he could not even succeed in obtaining the nomination of guardian to his own children without passing through a year of civil war. His power being almost nominal in the northern provinces, he vainly attempted to suppress the violence of the factions of Hoeks and Kaabeljauws. In Flanders his authority was openly resisted. The turbulent towns of that country, and particularly Bruges, taking umbrage at a government half German, half Burgundian, and altogether hateful to the people, rose up against Maximilian, seized on his person, imprisoned him in a house which still exists, and put to death his most faithful followers. But the fury of Ghent and other places becoming still more outrageous, Maximilian asked as a favor from his rebel subjects of Bruges to be guarded by them alone. Since 1486 he had been king of the Romans, and all Europe became interested in his fate. The Pope addressed a brief to the town of Bruges, demanding his deliverance. But the burghers were as inflexible as factious, and they at length released him, only after they had concluded with him and the assembled states a treaty which most amply secured the enjoyment of their privileges and the pardon of their rebellion.

But Maximilian was not slow in breaking the treaty thus forced upon him. He placed the command of his troops in the hands of an able leader, Albert of Saxe Meissen, the best general of his time, well fitted to cope with Philip of Cleves, the talented leader of the Flemings. Aided by the faction of the Kaabeljauws, Albert soon conquered Holland, 1489, and extinguished the weaker party of the Hoeks. Place after place was taken from the Flemings, and after the fall of Sluys Philip of Cleves fled to France. By 1492 Albert was able to announce to Maximilian that the Netherlands were completely subdued. The destruction of the parties which had so long rent Holland by their feuds enabled that province to recover from its exhaustion and insignificance and to assume a new and ever increasing importance in the Netherlands.

The situation of the Netherlands was still extremely precarious and difficult to manage during the unstable sway of a government so weak as Maximilian's. But he, having succeeded his father on the imperial throne in 1493, and his son Philip having been proclaimed the following year duke and count of the various provinces at the age of sixteen, a more pleasing prospect was offered to the people. Philip, young, handsome, and descended by his mother from the ancient sovereigns of the country, was joyfully hailed by all the towns. He did not belie the hopes so enthusiastically expressed. He had the good sense to renounce all pretensions to Friesland, the fertile source of many preceding quarrels and sacrifices. He reëstablished the ancient commercial relations with England, to which country Maximilian had given mortal offense by sustaining the imposture of Perkin Warbeck. Philip also consulted the states-general on his projects of a double alliance between himself and his sister with the son and daughter of Ferdinand, King of Aragon, and Isabella, Queen of Castile, and from this wise precaution the project soon became one of national partiality instead of private or personal interest. In this manner complete harmony was established between the young prince and the inhabitants of the Netherlands. All the ills produced by civil war disappeared with immense rapidity in Flanders and Brabant as soon as peace was thus consolidated. Even Holland, though it had particularly felt the scourge of these dissensions, and suffered severely from repeated inundations, began to recover.

The reign of Philip, unfortunately a short one, was rendered remarkable by two intestine quarrels, one in Friesland, the other in Guelders. The Frisons, who had been so isolated from the more important affairs of Europe that they were in a manner lost sight of by history for several centuries, had nevertheless their full share of domestic disputes; too long, too multifarious, and too minute to allow us to give more than this brief notice of their existence. But finally, about the period of Philip's accession, eastern Friesland had chosen for its count a gentleman of the country surnamed Edzart, who fixed the headquarters of his military government at Embden. The sight of such an elevation in an individual whose pretensions he thought far inferior to his own induced Albert of Saxony, who had well served Maximilian against the refractory Flemings, to demand as his reward the title of stadtholder, or hereditary governor, of Friesland. But it was far easier for the emperor to accede to this request than for his favorite to put the grant into effect. The Frisons, true to their character, held to their privileges, and fought for their maintenance with heroic courage. And Albert died, in 1500, without succeeding in subduing the province.

The war of Guelders was of a totally different nature. In this case it was not a question of popular resistance to a tyrannical nomination, but of patriotic fidelity to the reigning family. Adolphus, the duke who had dethroned his father, had died in Flanders, leaving a son who had been brought up almost a captive as long as Maximilian governed the states of his inheritance. This young man, called Charles of Egmont, and who is honored in the history of his country under the title of the Achilles of Guelders, fell into the hands of the French during the combat in which he made his first essay in arms. The towns of Guelders unanimously joined to pay his ransom, and as soon as he was at liberty they one and all proclaimed him duke. The Emperor Philip and the Germanic diet in vain protested against this measure, and declared Charles a usurper. The spirit of justice and of liberty spoke more loudly than the thunders of their ban, and the people resolved to support to the last this scion of an ancient race, glorious in much of its conduct, though often criminal in many of its members. Charles of Egmont found faithful friends in his devoted subjects, and he maintained his rights, sometimes with, sometimes without, the assistance of France—making up for his want of numbers by energy and enterprise. We cannot follow this warlike prince in the long series of adventures which consolidated his power, nor stop to depict his daring adherents on land, who caused the whole of Holland to tremble at their deeds; nor his pirates—the chief of whom, Long Peter, called himself king of the Zuyder Zee. But amid all the consequent troubles of such a struggle it is marvelous to find Charles of Egmont upholding his country in a state of high prosperity and leaving it at his death almost as rich as Holland itself.

The incapacity of Philip the Fair doubtless contributed to cause him the loss of this portion of his dominions. This prince, after his first acts of moderation and good sense, was remarkable only as being the father of Charles V. The remainder of his life was worn out in undignified pleasures, and he died suddenly, in the year 1506, at Burgos in Castile, whither he repaired to pay a visit to his father-in-law, the Regent of Spain.

Chapter VI

MARGARET OF AUSTRIA AND CHARLES V. OF SPAIN. 1506-1555

PHILIP being dead, and his wife, Joanna of Spain, having become mad from grief at his loss, after nearly losing her senses from jealousy during his life, the regency of the Netherlands reverted to Maximilian, who immediately named his daughter Margaret governant of the country. This princess, scarcely twenty-seven years of age, had been, like the celebrated Jacqueline of Bavaria, already three times married, and was now again a widow. Her first husband, Charles VIII. of France, had broken from his contract of marriage before its consummation; her second, the Infante of Spain, died immediately after their union; and her third, the Duke of Savoy, left her again a widow after three years of wedded life. She was a woman of talent and courage, and was received with the greatest joy by the people of the Netherlands, whom she governed as peaceably as circumstances allowed. Supported by England, she firmly maintained her authority against the threats of France, and she carried on in person all the negotiations between Louis XII., Maximilian, the Pope Jules II., and Ferdinand of Aragon, for the famous league against Venice. These negotiations took place in 1508, at Cambrai, where Margaret, if we are to credit an expression to that effect in one of her letters, was more than once on the point of having serious differences with the Cardinal of Amboise, minister of Louis XII. But, besides her attention to the interests of her father on this important occasion, she also succeeded in repressing the rising pretensions of Charles of Egmont, and assisted by the interference of the King of France, she obliged him to give up some places in Holland which he illegally held.

From this period the alliance between England and Spain raised the commerce and manufactures of the southern provinces of the Netherlands to a high degree of prosperity, while the northern parts of the country were still kept down by their various dissensions. Holland was at war with the Hanseatic towns. The Frisons continued to struggle for freedom against the heirs of Albert of Saxony. Utrecht was at variance with its bishop, and finally recognized Charles of Egmont as its protector. The consequence of all these circumstances was that the south took the start in a course of prosperity, which was, however, soon to become common to the whole nation.

A new rupture with France, in 1513, united Maximilian, Margaret, and Henry VIII. of England in one common cause. An English and Belgian army, in which Maximilian figured as a spectator (taking care to be paid by England), marched for the destruction of Therouenne, and defeated and dispersed the French at the Battle of the Spurs. But Louis XII. soon persuaded Henry to make a separate peace, and the unconquerable Duke of Guelders made Margaret and the emperor pay the penalty of their success against France. He pursued his victories in Friesland and forced the country to recognize him as stadtholder of Groningen, its chief town; while the Duke of Saxony at length renounced to another his unjust claim on a territory which engulfed both his armies and his treasure.

About the same epoch (1515) young Charles, son of Philip the Fair, having just attained his fifteenth year, was inaugurated Duke of Brabant and Count of Flanders and of Holland, having purchased the presumed right of Saxony to the sovereignty of Friesland. In the following year he was recognized as Prince of Castile, in right of his mother, who associated him with herself in the royal power—a step which soon left her merely the title of queen. Charles procured the nomination of Bishop of Utrecht for Philip, Bastard of Burgundy, which made that province completely dependent on him. But this event was also one of general and lasting importance on another account. This Philip of Burgundy was deeply affected by the doctrines of the Reformation, which had burst forth in Germany. He opposed himself to the observances of the Roman Church, and set his face against the celibacy of the clergy. His example soon influenced his whole diocese, and the new notions on points of religion became rapidly popular. It was chiefly, however, in Friesland that the people embraced the opinions of Luther, which were quite conformable to many of the local customs of which we have already spoken. The celebrated Edzard, Count of Eastern Friesland, openly adopted

THE ATTEMPT OF THE CHURCH TO RESTORE REASON TO JOANNA OF SPAIN
Painting by W. Geets

the Reformation. Erasmus, the famous scholar of Rotterdam, without actually pronouncing himself a disciple of Lutheranism, effected more than all its advocates to further the movement.

We may here remark that during the government of the house of Burgundy the clergy of the Netherlands had fallen into low estate, and the Reformation, therefore, in the first instance found but a slight obstacle in their opposition. Its progress was all at once prodigious. The refusal of the dignity of emperor by Frederick "the Wise," Duke of Saxony, to whom it was offered by the electors, was also an event highly favorable to the new opinions, for Francis I. of France, and Charles, already king of Spain and sovereign of the Netherlands, both claiming the succession to the empire, a sort of interregnum deprived the disputed dominions of a chief who might lay the heavy hand of power on the new-springing doctrines of Protestantism. At length the intrigues of Charles and his pretensions as grandson of Maximilian having caused him to be chosen emperor, a desperate rivalry resulted between him and the French king, which for a while absorbed his whole attention and occupied all his power.

From the earliest appearance of the Reformation the young sovereign of so many states, having to establish his authority at the two extremities of Europe, could not efficiently occupy himself in resisting the doctrines which, despite their dishonoring epithet of heresy, were doomed so soon to become orthodox for a great part of the Continent. While Charles vigorously put down the revolted Spaniards, Luther gained new proselytes in Germany, so that the very greatness of the sovereignty was the cause of his impotency; and while Charles's extent of dominion thus fostered the growing Reformation, his sense of honor proved the safeguard of its apostle. The intrepid Luther, boldly venturing to appear and plead its cause before the representative power of Germany assembled at the Diet of Worms, was protected by the guarantee of the emperor—unlike the celebrated and unfortunate John Huss, who fell a victim to his own confidence and the bad faith of Sigismund, in the year 1415.

Charles was nevertheless a zealous and rigid Catholic, and in the Low Countries, where his authority was undisputed, he proscribed the heretics, and even violated the privileges of the country by appointing functionaries for the express purpose of their pursuit and punishment. This imprudent stretch of power fostered a rising spirit of opposition, for, though entertaining the best disposition to their young prince, the people deeply felt and loudly complained of the government, and thus the germs of a mighty revolution gradually began to be developed.

Charles V. and Francis I. had been rivals for dignity and power, and they now became implacable personal enemies. Young, ambitious, and sanguine, they could not, without reciprocal resentment, pursue in the same field objects essential to both. Charles, by a short but timely visit to England in 1520, had the address to gain over to his cause and secure for his purpose the powerful interest of Cardinal Wolsey, and to make a most favorable impression on Henry VIII.; and thus strengthened, he entered on the struggle against his less wily enemy with infinite advantage. War was declared on frivolous pretexts in 1521. The French sustained it for some time with great valor, but Francis being obstinately bent on the conquest of the Milanais, his reverses secured the triumph of his rival, and he fell into the hands of the imperial troops at the battle of Pavia in 1525. Charles's dominions in the Netherlands suffered severely from the naval operations during the war for the French cruisers having on repeated occasions taken, pillaged, and almost destroyed the principal resources of the herring fishery, Holland and Zealand felt considerable distress, which was still further augmented by the famine which desolated these provinces in 1524.

While such calamities afflicted the northern portion of the Netherlands, Flanders and Brabant continued to flourish, in spite of temporary embarrassments. The Bishop of Utrecht having died, his successor found himself engaged in a hopeless quarrel with his new diocese, already more than half converted to Protestantism; and to gain a triumph over these enemies, even by the sacrifice of his dignity, he ceded to the emperor in 1527 the whole of his temporal power. The Duke of Guelders, who then occupied the city of Utrecht, redoubled his hostility at this intelligence, and after having ravaged the neighboring country he did not lay down his arms till the subsequent year, having first procured an honorable and advantageous peace. One year more witnessed the termination of this long continued state of warfare by the Peace of Cambrai, between Charles and Francis, which was signed on August 5, 1529.

This peace once concluded, the industry and perseverance of

the inhabitants of the Netherlands repaired in a short time the evils caused by so many wars, excited by the ambition of princes, but in scarcely any instance for the interest of the country. Little, however, was wanting to endanger this tranquillity and to excite the people against each other on the score of religious dissension. The sect of Anabaptists, whose wild opinions were subversive of all principles of social order and every sentiment of natural decency, had its birth in Germany, and found many proselytes in the Netherlands. John Bokelszoon, a tailor of Leyden, one of the number, caused himself to be proclaimed king of Jerusalem; and, making himself master of the town of Munster, sent out his disciples to preach in the neighboring countries. Mary, sister of Charles V., and queen dowager of Hungary, the governant of the Netherlands, proposed a crusade against this fanatic, which was, however, totally discountenanced by the states. Encouraged by impunity, whole troops of these sectarians, from the very extremities of Hainault, put themselves into motion for Munster, and notwithstanding the colds of February they marched along, quite naked, according to the system of their sect. The frenzy of these fanatics being increased by persecution, they projected attempts against several towns, and particularly against Amsterdam. They were easily defeated, and massacred without mercy, and it was only by multiplied and horrible executions that their numbers were at length diminished. John Bokelszoon held out at Munster, which was besieged by the bishop and the neighboring princes. This profligate fanatic, who had married no less than seventeen women, had gained considerable influence over the insensate multitude, but he was at length taken and imprisoned in an iron cage—an event which undeceived the greatest number of those whom he had persuaded of his superhuman powers.[1]

The prosperity of the southern provinces proceeded rapidly and uninterruptedly in consequence of the great and valuable traffic of the merchants of Flanders and Brabant, who exchanged their goods of native manufacture for the riches drawn from America and India by the Spaniards and Portuguese. Antwerp had succeeded to Bruges as the general mart of commerce, and was the most opulent town of the north of Europe. The expenses, estimated at 130,000 golden crowns, which this city voluntarily

[1] A very interesting account of the Anabaptist's rule at Munster will be found in S. Baring-Gould, "Freaks of Fanaticism."

incurred to do honor to the visit of Philip, son of Charles V., are cited as a proof of its wealth. The value of the wool annually imported for manufacture into the Low Countries from England and Spain was calculated at 4,000,000 pieces of gold. Their herring fishery was unrivaled, for even the Scotch, on whose coasts these fish were taken, did not attempt a competition with the Zealanders. But the chief seat of prosperity was the south. Flanders alone was taxed for one-third of the general burdens of the state. Brabant paid only one-seventh less than Flanders. So that these two rich provinces contributed thirteen out of twenty-one parts of the general contribution, and all the rest combined but eight. A search for further or minuter proofs of the comparative state of the various divisions of the country would be superfluous.

The perpetual quarrels of Charles V. with Francis I. and Charles of Guelders led, as may be supposed, to a repeated state of exhaustion, which forced the princes to pause till the people recovered strength and resources for each fresh encounter. Charles rarely appeared in the Netherlands, fixing his residence chiefly in Spain, and leaving to his sister the regulation of those distant provinces. One of his occasional visits was for the purpose of inflicting a terrible example upon them. The people of Ghent, suspecting an improper or improvident application of the funds they had furnished for a new campaign, offered themselves to march against the French, instead of being forced to pay their quota of some further subsidy. The government having rejected this proposal, a sedition was the result, at the moment when Charles and Francis had just negotiated one of their temporary reconciliations. On this occasion Charles formed the daring resolution of crossing the kingdom of France to promptly take into his own hands the settlement of this affair—trusting to the generosity of his scarcely reconciled enemy not to abuse the confidence with which he risked himself in his power. Ghent, taken by surprise, did not dare to oppose the entrance of the emperor when he appeared before the walls, and the city was punished with extreme severity. Twenty-seven leaders of the sedition were beheaded, the principal privileges of the city were withdrawn, and a citadel built to hold it in check for the future. Charles met with neither opposition nor complaint. The province had so prospered under his sway, and was so flattered by the greatness of the sovereign, who was born in the town he so severely punished, that his acts of despotic harshness were borne without a murmur. But in the north the people did not view his measures so complacently, and a wide separation in interests and opinions became manifest in the different divisions of the nation.

Yet the Dutch and the Zealanders signalized themselves beyond all his other subjects on the occasion of two expeditions which Charles undertook against Tunis and Algiers. The two northern provinces furnished a greater number of ships than the united quotas of all the rest of his states. But though Charles's gratitude did not lead him to do anything in return as peculiarly favorable to these provinces, he obtained for them nevertheless a great advantage in making himself master of Friesland and Guelders on the death of Charles of Egmont. His acquisition of the latter, which took place in 1543, put an end to the domestic wars of the northern provinces. From that period they might fairly look for a futurity of union and peace, and thus the latter years of Charles promised better for his country than his early ones, though he obtained less success in his new wars with France, which were not, however, signalized by any grand event on either side.

Toward the end of his career Charles redoubled his severities against the Protestants, and even introduced a modified species of inquisition into the Netherlands, but with little effect toward the suppression of the Reformed doctrines. The misunderstandings between his only son Philip and Mary of England, whom he had induced the prince to marry, together with the unamiable disposition of the latter, tormented him almost as much as he was humiliated by the victories of Henry II. of France, the successor of Francis I., and the successful dissimulation of Maurice, Elector of Saxony, by whom he was completely outwitted, deceived, and defeated. Influenced by these considerations, and others, perhaps, which are and must ever remain unknown, Charles at length decided on abdicating the whole of his immense possessions. He chose the city of Brussels as the scene of the solemnity, and the day fixed for it was October 25, 1555. It took place, accordingly, in the presence of the King of Bohemia, the Duke of Savoy, the dowager queens of France and Hungary, the Duchess of Lorraine, and an immense assemblage of nobility from various countries. Charles resigned the empire to his brother Ferdinand, already King of the Romans, and all the rest of his dominions to his son. Soon after the ceremony Charles embarked from Zealand on his voyage to Spain. He retired to the monastery of St. Justus, near the town of Placentia, in Estremadura. He entered this retreat in February, 1556, and died there on September 21, 1558, in the fifty-ninth year of his age.

The whole of the provinces of the Netherlands being now for the first time united under one sovereign, such a junction marks

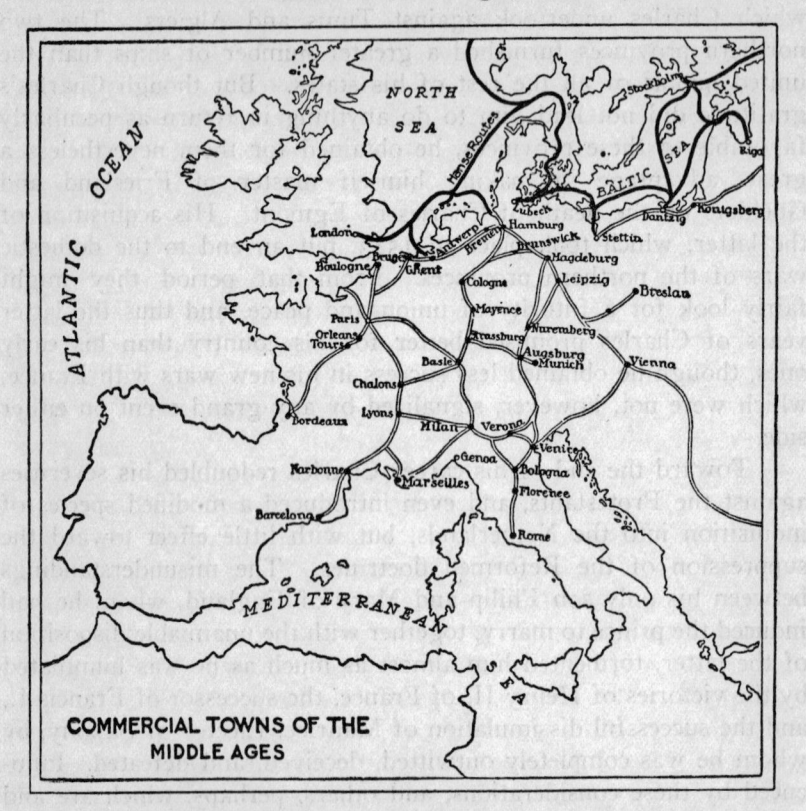

COMMERCIAL TOWNS OF THE MIDDLE AGES

the limits of a distinct epoch in their history. It would be a presumptuous and vain attempt to trace in a compass so confined as ours the various changes in manners and customs which arose in these countries during a period of one thousand years. The amazing increase of commerce was, above all other considerations, the cause of the growth of liberty in the Netherlands. The Reformation opened the minds of men to that intellectual freedom without which political enfranchisement is a worthless privilege. The invention of printing opened a thousand channels to the flow of erudition and talent, and sent them out from the reservoirs of individual possession to fertilize the whole domain of human nature. War, which seems to be an instinct of man, and which particular instances of heroism often raise to the dignity of a passion, was reduced to a science, and made subservient to those great principles of policy in which society began to perceive its only chance of durable good. Manufactures attained a state of high perfection, and went on progressively with the growth of wealth and luxury. The opulence of the towns of Brabant and Flanders was without any previous example in the state of Europe. A merchant of Bruges took upon himself alone the security for the ransom of John the Fearless, taken at the battle of Nicopolis, amounting to 200,000 ducats. A provost of Valenciennes repaired to Paris at one of the great fairs periodically held there, and purchased on his own account every article that was for sale. At a repast given by one of the counts of Flanders to the Flemish magistrates the seats they occupied were unfurnished with cushions. Those proud burghers folded their sumptuous cloaks and sat on them. After the feast they were retiring without retaining these important and costly articles of dress, and on a courtier reminding them of their apparent neglect, the burgomaster of Bruges replied: "We Flemings are not in the habit of carrying away the cushions after dinner!" The meetings of the different towns for the sports of archery were signalized by the most splendid display of dress and decoration. The archers were habited in silk, damask, and the finest linen, and carried chains of gold of great weight and value. Luxury was at its height among women. The queen of Philip the Fair of France, on a visit to Bruges, exclaimed, with astonishment not unmixed with envy, " I thought myself the only queen here; but I see six hundred others who appear more so than I."

The court of Philip the Good seemed to carry magnificence and splendor to their greatest possible height. The dresses of both men and women at this chivalric epoch were of almost incredible expense. Velvet, satin, gold, and precious stones seemed the ordinary materials for the dress of either sex, while the very housings of the horses sparkled with brilliants and cost immense sums. This absurd extravagance was carried so far that Charles V. found himself forced at length to proclaim sumptuary laws for its repression.

The style of the banquets given on grand occasions was regulated on a scale of almost puerile splendor. The banquet of vows given at Lille, in the year 1453, and so called from the obligations entered into by some of the nobles to accompany Philip in a new crusade against the infidels, showed a succession of costly fooleries, most amusing in the detail given by an eye-witness, the minutest of the chroniclers, but unluckily too long to find a place in our pages.[2]

Such excessive luxury naturally led to great corruption of manners and the commission of terrible crimes. During the reign of Philip de Mâle there were committed in the city of Ghent and its outskirts in less than a year above 1400 murders in gambling-houses and other resorts of debauchery. As early as the tenth century the petty sovereigns established on the ruins of the empire of Charlemagne began the independent coining of money, and the various provinces were during the rest of this epoch inundated with a most embarrassing variety of gold, silver, and copper. Even in ages of comparative darkness literature made feeble efforts to burst through the entangled weeds of superstition, ignorance, and war. In the fourteenth and fifteenth centuries history was greatly cultivated, and Froissart, Monstrelet, Olivier de la Marche, and Philip de Comines gave to their chronicles and memoirs a charm of style since their days almost unrivaled. Poetry began to be followed with success in the Netherlands, in the Dutch, Flemish, and French languages, and even before the institution of the Floral Games in France Belgium possessed its chambers of rhetoric (*rederykkamers*), which labored to keep alive the sacred flame of poetry with more zeal than success. In the fourteenth and fifteenth centuries these societies were established in almost every burgh of Flanders and Brabant, the principal towns possessing several at once.

The arts in their several branches made considerable progress in the Netherlands during this epoch. Architecture was greatly cultivated in the thirteenth and fourteenth centuries, most of the cathedrals and town houses being constructed in that age. Their vastness, solidity, and beauty of design and execution make them still speaking monuments of the stern magnificence and finished taste of the times. The patronage of Philip the Good, Charles the

---

[2] See Blok, "History of the Dutch People," vol. iii. p. 283 ff., from the chronicle of Olivier de la Marche.

Rash, and Margaret of Austria brought music into fashion and led to its cultivation in a remarkable degree. The first musicians of France were drawn from Flanders, and other professors from that country acquired great celebrity in Italy for their scientific improvements in their delightful art.

Painting, which had languished before the fifteenth century, sprung at once into a new existence from the invention of John Van Eyck, known better by the name of John of Bruges. His accidental discovery of the art of painting in oil quickly spread over Europe, and served to perpetuate to all time the records of the genius which has bequeathed its vivid impressions to the world. Painting on glass, polishing diamonds, the carillon, lace, and tapestry, were among the inventions which owed their birth to the Netherlands in these ages, when the faculties of mankind sought so many new channels for mechanical development. The discovery of a new world by Columbus and other eminent navigators gave a fresh and powerful impulse to European talent, by affording an immense reservoir for its reward. The town of Antwerp was, during the reign of Charles V., the outlet for the industry of Europe and the receptacle for the productions of all the nations of the earth. Its port was so often crowded with vessels that each successive fleet was obliged to wait long in the Scheldt before it could obtain admission for the discharge of its cargoes. The University of Louvain, that great nursery of science, was founded in 1425, and served greatly to the spread of knowledge, although it degenerated into the hotbed of fierce theological disputes.

Charles V. was the first to establish a solid plan of government instead of the constant fluctuations in the management of justice, police, and finance. He caused the edicts of the various sovereigns and the municipal usages to be embodied into a system of laws, and thus gave stability and method to the enjoyment of the prosperity in which he left his dominions.

The student and philosopher Erasmus belongs to this time. Induced at an early age to enter the monastic life, by the hope of its opportunities for study, he soon distinguished himself as a Latin scholar. Impelled by varying circumstances as well as by his own passion for travel, Erasmus visited many countries of Europe, never remaining long in one place. He journeyed to Italy, and for a while sojourned with Aldus and his companion scholars and printers in Venice, where the accurate scholarship of Erasmus eminently contributed to the Aldine restoration of classical letters. During the Lutheran Revolt Erasmus was suspected of heretical tendencies, but remained faithful to the church, though absolved from his monastic vows since 1516. The attitude he persistently maintained was that of mediator, preaching conciliation on the one hand and moderation on the other. Erasmus died while on a visit to Basel in 1536, but his life had left a permanent impression on the intellectual development of Europe.

PART II

THE STRUGGLE FOR LIBERTY. 1555-1648

Chapter VII

CONDITION OF THE NETHERLANDS UNDER PHILIP II. OF SPAIN. 1555-1566

IT has been shown that the Netherlands were never in a more flourishing state than at the accession of Philip II. The external relations of the country presented an aspect of prosperity and peace. England was closely allied to it by Queen Mary's marriage with Philip; France, fatigued with war, had just concluded with it a five years' truce; Germany, paralyzed by religious dissensions, exhausted itself in domestic quarrels; the other states were too distant or too weak to inspire any uneasiness, and nothing appeared wanting for the public weal. Nevertheless there was something dangerous and alarming in the situation of the Low Countries, but the danger consisted wholly in the connection between the monarch and the people, and the alarm was not sounded till the mischief was beyond remedy.

From the time that Charles V. was called to reign over Spain he may be said to have been virtually lost to the country of his birth. He was no longer a mere duke of Brabant or Limberg, a count of Flanders or of Holland; he was also king of Castile, Aragon, Leon, and Navarre, of Naples, and of Sicily. These various kingdoms had interests evidently opposed to those of the Low Countries, and forms of government far different. It was scarcely to be doubted that the absolute monarch of so many people would look with a jealous eye on the institutions of those provinces which placed limits to his power; and the natural consequence was that he who was a legitimate king in the south soon degenerated into a usurping master in the north.

But during the reign of Charles the danger was in some measure lessened, or at least concealed from public view, by the apparent facility with which he submitted to and observed the laws and customs of his native country. With Philip the case was far different, and the results too obvious. Uninformed on the Belgian character, despising the state of manners, and ignorant of the language, no sympathy attached him to the people. He brought with him to the throne all the hostile prejudices of a foreigner, without one of the kindly or considerate feelings of a compatriot.

Spain, where this young prince had hitherto passed his life, was in some degree excluded from European civilization. A contest of seven centuries between the Mohammedan tribes and the descendants of the Visigoths, cruel like all civil wars, and, like all those of religion, not merely a contest of rulers, but essentially of the people, had given to the manners and feelings of this country a deep stamp of barbarity, as well as a strong religious zeal and a crusading spirit unmatched in Europe. In Spain the Catholic Church had a mighty champion against the rising tide of Protestantism.

The new King of Spain, Philip II., had been bred in a school of superstition and despotism. Isolated by his station and taught to consider himself absolute ruler over his subjects, he was apparently insensible to affection or natural feeling. Of unbounded ambition, great natural ability, and an unsurpassed capacity for work, his suspicious nature, which trusted no man, led him to endeavor to control all the business of his huge empire to the minutest details; and it was this very devotion to an impossible task that aided materially in making his reign disastrous to his country. Above all things he was a devout Catholic to the very extremes of bigotry, feeling himself a chosen instrument for the extirpation of heresy throughout the world.

Nature had endowed Philip with wonderful penetration and unusual self-command. Although ignorant, he had a prodigious instinct of cunning. He lacked courage, but its place was supplied by a harsh obstinacy which never faltered. All the corruptions of intrigue were familiar to him; yet he often failed through a very excess of subtilty and bad faith. Not till recently have we learned that this narrow, cruel, and somber king was also capable of high ideals and noble feelings of belief.

Such was the man who now began that terrible reign which menaced utter ruin to the national prosperity of the Netherlands. His father had already sapped its foundations, by encouraging foreign manners and ideas among the nobility, and dazzling them with the hope of the honors and wealth which he had at his disposal abroad. His severe edicts against heresy had also begun to accustom the nation to religious discords and hatred. Philip soon enlarged on what Charles had commenced, and he unmercifully sacrificed the well-being of a people to the worst objects of his ambition.

Philip had only once visited the Netherlands before his accession to sovereign power. Being at that time twenty-two years of age, his opinions were formed and his prejudices deeply rooted. Everything that he observed on this visit was calculated to revolt both. The frank cordiality of the people appeared too familiar. The expression of popular rights sounded like the voice of rebellion. Even the magnificence displayed in his honor offended his jealous vanity. From that moment he seems to have conceived an implacable aversion to the country, in which alone, of all his vast possessions, he could not display the power or inspire the terror of despotism.

Philip knew well that force alone was insufficient to reduce such a people to slavery. He succeeded in persuading the states to grant him considerable subsidies, some of which were to be paid by instalments during a period of nine years. That was gaining a great step toward his designs, as it superseded the necessity of a yearly application to the three orders, the guardians of the public liberty. At the same time he sent secret agents to Rome, to obtain the approbation of the Pope to his insidious but most effective plan for placing the whole of the clergy in dependence upon the crown. He also kept up the army of Spaniards and Germans which his father had formed on the frontiers of France, and although he did not remove from their employments the functionaries already in place, he took care to make no new appointments to office among the natives of the Netherlands.

In the midst of these cunning preparations for tyranny Philip was suddenly attacked in two quarters at once—by Henry II. of France, and by Pope Paul IV. A prince less obstinate than Philip would in such circumstances have renounced, or at least postponed, his designs against the liberties of so important a part of his dominions as those to which he was obliged to have recourse for aid in support of this double war. But he seemed to make every foreign consideration subservient to the object of domestic aggression which he had so much at heart.

He, however, promptly met the threatened dangers from abroad. He turned his first attention toward his contest with the Pope, and he extricated himself from it with an adroitness that proved the whole force and cunning of his character. Having first publicly obtained the opinion of several doctors of theology that he was justified in taking arms against the Pontiff (a point on which he really had no doubt), he prosecuted the war with the utmost vigor, by the means of the afterwards notorious Duke of Alva, at that time viceroy of his Italian dominions. Paul soon yielded to superior skill and force, and demanded terms of peace, which were granted with a readiness and seeming liberality that astonished no one more than the defeated Pontiff. But Philip's moderation to his enemy was far outdone by his perfidy to his allies. He confirmed Alva's consent to the confiscation of the domains of the Roman nobles who had espoused his cause, and thus gained a stanch and powerful supporter to all his future projects in the religious authority of the successor of St. Peter.

His conduct in the conclusion of the war with France was not less base. His army, under the command of Philibert Emmanuel, Duke of Savoy, consisting of Belgians, Germans, and Spaniards, with a considerable body of English sent by Mary to the assistance of her husband, penetrated into Picardy and gained a complete victory over the French forces. The honor of this brilliant affair, which took place near St. Quentin, was almost wholly due to the Count of Egmont, a Belgian noble who commanded the light cavalry; but the king, unwilling to let any one man enjoy the glory of the day, piously pretended that he owed the entire obligation to St. Lawrence, on whose festival the battle was fought. His gratitude or hypocrisy found a fitting monument in the celebrated convent and palace of the Escurial, which he caused to be built in the form of a gridiron, the instrument of the saint's martyrdom. When the news of the victory reached Charles V. in his retreat, the old warrior inquired if Philip was in Paris, but the cautious victor had no notion of such prompt maneuvering, nor would he risk against foreign enemies the exhaustion of forces destined for the enslavement of his people.

The French in some measure retrieved their late disgrace by the capture of Calais, the only town remaining to England of all its French conquests, and which, consequently, had deeply interested the national glory of each people. In the early part of the year 1558 one of the generals of Henry II. made an irruption into western Flanders, but the gallant Count of Egmont once more proved his valor and skill by attacking and totally defeating the invaders near the town of Gravelines.

A general peace was concluded in April, 1559, which bore the name of Câteau-Cambresis, from that of the place where it was negotiated. Philip secured for himself various advantages in the treaty, but he sacrificed the interests of England by consenting to the retention of Calais by the French king, a cession deeply humiliating to the national pride of his allies; and, if general opinion be correct, a proximate cause of his consort's death. The alliance of France and the support of Rome, the important results of the two wars now brought to a close, were counterbalanced by the well-known hostility of Elizabeth, who had succeeded to the throne of England, and this latter consideration was an additional motive with Philip to push forward the design of consolidating his despotism in the Low Countries.

To lead his already deceived subjects the more surely into the snare, he announced his intended departure on a short visit to Spain; and created for the period of his absence a provisional government, chiefly composed of the leading men among the Belgian nobility. He flattered himself that the states, dazzled by the illustrious illusion thus prepared, would cheerfully grant to this provisional government the right of levying taxes during the temporary absence of the sovereign. He also reckoned on the influence of the clergy in the national assembly, to procure the revival of the edicts against heresy, which he had gained the merit of suspending. These, with many minor details of profound duplicity, formed the principal features of a plan which, if successful, would have reduced the Netherlands to the wretched state of colonial dependence by which Naples and Sicily were held in the tenure of Spain.

As soon as the states had consented to place the whole powers of government in the hands of the new administration for the period of the king's absence, Philip believed his scheme secure, and flattered himself he had established an instrument of durable despotism. The composition of this new government was a masterpiece of political machinery. It consisted of several councils, in which the most distinguished citizens were entitled to a place, in sufficient numbers to deceive the people with a show of representation, but not enough to command a majority, which was sure on any important question to rest with the titled creatures of the court. The edicts against heresy, soon adopted, gave to the clergy an almost unlimited power over the lives and fortunes of the people. But almost all the dignitaries of the church being men of great

Hist. Nat. XIII-6

respectability and moderation, chosen by the body of the inferior clergy, these extraordinary powers excited little alarm. Philip's project was suddenly to replace these ecclesiastics by others of his own choice as soon as the states broke up from their annual meeting, and for this intention he had procured the secret consent and authority of the court of Rome.

To complete the execution of his system, Philip convened an assembly of all the states at Ghent in the month of July, 1559. This meeting of the representatives of the three orders of the state offered no apparent obstacle to Philip's views. The clergy, alarmed at the progress of the new doctrines, gathered more closely round the government of which they required the support. The nobles had lost much of their ancient attachment to liberty, and had become, in various ways, dependent on the royal favor. Many of the first families were then represented by men possessed rather of courage and candor than of foresight and sagacity. That of Nassau, the most distinguished of all, seemed the least interested in the national cause. A great part of its possessions were in Germany and France, where it had recently acquired the sovereign principality of Orange. It was only from the third order—that of the commons—that Philip had to expect any opposition. Already during the war it had shown some discontent, and had insisted on the nomination of commissioners to control the accounts and the disbursements of the subsidies. But it seemed improbable that among this class of men any would be found capable of penetrating the manifold combinations of the king and disconcerting his designs.

Anthony Perrenot de Granvelle, Bishop of Arras, who was considered as Philip's favorite counselor, but who was in reality no more than his docile agent, was commissioned to address the assembly in the name of his master, who spoke only Spanish. His oration was one of cautious deception, and contained the most flattering assurances of Philip's attachment to the people of the Netherlands. It excused the king for not having nominated his only son, Don Carlos, to reign over them in his name, alleging, as a proof of his royal affection, that he preferred giving them as governant a Belgian princess, Madame Marguerite, Duchess of Parma, the natural daughter of Charles V. Fair promises and fine words were thus lavished in profusion to gain the confidence of the deputies.

But notwithstanding all the talent, the caution, and the mystery of Philip and his minister, there was among the nobles one man who saw through all. This individual, endowed with many of the highest attributes of political genius, and preëminently with judgment, the most important of all, entered fearlessly into the contest against tyranny—despising every personal sacrifice for the country's good. Without making himself suspiciously prominent, he privately warned some members of the states of the coming danger. Those in whom he confided did not betray the trust. They spread among the other deputies the alarm, and pointed out the danger to which they had been so judiciously awakened. The consequence was a reply to Philip's demand, in vague and general terms, without binding the nation by any pledge, and a unanimous entreaty that he would diminish the taxes, withdraw the foreign troops, and entrust no official employments to any but natives of the country. The object of this last request was the removal of Granvelle, who was born in Franche-Comté.

Philip was utterly astounded at all this. In the first moment of his vexation he imprudently cried out, " Would ye, then, also bereave me of my place; I, who am a Spaniard?" But he soon recovered his self-command, and resumed his usual mask, expressed his regret at not having sooner learned the wishes of the states, promised to remove the foreign troops within three months, and set off for Zealand, with assumed composure, but filled with fury.

A fleet under the command of Count Horn, the admiral of the United Provinces, waited at Flessingue to form his escort to Spain. At the very moment of his departure, William of Nassau, Prince of Orange and governor of Zealand, waited on him to pay his official respects. The king, taking him apart from the other attendant nobles, recommended him to hasten the execution of several gentlemen and wealthy citizens attached to the newly introduced religious opinions. Then quite suddenly, whether in the random impulse of suppressed rage, or that his piercing glance discovered William's secret feelings in his countenance, he accused him with having been the means of thwarting his designs. " Sire," replied Nassau, " it was the work of the national states." " No!" cried Philip, grasping him furiously by the arm; " it was not done by the states, but by you, and you alone!" [1]

[1] The words of Philip were: "*No, no los estados; ma vos, vos, vos!*" *Vos* thus used in Spanish is a term of contempt, equivalent to *toi* in French.

For some time after Philip's departure the Netherlands continued to enjoy considerable prosperity. From the period of the Peace of Câteau-Cambresis commerce and navigation had acquired new and increasing activity. The fisheries, but particularly that of herring, which alone occupied two thousand boats, became daily more important. While Holland, Zealand, and Friesland made this progress in their peculiar branches of industry, the southern provinces were not less active or successful. Spain and the colonies offered such a mart for the objects of their manufacture that in a single year they received from Flanders fifty large ships filled with articles of household furniture and utensils. The exportation of woolen goods amounted to enormous sums. Bruges alone sold annually to the amount of four million florins of stuffs of Spanish, and as much of English wool; and the least value of the florin then was quadruple its present worth. The commerce with England, though less important than that with Spain, was calculated yearly at twenty-four million florins, which was chiefly clear profit to the Netherlands, as their exportations consisted almost entirely of objects of their own manufacture. Their commercial relations with France, Germany, Italy, Portugal, and the Levant were daily increasing. Antwerp was the center of this prodigious trade. Several sovereigns, among others Elizabeth of England, had recognized agents in that city, equivalent to consuls of the present times, and loans of immense amount were frequently negotiated by them with wealthy merchants, who furnished them, not in negotiable bills or for unredeemable debentures, but in solid gold, and on a simple acknowledgment.[2]

Flanders and Brabant were still the richest and most flourishing portions of the state. Some municipal fêtes given about this time afford a notion of their opulence. On one of these occasions the town of Mechlin sent a deputation to Antwerp, consisting of 326 horsemen dressed in velvet and satin, with gold and silver ornaments; while those of Brussels consisted of 340, as splendidly equipped, and accompanied by 7 huge triumphal chariots and 78 carriages of various construction—a prodigious number for those days.

But the splendor and prosperity which thus sprung out of the national industry and independence, and which a wise or a gen-

[2] Elizabeth's agent was for long the famous Sir Thomas Gresham, founder of the Royal Exchange in London.

erous sovereign would have promoted, or at least have established on a permanent basis, were destined speedily to sink beneath the bigoted fury of Philip II. The new government which he had established was most ingeniously adapted to produce every imaginable evil to the state. The king, hundreds of leagues distant, could not himself issue an order but with a lapse of time ruinous to any object of pressing importance. The governant-general, who represented him, had but a nominal authority, and was forced to follow her instructions, and liable to have all her acts reversed; besides which, she had the king's orders to consult her private council on all affairs whatever, and the council of state on any matter of paramount importance. These two councils, however, contained the elements of a serious opposition to the royal projects, in the persons of the patriot nobles sprinkled among Philip's devoted creatures. Thus the influence of the crown was often thwarted, if not actually balanced, and the proposals which emanated from it were frequently opposed by the governant herself. She, although a woman of masculine appearance and habits, was possessed of no strength of mind. Her prevailing sentiment seemed to be dread of the king, yet she was at times influenced by a sense of justice and by the remonstrances of the well-judging members of her councils. But these were not all the difficulties that clogged the machinery of the state. After the king, the government, and the councils had deliberated on any measure, its execution rested with the provincial governors or stadtholders, or the magistrates of the towns. Almost every one of these, being strongly attached to the laws and customs of the nation, hesitated or refused to obey the orders conveyed to them when those orders appeared illegal. Some, however, yielded to the authority of the government, so it often happened that an edict, which in one district was carried into full effect, was in others deferred, rejected, or violated in a way productive of great confusion in the public affairs.

Philip was conscious that he had himself to blame for the consequent disorder. In nominating the members of the two councils he had overreached himself in his plan for silently sapping the liberty that was so obnoxious to his designs. But to neutralize the influence of the restive members he had left Granvelle the first place in the administration. This man, an immoral ecclesiastic, an eloquent orator, a supple courtier, and a profound politician, was the real head of the government. Next to him among the royalist party was Viglius, president of the privy council, an erudite schoolman, attached less to the broad principles of justice than to the letter of the laws, and thus carrying pedantry into the very councils of the state. Next in order came the Count de Barlaimont, head of the financial department,—a stern and intolerant satellite of the court, and a furious enemy to those national institutions which operated as checks upon fraud. These three individuals formed the governant's privy council. The remaining creatures of the king were mere subaltern agents.

A government so composed could scarcely fail to excite discontent and create danger to the public weal. The first proof of incapacity was elicited by the measures required for the departure of the Spanish troops. The period fixed by the king had already expired, and these obnoxious foreigners were still in the country, living in part on pillage, and each day committing some new excess. Complaints were carried in successive gradation from the government to the council, and from the council to the king. The Spaniards were removed to Zealand, but instead of being embarked at any of its ports, they were detained there on various pretexts. Money, ships, or, on necessity, a wind was professed to be still wanting for their final removal by those who found excuses for delay in every element of nature or subterfuge of art. In the meantime those ferocious soldiers ravaged a part of the country. The simple natives at length declared they would open the sluices of their dikes, preferring to be swallowed by the waters rather than remain exposed to the cruelty and rapacity of those Spaniards. Still the embarkation was postponed, until the king requiring his troops in Spain for some domestic project, they took their long desired departure in the beginning of the year 1561.

The public discontent at this just cause was soon, however, overwhelmed by one infinitely more important and lasting. The Belgian clergy had hitherto formed a free and powerful order in the state, governed and represented by four bishops chosen by the chapters of the towns, or elected by the monks of the principal abbeys. These bishops, possessing an independent territorial revenue, and not directly subject to the influence of the crown, had interests and feelings in common with the nation. But Philip had prepared, and the Pope had sanctioned, a new system of ecclesiastical organization, and the provisional government now put it into execution. Instead of four bishops, it was intended to appoint eighteen, their nominations being vested in the king. By a wily system of trickery the subserviency of the abbeys was also aimed at. The new prelates, on a pretended principle of economy, were endowed with the title of abbots of the chief monasteries of their respective dioceses.

The consequences of this vital blow to the integrity of the national institutions were evident, and the indignation of both clergy and laity was universal. Every legal means of opposition was resorted to, but the people were without leaders, the states were not in session. While the authority of the Pope and the king combined, the reverence excited by the very name of religion, and the address and perseverance of the government, formed too powerful a combination, and triumphed over the national discontents which had not yet been formed in resistance. The new bishops were appointed, Granvelle securing for himself the archiepiscopal see of Mechlin, with the title of Primate of the Low Countries. At the same time Paul IV. put the crowning point to the capital of his ambition by presenting him with a cardinal's hat.

The new bishops were to a man most violent, intolerant, and it may be conscientious, opponents to the wide-spreading doctrines of reform. The execution of the edicts against heresy was confided to them. The provincial governors and inferior magistrates were commanded to aid them with a strong arm, and the most unjust and frightful persecution immediately commenced. But still some of these governors and magistrates, considering themselves not only the officers of the prince, but the protectors of the people, and the defenders of the laws rather than of the faith, did not blindly conform to those harsh and illegal commands. The Prince of Orange, stadtholder of Holland, Zealand, and Utrecht, and the Count of Egmont, governor of Flanders and Artois, permitted no persecutions in those five provinces. But in various places the very people, even when influenced by their superiors, openly opposed it. Catholics as well as Protestants were indignant at the atrocious spectacles of cruelty presented on all sides. The public peace was endangered by isolated acts of resistance, and fears of a general insurrection soon became universal.

Among the various causes of the general confusion, the situation of Brabant gave to that province a peculiar share of suffering. Brussels, its capital, being the seat of government, had no particular chief magistrate, like the other provinces. The executive power was therefore wholly confided to the municipal authorities and the territorial proprietors. But these, though generally patriotic in their views, were divided into a multiplicity of different opinions. Rivalry and resentment produced a total want of union, ended in anarchy, and prepared the way for civil war. William of Orange penetrated the cause, and proposed the remedy in moving for the appointment of a provincial governor. This proposition terrified Granvelle, who saw, as clearly as did his sagacious opponent in the council, that the nomination of a special protector between the people and the government would have paralyzed all his efforts for hurrying on the discord and resistance which were meant to be the plausible excuses for the introduction of arbitrary power. He therefore energetically dissented from the proposed measure, and William immediately desisted from his demand. But he at the same time claimed, in the name of the whole country, the convocation of the states-general. This assembly alone was competent to decide what was just, legal, and obligatory for each province and every town. Governors, magistrates, and simple citizens would thus have some rule for their common conduct, and the government would be at least endowed with the dignity of uniformity and steadiness. The ministers endeavored to evade a demand which they were at first unwilling openly to refuse. But the firm demeanor and persuasive eloquence of the Prince of Orange carried before them all who were not actually bought by the crown, and Granvelle found himself at length forced to avow that an express order from the king forbade the convocation of the states, on any pretext, during his absence.

The veil was thus rent asunder, which had in some measure concealed the deformity of Philip's despotism. The result was a powerful confederacy among all who held it odious, for the overthrow of Granvelle, to whom they chose to attribute the king's conduct. Many of the royalist nobles united for the national cause, and even the governant joined her efforts to theirs, for an object which would relieve her from the tyranny which none felt more than she did. Those who composed this confederacy against the minister were actuated by a great variety of motives. The Duchess of Parma hated him, as a domestic spy robbing her of all real authority; the royalist nobles, as an insolent upstart at every instant mortifying their pride. The Counts Egmont and Horn, with nobler sentiments, opposed him as the author of their country's growing misfortunes. But it is doubtful if any of the confederates except the Prince of Orange clearly saw that they were putting themselves in direct and personal opposition to the king himself. William alone, clear-sighted in politics and profound in his views, knew in thus devoting himself to the public cause the adversary with whom he entered the lists.

This great man, for whom the national traditions still preserve the sacred title of "father" (*Vader-Willem*), and who was in truth not merely the parent, but the political creator of the country, was at this period in his thirtieth year. He already joined the vigor of manhood to the wisdom of age. Brought up under the eye of Charles V., whose sagacity soon discovered his precocious talents, he was admitted to the councils of the emperor, at a time of life which was little advanced beyond mere boyhood. He alone was chosen by this powerful sovereign to be present at the audiences which he gave to foreign ambassadors, which proves that in early youth he well deserved by his discretion the surname of "the Taciturn." It was on the arm of William, then twenty years of age, and already named by him to the command of the Belgian troops, that this powerful monarch leaned for support on the memorable day of his abdication; and he immediately afterwards employed him on the important mission of bearing the imperial crown to his brother Ferdinand, in whose favor he had resigned it. William's grateful attachment to Charles did not blind him to the demerits of Philip. He repaired to France, as one of the hostages on the part of the latter monarch for the fulfillment of the peace of Câteau-Cambresis, and he then learned from the lips of Henry II., who soon conceived a high esteem for him, the measures reciprocally agreed on by the two sovereigns for the oppression of their subjects. From that moment his mind was made up on the character of Philip, and on the part which he had himself to perform; and he never felt a doubt on the first point, nor swerved from the latter.

But even before his patriotism was openly displayed, Philip had taken a dislike to one in whom his shrewdness quickly discovered an intellect of which he was jealous. He could not actually remove William from all interference with public affairs, but he refused him the government of Flanders, and opposed in secret his projected marriage with a princess of the house of Lorraine, which was calculated to bring him a considerable accession of fortune, and consequently of influence.

It is, therefore, possible that William's subsequent conduct was influenced by feelings of personal enmity toward Philip. The secret impulses of conduct can never be known beyond the individual's own breast, but actions, however questionable, must be taken as the tests of motives. In all those of William's illustrious career we can detect none that might be supposed to spring from vulgar or base feelings. If his hostility to Philip was indeed increased by private dislike, he has at least set an example of unparalleled dignity in his method of revenge; but in calmly considering and weighing, without deciding on the question, we see nothing that should deprive William of an unsullied title to pure and perfect patriotism. The injuries done to him by Philip at this period were not of a nature to excite any violent hatred. Enough of public wrong was inflicted to arouse the patriot, but not of private ill to inflame the man. Neither was William of a vindictive disposition. He was never known to turn the knife of an assassin against his royal rival, even when the blade hired by the latter glanced from him reeking with his blood. And though William's enmity may have been kept alive or strengthened by the provocations he received, it is certain that, if a foe to the king, he was, as long as it was possible, the faithful counselor of the crown. He spared no pains to impress on the monarch who hated him the real means for preventing the coming evils, and had not a revolution been absolutely inevitable, it is he who would have prevented it.

Such was the chief of the patriot party, chosen by the silent election of general opinion and by that involuntary homage to genius which leads individuals in the train of those master-minds who take the lead in public affairs. Counts Egmont and Horn and some others largely shared with him the popular favor. The multitude could not for some time distinguish the uncertain and capricious opposition of an offended courtier from the determined resistance of a great man. William was still comparatively young, he had lived long out of the country, and it was little by little that his eminent public virtues were developed and understood.

The great object of immediate good was the removal of Cardinal Granvelle. William boldly put himself at the head of the confederacy. He wrote to the king, conjointly with Counts Egmont and Horn, faithfully portraying the state of affairs. The

Duchess of Parma backed this remonstrance with a strenuous request for Granvelle's dismissal. Philip's reply to the three noblemen was a mere tissue of duplicity to obtain delay, accompanied by an invitation to Count Egmont to repair to Madrid, to hear his sentiments at large by word of mouth. His only answer to the governant was a positive recommendation to use every possible means to disunite and breed ill-will among the three confederate lords. It was difficult to deprive William of the confidence of his friends, and impossible to deceive him. He saw the trap prepared by the royal intrigues, restrained Egmont for a while from the fatal step he was but too well inclined to take, and persuaded him and Horn to renew with him their firm but respectful representations, at the same time begging permission to resign their various employments, and simultaneously ceasing to appear at the court of the governant.

In the meantime every possible indignity was offered to the cardinal by private pique and public satire. Several lords, following Count Egmont's example, had a kind of capuchon or fool's cap embroidered on the liveries of their varlets, and it was generally known that this was meant as a practical parody on the cardinal's hat. The crowd laughed heartily at this stupid pleasantry, and the coarse satire of the times may be judged by a caricature, which was forwarded to the cardinal's own hands, representing him in the act of hatching a nestful of eggs, from which a crowd of bishops escaped, while overhead was the devil *in propriâ personâ,* with the following scroll: "This is my well-beloved son —listen to him!"

Philip, thus driven before the popular voice, found himself forced to the choice of throwing off the mask at once or of sacrificing Granvelle. An invincible inclination for maneuvering and deceit decided him on the latter measure, and the cardinal, recalled but not disgraced, quitted the Netherlands on March 10, 1564. The secret instructions to the governant remained unrevoked, the president, Viglius, succeeded to the post which Granvelle had occupied, and it was clear that the projects of the king had suffered no change.

Nevertheless some good resulted from the departure of the unpopular minister. The public fermentation subsided, the patriot lords reappeared at court, and the Prince of Orange acquired an increasing influence in the council and over the governant, who by his advice adopted a conciliatory line of conduct—a fallacious, but still a temporary hope for the nation. But the calm was of short duration. Scarcely was this moderation evinced by the government when Philip, obstinate in his designs and outrageous in his resentment, sent an order to have the edicts against heresy put into most rigorous execution, and to proclaim throughout the seventeen provinces the decrees of the Council of Trent.

The revolting cruelty of the first edicts were already admitted. As to the decrees of this memorable council—the nineteenth œcumenical council of the Catholic Church—they were received in the Netherlands with general reprobation. Even the new bishops loudly denounced them as unjust innovations, and thus Philip found zealous opponents in those on whom he had reckoned as his most useful tools. The governant was not the less urged to implicit obedience to the orders of the king by Viglius and De Barlaimont, who took upon themselves an almost menacing tone. The duchess assembled a council of state, and asked its advice as to her proceedings. The Prince of Orange at once boldly proposed disobedience to measures which he believed to be fraught with danger to the monarchy and ruin to the nation. The council could not resist his appeal to their best feelings. His proposal that fresh remonstrances should be addressed to the king met with almost general support. The president, Viglius, who had spoken in the opening of the council in favor of the king's orders, was overwhelmed by William's reasoning, and demanded time to prepare his reply. His agitation during the debate, and his despair of carrying the measures against the patriot party, brought on in the night an attack of apoplexy.

It was resolved to dispatch a special envoy to Spain to explain to Philip the views of the council, and to lay before him a plan proposed by the Prince of Orange for forming a junction between the two councils and that of finance, and forming them into one body. The object of this measure was at once to give greater union and power to the provisional government, to create a central administration in the Netherlands, and to remove from some obscure and avaricious financiers the exclusive management of the national resources. The Count of Egmont, chosen by the council for this important mission, set out for Madrid in the month of February, 1565. Philip received him with profound hypocrisy, loaded him with the most flattering promises, sent him back in the utmost elation, and when the credulous count returned to Brussels he found that the written orders, of which he was the bearer, were in direct variance with every word which the king had uttered.

These orders were chiefly concerning the reiterated subject of the persecution to be inflexibly pursued against the religious reformers. Not satisfied with the hitherto established forms of punishment, Philip now expressly commanded that the more revolting

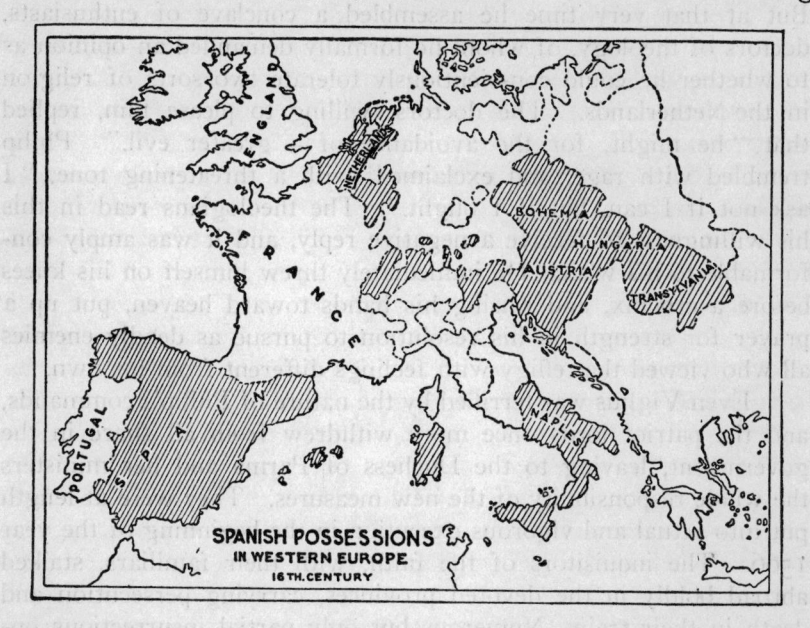

SPANISH POSSESSIONS IN WESTERN EUROPE 16TH. CENTURY

means decreed by his father in the rigor of his early zeal, such as burning, living burial, and the like, should be adopted; and he somewhat more obscurely directed that the victims should be no longer publicly immolated, but secretly destroyed. He endeavored by this vague phraseology to avoid the actual utterance of the word inquisition;[3] but he thus virtually established that tribunal, with attributes still more terrific than even in Spain, for there the condemned had at least the consolation of dying in open day and of displaying

[3] The Spanish Inquisition, which must not be confused with the Ecclesiastical Inquisition, was first appointed by Ferdinand and Isabella. This, although it cannot be considered as a mere State institution, was yet dependent on the temporal rulers. How little the apostolic chair approved of it, is seen from a letter written by Sixtus IV. on August 2, 1483. It should also be remembered that in both Inquisitions the trial only was conducted by the priestly order, the sentence and its execution belonging to secular jurisdiction.

the fortitude which is rarely proof against the horrors of a private execution.

Philip's design of establishing this terrible tribunal had been long suspected by the people of the Netherlands. The expression of those fears had reached him more than once. He as often replied by assurances that he had formed no such project, and particularly to the Count of Egmont during his visit to Madrid. But at that very time he assembled a conclave of enthusiasts, doctors of theology, of whom he formally demanded an opinion as to whether he could conscientiously tolerate two sorts of religion in the Netherlands. The doctors, willing to please, him, replied that "he might, for the avoidance of a greater evil." Philip trembled with rage, and exclaimed, with a threatening tone, " I ask not if I can, but if I ought." The theologians read in this his willingness to receive a negative reply, and it was amply conformable to his wish. He immediately threw himself on his knees before a crucifix, and raising his hands toward heaven, put up a prayer for strength in his resolution to pursue as deadly enemies all who viewed that effigy with feelings different from his own.

Even Viglius was terrified by the nature of Philip's commands, and the patriot lords once more withdrew from all share in the government, leaving to the Duchess of Parma and her ministers the whole responsibility of the new measures. They were at length put into actual and vigorous execution in the beginning of the year 1566. The inquisitors of the faith, with their familiars, stalked abroad boldly in the devoted provinces, carrying persecution and death in their train. Numerous but only partial insurrections opposed their advance. Every district and town became the scene of frightful executions or tumultuous resistance. The converts to the new doctrines multiplied, as usual, under the effects of persecution. "There was nowhere to be seen," says a contemporary author, "the meanest mechanic who did not find a weapon to strike down the murderers of his compatriots." Holland, Zealand, and Utrecht alone escaped from those fast accumulating horrors. William of Nassau was there.

Chapter VIII

COMMENCEMENT OF THE REVOLUTION. 1566

THE governant and her ministers now began to tremble. Philip's favorite counselors advised him to yield to the popular despair, but nothing could change his determination to pursue his bloody game to the last chance. He had foreseen the impossibility of reducing the country to slavery as long as it maintained its tranquillity and that union which forms in itself the elements and the cement of strength. It was from deep calculation that he had excited the troubles, and now kept them alive. He knew that the structure of illegal power could only be raised on the ruins of public rights and national happiness, and the materials of desolation found sympathy in his congenial mind.

And now in reality began the awful revolution of the Netherlands against their lord. In a few years this so lately flourishing and happy nation presented a frightful picture; and in the midst of European peace, prosperity, and civilization, the enthusiasm of one prince drew down on the country he ruled more suffering than it had endured for centuries from the worst effects of its foreign foes.

Up to the present moment the Prince of Orange and the Counts Egmont and Horn, with their partisans and friends, had sincerely desired the public peace, and acted in the common interest of the king and the people. But all the nobles had not acted with the same constitutional moderation. Many of those, disappointed on personal accounts, others professing the new doctrines, and the rest variously affected by manifold motives, formed a body of violent and sometimes of imprudent malcontents. The marriage of Alexander, Prince of Parma, son of the governant, which was at this time celebrated at Brussels, brought together an immense number of these dissatisfied nobles, who became thus drawn into closer connection, and whose national candor was more than usually brought out in the confidential intercourse of society. Politics and patriotism were the common subjects of conversation in the various convivial meetings that took place. Two German nobles, Counts Holle and Schwarzemberg, at that period in the Netherlands, loudly proclaimed the favorable disposition of the princes of the empire toward the Belgians. It was supposed even thus early that negotiations had been opened with several of those sovereigns. In short, nothing seemed wanting but a leader, to give consistency and weight to the confederacy which was as yet but in embryo. This was doubly furnished in the persons of Louis of Nassau and Henry de Brederode. The former, brother of the Prince of Orange, was possessed of many of those brilliant qualities which mark men as worthy of distinction in times of peril. Educated at Geneva, he was passionately attached to the Reformed religion and identified in his hatred the Catholic Church and the tyranny of Spain. Brave and impetuous, he was, to his elder brother, but as an adventurous partisan compared with a sagacious general. He loved William as well as he did their common cause, and his life was devoted to both.

Henry de Brederode, Lord of Vianen and Marquis of Utrecht, was descended from the ancient counts of Holland. This illustrious origin, which in his own eyes formed a high claim to distinction, had not procured him any of those employments or dignities which he considered his due. He was presumptuous and rash, and rather a fluent speaker than an eloquent orator. Louis of Nassau was thoroughly inspired by the justice of the cause he espoused, De Brederode espoused it for the glory of becoming its champion. The first only wished for action, the latter longed for distinction. But neither the enthusiasm of Nassau nor the vanity of De Brederode was allied with those superior attributes required to form a hero.

The confederation acquired its perfect organization in the month of February, 1566, on the 10th of which month its celebrated manifesto was signed by its numerous adherents. The first name affixed to this document was that of Philip de Marnix, Lord of St. Aldegonde, from whose pen it emanated—a man of great talents both as soldier and writer. Numbers of the nobility followed him on this muster-roll of patriotism, and many of the most zealous royalists were among them. This remarkable proclamation of general feeling consisted chiefly in a powerful reprehension of the illegal establishment of the Inquisition in the Low Countries, and a solemn obligation on the members of the confederacy to unite in the common cause against this detested nuisance. Men of all ranks and classes offered their signatures, and several Catholic priests among the rest. The Prince of Orange and the Counts Egmont, Horn, and Meghem declined becoming actual parties to this bold measure, and when the question was debated as to the most appropriate way of presenting an address to the governant, these noblemen advised the mildest and most respectful demeanor on the part of the purposed deputation.

At the first intelligence of these proceedings the Duchess of Parma, absorbed by terror, had no recourse but to assemble hastily such members of the council of state as were at Brussels, and she entreated, by the most pressing letters, the Prince of Orange and Count Horn to resume their places at this council. But three courses of conduct seemed applicable to the emergency—to take up arms, to grant the demands of the confederates, or to temporize and to amuse them with a feint of moderation, until the orders of the king might be obtained from Spain. It was not, however, till after a lapse of four months that the council finally met to deliberate on these important questions, and during this long interval at such a crisis the confederates gained constant accessions to their numbers, and completely consolidated their plans. The opinions in the council were greatly divided as to the mode of treatment toward those whom one party considered as patriots acting in their constitutional rights, and the other as rebels in open revolt against the king. The Prince of Orange and De Barlaimont were the principal leaders and chief speakers at either side. But the reasonings of the former, backed by the urgency of events, carried the majority of the suffrages, and a promised redress of grievances was agreed on beforehand, as the anticipated answer to the coming demands.

Even while the council of state held its sittings, the report was spread through Brussels that the confederates were approaching. And at length they did enter the city, to the amount of some hundreds of the representatives of the first families in the country. On the following day, April 5, 1566, they walked in solemn procession to the palace. Their demeanor was highly imposing, from their mingled air of forbearance and determination. All Brussels thronged out, to gaze and sympathize with this extraordinary spectacle of men whose resolute step showed they were no common suppliants, but whose modest bearing had none of the seditious air

Hist. Nat. xiii-7

of faction. The governant received the distinguished petitioners with courtesy, listened to their detail of grievances, and returned a moderate, conciliatory, but evasive answer.

The confederation, which owed its birth to, and was cradled in social enjoyments, was consolidated in the midst of a feast. The day following this first deputation to the governant De Brederode gave a grand repast to his associates in the Hotel de Cuilemburg. Three hundred guests were present. Inflamed by joy and hope, their spirits rose high under the influence of wine, and temperance gave way to temerity. In the midst of their carousing some of the members remarked that when the governant received the written petition, Count Barlaimont observed to her that "she had nothing to fear from such a band of beggars" (*tas de Gueux*). The fact was that many of the confederates were, from individual extravagance and mismanagement, reduced to such a state of poverty as to justify in some sort the sarcasm. The chiefs of the company being at that very moment debating on the name which they should choose for this patriotic league, the title of *Gueux* was instantly proposed, and adopted with acclamation. The reproach it was originally intended to convey became neutralized, as its general application to men of all ranks and fortunes concealed its effect as a stigma on many to whom it might be seriously applied. Neither were examples wanting of the most absurd and apparently dishonoring nicknames being elsewhere adopted by powerful political parties. "Long live the Gueux!" was the toast given and tumultuously drunk by this mad-brained company; and Brederode, setting no bounds to the boisterous excitement which followed, procured immediately, and slung across his shoulders, a wallet such as was worn by pilgrims and beggars, drank to the health of all present in a wooden cup or porringer, and loudly swore that he was ready to sacrifice his fortune and life for the common cause. Each man passed round the bowl, which he first put to his lips, repeated the oath, and thus pledged himself to the compact. The wallet next went the rounds of the whole assembly, and was finally hung upon a nail driven into the wall for the purpose, and gazed on with such emotions as the emblems of political or religious faith, however worthless or absurd, never fail to inspire in the minds of enthusiasts.

The tumult caused by this ceremony, so ridiculous in itself, but so sublime in its results, attracted to the spot the Prince of

Orange and Counts Egmont and Horn, whose presence is universally attributed by the historians to accident, but which was probably more than mere chance. They entered, and Brederode, who did the honors of the mansion, forced them to be seated, and to join in the festivity.[1] The appearance of three such distinguished personages heightened the general excitement, and the most important assemblage that had for centuries met together in the Netherlands mingled the discussion of affairs of state with all the burlesque extravagance of a debauch. But this frantic scene did not finish the affair. What they resolved on while drunk they prepared to perform when sober. Rallying signs and watchwords were adopted and soon displayed. It was thought that nothing better suited the occasion than the immediate adoption of the costume as well as the title of beggary. In a very few days the city streets were filled with men in gray cloaks, fashioned on the model of those used by mendicants and pilgrims. Each confederate caused this uniform to be worn by every member of his family, and replaced with it the livery of his servants. Several fastened to their girdles or their sword-hilts small wooden drinking-cups, clasp-knives, and other symbols of the begging fraternity, while all soon wore on their breasts a medal of gold or silver, representing on one side the effigy of Philip, with the words, " Faithful to the king "; and on the reverse, two hands clasped, with the motto, " *Jusqu'à la besace* " (Even to the wallet). From this origin arose the application of the word *Gueux* in its political sense as common to all the inhabitants of the Netherlands who embraced the cause of the Reformation and took up arms against their tyrant. Having presented two subsequent remonstrances to the governant, and obtained some consoling promises of moderation, the chief confederates quitted Brussels, leaving several directors to sustain their cause in the capital, while they themselves spread into the various provinces, exciting the people to join the legal and constitutional resistance with which they were resolved to oppose the march of bigotry and despotism.

[1] The following is Egmont's account of their conduct. "We drank a single glass of wine each, to shouts of 'Long live the king! long live the Gueux!' It was the first time I had heard the confederacy so named, and I avow that it displeased me; but the times were so critical that people were obliged to tolerate many things contrary to their inclinations, and I believed myself on this occasion to act with perfect innocence."—*Procès criminal du Comte d'Egmont.*

A new form of edict was now decided on by the governant and her council, and after various insidious and illegal but successful tricks, the consent of several of the provinces was obtained to the adoption of measures that, under a guise of comparative moderation, were little less abominable than those commanded by the king. These were formally signed by the council and dispatched to Spain to receive Philip's sanction, and thus acquire the force of law. The embassy to Madrid was confided to the Marquis of Bergen and the Baron de Montigny, the latter of whom was brother to Count Horn, and had formerly been employed on a like mission. Montigny appears to have had some qualms of apprehension in undertaking this new office. His good genius seemed for a while to stand between him and the fate which awaited him. An accident which happened to his colleague allowed an excuse for retarding his journey. But the governant urging him away, he set out, and reached his destination, not to defend the cause of his country at the foot of the throne, but to perish a victim to his patriotism.

The situation of the patriot lords was at this crisis peculiarly embarrassing. The conduct of the confederates was so essentially tantamount to open rebellion that the Prince of Orange and his friends found it almost impossible to preserve a neutrality between the court and the people. All their wishes urged them to join at once in the public cause, but they were restrained by a lingering sense of loyalty to the king, whose employments they still held, and whose confidence they were, therefore, nominally supposed to share. They seemed reduced to the necessity of coming to an explanation, and, perhaps, a premature rupture with the government, of joining in the harsh measures it was likely to adopt against those with whose proceedings they sympathized, or, as a last alternative, to withdraw, as they had done before, wholly from all interference in public affairs. Still their presence in the council of state was, even though their influence had greatly decreased, of vast service to the patriots, in checking the hostility of the court; and the confederates, on the other hand, were restrained from acts of open violence by fear of the disapprobation of these their best and most powerful friends. Be their individual motives or reasoning what they might, they at length adopted the alternative above alluded to, and resigned their places. Count Horn retired to his estates, Count Egmont repaired to Aix-la-Chapelle, under the pretext of being ordered thither by his physicians, and the Prince of Orange remained for a while at Brussels.

In the meanwhile the confederation gained ground every day. Its measures had totally changed the face of affairs in all parts of the nation. The general discontent now acquired stability, and consequent importance. The chief merchants of many of the towns enrolled themselves in the patriot band. Many active and ardent minds, hitherto withheld by the doubtful construction of the association, now freely entered into it when it took the form of union and respectability. Energy, if not excess, seemed legitimatized. The vanity of the leaders was flattered by the consequence they acquired, and weak minds gladly embraced an occasion of mixing with those whose importance gave both protection and concealment to their insignificance.

An occasion so favorable for the rapid promulgation of the new doctrines was promptly taken advantage of by the French Huguenots and their Protestant brethren of Germany. The disciples of Reform poured from all quarters into the Low Countries, and made prodigious progress, with all the energy of proselytes, and too often with the fury of fanatics. The three principal sects into which the reformers were divided were those of the Anabaptists, the Calvinists, and the Lutherans. The first and least numerous were chiefly established in Friesland. The second were spread over the eastern provinces. Their doctrines being already admitted into some kingdoms of the north, they were protected by the most powerful princes of the empire. The third, and by far the most numerous and wealthy, abounded in the southern provinces, and particularly in Flanders. They were supported by the zealous efforts of French, Swiss, and German ministers, and their dogmas were nearly the same with those of the established religion of England. The city of Antwerp was the central point of union for the three sects, but the only principle they held in common was their hatred against Catholicism, the Inquisition, and Spain.

The government had now issued orders to the chief magistrates to proceed with moderation against the heretics, orders which were obeyed in their most ample latitude by those to whose sympathies they were so congenial. Until then the Protestants were satisfied to meet by stealth at night, but under this negative protection of the authorities they now boldly assembled in public. Field preachings commenced in Flanders, and the minister who first set this example was Herman Stryker, a converted monk, a native of Overyssel, a powerful speaker, and a bold enthusiast. He soon drew together an audience of seven thousand persons. A furious magistrate rushed among this crowd and hoped to disperse them sword in hand, but he was soon struck down, severely wounded, with a shower of stones. Irritated and emboldened by this rash attempt, the Protestants assembled in still greater numbers near Alost, but on this occasion they appeared with poniards, guns, and halberds. They intrenched themselves under the protection of wagons and all sorts of obstacles to a sudden attack, placed outposts and videttes, and thus took the field in the doubly dangerous aspect of fanaticism and war. Similar assemblies soon spread over the whole of Flanders, inflamed by the exhortations of Stryker and another preacher, called Peter Dathen, of Poperingue. It was calculated that fifteen thousand men attended at some of these preachings, while a third apostle of Calvinism, Ambrose Ville, a Frenchman, successfully excited the inhabitants of Tournai, Valenciennes and Antwerp to form a common league for the promulgation of their faith. The sudden appearance of De Brederode at the latter place decided their plan, and gave the courage to fix on a day for its execution. An immense assemblage simultaneously quitted the three cities at a preconcerted time, and when they united their forces at the appointed rendezvous the preachings, exhortations, and psalm-singing commenced, under the auspices of several Huguenots and German ministers, and continued for several days in all the zealous extravagance which may be well imagined to characterize such a scene.

The citizens of Antwerp were terrified for the safety of the place, and courier after courier was dispatched to the governant at Brussels to implore her presence. The duchess, not daring to take such a step without the authority of the king, sent Count Meghem as her representative, with proposals to the magistrates to call out the garrison. The populace soon understood the object of this messenger, and assailing him with a violent outcry, forced him to fly from the city. Then the Calvinists petitioned the magistrates for permission to openly exercise their religion, and for the grant of a temple in which to celebrate its rites. The magistrates in this conjuncture renewed their application to the governant and entreated her to send the Prince of Orange, as the only person capable of saving the city from destruction. The duchess was forced to adopt this bitter alternative, and the prince, after repeated refusals to mix again in public affairs, yielded at length, less to the supplications of the governant than to his own wishes to do another service to the cause of his country. At half a league from the city he was met by De Brederode, with an immense concourse of people of all sects and opinions, who hailed him as a protector from the tyranny of the king and a savior from the dangers of their own excess. Nothing could exceed the wisdom, the firmness, and the benevolence with which he managed all conflicting interests, and preserved tranquillity amid a chaos of opposing prejudices and passions.

From the first establishment of the field preachings the governant had implored the confederate lords to aid her for the re-establishment of order. De Brederode seized this excuse for convoking a general meeting of the associates, which consequently took place at the town of St. Trond, in the district of Liege. Full two thousand of the members appeared on the summons. The language held in this assembly was much stronger and less equivocal than that formerly used. The delay in the arrival of the king's answer presaged ill as to his intentions, while the rapid growth of the public power seemed to mark the present as the time for successfully demanding all that the people required. Several of the Catholic members, still royalists at heart, were shocked to hear a total liberty of conscience spoken of as one of the privileges sought for. The young Count of Mansfield, among others, withdrew immediately from the confederation, and thus the first stone seemed to be removed from this imperfectly constructed edifice.

The Prince of Orange and Count Egmont were applied to, and appointed by the governant, with full powers to treat with the confederates. Twelve of the latter, among whom were Louis of Nassau, De Brederode, and De Kuilenburg, met them by appointment at Duffle, a village not far from Mechlin. The result of the conference was a respectful but firm address to the governant, repelling her accusations of having entered into foreign treaties, declaring their readiness to march against the French troops, should they set foot in the country, and claiming, with the utmost force of reasoning, the convocation of the states-general. This was replied to by an entreaty that they would still wait patiently for twenty-four days, in hopes of an answer from the king, and she sent the Marquis of Bergen in all speed to Madrid, to support

Montigny in his efforts to obtain some prompt decision from Philip. The king, who was then at Segovia, assembled his council, consisting of the Duke of Alva and eight other grandees. The two deputies from the Netherlands attended at the deliberations, which were held for several successive days; but the king was never present. The whole state of affairs being debated with what appears a calm and dispassionate view, considering the firm convictions of this council, it was decided to advise the king to adopt generally a more moderate line of conduct in the Netherlands, and to abolish the Inquisition, at the same time prohibiting under the most awful threats all confederation, assemblage, or public preaching under any pretext whatever.

The king's first care on receiving this advice was to order, in all the principal towns of Spain and the Netherlands, prayer and procession to implore the divine approbation on the resolutions which he had formed. He appeared then in person at the council of state, and issued a decree by which he refused his consent to the convocation of the states-general, and bound himself to take several German regiments into his pay. He ordered the Duchess of Parma, by private letter, to immediately cause to be raised 3000 cavalry and 10,000 foot, and he remitted to her for this purpose 300,000 florins in gold. He next wrote with his own hand to several of his partisans in the various towns, encouraging them in their fidelity to his purposes, and promising them his support. He rejected the adoption of the moderation recommended to him, but he consented to the abolition of the Inquisition in its most odious sense, reëstablishing the Episcopal Inquisition which had been introduced into the Netherlands by Charles V. The people of that devoted country were thus successful in obtaining one important concession from the king and in meeting unexpected consideration from this Spanish council. Whether these measures had been calculated with a view to their failure, it is not now easy to determine; at all events they came too late. When Philip's letters reached Brussels the Iconoclasts or image-breakers were abroad.

It requires no profound research to comprehend the impulse which leads a horde of fanatics to the most monstrous excesses. That the deeds of the Iconoclasts arose from the spontaneous outburst of mere vulgar fury admits of no doubt. The aspersion which would trace those deeds to the meeting of St. Trond, and fix the infamy on the body of nobility there assembled, is scarcely worthy of refutation. The very lowest of the people were the actors as well as the authors of the outrages, which were at once shocking to every friend of liberty, and injurious to that sacred cause. Artois and western Flanders were the scenes of the first exploits of the Iconoclasts. A band of peasants, intermixed with beggars and various other vagabonds, to the amount of about three hundred, urged by fanaticism and those baser passions which animate every lawless body of men, armed with hatchets, clubs, and hammers, forced open the doors of some of the village churches in the neighborhood of St. Omer, and tore down and destroyed not only the images and relics of saints, but those very ornaments which Christians of all sects hold sacred and essential to the most simple rites of religion.

The cities of Ypres, Lille, and other places of importance were soon subject to similar visitations, and the whole of Flanders was in a few days ravaged by furious multitudes, whose frantic energy spread terror and destruction on their route. Antwerp was protected for a while by the presence of the Prince of Orange, but an order from the governant having obliged him to repair to Brussels, a few nights after his departure the celebrated cathedral shared the fate of many a minor temple, and was utterly pillaged. The blind fury of the spoilers was not confined to the mere effigies which they considered the types of idolatry, nor even to the pictures, the vases, the sixty-six altars, and their richly wrought accessories; but it was equally fatal to the splendid organ, which was considered the finest at that time in existence. The rapidity and the order with which this torchlight scene was acted, without a single accident among the numerous doers, has excited the wonder of almost all its early historians. One of them does not hesitate to ascribe the "miracle" to the absolute agency of demons.[2] For three days and nights these revolting scenes were acted, and every church in the city shared the fate of the cathedral, which, next to St. Peter's at Rome, was the most magnificent in Christendom.

Ghent, Tournai, Valenciennes, Mechlin, and other cities were next the theaters of similar excesses, and in an incredibly short space of time above four hundred churches were pillaged in Flanders and Brabant. Zealand, Utrecht, and others of the northern provinces suffered more or less; Friesland, Guelders, and Holland alone escaped, and even the latter but in partial instances.

These terrible scenes extinguished every hope of reconciliation

[2] Strada, the Catholic historian of the revolt.

with the king. An inveterate and interminable hatred was now established between him and the people, for the whole nation was identified with deeds which were in reality only shared by the most base, and were loathsome to all who were enlightened. It was in vain that the patriot nobles might hope or strive to exculpate themselves; they were sure to be held criminal either in fact or by implication. No show of loyalty, no efforts to restore order, no personal sacrifice, could save them from the hatred or screen them from the vengeance of Philip.

The affright of the governant during the short reign of anarchy and terror was without bounds. She strove to make her escape from Brussels, and was restrained from so doing only by the joint solicitations of Viglius and the various knights of the Order of the Golden Fleece, consisting of the first among the nobles of all parties. But, in fact, a species of violence was used to restrain her from this most fatal step, for Viglius gave orders that the gates of the city should be shut and egress refused to anyone belonging to the court. The somewhat less terrified duchess now named Count Mansfield governor of the town, reinforced the garrison, ordered arms to be distributed to all her adherents, and then called a council to deliberate on the measures to be adopted. A compromise with the confederates and the reformers was unanimously agreed to. The Prince of Orange and Counts Egmont and Horn were once more appointed to this arduous arbitration between the court and the people. Necessity now extorted almost every concession which had been so long denied to reason and prudence. The confederates were declared absolved from all responsibility relative to their proceedings. The suppression of the Inquisition, the abolition of the edicts against heresy, and permission for the preachings were simultaneously granted.

The confederates, on their side, undertook to remain faithful to the service of the king, to do their best for the establishment of order, and to punish the Iconoclasts. A regular treaty to this effect was drawn up and executed by the respective plenipotentiaries, and formally approved by the governant, who affixed her sign-manual to the instrument. She only consented to this measure after a long struggle, and with tears in her eyes, and it was with a trembling hand that she wrote an account of these transactions to the king.

Soon after this the several governors repaired to their respective provinces, and their efforts for the reëstablishment of tranquillity were attended with various degrees of success. Several of the ringleaders in the late excesses were executed, and this severity was not confined to the partisans of the Catholic Church. The Prince of Orange and Count Egmont, with others of the patriot lords, set the example of this just severity. John Casambrot, Lord of Beckerzeel, Egmont's secretary, and a leading member of the confederation, put himself at the head of some others of the associated gentlemen, fell upon a refractory band of Iconoclasts near Grammont, in Flanders, and took thirty prisoners, of whom he ordered twenty-eight to be hanged on the spot.

Chapter IX

SURRENDER OF VALENCIENNES AND TYRANNY OF ALVA. 1566-1573

ALL the services just related in the common cause of the country and the king produced no effect on the vindictive spirit of the latter. Neither the lapse of time, the proofs of repentance, nor the fulfillment of their duty could efface the hatred excited by a conscientious opposition to even one design of despotism.

Philip was ill at Segovia when he received accounts of the excesses of the image-breakers and of the convention concluded with the heretics. Dispatches from the governant, with private advices from Viglius, Egmont, Mansfield, Meghem, De Barlaimont, and others, gave him ample information as to the real state of things, and they thus strove to palliate their having acceded to the convention. The emperor even wrote to his royal nephew, imploring him to treat his wayward subjects with moderation, and offered his mediation between them. Philip, though severely suffering, gave great attention to the details of this correspondence, which he minutely examined, and laid before his council of state, with notes and observations taken by himself.

Again the Spanish council appears to have interfered between the people of the Netherlands and the enmity of the monarch, and the offered mediation of the emperor was recommended to his acceptance, to avoid the appearance of a forced concession to the popular will. Philip was also strongly urged to repair to the scene of the disturbances, and a main question of debate was whether he should march at the head of an army or confide himself to the loyalty and good faith of his Belgian subjects. But the pride of Philip was too strong to admit of his taking so vigorous a measure, and all these consultations ended in two letters to the governant. In the first he declared his firm intention to visit the Netherlands in person, refused to convoke the states-general, passed in silence the treaties concluded with the Protestants and the confederates, and finished by a declaration that he would throw himself wholly on the fidelity of the country. In his second letter, meant for the governant alone, he authorized her to assemble the states-general if public opinion became too powerful for resistance, but on no account to let it transpire that he had under any circumstances given his consent.

During these deliberations in Spain the Reformers in the Netherlands amply availed themselves of the privileges they had gained. They erected numerous wooden churches with incredible activity. Young and old, noble and plebeian, of these energetic men, assisted in the manual labors of these occupations, and the women freely applied the produce of their ornaments and jewels to forward the pious work. But the furious outrages of the Iconoclasts had done infinite mischief to both political and religious freedom. Many of the Catholics, and particularly the priests, gradually withdrew themselves from the confederacy, which thus lost some of its most firm supporters. And on the other hand, the severity with which some of its members pursued the guilty offended and alarmed the body of the people, who could not distinguish the shades of difference between the love of liberty and the excess of license.

The governant and her satellites adroitly took advantage of this state of things to sow dissension among the patriots. Autograph letters from Philip to the principal lords were distributed among them with such artful and mysterious precautions as to throw the rest into perplexity and give each suspicions of the other's fidelity. The report of the immediate arrival of Philip had also considerable effect over the less resolute or more selfish, and the confederation was dissolved rapidly under the operations of intrigue, self-interest, and fear. Even the Count Egmont was not proof against the subtle seductions of the wily monarch, whose severe yet flattering letters half-frightened and half-soothed him into a relapse of royalism. But with the Prince of Orange Philip had no chance of success. It is unquestionable that he succeeded through a spy in his pay at the Spanish court in procuring minute intelligence of all that was going on in the king's most secret council. He had from time to time procured copies of the governant's dispatches, but the document which threw the most important light upon the real intentions of Philip was a confidential epistle to the governant from D'Alava, the Spanish minister at Paris, in which he spoke in terms too clear to admit any doubt as to the terrible example which the king was resolved to make among the patriot lords. Bergen and Montigny confirmed this by the accounts they sent home from Madrid of the alteration in the manner with which they were treated by Philip and his courtiers, and the Prince of Orange was more firmly decided in his opinions of the coming vengeance of the tyrant.

William summoned his brother Louis, the Counts Egmont, Horn, and Hoogstraeten, to a secret conference at Dendermonde, and he there submitted to them this letter of Alava's, with others which he had received from Spain, confirmatory of his worst fears. Louis of Nassau voted for open and instant rebellion. William recommended a cautious observance of the projects of government, not doubting that a fair pretext would soon be given to justify the most vigorous overt-acts of revolt; but Egmont at once struck a death-blow to the energetic project of one brother and the cautious amendment of the other, by declaring his present resolution to devote himself wholly to the service of the king, and on no inducement whatever to risk the perils of rebellion. He expressed his perfect reliance on the justice and the goodness of Philip, when once he should see the determined loyalty of those whom he had hitherto had so much reason to suspect, and he exhorted the others to follow his example. The two brothers and Count Horn implored him in their turn to abandon this blind reliance on the tyrant, but in vain. His new and unlooked-for profession of faith completely paralyzed their plans. He possessed too largely the confidence of both the soldiery and the people to make it possible to attempt any serious measure of resistance in which he would not take a part. The meeting broke up without coming to any decision. All those who bore a part in it were expected at Brussels to attend the council of state; Egmont alone repaired thither. The governant questioned him on the object of the conference at Dendermonde. He only replied by an indignant glance, at the same time presenting a copy of Alava's letter.

The governant now applied her whole efforts to destroy the union among the patriot lords. She in the meantime ordered levies of troops to the amount of some thousands, the command of which was given to the nobles on whose attachment she could reckon. The most vigorous measures were adopted. Noircarmes, governor of Hainault, appeared before Valenciennes, which being in the power of the Calvinists, had assumed a most determined attitude of resistance. He vainly summoned the place to submission and to admit a royalist garrison, and on receiving an obstinate refusal he commenced the siege in form. An undisciplined rabble of between 3000 and 4000 Gueux, under the direction of John de Soreas, gathered together in the neighborhood of Lille and Tournai, with a show of attacking these places. But the governor of the former town dispersed one party of them, and Noircarmes surprised and almost destroyed the main body—their leader falling in the action. These were the first encounters of the civil war which raged without cessation for upwards of forty years in these devoted countries, and which is universally allowed to be the most remarkable that ever desolated any isolated portion of Europe. The space which we have already given to the causes which produced this memorable revolution, now actually commenced, will not allow us to do more than rapidly sketch the fierce events that succeeded each other with frightful rapidity.

While Valenciennes prepared for a vigorous resistance, a general synod of the Reformers was held at Antwerp, and De Brederode undertook an attempt to see the governant and lay before her the complaints of this body, but she refused to admit him into the capital. He then addressed to her a remonstrance in writing, in which he reproached her with her violation of the treaties, on the faith of which the confederates had dispersed and the majority of the Protestants laid down their arms. He implored her to revoke the new proclamations, by which she prohibited them from the free exercise of their religion, and above all things he insisted on the abandonment of the siege of Valenciennes, and the disbanding of the new levies. The governant's reply was one of haughty reproach and defiance. The gauntlet was now thrown down, no possible hope of reconciliation remained, and the whole country flew to arms. A sudden attempt on the part of the royalists, under Count Meghem, against Bois-le-duc, was repulsed by 800 men, commanded by an officer named Bomberg, in the immediate service of De Brederode, who had fortified himself in his garrison town of Vienen.

The Prince of Orange maintained at Antwerp an attitude of extreme firmness and caution. His time for action had not yet arrived, but his advice and protection were of infinite importance on many occasions. John de Marnix, Lord of Toulouse, brother of Philip de St. Aldegonde, took possession of Osterweel on the Scheldt, a quarter of a league from Antwerp, and fortified himself in a strong position. But he was impetuously attacked by the Count de Lannoy with a considerable force, and perished, after a desperate defense, with full 1000 of his followers. Three hundred who laid down their arms were immediately after the action butchered in cold blood. Antwerp was on this occasion saved from the excesses of its divided and furious citizens, and preserved from the horrors of pillage, by the calmness and intrepidity of the Prince of Orange. Valenciennes at length capitulated to the royalists, disheartened by the defeat and death of De Marnix, and terrified by a bombardment of thirty-six hours. The governor, two preachers, and about forty of the citizens were hanged by the victors, and the Reformed religion prohibited. Noircarmes promptly followed up his success. Maastricht, Turnhout, and Bois-le-duc submitted at his approach and the insurgents were soon driven from all the provinces, Holland alone excepted. Brederode fled to Germany, where he died the following year.

The govenant showed in her success no small proofs of decision. She and her counselors, acting under orders from the king, were resolved on embarrassing to the utmost the patriot lords, and a new oath of allegiance, to be proposed to every functionary of the state, was considered as a certain means for attaining this object without the violence of an unmerited dismissal. The terms of this oath were strongly opposed to every principle of patriotism and toleration. Count Mansfield was the first of the nobles who took it. The Duke of Arschot, Counts Meghem, Barliamont, and Egmont followed his example. The Counts of Horn, Hoogstraeten, De Brederode, and others refused on various pretexts. Every artifice and persuasion was tried to induce the Prince of Orange to subscribe to this new test, but his resolution had been for some time formed. He saw that every chance of constitutional resistance to tyranny was for the present at an end. The time for petitioning was gone by. The confederation was dissolved. A royalist army was in the field; the Duke of Alva was notoriously approaching at the head of another, more numerous. It was worse than useless to conclude a hollow convention with the governant, of mock loyalty on his part and mock confidence on hers. Many other important considerations convinced William that his only honorable, safe, and wise course was to exile himself from the Netherlands altogether, until more propitious circumstances allowed of his acting openly, boldly, and with effect.

Before he put this plan of voluntary banishment into execution, he and Egmont had a parting interview at the village of Willebroek, between Antwerp and Brussels. Count Mansfield and Berti, secretary to the governant, were present at this memorable meeting. The details of what passed were reported to the confederates by one of their party, who contrived to conceal himself in the chimney of the chamber. Nothing could exceed the energetic warmth with which the two illustrious friends reciprocally endeavored to turn each other from their respective line of conduct; but in vain. Egmont's fatal confidence in the king was not to be shaken, nor was Nassau's penetrating mind to be deceived by the romantic delusion which led away his friend. They separated with most affectionate expressions, and Nassau was even moved to tears. His parting words were to the following effect: " Confide, then, since it must be so, in the gratitude of the king; but a painful presentiment (God grant it may prove a false one!) tells me that you will serve the Spaniards as the bridge by which they will enter the country, and which they will destroy as soon as they have passed over it!"

On April 11, a few days after this conference, the Prince of Orange set out for Germany, with his three brothers and his whole family, with the exception of his eldest son, Philip William, Count of Beuren, whom he left behind a student in the University of Louvain. He believed that the privileges of the college and the franchises of Brabant would prove a sufficient protection to the youth, and this appears the only instance in which William's vigilant prudence was deceived. The departure of the prince seemed to remove all hope of protection or support from the unfortunate Protestants, now left the prey of their implacable tyrant. The confederation of the nobles was completely broken up. The counts of Hoogstraeten, Bergen, and Kuilenburg followed the example of the Prince of Orange and escaped to Germany, and the greater number of those who remained behind took the new oath of allegiance and became reconciled to the government.

This total dispersion of the confederacy brought all the towns of Holland into obedience to the king. But the emigration which immediately commenced threatened the country with ruin. England and Germany swarmed with Dutch and Belgian refugees, and all the efforts of the governant could not restrain the thousands that took to flight. She was not more successful in her attempts to influence the measures of the king. She implored him, in repeated letters, to abandon his design of sending a foreign army into the country, which she represented as being now quite reduced to submission and tranquillity. She added that the mere report of this royal invasion (so to call it) had already deprived the Netherlands of many thousands of its best inhabitants, and that the appearance of the troops would change it into a desert. These arguments, meant to dissuade, were the very means of encouraging Philip in his design. He conceived his project to be now fully ripe for the complete suppression of freedom, and Alva soon began his march.

On May 5, 1567, this celebrated captain, whose reputation was so quickly destined to sink into the notoriety of an executioner, began his memorable march; and on August 22 he, with his two natural sons and his veteran army consisting of about 15,000 men, arrived at the walls of Brussels. The discipline observed on this march was a terrible forewarning to the people of the Netherlands of the influence of the general and the obedience of the troops. They had little chance of resistance against such soldiers so commanded.

Several of the Belgian nobility went forward to meet Alva to render him the accustomed honors and endeavor thus early to gain his good graces. Among them was the infatuated Egmont, who made a present to Alva of two superb horses, which the latter received with a disdainful air of condescension. Alva's first care was the distribution of his troops—several thousand of whom were placed in Antwerp, Ghent, and other important towns, and the remainder reserved under his own immediate orders at Brussels. His approach was celebrated by universal terror, and his arrival was thoroughly humiliating to the Duchess of Parma. He immediately produced his commission as commander-in-chief of the royal armies in the Netherlands, but he next showed her another, which confided to him powers infinitely more extended than any Marguerite herself had enjoyed, and which proved to her that an almost sovereign power over the country was virtually vested in him.

Alva first turned his attention to the seizure of those patriot lords whose pertinacious infatuation left them within his reach.

He summoned a meeting of all the members of the council of state and the knights of the Order of the Golden Fleece, to deliberate on matters of great importance. Counts Egmont and Horn attended, among many others; and at the conclusion of the council they were both arrested, as was also Van Straeten, burgomaster of Antwerp, and Casambrot, Egmont's secretary. The young Count of Mansfield appeared for a moment at this meeting, but, warned by his father of the fate intended him, as an original member of the confederation, he had time to fly. The Count of Hoogstraeten was happily detained by illness, and thus escaped the fate of his friends. Egmont and Horn were transferred to the citadel of Ghent, under an escort of 3000 Spanish soldiers. Several other persons of the first families were arrested, and those who had originally been taken in arms were executed without delay.

The next measures of the new governor were the reëstablishment of the Inquisition, the promulgation of the decrees of the Council of Trent, the revocation of the Duchess of Parma's edicts, and the royal refusal to recognize the terms of her treaties with the Protestants. He immediately established a special tribunal, composed of twelve members, with full powers to inquire into and pronounce judgment on every circumstance connected with the late troubles. He named himself president of this council, and appointed a Spaniard, named Vargas, as vice president—a wretch of the most diabolical cruelty. Several others of the judges were also Spaniards, in direct infraction of the fundamental laws of the country. This council, immortalized by its infamy, was named by the new governor (for so Alva was in fact, though not yet in name) the Council of Troubles. By the people it was soon designated the Council of Blood. In its atrocious procedings no respect was paid to titles, contracts, or privileges, however sacred. Its judgments were without appeal. Every subject of the state was amenable to its summons—clergy and laity, the first individuals of the country, as well as the most wretched outcasts of society. Its decrees were passed with outrageous rapidity and contempt of form. Contumacy was punished with exile and confiscation. Those who, strong in innocence, dared to brave a trial were lost without resource. The accused were forced to its bar without previous warning. Many a wealthy citizen was dragged to trial four leagues' distance, tied to a horse's tail. The number of victims was appalling. On one occasion the town of Valenciennes alone saw fifty-five of its citizens fall by the hands of the executioner. Hanging, beheading, quartering, and burning were the every-day spectacles. The enormous confiscations only added to the thirst for gold and blood by which Alva and his satellites were parched. History offers no example of parallel horrors, for while party vengeance on other occasions has led to scenes of fury and terror, they arose in this instance from the vilest cupidity and the most cold-blooded cruelty.

After three months of such atrocity Alva, fatigued rather than satiated with butchery, resigned his hateful functions wholly into the hands of Vargas, who was chiefly aided by the members Delrio and Dela Torre. One of these wretches, called Hesselts, used at length to sleep during the mock trials of the already doomed victims, and as often as he was roused up by his colleagues he used to cry out mechanically, "To the gibbet! to the gibbet!" so familiar was his tongue with the sounds of condemnation.

The despair of the people may be imagined from the fact that until the end of the year 1567 their only consolation was the prospect of the king's arrival! He never dreamed of coming. The good Duchess of Parma—for so she was in comparison with her successor—was not long left to oppose the feeble barrier of her prayers between Alva and his victims. She demanded her dismissal from the nominal dignity, which was now but a title of disgrace. Philip granted it readily, accompanied by a hypocritical letter, a present of 30,000 crowns, and the promise of an annual pension of 20,000 more. She left Brussels in the month of April, 1568, raised to a high place in the esteem and gratitude of the people, less by any actual claims from her own conduct than by its fortuitous contrast with the infamy of her successor. She retired to Italy, and died at Naples in the month of February, 1586.

Ferdinand Alvarez de Toledo, Duke of Alva, was of a distinguished family in Spain, and even boasted of his descent from one of the Moorish monarchs who had reigned in the insignificant kingdom of Toledo. When he assumed the chief command in the Netherlands he was sixty years of age, having grown old and obdurate in pride, ferocity, and avarice. His deeds must stand instead of a more detailed portrait, which, to be thoroughly striking, should be traced with a pen dipped in blood. He was a fierce and clever soldier, brought up in the school of Charles V., and trained to his profession in the wars of that monarch in Germany, and subsequently in that of Philip II. against France. In addition to the horrors acted by the Council of Blood, Alva committed many deeds of collateral but minor tyranny; among others, he issued a decree forbidding, under severe penalties, any inhabitant of the country to marry without his express permission. His furious edicts against emigration were attempted to be enforced in vain. Elizabeth of England opened all the ports of her kingdom to the Flemish refugees who carried with them those abundant stores of manufacturing knowledge which she wisely knew to be the elements of national wealth.

Alva soon summoned the Prince of Orange, his brothers, and all the confederate lords to appear before the council and answer to the charge of high treason. The prince gave a prompt and contemptuous answer, denying the authority of Alva and his council, and acknowledging for his judges only the emperor, whose vassal he was, or the King of Spain in person, as president of the Order of the Golden Fleece. The other lords made replies nearly similar. The trials of each were, therefore, proceeded on, by contumacy, confiscation of property being an object almost as dear to the tyrant viceroy as the death of his victims. Judgments were promptly pronounced against those present or absent, alive or dead. Witness the case of the unfortunate Marquis of Bergen, who had previously expired at Madrid, and his equally ill-fated colleague in the embassy, the Baron Montigny, who, for a while imprisoned at Segovia, was soon after secretly beheaded, on the base pretext of former disaffection.

The departure of the Duchess of Parma having left Alva undisputed as well as unlimited authority, he proceeded rapidly in his terrible career. The Count of Beuren was seized at Louvain and sent prisoner to Madrid, and wherever it was possible to lay hands on a suspected patriot the occasion was not neglected. It would be a revolting task to enter into a minute detail of all the horrors committed and impossible to record the names of the victims who so quickly fell before Alva's insatiate cruelty. The people were driven to frenzy. Bands of wretches fled to the woods and marshes, whence, half famished and perishing for want, they revenged themselves with pillage and murder. Pirates infested and ravaged the coast, and thus, from both sea and land, the whole extent of the Netherlands was devoted to carnage and ruin. The chronicles of Brabant and Holland, chiefly written in Flemish by contemporary authors, abound in thrilling details of the horrors of this general desolation, with long lists of those who perished. Suffice it to say, that on the recorded boast of Alva himself he caused 18,000 inhabitants of the Low Countries to perish by the hands of the executioner during his less than six years' sovereignty in the Netherlands.

The most important of these tragical scenes was now soon to be acted. The Counts Egmont and Horn, having submitted to some previous interrogatories by Vargas and others, were removed from Ghent to Brussels on June 3 under a strong escort. The following day they passed through the mockery of a trial before the Council of Blood; and on the 5th they were both beheaded in the great square of Brussels in the presence of Alva, who gloated on the spectacle from a balcony that commanded the execution. The same day Van Straelen and Casambrot shared the fate of their illustrious friends, in the castle of Vilvorde, with many others whose names only find a place in the local chronicles of the times. Egmont and Horn met their fate with the firmness expected from their well-proved courage.

These judicial murders excited in the Netherlands an agitation without bounds. It was no longer hatred or aversion that filled men's minds, but fury and despair. The outbreaking of a general revolt was hourly watched for. The foreign powers without exception expressed their disapproval of these executions. The Emperor Maximilian II. and all the Catholic princes condemned them. The former sent his brother expressly to the King of Spain, to warn him that without a cessation of his cruelties he could not restrain a general declaration from the members of the empire, which would, in all likelihood, deprive him of every acre of land in the Netherlands. The princes of the Protestant states held no limits to the expression of their disgust and resentment, and everything seemed now ripe, both at home and abroad, to favor the enterprise on which the Prince of Orange was determined to risk his fortune and his life. But his principal resources were to be found in his genius and courage and in the heroic devotion partaken by his whole family in the cause of their country. His brother, Count John, advanced him a considerable sum of money, the Flemings and Hollanders in England and elsewhere subscribed largely, and the prince himself, after raising loans in every possible way on his private means, sold his jewels, his plate, and even the furniture of his houses, and threw the amount into the common fund.

Two remarkable events took place this year in Spain and added to the general odium entertained against Philip's character throughout Europe. The first was the death of his son, Don Carlos, who, suspected by his father of treason, was imprisoned and either committed suicide or was poisoned by Philip's orders; the other was the death of the queen. Universal opinion assigned poison as the cause, and Charles IX. of France, her brother, who loved her with great tenderness, seems to have joined in this belief. Astonishment and horror filled all minds on the double *dénouément* of this romantic tragedy, and the enemies of the tyrant reaped all the advantages it was so well adapted to produce.

The Prince of Orange, having raised a considerable force in Germany, now entered on the war with all the well-directed energy by which he was characterized. The Queen of England, the French Huguenots, and the Protestant princes of Germany all lent him their aid in money or in men, and he opened his first campaign with great advantage. He formed his army into four several corps, intending to enter the country on as many different points, and by a sudden irruption on that most vulnerable to rouse at once the hopes and the coöperation of the people. His brothers Louis and Adolphus, at the head of one of these divisions, penetrated into Groningen, and there commenced the contest. The Count of Aremberg, governor of this province, assisted by the Spanish troops under Gonsalvo de Bracamonte, quickly opposed the invaders. They met on May 24, near the abbey of Heiligerlee, which gave its name to the battle, and after a short contest the royalists were defeated with great loss. The Count of Aremberg and Adolphus of Nassau encountered in single combat and fell by each other's hands. The victory was dearly purchased by the loss of this gallant prince, the first of his illustrious family who have on so many occasions freely shed their blood for the freedom and happiness of the country so emphatically called their own.

Alva immediately hastened to the scene of this first action, and soon forced Count Louis to another at a place called Jemmingen, near the town of Emden, on July 21. Their forces were nearly equal, about 14,000 at either side, but all the advantage of discipline and skill was in favor of Alva, and the consequence was the total rout of the patriots with a considerable loss in killed and the whole of the cannon and baggage. The entire province of Friesland was thus again reduced to obedience, and Alva hastened back to Brabant to make head against the Prince of Orange. The latter had now under his command an army of 28,000 men—an imposing force in point of numbers, being nearly double that which his rival was able to muster. He soon made himself master of the towns of Tongres and St. Trond, and the whole province of Liege was in his power. He advanced boldly against Alva, and for several months did all that maneuvering could do to force him to a battle. But the wily veteran knew his trade too well; he felt sure that in time the prince's force would disperse for want of pay and supplies, and he managed his resources so ably that with little risk and scarcely any loss he finally succeeded in his object. In the month of October the prince found himself forced to disband his large but undisciplined force, and he retired into France to recruit his funds and consider on the best measures for some future enterprise.

The insolent triumph of Alva knew no bounds. The rest of the year was consumed in new executions. The hotel of Kuilenburg, the early cradle of De Brederode's confederacy, was razed to the ground, and a pillar erected on the spot commemorative of the deed; while Alva, resolved to erect a monument of his success as well as of his hate, had his own statue in brass, formed of the cannons taken at Jemmingen, set up in the citadel of Antwerp, with various symbols of power and an inscription of inflated pride.

The following year was ushered in by a demand of unwonted and extravagant rapacity, the establishment of two taxes on property, personal and real, to the amount of the hundredth penny (or denier) on each kind, and at every transfer or sale ten per cent. on personal and five per cent. for real property. These taxes were based on a similar system long in use in Spain. They were not new in the Netherlands, but had never before been really enforced. The states-general, of whom this demand was made, were unanimous in their opposition, as well as the ministers, but particularly De Barlaimont and Viglius. Alva was so irritated that he even menaced the venerable president of the council, but could not succeed in intimidating him. He obstinately persisted in his design for a considerable period, resisting arguments and prayers, and even the more likely means tried for softening his cupidity, by furnishing him with sums from other sources equivalent to those which the new taxes were calculated to produce. To his repeated threats against Viglius the latter replied that "he was convinced the king would not condemn him unheard, but that at any rate his gray hairs saved him from any ignoble fear of death."

A deputation was sent from the states-general to Philip, explaining the impossibility of persevering in the attempted taxes, which were incompatible with every principle of commercial liberty. But Alva would not abandon his design till he had forced every province into resistance, and the king himself commanded him to desist. The northern provinces had hitherto suffered comparatively little from Alva's rule, but the attempts of the duke to enforce the obnoxious taxes, so ruinous to all commercial enterprise, did much to force them into open revolt. The events of this and the following year (1570) may be shortly summed up, none of any striking interest or eventual importance having occurred. The sufferings of the country were increasing from day to day under the intolerable tyranny which bore it down. The patriots attempted nothing on land, but their naval force began from this time to acquire that consistency and power which was so soon to render it the chief means of resistance and the great source of wealth. The privateers or corsairs which began to swarm from every port in Holland and Zealand, and which found refuge in all those of England, sullied many gallant exploits by instances of culpable excess; so much so that the Prince of Orange was forced to withdraw the command which he had delegated to the Lord of Dolhain, and to replace him by Gislain de Fiennes, for already several of the exiled nobles and ruined merchants of Antwerp and Amsterdam had joined these bold adventurers, and purchased or built, with the remnant of their fortunes, many vessels in which they carried on a most productive warfare against Spanish commerce through the whole extent of the English Channel, from the mouth of the Ems to the harbor of La Rochelle.

One of those frightful inundations to which the northern provinces were so constantly exposed occurred this year, carrying away the dikes and destroying lives and property to a considerable amount. In Friesland alone 20,000 men were victims to this calamity. But no suffering could affect the inflexible sternness of the Duke of Alva, and to such excess did he carry his persecution that Philip himself began to be discontented and thought his representative was overstepping the bounds of delegated tyranny. He even reproached him sharply in some of his dispatches. The governor replied in the same strain, and such was the effect of this correspondence that Philip resolved to remove him from his command. But the king's marriage with Anne of Austria, daughter of the Emperor Maximilian, obliged him to defer his intentions for a while, and he at length named John de la Cerda, Duke of Medina-Celi, for Alva's successor. Upward of a year, however, elapsed before this new governor was finally appointed, and he made his appearance on the coast of Flanders with a considerable fleet on July 11, 1572. He was afforded on this very day a specimen of the sort of people he came to contend with, for his fleet was suddenly attacked by that of the patriots, and many of his vessels burned and taken before his eyes, with their rich cargoes and considerable treasures which were intended for the service of the state.

The Duke of Medina-Celi proceeded rapidly to Brussels, where he was ceremoniously received by Alva, who, however, refused to resign the government, under the pretext that the term of his appointment had not expired, and that he was resolved first to completely suppress all symptoms of revolt in the northern provinces. He succeeded in effectually disgusting La Cerda, who almost immediately demanded and obtained his own recall to Spain. Alva, left once more in undisputed possession of his power, turned it with increased vigor into new channels of oppression. He was soon again employed in efforts to effect the levying of his favorite taxes, and such was the resolution of the tradesmen of Brussels, that sooner than submit they almost universally closed their shops altogether. Alva, furious at this measure, caused sixty of the citizens to be seized, and ordered them to be hanged opposite their own doors. The gibbets were actually erected, when, on the very morning of the day fixed for the executions, he received dispatches that wholly disconcerted him and he stopped their completion.

To avoid an open rupture with Spain, the Queen of England had just at this time interdicted the Dutch and Flemish privateers from taking shelter in her ports. William de Lumey, Count de la Marck, had now the chief command of this adventurous force. He was distinguished by an inveterate hatred against the Spaniards, and had made a wild and romantic vow never to cut his hair or beard till he had avenged the murders of Egmont and Horn.

Driven out of the harbors of England, he resolved on some desperate enterprise, and on April 1 he succeeded in surprising the little town of Briel, in the island of Voorn, situated between Zealand and Holland. This insignificant place acquired great celebrity from this event, which may be considered the first successful step toward the establishment of liberty and the republic.

Alva was confounded by the news of this exploit, but with his usual activity he immediately turned his whole attention toward the point of greatest danger. His embarrassment, however, became every day more considerable. Lumey's success was the signal of a general revolt. In a few days every town in Holland and Zealand declared for liberty, with the exception of Amsterdam and Middelburg, where the Spanish garrisons were too strong for the people to attempt their expulsion.

The Prince of Orange, who had been on the watch for a favorable moment, now entered Brabant at the head of 24,000 men, composed of French, German, and English, and made himself master of several important places, while his indefatigable brother Louis, with a minor force, suddenly appeared in Hainault, and, joined by a large body of French Huguenots under De Genlis, he seized on Mons, the capital of the province, on May 25.

Alva turned first toward the recovery of this important place, and gave the command of the siege to his son, Frederic of Toledo, who was assisted by the counsels of Noircarmes and Vitelli; but Louis of Nassau held out for upwards of three months, and only surrendered on an honorable capitulation in the month of September, his French allies having been first entirely defeated, and their brave leader, De Genlis, taken prisoner. The Prince of Orange had in the meantime secured possession of Louvain, Ruremonde, Mechlin, and other towns, carried Termonde and Oudenarde by assault, and made demonstrations which seemed to court Alva once more to try the fortune of the campaign in a pitched battle. But such were not William's real intentions, nor did the cautious tactics of his able opponent allow him to provoke such a risk. He, however, ordered his son Frederic to march with all his force into Holland, and he soon undertook the siege of Haarlem. By the time that Mons fell again into the power of the Spaniards sixty-five towns and their territories, chiefly in the northern provinces, had thrown off the yoke. The single port of Flushing contained one hundred and fifty vessels, well armed and equipped, and from that epoch may be dated the rapid growth of the first naval power in Europe, with the single exception of Great Britain.

It is here worthy of remark that all the horrors of which the people of Flanders were the victims, and in their full proportion, had not the effect of exciting them to revolt, but they rose up with fury against the payment of the new taxes. They sacrificed everything sooner than pay these unjust exactions. The next important event in these wars was the siege of Haarlem, before which place the Spaniards were arrested in their progress for seven months, and which they at length succeeded in taking with a loss of 10,000 men.

The details of this memorable siege are calculated to arouse every feeling of pity for the heroic defenders and of execration against the cruel assailants. A widow, named Catherine van Hasselaar, gained a niche in history by her remarkable valor at the head of a battalion of 300 of her townswomen, who bore a part in all the labors and perils of the siege. After the surrender, and in pursuance of Alva's common system, his son caused the governor and the other chief officers to be beheaded, and upwards of 1200 of the worn-out garrison and burghers were either put to the sword or tied two-and-two and drowned in the lake which gives its name to the town. Tergoes in South Beveland, Mechlin, Naerden, and other towns were about the same period the scenes of gallant actions, and of subsequent cruelties of the most revolting nature as soon as they fell into the power of the Spaniards. Horrors like these were sure to force reprisals on the part of the maddened patriots. De la Marck carried on his daring exploits with a cruelty which excited the indignation of the Prince of Orange, by whom he was removed from his command. The contest was for a while prosecuted with a decrease of vigor proportioned to the serious losses on both sides. Money and the munitions of war began to fail, and though the Spaniards succeeded in taking The Hague, they were repulsed before Alkmaar with great loss, and their fleet was almost entirely destroyed in a naval combat on the Zuyder Zee. The Count Bossu, their admiral, was taken in this fight, with about 300 of his best sailors.

Holland was now from one end to the other the theater of the most shocking events. While the people performed deeds of the greatest heroism, the perfidy and cruelty of the Spaniards had no bounds. The patriots seeing more danger in submission than in resistance, each town which was in succession subdued endured the last extremities of suffering before it yielded, and victory was frequently the consequence of despair. This unlooked-for turn in affairs decided the king to remove Alva, whose barbarous and rapacious conduct was now objected to even by Philip, when it produced results disastrous to his cause. Don Luis Zuniga y Requesens, commander of the Order of Malta, was named to the government of the Netherlands. He arrived at Brussels on November 17, 1573, and on the 18th of the following month Alva set out for Spain, loaded with the booty to which he had waded through oceans of blood, and with the curses of the country, which, however, owed its subsequent freedom to the impulse given by his intolerable cruelty. He repaired to Spain, and after various fluctuations of favor and disgrace at the hands of his master, he died in his bed, at Lisbon, in 1582, at the advanced age of seventy-four years. His last act had been the conquest of Portugal, one of the few great successes achieved by Philip.

Chapter X

APPOINTMENT OF REQUESENS AND PACIFICATION OF GHENT. 1573-1576

THE character of Requesens was not more opposed to that of his predecessor than were the instructions given to him for his government. He was an honest, well-meaning, and moderate man, and the King of Spain hoped that by his influence and a total change of measures he might succeed in recalling the Netherlands to obedience. But, happily for the country, this change was adopted too late for success, and the weakness of the new government completed the glorious results which the ferocity of the former had prepared.

Requesens performed all that depended on him to gain the confidence of the people. He caused Alva's statue to be removed, and hoped to efface the memory of the tyrant by dissolving the Council of Blood, and abandoning the obnoxious taxes which their inventor had suspended rather than abolished. A general amnesty was also promulgated against the revolted provinces, but they received it with contempt and defiance. Nothing then was left to Requesens but to renew the war, and this he found to be a matter of no easy execution. The finances were in a state of the greatest confusion, and the Spanish troops were in many places seditious, in some openly mutinous, Alva having left large arrears of pay due to almost all, notwithstanding the immense amount of his pillage and extortion. Middelburg, which had long sustained a siege against all the efforts of the patriots, was now nearly reduced by famine, notwithstanding the gallant efforts of its governor, Mondragon. Requesens turned his immediate attention to the relief of this important place, and he soon assembled, at Antwerp and Bergen-op-Zoom, a fleet of forty vessels for that purpose. But Louis Boisot, admiral of Zealand, promptly repaired to attack this force, and after a severe action he totally defeated it, and killed De Glimes, one of its admirals, under the eyes of Requesens himself, who, accompanied by his suite, stood during the whole affair on the dike of Schakerloo. This action took place January 29, 1574; and, on February 19 following, Middelburg surrendered, after a resistance of two years. The Prince of Orange granted such conditions as were due to the bravery of the governor, and thus set an example of generosity and honor which greatly changed the complexion of the war. All Zealand was now free, and the intrepid admiral, Boisot, gained another victory on May 30—destroying several of the Spanish vessels, and taking some others, with their admiral, Von Haemstede. Frequent naval enterprises were also undertaken against the frontiers of Flanders, and while the naval forces thus harassed the enemy on every vulnerable point, the unfortunate provinces of the interior were ravaged by the mutinous and revolted Spaniards, and by the native brigands, who pillaged both royalists and patriots with atrocious impartiality.

To these manifold evils was now added one more terrible, in the appearance of the plague, which broke out at Ghent in the month of October and devastated a great part of the Netherlands, not, however, with that violence with which it rages in more southern climates.

Requesens, overwhelmed by difficulties, yet exerted himself to the utmost to put the best face on the affairs of government. His chief care was to appease the mutinous soldiery, and he even caused his plate to be melted, and freely gave the produce toward the payment of their arrears. The patriots, well informed of this state of things, labored to turn it to their best advantage. They opened the campaign in the province of Guelders, where Louis of Nassau, with his younger brother, Henry, and the Prince Palatine, son of the Elector Frederick III., appeared at the head of 11,000 men. The Prince of Orange prepared to join him with an equal number, but Requesens promptly dispatched Sanchez d'Avila to prevent this junction. The Spanish commander quickly passed the Meuse near Nimeugen, and on April 14 he forced Count Louis to a battle, on the great plain called Mookerheyde, close to the village of Mook. The royalists attacked with their usual valor, and after two hours of hard fighting the confederates were totally defeated. The three gallant princes were among the slain, and their bodies were never afterward discovered. It has been stated, on doubtful authority, that Louis of Nassau, after having lain some time among the heaps of dead, dragged himself to the side of the River Meuse, and while washing his wounds was inhumanly murdered by some straggling peasants to whom he was unknown. The unfortunate fate of this enterprising prince was a severe blow to the patriot cause and a cruel affliction to the Prince of Orange. He had now already lost three brothers in the war, and remained alone to revenge their fate and sustain the cause for which they had perished.

D'Avila soon found his victory to be as fruitless as it was brilliant. The ruffian troops by whom it was gained became immediately self-disbanded, threw off all authority, hastened to possess themselves of Antwerp, and threatened to proceed to the most horrible extremities if their pay was longer withheld. The citizens succeeded with difficulty in appeasing them by the sacrifice of some money in part payment of their claims. Requesens took advantage of their temporary calm and dispatched them promptly to take part in the siege of Leyden.

This siege formed another of those numerous instances which became so memorable from the mixture of heroism and horror. John van der Duye, known in literature by the name of Dousa, and celebrated for his Latin poems, commanded the place. Valdez, who conducted the siege, urged Dousa to surrender, when the latter replied, in the name of the inhabitants, that "when provisions failed them they would devour their left hands, reserving the right to defend their liberty." A party of the inhabitants, driven to disobedience and revolt by the excess of misery to which they were shortly reduced, attempted to force the burgomaster, Vanderwerf, to supply them with bread or yield up the place. But he sternly made the celebrated answer, which cannot be remembered without shuddering: "Bread I have none; but if my death can afford you relief, tear my body in pieces, and let those who are most hungry devour it!"

But in this extremity relief at last was afforded by the decisive measures of the Prince of Orange, who ordered all the neighboring dikes to be opened and the sluices raised, thus sweeping away the besiegers on the waves of the ocean. The inhabitants of Leyden were apprised of this intention by means of letters intrusted to the safe carriage of pigeons trained for the purpose. The inundation was no sooner effected than hundreds of flat-bottomed boats brought abundance of supplies to the half-famished town, while a violent storm carried the sea across the country for twenty leagues around, and destroyed the Spanish camp, with above 1000 soldiers, who were overtaken by the flood. This deliverance took place on October 3, on which day it is still annually celebrated by the descendants of the grateful citizens.

It was now for the first time that Spain would consent to listen to advice or mediation which had for its object the termination of this frightful war. The Emperor Maximilian II. renewed at this epoch his efforts with Philip, and under such favorable auspices conferences commenced at Breda, where the Counts Schwartzenburg and Hohenloe, brothers-in-law of the Prince of Orange, met, on the part of the emperor, the deputies from the King of Spain and the patriots, and hopes of a complete pacification were generally entertained. But three months of deliberation proved their fallacy. The patriots demanded toleration for the Reformed religion. The point was referred to Spain, and Philip utterly refused any real concessions. The congress was therefore broken up, and both oppressors and oppressed resumed their arms with increased vigor and tenfold desperation.

Requesens had long fixed his eyes on Zealand as the scene of an expedition by which he hoped to repair the failure before Leyden, and he caused an attempt to be made on the town of Zuriczee, in the Island of Scauwen, which merits record as one of the boldest and most original enterprises of the war.

The little islands of Zealand are separated from each other by narrow branches of the sea which are fordable at low water; and it was by such a passage, two leagues in breadth, and till then untried, that the Spanish detachment of 1750 men, under Ulloa and other veteran captains, advanced to their exploit in the midst of dangers greatly increased by a night of total darkness. Each man carried round his neck two pounds of gunpowder, with a sufficient supply of biscuit for two days, and holding their swords and muskets high over their heads, they boldly waded forward, three abreast, in some places up to their shoulders in water. The alarm was soon given, and a shower of balls was poured upon the gallant band from upwards of forty boats which the Zealanders sent rapidly toward the spot. The only light afforded to either party was from the flashes of their guns, and while the adventurers advanced with undaunted firmness, their equally daring assailants, jumping from their boats into the water, attacked them with oars and hooked handspikes, by which many of the Spaniards were destroyed. The rear guard in this extremity, cut off from their

Hist. Nat. XIII-9

companions, was obliged to retreat; but the rest, after a considerable loss, at length reached the land, and thus gained possession of the island, on the night of September 28, 1575.

Requesens quickly afterward repaired to the scene of this gallant exploit and commenced the siege of Zuriczee, which he did not live to see completed. After having passed the winter months in preparations for the success of this object which he had so much at heart, he was recalled to Brussels by accounts of new mutinies in the Spanish cavalry, and the very evening before he reached the city he was attacked by a violent fever, which carried him off five days afterward, on March 5, 1576.

The suddenness of Requesen's illness had not allowed time for even the nomination of a successor, to which he was authorized by letters patent from the king. It is believed that his intention was to appoint Count Mansfield to the command of the army, and Barlaimont to the administration of civil affairs. The government, however, now devolved entirely into the hands of the council of state, which was at that period composed of nine members. The principal of these was Philip de Croi, Duke of Aerschot; the other leading members were Giglius, Counts Mansfield and Barlaiment, and the council was degraded by numbering, among the rest, Debris and De Roda, two of the notorious Spaniards who had formed part of the Council of Blood.

The king resolved to leave the authority in the hands of this incongruous mixture until the arrival of Don John of Austria, his natural brother, whom he had already named to the office of governor-general. But in the interval the government assumed an aspect of unprecedented disorder, and widespread anarchy embraced the whole country. The royal troops openly revolted and fought against each other like deadly enemies. The nobles, divided in their views, arrogated to themselves in different places the titles and powers of command. Public faith and private probity seemed alike destroyed. Pillage, violence, and ferocity were the commonplace characteristics of the times.

Circumstances like these may be well supposed to have revived the hopes of the Prince of Orange, who quickly saw amid this chaos the elements of order, strength, and liberty. Such had been his previous affliction at the harrowing events which he witnessed, and despaired of being able to relieve, that he had proposed to the patriots of Holland and Zealand to destroy the dikes, submerge the whole country, and abandon to the waves the soil which refused security to freedom. But Providence destined him to be the savior, instead of the destroyer, of his country. The chief motive of this excessive desperation had been the apparent desertion by Queen Elizabeth of the cause which she had hitherto so mainly assisted. Offended at the capture of some English ships by the Dutch, who asserted that they carried supplies for the Spaniards, she withdrew from them her protection, but by timely submission they appeased her wrath, and it is thought by some historians that even thus early the Prince of Orange proposed to place the revolted provinces wholly under her protection. This, however, she for the time refused, but she strongly solicited Philip's mercy for these unfortunate countries, through the Spanish ambassador at her court.

In the meantime the council of state at Brussels seemed disposed to follow up as far as possible the plans of Requesens. The siege of Zuriczee was continued, but speedy dissensions among the members of the government rendered their authority contemptible, if not utterly extinct, in the eyes of the people. The exhaustion of the treasury deprived them of all power to put an end to the mutinous excesses of the Spanish troops, and the latter carried their licentiousness to the utmost bounds. Zuriczee, admitted to a surrender, and saved from pillage by the payment of a large sum, was lost to the loyalists within three months from the want of discipline in its garrison, and the towns and burghs of Brabant suffered as much from the excesses of their nominal protectors as could have been inflicted by the enemy. The mutineers at length, to the number of some thousands, attacked and carried by force the town of Alost, at equal distances between Brussels, Ghent, and Antwerp, imprisoned the chief citizens, and levied contributions on all the country round. It was then that the council of state found itself forced to proclaim them rebels, traitors, and enemies to the king and the country, and called on all loyal subjects to pursue and exterminate them wherever they were found in arms.

This proscription of the Spanish mutineers was followed by the convocation of the states-general, and the government thus hoped to maintain some show of union and some chance of authority. But a new scene of intestine violence completed the picture of executive inefficiency. On September 4 the grand bailiff of

Brabant, as lieutenant of the Baron de Hèze, governor of Brussels, entered the council-chamber by force and arrested all the members present on suspicion of treacherously maintaining intelligence with the Spaniards. Counts Mansfield and Barlaimont were imprisoned, with some others. Viglius escaped this indignity by being absent from indisposition. This bold measure was hailed by the people with unusual joy, as being the signal for that total change in the government which they reckoned on as the prelude to complete freedom.

The states-general were all at this time assembled, with the exception of those of Flanders, who joined the others with but little delay. The general reprobation against the Spaniards procured a second decree of proscription, and their desperate conduct justified the utmost violence with which they might be pursued. They still held the citadels of Ghent and Antwerp, as well as Maestricht, which they had seized on, sacked, and pillaged with all the fury which a barbarous enemy inflicts on a town carried by assault. On November 3 the other body of mutineers, in possession of Alost, marched to the support of their fellow-brigands in the citadel of Antwerp, and both, simultaneously attacking this magnificent city, became masters of it in all points, in spite of a vigorous resistance on the part of the citizens. They then began a scene of rapine and destruction unequaled in the annals of these desperate wars. More than five hundred private mansions and the splendid town-house were delivered to the flames, and seven thousand citizens perished by the sword or in the waters of the Scheldt. For three days the carnage and the pillage went on with unheard-of fury, and the most opulent town in Europe was thus reduced to ruin and desolation by a few thousand frantic ruffians. The loss was valued at above two million golden crowns. Vargas and Romero were the principal leaders of this infernal exploit, which has taken its place in history under the significant name of the "Spanish Fury."

The states-general, assembled at Ghent, were solemnly opened on September 14. Being apprehensive of a sudden attack from the Spanish troops in the citadel, they proposed a negotiation, and demanded a protecting force from the Prince of Orange, who immediately entered into a treaty with their envoy, and sent to their assistance eight companies of infantry and seventeen pieces of cannon under the command of the English colonel, Temple. In the midst of this turmoil and apparent insecurity the states-general proceeded in their great work and assumed the reins of government in the name of the king. They allowed the council of state still nominally to exist, but they restricted its powers far within those it had hitherto exercised; and the government, thus absolutely assuming the form of a republic, issued manifestos in justification of its conduct and demanded succor from all the foreign powers. To complete the union between the various provinces, it was resolved to resume the negotiations commenced the preceding year at Breda, and October 10 was fixed for this new congress to be held in the town-house of Ghent.

On the day appointed the congress opened its sittings, and rapidly arriving at the termination of its important object, the celebrated treaty known by the title of "The Pacification of Ghent" was published on November 8, to the sound of bells and trumpets, while the ceremony was rendered still more imposing by the thunder of the artillery which battered the walls of the besieged citadel. It was even intended to have delivered a general assault against the place at the moment of the proclamation, but the mutineers demanded a capitulation, and finally surrendered three days afterward. It was the wife of the famous Mondragon who commanded the place in her husband's absence, and by her heroism gave a new proof of the capability of the sex to surpass the limits which nature seems to have fixed for their conduct.

The "Pacification" contained twenty-five articles. Among others, it was agreed:

That a full amnesty should be passed for all offenses whatsoever.

That the estates of Brabant, Flanders, Hainault, Artois, and others, on the one part; the Prince of Orange and the states of Holland and Zealand and their associates, on the other; promised to maintain good faith, peace, and friendship, firm and inviolable; to mutually assist each other, at all times, in council and action; and to employ life and fortune, above all things, to expel from the country the Spanish soldiers and other foreigners.

That no one should be allowed to injure or insult, by word or deed, the exercise of the Catholic religion, on pain of being treated as a disturber of the public peace.

That the edicts against heresy and the proclamations of the Duke of Alva should be suspended.

That all confiscations, sentences, and judgments rendered since 1566 should be annulled.

That the inscriptions, monuments, and trophies erected by the Duke of Alva should be demolished.

Such were the general conditions of the treaty. The remaining articles chiefly concerned individual interests. The promulgation of this great charter of union, which was considered as the fundamental law of the country, was hailed in all parts of the Netherlands with extravagant demonstrations of joy.

Chapter XI

REVOLT FROM SOVEREIGNTY AND DECLARATION OF INDEPENDENCE. 1576-1580

ON the very day of the sack of Antwerp Don John of Austria arrived at Luxemburg. This ominous commencement of his viceregal reign was not belied by the events which followed, and the hero of Lepanto, the victor of the Turks, the idol of Christendom, was destined to have his reputation and well-won laurels tarnished in the service of the despotism to which he now became an instrument. Don John was a natural son of Charles V., and to fine talents and a good disposition united the advantages of hereditary courage and a liberal education. He was born at Ratisbon on February 24, 1553.[1] His mother was a woman of humble birth, Barbara Blomberg, with whom Charles had a brief intrigue. The prince, having passed through France, disguised, for greater secrecy or in a youthful frolic, as a negro valet to Prince Octavo Gonzaga, entered on the limits of his new government and immediately wrote to the council of state in the most condescending terms to announce his arrival.

Nothing could present a less promising aspect to the prince than the country at the head of which he was now placed. He found all its provinces, with the sole exception of Luxemburg, in the anarchy attendant on a ten years' civil war, and apparently resolved on a total breach of their allegiance to Spain. He found his best, indeed his only, course to be that of moderation and management, and it is most probable that at the outset his intentions were really honorable and candid.

The states-general were not less embarrassed than the prince. His sudden arrival threw them into great perplexity, which was increased by the conciliatory tone of his letter. They had now removed from Ghent to Brussels, and first sending deputies to pay the honors of a ceremonious welcome to Don John, they wrote to

[1] The best life of Don John of Austria, whose career was one of the most romantic in history, is by Stirling Maxwell.

the Prince of Orange, then in Holland, for his advice in this difficult conjuncture. The prince replied by a memorial of considerable length, dated Middelburg, November 30, in which he gave them the most wise and prudent advice, the substance of which was to receive any propositions coming from the wily and perfidious Philip with the utmost suspicion, and to refuse all negotiation with his deputy if the immediate withdrawal of the foreign troops was not at once conceded and the acceptance of the pacification guaranteed in its most ample extent.

This advice was implicitly followed, the states in the meantime taking the precaution of assembling a large body of troops at Wavre, between Brussels and Namur, the command of which was given to the Count of Lalain. A still more important measure was the dispatch of an envoy to England to implore the assistance of Elizabeth. She acted on this occasion with frankness and intrepidity, giving a distinguished reception to the envoy, De Sweveghem, and advancing a loan of £100,000 sterling, on condition that the states made no treaty without her knowledge or participation.

To secure still more closely the federal union that now bound the different provinces, a new compact was concluded by the deputies on January 9, 1577, known by the title of "The Union of Brussels," and signed by the prelates, ecclesiastics, lords, gentlemen, magistrates, and others, representing the estates of the Netherlands. A copy of this act of union was transmitted to Don John, to enable him thoroughly to understand the present state of feeling among those with whom he was now about to negotiate. He maintained a general tone of great moderation throughout the conference which immediately took place, and after some weeks of cautious parleying, in the latter part of which the candor of the prince seemed doubtful, and which the native historians do not hesitate to stigmatize as merely assumed, a treaty was signed at Marche-en-Famenne, a place between Namur and Luxemburg, in which every point insisted on by the states was, to the surprise and delight of the nation, fully consented to and guaranteed. This important document called "The Perpetual Edict," bears date February 12, 1577, and contains nineteen articles. They were based on the acceptance of the "Pacification," but one expressly stipulated that the Count of Beuren should be set at liberty as soon as the Prince of Orange, his father, had on his part ratified the treaty. An important change, however, was the stipulation for the maintenance of the Catholic religion everywhere.

Don John made his solemn entry into Brussels on May 1 and assumed the functions of his limited authority. The conditions of the treaty were promptly and regularly fulfilled. The citadels occupied by the Spanish soldiers were given up to the Flemish and Walloon troops, and the departure of these ferocious foreigners took place at once. The large sums required to facilitate this measure made it necessary to submit for a while to the presence of the German mercenaries. It seems evident that both Don John and the king were anxious for peace at this time. But the impetuous nature of the prince could ill brook the almost total deprivation of his authority by the states-general. He at once demanded from the council of state the command of the troops and the disposal of the revenues. The answer was a simple reference to the " Pacification of Ghent," and the prince's rejoinder was an apparent submission, and the immediate dispatch of letters in cipher to the king, demanding a supply of troops sufficient to restore his ruined authority. These letters were intercepted by the King of Navarre, afterward Henry IV. of France, who immediately transmitted them to the Prince of Orange, his old friend and fellow-soldier.

Public opinion, to the suspicions of which Don John had been from the first obnoxious, was now unanimous in attributing to design all that was unconstitutional and unfair. His impetuous character could no longer submit to the restraint of his authority, and he resolved to take some bold and decided measure. A very favorable opportunity was presented in the arrival of the Queen of Navarre, Marguerite of Valois, at Namur, on her way to Spa. The prince, numerously attended, hastened to the former town under pretense of paying his respects to the queen. As soon as she left the place he repaired to the glacis of the town, as if for the mere enjoyment of a walk, admired the external appearance of the citadel, and expressed a desire to be admitted inside. The young Count of Barlaimont, in the absence of his father, the governor of the place, and an accomplice in the plot with Don John, freely admitted him. The prince immediately drew forth a pistol, and exclaiming that that was the first moment of his government, took possession of the place with his immediate guard, and instantly formed them into a devoted garrison.

The Prince of Orange immediately made public the intercepted letters, and at the solicitation of the states-general repaired to Brussels, into which city he made a truly triumphant entry on September 23, and was immediately nominated governor, protector or *ruward* of Brabant—a dignity which had fallen into disuse, but was revived on this occasion, and which was little inferior in power to that of the dictators of Rome. His authority, now almost unlimited, extended over every province of the Netherlands, except Namur and Luxemburg, both of which acknowledged Don John.

The first care of the liberated nation was to demolish the various citadels rendered celebrated and odious by the excesses of the Spaniards. This was done with an enthusiastic industry in which every age and sex bore a part and which promised well for liberty. Among the ruins of that of Antwerp the statue of the Duke of Alva was discovered, dragged through the filthiest streets of the town, and, with all the indignity so well merited by the original, it was finally broken into a thousand pieces.

The country in conferring such extensive powers on the Prince of Orange had certainly gone too far, not for his desert, but for its own tranquillity. It was impossible that such an elevation should not excite the discontent and awaken the energy of the haughty aristocracy of Flanders and Brabant, and particularly of the house of Croi, the ancient rivals of that of Nassau. The then representative of that family seemed the person most suited to counterbalance William's excessive power. The Duke of Aerschot was therefore named governor of Flanders, and he immediately put himself at the head of a confederacy of the Catholic party, which quickly decided to offer the chief government of the country, still in the name of Philip, to the Archduke Mathias, brother of Emperor Rudolf II. and cousin german to Philip of Spain, a youth only nineteen years of age. A Flemish gentleman named Maelsted was intrusted with the proposal. Mathias joyously consented, and, quitting Vienna with the greatest secrecy, he arrived at Maestricht without any previous announcement, and expected only by the party that had invited him, at the end of October, 1577.

The Prince of Orange, instead of showing the least symptom of dissatisfaction at this underhand proceeding aimed at his personal authority, announced his perfect approval of the nomination, and was the foremost in recommending measures for the honor of the archduke and the security of the country. He drew up the basis of a treaty for Mathias's acceptance, on terms which guaranteed to the council of state and the states-general the virtual sovereignty, and left to the young prince little beyond the fine title which had dazzled his boyish vanity. The Prince of Orange was appointed his lieutenant in all the branches of the administration, civil, military, or financial, and the Duke of Aerschot, who had hoped to obtain an entire domination over the puppet he had brought upon the stage, saw himself totally foiled in his project and left without a chance or a pretext for the least increase to his influence.

But a still greater disappointment attended this ambitious nobleman in the very stronghold of his power. The Flemings, driven by persecution to a state of fury almost unnatural, had, in their antipathy to Spain, adopted a hatred against Catholicism which had its source only in political frenzy, while the converts imagined it to arise from reason and conviction. Two men had taken advantage of this state of the public mind and gained over it an unbounded ascendency. They were Francis de Kethulle, Lord of Ryhove, and John Hembyse, and each seemed formed to realize the beau-ideal of a factious demagogue. They had acquired supreme power over the people of Ghent, and had at their command a body of 20,000 resolute and well-armed supporters. The Duke of Aerschot vainly attempted to oppose his authority to that of these men, and on one occasion imprudently exclaimed that he would have them hanged, even though they were protected by the Prince of Orange himself. The same night Ryhove summoned the leaders of his bands, and quickly assembling a considerable force, they repaired to the duke's hotel, made him prisoner, and, without allowing him time to dress, carried him away in triumph. At the same time the bishops of Bruges and Ypres, the high bailiffs of Ghent and Courtrai, the governor of Oudenarde, and other important magistrates were arrested—accused of complicity with the duke, but of what particular offense the lawless demagogues did not deign to specify. The two tribunes immediately divided the whole honors and authority of administration, Ryhove as military, and Hembyse as civil, chief.

The latter of these legislators completely changed the forms of the government. He revived the ancient privileges destroyed by Charles V. and took all preliminary measures for forcing the various provinces to join with the city of Ghent in forming a federative republic. The states-general and the Prince of Orange were alarmed lest these troubles might lead to a renewal of the anarchy from the effects of which the country had but just obtained breathing-time. Ryhove consented, at the remonstrance of the Prince of Orange, to release the Duke of Aerschot, but William was obliged to repair to Ghent in person in the hope of establishing order. He arrived on December 29 and entered on a strict inquiry with his usual calmness and decision. He could not succeed in obtaining the liberty of the other prisoners, though he pleaded for them strongly. Having severely reprimanded the factious leaders, and pointed out the dangers of their illegal course, he returned to Brussels, leaving the factious city in a temporary tranquillity which his firmness and discretion could alone have obtained.

The Archduke Mathias, having visited Antwerp and acceded to all the conditions required of him, made his public entry into Brussels on January 18, 1578, and was installed in his dignity of governor-general amid the usual fêtes and rejoicings. Don John of Austria was at the same time declared an enemy to the country, with a public order to quit it without delay, and a prohibition was issued against any inhabitant acknowledging his forfeited authority.

War was now once more openly declared, some fruitless negotiations having afforded a fair pretext for hostilities. The rapid appearance of a numerous army under the orders of Don John gave strength to the suspicions of his former dissimulation. It was currently believed that large bodies of the Spanish troops had remained concealed in the forests of Luxemburg and Lorraine, while several regiments, which had remained in France in the service of the league, immediately reëntered the Netherlands. Alexander Farnese, Prince of Parma, son of the former governant, came to the aid of his uncle, Don John, at the head of a large force of Italians, and these several reinforcements, with the German auxiliaries still in the country, composed an army of 20,000 men. The army of the states-general was still larger, but far inferior in point of discipline. It was commanded by Antoine de Goignies, a gentleman of Hainault and an old soldier of the school of Charles V.

After a sharp affair at the village of Riminants, in which the royalists had the worst, the two armies met at Gemblours, on January 31, 1578, and the Prince of Parma gained a complete victory, almost with his cavalry only, taking De Goignies prisoner, with the whole of his artillery and baggage. The account of his victory is almost miraculous. The royalists, if we are to credit their most minute but not impartial historian, had only 1200 men engaged, by whom 6000 were put to the sword, with the loss of but 12 men and little more than an hour's labor.

The news of this battle threw the states into the utmost consternation. Brussels being considered insecure, the Archduke Mathias and his council retired to Antwerp, but the victors did not feel their forces sufficient to justify an attack upon the capital. They, however, took Louvain, Tirlemont, and several other towns, but these conquests were of little import in comparison with the loss of Amsterdam, which declared openly and unanimously for the patriot cause. The states-general recovered their courage and prepared for a new contest. They sent deputies to the Diet of Worms to ask succor from the princes of the empire. The Count Palatine, John Casimir, repaired to their assistance with a considerable force of Germans and English, all equipped and paid by Queen Elizabeth. The Duke of Anjou, brother of Henry III. of France, hovered on the frontiers of Hainault with a respectable army, and the cause of liberty seemed not quite desperate.

But all the various chiefs had separate interests and opposite views, while the fanatic violence of the people of Ghent sapped the foundations of the pacification to which the town had given its name. The Walloon provinces, deep-rooted in their attachment to the Catholic religion, which they loved still better than political freedom, and full of hatred for the Calvinists of Ghent, gradually withdrew from the common cause, and without yet openly becoming reconciled with Spain, they adopted a neutrality which was tantamount to it. Don John was, however, deprived of all chance of reaping any advantage from these unfortunate dissensions. He was suddenly taken ill in his camp at Bougy, and died, after a fortnight's suffering, on October 1, 1578, in the thirty-third year of his age.

This unlooked-for close to a career which had been so brilliant, and to a life from which so much was yet to be expected, makes us pause to consider for a moment the different opinions of his times and of history on the fate of a personage so remarkable. The contemporary Flemish memoirs say that he died of the plague; those of Spain call his disorder the purple fever. Contemporary opinion was largely to the effect that he was poisoned by Philip, who was jealous of Don John's popularity and ambition. But there seems to be no doubt that he died of the camp fever, weakened as he was by the mental and physical strain of his difficult position.

The Prince of Parma, who now succeeded by virtue of Don John's testament to the post of governor-general in the name of the king, remained intrenched in his camp. He expected much from the disunion of his various opponents, and what he foresaw very quickly happened. The Duke of Anjou disbanded his troops

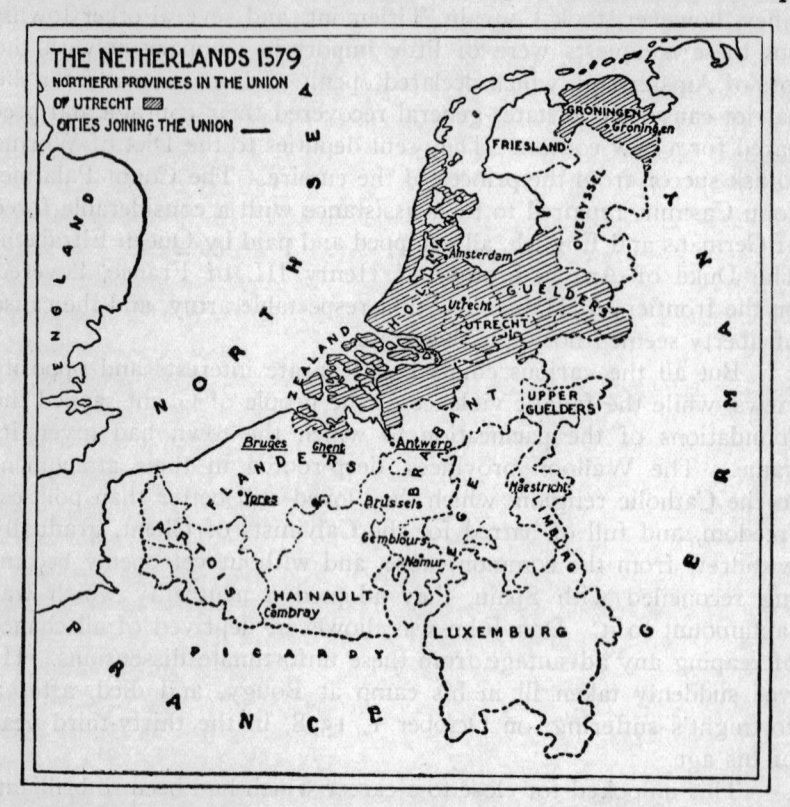

THE NETHERLANDS 1579
NORTHERN PROVINCES IN THE UNION OF UTRECHT
CITIES JOINING THE UNION

and retired to France, and the Count Palatine, following his example, withdrew to Germany, having first made an unsuccessful attempt to engage the Queen of England as a principal in the confederacy. In this perplexity the Prince of Orange saw that the real hope for safety was in uniting still more closely the northern provinces of the union, for he discovered the fallacy of reckoning on the cordial and persevering fidelity of the Walloons. He therefore convoked a new assembly at Utrecht, and the deputies of

Holland, Guelders, Zealand, Utrecht, and Groningen signed, January 29, 1579, the famous act called the "Union of Utrecht," the real basis or fundamental pact of the republic of the United Provinces. It makes no formal renunciation of allegiance to Spain, but this is virtually done by the omission of the king's name. The twenty-six articles of this act consolidate the indissoluble connection of the United Provinces, each preserving its separate franchises, and following its own good pleasure on the subject of religion. The towns of Ghent, Antwerp, Bruges, and Ypres soon after acceded to and joined the union.

The Prince of Parma now assumed the offensive, and marched against Maestricht with his whole army. He took the place in the month of June, 1579, after a gallant resistance, and delivered it to sack and massacre for three entire days. About the same time Mechlin and Bois-le-duc returned to their obedience to the king. Hembyse, having renewed his attempts against the public peace at Ghent, the Prince of Orange repaired to that place with speed, and having reëstablished order, and frightened the inveterate demagogue into secret flight, Flanders was once more restored to tranquillity.

An attempt was made this year at a reconciliation between the king and the states. The Emperor Rudolf II. and Pope Gregory XIII. offered their mediation, and on April 5 a congress assembled at Cologne, where a number of the most celebrated diplomatists in Europe were collected. But it was early seen that no settlement would result from the apparently reciprocal wish for peace. One point—that of religion, the main, and indeed the only one in debate—was now maintained by Philip's ambassador in the same unyielding spirit, as if torrents of blood and millions of treasure had never been sacrificed in the cause. Philip was inflexible in his resolution never to concede the exercise of the Reformed worship, and after nearly a year of fruitless consultation and the expenditure of immense sums of money, the congress separated on November 17 without having effected anything. There were several other articles intended for discussion, had the main one been adjusted, on which Philip was fully as determined to make no concession; but his obstinacy was not put to these new tests.

The time had now arrived for the execution of the great and decisive step for independence, the means of effecting which had been so long the object of exertion and calculation on the part of the Prince of Orange. He now resolved to assemble the states of the United Provinces, solemnly abjure the dominion of Spain, and depose King Philip from the sovereignty he had so justly forfeited. Much has been written both for and against this measure, which involved every argument of natural rights and municipal privilege. The natural rights of man may seem to comprise only those which he enjoys in a state of nature; but he carries several of those with him into society, which is based upon the very principle of their preservation. The great precedent which so many subsequent revolutions have acknowledged and confirmed is that which we now record. The states-general assembled at Antwerp early in the year 1580, and, in spite of all the opposition of the Catholic deputies, the authority of Spain was revoked forever, and the United Provinces declared a free and independent state. At the same time was debated the important question as to whether the protection of the new state should be offered to England or to France. Opinions were divided on this point, but that of the Prince of Orange being in favor of the latter country, from many motives of sound policy it was decided to offer the sovereignty to the Duke of Anjou. The Archduke Mathias, who was present at the deliberations, was treated with little ceremony, but he obtained the promise of a pension when the finances were in a situation to afford it. The definite proposal to be made to the Duke of Anjou was not agreed upon for some months afterward, and it was in the month of August following that St. Aldegonde and other deputies waited on the duke at the château of Plessis-le-Tours, when he accepted the offered sovereignty on the proposed conditions, which set narrow bounds to his authority and gave ample security to the United Provinces. The articles were formally signed on September 19, and the duke not only promised quickly to lead a numerous army to the Netherlands, but he obtained a letter from his brother, Henry III., dated December 26, by which the king pledged himself to give further aid as soon as he might succeed in quieting his own disturbed and unfortunate country. The states-general, assembled at Delft, ratified the treaty on December 30, and the year which was about to open seemed to promise the consolidation of freedom and internal peace.

THE SPANISH FURY IN ANTWERP, NOVEMBER 4, 1576
Painting by K. Ooms

—page 122

Chapter XII

EDICT OF PHILIP AND MURDER OF PRINCE OF ORANGE. 1580-1584

PHILIP might be well excused the utmost violence of resentment on this occasion, had it been bounded by fair and honorable efforts for the maintenance of his authority. But every general principle seemed lost in the base inveteracy of private hatred. The ruin of the Prince of Orange was his main object, and his industry and ingenuity were taxed to the utmost to procure his murder.[1] Existing documents prove that he first wished to accomplish this in such a way that the responsibility and odium of the act might rest on the Prince of Parma, but the mind of the prince was too magnanimous to allow of a participation in the crime.

The correspondence on the subject is preserved in the archives, and the date of Philip's first letter, November 30, 1579, proves that even before the final disavowal of his authority by the United Provinces he had harbored his diabolical design. The prince remonstrated, but with no effect. It even appears that Philip's anxiety would not admit of the delay necessary for the prince's reply. The infamous edict of proscription against William bears date of March 15, and the most pressing letters commanded the Prince of Parma to make it public. It was not, however, till June 15 that he sent forth the fatal ban.

The edict, under Philip's own signature, is a tissue of invective and virulence. The illustrious object of its abuse is accused of having engaged the heretics to profane the churches and break the images; of having persecuted and massacred the Catholic priests; of hypocrisy, tyranny, and perjury; and, as the height of atrocity, of having introduced liberty of conscience into his country. For these causes, and many others, the king declares him

[1] The project of the murder of William did not, however, originate with Philip, but was proposed by Cardinal Granvelle.

"proscribed and banished as a public pest!" and it is permitted to all persons to assail him "in his fortune, person, and life, as an enemy to human nature." Philip also, "for the recompense of virtue and the punishment of crime," promises to whoever will deliver up William of Nassau, dead or alive, " in lands or money, at his choice, the sum of 25,000 golden crowns; to grant a free pardon to such persons for all former offenses of what kind soever, and to invest him with letters patent of nobility."

In reply to this brutal document William published all over Europe his famous "Apology," of which it is enough to say that language could not produce a more splendid refutation of every charge or a more terrible recrimination against the guilty tyrant. It was attributed to the pen of Pierre de Villars, a Protestant minister. William from the hour of his proscription became at once the equal in worldly station, as he had ever been the superior in moral worth, of his royal calumniator. He took his place as a prince of an imperial family, not less ancient or illustrious than that of the house of Austria, and he stood forward at the supreme tribunal of public feeling and opinion as the accuser of a king who disgraced his lineage and his throne.

By a separate article in the treaty with the states, the Duke of Anjou secured to William the sovereignty of Holland and Zealand, as well as the lordship of Friesland, with his title of stadtholder, retaining to the duke his claim on the prince's faith and homage. The exact nature of William's authority was finally ratified on July 24, 1581, on which day he took the prescribed oath and entered on the exercise of his well-earned rights.

Philip now formed the design of sending back the Duchess of Parma to resume her former situation as governant and exercise the authority conjointly with her son. But the latter positively declined this proposal of divided power, and he consequently was left alone to its entire exercise. Military affairs made but slow progress this year. The most remarkable event was the capture of La Noue, a native of Bretagne, one of the bravest officers, and certainly the cleverest, in the service of the states, into which he had passed after having given important aid to the Huguenots of France. He was considered so important a prize that Philip refused all proposals for his exchange, and detained him in the castle of Limburg for five years.

The siege of Cambray was now undertaken by the Prince of

Parma in person, while the Duke of Anjou, at the head of a large army and the flower of the French nobility, advanced to its relief, and soon forced his rival to raise the siege. The new sovereign of the Netherlands entered the town and was received with tumultuous joy by the half-starved citizens and garrison. The Prince of Parma sought an equivalent for this check in the attack of Tournay, which he immediately afterward invested. The town was but feebly garrisoned, but the Protestant inhabitants prepared for a desperate defense, under the exciting example of the Princess of Epinoi, wife of the governor, who was himself absent. This remarkable woman furnishes another proof of the female heroism which abounded in these wars. Though wounded in the arm, she fought in the breach sword in hand, braving peril and death. And when at length it was impossible to hold out longer, she obtained an honorable capitulation, and marched out, on November 29, on horseback, at the head of the garrison, with an air of triumph rather than of defeat.

The Duke of Anjou had repaired to England in hopes of completing his project of marriage with Elizabeth. After three months of almost confident expectation the Virgin Queen, at this time fifty years of age, with a caprice not quite justifiable, broke all her former engagements, and, happily for herself and her country, declined the marriage. Anjou burst out into all the violence of his turbulent temper and set sail for the Netherlands. Elizabeth made all the reparation in her power, by the honors paid him on his dismissal. She accompanied him as far as Canterbury, and sent him away under the convoy of the Earl of Leicester, her chief favorite, and with a brilliant suite and a fleet of fifteen sail. Anjou was received at Antwerp with equal distinction, and was inaugurated there on February 19 as Duke of Brabant, Lothier, Limburg, and Guelders, with many other titles, of which he soon proved himself unworthy. When the Prince of Orange at the ceremony placed the ducal mantle on his shoulders Anjou said to him, "Fasten it so well, prince, that they cannot take it off again!"

During the rejoicings which followed this ceremony Philip's proscription against the Prince of Orange put forth its first fruits. The latter gave a grand dinner in the château of Antwerp, which he occupied, on March 18, the birthday of the Duke of Anjou, and as he was quitting the dining-room on his way to his private chamber a young man stepped forward and offered a pretended petition, William being at all times of easy access for such an object. While he read the paper the treacherous suppliant discharged a pistol at his head, the ball striking him under the left ear and passing out at the right cheek. As he tottered and fell, the assassin drew a poniard to add suicide to the crime, but he was instantly put to death by the attendant guards. The young Count Maurice, William's second son, examined the murderer's body, and the papers found on him and subsequent inquiries revealed that his name was John Jaureguay, he was twenty-three years of age, a native of Biscay, and clerk to a Spanish merchant of Antwerp called Gaspar Anastro. This man had instigated him to the crime, having received a promise signed by King Philip, engaging to give him 28,000 ducats and other advantages if he would undertake to assassinate the Prince of Orange. The inducements held out by Anastro to his simple dupe were backed strongly by the persuasions of Antony Timmerman, a Dominican monk, and by Venero, Anastro's cashier, who had from fear declined becoming himself the murderer. Jaureguay had duly heard mass and received the sacrament before executing its attempt, and in his pockets were found a catechism of the Jesuits, with tablets filled with prayers in the Spanish language, one in particular being addressed to the Angel Gabriel, imploring his intercession with God and the Virgin to aid him in the consummation of his object. Timmerman and Venero made a full avowal and suffered death in the barbarous manner of the times. Anastro, however, effected his escape.

The alarm and indignation of the people of Antwerp knew no bounds. Their suspicions at first fell on the Duke of Anjou and the French party, but the truth was soon discovered, and the rapid recovery of the Prince of Orange from his desperate wound set everything once more to rights. But a premature report of his death flew rapidly abroad, and he had anticipated proofs of his importance in the eyes of all Europe in the frantic delight of the base and the deep affliction of the good. Within three months William was able to accompany the Duke of Anjou in his visits to Ghent, Bruges, and the other chief towns of Flanders, in each of which the ceremony of inauguration was repeated. Several military exploits now took place, and various towns fell into the hands of the opposing parties, changing masters with a rapidity, as well as a previous endurance of suffering, that must have carried confusion on the contending principles of allegiance into the hearts and heads of the harassed inhabitants.

The Duke of Anjou, intemperate, inconstant, and unprincipled, saw that his authority was but the shadow of power compared to the deep-fixed practices of despotism which governed the other nations of Europe. The French officers who formed his suite and possessed all his confidence had no difficulty in raising his discontent into treason against the people with whom he had made a solemn compact. The result of their councils was a deep-laid plot against Flemish liberty, and its execution was ere long attempted. He sent secret orders to the governors of Dunkirk, Bruges, Termonde, and other towns to seize on and hold them in his name, reserving for himself the infamy of the enterprise against Antwerp. To prepare for its execution he caused his numerous army of French and Swiss to approach the city, and they were encamped in the neighborhood, at a place called Borgerhout.

On January 17, 1583, the duke dined somewhat earlier than usual, under the pretext of proceeding afterward to review his army in their camp. He set out at noon, accompanied by his guard, of two hundred horse, and when he reached the second drawbridge one of his officers gave the preconcerted signal for an attack on the Flemish guard by pretending that he had fallen and broken his leg. The duke called out to his followers, "Courage, courage! the town is ours!" The guard at the gate was all soon dispatched, and the French troops, which waited outside to the number of 3000, rushed quickly in, furiously shouting the war-cry, "Town taken! town taken! kill! kill!" The astonished but intrepid citizens, recovering from their confusion, instantly flew to arms. All differences in religion or politics were forgotten in the common danger to their freedom. Catholics and Protestants, men and women, rushed alike to the conflict. The ancient spirit of Flanders seemed to animate all. Workmen, armed with the instruments of their various trades, started from their shops and flung themselves upon the enemy. A baker sprang from the cellar where he was kneading his dough and with his oven shovel struck a French dragoon to the ground. Those who had firearms, after expending their bullets, took from their pouches and pockets pieces of money, which they bent between their teeth and used for charging their arquebuses. The French were driven successively from the streets and ramparts, and the cannons planted on the latter were immediately turned against the reinforcements which attempted to enter the town. The French were everywhere beaten; the Duke of Anjou saved himself by flight and reached Dendermonde after the perilous necessity of passing through a large tract of inundated country, for the citizens of Mechlin had cut the dikes to impede his retreat. His loss in this base enterprise amounted to 1500, while that of the citizens did not exceed 80 men. The attempts simultaneously made on the other towns succeeded at Dunkirk and Dendermonde, but all the others failed.

The character of the Prince of Orange never appeared so thoroughly great as at this crisis. With wisdom and magnanimity rarely equaled and never surpassed, he threw himself and his authority between the indignation of the country and the guilt of Anjou, saving the former from excess and the latter from execration. The disgraced and discomfited duke proffered to the states excuses as mean as they were hypocritical, and his brother, the King of France, sent a special envoy to intercede for him. But it was the influence of William that screened the culprit from public reprobation and ruin, and regained for him the place and power which he might easily have secured for himself had he not prized the welfare of his country far above all objects of private advantage. A new treaty was negotiated, confirming Anjou in his former station, with renewed security against any future treachery on his part. He in the meantime retired to France, to let the public indignation subside, but before he could assume sufficient confidence to again face the country he had so basely injured his worthless existence was suddenly terminated, some thought by poison—the common solution of all such doubtful questions in those days—in the month of June, 1584. He expired in his twenty-ninth year.

A distressing proof of public ingratitude and want of judgment had previously been furnished by the conduct of the people of Antwerp against him who had been so often their deliverer from such various dangers. Unable to comprehend the greatness of his mind, they openly accused the Prince of Orange of having joined with the French for their subjugation and of having concealed a body of that detested nation in the citadel. The populace rushed to the place, and having minutely examined it, were convinced of their own absurdity and the prince's innocence. He scorned to demand their punishment for such an outrageous calumny, but was none the less affected by it. He took the resolution of quitting Flanders, as it turned out, forever, and retired into Zealand, where he was better known and presumably better trusted.

In the midst of the consequent confusion in the former of these provinces, the Prince of Parma, with indefatigable vigor, made himself master of town after town, and turned his particular attention to the creation of a naval force, which was greatly favored by the possession of Dunkirk, Nieuport, and Gravelines. Native treachery was not idle in this time of tumult and confusion. Count Van den Bergh, brother-in-law of William of Orange, now governor of Friesland and Groningen, had set the basest example and gone over to the Spaniards. The Prince of Chimay, son of the Duke of Aerschot and governor of Bruges, yielded to the persuasions of his father and gave up the place to the Prince of Parma. Hembyse also, amply confirming the bad opinion in which the Prince of Orange always held him, returned to Ghent, where he regained a great portion of his former influence, and immediately commenced a correspondence with the Prince of Parma, offering to deliver up both Ghent and Dendermonde. An attempt was consequently made by the Spaniards to surprise the former town, but the citizens were prepared for this, having intercepted some of the letters of Hembyse, and the traitor was seized, tried, condemned, and executed on August 4, 1584. He was upwards of seventy years of age. Ryhove, his celebrated colleague, who had caused the arrest of his old ally, died in Holland some years later.

But the fate of so insignificant a person as Hembyse passed almost unnoticed in the agitation caused by an event which shortly preceded his death.

From the moment of their abandonment by the Duke of Anjou the United Provinces considered themselves independent, and although they consented to renew his authority over the country at large, at the solicitation of the Prince of Orange, they were resolved to confirm the influence of the latter over their particular interests, which they were now sensible could acquire stability only by that means. The death of Anjou left them without a sovereign, and they did not hesitate in the choice which they were now called upon to make. On whom, indeed, could they fix but William of

Nassau, without the utmost injustice to him and the deepest injury to themselves? To whom could they turn, in preference to him who had given consistency to the early explosion of their despair; to him who helped to give the country political existence, then nursed it into freedom, and now beheld it in the vigor and prime of independence? He had seen the necessity, but certainly overrated the value, of foreign support, to enable the new state to cope with the tremendous tyranny from which it had broken. He had tried successively Germany, England, and France. From the first and the last of these powers he had received two governors, to whom he cheerfully resigned the title. The incapacity of both, and the treachery of the latter, proved to the states that their only chance for safety was in the consolidation of William's authority, and they contemplated the noblest reward which a grateful nation could bestow on a glorious liberator.

Yet William still refused the proffered honor, still feeling that the only chance of union and independence lay in the sovereignty of a foreign prince. After the death of Anjou, however, his resolution wavered and he consented to assume a limited authority. That William had no desire for despotic power, as he has been accused, is amply proved by the articles drawn up between him and the states. This capitulation exists at full length, but was never formally executed. Its conditions are founded on the same principles and conceived in nearly the same terms as those accepted by the Duke of Anjou, and the whole compact is one of the most thoroughly liberal that history has on record. The prince repaired to Delft for the ceremony of his inauguration, the price of his long labors; but there, instead of anticipated dignity, he met the sudden stroke of death.

On July 10 as he left his dining-room, and while he placed his foot on the first step of the great stair leading to the upper apartments of his house, a man named Balthasar Gerard discharged a pistol at his body, three balls entering it. He fell into the arms of an attendant and cried out faintly, in the French language, " God pity me! I am sadly wounded—God have mercy on my soul, and on this unfortunate nation!" His sister, the Countess of Schwartzenburg, who now hastened to his side, asked him in German if he did not recommend his soul to God. He answered, " Yes," in the same language, but with a feeble voice. He was carried into the dining-room, where he immediately expired. His sister closed his eyes. His wife, too, was on the spot—Louisa, daughter of the illustrious Coligny and widow of the gallant Count of Teligny, both of whom were also murdered almost in her sight in the frightful massacre of St. Bartholomew. We may not enter on a description of the affecting scene which followed, but the mind is pleased in picturing the bold solemnity with which Prince Maurice, then eighteen years of age, swore—not vengeance or hatred against his father's murderers—but that he would faithfully and religiously follow the glorious example he had given him.

There is one important feature in the character of William which we have hitherto left untouched, but which the circumstances of his death seemed to sanctify and point out for record in the same page with it. We mean his religious opinions, and we shall dispatch a subject which is, in regard to all men, so delicate, indeed so sacred, in a few words. He was born a Lutheran. When he arrived, a boy, at the court of Charles V., he was initiated into the Catholic creed, in which he was thenceforward brought up. Not till after the beginning of the revolt did he embrace the doctrines of Calvin. His whole public conduct seems to prove that he viewed sectarian principles chiefly in the light of political instruments, and that, himself a conscientious Christian, in the broad sense of the term, he was deeply imbued with the spirit of universal toleration and considered the various shades of belief as subservient to the one grand principle of civil and religious liberty for which he had long devoted and at length laid down his life. His assassin was taken alive, and four days afterward executed with terrible circumstances of cruelty, which he bore as a martyr might have borne them. He was a native of Burgundy, and had for some months lingered near his victim, and insinuated himself into his confidence by a feigned attachment to liberty and an apparent zeal for the Reformed faith. He was nevertheless a Catholic, and claimed in his confession to have communicated his design to, and received encouragement from, more than one minister of his faith. His avowal incriminated one whose character stands so high in history that it behooves us to examine thoroughly the truth of the accusation and the nature of the collateral proofs by which it is supported. Most writers on this question have leaned to the side which all would wish to adopt. But an original letter exists in the archives of Brussels, from the Prince of Parma himself to Philip of Spain, in which he admits that Balthazar Gerard had communicated to him his intention of murdering the Prince of Orange, some months before the deed was done; and he mixes phrases of compassion for "the poor man" (the murderer) and of praise for the act, which, if the document be authentic, furnishes a striking example of the influence the religious feeling of the time had on the minds of the most eminent men.

Chapter XIII

ALEXANDER, DUKE OF PARMA. 1584-1592

THE death of William of Nassau not only closes the scene of his individual career, but throws a deep gloom over the history of a revolution that was sealed by so great a sacrifice. The animation of the story seems suspended. Its events lose for a time their excitement. The last act of the political drama is performed. The great hero of the tragedy is no more. Most of the other memorable actors have one by one passed away. A whole generation has fallen in the contest, and it is with feelings less intense that we resume the details of war and blood which seem no longer sanctified by the grander movements of heroism. The stirring impulse of slavery breaking its chains yields to the colder inspiration of independence maintaining its rights. The men we have now to depict were born free, and the deeds they did were those of stern resolve rather than of frantic despair. The present picture may be as instructive as the last, but it is less thrilling. Passion gives place to reason, and that which wore the air of fierce romance is superseded by what bears the stamp of calm reality.

The consternation caused by the news of William's death soon yielded to the firmness natural to a people inured to suffering and calamity. The United Provinces rejected at once the overtures made by the Prince of Parma to induce them to obedience. They seemed proud to show that their fate did not depend on that of one man. He therefore turned his attention to the most effective means of obtaining results by force, which he found it impossible to secure by persuasion. He proceeded vigorously to the reduction of the chief towns of Flanders, the conquest of which would give him possession of the entire province, no army now remaining to oppose him in the field. He soon obliged Ypres and Dendermonde to surrender, and Ghent, forced by famine, at length yielded on reasonable terms. The most severe was the utter abolition of the Reformed religion—by which a large portion of the population was driven to the alternative of exile, and they passed over in crowds to Holland and Zealand, not half of the inhabitants remaining behind. Mechlin, and finally Brussels, worn out by a fruitless resistance, followed the example of the rest in the spring of 1586, and thus within a year after the death of William of Nassau the power of Spain was again established in the whole province of Flanders and the others which comprise to-day the kingdom of Belgium.

But these domestic victories of the Prince of Parma were barren in any of those results which humanity would love to see in the train of conquest. The reconciled provinces presented the most deplorable spectacle. The chief towns were almost depopulated. The inhabitants had in a great measure fallen victims to war, pestilence, and famine. The thousands of villages which had covered the face of the country were absolutely abandoned to the wolves, which had so rapidly increased that they attacked not merely cattle and children, but grown-up persons. The dogs, driven abroad by hunger, had become as ferocious as other beasts of prey, and joined in large packs to hunt down brutes and men. Neither fields nor woods nor roads were now to be distinguished by any visible limits. All was an entangled mass of trees, weeds, and grass. The prices of the necessaries of life were so high that people of rank, after selling everything to buy bread, were obliged to have recourse to open beggary in the streets of the great towns.

From this frightful picture and the numerous details which imagination may readily supply, we gladly turn to the contrast afforded by the northern states. Those we have just described have a feeble hold upon our sympathies; we cannot pronounce their sufferings to be unmerited. The want of firmness or enlightenment which preferred such an existence to the risk of entire destruction only heightens the glory of the people whose unyielding energy and courage gained them so proud a place among the independent nations of Europe.

The murder of William seemed to carry to the United Provinces conviction of the weakness as well as the atrocity of Spain, and the indecent joy excited among the royalists added to their courage. An immediate council was created, composed of eighteen members, at the head of which was unanimously placed Prince Maurice of Nassau (who even then gave striking indications of talent and prudence), with the title of stadtholder, his elder brother, the Count of Beuren, now Prince of Orange, being still kept captive in Spain. Count Hohenloe was appointed lieutenant general, and several other measures were promptly adopted to consolidate the power of the infant republic. But its forces were small compared to the 80,000 men which Parma had under his command. With such means of carrying on his conquests Parma sat down regularly before Antwerp and commenced the operations of one of the most celebrated among the many memorable sieges of those times. He completely surrounded the city with troops, placing a large portion of his army on the left bank of the Scheldt, the other on the right, and causing to be attacked at the same time the two strong forts of Liefkinshoek and Lillo. Repulsed on the latter important point, his only hope of gaining the command of the navigation of the river, on which the success of the siege depended, was by throwing a bridge across the stream. Neither its great rapidity, nor its immense width, nor the want of wood and workmen could deter him from this vast undertaking. He was assisted, if not guided, in all his projects on the occasion by Barroccio, a celebrated Italian engineer sent to him by Philip, and the merit of all that was done ought fairly to be, at least, divided between the general and the engineer. If enterprise and perseverance belonged to the first, science and skill were the portion of the latter. They first caused two strong forts to be erected at opposite sides of the river, and adding to their resources by every possible means they threw forward a pier on each side of, and far into, the stream. The stakes, driven firmly into the bed of the river and cemented with masses of earth and stones, were at a proper height covered with planks and defended by parapets. These estoccades, as they were called, reduced the river to half its original breadth, and the cannon with which they were mounted rendered the passage extremely dangerous to hostile vessels. But to fill up this strait a considerable number of boats were fastened together by chain-hooks and anchors, and being manned and armed with cannon, they were moored in the interval between the estoccades. During these operations a canal was cut between the Moer and Calloo, by which means a communication was formed with Ghent, which insured a supply of ammunition and provisions. The works of the bridge, which was 2400 feet in length, were constructed with such strength and solidity that they braved the winds, the floods, and the ice of the whole winter.

The people of Antwerp at first laughed to scorn the whole of these stupendous preparations, but when they found that the bridge resisted the natural elements, by which they doubted not it would have been destroyed, they began to tremble in the anticipation of famine; yet they vigorously prepared for their defense, and rejected the overtures made by the Prince of Parma even at this advanced stage of his proceedings. Ninety-seven pieces of cannon now defended the bridge, besides which thirty large barges at each side of the river guarded its extremities, and forty ships of war formed a fleet of protection constantly ready to meet any attack from the besieged. They, seeing the Scheldt thus really closed up and all communication with Zealand impossible, felt their whole safety to depend on the destruction of the bridge. The states of Zealand now sent forward an expedition, which, joined with some ships from Lillo, gave new courage to the besieged, and everything was prepared for their great attempt. An Italian engineer named Giambelli was at this time in Antwerp, and by his talents had long protracted the defense. He has the distinction of being the inventor of those terrible fire-ships which gained the title of "infernal machines," and with some of these formidable instruments and the Zealand fleet the long-projected attack was at length made.

Early on the night of April 4 the Prince of Parma and his army were amazed by the spectacle of three huge masses of flame floating down the river, accompanied by numerous lesser appearances of a similar kind, and bearing directly against the prodigious barrier which had cost months of labor to him and his troops and immense sums of money to the state. The whole surface of the Scheldt presented one sheet of fire; the country all round was as visible as at noon; the flags, the arms of the soldiers, and every object on the bridge, in the fleet, or the forts, stood out clearly to view, and the pitchy darkness of the sky gave increased effect to the marked distinctness of all. Astonishment was soon succeeded by consternation, when one of the three machines burst with a terrific noise before they reached their intended mark, but time enough to offer a sample of their nature. The Prince of Parma with numerous officers and soldiers rushed to the bridge to witness the effects of this explosion, and just then a second and still larger fire-ship, having burst through the flying bridge of boats, struck against one of the estoccades. Alexander, unmindful of danger, used every exertion of his authority to stimulate the sailors in their attempts to clear away the monstrous machine which threatened destruction to all within its reach. Happily for him an ensign who was near, forgetting in his general's peril all rules of discipline and forms of ceremony, actually forced him from the estoccade. He had not put his foot on the river bank when the machine blew up. The effects were such as really baffle description. The bridge was burst through, the estoccade was shattered almost to atoms, and, with all that it supported—men, cannon, and the huge machinery employed in the various works—dispersed in the air. The Marquis of Roubais, many other officers, and 800 soldiers perished in all varieties of death—by flood, or flame, or the horrid wounds from the missiles with which the terrible machine was overcharged. Fragments of bodies and limbs were flung far and wide, and many gallant soldiers were destroyed without a vestige of the human form being left to prove that they had ever existed. The river, forced from its bed at either side, rushed into the forts and drowned numbers of their garrisons, while the ground far beyond shook as in an earthquake. The prince was struck down by a beam and lay for some time senseless, together with two generals, Delvasto and Gajitani, both more seriously wounded than he, and many of the soldiers were burned and mutilated in the most frightful manner. Alexander soon recovered, and by his presence of mind, humanity, and resolution he endeavored with incredible quickness to repair the mischief, and raised the confidence of his army as high as ever. Had the Zealand fleet come in time to the spot the whole plan might have been crowned with success; but by some want of concert, or accidental delay, it did not appear, and consequently the beleaguered town received no relief.

One last resource was left to the besieged, that which had formerly been resorted to at Leyden, and by which the place was saved. To enable them to inundate the immense plain which stretched between Lillo and Stabrock up to the walls of Antwerp, it was necessary to cut through the dike which defended it against the irruptions of the eastern Scheldt. This plain was traversed by a high and wide counter-dike, called the dike of Couvestien, and Alexander, knowing its importance, had early taken possession of and strongly defended it by several forts. Two attacks were made by the garrison of Antwerp on this important construction, the latter of which led to one of the most desperate encounters of the war. The prince, seeing that on the results of this day depended the whole consequence of his labors, fought with a valor that even he had never before displayed, and he was finally victorious. The confederates were therefore forced to abandon the attack, leaving 3000 dead upon the dike or at its base, and the Spaniards lost fully 800 men.

One more fruitless attempt was made to destroy the bridge and raised the siege, by means of an enormous vessel bearing the presumptuous title of *The End of the War*. But this floating citadel ran aground without producing any effect, and the gallant governor of Antwerp, the celebrated Philip de Saint Aldegonde, was forced to capitulate on August 16, 1585, after a siege of fourteen months. The reduction of Antwerp was considered a miracle of perseverance and courage. The Prince of Parma was elevated by his success to the highest pinnacle of renown, and Philip, on receiving the news, displayed a burst of joy such as rarely varied his cold and gloomy reserve.

Even while the fate of Antwerp was undecided the United Provinces, seeing that they were still too weak to resist alone the undivided force of the Spanish monarchy, had opened negotiations with France and England at once, in the hope of gaining one or the other for an ally and protector. Henry III. gave a most honorable reception to the ambassadors sent to his court, and was evidently disposed to accept their offers had not the distracted state of his own country, still torn by civil war, quite disabled him from any effective coöperation. The deputies sent to England were also well received. Elizabeth listened to the proposals of the states, sent them an ambassador in return, and held out the most flattering hopes of succor. But her cautious policy would not suffer her to accept the sovereignty, though she by no means made a final rejection of it, and she declared that she would in no ways interfere with the negotiations, which might end in its being accepted by the King of France. She gave prompt evidence of her sincerity by an advance of considerable sums of money, and by sending to Holland a body of 6000 troops, under the command of her favorite, Robert Dudley, Earl of Leicester, and as security for the repayment of her loan the towns of Flushing and Brille and the castle of Rammekins were given up to her.

The Earl of Leicester was accompanied by a splendid retinue of noblemen and a select troop of 500 followers. He was received at Flushing by the governor, Sir Philip Sidney, his nephew, the model of manners and conduct for the young men of his day. But Leicester possessed neither courage nor capacity equal to the trust reposed in him, and his arbitrary and indolent conduct soon disgusted the people whom he was sent to assist. They had in the first impulse of their gratitude given him the title of governor and captain-general of the provinces, in the hope of flattering Elizabeth. But this had a far contrary effect. She was equally displeased with the states and with Leicester, and it was with difficulty that, after many humble submissions, they were able to appease her.

To form a counterpoise to the power so lavishly conferred on Leicester, Prince Maurice was, according to the wise advice of Olden Barneveldt, raised to the dignity of stadtholder, captain-general, and admiral of Holland and Zealand. This is the first instance of these states taking on themselves the nomination to the dignity of stadtholder, for even William had held his commission from Philip, or in his name; but Friesland, Groningen, and Guelders had already appointed their local governors, under the same title, by the authority of the states-general, the Archduke Mathias, or even of the provincial states. Holland had now also at the head of its civil government a citizen full of talent and probity, who was thus able to contend with the insidious designs of Leicester against the liberty he nominally came to protect. This was John of Olden Barneveldt, who was promoted from his office of pensionary of Rotterdam to that of Holland, and who accepted the dignity only on condition of being free to resign it if any accommodation of differences should take place with Spain.

Alexander of Parma had, by the death of his mother, in February, 1586, exchanged his title of prince for the superior one of Duke of Parma, and soon resumed his enterprises with his usual energy and success. Various operations took place, in which the English on every opportunity distinguished themselves, particularly in an action near the town of Grave, in Brabant, and in the taking of Axtel by escalade, under the orders of Sir Philip Sidney. A more important affair occurred near Zutphen, at a place called Wernsfeld, both towns having given names to the action. On this occasion the veteran Spaniards under the Marquis of Guasto were warmly attacked and defeated by the English, but the victory was dearly purchased by the death of Sir Philip Sidney, who was

Hist. Nat. XIII-11

mortally wounded in the thigh, and expired a few days afterward, at the early age of thirty-two years. In addition to the valor, talent, and conduct, which had united to establish his fame, he displayed on this last opportunity of his short career an instance of humanity that sheds a new luster on even a character like his. Stretched on the battlefield, in all the agony of his wound, and parched with thirst, his afflicted followers brought him some water, procured with difficulty at a distance and during the heat of the fight. But Sidney, seeing a soldier lying near, mangled like himself and apparently expiring, refused the water, saying, " Give it to that poor man; his sufferings are greater than mine."

Leicester's conduct was now become quite intolerable to the states. His incapacity and presumption were every day more evident and more revolting. He seemed to consider himself in a province wholly reduced to English authority, and paid no sort of attention to the very opposite character of the people. An eminent Dutch author accounts for this, in terms which may make an Englishman of this age not a little proud of the contrast which his character presents to what it was then considered. " The Englishman," says Grotius, " obeys like a slave and governs like a tyrant; while the Belgian knows how to serve and to command with equal moderation." The dislike between Leicester and those he insulted and misgoverned soon became mutual. He retired to the town of Utrecht, and pushed his injurious conduct to such an extent that he became an object of utter hatred to the provinces. All the friendly feelings toward England were gradually changed into suspicion and dislike. Conferences took place at The Hague between Leicester and the states, in which Barneveld overwhelmed his contemptible shuffling by the force of irresistible eloquence and well-deserved reproaches, and after new acts of treachery, still more odious than his former, this unworthy favorite at last set out for England, to lay an account of his government at the feet of the queen.

The growing hatred against England was fomented by the true patriots, who aimed at the liberty of their country, and may be excused from the various instances of treachery displayed, not only by the commander-in-chief, but by several of his inferiors in command. A strong fort near Zutphen, under the government of Roland York, the town of Deventer under that of William Stanley, and subsequently Guelders under a Scotchman named Pallot, were delivered up to the Spaniards by these men, and about the same time the English cavalry committed some excesses in Guelders and Holland which added to the prevalent prejudice against the nation in general. This enmity was no longer to be concealed. The partisans of Leicester were one by one, under plausible pretexts, removed from the council of state, and Elizabeth having required from Holland the exportation into England of a large quantity of rye, it was firmly but respectfully refused, as inconsistent with the wants of the provinces.

Prince Maurice, from the caprice and jealousy of Leicester, now united in himself the whole power of command, and commenced that brilliant course of conduct which consolidated the independence of his country and elevated him to the first rank of military glory. His early efforts were turned to the suppression of the partiality which in some places existed for English domination, and he never allowed himself to be deceived by the hopes of peace held out by the emperor and the kings of Denmark and Poland. Without refusing their mediation, he labored incessantly to organize every possible means for maintaining the war. His efforts were considerably favored by the measures of Philip for the support of the league formed by the House of Guise against Henry III. and Henry IV. of France; but still more by the formidable enterprise which the Spanish monarch was now preparing against England.

Philip had for some years nourished the project of conquering England, hoping afterward to effect with ease the subjugation of the Netherlands. He caused to be built, in almost every port of Spain and Portugal, galleons, carricks, and other ships of war of the largest dimensions, and at the same time gave orders to the Duke of Parma to assemble in the harbors of Flanders as many vessels as he could collect together. The Spanish fleet, consisting of more than 140 ships of the line, and manned by 20,000 sailors, assembled at Lisbon under the orders of the Duke of Medina Sidonia, while the Duke of Parma, uniting his forces, held himself ready on the coast of Flanders, with an army of 30,000 men and 400 transports. This prodigious force obtained, in Spain, the ostentatious title of the Invincible Armada. Its destination was for a while attempted to be concealed, under pretext that it was meant for India, or for the annihilation of the United Provinces; but the mystery was soon discovered. At the end of May the principal fleet sailed from the port of Lisbon, and, being reinforced off Corunna by a considerable squadron, the whole armament steered its course for the shores of England.

The details of the progress and the failure of this celebrated attempt are so thoroughly the province of English history that they would be in this place superfluous. But it must not be forgotten that the glory of the proud result was amply shared by the new republic, whose existence depended on it. While Howard and Drake held the British fleet in readiness to oppose the Spanish armada, that of Holland, consisting of but twenty-five ships, under the command of Justin of Nassau, prepared to take a part in the conflict. This gallant though illegitimate scion of the illustrious house whose name he upheld on many occasions, proved himself on the present worthy of such a father as William and such a brother as Maurice. While the Duke of Medina Sidonia, ascending the Channel as far as Dunkirk, there awaited the junction of the Duke of Parma with his important reinforcement, Justin of Nassau, by a constant activity and a display of intrepid talent, contrived to block up the whole expected force in the ports of Flanders from Lillo to Dunkirk. The Duke of Parma found it impossible to force a passage on any one point, and was doomed to the mortification of knowing that the attempt was frustrated and the whole force of Spain frittered away, discomfited, and disgraced from the want of a coöperation which he could not, however, reproach himself for having withheld. The issue of the memorable expedition which cost Spain years of preparation, thousands of men, and millions of treasure was received in the country which sent it forth with consternation and rage. Philip alone possessed or affected an apathy which he covered with a veil of devotion that few were deceived by. At the news of the disaster he fell on his knees and, rendering thanks for that gracious dispensation of Providence, expressed his joy that the calamity was not greater.

The people, the priests, and the commanders of the expedition were not so easily appeased, or so clever as their resourceful master in concealing their mortification. The priests accounted for this triumph of heresy as a punishment on Spain for suffering the existence of the infidel Moors in some parts of the country. The defeated admirals threw the whole blame on the Duke of Parma. He, on his part, sent an ample remonstrance to the king, and Philip declared that he was satisfied with the conduct of his nephew. Leicester died four days after the final defeat and dispersion of the armada.

The war in the Netherlands had been necessarily suffered to languish, while every eye was fixed on the progress of the armada, from formation to defeat. But new efforts were soon made by the Duke of Parma to repair the time he had lost, and soothe by his successes the disappointed pride of Spain. Several officers now came into notice, remarkable for deeds of great gallantry and skill. None among these was so distinguished as Martin Schenck, a soldier of fortune, a man of ferocious activity, who began his career in the service of tyranny and ended it by chance in that of independence. He changed sides several times, but no matter who he fought for he did his duty well, from that unconquerable principle of pugnacity which seemed to make his sword a part of himself.

Schenck had lately, for the last time, gone over to the side of the states and had caused a fort to be built in the Isle of Betewe—that possessed of old by the Batavians—which was called by his name, and was considered the key to the passage of the Rhine. From this stronghold he constantly harassed the Archbishop of Cologne, and had as his latest exploit surprised and taken the strong town of Bonn. While the Duke of Parma took prompt measures for the relief of the prelate, making himself master in the meantime of some places of strength, the indefatigable Schenck resolved to make an attempt on the important town of Nimeugen. He with great caution embarked a chosen body of troops on the Waal and arrived under the walls of Nimeguen at sunrise on the morning chosen for the attack. His enterprise seemed almost crowned with success, when the inhabitants, recovering from their fright, precipitated themselves from the town, forced the assailants to retreat to their boats, and, carrying the combat into those overcharged and fragile vessels, upset several, and among others that which contained Schenck himself, who, covered with wounds and fighting to the last gasp, was drowned with the greater part of his followers. His body, when recovered, was treated at first with the utmost indignity, quartered, and hung in portions over the different gates of the city, but was later accorded honorable burial by the orders of the Spanish commander. In Schenck the states lost their bravest and most enterprising leader.

The following year was distinguished by another daring attempt on the part of the Hollanders, but followed by a different result. A captain named Haranguer concerted with one Adrien Vandenberg a plan for the surprise of Breda, on the possession of which Prince Maurice had set a great value. The associates contrived to conceal in a boat laden with turf (which formed the principal fuel of the inhabitants of that part of the country), and of which Vandenberg was master, eighty determined soldiers, and succeeded in arriving close to the city without any suspicion being excited. One of the soldiers, named Mathew Helt, being suddenly affected with a violent cough, implored his comrades to put him to death to avoid the risk of a discovery. But a corporal of the city guard having inspected the cargo with unsuspecting carelessness, the immolation of the brave soldier became unnecessary, and the boat was dragged into the basin by the assistance of some of the very garrison who were so soon to fall victims to the stratagem. At midnight the concealed soldiers quitted their hiding-places, leaped on shore, killed the sentinels, and easily became masters of the citadel. Prince Maurice, following close with his army, soon forced the town to submit, and put it into so good a state of defense that Count Mansfield, who was sent to retake it, was obliged to retreat after useless efforts to fulfill his mission.

The Duke of Parma, whose constitution was severely injured by the constant fatigues of war and the anxieties attending on the late transactions, had snatched a short interval for the purpose of recruiting his health at the waters of Spa. While at that place he received urgent orders from Philip to abandon for a while all his proceedings in the Netherlands and to hasten into France with his whole disposable force to assist the army of the league. The battle of Yvri (in which the son of the unfortunate Count Egmont met his death while fighting in the service of his father's royal murderer) had raised the prospects and hopes of Henry IV. to a high pitch, and Paris, which he closely besieged, was on the point of yielding to his arms. The Duke of Parma received his uncle's orders with great repugnance, and lamented the necessity of leaving the field of his former exploits open to the enterprise and talents of Prince Maurice. He nevertheless obeyed, and, leaving Count Mansfield at the head of the government, he conducted his troops against the royal opponent, who alone seemed fully worthy of coping with him.

The attention of all Europe was now fixed on the exciting

spectacle of a contest between these two greatest captains of the age. The glory of success, the fruit of consummate skill, was gained by Alexander, who by an admirable maneuver got possession of the town of Lagny-sur-Seine under the very eyes of Henry and his whole army, and thus acquired the means of providing Paris with everything requisite for its defense. The French monarch saw all his projects baffled and his hopes frustrated, while his antagonist, having fully completed his object, drew off his army through Champagne and made a fine retreat through an enemy's country, harassed at every step, but with scarcely any loss.

But while this expedition added greatly to the renown of the general, it considerably injured the cause of Spain in the Low Countries. Prince Maurice, taking prompt advantage of the absence of his great rival, had made himself master of several fortresses, and some Spanish regiments having mutinied against the commanders left behind by the Duke of Parma, others, encouraged by the impunity they enjoyed, were ready on the slightest pretext to follow their example. Maurice did not lose a single opportunity of profiting by circumstances so favorable, and even after the return of Alexander he seized on Zutphen, Deventer, and Nimeugen in spite of all the efforts of the Spanish army. The Duke of Parma, daily breaking down under the progress of disease and agitated by these reverses, repaired again to Spa, taking at once every possible means for the recruitment of his army and the recovery of his health, on which its discipline and the chances of success now so evidently depended.

But all his plans were again frustrated by a renewal of Philip's peremptory orders to march once more into France to uphold the failing cause of the league against the intrepidity and talent of Henry IV. At this juncture the Emperor Rudolf again offered his mediation between Spain and the United Provinces. But it was not likely that the confederated states, at the very moment when their cause began to triumph, and their commerce was every day becoming more and more flourishing, would consent to make any compromise with the tyranny they were at length in a fair way of crushing.

The Duke of Parma again appeared in France in the beginning of the year 1592, and, having formed his communications with the army of the league, marched to the relief of the city of

Rouen, at that period pressed to the last extremity by the Huguenot forces. After some sharp skirmishes—and one in particular, in which Henry IV. suffered his valor to lead him into a too rash exposure of his own and his army's safety—a series of maneuvers took place which displayed the talents of the rival generals in the most brilliant aspect. Alexander at length succeeded in raising the siege of Rouen and made himself master of Condebec, which commanded the navigation of the Seine. Henry, taking advantage of what appeared an irreparable fault on the part of the duke, invested his army in the hazardous position he had chosen, but while believing that he had the whole of his enemies in his power, he found that Alexander had passed the Seine with his entire force—raising his military renown to the utmost possible height by a retreat which it was deemed utterly impossible to effect.

On his return to the Netherlands the duke found himself again under the necessity of repairing to Spa in search of some relief from his suffering, which was considerably increased by the effects of a wound received in this last campaign. In spite of his shattered constitution he maintained to the latest moment the most active endeavors for the reorganization of his army, and he was preparing for a new expedition into France when, fortunately for the good cause in both countries, he was surprised by death on December 3, 1592, at the abbey of St. Vaast, near Arras, at the age of forty-seven years. Incredible as it may seem, Philip II. had been suspicious of the fidelity of his great captain, as well as jealous of his fame, and had already sent the Count of Fuentes to supersede him.

Alexander of Parma was certainly one of the most remarkable and, it may be added, one of the greatest, characters of his day. Most historians have upheld him even higher perhaps than he should be placed on the scale, asserting that he can be reproached with very few of the vices of the age in which he lived. Others consider this judgment too favorable, and accuse him of participation in all the crimes of Philip, whom he served so zealously. His having excited the jealousy of the tyrant, or even having been put to death by his orders, would little influence the question, for Philip was quite capable of ingratitude or murder to either an accomplice or an opponent of his baseness. But even allowing that Alexander's fine qualities were sullied by his complicity in these odious measures, we must still in justice admit that they were too much in the spirit of the times, and particularly of the school in which he was trained; and while we lament that his political or private faults place him on so low a level, we must rank him as one of the very first masters in the art of war in his own or any other age. In his fourteen years as governor he had recovered for his master all the southern provinces of the Netherlands, which on his arrival had seemed hopelessly lost to Spain.

Chapter XIV

SUCCESSES OF PRINCE MAURICE AND DEATH OF PHILIP II. 1592-1599

THE Duke of Parma had chosen the Count of Mansfield for his successor, and the nomination was approved by the king. He entered on his government under most disheartening circumstances. The rapid conquests of Prince Maurice in Brabant and Flanders were scarcely less mortifying that the total disorganization into which those two provinces had fallen. They were ravaged by bands of robbers called Picaroons, whose audacity reached such a height that they opposed in large bodies the forces sent for their suppression by the government. They on one occasion killed the provost of Flanders and burned his lieutenant in a hollow tree, and on another they mutilated a whole troop of the national militia and their commander with circumstances of most revolting cruelty.

The authority of governor-general, though not the title, was now fully shared by the Count of Fuentes, who was sent to Brussels by the King of Spain, and the ill effects of this double viceroyalty was soon seen in the brilliant progress of Prince Maurice and the continual reverses sustained by the royalist armies. The king sacrificed without scruple men and treasure for the overthrow of Henry IV. and the success of the league. The affairs of the Netherlands seemed now a secondary object, and he drew largely on his forces in that country for reinforcements to the ranks of his tottering allies. A final blow was, however, struck against the hopes of intolerance in France, and to the existence of the league, by the conversion of Henry IV. to the Catholic religion, he deeming theological disputes which put the happiness of a whole kingdom in jeopardy as quite subordinate to the public good.

Such was the prosperity of the United Provinces that they had been enabled to send a considerable supply, both of money and men, to the aid of Henry, their constant and generous ally. And notwithstanding this, their armies and fleets, so far from suffering diminution, were augmented day by day. Philip, resolved to summon up all his energy for the revival of the war against the republic, now appointed the Archduke Ernest, brother of the Emperor Rudolf, to the post which the disunion of Mansfield and Fuentes rendered as embarrassing as it had become inglorious. This prince, of a gentle and conciliatory character, was received at Brussels with great magnificence and general joy, his presence reviving the deep-felt hopes of peace entertained by the suffering people. Such were also the cordial wishes of the prince, but more than one design formed at this period against the life of Prince Maurice frustrated every expectation of the kind. A priest of the province of Namur, named Michael Renichon, disguised as a soldier, was the new instrument meant to strike another blow at the greatness of the house of Nassau in the person of its gallant representative, Prince Maurice, as also in that of his brother, Frederic Henry, then ten years of age. On the confession of the intended assassin he was employed by Count Barlaimont to murder the two princes. Renichon happily mismanaged the affair and betrayed his intention. He was arrested at Breda, conducted to The Hague, and there tried and executed on June 3, 1594. This miserable wretch accused the Archduke Ernest of having countenanced his attempt, but nothing whatever tends to incriminate, while every probability acquits, that prince of such a participation.

In this same year a soldier named Peter Dufour embarked in a like atrocious plot. He, too, was seized and executed before he could carry it into effect, and to his dying hour persisted in accusing the archduke of being his instigator. But neither the judges who tried nor the best historians who record his intended crime gave any belief to this accusation. The mild and honorable disposition of the prince held a sufficient guarantee against its likelihood, and it is not less pleasing to be able to fully join in the prevalent opinion than to mark a spirit of candor and impartiality break forth through the mass of bad and violent passions which crowd the records of that age.

But all the esteem inspired by the personal character of Ernest could not overcome the repugnance of the United Provinces to trust to the apparent sincerity of the tyrant in whose name he made his overtures for peace. They were all respectfully and firmly rejected, and Prince Maurice in the meantime, with his usual activity, passed the Meuse and the Rhine and invested and quickly took the town of Groningen, by which he consummated the establishment of the republic and secured its rank among the principal powers of Europe.[1]

The Archduke Ernest, finding all his efforts for peace frustrated and all hopes of gaining his object by hostility to be vain, became a prey to disappointment and regret, and died from the effects of a slow fever on February 21, 1595, leaving to the Count of Fuentes the honors and anxieties of the government, subject to the ratification of the king. This nobleman began the exercise of his temporary functions by an irruption into France at the head of a small army, war having been declared against Spain by Henry IV., who, on his side, had dispatched the Admiral de Villars to attack Philip's possessions in Hainault and Artois. This gallant officer lost a battle and his life in the contest, and Fuentes, encouraged by the victory, took some frontier towns and laid siege to Cambray, the object of his plans. The citizens, who detested their governor, the Marquis of Baligny, who had for some time assumed an independent tyranny over them, gave up the place to the besiegers, and the citadel surrendered some days later. After this exploit Fuentes returned to Brussels, where, notwithstanding his success, he was extremely unpopular. He had placed a part of his forces under the command of Mondragon, one of the oldest and cleverest officers in the service of Spain. Some trifling affairs took place in Brabant, but the arrival of the Archduke Albert, whom the king had appointed to succeed his brother Ernest in the office of governor-general, deprived Fuentes of any further opportunity of signalizing his talents for supreme command. Albert arrived at Brussels on February 11, 1596, accompanied by the Prince of Orange, who, when Count of Beuren, had been carried off from the University of Louvain, twenty-eight years previously, and held captive in Spain during the whole of that period.

The Archduke Albert, fifth son of the Emperor Maximilian II. and brother of Rudolf, stood high in the opinion of Philip, his uncle, and merited his reputation for talents, bravery, and prudence. He had early been made Archbishop of Toledo and afterward cardinal, but his profession was not that of these nominal dignities. He was a warrior and politician of considerable capacity, and had for some years faithfully served the king as viceroy of Portugal. But Philip meant him for the more independent situation of sov-

---

[1] In May, 1596, the states were admitted as equals into a triple alliance with France and England against Spain. They had already been invited by King James of Scotland to stand as sponsors to his heir, Prince Henry.

ereign of the Netherlands, and at the same time destined him to be the husband of his daughter Isabella. He now sent him, in the capacity of governor-general, to prepare the way for the important change, at once to gain the good graces of the people, and soothe, by this removal from Philip's too close neighborhood, the jealousy of his son, the hereditary prince of Spain. Albert brought with him to Brussels a small reinforcement for the army, with a large supply of money, more needed at this conjuncture than men. He highly praised the conduct of Fuentes in the operations just finished, and resolved to continue the war on the same plan, but with forces much superior.

He opened his first campaign early, and by a display of clever maneuvering, which threatened an attempt to force the French to raise the siege of La Fère, in the heart of Picardy, he concealed his real design—the capture of Calais; and he succeeded in its completion almost before it was suspected. The Spanish and Walloon troops, led by De Roene, a distinguished officer, carried the first defenses. After nine days of siege the place was forced to surrender, and in a few more the citadel followed the example. The archduke soon after took the towns of Ardres and Hulst, and by prudently avoiding a battle, to which he was constantly provoked by Henry IV., who commanded the French army in person, he established his character for military talent of no ordinary degree.

He at the same time made overtures of reconciliation to the United Provinces, and hoped that the return of the Prince of Orange would be a means of effecting so desirable a purpose. But the Dutch were not to be deceived by the apparent sincerity of Spanish negotiation. They even doubted the sentiments of the Prince of Orange, whose attachments and principles had been formed in so hated a school, and nothing passed between them and him but mutual civilities. They clearly evinced their disapprobation of his intended visit to Holland, and he consequently fixed his residence in Brussels, passing his life in an inglorious neutrality.

A naval expedition formed in this year by the English and Dutch against Cadiz, commanded by the Earl of Essex and Counts Louis and William of Nassau, cousins of Prince Maurice, was crowned with brilliant success and somewhat consoled the provinces for the contemporary exploits of the archduke. But the following year opened with an affair which at once proved his unceasing activity and added largely to the reputation of his rival, Prince

Maurice. The former had detached the Count of Varas, with about 6000 men, for the purpose of invading the province of Holland; but Maurice, with equal energy and superior talent, followed his movements, came up with him near Turnhout, on January 24, 1597, and after a sharp action, of which the Dutch cavalry bore the whole brunt, Varas was killed and his troops defeated with considerable loss.

This was in its consequences a most disastrous affair to the archduke. His army was disorganized and his finances exhausted, while the confidence of the states in their troops and their general was considerably raised. But the taking of Amiens by Portocarrero, one of the most enterprising of the Spanish captains, gave a new turn to the failing fortunes of Albert. This gallant officer, whose greatness of mind, according to some historians, was much disproportioned to the smallness of his person, gained possession of that important town by a well-conducted stratagem and maintained his conquest valiantly till he was killed in its defense. Henry IV. made prodigious efforts to recover the place, the chief bulwark on that side of France, and having forced Montenegro, the worthy successor of Portocarrero, to capitulate, granted him and his garrison most honorable conditions. Henry, having secured Amiens against any new attack, returned to Paris and made a triumphal entry into the city.

During this year Prince Maurice took a number of towns in rapid succession, and the states, according to their custom, caused various medals, in gold, silver, and copper, to be struck to commemorate the victories which had signalized their arms.

Philip II., feeling himself approaching the termination of his long and agitating career, now wholly occupied himself in negotiations for peace with France. Henry IV. desired it as anxiously. The Pope, Clement VIII., encouraged by his exhortations this mutual inclination. The King of Poland sent ambassadors to The Hague and to London to induce the states and Queen Elizabeth to become parties in a general pacification. These overtures led to no conclusion, but the conferences between France and Spain went on with apparent cordiality and great promptitude, and a peace was concluded between these powers at Vervins on May 2, 1598.

Shortly after the publication of this treaty another important act was made known to the world, by which Philip ceded to Albert and Isabella, on their being formally affianced—a ceremony which now took place—the sovereignty of Burgundy and the Netherlands. This act bears date of May 6, and was proclaimed with all the solemnity due to so important a transaction. It contained thirteen articles, and was based on the misfortunes which the absence of the sovereign had hitherto caused to the Low Countries. The Catholic religion was declared that of the state, in its full integrity. The provinces were guaranteed against dismemberment. The archdukes, by which title the joint sovereigns were designated without any distinction of sex, were secured in the possession, with right of succession to their children, and a provision was added that, in default of posterity, their possessions should revert to the Spanish crown. The Infanta Isabella soon sent her procuration to the archduke, her affianced husband, giving him full power and authority to take possession of the ceded dominions in her name as in his own, and Albert was inaugurated with great pomp at Brussels on August 22. Having put everything in order for the regulation of the government during his absence, he set out for Italy for the purpose of accomplishing his espousals and bringing back his bride to the chief seat of their joint power. But before his departure he wrote to the various states of the republic, and to Prince Maurice himself, strongly recommending submission and reconciliation. These letters received no answer, a new plot against the life of Prince Maurice by a wretched individual named Peter Pann having aroused the indignation of the country and determined it to treat with suspicion and contempt every insidious proposition from the tyranny it defied.

Albert placed his uncle, Cardinal Andrew of Austria, at the head of the temporary government and set out on his journey, taking the little town of Halle in his route, and deposing at the altar of the Virgin, who is there held in particular honor, his cardinal's hat as a token of his veneration. He had not made much progress when he received accounts of the demise of Philip II., who died, after long suffering and with great resignation, on September 13, 1598, at the age of seventy-two. Albert was several months on his journey through Germany, and the ceremonials of his union with the Infanta did not take place till April 18, 1599, when it was finally solemnized in the city of Valencia in Spain.

By this transaction the Netherlands were positively erected into a separate sovereignty. Indeed, it completely decided the division between the northern and southern provinces, which, although it had virtually taken place long previous to this period, could scarcely be considered as formally consummated until then. Here then we shall pause anew and take a rapid view of the social state of the Netherlands during the last half century, which constitutes beyond all doubt the most important period of their history, from the earliest times till the present.

It has been seen that when Charles V. resigned his throne and the possession of his vast dominions to his son, arts, commerce, and manufactures had risen to a state of considerable perfection throughout the Netherlands. The revolution, of which we have traced the rise and progress, naturally produced to these provinces which relapsed into slavery a most lamentable change in every branch of industry, and struck a blow at the general prosperity, the effects of which are felt to this very day. Arts, science, and literature were sure to be checked and withered in the blaze of civil war, and we have now to mark the retrograde movements of most of those charms and advantages of civilized life in which Flanders and the other southern states were so rich.

The rapid spread of liberalism in religious subjects soon converted the manufactories and workshops of Flanders into so many conventicles of the Reform, and the clear-sighted artisans fled in thousands from the tyranny of Alva into England, Germany, and Holland. Commerce followed the fate of manufactures. The foreign merchants one by one abandoned the theater of bigotry and persecution, and even Antwerp, which had succeeded Bruges as the great mart of European traffic, was ruined by the horrible excesses of the Spanish soldiery and never recovered from the shock. Its trade, its wealth, and its prosperity were gradually transferred to Amsterdam, Rotterdam, and the towns of Holland and Zealand, and the growth of Dutch commerce attained its proud maturity in the establishment of the India Company in 1596, the effects of which we shall have hereafter more particularly to dwell on.

The exciting and romantic enterprises of the Portuguese and Spanish navigators in the fifteenth and sixteenth centuries roused all the ardor of other nations for those distant adventures, and the people of the Netherlands were early influenced by the general spirit of Europe. If they were not the discoverers of new worlds, they were certainly the first to make the name of European respected and venerated by the natives.

Animated by the ardor which springs from the spirit of freedom and the enthusiasm of success, the United Provinces labored for the discovery of new outlets for their commerce and navigation. The government encouraged the speculation of individuals, which promised fresh and fertile sources of revenue, so necessary for the maintenance of the war. Until the year 1581 the merchants of Holland and Zealand were satisfied to find the productions of India at Lisbon, which was the mart of that branch of trade from the time the Portuguese discovered the passage by the Cape of Good Hope. But Philip II., having conquered Portugal, excluded the United Provinces from the ports of that country, and their enterprising mariners were from that time driven to those efforts which rapidly led to private fortune and general prosperity.

The year 1595 marks the expansion of Dutch commerce into the East Indies and the beginning of the great colonial empire of the Netherlands. The closing of the Spanish ports to Dutch ships in 1586 drove the adventurous merchants of Holland and Zealand far afield in search of new markets, while the fame of the English and Portuguese discoveries roused them to emulation. In 1595 one Cornelis Houtman and others formed a company for trade with the Indies. An expedition sailed from the Texel in April and reached the Island of Java in June of the following year. In spite of Portuguese opposition a brisk trade was established, and in 1597 three ships returned to Holland laden with spice. Thenceforth an ever-increasing commerce was driven with the Indies, and almost every year a Dutch fleet sailed for the far East. Nor was the activity of the Dutch sailors confined to the Indian trade. Incited by offers of reward from the states-general for the discovery of a northern passage to the Indies, numerous expeditions were fitted out for Arctic exploration. In one of these adventurous voyages Rijp and Heemskirk discovered Spitzbergen, and some years later in a similar attempt Henry Hudson discovered the bay and the river in America which bear his name.

In 1602 the famous Dutch East India Company, the source of immense wealth to Holland, was founded. Since 1595 several companies had been founded in the Netherlands for trade with the Indies. Treaties had been made with the rulers of Banda, Ternate, and Achin in Sumatra, and the Dutch captains found themselves able to compete with their Spanish and Portuguese rivals. But the several companies soon saw that still greater prosperity could be gained by union, and the states-general authorized the formation of a single East India Company, with exclusive privileges in the Indies for twenty-one years. The new company entered on a career of almost uninterrupted prosperity and power; and the capture of the Portuguese stronghold of Amboyna in India, 1603, laid the foundations for the future colonial empire.

The United Provinces were soon without any rival on the seas. In Europe alone they had 1200 merchant ships in activity and upward of 70,000 sailors constantly employed. They built annually 2000 vessels. In the year 1598 eighty ships sailed from their ports for the Indies or America. They carried on, besides, an extensive trade on the coast of Guinea, whence they brought large quantities of gold dust, and found, in short, in all quarters of the globe the reward of their skill, industry, and courage.

The spirit of conquest soon became grafted on the habits of trade. Expedition succeeded to expedition. Failure taught wisdom to those who did not want bravery. The random efforts of individuals were succeeded by organized plans, under associations well constituted and wealthy, and these soon gave birth to those eastern and western companies before alluded to. The disputes between the English and the Hanseatic towns were carefully observed by the Dutch, and turned to their own advantage. The English manufacturers, who quickly began to flourish from the influx of Flemish workmen under the encouragement of Elizabeth, formed companies in the Netherlands and sent their cloths into those very towns of Germany which formerly possessed the exclusive privilege of their manufacture. These towns naturally felt dissatisfied, and their complaints were encouraged by the King of Spain. The English adventurers received orders to quit the empire, and, invited by the states-general, many of them fixed their residence in Middelburg, which became the most celebrated woolen market in Europe.

The establishment of the Jews in the towns of the republic forms a remarkable epoch in the annals of trade. This people, so outraged by religious persecution, so far from being depressed, seemed to find it a fresh stimulus to the exertion of their industry. To escape death in Spain and Portugal they took refuge in Holland, where toleration encouraged and just principles of state maintained them. They were at first taken for Catholics, and subjected to suspicion, but when their real faith was understood they were no longer molested.

Astronomy and geography, two sciences so closely allied with and so essential to navigation, flourished now throughout Europe. Ortelius of Antwerp and Gerard Mercator of Rupelmonde were two of the greatest geographers of the sixteenth century, and the reform in the calendar at the end of that period gave stability to the calculations of time, which had previously suffered all the inconvenient fluctuations attendant on the old style.

Literature had assumed during the revolution in the Netherlands the almost exclusive aspect of controversial learning. The University of Douay, founded in 1562 by Philip II., quickly became a stronghold of the Catholic religion. That of Leyden, established by the efforts of the Prince of Orange, soon after the famous siege of that town in 1574, was on a less exclusive plan—its professors being in the first instance drawn from Germany. Many Flemish historians succeeded in this century to the ancient and uncultivated chroniclers of preceding times, the civil wars drawing forth many writers, who recorded what they witnessed, but often in a spirit of partisanship and want of candor which seriously embarrasses him who desires to learn the truth on both sides of an important question. Poetry declined and drooped in these times of tumult and suffering, and the chambers of rhetoric, to which its cultivation had been chiefly due, gradually lost their influence and finally ceased to exist.

In fixing our attention on the republic of the United Provinces during the epoch now completed we feel the desire and lament the impossibility of entering on the details of government in that most remarkable state. For these we must refer to what appears to us the best authority for clear and ample information on the prerogative of the stadtholder, the constitution of the states-general, the privileges of the tribunals and local assemblies, and other points of moment concerning the principles of the Belgic confederation.[2]

[2] Blok, "History of the Dutch People," vol. iii. ch. xiii.

Chapter XV

PRINCE MAURICE AND SPINOLA. 1599-1605

PREVIOUS to his departure for Spain the Archduke Albert had placed the government of the provinces which acknowledged his domination in the hands of his uncle, the Cardinal Andrew of Austria, leaving in command of the army Francisco Mendoza, Admiral of Aragon. The troops at his disposal amounted to 22,000 fighting men, a formidable force, and enough to justify the serious apprehensions of the republic. Albert, whose finances were exhausted by payments made to the numerous Spanish and Italian mutineers, had left orders with Mendoza to secure some place on the Rhine which might open a passage for free quarters in the enemy's country. But this unprincipled officer forced his way into the neutral districts of Cleves and Westphalia, and with a body of executioners ready to hang up all who might resist, and of priests to prepare them for death, he carried such terror on his march that no opposition was ventured. The atrocious cruelties of Mendoza and his troops baffle all description. On one occasion they murdered in cold blood the Count of Walkenstein, who surrendered his castle on the express condition of his freedom, and they committed every possible excess that may be imagined of ferocious soldiery encouraged by a base commander.

Prince Maurice soon put into motion, to oppose this army of brigands, his small disposable force of about 7000 men. With these, however, and a succession of masterly maneuvers, he contrived to preserve the republic from invasion and to paralyze and almost destroy an army three times superior in numbers to his own. The horrors committed by the Spaniards in the midst of peace and without the slightest provocation could not fail to excite the utmost indignation in a country so fond of liberty and so proud as Germany. The duchy of Cleves felt particularly aggrieved, and Sybilla, the sister of the duke, a real heroine in a glorious cause, so worked on the excited passions of the people by her eloquence and her tears that she persuaded all the orders of the state to unite against the odious enemy. A diet of princes sitting at Coblenz determined to raise troops for the protection of the Rhine Circle. The Count of Lippe was chosen general of their united forces, and the choice could not have fallen on one more certainly incapable or more probably treacherous.

The German army, with its usual want of activity, did not open the campaign till the month of June. It consisted of 14,000 men, and never was an army so badly conducted. Without money, artillery, provisions, or discipline, it was at any moment ready to break up and abandon its incompetent general. On the very first encounter with the enemy, and after a loss of a couple of hundred men, it became self-disbanded, and, flying in every direction, not a single man could be rallied to clear away this disgrace.

The states-general, cruelly disappointed at this result of measures from which they had looked for so important a diversion in their favor, now resolved on a vigorous exertion of their own energies, and determined to undertake a naval expedition of a magnitude greater than any they had hitherto attempted. The force of public opinion was at this period more powerful than it had ever yet been in the United Provinces, for a great number of the inhabitants, who during the life of Philip II. conscientiously believed that they could not lawfully abjure the authority once recognized and sworn to, became now liberated from those respectable although absurd scruples, and the death of one unfeeling despot gave thousands of new citizens to the state.

A fleet of seventy-three vessels, carrying 8000 men, was soon equipped, under the order of Admiral Van der Does, and after a series of attempts on the coasts of Spain, Portugal, Africa, and the Canary Isles, this expedition, from which the most splendid results were expected, was shattered, dispersed, and reduced to nothing by a succession of unheard-of mishaps.

To these disappointments were now added domestic dissensions in the republic in consequence of the new taxes absolutely necessary for the exigencies of the state. The conduct of Queen Elizabeth greatly added to the general embarrassment. She called for the payment of her former loans, insisted on the recall of the English troops, and declared her resolution to make peace with Spain. Several German princes promised aid in men and money, but never furnished either, and in this most critical juncture Henry IV. was the only foreign sovereign who did not abandon the republic. He sent them 1000 Swiss troops whom he had in his pay, allowed them to levy 3000 more in France, and gave them a loan of 200,000 crowns—a very convenient supply in their exhausted state.

The Archdukes Albert and Isabella arrived in the Netherlands in September, 1599, and made their entrance into Brussels with unexampled magnificence. They soon found themselves in a situation quite as critical as was that of the United Provinces, and both parties displayed immense energy to remedy their mutual embarrassments. The winter was extremely rigorous, so much so as to allow of military operations being undertaken on the ice. Prince Maurice soon commenced a Christmas campaign by taking the town of Wachtendenck, and he followed up his success by obtaining possession of the important forts of Crevecœur and St. Andrew in the Island of Bommel. A most dangerous mutiny at the same time broke out in the army of the archdukes, and Albert seemed left without troops or money at the very beginning of his sovereignty.

But these successes of Prince Maurice were only the prelude to an expedition of infinitely more moment, arranged with the utmost secrecy, and executed with an energy scarcely to be looked for from the situation of the states. This was nothing less than an invasion poured into the very heart of Flanders, thus putting the archdukes on the defense of their own and most vital possessions and changing completely the whole character of the war. The whole disposable troops of the republic, amounting to about 17,000 men, were secretly assembled in the Island of Walcheren, in the month of June; and setting sail for Flanders, they disembarked near Ghent and arrived on the 20th of that month under the walls of Bruges. Some previous negotiations with that town had led the prince to expect that it would have opened its gates at his approach. In this he was, however, disappointed, and after taking possession of some forts in the neighborhood he continued his march to Nieuport, which place he invested on July 1.

At the news of this invasion the archdukes, though taken by surprise, displayed a promptness and decision that proved them worthy of the sovereignty which seemed at stake. With incredible activity they mustered in a few days an army of 12,000 men, which they passed in review near Ghent. On this occasion Isabella, proving her title to a place among those heroic women with whom the age abounded, rode through the royalist ranks and harangued them in a style of inspiring eloquence that inflamed their courage and secured their fidelity. Albert, seizing the moment of this excitement, put himself at their head and marched to seek the enemy, leaving his intrepid wife at Bruges, the nearest town to the scene of the action he was resolved on. He gained possession of all the forts taken and garrisoned by Maurice a few days before, and, pushing forward with his apparently irresistible troops, he came up on the morning of July 1 with a large body of those of the states, consisting of about 3000 men, sent forward under the command of Count Ernest of Nassau to reconnoiter and judge of the extent of this most unexpected movement. Prince Maurice was, in his turn, completely surprised, and not merely by one of those maneuvers of war by which the best generals are sometimes deceived, but by an exertion of political vigor and capacity of which history offers few more striking examples. Such a circumstance, however, served only to draw forth a fresh display of those uncommon talents which in so many various accidents of war had placed Maurice in the highest rank for military talent. The detachment under Count Ernest of Nassau was chiefly composed of Scottish infantry, and this small force stood firmly opposed to the impetuous attack of the whole royalist army—thus giving time to the main body under the prince to take up a position and form in order of battle. Count Ernest was at length driven back, with the loss of 800 men killed, almost all Scottish, and, being cut off from the rest of the army, was forced to take refuge in Ostend, which town was in possession of the troops of the states.

The army of Albert now marched on, flushed with this first success and confident of final victory. Prince Maurice received them with the courage of a gallant soldier and the precaution of a consummate general. He had caused the fleet of ships of war and transports which had sailed along the coast from Zealand and landed supplies of ammunition and provisions, to retire far from the shore, so as to leave to his army no chance of escape but in victory. The commissioners from the states, who always accompanied the prince as a council of observation rather than of war, had retired to Ostend in great consternation, to wait the issue of the battle which now seemed inevitable. A scene of deep feeling and heroism was the next episode of this memorable day, and throws the charm of natural affection over those circumstances in which glory too seldom leaves a place for the softer emotions of the heart. When the patriot army was in its position and firmly awaiting the advance of the foe, Prince Maurice turned to his brother, Frederick Henry, then sixteen years of age, and several young noblemen, English, French, and German, who, like him, attended on the great captain to learn the art of war; he pointed out in a few words the perilous situation in which he was placed, declared his resolution to conquer or perish on the battlefield, and recommended the boyish band to retire to Ostend and wait for some less desperate occasion to share his renown or revenge his fall. Frederick Henry spurned the affectionate suggestion, and swore to stand by his brother to the last; and all his young companions adopted the same generous resolution.

The army of the states was placed in order of battle, about a league in front of Nieuport, in the sand-hills with which the neighborhood abounds, its left wing resting on the seashore. Its losses of the previous day and of the garrison left in the forts near Bruges reduced it to an almost exact equality with that of the archduke. Each of these armies was composed of that variety of troops which made them respectively an epitome of the various nations of Europe.

The patriot force contained Dutch, English, French, German, and Swiss, under the orders of Count Louis of Nassau, Sir Francis and Sir Horace Vere, brothers and English officers of great celebrity, with other distinguished captains. The archduke mustered Spaniards, Italians, Walloons, and Irish in his ranks, led on by Mendoza, La Berlotta, and their fellow-veterans. Both armies were in the highest state of discipline, trained to war by long service, and enthusiastic in the several causes which they served, the two highest principles of enthusiasm urging them on—religious fanaticism on the one hand and the love of freedom on the other. The rival generals rode along their respective lines, addressed a few brief sentences of encouragement to their men, and presently the bloody contest began.

It was three o'clock in the afternoon when the archduke commenced the attack. His advanced guard, commanded by Mendoza and composed of those former mutineers who now resolved to atone for their misconduct, marched across the sand-hills with desperate resolution. They soon came in contact with the English contingent under Francis Vere, who was desperately wounded in the shock. The assault was almost irresistible. The English, borne down by numbers, were forced to give way, but the main body pressed on to their support. Horace Vere stepped forward to supply his brother's place. Not an inch of ground more was gained or lost; the firing ceased and pikes and swords crossed each other in the resolute conflict of man to man. The action became general along the whole line. The two commanders-in-chief were at all points. Nothing could exceed their mutual display of skill and courage. At length the Spanish cavalry, broken by the well-directed fire of the patriot artillery, fell back on their infantry and threw it into confusion. The archduke at the same instant was wounded by a lance in the cheek, unhorsed, and forced to quit the field. The report of his death and the sight of his war-steed galloping alone across the field spread alarm through the royalist ranks. Prince Maurice saw and seized on the critical moment. He who had so patiently maintained his position for three hours of desperate conflict now knew the crisis for a prompt and general advance. He gave the word and led on to the charge, and the victory was at once his own.

The defeat of the royalist army was complete. The whole of the artillery, baggage, standards, and ammunition fell into the possession of the conquerors. Night coming on saved those who fled, and the nature of the ground prevented the cavalry from consummating the destruction of the whole. As far as the conflicting accounts of the various historians may be compared and calculated on, the royalists had 3000 killed, and among them several officers of rank, while the patriot army, including those who fell on the previous day, lost about the same number. The archduke, furnished with a fresh horse, gained Bruges in safety, but he waited there only long enough to join his heroic wife, with whom he proceeded rapidly to Ghent, and thence to Brussels. Mendoza was wounded and taken prisoner, and with difficulty saved by Prince Maurice from the fury of the German auxiliaries.

The moral effects produced by this victory on the vanquishers and vanquished, and on the state of public opinion throughout Europe, was immense, but its immediate consequences were incredibly trifling. Not one result in a military point of view followed an event which appeared almost decisive of the war. Nieuport was again invested three days after the battle, but a strong reinforcement entered the place and saved it from all danger, and Maurice found himself forced for want of supplies to abandon the scene of his greatest exploit. He returned to Holland, welcomed by the acclamations of his grateful country, and exciting the jealousy and hatred of all who envied his glory or feared his power. Among the sincere and conscientious republicans who saw danger to the public liberty in the growing influence of a successful soldier, placed at the head of affairs and endeared to the people by every hereditary and personal claim, was Olden Barneveldt, the pensionary; and from this period may be traced the growth of the mutual antipathy which led to the sacrifice of the most virtuous statesman of Holland and the eternal disgrace of its hitherto heroic chief.

The states of the Catholic provinces assembled at Brussels now gave the archdukes to understand that nothing but peace could satisfy their wishes or save the country from exhaustion and ruin. Albert saw the reasonableness of their remonstrances and attempted to carry the great object into effect. The states-general listened to his proposals. Commissioners were appointed on both sides to treat of terms. They met at Bergen-op-Zoom, but their conferences were broken up almost as soon as commenced. The deputies of the states-general proposed that the Belgians should unite with them. This they refused to do, and, as the Netherlands were equally firm in refusing to recognize the archdukes, the negotiations went no further. Preparations for hostilities were therefore commenced on both sides, and the whole of the winter was thus employed.

Early in the spring Prince Maurice opened the campaign at the head of 16,000 men, chiefly composed of English and French, who seemed throughout the contest to forget their national animosities and to know no rivalry but that of emulation in the cause of liberty. The town of Rheinberg soon fell into the hands of the prince. His next attempt was against Bois-le-duc, and the siege of this place was signalized by an event that flavored of the chivalric contests characteristic of the times. A Norman gentleman of the name of Bréauté, in the service of Prince Maurice, challenged the royalist garrison to meet him and twenty of his comrades in arms under the walls of the place. The cartel was accepted by a Fleming named Abramzoom, but better known by the epithet *Leckerbeetje* (savory bit), who, with twenty more, met Bréauté and his friends. The combat was desperate. The Flemish champion was killed at the first shock by his Norman challenger, but the latter falling into the hands of the enemy, they treacherously and cruelly put him to death, in violation of the strict conditions of the fight. Prince Maurice was forced to raise the siege of Bois-le-duc and turn his attention in another direction.

The Archduke Albert had now resolved to invest Ostend, a place of great importance to the United Provinces, but little worth to either party in comparison with the dreadful waste of treasure and human life which was the consequence of its memorable siege. Sir Francis Vere commanded in the place at the period of its final investment, but governors, garrisons, and besieging forces were renewed and replaced with a rapidity which gives one of the most frightful instances of the ravages of war. The siege of Ostend lasted upwards of three years. It became a school for the young nobility of all Europe, who repaired to either one or the other party to learn the principles and the practice of attack and defense. Everything that the art of strategy could devise was resorted to on either side. The slaughter in the various assaults, sorties, and bombardments was enormous. Squadrons at sea gave a double interest to the land operations, and the celebrated brothers, Frederick and Ambrose Spinola, founded their reputation on these opposing elements. Frederick was killed in one of the naval combats with the Dutch galleys, and the fame of reducing Ostend was reserved for Ambrose. This afterward celebrated general had undertaken the command at the earnest entreaties of the archduke and the King of Spain, and by the firmness and vigor of his measures he revived the courage of the worn-out assailants of the place. Redoubled attacks and multiplied mines at length reduced the town to a mere mass of ruin, and scarcely left its still undaunted garrison sufficient footing on which to prolong their desperate defense. Ostend at length surrendered, on September 22, 1604, and the victors marched in over its crumbled walls and shattered batteries. Scarcely a vestige of the place remained beyond those terrible evidences of destruction. Its ditches, filled with the rubbish of ramparts, bastions, and redoubts, left no distinct line of separation between the operations of its attack and its defense. It resembled rather a vast sepulcher than a ruined town, a mountain of earth and rubbish, without a single house in which the wretched remnant of the inhabitants could hide their heads—a monument of desolation on which victory might have sat and wept.

During the progress of this memorable siege Queen Elizabeth of England had died, after a long and, it must be pronounced, a glorious reign, though the glory belongs rather to the nation than to the monarch, whose memory is marked with indelible stains of private cruelty, as in the cases of Essex and Mary Queen of Scots, and of public wrongs, as in that of her whole system of tyranny in Ireland. With respect to the United Provinces she was a harsh protectress and a capricious ally. She in turns advised them to remain faithful to the established forms in religion and to their intolerable king, refused to incorporate them with her own states, and then used her best efforts for subjecting them to her sway. She seemed to take pleasure in the uncertainty to which she reduced them by constant demands for payment of her loans and threats of making peace with Spain. Thus the states-general were not much affected by the news of her death; and so rejoiced were they at the accession of James I. to the throne of England that all the bells of Holland rang out merry peals, bonfires were set blazing all over the country, a letter of congratulation was dispatched to the new monarch, and it was speedily followed by a solemn embassy, composed of Prince Frederick Henry, the grand pensionary Barneveldt, and others of the first dignitaries of the republic. These ambassadors were grievously disappointed at the reception given to them by James, who treated them as little better than rebels to their lawful king. But this first disposition to contempt and insult was soon overcome by the united talents of Barneveldt and the great Duke of Sully, who was at the same period ambassador from France at the English court. The result of the negotiations was an agreement between these two powers to take the republic under their protection and use their best efforts for obtaining the recognition of its independence by Spain.

The states-general considered themselves amply recompensed for the loss of Ostend by the taking of Sluis, Rheinberg, and Grave, all of which had in the interval surrendered to Prince Maurice; but they were seriously alarmed on finding themselves abandoned by King James, who concluded a separate peace with Philip III. of Spain in the month of August this year.

The two monarchs stipulated in the treaty that neither was to give support of any kind to the revolted subjects of the other. It is nevertheless true that James did not withdraw his troops from the service of the states, but he authorized the Spaniards to levy soldiers in England. He refused to give up the cautionary towns to Spain, but he promised that no aid should be given to the Netherlands through them. The news of the treaty was received with mingled consternation and indignation by the provinces, and Barneveldt despaired of ultimate success without the aid of England. In their first burst of indignation the states-general ordered the closing of the Scheldt to the English. They even arrested the progress of several of their merchant ships. But soon after, gratified at finding that James received their deputy with the title of ambassador, they resolved to dissimulate their resentment.

Prince Maurice and Spinola now took the field with their respective armies, and a rapid series of operations placing them in direct contact, displayed their talents in the most striking points of view. The first steps on the part of the prince were a new invasion of Flanders and an attempt on Antwerp, which he hoped to carry before the Spanish army could arrive to its succor. But the promptitude and sagacity of Spinola defeated this plan, which Maurice was obliged to abandon after some loss, while the royalist general resolved to signalize himself by some important movement, and, ere his design was suspected, he had penetrated into the province of Overyssel, and thus retorted his rival's favorite measure of carrying the war into the enemy's country. Several towns were rapidly reduced, but Maurice flew toward the threatened provinces and by his active measures forced Spinola to fall back on the Rhine and take up a position near Ruhrart, where he was impetuously attacked by the Dutch army. But the cavalry having followed up too slowly the orders of Maurice, his hopes of surprising the royalists were frustrated, and the Spanish forces, gaining time by this hesitation, soon changed the fortune of the day. The Dutch cavalry shamefully took to flight, despite the gallant endeavors of both Maurice and his brother, Frederick Henry, and at this juncture a large reinforcement of Spaniards arrived under the command of Velasco. Maurice now brought forward some companies of English and French infantry under Horatio Vere and D'Omerville, also a distinguished officer. The battle was again fiercely renewed, and the Spaniards now gave way, and would have been completely defeated had not Spinola put in practice an old and generally successful stratagem. He caused almost all the drums of his army to beat in one direction, so as to give the impression that a still larger reinforcement was approaching. Maurice, apprehensive that the former panic might find a parallel in a fresh one, prudently ordered a retreat, which he was able to effect in good order, in preference to risking the total disorganization of his troops. The loss on each side was nearly the same, but the glory of this hard-fought day remained on the side of **Spinola,** who proved himself a worthy successor of the great Duke of Parma, and an antagonist with whom Maurice might contend without dishonor.

The naval transactions of this year restored the balance which Spinola's successes had begun to turn in favor of the royalist cause. A squadron of ships, commanded by Haultain, Admiral of Zealand, attacked a superior force of Spanish vessels close to Dover and defeated them, with considerable loss. But the victory was sullied by an act of great barbarity. All the soldiers found on board the captured ships were tied two and two and mercilessly flung into the sea. Some contrived to extricate themselves and gained the shore by swimming; others were picked up by the English boats, whose crews witnessed the scene and hastened to their relief. The generous British seamen could not remain neutral in such a moment, nor repress their indignation against those whom they had hitherto so long considered as friends. The Dutch vessels pursuing those of Spain which fled into Dover harbor were fired on by the cannon of the castle and forced to give up the chase. The English loudly complained that the Dutch had on this occasion violated their territory, and this transaction laid the foundation of the quarrel which subsequently broke out between England and the republic, and which the jealousies of rival merchants in either state unceasingly fomented. In this year also the Dutch succeeded in capturing the chief of the Dunkirk privateers which had so long annoyed their trade, and they cruelly ordered sixty of the prisoners to be put to death. But the people, more humane than the authorities, rescued them from the executioners and set them free.

But these domestic instances of success and inhumanity were trifling in comparison with the splendid train of distant events, accompanied by a course of wholesale benevolence, that redeemed the traits of petty guilt. The maritime enterprises of Holland, forced by the imprudent policy of Spain to seek a wider career than in the narrow seas of Europe, were day by day extending in the Indies.

To ruin, if possible, their increasing trade, Philip III. sent out the Admiral Hurtado, with a fleet of eight galleons and thirty-two galleys. The Dutch squadron of five vessels, commanded by Wolfert Hermanszoon, attacked them off the coast of Malabar, and his temerity was crowned with great success. He took two of their vessels and completely drove the remainder from the Indian seas. He then concluded a treaty with the natives of the Isle of Banda, by which he promised to support them against the Spaniards and Portuguese on condition that they were to give his fellow-countrymen the exclusive privilege of purchasing the spices of the island. This treaty was the foundation of the influence which the Dutch so soon succeeded in forming in the East Indies, and they established it by a candid, mild, and tolerant conduct, strongly contrasted with the pride and bigotry which had signalized every act of the Portuguese and Spaniards.

Chapter XVI

DUTCH DISASTERS AND THE TWELVE YEARS' PEACE
1606-1619

THE states-general now resolved to confine their military operations to a war merely defensive, for the burden of the war was becoming well-nigh unbearable. Spinola had by his conduct during the late campaign completely revived the spirits of the Spanish troops and excited at least the caution of the Dutch. He now threatened the United Provinces with invasion, and he exerted his utmost efforts to raise the supplies necessary for the execution of his plan. He not only exhausted the resources of the King of Spain and the archduke, but obtained money on his private account from all those usurers who were tempted by his confident anticipations of conquest. He soon equipped two armies of about 12,000 men each. At the head of one of these he took the field; the other, commanded by the Count of Bucquoi, was destined to join him in the neighborhood of Utrecht, and he was then resolved to push forward with the whole united force into the very heart of the republic.

Prince Maurice in the meantime concentrated his army, amounting to 12,000 men, and prepared to make head against his formidable opponents. By a succession of the most prudent maneuvers he contrived to keep Spinola in check, disconcerted all his projects and forced him to content himself with the capture of two or three towns—a comparatively insignificant conquest. Desiring to wipe away the disgrace of this discomfiture, and to risk everything for the accomplishment of his grand design, Spinola used every method to provoke the prince to a battle, even though a serious mutiny among his troops and the impossibility of forming a junction with Bucquoi had reduced his force below that of Maurice; but the latter, to the surprise of all who expected a decisive blow, retreated from before the Italian general—abandoning the town of Grol, which immediately fell into Spinola's power, and giving rise to manifold conjectures and infinite discontent at conduct so little in unison with his wonted enterprise and skill. Even Henry IV. acknowledged it did not answer the expectation he had formed from Maurice's splendid talents for war. The fact seems to be that the prince, much as he valued victory, dreaded peace more, and that he was resolved to avoid a decisive blow, which, in putting an end to the contest, would at the same time have decreased that individual influence in the state which his ambitions now urged him to augment by every possible means.

The Dutch naval expeditions this year were not more brilliant than those on land. Admiral Haultain, with fifteen ships, was surprised off Cape St. Vincent by the Spanish fleet. The formidable appearance of their galleons inspired on this occasion a perfect panic among the Dutch sailors. They hoisted their sails and fled, with the exception of one ship, commanded by Vice Admiral Klaazoon, whose desperate conduct saved the national honor. Having held out until his vessel was quite unmanageable, and almost his whole crew killed or wounded, he prevailed on the rest to agree to the resolution he had formed, knelt down on the deck, and putting up a brief prayer for pardon for the act, thrust a light into the powder magazine and was instantly blown up with his companions. Only two men were snatched from the sea by the Spaniards, and even these, dreadfully burned and mangled, died in the utterance of curses on the enemy.

This disastrous occurrence was soon, however, forgotten in the rejoicings for a brilliant victory gained the following year by Heemskirk, so celebrated for his voyage to Nova Zembla and by his conduct in the East. He set sail from the ports of Holland in the month of March, determined to signalize himself by some great exploit, now necessary to redeem the disgrace which had begun to sully the reputation of the Dutch navy. He soon got intelligence that the Spanish fleet lay at anchor in the Bay of Gibraltar, and he speedily prepared to offer them battle. Before the combat began he held a council of war, and addressed the officers in an energetic speech, in which he made an imperative call on their valor to conquer or die in the approaching conflict. He led on to the action in his own ship, and, to the astonishment of both fleets, he bore right down against the enormous galleon in which the flag of the Spanish admiral-in-chief was hoisted. D'Avila could scarcely believe the evidence of his eyes at this audacity. He at first burst into laughter

Hist. Nat. XIII-13

at the notion, but as Heemskirk approached he cut his cables and attempted to escape under the shelter of the town. The heroic Dutchman pursued him through the whole of the Spanish fleet and soon forced him to action. At the second broadside Heemskirk had his left leg carried off by a cannon ball, and he almost instantly died, exhorting his crew to seek for consolation in the defeat of the enemy. Verhoef, the captain of the ship, concealed the admiral's death, and the whole fleet continued the action with a valor worthy the spirit in which it was commenced. The victory was soon decided. Four of the Spanish galleons were sunk or burned, the remainder fled, and the citizens of Cadiz trembled with the apprehension of sack and pillage. But the death of Heemskirk, when made known to the surviving victors, seemed completely to paralyze them. They attempted nothing further, but sailing back to Holland with the body of their lamented chief thus paid a greater tribute to his importance than was to be found in the mausoleum erected to his memory in the city of Amsterdam.

The news of this battle, reaching Brussels before it was known in Holland, contributed not a little to quicken the anxiety of the archdukes for peace. The King of Spain, worn out by the war which drained his treasury, had for some time ardently desired it. The Portuguese made loud complaints of the ruin that threatened their trade and their East Indian colonies. The Spanish ministers were fatigued with the apparently interminable contest which baffled all their calculations. Spinola, even in the midst of his brilliant career, found himself so overwhelmed with debts and so oppressed by the reproaches of the numerous creditors who were ruined by his default of payment, that he joined in the general demand for repose. In the month of May, 1607, proposals were made by the archdukes, in compliance with the general desire, and their two plenipotentiaries, Van Wittenhorst and Gevaerts, repaired to The Hague.

Public opinion in the United Provinces was divided on this important question. An instinctive hatred against the Spaniards and long habits of warfare influenced the great mass of the people to consider any overture for peace as some wily artifice aimed at their religion and liberty. War seemed to open inexhaustible sources of wealth, while peace seemed to threaten the extinction of the courage which was now as much a habit as war appeared to be a want. This reasoning was particularly convincing to Prince Maurice, whose fame, with a large portion of his authority and revenues, depended on the continuance of hostilities. It was also strongly relished and supported in Zealand generally and in the chief towns which dreaded the rivalry of Antwerp. But those who bore the burden of the war saw the subject under a different aspect. They feared that the present state of things would lead to their conquest by the enemy or to the ruin of their liberty by the growing power of Maurice. They hoped that peace would consolidate the republic and cause the reduction of the debt, which amounted to twenty-six millions of florins for the state of Holland alone. At the head of the party who so reasoned was Barneveldt, and his name is a guarantee with posterity for the wisdom of the opinion.

To allow the violent opposition to subside and to prevent any explosion of party feuds, the prudent Barneveldt suggested a mere suspension of arms, during which the permanent interests of both states might be calmly discussed. He even undertook to obtain Maurice's consent to the armistice. The prince listened to his arguments, and was apparently convinced by them. He at any rate sanctioned the proposal, but he afterward complained that Barneveldt had deceived him, in representing the negotiation as a feint for the purpose of persuading the kings of France and England to give greater aid to the republic. It is more than likely that Maurice reckoned on the improbability of Spain's consenting to the terms of the proposed treaty, and on that chance withdrew an opposition which could scarcely be ascribed to any but motives of personal ambition. It is, however, certain that his discontent at this transaction, either with himself or Barneveldt, laid the foundation of that bitter enmity which proved fatal to the life of the latter, and covered his own name, otherwise glorious, with undying reproach.

The United Provinces positively refused to admit even the commencement of a negotiation without the absolute recognition of their independence by the archdukes. A new ambassador was accordingly chosen on the part of these sovereigns, and empowered to concede this important admission. This person attracted considerable attention from his well-known qualities as an able diplomatist. He was a monk of the Order of St. Francis, named John de Neyen, a native of Antwerp, and a person as well versed in court intrigue as in the studies of the cloister. He in the first instance repaired secretly to The Hague, and had several private interviews with Prince Maurice and Barneveldt before he was regularly introduced to the states-general in his official character. Two different journeys were undertaken by this agent between The Hague and Brussels, before he could succeed in obtaining a perfect understanding as to the specific views of the archdukes. The suspicions of the states-general seemed fully justified by the dubious tone of the various communications, which avoided the direct admission of the required preliminary as to the independence of the United Provinces. It was at length concluded in explicit terms, and a suspension of arms for eight months was the immediate consequence.

But the negotiation for peace was on the point of being completely broken, in consequence of the conduct of Neyen, who justified every doubt of his sincerity by an attempt to corrupt Aarsens, the greffier of the states-general, or at least to influence his conduct in the progress of the treaty. Neyen presented him in the name of the archdukes, and as a token of his esteem, with a diamond of great value and a bond for 50,000 crowns. Aarsens accepted these presents with the approbation of Prince Maurice, to whom he had confided the circumstance, and who was no doubt delighted at what promised a rupture to the negotiations. Verreiken, a counselor of state who assisted Neyen in his diplomatic labors, was formally summoned before the assembled states-general, and there Barneveldt handed to him the diamond and the bond, and at the same time read him a lecture of true republican severity on the subject. Verreiken was overwhelmed by the violent attack. He denied the authority of Neyen for the measure he had taken, and remarked that it was not surprising that monks, naturally interested and avaricious, judged others by themselves. This repudiation of Neyen's suspicious conduct seems to have satisfied the stern resentment of Barneveldt and the party which so earnestly labored for peace. In spite of all the opposition of Maurice and his partisans the negotiations went on.

In the month of January, 1608, the various ambassadors were assembled at The Hague. Spinola was the chief of the plenipotentiaries appointed by the King of Spain, and Jeannin, president of the parliament of Dijon, a man of rare endowments, represented France. Prince Maurice, accompanied by his brother Frederick Henry, the various counts of Nassau, his cousins, and a numerous escort, advanced some distance to meet Spinola, conveyed him to The Hague in his own carriage, and lavished on him all the attentions reciprocally due between two such renowned captains during the suspension of their rivalry. The president, Richardot, was, with Neyen and Verreiken, ambassador from the archdukes, but Barneveldt and Jeannin appear to have played the chief parts in the important transaction which now filled all Europe with anxiety. Every state was more or less concerned in the result, and the three great monarchies of England, France, and Spain had all a vital interest at stake. The conferences were therefore frequent, and the debates assumed a great variety of aspects, which long kept the civilized world in suspense.

King James was extremely jealous of the more prominent part taken by the French ambassadors and of the subaltern consideration held by his own envoys, Winwood and Spencer, in consequence of the disfavor in which he himself was held by the Dutch people. It appears evident that, whether deservedly or the contrary, England was at this period unpopular in the United Provinces, while France was looked up to with the greatest enthusiasm. This is not surprising, when we compare the characters of Henry IV. and James I., bearing in mind how much of national reputation at the time depended on the personal conduct of kings, and how political situations influence, if they do not create, the virtues and vices of a people. Independent of the suspicions of his being altogether unfavorable to the declaration required by the United Provinces from Spain, to which James's conduct had given rise, he had established some exactions which greatly embarrassed their fishing expeditions on the coasts of England.

The main points for discussion, and on which depended the decision for peace or war, were those which concerned religion, and the demand on the part of Spain that the United Provinces should renounce all claims to the navigation of the Indian seas. Philip required for the Catholics of the United Provinces the free exercise of their religion. This was opposed by the states-general, and the Archduke Albert, seeing the impossibility of carrying that point, dispatched his confessor, Fra Inigo de Briznella, to Spain. This Dominican was furnished with the written opinion of several theologians, that the king might conscientiously slur over the article of religion, and he was the more successful with Philip, as the Duke of Lerma, his prime minister, was resolved to accomplish the peace at any price. The conferences at The Hague were therefore not interrupted on this question, but they went on slowly, months being consumed in discussions on articles of trifling importance. They were, however, resumed in the month of August with greater vigor. It was announced that the King of Spain abandoned the question respecting religion, but that it was in the certainty that his moderation would be recompensed by ample concessions on that of the Indian trade, on which he was inexorable. This article became the rock on which the whole negotiation eventually split. The court of Spain on the one hand and the states-general on the other inflexibly maintained their opposing claims. It was in vain that the ambassadors turned and twisted the subject with all the subtleties of diplomacy. Every possible expedient was used to shake the determination of the Dutch. But the influence of the East India Company, the islands of Zealand, and the city of Amsterdam prevailed over all. Reports of the avowal on the part of the King of Spain that he would never renounce his title to the sovereignty of the United Provinces unless they abandoned the Indian navigation and granted the free exercise of religion threw the whole diplomatic corps into confusion, and on August 25 the states-general announced to the Marquis of Spinola and the other ambassadors that the congress was dissolved and that all hopes of peace were abandoned.[1]

Nothing seemed now likely to prevent the immediate renewal of hostilities, when the ambassadors of France and England proposed the mediation of their respective masters for the conclusion of a truce for several years. The King of Spain and the archdukes were well satisfied to obtain even this temporary cessation of the war, but Prince Maurice and a portion of the provinces strenuously opposed the proposition. The French and English ambassadors, however, in concert with Barneveldt, who steadily maintained his influence, labored incessantly to overcome those difficulties, and finally succeeded in overpowering all opposition to the truce. A new congress was agreed on, to assemble at Antwerp for the consideration of the conditions, and the states-general agreed to remove from The Hague to Bergen-op-Zoom, to be more within reach and ready to coöperate in the negotiation.

But before matters assumed this favorable turn discussions and disputes had intervened on several occasions to render fruitless every effort of those who so incessantly labored for the great causes of humanity and the general good. On one occasion Barneveldt,

---

[1] The states-general were the less disposed to give up the Indian trade as their fleet in the East had won several important successes.

disgusted with the opposition of Prince Maurice and his partisans, had actually resigned his employments, but brought back by the solicitations of the states-general, and reconciled to Maurice by the intervention of Jeannin, the negotiations for the truce were resumed, and under the auspices of the ambassadors they were happily terminated. After two years' delay this long-wished-for truce was concluded and signed on April 9, 1609, to continue for the space of twelve years.

This celebrated treaty contained thirty-four articles, and its fulfillment on either side was guaranteed by the kings of France and England. Notwithstanding the time taken up in previous discussions, the treaty is one of the most vague and unspecific state papers that exist. The archdukes, in their own names and in that of the King of Spain, declared the United Provinces to be free and independent states on which they renounced all claim whatever. By the third article each party was to hold respectively the places which each possessed at the commencement of the armistice. The fourth and fifth articles grant to the republic, but in a phraseology obscure and even doubtful, the right of navigation and free trade to the Indies. The eighth contains all that regards the exercise of religion; and the remaining clauses are wholly relative to points of internal trade, custom-house regulations, and matters of private interests.

Ephemeral and temporary as this peace appeared, it was received with almost universal demonstrations of joy by the population of the Netherlands in their two grand divisions. Everyone seemed to turn toward the enjoyment of tranquillity with the animated composure of tired laborers looking forward to a day of rest and sunshine. This truce brought a calm of comparative happiness upon the country, which an almost unremitting tempest had desolated for nearly half a century; and, after so long a series of calamity, all the national advantages of social life seemed about to settle on the land. The attitude which the United Provinces assumed at this period was indeed a proud one. They were not now compelled to look abroad and solicit other states to become their masters. They had forced their old tyrants to acknowledge their independence, to come and ask for peace on their own ground, and to treat with them on terms of no doubtful equality. They had already become so flourishing, so powerful, and so envied that they who had so lately excited but compassion from the neighboring states were now regarded with such jealousy as rivals, unequivocally equal, may justly inspire in each other.

The ten southern provinces, now confirmed under the sovereignty of the house of Austria, and from this period generally distinguished by the name of Belgium, immediately began, like the northern division of the country, to labor for the great object of repairing the dreadful sufferings caused by their long and cruel

THE UNITED PROVINCES AND THE AUSTRIAN NETHERLANDS 1609

war. Their success was considerable. Albert and Isabella, their sovereigns, joined to considerable probity of character and talents for government a fund of humanity which led them to unceasing acts of benevolence. The whole of their dominions quickly began to recover from the ravages of war. Agriculture and the minor operations of trade resumed all their wonted activity. But the manufactures of Flanders were no more, and the refusal of the United Provinces to reopen the River Scheldt and thus permit the revival of the Antwerp trade had the effect of transferring the commercial center of the Netherlands to Amsterdam and the other chief towns of Holland.

The tranquil course of prosperity in the Belgian provinces was only once interrupted during the whole continuance of the twelve years' truce, and that was in the year following its commencement. The death of the Duke of Cleves and Juliers in this year gave rise to serious disputes for the succession to his states, which was claimed by several of the princes of Germany. The Elector of Brandenburg and the Duke of Neuburg were seconded both by France and the United Provinces, and a joint army of both nations, commanded by Prince Maurice and the Marshal de la Châtre, was marched into the duchy of Cleves. After taking possession of the town of Juliers, the allies retired, leaving the two princes above mentioned in a partnership possession of the disputed states. But this joint sovereignty did not satisfy the ambition of either, and serious divisions arose between them, each endeavoring to strengthen himself by foreign alliances. The Archdukes Albert and Isabella were drawn into the quarrel, and they dispatched Spinola at the head of 20,000 men to support the Duke of Neuburg, whose pretensions they countenanced. Prince Maurice, with a Dutch army, advanced on the other hand to uphold the claims of the Elector of Brandenburg. Both generals took possession of several towns, and this double expedition offered the singular spectacle of two opposing armies, acting in different interests, making conquests and dividing an important inheritance without the occurrence of one act of hostility to each other. The Treaty of Xanten, 1614, finally provided that the Elector of Brandenburg should hold Cleves and Mark, while the Duke of Neuburg should administer Julich and Berg. But the interference of the court of Madrid had nearly been the cause of a new rupture. The greatest alarm was excited in the Belgic provinces, and nothing but the prudence of the archdukes and the forbearance of the states-general could have succeeded in averting the threatened evil.

With the exception of this bloodless mimicry of war, the United Provinces presented for the space of twelve years a long continued picture of peace, as the term is generally received, but a peace so disfigured by intestine troubles and so stained by actions of despotic cruelty that the period which should have been that of its greatest happiness becomes but an example of its worst disgrace.

The assassination of Henry IV., in the year 1610, was a new instance of the intolerant spirit which reigned paramount in Europe at the time, and while robbing France of one of its best monarchs, it deprived the United Provinces of their truest and most powerful friend. Henry has, from his own days to the present, found a ready eulogy in all who value kings in proportion as they are distinguished by heroism, without ceasing to evince the feelings of humanity. Henry seems to have gone as far as man can go to combine wisdom, dignity, and courage with all those endearing qualities of private life which alone give men a prominent hold upon the sympathies of their kind. We acknowledge his errors, his faults, his follies, only to love him the better. We admire his valor and generosity, without being shocked by cruelty or disgusted by profusion. We look on his greatness without envy, and in tracing his whole career we seem to walk hand in hand beside a dear companion rather than to follow the footsteps of a mighty monarch.

But the death of this powerful supporter of their efforts for freedom and the chief guarantee for its continuance was a trifling calamity to the United Provinces in comparison with the rapid fall from the true point of glory so painfully exhibited in the conduct of their own domestic champion. It had been well for Prince Maurice of Nassau that the last shot fired by the defeated Spaniards in the battle of Nieuport had struck him dead in the moment of his greatest victory and on the summit of his fame. From that celebrated day he had performed no deed of war that could raise his reputation as a soldier, and all his acts as stadtholder were calculated to sink him below the level of civil virtue and just government. His two campaigns against Spinola had redounded more to the credit of his rival than to his own, and his whole conduct during the negotiation for the truce too plainly betrayed the unworthy nature of his ambition, founded on despotic principles. It was his misfortune to have been so completely thrown out of the career for which he had been designed by nature and education. War was his element. By his genius he improved it as a science; by his valor he was one of those who raised it from the degradation of a trade to the dignity of a passion. But when removed from the camp to the council-room he became all at once a common man. His frankness degenerated into roughness, his decision into despotism, his courage into cruelty. He gave a new proof of the melancholy fact that circumstances may transform the most apparent qualities of virtue into those opposite vices between which human wisdom is baffled when it attempts to draw a decided and invariable line.

Opposed to Maurice in almost every one of his acts was, as we have already seen, Barneveldt, one of the truest patriots of any time or country, and, with the exception of William, the great Prince of Orange, the most eminent citizen to whom the affairs of the Netherlands have given celebrity. Yet with all our admiration for this great man, we must not forget that he stood for no liberal or popular movement. In his desire for religious tolerance he stood with the minority, while politically he was the champion of aristrocracy, as Maurice was the leader of the populace. We cannot enter minutely into the train of circumstances which for several years brought Maurice and Barneveldt into perpetual concussion with each other. Long after the completion of the truce, which the latter so mainly aided in accomplishing, every minor point in the domestic affairs of the republic seemed merged in the conflict between the stadtholder and the pensionary. Without attempting to specify these, we may say generally that almost every one redounded to the disgrace of the prince and the honor of the patriot. But the main question of agitation was the fierce dispute which soon broke out between two professors of theology of the University of Leyden, Francis Gomarus and Jacob Arminius. We do not regret on this occasion that our confined limits spare us the task of recording in detail controversies on points of speculative doctrine. The whole strength of the intellects which had long been engaged in the conflict for national and religious liberty was now directed to metaphysical theology and wasted upon interminable disputes about predestination and grace. Barneveldt enrolled himself among the partisans of Arminius; Maurice became a Gomarist.

It was, however, scarcely to be wondered at, that a country so recently changed in organization both in church and state should run into wild excesses of intolerance before sectarian principles were thoroughly understood and definitively fixed. Persecutions of various kinds were indulged in against all the shades of doctrine into which Christianity had split. Every minister who strove to moderate the rage of Calvinistic enthusiasm was openly denounced by its partisans, and one, named Gaspard Koolhaas, was actually excommunicated by a synod and denounced in plain terms to the devil. Arminius had been appointed professor at Leyden in 1603, for the mildness of his doctrines, which were joined to most affable manners, a happy temper, and a purity of conduct which no calumny could successfully traduce.

His colleague, Gomarus, a native of Bruges, learned, violent, and rigid in sectarian points, soon became jealous of the more popular professor's influence. A furious attack on the latter was answered by recrimination, and the whole battery of theological authorities was reciprocally discharged by one or other of the disputants. The states-general interfered between them. They were summoned to appear before the council of state, and grave politicians listened for hours to the dispute. Arminius obtained the advantage, by the gentleness and moderation of his conduct. He was meek, while Gomarus was furious, and many of the listeners declared that they would rather die with the charity of the former than in the faith of the latter. A second hearing was allowed them before the states of Holland. Again Arminius took the lead, and the controversy went on unceasingly, till this amiable man, worn out by his exertions and the presentiment of the evil which these disputes were engendering for his country, expired in his forty-ninth year, still persisting in his opinions.

The Gomarists now loudly called for a national synod to regulate the points of faith. The Arminians remonstrated on various grounds, and thus acquired the name of Remonstrants, by which they were soon generally distinguished. The most deplorable contests ensued. Serious riots occurred in several of the towns of Holland, and James I. of England could not resist the temptation of entering the polemical lists, as a champion of orthodoxy and a decided Gomarist. His hostility was chiefly directed against Vorstius, the successor and disciple of Arminius, whom he strongly recommended the states-general to have burned for heresy. His inveterate intolerance knew no bounds, and it completed the melancholy picture of absurdity which the whole affair presents to the modern students of the times.

In this dispute, which occupied and agitated all, it was impossible that Barneveldt should not choose the congenial temperance and toleration of Arminius. Maurice, with probably no distinct conviction or much interest in the abstract differences on either side, joined the Gomarists. His motives were purely temporal, for the party espoused was now decidedly as much political as religious.

King James rewarded him by conferring on him the ribbon of the Order of the Garter, vacant by the death of Henry IV. of France. The ceremony of investment was performed with great pomp by the English ambassador at The Hague, and James and Maurice entered from that time into a closer and more uninterrupted correspondence than before.

During the long continuance of the theological disputes the United Provinces had nevertheless made rapid strides toward commercial greatness. Commercial treaties with Denmark, Sweden, Russia, and the Hanse towns insured their enormous trade and fisheries in the northern seas. In 1609 the famous Bank of Amsterdam, for years the leading institution of its kind in Europe, was established. And the year 1616 witnessed the completion of an affair which was considered the consolidation of their independence. This important matter was the recovery of the towns of Brill and Flushing, and the fort of Rammekins, which had been placed in the hands of the English as security for the loan granted to the republic by Queen Elizabeth. The whole merit of the transaction was due to the perseverance and address of Barneveldt acting on the weakness and the embarrassments of King James. Religious contention did not so fully occupy Barneveldt but that he kept a constant eye on political concerns. He was well informed on all that passed in the English court. He knew the wants of James, and was aware of his efforts to bring about the marriage of his son with the Infanta of Spain. The danger of such an alliance was evident to the penetrating Barneveldt, who saw in perspective the probability of the wily Spaniard's obtaining from the English monarch possession of the strong places in question. He therefore resolved on obtaining their recovery, and his great care was to get them back with a considerable abatement of the enormous debt for which they stood pledged, and which now amounted to 8,000,000 florins.

Barneveldt commenced his operations by sounding the needy monarch through the medium of Noel Caron, the ambassador from the states-general, and he next managed so that James himself should offer to give up the towns, thereby allowing a fair pretext to the states for claiming a diminution of the debt. The English garrisons were unpaid, and their complaints brought down a strong remonstrance from James, and excuses from the states, founded on the poverty of their financial resources. The negotiation rapidly went on, in the same spirit of avidity on the part of the king and of good management on that of his debtors. It was finally agreed that the states should pay in full of the demand 2,728,000 florins, being about one-third of the debt. Prince Maurice repaired to the cautionary towns in the month of June, and received them at the hands of the English governors, the garrisons at the same time entering into the service of the republic.

The accomplishment of this measure afforded the highest satisfaction to the United Provinces. It caused infinite discontent in England, and James, with the common injustice of men who make a bad bargain (even though its conditions be of their own seeking, and suited to their own convenience), turned his own self-dissatisfaction into bitter hatred against him whose watchful integrity had successfully labored for his country's good. Barneveldt's leaning toward France and the Arminians filled the measure of. James's unworthy enmity. Its effects were soon apparent, on the arrival at The Hague of Carleton, who succeeded Winwood as James's ambassador. The haughty pretensions of this diplomatist, whose attention seemed turned to theological disputes rather than politics, gave great disgust, and he contributed not a little to the persecution which led to the tragical end of Barneveldt's valuable life.

While this indefatigable patriot was busy in relieving his country from its dependency on England, his enemies accused him of the wish to reduce it once more to Spanish tyranny. Francis Aarsens, son to him who proved himself so incorruptible when attempted to be bribed by Neyen, was one of the foremost of the faction who now labored for the downfall of the pensionary. He was a man of infinite dissimulation, versed in all the intrigues of courts, and so deep in all their tortuous tactics that Cardinal Richelieu, well qualified to prize that species of talent, declared that he knew only three great political geniuses, of whom Francis Aarsens was one.

Though there is little evidence to show that Prince Maurice actually aimed at the sovereignty of the Netherlands, still he felt himself aggrieved at the secondary position in the state to which he had been reduced since the truce which he had so bitterly opposed. The descendant of an imperial house, the son of the "father of his country," and himself its preserver, the first position in the state, if not the sovereignty itself, was only his just recompense. Secure in the support of the people, who had no share in the government, and of the Calvinist party, Maurice saw but one obstacle in his path—the domineering Barneveldt, leader of the aristocracy. He was for a while diverted from his pursuit by the preparation made to afford assistance to some of the allies of the republic. Fifty thousand florins a month were granted to the Duke of Savoy, who was at war with Spain, and 4000 men, with nearly forty ships, were dispatched to the aid of the republic of Venice in its contest with Ferdinand, Archduke of Styria, who was afterward elected emperor. The honorary empire of the seas seems at this time to have been successfully claimed by the United Provinces. They paid back with interest the haughty conduct with which they had been long treated by the English, and they refused to pay the fishery duties to which the inhabitants of Great Britain were subject. The Dutch sailors had even the temerity, under pretext of pursuing pirates, to violate the British territory, and they set fire to the town of Crookhaven, in Ireland, and massacred several of the inhabitants.

King James, immersed in theological studies, appears to have passed slightly over this outrage. But he took fire at the news that the states had prohibited the importation of cloth dyed and dressed in England. It required the best exertion of Barneveldt's talents to pacify him, and it was not easy to effect this through the jaundiced medium of the ambassador Carleton. But it was unanswerably argued by the pensionary that the manufacture of cloth was one of those ancient and natural sources of wealth which England had ravished from the Netherlands, and which the latter was justified in recovering by every effort consistent with national honor and fair principles of government.

The influence of Prince Maurice had gained complete success for the Calvinist party in its various titles of Gomarists, non-Remonstrants, etc. The audacity and violence of these ferocious sectarians knew no bounds. Outrages, too many to enumerate, became common through the country, and Arminianism was on all sides assailed and persecuted. Barneveldt frequently appealed to Maurice without effect, and all the efforts of the former to obtain justice by means of the civil authorities were paralyzed by the inaction in which the prince retained the military force. In this juncture the magistrates of various towns, spurred on by Barneveldt, called out the national militia, called Waardegelders, which possessed the right of arming at its own expense for the protection of the public peace. Schism upon schism was the consequence, and the whole country was reduced to that state of anarchy so favorable to the designs of an ambitious soldier already in the enjoyment of almost absolute power. Maurice possessed all the hardihood and vigor suited to such an occasion. At the head of two companies of infantry, and accompanied by his brother Frederick Henry, he suddenly set out at night from The Hague, arrived at the Brill, and in defiance of the remonstrances of the magistrates and in violation of the rights of the town he placed his devoted garrison in that important place. To justify this measure reports were spread that Barneveldt intended to deliver it up to the Spaniards, and the ignorant, insensate, and ungrateful people swallowed the calumny.

This and such minor efforts were, however, all subservient to the one grand object of utterly destroying, by a public proscription, the whole of the party of Barneveldt, now identified with Arminianism. A national synod was loudly clamored for by the Gomarists, and in spite of all opposition on constitutional grounds it was finally proclaimed. Uyttenbogaert, the enlightened pastor and friend of Maurice, who on all occasions labored for the general good, now moderated as much as possible the violence of either party. But he could not persuade Barneveldt to render himself, by compliance, a tacit accomplice with a measure that he conceived fraught with violence to the public privileges. He had an inflexible enemy in Carleton, the English ambassador. His interference carried the question, and it was at his suggestion that Dordrecht, or Dort, was chosen for the assembling of the synod. Du Maurier, the French ambassador, acted on all occasions as a mediator, but to obtain influence at such a time it was necessary to become a partisan. Several towns —Leyden, Gouda, Rotterdam, and some others—made a last effort for their liberties, and formed a fruitless confederation.

Barneveldt solicited the acceptance of his resignation of all his offices. The states-general implored him not to abandon the country at such a critical moment. He consequently maintained his post. Libels the most vindictive and atrocious were published and circulated against him, and at last, forced from his silence by these multiplied calumnies, he put forward his " Apology," addressed to the states of Holland.

This dignified vindiction only produced new outrages. Maurice, now become Prince of Orange by the death of his elder brother without children, employed his whole authority to carry his object and crush Barneveldt. The states-general were now completely under the prince's control. They thanked him, they consented to disband the militia; they formally invited foreign powers to favor and protect the synod about to be held at Dort. The return of Carleton from England, where he had gone to receive the more positive promises of support from King James, was only wanting to decide Maurice to take the final step, and no sooner did the ambassador arrive at The Hague than Barneveldt and his most able friends, Grotius, Hoogerbeets, and Ledenberg, were arrested in the name of the states-general.

The country was taken by surprise, no resistance being offered. The concluding scenes of the tragedy were hurried on. Violence was succeeded by violence, against public feeling and public justice. Maurice became completely absolute in everything but in name. The supplications of ambassadors, the protests of individuals, the arguments of statesmen, were alike unavailing to stop the torrent of despotism and injustice. The synod of Dort was opened on November 13, 1618. Theology was mystified, religion disgraced, Christianity outraged. And after 152 sittings, during six months' display of ferocity and fraud, the solemn mockery was closed on May 9, 1619, by the declaration of its president that "its miraculous labors had made hell tremble."

Proscriptions, banishments, and death were the natural consequences of this synod. The divisions which it had professed to extinguish were rendered a thousand times more violent than before. Its decrees did incalculable ill to the cause they were meant to promote. But the moral effects of this memorable conclave were too remote to prevent the sacrifice which almost immediately followed the celebration of its rites. A trial by twenty-four prejudiced enemies, by courtesy called judges, ended in the condemnation of Barneveldt and his fellow-patriots for treason against the liberties they had vainly labored to save. Barneveldt died on the scaffold by the hands of the executioner on May 13, 1619, in the seventy-second year of his age. Grotius and Hoogerbeets were sentenced to perpetual imprisonment. Ledenberg committed suicide in his cell sooner than brave the tortures which he anticipated at the hands of his enemies.

Many more pages than we are able to afford sentences might be devoted to the details of these iniquitous proceedings and an account of their consummation. The heroism of Barneveldt was never excelled by any martyr to the most holy cause. He appealed to Maurice against the unjust sentence which condemned him to

Hist. Nat. XIII-14

death, but he scorned to beg his life. He met his fate with such temperate courage as was to be expected from the dignified energy of his life. His last words were worthy a philosopher whose thoughts, even in his latest moments, were superior to mere personal hope or fear, and turned to the deep mysteries of his being. "O God!" cried Barneveldt, "what then is man?" as he bent his head to the sword that severed it from his body and sent the inquiring spirit to learn the great mystery for which it longed.

Chapter XVII

RENEWAL OF WAR WITH SPAIN AND THE DESPOTISM OF PRINCE MAURICE. 1619-1625

WITH the death of Barneveldt the troubles of the truce were ended, and Prince Maurice was supreme in the state. Both sides have to bear their share of the blame, though the greater wrong rests with the party which committed the judicial murder of the greatest of Dutch statesmen. Honoring after his death the man whom they had failed in life, the states of Holland recorded of him: "A man of great activity, diligence, memory, and conduct; yea, remarkable in every respect. Let him that thinketh he standeth, take heed lest he fall; and may God be merciful to his soul."

Grotius and Hoogerbeets were confined in the castle of Louvestein. Moersbergen, a leading patriot of Utrecht, De Haan, pensionary of Haarlem, and Uyttenbogaert, the chosen confidant of Maurice, but the friend of Barneveldt, were next accused and sentenced to imprisonment or banishment. And thus Arminianism, deprived of its chiefs, was for the time completely stifled. The Remonstrants, thrown into utter despair, looked to emigration as their last resource. Gustavus Adolphus, King of Sweden, and Frederick, Duke of Holstein, offered them shelter and protection in their respective states. Several availed themselves of these offers, but the states-general, alarmed at the progress of self-expatriation, moderated their rigor and thus checked the desolating evil. Several of the imprisoned Arminians had the good fortune to elude the vigilance of their jailers; but the escape of Grotius is the most remarkable of all, both from his own celebrity as one of the first writers of his age in the most varied walks of literature, and from its peculiar circumstances.

Grotius was freely allowed during his close imprisonment all the relaxations of study. His friends supplied him with quantities of books, which were usually brought into the fortress in a trunk two feet two inches long, which the governor regularly and carefully examined during the first year. But custom brought relaxation in the strictness of the prison rules, and the wife of the illustrious prisoner, his faithful and constant visitor, proposed the plan of his escape, to which he gave a ready and, all hazards considered, a courageous assent. Shut up in this trunk for two hours, and with all the risk of suffocation, and of injury from the rude handling of the soldiers who carried it out of the fort, Grotius was brought clear off by the very agents of his persecutors, and safely delivered to the care of his devoted and discreet female servant, who knew the secret and kept it well. She attended the important consignment in the barge to the town of Gorkum, and after various risks of discovery, providentially escaped, Grotius at length found himself safe beyond the limits of his native land. His wife, whose torturing suspense may be imagined the while, concealed the stratagem as long as it was possible to impose on the jailer with the pardonable and praiseworthy fiction of her husband's illness and confinement to his bed. The government, outrageous at the result of the affair, at first proposed to hold this courageous prisoner in place of the prey they had lost, and to proceed criminally against her. But after a fortnight's confinement she was restored to liberty, and the country saved from the disgrace of so ungenerous and cowardly a proceeding. Grotius repaired to Paris, where he was received in the most flattering manner, and distinguished by a pension of one thousand crowns allowed by the king. He soon published his vindication—one of the most eloquent and unanswerable productions of its kind, in which those times of unjust accusations and illegal punishments were so fertile.

The expiration of the twelve years' truce was now at hand, and the United Provinces after that long period of intestine trouble and disgrace had once more to recommence a more congenial struggle against foreign enemies, for a renewal of the war with Spain might be fairly considered a return to the regimen best suited to the constitution of the people. The republic saw, however, with considerable anxiety the approach of this new contest. It was fully sensible of its own weakness. Exile had reduced its population; patriotism had subsided; foreign friends were dead; the troops were unused to warfare; the hatred against Spanish cruelty had lost its excitement; the finances were in confusion; Prince Maurice had no longer the activity of youth; and the still more vigorous impulse of fighting for his country's liberty was changed to the less honorable task of upholding his own authority.

The archdukes, encouraged by these considerations, had hopes of bringing back the United Provinces to their domination. They accordingly sent an embassy to Holland with proposals to that effect. It was received with indignation, and the ambassador, Peckius, was obliged to be escorted back to the frontiers by soldiers, to protect him from the insults of the people. Military operations were, however, for a while refrained from on either side, in consequence of the deaths of Philip III. of Spain and the Archduke Albert. Philip IV. succeeded his father at the age of sixteen, and the Archduchess Isabella found herself alone at the head of the government in the Belgian provinces. Olivarez became as sovereign a minister in Spain as his predecessor, the Duke of Lerma, had been; but the archduchess, though now with only the title of governant of the Netherlands, held the reins of power with a firm and steady hand.

In the celebrated Thirty Years' War which had commenced between the Protestants and Catholics of Germany the former had met with considerable assistance from the United Provinces. Barneveldt, who foresaw the embarrassments which the country would have to contend with on the expiration of that truce, had strongly opposed its meddling in the quarrel. But his ruin and death left no restraint on the policy which prompted the republic to aid the Protestant cause. Fifty thousand florins a month to the revolted Protestants, and a like sum to the princes of the union, were for some time advanced. Frederick, the Elector Palatine, son-in-law of the King of England and nephew of the prince, was chosen by the Bohemians for their king, but in spite of the enthusiastic wishes of the English nation James persisted in refusing to interfere in Frederick's favor. France, governed by De Luynes, a favorite whose influence was deeply pledged, and, it is said, dearly sold, to Spain, abandoned the system of Henry IV. and upheld the house of Austria. Thus the new monarch, only aided by the United Provinces, and that feebly, was soon driven from his temporary dignity, his hereditary dominions in the Palatinate were overrun by the Spanish army under Spinola, and Frederick, utterly defeated at the battle of Prague, was obliged to take refuge in Holland. James's abandonment of his son-in-law has been universally blamed by almost every historian. He certainly allowed a few generous individuals to raise a regiment in England of 2400 chosen soldiers, who, under the command of the gallant Sir Horace Vere, could only vainly regret the impossibility of opposition to ten times their number of veteran troops.

This contest was carried on at first with almost all the advantages on the side of the house of Austria. Two men of extraordinary character, which presented a savage parody of military talent, and a courage chiefly remarkable for the ferocity into which it degenerated, struggled for a while against the imperial arms. These were the Count of Mansfeld and Christian of Brunswick. At the head of two desperate bands, which, by dint of hard fighting, acquired something of the consistency of regular armies, they maintained a long resistance; but the imperial commanders, the Duke of Bavaria and Count Tilly, completed in the year 1622 the defeat of their daring and semi-barbarous opponents.

Spinola was resolved to commence the war against the republic by some important exploit. He therefore laid siege to Bergen-op-Zoom, a place of great consequence, commanding the navigation of the Meuse and the coasts of all the islands of Zealand. But Maurice, roused from the lethargy of despotism which seemed to have wholly changed his character, repaired to the scene of threatened danger, and succeeded, after a series of desperate efforts on both sides, in raising the siege, and forced Spinola to abandon his attempt with a loss of upwards of 12,000 men. Frederick Henry in the meantime had made an incursion into Brabant with a body of light troops, and, ravaging the country up to the very gates of Mechlin, Louvain, and Brussels, levied contributions to the amount of 600,000 florins. The states completed this series of good fortune by obtaining the possession of West Friesland by means of Count Mansfeld, whom they had dispatched thither at the head of his formidable army, and who had, in spite of the opposition of Count Tilly, successfully performed his mission.

We must now turn from these brief records of military affairs, the more pleasing theme for the historian of the Netherlands in comparison with domestic events, which claim attention but to create sensations of regret and censure. Prince Maurice had enjoyed without restraint the fruits of his ambitious daring. His power was uncontrolled and unopposed, but it was publicly odious, and private resentments were only withheld by fear, and, perhaps, in some measure by the moderation and patience which distinguished the disciples of Arminianism. In the midst, however, of the apparent calm a deep conspiracy was formed against the life of the prince. William van Stoutenburg and Regnier van Groeneveldt were the two sons of the great pensionary of Holland. The former was the younger, but, of more impetuous character than his brother, he was the principal in the plot. Instead of any efforts to soften down the hatred of this unfortunate family, these brothers had been removed from their employments, their property was confiscated, and despair soon urged them to desperation. In such a time of general discontent it was easy to find accomplices. Seven or eight determined men readily joined in the plot. Of these, two were Catholics, the rest Arminians, the chief of whom was Henry Slatius, a preacher of considerable eloquence, talent, and energy. It was first proposed to attack the prince at Rotterdam, but the place was soon after changed for Ryswick, a village near The Hague, and afterward celebrated by the treaty of peace signed there and which bears its name. Ten other associates were soon engaged by the exertions of Slatius. These were Arminian artisans and sailors, to whom the actual execution of the murder was to be confided, and they were persuaded that it was planned with the connivance of Prince Frederick Henry, who was considered by the Arminians as the secret partisan of their sect. February 6 was fixed on for the accomplishment of the deed. The better to conceal the design, the conspirators agreed to go unarmed to the place, where they were to find a box containing pistols and poniards in a spot agreed upon. The death of the Prince of Orange was not the only object intended. During the confusion subsequent to the hoped-for success of that first blow, the chief conspirators intended to excite simultaneous revolts at Leyden, Gouda, and Rotterdam, in which town the Arminians were most numerous. A general revolution throughout Holland was firmly reckoned on as the infallible result, and success was enthusiastically looked forward to.

But the plot, however, cautiously laid and resolutely persevered in, was doomed to the fate of many another, and the horror of a second murder (but with far different provocation from the first) averted from the illustrious family to whom was still destined the glory of consolidating the country it had formed. Two brothers named Blansaart, and one Parthy, having procured a considerable sum of money from the leading conspirators, repaired to The Hague, as they asserted, for the purpose of betraying the plot; but they were forestalled in this purpose. Four of the sailors had gone out to Ryswick the preceding evening, and laid the whole of the project, together with the wages of their intended crime, before the prince, who, it would appear, then occupied the ancient château, which no longer exists at Ryswick. The box of arms was found in the place pointed out by the informers, and measures were instantly taken to arrest the various accomplices. Several were seized. Groeneveldt had escaped along the coast disguised as a fisherman, and had nearly effected his passage to England when he was recognized and arrested in the Island of Vlieland. Slatius and others were also intercepted in their attempts at escape. Stoutenburg, the most culpable of all, was the most fortunate—probably from the energy of character which marks the difference between a bold adventurer and a timid speculator. He is believed to have passed from The Hague in the same manner as Grotius quitted his prison, and, by the aid of a faithful servant, he accomplished his escape through various perils, and finally reached Brussels, where the Archduchess Isabella took him under her special protection. He for several years made efforts to be allowed to return to Holland, but finding them hopeless, even after the death of Maurice, he embraced the Catholic religion and obtained the command of a troop of Spanish cavalry, at the head of which he made incursions into his native country, carrying before him a black flag with the effigy of a death's-head, to announce the mournful vengeance which he came to execute.

Fifteen persons were executed for the conspiracy. If ever mercy was becoming to a man, it would have been preëminently so to Maurice on this occasion; but he was inflexible as adamant. The mother, the wife, and the son of Groeneveldt threw themselves at his feet, imploring pardon. Prayers, tears, and sobs were alike ineffectual. It is even said that Maurice asked the wretched mother why she begged mercy for her son, having refused to do as much for her husband? To which cruel question she is reported to have made the sublime answer: "Because my son is guilty, and my husband was not."

These bloody executions caused a deep sentiment of gloom. The conspiracy excited more pity for the victims than horror for the intended crime. Maurice, from being the idol of his countrymen, was now become an object of their fear and dislike. When he moved from town to town the people no longer hailed him with acclamations, and even the common tokens of outward respect were at times withheld. The Spaniards, taking advantage of the internal weakness consequent on this state of public feeling in the states, made repeated incursions into the provinces, which were now united but in title, not in spirit. Spinola was once more in the field, and had invested the important town of Breda, which was the patrimonial inheritance of the princes of Orange. Maurice was oppressed with anxiety and regret, and, for the sake of his better feelings, it may be hoped, with remorse. He could effect nothing against his rival, and he saw his own laurels withering from his care-worn brow. The only hope left of obtaining the so much wanted supplies of money was in the completion of a new treaty with France and England. Cardinal Richelieu, desirous of setting bounds to the ambition and the successes of the house of Austria, readily came into the views of the states, and an obligation for a loan of 1,200,000 livres during the year 1624 and 1,000,000 more for each of the two succeeding years was granted by the King of France, on condition that the republic made no new truce with Spain without his mediation.

An alliance nearly similar was at the same time concluded with England. The failure of his son's intended marriage with the Infanta of Spain had opened the eyes of King James to the way in which he was despised by those who seemed so much to respect him. He was highly indignant, and undertook to revenge himself by aiding the republic. He agreed to furnish 6000 men, and supply the funds for their pay, with a provision for repayment by the states at the conclusion of a peace with Spain.

Prince Maurice had no opportunity of reaping the expected advantages from these treaties. Baffled in all his efforts for relieving Breda, and being unsuccessful in a new attempt upon Antwerp, he returned to The Hague, where a lingering illness, that had for some time exhausted him, terminated in his death on April 23, 1625, in his fifty-ninth year. Most writers attribute this event to agitation at being unable to relieve Breda from the attack of Spinola. It is in any case absurd to suppose that the loss of a single town could have produced so fatal an effect on one whose life had been an almost continual game of the chances of war. But cause enough for Maurice's death may be found in the wearing effects of thirty years of active military service, and the more wasting ravages of half as many of domestic despotism.

Chapter XVIII

FREDERICK HENRY AND THE PEACE OF WESTPHALIA
1625-1648

FREDERICK HENRY succeeded to almost all his brother's titles and employments, and found his new dignities clogged with an accumulation of difficulties sufficient to appall the most determined spirit. Everything seemed to justify alarm and despondency. If the affairs of the republic in India wore an aspect of prosperity, those in Europe presented a picture of past disaster and approaching peril. Disunion and discontent, an almost insupportable weight of taxation, and the disputes of which it was the fruitful source, formed the subjects of internal ill. Abroad was to be seen navigation harassed and trammeled by the pirates of Dunkirk, and the almost defenseless frontiers of the republic exposed to the irruptions of the enemy. The King of Denmark, who endeavored to make head against the imperialist and Spanish forces, was beaten by Tilly and made to tremble for the safety of his own states. England did nothing toward the common cause of Protestantism, in consequence of internal troubles, and civil dissensions for a while disabled France from resuming the system of Henry IV. for humbling the house of Austria.

Frederick Henry was at this period in his forty-second year. His military reputation was well established; he soon proved his political talents. He commenced his career by a total change in the tone of government on the subject of sectarian differences. He exercised several acts of clemency in favor of the imprisoned and exiled Arminians at the same time that he upheld the dominant religion. By these measures he conciliated all parties, and by degrees the fierce spirit of intolerance became subdued. The foreign relations of the United Provinces now presented the anomalous policy of a fleet furnished by the French king, manned by rigid Calvinists, and commanded by a grandson of Admiral Coligny, for the purpose of combating the remainder of the French Huguenots. whom they considered as brothers in religion, though political foes; and during the joint expedition which was undertaken by the allied French and Dutch troops against Rochelle, the stronghold of Protestantism, the preachers of Holland put up prayers for the protection of those whom their army was marching to destroy. The states-general, ashamed of this unpopular union, recalled their fleet, after some severe fighting with that of the Huguenots. Cardinal Richelieu and the King of France were for a time furious in their displeasure; but interests of state overpowered individual resentments, and no rupture took place.

Charles I. had now succeeded his father on the English throne. He renewed the treaty with the republic, who furnished him with twenty ships to assist his own formidable fleet in his war against Spain. Frederick Henry had, soon after his succession to the chief command, commenced an active course of martial operations, and was successful in almost all his enterprises. He took Grol and several other towns, and it was hoped that his successes would have been pushed forward upon a wider field of action against the imperial arms, but the states prudently resolved to act on the defensive by land, choosing the sea for the theater of their more active operations. All the hopes of a powerful confederation against the emperor and the King of Spain seemed frustrated by the war which now broke out between France and England. The states-general contrived by great prudence to maintain a strict neutrality in this quarrel. They even succeeded in mediating a peace between the rival powers, which was concluded the following year; and in the meantime they obtained a more astonishing and important series of triumphs against the Spanish fleets than had yet been witnessed in naval conflicts.

The West India Company had confided the command of their fleet to Peter Heyn, a most intrepid and intelligent sailor, who proved his own merits and the sagacity of his employers on many occasions, two of them of an extraordinary nature. In 1627 he defeated a fleet of twenty-six vessels with a much inferior force. In the following year he had the still more brilliant good fortune, near Havana, in the island of Cuba, in an engagement with the great Spanish armament called the Silver Fleet, to indicate the immense wealth which it contained. The booty was safely carried to Amsterdam, and the whole of the treasure, in money, precious stones, indigo, etc., was estimated at the value of twelve million florins. This was indeed a victory worth gaining, won almost without bloodshed, and raising the republic far above the manifold difficulties by which it had been embarrassed. Heyn perished in the following year in a combat with some of the pirates of Dunkirk —those terrible freebooters whose name was a watchword of terror during the whole continuance of the war.

The year 1629 brought three formidable armies at once to the frontiers of the republic, and caused a general dismay all through the United Provinces; but the immense treasures taken from the Spaniards enabled them to make preparations suitable to the danger, and Frederick Henry, supported by his cousin, William of Nassau, his natural brother, Justin, and other brave and experienced officers, defeated every effort of the enemy. He took many towns in rapid succession, and finally forced the Spaniards to abandon all notion of invading the territories of the republic. Deprived of the powerful talents of Spinola, who was called to command the Spanish troops in Italy, the armies of the archduchess, under the Count of Berg, were not able to cope with the genius of the Prince of Orange. The consequence was the renewal of negotiations for a second truce. But these were received on the part of the republic with a burst of opposition. All parties seemed decided on that point, and every interest, however opposed on minor questions, combined to give a positive negative on this.

The gratitude of the country for the services of Frederick Henry induced the provinces of which he was stadtholder to grant the reversion in this title to his son, a child of three years, and this dignity had every chance of becoming as absolute as it was now pronounced almost hereditary, by the means of an army of 120,000 men devoted to their chief. However, few military occurrences took place, the sea being still chosen as the element best suited to the present enterprises of the republic. In the widely distant settlements of Brazil and Batavia the Dutch were equally successful, and the East and West India companies acquired eminent power and increasing solidity.

The year 1631 was signalized by an expedition into Flanders consisting of 18,000 men, intended against Dunkirk, but hastily abandoned, in spite of every probability of success, by the commissioners of the states-general, who accompanied the army and thwarted all the ardor and vigor of the Prince of Orange. But another great naval victory in the narrow seas of Zealand recompensed the disappointments of this inglorious affair.

The splendid victories of Gustavus Adolphus against the imperial arms in Germany changed the whole face of European affairs. Protestantism began once more to raise its head, and the important conquests by Frederick Henry of almost all the strong places on the Meuse, including Maestricht, the strongest of all, gave the United Provinces their ample share in the glories of the war. The death of the Archduchess Isabella, which took place at Brussels in the year 1633, added considerably to the difficulties of Spain in the Belgian provinces. The defection of the Count of Berg, the chief general of their armies, who was actuated by resentment on the appointment of the Marquis of St. Croix over his head, threw everything into confusion, in exposing a widespread confederacy among the nobility of these provinces to erect themselves into an independent republic, strengthened by a perpetual alliance with the United Provinces against the power of Spain. After the death of Isabella the Duke of Brabançon was arrested. The Prince of Epinoi and the Duke of Burnonville made their escape, and the Duke of Aerschot, who was arrested in Spain, was soon liberated, in consideration of some discoveries into the nature of the plot. An armistice, published in 1634, threw this whole affair into complete oblivion.

The King of Spain appointed his brother Ferdinand, a cardinal and Archbishop of Toledo, to the dignity of governor-general of the Netherlands. He repaired to Germany at the head of 17,000 men, and bore his share in the victory of Nordlingen, after which he hastened to the Netherlands and made his entry into Brussels in 1634. Richelieu had hitherto only combated the house of Austria in these countries by negotiation and intrigue, but he now entered warmly into the proposals made by Holland for a treaty offensive and defensive between Louis XIII. and the republic. By a treaty soon after concluded (February 8, 1635), the King of France engaged to invade the Belgian provinces with an army of 30,000 men, in concert with a Dutch force of equal number. It was agreed that if Belgium would consent to break from the Spanish yoke it was to be erected into a free state; if, on the contrary, it would not coöperate for its own freedom, France and Holland were to dismember and to divide it equally.

The plan of these combined measures was soon acted on. The French army took the field under the command of the Marshals De Châtillon and De Brèze and defeated the Spaniards in a bloody battle near Avein, in the province of Luxemburg, on May 20, 1635, with the loss of 4000 men. The victors soon made a junction with the Prince of Orange, and the towns of Tirlemont, St. Trond, and some others were quickly reduced. The former of these places was taken by assault and pillaged with circumstances of cruelty that recall the horrors of the early transactions of the war. The Prince of Orange was forced to punish severely the authors of these offenses. The consequences of this event were highly injurious to the allies. A spirit of fierce resistance was excited throughout the invaded provinces. Louvain set the first example. The citizens and students took arms for its defense, and the combined forces of France and Holland were repulsed and forced by want of supplies to abandon the siege and rapidly retreat. The Prince-Cardinal, as Ferdinand was called, took advantage of this reverse to press the retiring French, recovered several towns, and gained all the advantages as well as glory of the campaign. The remains of the French army, reduced by continual combats, and still more by sickness, finally embarked at Rotterdam to return to France in the ensuing spring, a sad contrast to its brilliant appearance at the commencement of the campaign.

The military events for several ensuing years present nothing of sufficient interest to induce us to record them in detail. A perpetual succession of sieges and skirmishes afford a monotonous picture of isolated courage and skill, but we see none of those great conflicts which bring out the genius of opposing generals and show war in its grand results as the decisive means of enslaving or emancipating mankind. The Prince-Cardinal, one of the many who on this bloody theater displayed consummate military talents, incessantly employed himself in incursions into the bordering provinces of France, ravaged Picardy, and filled Paris with fear and trembling. He, however, reaped no new laurels when he came into contact with Frederick Henry, who on almost every occasion, particularly that of the siege of Breda in 1637, carried his object in spite of all opposition. The triumphs of war were balanced, but Spain and the Belgian provinces, so long upheld by the talent of the governor-general, had gradually become exhausted. The revolution in Portugal and the succession of the Duke of Braganza, under the title of John IV., to the throne of his ancestors struck a fatal blow to the power of Spain. A strict alliance was concluded between the new monarch of France and

Holland, and hostilities against the common enemy were on all sides vigorously continued.

The successes of the republic at sea and in their distant enterprises were continual, and in some instances brilliant. Brazil was gradually falling into the power of the West India Company. The East India possessions were secure. The great victory of Van Tromp, known by the name of the Battle of the Downs, from being fought off the coast of England, on October 21, 1639, raised the naval reputation of Holland as high as it could well be carried. Fifty ships taken, burned, and sunk were the proofs of their admiral's triumph, and the Spanish navy never recovered the loss. The victory was celebrated throughout Europe, and Van Tromp was the hero of the day. The King of England was, however, highly indignant at the hardihood with which the Dutch admiral broke through the etiquette of territorial respect and destroyed his country's bitter foes under the very sanction of English neutrality. But the subjects of Charles I. did not partake their monarch's feelings. They had no sympathy with arbitrary and tyrannic government, and their joy at the misfortune of their old enemies, the Spaniards, gave a fair warning of the spirit which afterward proved so fatal to the infatuated king, who on this occasion would have protected and aided them.

In an unsuccessful enterprise in Flanders, Count Henry Casimir of Nassau was mortally wounded, adding another to the list of those of that illustrious family whose lives were lost in the service of their country. His brother, Count William Frederick, succeeded him in his office of stadtholder of Friesland, but the same dignity in the provinces of Groningen and Drenthe devolved on the Prince of Orange. The latter had conceived the desire of a royal alliance for his son William. Charles I. readily assented to the proposal of the states-general, that this young prince should receive the hand of his daughter Mary. Embassies were exchanged, the conditions of the contract agreed on, but it was not till two years later that Van Tromp, with an escort of twenty ships, conducted the princess, then twelve years old, to the country of her future husband. The republic did not view with an eye quite favorable this advancing aggrandizement of the house of Orange. Frederick Henry had shortly before been dignified by the King of France, at the suggestion of Richelieu, with the title of "highness," instead of the inferior one of "excellency," and the states-general, jealous of this distinction granted to their chief magistrate, adopted for themselves the sounding appellation of "high and mighty lords." The Prince of Orange, whatever might have been his private views of ambition, had, however, the prudence to silence all suspicion by the mild and moderate use which he made of the power which he might perhaps have wished to increase, but never attempted to abuse.

On November 9, 1641, the Prince-Cardinal Ferdinand died at Brussels in his thirty-third year, another instance of those who were cut off in the very vigor of manhood from worldly dignities and the exercise of the painful and inauspicious duties of governor-general of the Netherlands. Don Francisco de Mello, a nobleman of highly reputed talents, was the next who obtained this onerous situation. He commenced his governorship by a succession of military operations, by which, like most of his predecessors, he is alone distinguished. Acts of civil administration are scarcely noticed by the historians of these men. Not one of them, with the exception of the Archduke Albert, seems to have valued the internal interests of the government, and he alone, perhaps, because they were declared and secured as his own. De Mello, after taking some towns and defeating the Marshal de Guiche in the battle of Hannecourt, tarnished all his fame by the great faults which he committed in the famous battle of Rocroy. The Duke of Enghien, then twenty-one years of age, and subsequently so celebrated as the great Condé, completely defeated De Mello, and nearly annihilated the Spanish and Walloon infantry. The military operations of the Dutch army were this year only remarkable by the gallant conduct of Prince William, son of the Prince of Orange, who, not yet seventeen years of age, defeated near Hulst, under the eyes of his father, a Spanish detachment in a very warm skirmish.

Considerable changes were now insensibly operating in the policy of Europe. Cardinal Richelieu had finished his dazzling but tempestuous career of government, in which the hand of death arrested him on December 4, 1642. Louis XIII. soon followed to the grave him who was rather his master than his minister. Anne of Austria was declared regent during the minority of her son, Louis XIV., then only five years of age, and Cardinal Mazarin succeeded to the station from which death alone had power to remove his predecessor.

The civil wars in England now broke out, and their terrible

results seemed to promise to the republic the undisturbed sovereignty of the seas. The Prince of Orange received with great distinction the mother-in-law of his son, when she came to Holland under pretext of conducting her daughter, but her principal purpose was to obtain, by the sale of the crown jewels and the assistance of Frederick Henry, funds for the supply of her unfortunate husband's cause. The prince and several private individuals contributed largely in money, and several experienced officers passed over to serve in the royalist army of England. The provincial states of Holland, however, sympathizing wholly with Parliament, remonstrated with the stadtholder, and the Dutch colonists encouraged the hostile efforts of their brethren, the Puritans of Scotland, by all the absurd exhortations of fanatic zeal. Boswell, the English resident in the name of the king, and Strickland, the ambassador from Parliament, kept up a constant succession of complaints and remonstrances on occasion of every incident which seemed to balance the conduct of the republic in the great question of English politics. Considerable differences existed. The province of Holland and some others leaned toward the Parliament, the Prince of Orange favored the king, and the states-general endeavored to continue neutral.

The struggle was still furiously maintained in Germany. Generals of the first order of military talent were continually appearing, and successively eclipsing each other by their brilliant actions: Gustavus Adolphus was killed in the midst of his glorious career, at the battle of Lutzen; Bernard of Saxe-Weimar succeeded to the command, and proved himself worthy of the place; Tilly and the celebrated Wallenstein were no longer on the scene. The Emperor Ferdinand II. was dead, and his son, Ferdinand III., saw his victorious enemies threaten, at last, the existence of the empire. Everything tended to make peace necessary to some of the contending powers, as it was at length desirable for all. Sweden and Denmark were engaged in a bloody and wasteful conflict. The United Provinces sent an embassy, in the month of June, 1644, to each of those powers, and by a vigorous demonstration of their resolution to assist Sweden, if Denmark proved refractory, a peace was signed the following year, which terminated the disputes of the rival nations.

Negotiations were now opened at Munster between the several belligerents. The republic was, however, the last to send its plenipotentiaries there, having signed a new treaty with France, by which they mutually stipulated to make no peace independent of each other. It behooved the republic, however, to contribute as much as possible toward the general object, for, among other strong motives to that line of conduct, the finances of Holland were in a state nothing short of deplorable.

Every year brought the necessity of a new loan, and the public debt of the provinces now amounted to 150,000,000 florins, bearing interest at $6\frac{1}{4}$ per cent. Considerable alarm was excited at the progress of the French army in the Belgian provinces, and escape from the tyranny of Spain seemed only to lead to the danger of submission to a nation too powerful and too close at hand not to be dangerous, either as a foe or an ally. These fears were increased by the knowledge that Cardinal Mazarin projected a marriage between Louis XIV. and the Infanta of Spain, with the Belgian provinces, or Spanish Netherlands, as they were now called, for her marriage portion. This project was confided to the Prince of Orange, under the seal of secrecy, and he was offered the marquisate of Antwerp as the price of his influence toward effecting the plan. The prince revealed the whole to the states-general. Great fermentation was excited—the stadtholder himself was blamed, and suspected of complicity with the designs of the cardinal. Frederick Henry was deeply hurt at this want of confidence, and the injurious publications which openly assailed his honor in a point where he felt himself entitled to praise instead of suspicion.

The French labored to remove the impression which this affair excited in the republic, but the states-general felt themselves justified by the intriguing policy of Mazarin in entering into a secret negotiation with the King of Spain, who offered very favorable conditions. The negotiations were considerably advanced by the marked disposition evinced by the Prince of Orange to hasten the establishment of peace. Yet at this very period, and while anxiously wishing this great object, he could not resist the desire for another campaign, one more exploit, to signalize the epoch at which he finally placed his sword in the scabbard. Frederick Henry was essentially a soldier, with all the spirit of his race, and this evidence of the ruling passion, while he touched the verge of the grave, is one of the most striking points of his character. He accordingly took the field, but with a constitution broken by a lingering disease, he was little fitted to accomplish any feat worthy of his splendid reputation. He failed in an attempt on Venlo, and another on Antwerp, and retired to The Hague, where for some months he rapidly declined. On March 14, 1647, he expired, in his sixty-third year, leaving behind him a character of unblemished integrity, prudence, toleration, and valor. He was not of that impetuous stamp which leads men to heroic deeds and brings danger to the states whose liberty is compromised by their ambition. He was a striking contrast to his brother Maurice, and more resembled his father in many of those calmer qualities of the mind which make men more beloved without lessening their claims to admiration. Frederick Henry had the honor of completing the glorious task which William began and Maurice followed up. He saw the oppression they had combated now humbled and overthrown, and he forms the third in a sequence of family renown, the most surprising and the least checkered afforded by the annals of Europe.

William II. succeeded his father in his dignities, and his ardent spirit longed to rival him in war. He turned his endeavors to thwart all the efforts for peace. But the interests of the nation and the dying wishes of Frederick Henry were of too powerful influence with the states to be overcome by the martial yearnings of an inexperienced youth. The negotiations were pressed forward, and, despite the complaints, the murmurs, and the intrigues of France, the Treaty of Munster was finally signed by the respective ambassadors of the United Provinces and Spain on January 30, 1648. This celebrated treaty contains seventy-nine articles. Three points were of main and vital importance to the republic: the first acknowledges an ample and entire recognition of the sovereignty of the states-general and a renunciation forever of all claims on the part of Spain; the second confirms the rights of trade and navigation in the East and West Indies, with the possession of the various countries and stations then actually occupied by the contracting powers; the third guarantees a like possession of all the provinces and towns of the Netherlands, as they then stood in their respective occupation—a clause highly favorable to the republic, which had conquered several considerable places in Brabant and Flanders. The ratifications of the treaty were exchanged at Munster with great solemnity on May 15, following the signature; the peace was published in that town and in Osnaburg on the 19th, and in all the different states of the King of Spain and the United

Provinces as soon as the joyous intelligence could reach such various and widely separated destinations. Thus, after eighty years of unparalleled warfare, only interrupted by the truce of 1609, during which hostilities had not ceased in the Indies, the new republic rose from the horrors of civil war and foreign tyranny to its uncontested rank as a free and independent state among the

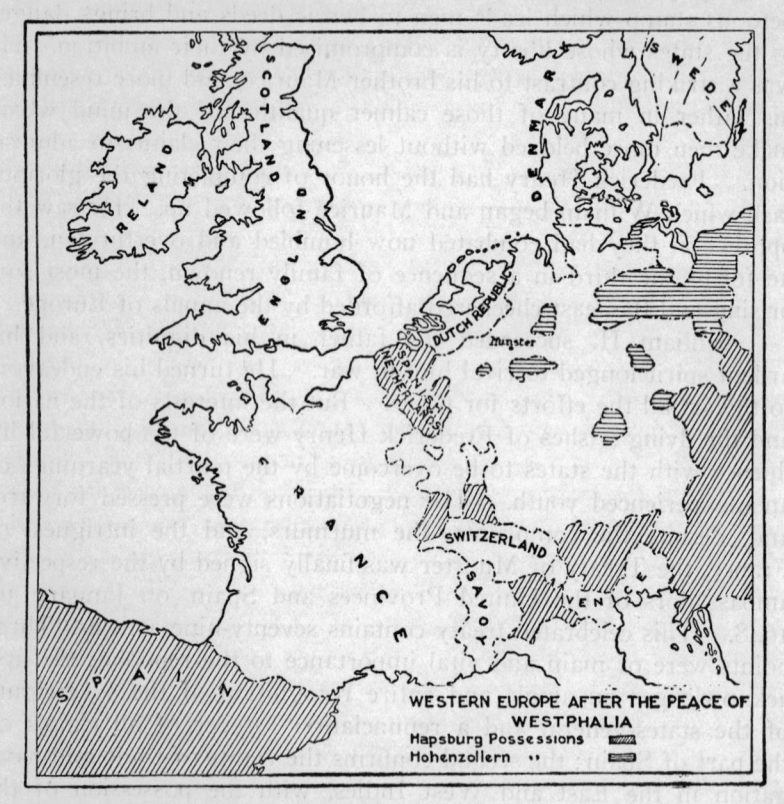

WESTERN EUROPE AFTER THE PEACE OF WESTPHALIA
Hapsburg Possessions
Hohenzollern "

most powerful nations of Europe. No country had ever done more for glory, and the result of its efforts was the irrevocable guarantee of civil and religious liberty, the great aim and end of civilization.

The King of France alone had reason to complain of this treaty, and his resentment was strongly pronounced. But the United Provinces flung back the reproaches of his ambassador on Cardinal Mazarin, and the anger of the monarch was smothered by the policy of the minister.

PEACE OF WESTPHALIA

The internal tranquillity of the republic was secured from all future alarm by the conclusion of the general Peace of Westphalia, definitely signed October 24, 1648. This treaty was long considered not only as the fundamental law of the empire, but as the basis of the political system of Europe. As numbers of conflicting interests were reconciled, Germanic liberty secured, and a just equilibrium established between the Catholics and Protestants, France and Sweden obtained great advantages; and the various princes of the empire saw their possessions regulated and secured, at the same time that the powers of the emperor were strictly defined.

This great epoch in European history naturally marks the conclusion of another in that of the Netherlands, and this period of general repose allows a brief consideration of the progress of arts, sciences, and manners during the half century just now completed.

The Archdukes Albert and Isabella during the whole course of their sovereignty labored to remedy the abuses which had crowded the administration of justice. The "perpetual edict," in 1611, regulated the form of judicial proceedings, but several provinces received new charters, by which the privileges of the people were placed on a footing in harmony with their wants. Anarchy, in short, gave place to regular government, and the archdukes, in swearing to maintain the celebrated pact known by the name of the "*Joyeuse Entrée*," did all in their power to satisfy their subjects, while securing their own authority. The piety of the archdukes gave an example to all classes. This, although degenerating in the vulgar to superstition and bigotry, formed a severe check, which allowed their rulers to restrain popular excess and enabled them in the internal quiet of their despotism to soften the people by the encouragement of the sciences and arts. Medicine, astronomy, and mathematics made prodigious progress during this epoch. Several eminent men flourished in the Netherlands. But the glory of others, in countries presenting a wider theater for their renown, in many instances eclipsed them; and the inventors of new methods and systems in anatomy, optics, and music were almost forgotten in the splendid improvements of their followers.

In literature, Hugo de Groot, or Grotius (his Latinized name, by which he is better known), was the most brilliant star of his country or his age, as Erasmus was of that which preceded. He was at once eminent as jurist, poet, theologian, and historian. His erudition was immense, and he brought it to bear in his political capacity, as ambassador from Sweden to the court of France, when the violence of party and the injustice of power condemned him to perpetual imprisonment in his native land. The religious disputations in Holland had given a great impulse to talent. They were not solely theological arguments, but often blended various illustrations from history, art, and science, and a tone of keen and delicate satire at once refined and made them readable. It is remarkable that almost the whole of the Latin writings of this period abound in good taste, while those written in the vulgar tongue are chiefly coarse and trivial. Vondel, the greatest of all Dutch writers, is celebrated for his tragedies, and Hooft for his lyrical verse. The latter of these writers was also distinguished for his prose works, in honor of which Louis XIII. dignified him with letters patent of nobility and decorated him with the Order of St. Michael.

But while Holland was more particularly distinguished by the progress of the mechanical arts, to which Prince Maurice afforded unbounded patronage, the Belgian provinces gave birth to that galaxy of genius in the art of painting which no equal period of any other country has even rivaled, artists who now flourished in Belgium at once founding, perfecting, and immortalizing the Flemish school of painting. Rubens, Vandyke, Teniers, Crayer, Jordaens, Sneyders, and a host of other great names crowd on us, with claims for notice that almost make the mention of any an injustice to the rest. But the world is familar with their fame, and the widespread taste for their wonderful art makes them independent of other record than the combination of their own exquisite touch, undying tints, and unequaled knowledge of nature. Engraving, carried at the same time to great perfection, has multiplied some of the merits of the celebrated painters, while stamping the reputation of its own professors. Sculpture also had its votaries of considerable note. Among these, Des Jardins and Quesnoy held the foremost station. Architecture also produced some remarkable names. Nor was the Dutch school of art far behind the Flemish, with the names of Frans Hals, Terburg, Rysdael, and, towering above them all, Rembrandt, the most human and original artist of his time.

The arts were, in short, never held in higher honor than at this brilliant epoch. Otto-Venire, the master of Rubens, held most important employments. Rubens himself, appointed secretary to the privy council of the archdukes, was subsequently sent to England, where he negotiated the peace between that country and Spain. The unfortunate King Charles so highly esteemed his merit that he knighted him in full Parliament, and presented him with the diamond ring he wore on his own finger and a chain enriched with brilliants. David Teniers, the great pupil of this distinguished master, met his due share of honor. He has left several portraits of himself, one of which hands him down to posterity, in the costume and with the decorations of the belt and key, which he wore in his capacity of chamberlain to the Archduke Leopold, governor-general of the Spanish Netherlands.

The intestine disturbances of Holland during the twelve years' truce, and the enterprises against Friesland and the duchy of Cleves, had prevented that wise economy which was expected from the republic. The annual ordinary cost of the military establishment at that period amounted to 13,000,000 florins. To meet the enormous expenses of the state, taxes were raised on every material. They produced about 30,000,000 florins a year, independent of 5,000,000 each for the East and West India companies. The population in 1620, in Holland, was about 600,000, and the other provinces contained about the same number.

It is singular to observe the fertile erections of monopoly in a state founded on principles of commercial freedom. The East and West India companies, the Greenland company, and others were successively formed. By the effect of their enterprise, industry, and wealth conquests were made and colonies founded with surprising rapidity. In America the town of Amsterdam, now New York, was founded in 1624; the East saw Batavia rise up from the ruins of Jacatra, which was sacked and razed by the Dutch adventurers, while the West India Company conquered Curaçao and a large part of Brazil from the Portuguese.

The Dutch and English East India companies, repressing their mutual jealousy, formed a species of partnership in 1619 for the reciprocal enjoyment of the rights of commerce. But four years later than this date an event took place so fatal to national confidence that its impressions are scarcely yet effaced—this was the torturing and execution of several Englishmen in the island of Amboyna, on pretense of an unproved plot, of which every probability leads to the belief that they were wholly innocent. This circumstance was the strongest stimulant to the hatred so evident in the bloody wars which not long afterward took place between the two nations, and the lapse of two centuries has been necessary to efface its effects. Much has been written at various periods for and against the establishment of monopolizing companies, by which individual wealth and skill are excluded from their chances of reward. With reference to those of Holland at this period of its history it is sufficient to remark that the great results of their formation could never have been brought about by isolated enterprises, and the justice or wisdom of their continuance are questions wholly dependent on the fluctuations in trade and the effects produced on that of any given country by the progress and the rivalry of others.

With respect to the state of manners in the republic, it is clear that the jealousies and emulation of commerce were not likely to lessen the vice of avarice with which the natives have been reproached. Drunkenness was a vice considered scarcely scandalous, but the intrigues of gallantry were concealed with the most scrupulous mystery—giving evidence of good taste, at least, if not of strict morality. Court etiquette began to be of infinite importance. But a characteristic more noble and worthy was the full enjoyment of the liberty of the press in the United Provinces. The thirst of gain, the fury of faction, the federal independence of the minor towns, the absolute power of Prince Maurice, all the combinations which might carry weight, were totally ineffectual to prevail over this grand principle, and the republic was, on this point, proudly preëminent among surrounding nations.

PART III

THE DUTCH REPUBLIC. 1648-1813

Chapter XIX

WAR WITH ENGLAND. 1648-1678

THE completion of the Peace of Munster opens a new scene in the history of the republic. Its political system experienced considerable changes. Its ancient enemies became its most ardent friends, and its old allies loosened the bonds of long continued amity. The other states of Europe, displeased at its imperious conduct or jealous of its success, began to wish its humiliation; but it was little thought that the consummation was to be effected at the hands of England.

While Holland prepared to profit by the peace so brilliantly gained, England, torn by civil war, was hurried on in crime and misery to the final act which has left an indelible stain on her annals. The United Provinces had preserved a strict neutrality while the contest was undecided. The Prince of Orange warmly strove to obtain a declaration in favor of his father-in-law, Charles I. The Prince of Wales and the Duke of York, his sons, who had taken refuge at The Hague, earnestly joined in the entreaty, but all that could be obtained from the states-general was their consent to an embassy to interpose with the uncompromising men who doomed the hapless monarch to the block. Pauw and Joachimi, the one sixty-four years of age, the other eighty-eight, the most able men of the republic, undertook the task of mediation. They were scarcely listened to by the Parliament, and the bloody sacrifice took place.

The details of this event and its immediate consequences belong to English history, and we must hurry over the brief, turbid, and inglorious stadtholderate of William II., to arrive at the more interesting contest between the Dutch Republic and the rival Commonwealth of England.

William II. was now in his twenty-fourth year. He had early evinced that heroic disposition which was common to his race. He panted for military glory. All his pleasures were those usual to ardent and high-spirited men, although his delicate constitution seemed to forbid the indulgence of hunting, tennis, and the other violent exercises in which he delighted. He was highly accomplished, spoke five different languages with elegance and fluency, and had made considerable progress in mathematics and other abstract sciences. His ambition knew no bounds. Had he reigned over a monarchy as absolute king he would most probably have gone down to posterity a conqueror and a hero. But, unfitted to direct a republic as its first citizen, he has left but the name of a rash and unconstitutional magistrate. From the moment of his accession to power he was made sensible of the jealousy and suspicion with which his office and his character were observed by the provincial states of Holland. Many instances of this disposition were accumulated to his great disgust, and he was not long in evincing his determination to brave all the odium and reproach of despotic designs and to risk everything for the establishment of absolute power. The province of Holland, arrogating to itself the greatest share in the reforms of the army, and the financial arrangements called for by the transition from war to peace, was soon in fierce opposition with the states-general, which supported the prince in his early views. Cornelius Bikker, one of the burgomasters of Amsterdam, was the leading person in the states of Holland, and a circumstance soon occurred which put him and the stadtholder in collision, and quickly decided the great question at issue.

The admiral Cornelius de Witt arrived from Brazil with the remains of his fleet, and without the consent of the council of regency there established by the states-general. He was instantly arrested by order of the Prince of Orange, in his capacity of high admiral. The admiralty of Amsterdam was at the same time ordered by the states-general to imprison six of the captains of this fleet. The states of Holland maintained that this was a violation of their provincial rights, and an illegal assumption of power on the part of the states-general, and the magistrates of Amsterdam forced the prison doors and set the captains at liberty. William, backed by the authority of the states-general, now put himself at the head of a deputation from that body, and made a rapid tour of visitation to the different chief towns of the republic to sound the depths of public opinion on the matters in dispute. The deputation met with varied success, but the results proved to the irritated prince that no measures of compromise were to be expected, and that force alone was to arbitrate the question. The army was to a man devoted to him. The states-general gave him their entire and somewhat servile, support. He therefore on his own authority arrested the six deputies of Holland, in the same way that his uncle Maurice had seized on Barneveldt, Grotius, and the others, and they were immediately conveyed to the castle of Louvestein.

In adopting this bold and unauthorized measure he decided on an immediate attempt to gain possession of the city of Amsterdam, the central point of opposition to his violent designs. William Frederick, Count of Nassau, stadtholder of Friesland, at the head of a numerous detachment of troops, marched secretly and by night to surprise the town, but the darkness and a violent thunder storm having caused the greater number to lose their way, the count found himself at dawn at the city gates with a very insufficient force, and had the further mortification to see the walls well manned, the cannon pointed, the drawbridges raised, and everything in a state of defense. The courier from Hamburg, who had passed through the scattered bands of soldiers during the night, had given the alarm. The first notion was that a roving band of Swedish or Lorraine troops, attracted by the opulence of Amsterdam, had resolved on an attempt to seize and pillage it. The magistrates could scarcely credit the evidence of day, which showed them the Count of Nassau and his force on their hostile mission. A short conference with the deputies from the citizens convinced him that a speedy retreat was the only measure of safety for himself and his force, as the sluices of the dikes were in part opened, and a threat of submerging the intended assailants only required a moment more to be enforced.

Nothing could exceed the disappointment and irritation of the Prince of Orange consequent on this transaction. He at first threatened, then negotiated, and finally patched up the matter in a manner the least mortifying to his wounded pride. Bikker nobly offered himself for a peace-offering, and voluntarily resigned his employments in the city he had saved; and De Witt and his officers were released. William was in some measure consoled for his disgrace by the condolence of the army, the thanks of the province of Zealand, and a new treaty with France, strengthened by promises of future support from Cardinal Mazarin; but before he could profit by these encouraging symptoms, domestic and foreign, a premature death cut short all his projects of ambition. Over-violent exercise in a shooting party in Guelders brought on a fever, which soon terminated in an attack of small-pox. On the first appearance of his illness he was removed to The Hague, and he died there on November 6, 1650, aged twenty-four years and six months.

The death of this prince left the state without a stadtholder and the army without a chief. The whole of Europe shared more or less in the joy or the regret it caused. The republican party, both in Holland and in England, rejoiced in a circumstance which threw back the sovereign power into the hands of the nation; the partisans of the house of Orange deeply lamented the event. But the birth of a son, of which the widowed Princess of Orange was delivered within a week of her husband's death, revived the hopes of those who mourned his loss, and offered her the only consolation which could assuage her grief. The guardianship of the child was after some dispute given to his uncle, the Elector of Brandenburg. The states of Holland soon exercised their influence on the other provinces. Many of the prerogatives of the stadtholder were now assumed by the people, and, with the exception of Zealand, which made an ineffectual attempt to name the infant prince to the dignity of his ancestors under the title of William III., a perfect unanimity seemed to have reconciled all opposing interests. The various towns secured the privileges of appointing their own magistrates, and the direction of the army and navy devolved to the states-general.

The time was now arrived when the wisdom, the courage, and the resources of the republic were to be put once more to the test, in a contest hitherto without example, and never since equaled in its nature. The naval wars between Holland and England had their real source in the inveterate jealousies and unbounded ambition of both countries, reciprocally convinced that a joint supremacy at sea was incompatible with their interests and their honor, and each resolved to risk everything for their mutual pretensions—to perish rather than yield. The United Provinces were assuredly not the aggressors in this quarrel. They had made sure of their capability to meet it, by the settlement of all questions of internal government and the solid peace which secured them against any attack on the part of their old and inveterate enemy; but they did not seek a rupture. They at first endeavored to ward off the threatened danger by every effort of conciliation, and they met with temperate management even the advances made by Cromwell at the instigation of St. John, the chief justice, for a proposed yet impracticable coalition between the two republics, which was to make them one and indivisible. An embassy to The Hague, with St. John and Strickland at its head, was received with all public honors, but the partisans of the families of Orange and Stuart, and the populace generally, openly insulted the ambassadors. About the same time Dorislaus, a Dutchman naturalized in England, and sent on a mission from the Parliament, was murdered at The Hague by some Scotch officers, friends of the banished king; the massacre of Amboyna, thirty years before, was made a cause of revived complaint; and altogether a sum of injuries was easily made up to turn the proposed coalition into a fierce and bloody war.

The Parliament of England soon found a pretext in an outrageous measure, under pretense of providing for the interests of commerce. They passed the celebrated Navigation Act, which prohibited all nations from importing into England in their ships any commodity which was not the growth and manufacture of their own country. This law, though worded generally, was aimed directly at the Dutch, who were the general factors and carriers of Europe. Ships were seized, reprisals made, the mockery of negotiation carried on, fleets equipped, and at length the war broke out.

In the month of May, 1652, the Dutch admiral Tromp, commanding forty-two ships of war, met with the English fleet under Blake in the straits of Dover. The latter, though much inferior in number, gave a signal to the Dutch admiral to strike, the usual salutation of honor accorded to the English during the monarchy. Totally different versions have been given by the two admirals of what followed. Blake insisted that Tromp, instead of complying, fired a broadside at his vessel; Tromp stated that a second and a third bullet were sent promptly from the British ship while he was preparing to obey the admiral's claim. The discharge of the first broadside is also a matter of contradiction, and of course of doubt. But it is of small consequence, for whether hostilities had been hurried on or delayed, they were ultimately inevitable. A bloody battle began, and it lasted five hours. The inferiority in number on the side of the English was balanced by the larger size of their ships. One Dutch vessel was sunk, another taken, and night parted the combatants.

The states-general heard the news with consternation. They dispatched the grand pensionary, Pauw, on a special embassy to London. The imperious Parliament would hear of neither reason nor remonstrance. Right or wrong, they were resolved on war. Blake was soon at sea again with a numerous fleet, Tromp following with a hundred ships, but a violent tempest separated these furious enemies, and retarded for a while the reëncounter they mutually longed for. On August 16 a battle took place between Sir George Ayscue and the renowned De Ruyter, near Plymouth, each with about forty ships, but with no decisive consequences. On October 28 Blake, aided by Bourn and Penn, met a Dutch squadron of nearly equal force off the coast of Kent under De Ruyter and De Witt. The fight which followed was also severe, but not decisive, though the Dutch had the worst of the day. In the Mediterranean the Dutch admiral, Van Galen, defeated the English captain, Appleton, but bought the victory with his life. And on December 10 another bloody conflict took place between Blake and Tromp, seconded by De Ruyter, near the Goodwin Sands. In this determined action Blake was wounded and defeated, five English ships taken, burned, or sunk, and night saved the fleet from destruction.

Great preparations were made in England to recover this disgrace. Eighty sail put to sea under Blake, Dean, and Monk, so celebrated subsequently as the restorer of the monarchy. Tromp and De Ruyter, with seventy-six vessels, were descried on February 28 escorting three hundred merchantmen up the Channel. Three days of desperate fighting ended in a drawn battle, the Dutch losing ten ships and 600 men, while the English lost six ships but over 2000 men. Tromp acquired prodigious honor by this battle, having succeeded in saving almost the whole of his immense convoy. It was after this engagement that Tromp is said to have placed a broom at his masthead to intimate that he would sweep the Channel clear of English ships. On June 12 and the day following two other actions were fought, in the first of which the English admiral, Dean, was killed; in the second, Monk, Penn, and Lawson amply revenged his death by forcing the Dutch to regain their harbors with great loss.

July 21 was the last of these bloody and obstinate conflicts for superiority. Tromp issued out once more, determined to conquer or die. He met the enemy off Scheveling, commanded by Monk. Both fleets rushed to the combat. The heroic Dutchman, animating his sailors with his sword drawn, was shot through the heart with a musket-ball. This battle, the bloodiest of the war, was as indecisive as most of the others. Both sides claimed the victory, but neither fleet kept the sea. The body of Tromp was carried with great solemnity to the church of Delft, where a magnificent mausoleum was erected over the remains of this eminently brave and distinguished man.

This memorable battle, and the death of this great naval hero, added to the injury done to their trade, induced the states-general to seek terms from their too powerful enemy. The want of peace was felt throughout the whole country. Cromwell was not averse to granting it, but insisted on conditions every way disadvantageous and humiliating. He had revived his chimerical scheme of a total conjunction of government, privileges, and interests between the two republics. This was firmly rejected by John de Witt, now grand pensionary of Holland, and by the states under his influence. But the Dutch consented to a defensive league; to punish the survivors of those concerned in the massacre of Amboyna, to pay £9000 of indemnity for vessels seized in the Sound, £5000 for the affair of Amboyna, and £85,000 to the English East India Company; to cede to them the island of Polerone in the East; to yield the honor of the national flag to the English; and, finally, that neither the young Prince of Orange nor any of his family should ever be invested with the dignity of stadtholder. These two latter conditions were certainly degrading to Holland, and the conditions of the treaty prove that an absurd point of honor was the only real cause for the short but bloody and ruinous war which plunged the Provinces into overwhelming difficulties.[1]

For several years after the conclusion of this inglorious peace universal discontent and dissension spread throughout the republic. The supporters of the house of Orange and every impartial friend of the national honor were indignant at the act of exclusion. Murmurs and revolts broke out in several towns, and all was once more tumult, agitation, and doubt. No event of considerable importance marks particularly this epoch of domestic trouble. A new war was at last pronounced inevitable, and was the means of appeasing the distractions of the people and reconciling by degrees contending parties. Denmark, the ancient ally of the republic, was threatened with destruction by Charles Gustavus, King of Sweden, who held Copenhagen in blockade. The interests of Holland were in imminent peril should the Swedes gain the passage of the Sound. This

---

[1] During the English war the Dutch West India Company lost its last strongholds in Brazil, which was now wholly in the hands of the Portuguese.

Hist. Nat. xiii-16

double motive influenced De Witt, and he persuaded the states-general to send Admiral Opdam with a considerable fleet to the Baltic. This intrepid successor of the immortal Tromp soon came to blows with a rival worthy to meet him. Wrangel, the Swedish admiral, with a superior force, defended the passage of the Sound, and the two castles of Kronenberg and Elsenberg supported his fleet with their tremendous fire. But Opdam resolutely advanced. Though suffering extreme anguish from an attack of gout, he had himself carried on deck, where he gave his orders with the most admirable coolness and precision, in the midst of danger and carnage. The rival monarchs witnessed the battle—the King of Sweden from the castle of Kronenberg and the King of Denmark from the summit of the highest tower in his besieged capital. A brilliant victory crowned the efforts of the Dutch admiral, dearly bought by the death of his second in command, the brave De Witt, and Peter Florizon, another admiral of note. Relief was poured into Copenhagen. Opdam was replaced in the command, too arduous for his infirmities, by the still more celebrated De Ruyter, who was greatly distinguished for his valor in several successive affairs, and, after the death of Charles Gustavus, the Swedes made peace, restoring their conquests in Denmark.

These transactions placed the United Provinces on a still higher pinnacle of glory than they had ever reached. Intestine disputes were suddenly calmed. The Algerines and other pirates were swept from the seas by a succession of small but vigorous expeditions. The mediation of the states reëstablished peace in several of the petty states of Germany. England and France were both held in check, if not preserved in friendship, by the dread of their recovered power. Trade and finance were reorganized. Everything seemed to promise a long-continued peace and growing greatness, much of which was owing to the talents and persevering energy of De Witt; and, to complete the good work of European tranquillity, the French and Spanish monarchs concluded in this year the treaty known by the name of the "Peace of the Pyrenees."

Cromwell had now closed his career, and Charles II. was restored to the throne from which he had so long been excluded. The complimentary entertainments rendered to the restored king in Holland were on the proudest scale of expense. He left the country which had given him refuge in misfortune, and done him honor in his prosperity, with profuse expressions of regard and gratitude. Scarcely was he established in his recovered kingdom when a still greater testimony of deference to his wishes was paid by the states-general formally annulling the act of exclusion against the house of Orange. A variety of motives, however, acting on the easy and plastic mind of the monarch, soon effaced whatever of gratitude he had at first conceived. He readily entered into the views of the English nation, which was irritated by the great commercial superiority of Holland, and a jealousy excited by its close connection with France at this period.

It was not till February 22, 1665, that war was formally declared against the Dutch, but many previous acts of hostility had taken place in expeditions against their settlements on the coast of Africa and in America, which were retaliated by De Ruyter with vigor and success. The Dutch used every possible means of avoiding the last extremities. De Witt employed all the powers of his great capacity to avert the evil of war, but nothing could finally prevent it, and the sea was once more to witness the conflict between those who claimed its sovereignty. A great battle was fought on June 13. The Duke of York, afterward James II., commanded the British fleet, and had under him the Earl of Sandwich and Prince Rupert. The Dutch were led on by Opdam, and the victory was decided in favor of the English by the blowing up of that admiral's ship, with himself and his whole crew. The loss of the Dutch was altogether nineteen ships.[2] De Witt, the pensionary, then took in person the command of the fleet, which was soon equipped, and he gave a high proof of the adaptation of genius to a pursuit previously unknown, by the rapid knowledge and the practical improvements he introduced into some of the most intricate branches of naval tactics.

Immense efforts were now made by England, but with a very questionable policy, to induce Louis XIV. to join in the war. Charles offered to allow of his acquiring the whole of the Spanish Netherlands, provided he would leave him without interruption to destroy the Dutch navy (and, consequently, their commerce), in the by no means certain expectation that its advantages would all fall to the share of England. But the King of France resolved to support the republic. The King of Denmark, too, formed an alliance with them,

[2] The best account of this and the succeeding battles in the naval wars between Holland and England will be found in Captain Mahan's "Influence of Sea Power on History, 1660-1783."

after a series of the most strange tergiversations. Spain, reduced to feebleness and menaced with invasion by France, showed no alacrity to meet with Charles's overtures for an offensive treaty. Van Galen, Bishop of Munster, a restless prelate, was the only ally he could acquire. This bishop, at the head of a tumultuous force of 20,000 men, penetrated into Friesland, but 6000 French were dispatched by Louis to the assistance of the republic, and this impotent invasion was easily repelled.

The republic, encouraged by all these favorable circumstances, resolved to put forward its utmost energies. Internal discords were once more appeased, the harbors were crowded with merchant ships, the young Prince of Orange had put himself under the tuition of the states of Holland and of De Witt, who faithfully executed his trust, and De Ruyter was ready to lead on the fleet. The English, in spite of the dreadful calamity of the great fire of London, the plague which desolated the city, and a declaration of war on the part of France, prepared boldly for the shock.

The Dutch fleet of one hundred ships, commanded by De Ruyter and Tromp, were soon at sea. The English, under Prince Rupert and Monk, now Duke of Albemarle, did not lie idle in port. A battle of four days' continuance, one of the most determined and terrible on record up to this period, was the consequence. De Ruyter won a decided victory, for the English lost seventeen ships and 8000 men, while the Dutch lost but four ships and less than 2000 men. The English and Dutch fleets met again on August 4, and this time the victory inclined to the English. De Ruyter, separated from the rest of his squadron and surrounded by twenty English ships, for the moment despaired of escape, but recovering his composure he succeeded in extricating himself by a masterly retreat which won the admiration of his contemporaries.

The King of France hastened forward in this crisis to the assistance of the republic, and De Witt, by a deep stroke of policy, amused the English with negotiation while a powerful fleet was fitted out. It suddenly appeared in the Thames, under the command of De Ruyter, and all England was thrown into consternation. The Dutch took Sheerness and burned many ships of war, almost insulting the capital itself in their predatory incursion. Had the French power joined that of the provinces at this time and invaded England, the most fatal results to that kingdom might have taken place. But the alarm soon subsided with the disappearance of the hostile fleet, and the signing of the Peace of Breda, on July 10, 1667, extricated Charles from his present difficulties. The island of Polerone was restored to the Dutch, and the point of maritime superiority was, on this occasion, undoubtedly theirs. A more lasting and important result was the loss of the Dutch colony of New Amsterdam in America, transferred to England under the treaty.

While Holland was preparing to indulge in the novelty of national repose, the death of Philip IV. of Spain, and the startling ambition of Louis XIV., brought war once more to their very doors, and soon even forced it across the threshold of the republic. The King of France, setting at nought his solemn renunciation at the Peace of the Pyrenees of all claims to any part of the Spanish territories in right of his wife, who was daughter of the late king, found excellent reasons (for his own satisfaction) to invade a material portion of that declining monarchy. Well prepared by the financial and military foresight of Colbert for his great design, he suddenly poured a powerful army, under Turenne, into Brabant and Flanders, quickly overran and took possession of these provinces, and in the space of three weeks added Franche-Comté[3] to his conquests. Europe was in universal alarm at these unexpected measures, and no state felt more terror than the republic of the United Provinces. The interests of all Europe seemed now to require a coalition against the aggressions of the French monarchy, which had grasped the overweening power that had fallen from the hands of the house of Austria. The first measure to this effect was the signing of a triple alliance between England, Sweden, and the United Provinces, at The Hague, January 13, 1668. The alliance forced Louis to relax his hold on the Spanish Netherlands, but his wrath now turned against the little republic which had thwarted his projects. The triple alliance soon fell to pieces. Sweden withdrew at the persuasion of the French ministers, and Charles II., perfidiously deserting his ally, made a secret treaty with France for the partition of the United Provinces, which soon found themselves involved in a double war for life with their late allies.

A base and piratical attack on the Dutch Smyrna fleet by a large force under Sir Robert Holmes, on March 23, 1672, was the first overt act of treachery on the part of the English government. The attempt completely failed, through the prudence and valor of

[3] Franche-Comté was the Spanish portion of the old Duchy of Burgundy.

the Dutch admirals, and Charles reaped only the double shame of perfidy and defeat. He instantly issued a declaration of war against the republic, on reasoning too palpably false to require refutation, and too frivolous to merit record.

Louis at least covered with the semblance of dignity his unjust coöperation in this violence. He soon advanced with his army and the contingents of Munster and Cologne, his allies, amounting altogether to nearly 170,000 men, commanded by Condé, Turenne, Luxembourg, and others of the greatest generals of France. Never was any country less prepared than were the United Provinces to resist this formidable aggression. Their army was as nought, their long cessation of military operations by land having totally demoralized that once invincible branch of their forces. No general existed who knew anything of the practice of war. Their very stores of ammunition had been delivered over, in the way of traffic, to the enemy who now prepared to overwhelm them. De Witt was severely, and not quite unjustly, blamed for having suffered the country to be thus taken by surprise, utterly defenseless, and apparently without resource. Envy of his uncommon merit aggravated the just complaints against his error. But, above all things, the popular affection for the young prince threatened, in some great convulsion, the overthrow of the pensionary, who was considered eminently hostile to the illustrious house of Orange.

William III., Prince of Orange, now twenty-two years of age, was amply endowed with those hereditary qualities of valor and wisdom which only required experience to give him rank with the greatest of his ancestors. The Louvenstein party, as the adherents of the house of Orange were called, now easily prevailed in their long-conceived design of placing him at the head of affairs, with the titles of captain-general and high admiral. De Witt, anxious from personal considerations, as well as patriotism, to employ every means of active exertion, attempted the organization of an army, and hastened the equipment of a formidable fleet of nearly a hundred ships of the line and half as many fire-ships. De Ruyter, now without exception the greatest commander of the age, set sail with this force in search of the combined fleets of England and France, commanded by the Duke of York and Marshal d'Estrees. He encountered them, on June 7, 1672, at Solebay. A most bloody engagement was the result of this meeting. Sandwich, on the side of the English, and Van Ghent, a Dutch admiral, were slain. The results of the battle were indecisive, though the glory of the day rested with De Ruyter; but the sea was not the element on which the fate of Holland was to be decided.

The French armies poured like a torrent into the territories of the republic. Rivers were passed, towns taken, and provinces overrun with a rapidity much less honorable to France than disgraceful to Holland. No victory was gained—no resistance offered, and it is disgusting to look back on the fulsome panegyrics with which courtiers and poets lauded Louis for those facile and inglorious triumphs. The Prince of Orange had received the command of a nominal army of 70,000 men, but with this undisciplined and discouraged mass he could attempt nothing. He prudently retired into the province of Holland, vainly hoping that the numerous fortresses on the frontiers would have offered some resistance to the enemy. Guelders, Overyssel, and Utrecht were already in Louis's hands. Groningen and Friesland were threatened. Holland and Zealand opposed obstruction to such rapid conquest from their natural position, and Amsterdam set a noble example to the remaining towns—forming a regular and energetic plan of defense and endeavoring to infuse its spirit into the rest. The sluices, those desperate sources at once of safety and desolation, were opened, the whole country submerged, and the other provinces following this example, extensive districts of fertility and wealth were given to the sea, for the exclusion of which so many centuries had scarcely sufficed.

The states-general now assembled, and it was decided to supplicate for peace at the hands of the combined monarchs. The haughty insolence of Louvois, coinciding with the temper of Louis himself, made the latter propose the following conditions as the price of peace: To take off all duties on commodities exported into Holland; to grant the free exercise of the Catholic religion in the United Provinces; to share the churches with the Catholics, and to pay their priests; to yield up all the frontier towns, with several in the heart of the republic; to pay him 20,000,000 livres; to send him every year a solemn embassy, accompanied by a present of a golden medal, as an acknowledgment that they owed him their liberty; and, finally, that they should give entire satisfaction to the King of England.

Charles, on his part, after the most insulting treatment of the ambassadors sent to London, required, among others terms, that the Dutch should give up the honor of the flag without reserve, whole fleets being expected, even on the coasts of Holland, to lower their topsails to the smallest ship under British colors; that the Dutch should pay £1,000,000 sterling toward the charges of the war, and £10,000 a year for permission to fish in the British seas; that they should share the Indian trade with the English; and that Walcheren and several other islands should be put into the king's hands as security for the performance of the articles.

The insatiable monarchs overshot the mark. Existence was not worth preserving on these intolerable terms. Holland was driven to desperation, and even the people of England were inspired with indignation at this monstrous injustice. In the republic a violent explosion of popular excess took place. The people now saw no safety but in the courage and talents of the Prince of Orange. He was tumultuously proclaimed stadtholder. De Witt and his brother Cornelius, the conscientious but too obstinate opponents of this measure of salvation, fell victims to the popular frenzy. The latter, condemned to banishment on an atrocious charge of intended assassination against the Prince of Orange, was visited in his prison at The Hague by the grand pensionary. The rabble, incited to fury by the calumnies spread against these two virtuous citizens, broke into the prison, forced the unfortunate brothers into the street, and there literally tore them to pieces with circumstances of the most brutal ferocity. This scene took place on August 27, 1672.[4]

The massacre of the De Witts completely destroyed the party of which they were the head. All men now united under the only leader left to the country. William showed himself well worthy of the trust, and of his heroic blood. He turned his whole force against the enemy. He sought nothing for himself but the glory of saving his country, and taking his ancestors for models, in the best points of their respective characters, he combined prudence with energy and firmness with moderation. His spirit inspired all ranks of men. The conditions of peace demanded by the partner kings were rejected with scorn. The whole nation was moved by one concentrated principle of heroism, and it was even resolved to put

[4] Though William's complicity in the murder has never been proved, yet he made no attempt to avenge the crime from which he gained so much; indeed, one of the leaders of the mob enjoyed a pension granted by him. The murder of the De Witts, like the Glencoe massacre, has cast an indelible stain on his character which admirers have vainly sought to remove.

WAR WITH ENGLAND

the ancient notion of the first William into practice, and abandon the country to the waves, sooner than submit to the political annihilation with which it was threatened. The capability of the vessels in their harbors was calculated, and they were found sufficient to transport 200,000 families to the Indian settlements. We must hasten from this sublime picture of national desperation. The hero who stands in its foreground was inaccessible to every overture of corruption. Buckingham, the English ambassador, offered him, on the part of England and France, the independent sovereignty of Holland if he would abandon the other provinces to their grasp, and, urging his consent, asked him if he did not see that the republic was ruined. "There is one means," replied the Prince of Orange, "which will save me from the sight of my country's ruin —I will die in the last ditch."

Action soon proved the reality of the prince's profession. He took the field, having first punished with death some of the cowardly commanders of the frontier towns. He besieged and took Naarden, an important place, and by a masterly movement formed a junction with Montecuculi, whom the Emperor Leopold had at length sent to his assistance with 20,000 men. Groningen repulsed the Bishop of Munster, the ally of France, with a loss of 12,000 men. The King of Spain (such are the strange fluctuations of political friendship and enmity) sent the Count of Monterey, governor of the Belgian provinces, with 10,000 men to support the Dutch army. The Elector of Brandenburg also lent them aid. The whole face of affairs was changed, and Louis was obliged to abandon all his conquests with more rapidity than he had made them. Two desperate battles at sea, on May 28 and June 4, in which De Ruyter and Prince Rupert again distinguished themselves, only proved the valor of the combatants, leaving victory still doubtful. England was with one common feeling ashamed of the odious war in which the king and his unworthy ministers had engaged the nation. Charles was forced to make peace on the conditions proposed by the Dutch. The honor of the flag was yielded to the English, a regulation of trade was agreed to, all possessions were restored to the same condition as before the war, and the states-general agreed to pay the king 800,000 patacoons, or nearly £300,000 ($15,000,000).

With these encouraging results from the Prince of Orange's influence and example, Holland persevered in the contest with

France. He, in the first place, made head, during a winter campaign in Holland, against Marshal Luxembourg, who had succeeded Turenne in the Low Countries, the latter being obliged to march against the imperialists in Westphalia. He next advanced to oppose the great Condé, who occupied Brabant with an army of 45,000 men. After much maneuvering, in which the Prince of Orange displayed consummate talent, he on only one occasion exposed a part of his army to a disadvantageous contest. Condé seized on the error, and of his own accord gave the battle to which his young opponent could not succeed in forcing him. The battle of Senef is remarkable not merely for the fury with which it was fought, or for its leaving victory undecided, but as being the last combat of one commander and the first of the other. "The Prince of Orange," said the veteran Condé (who had that day exposed his person more than on any previous occasion), "has acted in everything like an old captain, except venturing his life too like a young soldier."

The campaign of 1675 offered no remarkable event, the Prince of Orange with great prudence avoiding the risk of a battle. But the following year was rendered fatally remarkable by the death of the great De Ruyter,[5] who was killed in an action against the French fleet in the Mediterranean; and about the same time the not less celebrated Turenne met his death from a cannon-ball in the midst of his triumphs in Germany. This year was doubly occupied in a negotiation for peace and an active prosecution of the war. Louis, at the head of his army, took several towns in Belgium; William was unsuccessful in an attempt on Maestricht. About the beginning of winter the plenipotentiaries of the several belligerents assembled at Nimeguen, where the congress for peace was held. The Hollanders, loaded with debts and taxes, and seeing the weakness and slowness of their allies, the Spaniards and Germans, prognosticated nothing but misfortunes. Their commerce languished, while that of England, now neutral amid all these quarrels, flourished extremely. The Prince of Orange, however, ambitious of glory, urged another campaign, and it commenced accordingly.

In the middle of February Louis carried Valenciennes by

[5] The council of Spain gave De Ruyter the title and letters patent of duke. The latter arrived in Holland after his death, and his children, with true republican spirit, refused to adopt the title.

storm and laid siege to St. Omer and Cambrai. William, though full of activity, courage, and skill, was, nevertheless, almost always unsuccessful in the field, and never more so than in this campaign. Several towns fell almost in his sight, and he was completely defeated in the great battle of Cassel by the Duke of Orleans and Marshal Luxembourg. But the period for another peace was now approaching. Louis offered fair terms for the acceptance of the United Provinces at the Congress of Nimeguen, April, 1678, as he now considered his chief enemies Spain and the Empire, who had at first only entered into the war as auxiliaries. He was no doubt principally impelled in his measures by the marriage of the Prince of Orange with the Lady Mary, eldest daughter of the Duke of York and heir presumptive to the English crown, which took place on October 23, to the great joy of both the Dutch and English nations. Charles was at this moment the arbiter of the peace of Europe, and though several fluctuations took place in his policy in the course of a few months, as the urgent wishes of the Parliament and the large presents of Louis differently actuated him, still the wiser and more just course prevailed, and he finally decided the balance by vigorously declaring his resolution for peace. The treaty was consequently signed at Nimeguen on August 10, 1678. The Prince of Orange, from private motives of spleen, or a most unjustifiable desire for fighting, took the extraordinary measure of attacking the French troops under Luxembourg, near Mons, four days after the signing of this treaty. He must have known it, even though it were not officially notified to him, and he certainly had to answer for all the blood so wantonly spilled in the sharp though undecisive action which ensued. Spain, abandoned to her fate, was obliged to make the best terms she could, and on September 17 she also concluded a treaty with France, on conditions entirely favorable to the latter power.

The war with France marks the beginning of the decline of the United Provinces as a great naval power. The Prince of Orange, the inveterate enemy of Louis XIV., devoted his life and the resources of the state to the land struggle with the great French monarchy, and the sea power of Holland was henceforth allowed to sink before that of her ally, England. From this time we may begin to date the decline of the Dutch Republic as a power of the first rank.

Chapter XX

WILLIAM III AND LOUIS XIV. 1678-1713

A FEW years passed over after this period without the occurrence of any transaction sufficiently important to require a mention here. Each of the powers so lately at war followed the various bent of their respective ambition. Charles of England was sufficiently occupied by disputes with Parliament, and the discovery, fabrication, and punishment of plots, real or pretended. Louis XIV., by a stretch of audacious pride hitherto unknown, arrogated to himself the supreme power of regulating the rest of Europe, as if all the other princes were his vassals. He established courts, or chambers of reunion, as they were called, in Metz and Breisach, which cited princes, issued decrees, and authorized spoliation in the most unjust and arbitrary manner. Louis chose to award to himself Luxemburg, part of Alsace, and a considerable portion of Brabant and Flanders. He marched a considerable army into Belgium, which the Spanish governors were unable to oppose. The Prince of Orange, who labored incessantly to excite a confederacy among the other powers of Europe against the unwarrantable aggressions of France, was unable to arouse his countrymen to actual war, and was forced, instead of gaining the glory he longed for, to consent to a truce for twenty years, which the states-general, now wholly pacific and not a little cowardly, were too happy to obtain from France. The emperor and the King of Spain gladly entered into a like treaty. The fact was that the Peace of Nimeguen had disjoined the great confederacy which William had so successfully brought about, and the various powers were laid utterly prostrate at the feet of the imperious Louis, who for a while held the destinies of Europe in his hands.

Charles II. died most unexpectedly in the year 1685, and his unfortunate and untalented brother and successor, James II., seemed, during a reign of not four years' continuance, to rush willfully headlong to ruin. During this period the Prince of Orange had maintained a most circumspect, though hardly unexceptional, line of conduct. He seems to have favored the rash enterprise of the unfortunate Duke of Monmouth, at least till the latter proclaimed himself king; and he was in constant communication with the English malcontents headed by Gilbert Burnet. But his chief energies were devoted to the formation of another league against France. Louis XIV. had aroused a new feeling throughout Protestant Europe by the revocation of the Edict of Nantes. The refugees whom he had driven from their native country inspired in those in which they settled hatred of his persecution as well as alarm of his power. Holland now entered into all the views of the Prince of Orange. By his immense influence he succeeded in forming the great confederacy called the League of Augsburg, to which the emperor, Spain, and almost every European power but England became parties.

James gave the prince reason to believe that he too would join in this great project, if William would in return concur in his views of domestic tyranny, but William wisely refused. James, much disappointed and irritated by the moderation which showed his own violence in such striking contrast, expressed his displeasure against the prince, and against the Dutch generally, by various vexatious acts. William resolved to maintain a high attitude, and many applications were made to him by the most considerable persons in England for relief against James's violent measures, and which there was but one method of making effectual. That method was force. But as long as the Princess of Orange was certain of succeeding to the crown on her father's death, William hesitated to join in an attempt that might possibly have failed and lost her her inheritance. But the birth of a son, which, in giving James a male heir, destroyed all hope of redress for the kingdom, decided the wavering and rendered the determined desperate. The prince chose the time for his enterprise with the sagacity, arranged its plan with the prudence, and put it into execution with the vigor which were habitual qualities of his mind.

Louis XIV., menaced by the League of Augsburg, had resolved to strike the first blow against the allies. He invaded Germany, so that the Dutch preparations seemed in the first instance intended as measures of defense against the progress of the French. But Louis's envoy at The Hague could not be long deceived. He gave notice to his master, who in his turn warned James. But that infatuated monarch not only doubted the intelligence, but refused the French king's offers of assistance and coöperation. On October 21 the Prince of Orange, with an army of 14,000 men and a fleet of 500 vessels of all kinds, set sail from Helvoetsluys, and after some delays from bad weather he safely landed his army in Torbay, on November 5, 1688. The desertion of James's best friends, his own consternation, flight, seizure, and second escape, and the solemn act by which he was deposed, were the rapid occurrences of a few weeks. And thus the grandest revolution that England had ever seen was happily consummated. Without entering here on legislative reasonings or party sophisms, it is enough to record the act itself and to say, in reference to our more immediate subject, that without the assistance of Holland and her chief England might have still remained enslaved, or have had to purchase liberty by oceans of blood. By the bill of settlement the crown was conveyed jointly to the Prince and Princess of Orange, the sole administration of government to remain in the prince, and the new sovereigns were proclaimed on February 23, 1689. The convention which had arranged this important point annexed to the settlement a declaration of rights by which the powers of royal prerogative and the extent of popular privilege were defined and guaranteed.

William, now become King of England, still preserved his title of stadtholder of Holland, and presented the singular instance of a monarchy and a republic being at the same time governed by the same individual. But whether as a king or a citizen, William was actuated by one grand and powerful principle, to which every act of private administration was made subservient, although it certainly called for no sacrifice that was not required for the political existence of the two nations of which he was the head. Inveterate opposition to the power of Louis XIV. was this all-absorbing motive. A sentiment so mighty left William but little time for inferior points of government, and everything but that seems to have irritated and disgusted him. He was soon again on the Continent, the chief theater of his efforts. He put himself in front of the confederacy which resulted from the Congress of Utrecht in 1690. He took the command of the allied army, and till the hour of his death he never ceased his indefatigable course of hostility, whether in the camp or the cabinet, at the head of the allied armies, or as the guiding spirit of the councils which gave them force and motion.

Several campaigns were expended and bloody combats fought, almost all to the disadvantage of William, whose genius for war was never seconded by that good fortune which so often decides the fate of battles in defiance of all the calculations of talent. But no reverse had power to shake the constancy and courage of William. He always appeared as formidable after defeat as he was before action. His conquerors gained little but the honor of the day. Fleurus, Steenkirk, Neerwinden, were successively the scenes of his evil fortune and the sources of his fame. His retreats were master strokes of vigilant activity and profound combinations. Many eminent sieges took place during this war. Among other towns, Mons and Namur were taken by the French, and Huy by the allies, and the army of Marshal Villeroi bombarded Brussels during three days, in August, 1695, with such fury that the townhouse, fourteen churches, and four thousand houses were reduced to ashes. The year following this event saw another undecisive campaign. During the continuance of this war the naval transactions present no grand results, though the allied English and Dutch fleets defeated the French in a great battle off Cape la Hogue. Du Bart, a celebrated adventurer of Dunkirk, occupies the leading place in these affairs, in which he carried on a desultory but active warfare against the Dutch and English fleets, and generally with great success.

All the nations which had taken part in so many wars were now becoming exhausted by the contest, but none so much so as France. The great despot who had so long wielded the energies of that country with such wonderful splendor and success found that his unbounded love of dominion was gradually sapping all the real good of his people in chimerical schemes of universal conquest. England, though with much resolution voting new supplies, and in every way upholding William in his plans for the continuance of war, was rejoiced when Louis accepted the mediation of Charles XI., King of Sweden, and agreed to concessions which made peace feasible. The emperor and Charles II. of Spain were less satisfied with those concessions, but everything was finally arranged to meet the general views of the parties, and negotiations were opened at Ryswick. The death of the King of Sweden and the minority of his son and successor, the celebrated Charles XII., retarded them on points of form for some time. At length, on September 20, 1697, the articles of the treaty were subscribed by the Dutch, English, Spanish, and French ambassadors. The treaty consisted of seventeen articles. The French king declared he would not disturb or disquiet the King of Great Britain, whose title he now for the first time acknowledged. Between France and Holland were declared a general armistice, perpetual amity, a mutual restitution of towns, a reciprocal renunciation of all pretensions upon each other, and a treaty of commerce which was immediately put into execution.

Thus, after this long, expensive, and sanguinary war things were established just on the footing they had been by the Peace of Nimeguen, and a great, though unavailable, lesson read to the world on the futility and wickedness of those quarrels in which the personal ambition of kings leads to the misery of the people. Had the allies been true to each other throughout, Louis would certainly have been reduced much lower than he now was. His pride was humbled and his encroachments stopped. But the sufferings of the various countries engaged in the war were too generally reciprocal to make its result of any material benefit to either. The emperor held out for a while, encouraged by the great victory gained by his general, Prince Eugene of Savoy, over the Turks at Zenta in Hungary, but he finally acceded to the terms offered by France. The peace, therefore, became general, but unfortunately for Europe of very short duration.

France, as if looking forward to the speedy renewal of hostilities, still kept her armies undisbanded. Let the foresight of her politicians have been what it might, this negative proof of it was justified by events. The King of Spain, a weak prince, without any direct heir for his possessions, considered himself authorized to dispose of their succession by will. The leading powers of Europe thought otherwise, and took this right upon themselves. Charles died on November 1, 1700, and thus put the important question to the test. By a solemn testament he declared Philip, Duke of Anjou, second son of the Dauphin and grandson of Louis XIV., his successor to the whole of the Spanish monarchy. Louis immediately renounced his adherence to the treaties of partition executed at The Hague and in London in 1698 and 1700, and to which he had been a contracting party, and prepared to maintain the act by which the last of the descendants of Charles V. bequeathed the possessions of Spain and the Indies to the family which had so long been the inveterate enemy and rival of his own.

The Emperor Leopold, on his part, prepared to defend his claims, and thus commenced the new war between him and France, which took its name from the succession which formed the object of dispute. Hostilities were commenced in Italy, where Prince Eugene, the conqueror of the Turks, commanded for Leopold, and every day made for himself a still more brilliant reputation. Louis sent his grandson to Spain to take possession of the inheritance, for which so hard a fight was yet to be maintained, with the striking expression at parting: " My child, there are no longer any Pyrenees.! " an expression most happily unprophetic for the future independence of Europe, for the moral force of the barrier has long existed after the expiration of the family compact which was meant to deprive it of its strength.

Louis prepared to act vigorously. Among other measures, he caused part of the Dutch army that was quartered in Luxemburg and Brabant to be suddenly made prisoners of war, because they would not own Philip V. as King of Spain. The states-general, who were dreadfully alarmed, immediately made the required acknowledgment, and in consequence had their soldiers released. They quickly reinforced their garrisons, purchased supplies, solicited foreign aid, and prepared for the worst that might happen. They wrote to King William, professing the most inviolable attachment to England, and he met their application by warm assurances of support and an immediate reinforcement of three regiments.

William followed up these measures by the formation of the celebrated treaty called the Grand Alliance, by which England, the states, and the emperor covenanted for the support of the pretensions of the latter to the Spanish monarchy. William was preparing, in spite of his declining health, to take his usual lead in the military operations now decided on, and almost all Europe was again looking forward to his guidance, when he died on March 8, 1701, leaving his great plans to receive their execution from still more able adepts in the art of war.

William's character has been traced by many hands. In his capacity of King of England it is not our province to judge him in this place. As stadtholder of Holland he merits unqualified praise. Like his great ancestor, William I., whom he more resembled than any other of his race, he saved the country in a time

Hist. Nat. XIII-17

of such imminent peril that its abandonment seemed the only resource left to the inhabitants, who preferred self-exile to slavery. All his acts were certainly merged in the one overwhelming object of a great ambition—that noble quality, which, if coupled with the love of country, is the very essence of true heroism. Yet his cold and haughty temperament and his indifference to others prevented him from gaining the affections of his subjects, and he died respected rather than lamented by the peoples over whom he had ruled. William was the last of that illustrious line which for a century and a half had filled Europe with admiration. He never had a child, and being himself an only one, his title as Prince of Orange passed into another branch of the family. He left his cousin, Prince Frison of Nassau, the stadtholder of Friesland, his sole and universal heir, and appointed the states-general his executors.

William's death filled Holland with mourning and alarm. The meeting of the states-general after this sad intelligence was of a most affecting description, but William, like all master-minds, had left the mantle of his inspiration on his friends and followers. Heinsius, the grand pensionary, followed up the views of the stadtholder with considerable energy, and was answered by the unanimous exertions of the country. Strong assurances of support from Queen Anne, William's successor, still further encouraged the republic, which now vigorously prepared for war. But it did not lose this occasion of recurring to the form of government of 1650. No new stadtholder was now appointed, the supreme authority being vested in the general assembly of the states, and the active direction of affairs confided to the grand pensionary. This departure from the form of government which had been on various occasions proved to be essential to the safety, although at all times hazardous to the independence, of the states, was not attended with any evil consequences. The factions and the anarchy which had before been the consequence of the course now adopted, were prevented by the potent influence of national fear lest the enemy might triumph and crush the hopes, the jealousies, and the enmities of all parties in one general ruin. Thus the common danger awoke a common interest, and the splendid successes of her allies kept Holland steady in the career of patriotic energy which had its rise in the dread of her redoubtable foe.

The joy in France at William's death was proportionate to the grief it created in Holland, and the arrogant confidence of Louis seemed to know no bounds. "I will punish these audacious merchants," said he, with an air of disdain, when he read the manifesto of Holland, not foreseeing that those he affected to despise so much would, ere long, command in a great measure the destinies of his crown. Queen Anne assured the states of her determination to maintain all the alliances formed by the late king. Efforts were made by the English ministry and the states-general to mediate between the kings of Sweden and Poland. But Charles XII., enamored of glory and bent on the one great object of his designs against Russia, would listen to nothing that might lead him from his immediate career of victory. Many other of the northern princes were withheld by various motives from entering into the contest with France, and its whole brunt devolved on the original members of the grand alliance. The generals who carried it on were Marlborough and Prince Eugene. The former, at its commencement an earl, and subsequently raised to the dignity of duke, was declared generalissimo of the Dutch and English forces. He was a man of most powerful genius, both as warrior and politician. A pupil of the great Turenne, his exploits left those of his master in the shade. No commander ever possessed in a greater degree the faculty of forming vast designs and of carrying them into effect with consummate skill; no one displayed more coolness and courage in action, saw with a keener eye the errors of the enemy, or knew better how to profit by success. He never laid siege to a town that he did not take, and never fought a battle that he did not gain.

Prince Eugene joined to the highest order of personal bravery a profound judgment for the grand movements of war and a capacity for the most minute of the minor details on which their successful issue so often depends. United in the same cause, these two great generals pursued their course without the least misunderstanding. At the close of each of those successive campaigns in which they reaped such a full harvest of renown they retired together to The Hague to arrange in the profoundest secrecy the plans for the next year's operations with one other person who formed the great point of union between them, and completed a triumvirate without a parallel in the history of political affairs. This third was Heinsius, one of those great men produced by the republic whose names are tantamount to the most detailed eulogium for talent and patriotism. Every enterprise projected by the confederates was deliberately examined, rejected, or approved by these three associates, whose strict union of purpose, disowning all petty rivalry, formed the center of counsels and the source of circumstances finally so fatal to France.

Louis XIV., now sixty years of age, could no longer himself command his armies, or probably did not wish to risk the reputation he was conscious of having gained by the advice and services of Turenne, Condé, and Luxembourg. Louvois, his great war minister, too, was dead, and Colbert no longer managed his finances. A council of rash and ignorant ministers hung like a dead weight on the talent of the generals who succeeded the great men above mentioned. Favor and not merit too often decided promotion and lavished command. Vendôme, Villars, Boufflers, and Berwick were set aside to make way for Villeroi, Tallard, and Marsin, men every way inferior.

The war began in 1702 in Italy, and Marlborough opened his first campaign in Brabant also in that year. For several succeeding years the confederates pursued a career of brilliant success, the details of which do not properly belong to this work. A mere chronology of celebrated battles would be of little interest, and the pages of history abound in records of those deeds. Blenheim, Ramillies, Oudenarde, and Malplaquet are names that speak for themselves, and tell their own tale of glory. The utter humiliation of the French monarchy was the result of the brilliant campaigns to whose success the courage and devotion of the Dutch largely contributed. The naval affairs of Holland offered nothing very remarkable. The states had always a fleet ready to support the English in their enterprises, but no eminent admiral arose to rival the renown of Rook, Byng, Benbow, and others of their allies. The first of these admirals took Gibraltar, which has ever since remained in the possession of England. The Earl of Peterborough carried on the war with splendid success in Portugal and Spain, supported occasionally by the English fleet under Sir Cloudesley Shovel, and that of Holland under Admirals Allemonde and Wapenaer.

During the progress of the war the haughty and long-time imperial Louis was reduced to a state of humiliation that excited a compassion so profound as to prevent its own open expression—the most galling of all sentiments to a proud mind. In the year 1709 he solicited peace on terms of most abject submission. The states-general, under the influence of the Duke of Marlborough and Prince

Eugene, rejected all his supplications, retorting unsparingly the insolent harshness with which he had formerly received similar proposals from them. France, roused to renewed exertions by the insulting treatment experienced by her humiliated but still haughty despot, made prodigious and not altogether vain efforts to repair her ruinous losses. In the following year Louis renewed his attempts to obtain some tolerable conditions, offering to renounce his grandson, and to comply with all the former demands of the confederates. Even these overtures were rejected, Holland and England appearing satisfied with nothing short of, what was after all impracticable, the total destruction of the great power which Louis had so long proved to be incompatible with their welfare. The war still went on, and the taking of Bouchain on August 30, 1711, closed the almost unrivaled military career of Marlborough by the success of one of the boldest and best-conducted exploits. Party intrigue had accomplished the disgrace of this great soldier. The new ministry, who hated the Dutch, now entered seriously into negotiations with France. The queen acceded to these views, and sent special envoys to communicate with the court of Versailles. The states-general finding it impossible to continue hostilities if England withdrew from the coalition, conferences were consequently opened at Utrecht in the month of January, 1712. England took the important station of arbiter in the great question there debated. The only essential conditions which she demanded individually were the renunciation of all claims to the crown of France by Philip V. and the demolition of the harbor of Dunkirk. The first of these was the more readily acceded to, as the great battles of Almanza and Villaviciosa, gained by Philip's generals, the Dukes of Berwick and Vendôme, had steadily fixed him on the throne of Spain—a point still more firmly secured by the death of the Emperor Joseph I., son of Leopold, and the elevation of his brother Charles, Philip's competitor for the crown of Spain, to the imperial dignity by the title of Charles VI.

The peace was not definitively signed until April 11, 1713, and France obtained far better conditions than those which were refused her a few years previously. The Belgian provinces were given to the new emperor, and must henceforth be called the Austrian instead of the Spanish Netherlands. The gold and the blood of Holland had been profusely expended during this contest, it might seem for no positive results. But the exhaustion produced to every one of the other belligerents was a source of peace and prosperity to the republic. Its commerce was reëstablished, its financial resources recovered their level, and altogether we must fix on the epoch now before us as that of its utmost point of influence and greatness. France, on the contrary, was now reduced from its palmy state of almost European sovereignty to one of the deepest misery, and its monarch in his old age found little left of his former power but those records of poetry, painting, sculpture, and architecture which tell posterity of his magnificence, and the splendor of which throw his faults and his misfortunes into the shade.

The great object now to be accomplished by the United Provinces was the regulation of a distinct and guaranteed line of frontier between the republic and France. This object had become by degrees, ever since the Peace of Munster, a fundamental maxim of their politics. The interposition of the Belgian provinces between the republic and France was of serious inconvenience to the former in this point of view. It was made the subject of a special article in "the grand alliance." In the year 1707 it was particularly discussed between England and the states, to the great discontent of the emperor, who was far from wishing its definitive settlement. But it was now become an indispensable item in the total of important measures whose accomplishment was called for by the Peace of Utrecht. Conferences were opened on the sole question at Antwerp in the year 1714, and, after protracted and difficult discussions, the Treaty of the Barrier was concluded on November 15, 1715, by which the emperor ceded to the states several places which they considered essential for their safety.

This treaty was looked on with an evil eye in the Austrian Netherlands. The clamor was great and general, jealousy of the commercial prosperity of Holland being the real motive. Long negotiations took place on the subject of the treaty, and in December, 1718, the republic consented to modify some of the articles. The Pragmatic Sanction, published at Vienna in 1713 by Charles VI., regulated the succession to all the imperial hereditary possessions, and, among the rest, the provinces of the Netherlands. But this arrangement, though guaranteed by the chief powers of Europe, was, in the sequel, little respected, and but indifferently executed.

Chapter XXI

DECLINE OF THE REPUBLIC. 1713-1794

DURING a period of thirty years following the Treaty of Utrecht the republic enjoyed the unaccustomed blessing of profound peace. While the discontents of the Austrian Netherlands on the subject of the Treaty of the Barrier were in debate, the Quadruple Alliance was formed between Holland, England, France, and the emperor for reciprocal aid against all enemies, foreign and domestic. It was in virtue of this treaty that the pretender to the English throne received orders to remove from France; and the states-general about the same time arrested the Swedish ambassador, Baron Gortz, whose intrigues excited some suspicion. The death of Louis XIV. had once more changed the political system of Europe, and the commencement of the eighteenth century was fertile in negotiations and alliances in which we have at present but little direct interest. The rights of the republic were in all instances respected, and Holland did not cease to be considered as a power of the first distinction and consequence. The establishment of an East India Company at Ostend, by the Emperor Charles VI., in 1722, was the principal cause of disquiet to the United Provinces, and the most likely to lead to a rupture. But by the Treaty of Hanover in 1726 the rights of Holland resulting from the Treaty of Munster, by which the inhabitants of the Spanish Netherlands had been excluded from the trade with the Indies, were guaranteed, and in consequence the emperor abolished the company of his creation by the Treaty of Seville in 1729, and that of Vienna in 1731.

The peace which now reigned in Europe allowed the United Provinces to direct their whole efforts toward the reform of those internal abuses resulting from feudality and fanaticism. Confiscations were reversed and property secured throughout the republic. It received into its protection the persecuted sectarians of France, Germany, and Hungary, and the tolerant wisdom which it exercised in these measures gives the best assurance of its justice and prudence. A solitary exception to them was the expulsion of the Jesuits, whose doctrines had long caused uneasiness to the Protestant states of Europe.

In the year 1732 the United Provinces were threatened with imminent peril, which accident alone prevented from becoming fatal to their very existence. It was perceived that the dikes, which had for ages preserved the coasts, were in many places crumbling to ruin, in spite of the enormous expenditure of money and labor devoted to their preservation. By chance it was discovered that the beams, piles, and other timber works employed in the construction of the dikes were eaten through in all parts by a species of sea-worm hitherto unknown. The terror of the people was, as may be supposed, extreme. Every available resource was applied which possibly could remedy the evil, when a hard frost providentially set in and destroyed the formidable reptiles, and the country was thus saved from a danger tenfold greater than that involved in a dozen wars.

The peace of Europe was once more disturbed in 1733. Poland, Germany, France, and Spain were all embarked in the new war. Holland and England stood aloof, and another family alliance of great consequence drew still closer than ever the bonds of union between them. The young Prince of Orange, who in 1728 had been elected stadtholder of Groningen and Guelders, in addition to that of Friesland, which had been enjoyed by his father, had in the year 1734 married the Princess Anne, daughter of George II. of England, and by thus adding to the consideration of the house of Nassau had opened a field for the recovery of all its old distinctions.

The death of Emperor Charles VI., in October, 1740, left his daughter, the Archduchess Maria Theresa, heiress of his throne and possessions. Young, beautiful, and endowed with qualities of the highest order, she was surrounded with enemies whose envy and ambition would have despoiled her of her splendid rights. Frederick of Prussia, surnamed the Great, the electors of Bavaria and Saxony, and the kings of Spain and Sardinia all pressed forward to the spoliation of an inheritance which seemed a fair play for all comers. But Maria Theresa, first joining her husband, Duke Francis of Lorraine, in her sovereignty, but without prejudice to it, under the title of co-regent, took an attitude truly heroic. When everything seemed to threaten the dismemberment of her states she threw herself upon the generous fidelity of her Hungarian subjects with a dignified resolution that has few examples. There was imperial grandeur even in her appeal to their compassion. The results were electrical, and the whole tide of fortune was rapidly turned.

England and Holland were the first to come to the aid of the young empress. George II., at the head of his army, gained the victory of Dettingen, in support of her quarrel, in 1743. Louis XV. resolved to throw his whole influence into the scale against these generous efforts in the princess's favor, and he invaded the Austrian Netherlands in the following year. Marshal Saxe commanded under him, and at first carried everything before him. Holland, having furnished 20,000 troops and six ships of war to George II. on the invasion of the young pretender, was little in a state to oppose any formidable resistance to the enemy that threatened her own frontiers. The republic, wholly attached for so long a period to pursuits of peace and commerce, had no longer good generals nor effective armies, nor could it even put a fleet of any importance to sea. Yet with all these disadvantages it would not yield to the threats nor the demands of France, resolving to risk a new war rather than succumb to an enemy it had once so completely humbled and given the law to.

Conferences were opened at Breda, but interrupted almost as soon as commenced. Hostilities were renewed. The memorable battle of Fontenoy was offered and gloriously fought by the allies; accepted and splendidly won by the French. Never did the English and Dutch troops act more nobly in concert than on this remarkable occasion. The valor of the French was not less conspicuous, and the success of the day was in a great measure decided by the Irish battalions, sent, by the lamentable politics of those and much later days, to swell the ranks and gain the battles of England's enemies. Marshal Saxe followed up his advantage the following year, taking Brussels and many other towns. Almost the whole of the Austrian Netherlands being now in the power of Louis XV., and the United Provinces again exposed to invasion and threatened with danger, they had once more recourse to the old expedient of the elevation of the house of Orange, which in times of imminent peril seemed to present a never-failing palladium. Zealand was the first to give the impulsion; the other provinces soon followed the example and William IV. was proclaimed stadtholder and captain-general amid the almost unanimous rejoicings of all. These dignities were soon after declared hereditary both in the male and female line of succession of the house of Orange-Nassau.

The year 1748 saw the termination of the brilliant campaigns of Louis XV. during this bloody war of eight years' continuance. The treaty of Aix-la-Chapelle, definitively signed on October 18, put an end to hostilities. Maria Theresa was established in her rights and power, and Europe saw a fair balance of the nations, which gave promise of security and peace. But the United Provinces, when scarcely recovering from struggles which had so checked their prosperity, were employed in new and universal grief and anxiety by the death of their young stadtholder, which happened at The Hague, October 13, 1751. He had long been kept out of the government, though by no means deficient in the talents suited to his station. His son, William V., not yet four years old, succeeded him, under the guardianship of his mother, Anne of England, daughter of George II., a princess represented to be of a proud and ambitious temper, who immediately assumed a high tone of authority in the state.

The Seven Years' War, which agitated the north of Europe and deluged its plains with blood, was almost the only one in which the republic was able to preserve a strict neutrality throughout. But this happy state of tranquillity was not, as on former occasions, attended by that prodigious increase of commerce and that accumulation of wealth which had so often astonished the world. Differing with England on the policy which led the latter to weaken and humiliate France, jealousies sprang up between the two countries, and Dutch commerce became the object of the most vexatious and injurious efforts on the part of England. Remonstrance was vain, resistance impossible, and the decline of the republic hurried rapidly on. The Hanseatic towns, the American colonies, the northern states of Europe, and France itself all entered into the rivalry with Holland, in which, however, England carried off the most important prizes. Several private and petty encounters took place between the vessels of England and Holland, in consequence of the pretensions of the former to the right of search, and had the republic possessed the strength of former periods, and the talents of a Tromp or a De Ruyter, a new war would no doubt have been the result. But it was forced to submit, and a degrading but irritating tranquillity was the consequence for several years, the national feeling receiving a salve for home decline by some extension of colonial settlements in the East, in which the Island of Ceylon was included.

In the midst of this inglorious state of things, and the domestic abundance which was the only compensation for the gradual loss of national influence, the installation of William V. in 1766, his marriage with the Princess of Prussia, niece of Frederick the Great, in 1768, and the birth of two sons, the eldest on August 24, 1772, successively took place. Magnificent fêtes celebrated these events, the satisfied citizens little imagining, amid their indolent rejoicings, the dismal futurity of revolution and distress which was silently but rapidly preparing for their country.

Maria Theresa, reduced to widowhood by the death of her husband, whom she had elevated to the imperial dignity by the title of Francis I., continued for a while to rule singly her vast possessions, and had profited so little by the sufferings of her own early reign that she joined in the iniquitous dismemberment of Poland, which has left an indelible stain on her memory, and on that of Frederick of Prussia and Catherine of Russia. In her own dominions she was adored, and her name is to this day cherished in Belgium among the dearest recollections of the people.

The shock given to the political mind of Europe by the American Revolution was soon felt in the Netherlands. The wish for reform was not merely confined to the people. A memorable instance was offered by Joseph II., son and successor of Maria Theresa, that sovereigns were not only susceptible of rational notions of change, but that the infection of radical extravagance could penetrate even to the imperial crown. Joseph commenced his reign by measures aimed at the authority of the clergy of Belgium. The desperate spirit of hostility in the priesthood soon spread among the mass of the people. Miscalculating his own power, and undervaluing that of the priests, the emperor issued decrees and edicts with a sweeping violence that shocked every prejudice and roused every passion perilous to the country. Toleration to the Protestants, emancipation of the clergy from the Papal rule, application of the principles of the Reformation in the system of theological instruction, were among the wholesale measures of the emperor's enthusiasm, so imprudently attempted and so virulently opposed.

But ere the deep-sown seeds ripened to revolt, or produced the fruit of active resistance in Belgium, Holland had to endure the mortification of another war with England. The republic resolved on a futile imitation of the northern powers, who had adopted the difficult and anomalous system of an armed neutrality, for the prevention of English domination on the seas. The right of search, so proudly established by this power, was not likely to be wrenched from it by manifestoes or remonstrances, and Holland was not capable of a more effectual warfare. In the year 1781 St. Eustache, Surinam, Essequibo, and Demerara, Dutch colonies in the West Indies, were taken by British valor, and in the following year several of the Dutch colonies in the East, well fortified but ill defended, also fell into the hands of England. Almost the whole of these colonies, the remnants of prodigious power acquired by such incalculable instances of enterprise and courage, were one by one assailed and taken. But this did not suffice for the satisfaction of English objects in the prosecution of the war. It was also resolved to deprive Holland of the Baltic trade. A squadron of seven vessels, commanded by Sir Hyde Parker, was encountered on the Dogger Bank by a squadron of Dutch ships of the same force under Admiral Zoutman. An action of four hours was maintained with all the ancient courage which made so many of the memorable sea-fights between Tromp, DeRuyter, Blake, and Monk drawn battles. A storm separated the combatants and saved the honor of each, for both had suffered alike, and victory had belonged to neither. The peace of 1784 terminated this short, but, to Holland, fatal war, the two latter years of which had been, in the petty warfare of privateering, most disastrous to the commerce of the republic. Negapatam, on the coast of Coromandel, and the free navigation of the Indian seas were ceded to England, who occupied the other various colonies taken during the war.

Opinion was now rapidly opening out to that spirit of intense inquiry which arose in France, and threatened to sweep before it not only all that was corrupt, but everything that tended to corruption. It was in the very essence of all kinds of power to have that tendency, and, if not checked by salutary means, to reach that end. But the reformers of the last century, new in the desperate practice of revolutions, seeing its necessity, but ignorant of its nature, could place no bounds on the whirlwind that they raised. The well-meaning but intemperate changes essayed by Joseph II. in Belgium had a considerable share in the development of free principles, although they at first seemed only to excite the resistance of bigotry and strengthen the growth of superstition. Holland was always alive to those feelings of resistance to established authority which characterized republican opinions, and the general discontent at the conduct of the war with England and the unpatriotic attitude of the Orange party strengthened the general demand for change and reform. The stadtholder saw clearly the storm which was gathering and which menaced his power. Anxious for the present and uncertain for the future, he listened to the suggestions of England and resolved to secure and extend by foreign force the rights of which he risked the loss from domestic faction.

In the divisions which were now loudly proclaimed among the states in favor of or opposed to the house of Orange, the people, despising all new theories which they did not comprehend, took open part with the family so closely connected with every practical feeling of good which their country had yet known. The states of Holland soon proceeded to measures of violence. Resolved to limit the power of the stadtholder, they deprived him of the command of the garrison of The Hague, and of all the other troops of the province, and shortly afterward declared him removed from all his employments. The violent disputes and vehement discussions consequent upon this measure, throughout the republic, announced an inevitable commotion. The advance of a Prussian army toward the frontiers inflamed the passions of one party and strengthened the confidence of the other. An incident which now happened brought about the crisis even sooner than was expected. The Princess of Orange left her palace at Loo to repair to The Hague, and, traveling with great simplicity and slightly attended, she was arrested and detained by a military post on the frontiers of the province of Holland. The neighboring magistrates of the town of Woerden refused her permission to continue her journey, and forced her to return to Loo under such surveillance as was usual with a prisoner of state. The stadtholder and the English ambassador loudly complained of this outrage. The complaint was answered by the immediate advance of the Duke of Brunswick with 20,000 Prussian soldiers. Some demonstrations of resistance were made by the astonished party whose conduct had provoked the measure, but in three weeks' time the whole of the republic was in perfect obedience to the authority of the stadtholder, who resumed all his functions as chief magistrate, with the additional influence which was sure to result from a vain attempt to reduce his former power.

By this time the discontent and agitation in Belgium had attained a most formidable height. The attempted reorganization in religion and reform of judicial abuses persisted in by the emperor were violently opposed by the Belgians, who, conservative and devoted to their church, feared an overthrow of the old régime to which they were so strongly attached. Remonstrances and strong complaints were soon succeeded by tumultuous assemblages and open insurrection. A lawyer of Brussels named Van der Noot put himself at the head of the malcontents. The states-general of Brabant declared the new measures of the emperor to be in opposition to the constitution and privileges of the country. The other Belgian provinces soon followed this example. The Prince Albert of Saxe-Teschen and the Archduchess Maria Theresa, his wife, were at this period joint governors-general of the Austrian Netherlands. At the burst of rebellion they attempted to temporize, but this only strengthened the revolutionary party, while the emperor wholly disapproved their measures and recalled them to Vienna.

Count Murray was now named governor-general, and it was evident that the future fate of the provinces was to depend on the issues of civil war. Count Trautmansdorff, the imperial minister at Brussels, and Count d'Alten, who commanded the Austrian troops, took a high tone and evinced a peremptory resolution. The soldiery and the citizens soon came into contact on many points, and blood was spilled at Brussels, Mechlin, and Antwerp.

The provincial states were convoked for the purpose of voting the usual subsidies. Brabant, after some opposition, consented, but the states of Hainault unanimously refused the vote. The emperor saw, or supposed, that the necessity for decisive measures was now inevitable. The refractory states were dissolved, and arrests and imprisonments were multiplied in all quarters. Van der Noot, who had escaped to England, soon returned to the Netherlands and established a committee at Breda, which conferred on him the imposing title of agent-plenipotentiary of the people of Brabant. He hoped, under this authority, to interest the English, Prussian, and Dutch governments in favor of his views, but his proposals were coldly received. Protestant states had little sympathy for a people whose resistance was excited, not by tyrannical efforts against freedom, but by broad measures of civil and religious reorganization, the only fault of which was their attempted application to minds wholly incompetent to comprehend their value.

Left to themselves, the Belgians soon gave a display of that energetic valor which is natural to them, and which would be entitled to still greater admiration had it been evinced in a worthier cause. During the fermentation which led to a general rising in the provinces on the impulse of fanatic zeal, the truly enlightened portion of the people conceived the project of raising, on the ruins of monastic influence and aristocratical power, an edifice of constitutional freedom. Vonck, also an advocate of Brussels, took the lead in this splendid design, and he and his friends proved themselves to have reached the level of that true enlightenment which distinguished the close of the eighteenth century. But the Vonckists, as they were called, formed but a small minority compared with the mass, and, overwhelmed by fanaticism on the one hand and despotism on the other, they were unable to act effectually for the public good. Francis Van der Mersch, a soldier of fortune and a man of considerable talents, who had raised himself from the ranks to the command of a regiment, and had been formed in the school of the Seven Years' War, was appointed to the command of the patriot forces. Joseph II. was declared to have forfeited his sovereignty in Brabant, and hostilities soon commenced by a regular advance of the insurgent army upon that province. Van der Mersch displayed consummate ability in this crisis, where so much depended upon the prudence of the military chief. He made no rash attempt, to which commanders are sometimes induced by reliance upon the enthusiasm of a newly revolted people. He, however, took the earliest safe opportunity of coming to blows with the enemy, and, having cleverly induced the Austrians to follow him into the very streets of the town of Turnhout, he there entered on a bloody contest, and finally defeated the imperialists with considerable loss. He next maneuvered with great ability, and succeeded in making his way into the province of Flanders, took Ghent by assault, and soon reduced Bruges, Ypres, and Ostend. At the news of these successes the governors-general quitted Brussels in all haste. The states of Flanders assembled, in junction with those of Brabant. Both provinces were freed from the presence of the Austrian troops. Van der Noot and the committee of Breda made an entrance into Brussels with all the pomp of royalty, and in the early part of the following year (1790) a treaty of union was signed by the seven revolted provinces, now formed into a confederation under the name of the United Belgian States.

All the hopes arising from these brilliant events were soon, however, to be blighted by the scorching heats of faction. Joseph II., whose temperament appears to have been too sensitive to support the shock of disappointment in plans which sprung from the purest motives, saw, in addition to this successful insurrection against his power, his beloved sister, the Queen of France, menaced with the horrors of an inevitable revolution. His over-sanguine expectations of successfully rivaling the glory of Frederick and Catherine, and the ill success of his war against the Turks, all tended to break down his enthusiastic spirit, which only wanted the elastic resistance of fortitude to have made him a great character. He sank for some time into a profound melancholy, and expired on January 20, 1791, accusing his Belgian subjects of having caused his premature death.

Leopold, the successor of his brother, displayed much sagacity and moderation in the measures which he adopted for the recovery of the revolted provinces, but their internal disunion was the best ally of the new emperor. The violent party which now ruled at Brussels had ungratefully forgotten the eminent services of Van der Mersch, and accused him of treachery, merely from his attachment to the noble views and principles of the widely increasing party of the Vonckists. Induced by the hope of reconciling the opposing parties, he left his army in Namur, and imprudently ventured into the power of General Schoenfeld, who commanded the troops of the states. Van der Mersch was instantly arrested and thrown into prison, where he lingered for months, until set free by the overthrow of the faction he had raised to power. But he did not recover his liberty to witness the realization of his hopes for that of his country. The states-general, in their triumph over all that was truly patriotic, occupied themselves in restoring the old conditions and suppressing the liberal party. The overtures of the new emperor were rejected with scorn, and, as might be expected from this combination of bigotry and rashness, the imperial troops under General Bender marched quietly to the conquest of the whole country, town after town opening their gates, while Van der Noot and his partisans betook themselves to rapid and disgraceful flight. On December 10, 1791, the ministers of the emperor concluded a convention with those of England, Russia, and Holland (which powers guaranteed its execution), by which Leopold granted an amnesty for all past offenses, and confirmed to all his recovered provinces their ancient constitution and privileges. Thus returning under the domination of Austria, Belgium saw its best chance for successfully following the noble example of the United Provinces paralyzed by the shortsighted bigotry which deprived the national courage of all moral force.

Leopold enjoyed but a short time the fruits of his well-measured indulgences. He died suddenly, March 1, 1792, and was succeeded by his son, Francis II., whose fate it was to see those provinces of Belgium which had cost his ancestors so many struggles to maintain wrested forever from the imperial power. Belgium presented at this period an aspect of paramount interest to the world, less owing to its intrinsic importance than to its becoming at once the point of contest between the contending powers and the theater of the terrible struggle between republican France and the monarchs she braved and battled with. The whole combinations of European policy were staked on the question of the French possession of this country.

This war between France and Austria began its earliest operations on the very first days after the accession of Francis II. The victory of Jemappes, gained by Dumouriez, was the first great event of the campaign. The Austrians were on all sides driven out. Dumouriez made his triumphal entry into Brussels on November 13, and immediately after the occupation of this town the whole of Flanders, Brabant, and Hainault, with the other Belgian provinces, were subjected to France. Soon afterward several pretended deputies from the Belgian people hastened to Paris and implored the convention to grant them a share of that liberty and equality which was to confer such inestimable blessings on France. Various decrees were issued in consequence, and after the mockery of a public choice, hurried on in several of the towns by hired Jacobins and well-paid patriots, the incorporation of the Austrian Netherlands with the French republic was formally pronounced.

The next campaign destroyed this whole fabric of revolution. Dumouriez, beaten at Neerwinden by Prince Frederick of Saxe-Coburg, abandoned not only his last year's conquest, but fled from his own army to pass the remainder of his life on a foreign soil and leave his reputation a doubtful legacy to history. Belgium, once again in the possession of Austria, was placed under the government of the Archduke Charles, the emperor's brother, who was destined to a very brief continuance in this precarious authority.

During this and the succeeding year the war was continued with unbroken perseverance and a constant fluctuation in its results. In the various battles which were fought, and the sieges which took

Hist. Nat. xiii-18

place, the English army was, as usual, in the foremost ranks, under the Duke of York, second son of George III. The Prince of Orange, at the head of the Dutch troops, proved his inheritance of the valor which seems inseparable from the name of Nassau. The Archduke Charles laid the foundation of his subsequent high reputation. The Emperor Francis himself fought valiantly at the head of his troops. But all the coalesced courage of these princes and their armies could not effectually stop the progress of the republican arms. The battle of Fleurus rendered the French completely masters of Belgium, and the representatives of the city of Brussels once more repaired to the national convention of France to solicit the reincorporation of the two countries. This was not, however, finally pronounced till October 1, 1795, by which time the violence of an arbitrary government had given the people a sample of what they were to expect. The Austrian Netherlands and the province of Liege were divided into nine departments, forming an integral part of the French republic, and this new state of things was consolidated by the preliminaries of peace, signed at Leoben in Styria, between the French general, Bonaparte, and the Archduke Charles, and confirmed by the Treaty of Campo Formio on October 17, 1797.

Chapter XXII

THE FRENCH INVASION. 1794-1813

WHILE the fate of Belgium was decided on the plains of Fleurus, Pichegru prepared to carry the triumphant arms of France into the heart of Holland. He crossed the Meuse at the head of 100,000 men, and soon gained possession of most of the chief places of Flanders. An unusually severe winter was setting in, but a circumstance which in common cases retards the operations of war was in the present instance the means of hurrying on the conquest on which the French general was bent. The arms of the sea, which had hitherto been the best defenses of Holland, now became solid masses of ice, battlefields on which the soldiers maneuvered and the artillery thundered, as if the laws of the elements were repealed to hasten the fall of the once proud and long flourishing republic. Nothing could arrest the ambitious ardor of the invaders. The English army in Holland, commanded by the Duke of York, made but a feeble resistance; and borne down by numbers, was driven from position to position. Batteries, cannon, and magazines were successively taken, and Pichegru was soon at the term of his brilliant exploits.

But Holland speedily ceased to be a scene of warfare. The discontented portion of the citizens, now the majority, rejoiced to retaliate the revolution of 1787 by another, received the French as liberators. Reduced to extremity, yet still capable by the aid of his allies of making a long and desperate resistance, the stadtholder took the nobler resolution of saving his fellow-citizens from the horrors of prolonged warfare. He repaired to The Hague, presented himself in the assembly of the states-general, and solemnly deposed in their hands the exercise of the supreme power, which he found he could no longer wield but to entail misery and ruin on his conquered country. After this splendid instance of true patriotism and rare virtue, he quitted Holland and took refuge in England. The states-general dissolved a national assembly installed at The Hague, and, the stadtholderate abolished, the United

Provinces now changed their form of government, their long-cherished institutions, and their very name, and were christened the Batavian republic.

Assurances of the most flattering nature were profusely showered on the new state by the sister republic which had effected this new revolution. But the first measure of regeneration was the necessity of paying for the recovered independence, which was effected for the sum of 100,000,000 florins. The new constitution was almost entirely modeled on that of France, and the promised independence soon became a state of deplorable suffering and virtual slavery. Incalculable evils were the portion of Holland in the part which she was forced to take in the war between France and England. Her marine was nearly annihilated, and some of her most valuable possessions in the Indies ravished from her by the British arms. Cape Colony, held by the Dutch since 1652, was seized by the English in 1795 in behalf of the Prince of Orange, and during the progress of the war Java, the Celebes and most of the other Dutch colonies in the East passed into British hands. Holland was at the same time obliged to cede to her ally the whole of Dutch Flanders, Maastricht, Venloo, and their dependencies, and to render free and common to both nations the navigation of the Rhine, the Meuse, and the Scheldt.

The internal situation of the unfortunate republic was deplorable. Under the weight of an enormous and daily increasing debt, all the resources of trade and industry were paralyzed. Universal misery took the place of opulence, and not even the consolation of a free constitution remained to the people. They vainly sought that blessing from each new government of the country whose destinies they followed, but whose advantages they did not share. They saw themselves successively governed by the states-general, a national assembly, and the directory. But these ephemeral authorities had not sufficient weight to give the nation domestic happiness, nor consideration among the other powers.

On October 11, 1797, the English admiral, Sir Adam Duncan, with a superior force, encountered the Dutch fleet under De Winter off Camperdown, and in spite of the bravery of the latter he was taken prisoner, with nine ships of the line and a frigate. An expedition on an extensive scale was soon after fitted out in England to coöperate with a Russian force for the establishment of the house of Orange. The Helder was the destination of this armament, which was commanded by Sir Ralph Abercrombie. The Duke of York soon arrived in the Texel with a considerable reinforcement. A series of severe and well-contested actions near Bergen ended in the defeat of the allies and the abandonment of the enterprise, the only success of which was the capture of the remains of the Dutch fleet, which was safely conveyed to England.

From this period the weight of French oppression became every day more intolerable in Holland. Ministers, generals, and every other species of functionary, with swarms of minor tyrants, while treating the country as a conquered province, deprived it of all share in the brilliant though checkered glories gained by that to which it was subservient. The Dutch were robbed of national independence and personal freedom. While the words "liberty" and "equality" were everywhere emblazoned, the French ambassador assumed an almost Oriental despotism. The language and forms of a free government were used only to sanction a foreign tyranny, and the Batavian republic, reduced to the most hopeless and degraded state, was in fact but a forced appendage chained to the triumphal car of France.

Napoleon Bonaparte, creating by the force of his prodigious talents the circumstances of which inferior minds are but the creatures, now rapidly rose to the topmost height of power. Soon after his creation as First Consul he had made a tour of the Belgian provinces, whose importance he fully appreciated. The results of his visit seemed at first to promise a return of prosperity—over fifty millions of francs were spent on Antwerp alone. But the continuation of the war, interrupted for barely a year by the Peace of Amiens in 1802, and the disastrous results of the continental blockade which kept all the ports of the Netherlands closed, rendered any real prosperity impossible. The new Batavian republic was not destined to have a long existence. After the victory of Austerlitz Napoleon determined to create another kingdom for his family in Holland. Louis Bonaparte, in spite of his objections, was obliged by his brother to accept the crown, and ascended the throne of Holland in 1806.

The character of Louis Bonaparte was gentle and amiable, his manners easy and affable. He entered on his new rank with the best intentions toward the country over which he was sent to reign, and though he felt acutely when the people refused him marks of respect and applause, which was frequently the case, his temper was not soured and he conceived no resentment. He endeavored to merit popularity, and though his power was scanty, his efforts were not wholly unsuccessful. He labored to revive the ruined trade, which he knew to be the staple of Dutch prosperity. But the measures springing from this praiseworthy motive were totally opposed to the policy of Napoleon, and in proportion as Louis made friends and partisans among his subjects he excited bitter enmity in his imperial brother. Louis was so averse to the Continental system, or exclusion of British manufactures, that during his short reign every facility was given to his subjects to elude it, even in defiance of the orders conveyed to him from Paris through the medium of the French ambassador at The Hague. He imposed no restraints on public opinion, nor would he establish the odious system of espionage cherished by the French police. But he was fickle in his purposes and prodigal in his expenses. The profuseness of his expenditure was very offensive to the Dutch notions of respectability in matters of private finance and injurious to the existing state of the public means. The tyranny of Napoleon became soon quite insupportable to him, so much so that it is believed that had the ill-fated English expedition to Walcheren in 1809 succeeded, and the army advanced into the country, he would have declared war against France. After an ineffectual struggle of more than three years he chose rather to abdicate his throne than retain it under the degrading conditions of proconsulate subserviency. This measure excited considerable regret, and much esteem for the man who preferred the retirement of private life to the meanness of regal slavery. But Louis left a galling memento of misplaced magnificence, in an increase of ninety millions of florins (equivalent to about thirty-six millions of dollars) to the already oppressive amount of the national debt of the country.

The annexation of Holland to the French empire was immeditely pronounced by Napoleon. Two-thirds of the national debt were abolished, the conscription law was introduced, and the Berlin and Milan decrees against the introduction of British manufactures were rigidly enforced. The nature of the evils inflicted on the Dutch people by this annexation and its consequences demands a somewhat minute examination. The kingdom of Holland consisted of the departments of the Zuyder Zee, the mouths of the Meuse, the Upper Yssel, the mouths of the Yssel, Friesland, and the Western and Eastern Ems; and the population of the whole did not exceed 1,800,000 souls. When Louis abdicated his throne he left a military and naval force of 18,000 men, who were immediately taken into the service of France, and in three years and a half after that event this number was increased to 50,000, by the operation of the French naval and military code. Thus about a thirty-sixth part of the whole population was employed in arms. The forces included in the maritime conscription were wholly employed in the navy. The national guards were on constant duty in the garrisons or naval establishments. The cohorts were by law only liable to serve in the interior of the French empire—that is to say, from Hamburg to Rome. But after the Russian campaign this limitation was disregarded, and they formed a part of Napoleon's army at the battle of Bautzen.

The conscription laws now began to be executed with the greatest rigor, and though the strictest justice and impartiality were observed in the ballot and other details of this most oppressive measure, yet it has been calculated that on an average nearly one-half of the male population of the age of twenty years was annually taken off. The conscripts were told that their service was not to extend beyond the term of five years, but as few instances occurred of a French soldier being discharged without his being declared unfit for service, it was always considered in Holland that the service of a conscript was tantamount to an obligation during life. Besides, the regulations respecting the conscription were annually changed, by which means the code became each year more intricate and confused, and as the explanation of any doubt rested with the functionaries to whom the execution of the law was confided, there was little chance of their constructions mitigating its severity.

The various taxes were laid on and levied in the most oppressive manner, those on land usually amounting to twenty-five, and those on houses to thirty per cent. of the clear annual rent. Other direct taxes were levied on persons and movable property, and all were regulated on a scale of almost intolerable severity. The whole sum annually obtained from Holland by these means amounted to about thirty million of florins, or about fifteen million dollars.

The operation of what was called the Continental system created an excess of misery in Holland only to be understood by those who witnessed its lamentable results. In other countries,

Belgium, for instance, where great manufactories existed, the loss of maritime communication was compensated by the exclusion of English goods. In states possessed of large and fertile territories, the population which could no longer be employed in commerce might be occupied in agricultural pursuits. But in Holland, whose manufactures were inconsiderable, and whose territory is insufficient to support its inhabitants, the destruction of trade threw innumerable individuals wholly out of employment and produced a graduated scale of poverty in all ranks. A considerable part of the population had been employed in various branches of the traffic carried on by means of the many canals which conveyed merchandise from the seaports into the interior and to the different Continental markets. When the communication with England was cut off principals and subordinates were involved in a common ruin.

In France the effect of the Continental system was somewhat alleviated by the license trade, the exportation of various productions forced on the rest of Continental Europe, and the encouragement given to home manufactures. But all this was reversed in Holland. The few licenses granted to the Dutch were clogged with duties so exorbitant as to make them useless, the duties on one ship which entered the Meuse, loaded with sugar and coffee, amounting to about $250,000. At the same time every means was used to crush the remnant of Dutch commerce and sacrifice the country to France. The Dutch troops were clothed and armed from French factories, the frontiers were opened to the introduction of French commodities duty free, and the Dutch manufacturer was undersold in his own market.

The population of Amsterdam was reduced from 220,000 souls to 190,000, of which a fourth part derived their whole subsistence from charitable institutions, while another fourth part received partial succor from the same sources. At Haarlem, where the population had been chiefly employed in bleaching and preparing linen made in Brabant, whole streets were leveled with the ground and more than five hundred houses destroyed. At The Hague, at Delft, and in other towns many inhabitants had been induced to pull down their houses from inability to keep them in repair or pay the taxes. The preservation of the dikes, requiring an annual expense of $3,000,000, was everywhere neglected. The sea inundated the country and threatened to resume its ancient dominion. No object of ambition, no source of professional wealth or distinction, remained to which a Hollander could aspire. None could voluntarily enter the army or navy to fight for the worst enemy of Holland. The clergy were not provided with a decent competency. The ancient laws of the country, so dear to its pride and its prejudices, were replaced by the *Code Napoléon,* so that old practitioners had to recommence their studies, and young men were disgusted with the drudgery of learning a system which was universally pronounced unfit for a commercial country.

Independent of this mass of positive ill, it must be borne in mind that in Holland trade was not merely a means of gaining wealth, but a passion long and deeply grafted on the national mind —so that the Dutch felt every aggravation of calamity, considering themselves degraded and sacrificed by a power which had robbed them of all which attaches a people to their native land, and, for an accumulated list of evils, only offered them the empty glory of appertaining to the country which, with the sole exception of England, gave the law to all the nations of Europe.

Those who have considered the events noted in this history for the last two hundred years, and followed the fluctuations of public opinion depending on prosperity or misfortune, will have anticipated that in the present calamitous state of the country all eyes were turned toward the family whose memory was revived by every pang of slavery and associated with every throb for freedom. The presence of the Prince of Orange, William IV., who had on the death of his father succeeded to the title, though he had lost the revenues of his ancient house and the reëstablishment of the connection with England, were now the general desire. The leaders of the various parties into which the country was divided became by degrees more closely united. Approaches toward a better understanding were reciprocally made, and they ended in a general anxiety for the expulsion of the French, with the establishment of a free constitution and a cordial desire that the Prince of Orange should be at its head. It may be safely affirmed that at the close of the year 1813 these were the unanimous wishes of the Dutch nation.

Napoleon, lost in the labyrinths of his exorbitant ambition, afforded at length a chance of redress to the nations he had enslaved. Elevated so suddenly and so high, he seemed suspended between two influences, and unfit for either. He might in a moral view be said to have breathed badly in a station which was beyond the atmosphere of his natural world, without being out of its attraction; and having reached the pinnacle, he soon lost his balance and fell. Driven from Russia by the junction of human with elemental force in 1812, he made some grand efforts in the following year to recover from his irremediable reverses. The battles of Bautzen and Lutzen were the expiring efforts of his greatness. That of Leipzig put a fatal negative upon the hopes that sprang from the two former, and the obstinate ambition which at this epoch made him refuse the most liberal offers of the allies was justly punished by humiliation and defeat. Almost all the powers of Europe now leagued against him, and, France itself being worn out by his wasteful expenditure of men and money, he had no longer a chance in resistance. The empire was attacked at all points. The French troops in Holland were drawn off to reinforce the armies in distant directions, and the whole military force in that country scarcely exceeded 10,000 men. The advance of the combined armies toward the frontiers became generally known, and parties of Cossacks had entered the north of Holland in November and were scouring the country beyond the Yssel. The moment for action on the part of the Dutch confederate patriots had now arrived, and it was not lost or neglected.

A people inured to revolutions for upwards of two centuries, filled with proud recollections and urged on by well-digested hopes, were the most likely to understand the best period and the surest means for success. An attempt that might have appeared to other nations rash was proved to be wise both by the reasonings of its authors and its own results. The intolerable tyranny of France had made the population not only ripe, but eager, for revolt. This disposition was acted on by a few enterprising men, at once partisans of the house of Orange and patriots in the truest sense of the word. The leaders of the movement were the Counts Van Hogendorp and Stirum. These bold men, at the head of a hasty levy of 800 poorly armed men, proclaimed the Prince of Orange at The Hague November 17, 1813.

While a few gentlemen thus boldly came forward at their own risk, with no funds but their private fortunes, and aided only by an unarmed populace, to declare war against the French emperor, they did not even know the residence of the exiled prince in whose cause they were now so completely compromised. The other towns of Holland were in a state of the greatest incertitude. Rotterdam did not move, and the French troops were concentrated at Utrecht. In Amsterdam, however, 1500 of the national guard mounted the yellow cockade with cries of "*Orange bouen,*" but they had no leaders and the town corporation moved cautiously.

The subsequent events at The Hague furnish an inspiring lesson for all people who would learn that to be free they must be resolute and daring. The only hope of the confederates was from the British government and the combined armies then acting in the north of Europe. But many days were to be lingered through before troops could be embarked and make their way from England in the teeth of the easterly winds then prevailing, while a few Cossacks, hovering on the confines of Holland, gave the only evidence of the proximity of the allied forces. The French, however, thought only of retreat. The prefect at The Hague, M. de Stassart, fled at the first alarm and the small French garrison soon followed his example.

Unceasing efforts were now made to remedy the want of arms and men. A quantity of pikes were rudely made and distributed to the volunteers who crowded in, and numerous fishing boats were dispatched in different directions to inform the British cruisers of the passing events. An individual named Pronck, an inhabitant of Schævening, a village of the coast, rendered great services in this way, from his influence among the sailors and fishermen in the neighborhood.

The confederates spared no exertion to increase the confidence of the people under many contradictory and disheartening contingencies. An officer who had been dispatched for advice and information to Baron Bentinck, at Zwolle, who was in communication with the allies, returned with the discouraging news that General Bülow had orders not to pass the Yssel, the allies having decided not to advance into Holland beyond the line of that river. A meeting of the ancient regents of The Hague was convoked by the proclamation of the confederates, and took place at the house of Count Van Hogendorp, the ancient residence of the De Witts. The wary magistrates absolutely refused all coöperation in the daring measures of the confederates, who had now the whole responsibility on their heads, with little to cheer them on in their perilous career but their own resolute hearts and the recollection of those days when their ancestors, with odds as fearfully against them, rose up and shivered to atoms the yoke of their oppressors.

Some days of intense anxiety now elapsed, and various incidents occurred to keep up the general excitement. Reinforcements came gradually in, no hostile measure was resorted to by the French troops, yet the want of success, as rapid as was proportioned to the first movements of the revolution, threw a gloom over all. Amsterdam and Rotterdam still held back, but the nomination of Messrs. Van Hogendorp and Van der Duyn Van Maesdam to be heads of the government until the arrival of the Prince of Orange, and a formal abjuration of the Emperor Napoleon, inspired new vigor into the public mind. Two nominal armies mustering barely 1200 men were set on foot and received the grandiloquent titles of the army of Utrecht and the army of Gorcum.

The "army of Gorcum" marched on the 22d on Rotterdam. Its arrival was joyfully hailed by the people, who contributed 300 volunteers to swell its ranks. The "army of Utrecht" advanced on Leyden and raised the spirits of the people by the display of even so small a force. But still the contrary winds kept back all appearance of succor from England, and the enemy was known to meditate a general attack on the patriot lines from Amsterdam to Dordrecht. The bad state of the roads still retarded the approach of the far distant armies of the allies, and alarms, true and false, were spread on all hands, when the appearance of 300 Cossacks, detached from the Russian armies beyond the Yssel, prevailed over the hesitation of Amsterdam and the other towns, and they at length declared for the Prince of Orange.

But this somewhat tardy determination seemed to be the signal for various petty events which at an epoch like that were magnified into transactions of the most fatal import. A reinforcement of 1500 French troops reached Gorcum from Antwerp, a detachment of twenty-five Dutch, with a piece of cannon, were surprised at one of the outposts of Woerden, which had been previously evacuated by the French, and the recapture of the town was accompanied by some excesses. The numbers and the cruelties of the enemy were greatly exaggerated. Consternation began to spread over all the country. The French, who seemed to have recovered from their panic, had resumed on all sides offensive operations. The garrison of Gorcum made a sortie, repulsed the force under General Van Landas, entered the town of Dordrecht, and levied contributions. But the inhabitants soon expelled them, and the army was enabled to resume its position.

Still the wind continued adverse to arrivals from the English coast, the Cossacks, so often announced, had not yet reached The Hague, and the small unsupported parties in the neighborhood of Amsterdam were in daily danger of being cut off.

In this crisis the confederates were placed in a most critical position. On the eve of failure, and with the certainty, in such a result, of being branded as rebels and zealots, whose rashness had drawn down ruin on themselves, their families, and their country, it required no common share of fortitude to bear up against the danger that threatened them. Aware of its extent, they calmly and resolutely opposed it, and each seemed to vie with the others in energy and firmness.

On November 27 a messenger arrived from England with a letter from the Prince of Orange announcing his immediate coming; and finally the disembarkation of 200 English marines, on the 29th, was followed the next day by the landing of the prince, whose impatience to throw himself into the open arms of his country made him spurn every notion of risk and every reproach for rashness. He was received with indescribable enthusiasm. The generous flame rushed through the whole country. No bounds were set to the affectionate confidence of the nation, and no prince ever gave a nobler example of gratitude. As the people everywhere proclaimed William I. sovereign prince, it was proposed that he should everywhere assume that title. It was, however, after some consideration decided that no step of this nature should be taken till he had visited the capital. On December 1 the prince issued a proclamation to his countrymen, in which he stated his hopes of becoming, by the blessing of Providence, the means of restoring them to their former state of independence and prosperity. "This," continued he, "is my only object, and I have the satisfaction of assuring you that it is also the object of the combined powers. This is particularly the wish of the prince regent and the British nation, and it will be proved to you by the succor which that powerful people will immediately afford you, and which will, I hope, restore those ancient bonds of alliance and friendship which were a source of prosperity and happiness to both countries." This address being distributed at Amsterdam, a proclamation, signed by the commissioners of the confederate patriots, was published there the same day. It contained the following passages, remarkable as being the first authentic declaration of the sovereignty subsequently conferred on the Prince of Orange: "The uncertainty which formerly existed as to the executive power will no longer paralyze your efforts. It is not William, the sixth stadtholder, whom the nation recalls, without knowing what to hope or expect from him; but William I., who offers himself as sovereign prince of this free country." The following day, December 2, the prince made his entry into Amsterdam. On December 3 he published an address, from which we shall quote one paragraph: "You desire, Netherlanders, that I should be intrusted with a greater share of power than I should have possessed but for my absence. Your confidence, your affection, offer me the sovereignty; and I am called upon to accept it, since the state of my country and the situation of Europe require it. I accede to your wishes. I overlook the difficulties which may attend such a measure; I accept the offer which you have made me, but I accept it only on one condition—that it shall be accompanied by a wise constitution, which shall guarantee your liberties, and secure them against every attack. My ancestors sowed the seeds of your independence; the preservation of that independence shall be the constant object of the efforts of myself and those around me."

PART IV

THE KINGDOMS OF HOLLAND AND BELGIUM. 1814-1935

Chapter XXIII

WILLIAM I. AS PRINCE AND SOVEREIGN OF THE NETHERLANDS. 1814-1815

THE regeneration of Holland was rapid and complete. Within four months an army of 25,000 men was raised, and in the midst of financial, judicial, and commercial arrangements the grand object of the constitution was calmly and seriously debated. A committee consisting of fourteen persons of the first importance in the several provinces furnished the result of three months' labors in the plan of a political code, which was immediately printed and published for the consideration of the people at large. Twelve hundred names were next chosen from among the most respectable householders in the different towns and provinces, including persons of every religious persuasion, whether Jews or Christians. A special commission was then formed, who selected from this number 600 names, and every housekeeper was called on to give his vote for or against their election. A large majority of the 600 notables thus chosen met at Amsterdam on March 28, 1814. The following day they assembled with an immense concourse of people, in the great church, which was splendidly fitted up for the occasion, and then and there the prince, in an impressive speech, solemnly offered the constitution for acceptance or rejection. After a few hours' deliberation a discharge of artillery announced to the anxious population that the constitution had been accepted. The numbers present were 483, and the votes as follows: ayes, 458; noes, 25.

There were 117 members absent, several of whom were kept away by unavoidable obstacles. The majority among them was considered as dissentients, but it was calculated that if the whole body of 600 had voted, the adoption of the constitution would have been carried by a majority of five-sixths. The dissentients chiefly objected to the power of declaring war and concluding treaties of peace being vested in the sovereign. Some individuals urged that the Protestant interest was endangered by the admission of persons of every persuasion to all public offices, and the Catholics complained that the state did not sufficiently contribute to the support of their religious establishments.

Such objections as these were to be expected from individual interest or sectarian prejudices. But they prove that the whole plan was fairly considered and solemnly adopted, that so far from being the dictation of a government, it was the freely chosen charter of the nation at large, offered and sworn to by the prince, whose authority was only exerted in restraining and modifying the over-ardent generosity and confidence of the people.

Only one day more elapsed before the new sovereign was solemnly inaugurated and took the oath prescribed by the constitution: "I swear that first and above all things I will maintain the constitution of the United Netherlands, and that I will promote, to the utmost of my power, the independence of the state, and the liberty and prosperity of its inhabitants."

While Holland thus resumed its place among free nations, and France was restored to the Bourbons by the abdication of Napoleon, the allied armies had taken possession of and occupied the remainder of the Low Countries, or those provinces distinguished by the name of Belgium (but then still forming departments of the French empire), and the provisional government was vested in Baron Vincent, the Austrian general. This choice seemed to indicate an intention of restoring Austria to her ancient domination over the country. Such was certainly the common opinion among those who had no means of penetrating the secrets of European policy at that important epoch. It was, in fact, quite conformable to the principle of *status quo ante bellum* adopted toward France. Baron Vincent himself seemed to have been impressed with the false notion, and there did not exist a doubt throughout Belgium of the reëstablishment of the old institutions.

But the intentions of the allied powers were of a nature far different. The necessity of a consolidated state capable of offering a barrier to French aggression on the Flemish frontier seemed evident to the various powers who had so long suffered from its want. By England particularly such a field was required for the operations of her armies; and Prussia, and even France, in the person of Talleyrand, favored the formation of this "buffer" state, which well suited the ambitious views of the Prince of Orange.

The treaty of Paris (May 30, 1814) was the first act which gave an open manifestation of this principle. It was stipulated by its sixth article that "Holland, placed under the sovereignty of the house of Orange, should receive an increase of territory." In this was explained the primitive notion of the creation of the kingdom of the Netherlands, based on the necessity of augmenting the power of a nation which was destined to hold the balance between France and Germany. The following month witnessed the execution of the treaty of London, which prescribed the precise nature of the projected increase.

It was wholly decided, without subjecting the question to the approbation of the Belgians,[1] that that country and Holland should form one united state, and the rules of government in the chief branches of its administration were completely fixed. The Prince of Orange and the plenipotentiaries of the great allied powers covenanted by this treaty, first, that the union of the two portions forming the kingdom of the Netherlands should be as perfect as possible, forming one state, governed in conformity with the fundamental law of Holland, which might be modified by common consent; secondly, that religious liberty and the equal right of citizens of all persuasions to fill all the employments of the state should be maintained; thirdly, that the Belgian provinces should be fairly represented in the assembly of the states-general, and that the sessions of the states in time of peace should be held alternately in Belgium and in Holland; fourthly and fifthly, that all the commercial privileges of the country should be common to the citizens at large, that the Dutch colonies should be considered as belonging equally to Belgium, and finally, that the public debt of the two countries, and the expenses of its interest, should be borne in common.

We shall now briefly recapitulate some striking points in the materials which were thus meant to be amalgamated. Holland, wrenched from the Spanish yoke by the genius and courage of the early princes of Orange, had formed for two centuries an independent republic, to which the extension of maritime commerce had given immense wealth. The form of government was remarkable. It was composed of seven provinces, mutually independent of each other. These provinces possessed during the Middle Ages constitutions nearly similar to that of England—a sovereign with limited power, representatives of the nobles and

[1] "Because," says the protocol, "they had not done enough on their own behalf to justify independence being conferred upon them."

commons, whose concurrence with the prince was necessary for the formation of laws, and, finally, the existence of municipal privileges, which each town preserved and extended by means of its proper force. This state of things had known but one alteration, —but that a mighty one—the forfeiture of Philip II. at the latter end of the sixteenth century, and the total abolition of monarchical power.

The remaining forms of the government were hardly altered, so that the state was wholly regulated by its ancient usages, and, like some Gothic edifice, its beauty and solidity were original to itself and different from the general rules and modern theories of surrounding nations. The country loved its liberty, such as it found it, and not in the fashion of any Utopian plan traced by some new-fangled system of political philosophy. Inherently Protestant and commercial, the Dutch abhorred every yoke but that of their own laws, of which they were proud even in their abuse. They held in particular detestation all French customs, in remembrance of the wretchedness they had suffered from French tyranny, and had unbounded confidence in the house of Orange, from long experience of its hereditary virtues. The main strength of Holland was, in fact, in its recollection; but these, perhaps, generated a germ of discontent, in leading it to expect a revival of all the influence it had lost, and was little likely to recover, in the total change of systems and the variations of trade. There nevertheless remained sufficient capital in the country, and the people were sufficiently enlightened, to give just and extensive hope for the future which now dawned on them. The obstacles offered by the Dutch character to the proposed union were chiefly to be found in the dogmatical opinions consequent on the isolation of the country from all the principles that actuated other states, and particularly that with which it was now joined, while long-cherished sentiments of opposition to the Catholic religion were little likely to lead to feelings of accommodation and sympathy with its new fellow-citizens.

The inhabitants of Belgium, accustomed to foreign domination, were little shocked by the fact of the allied powers having disposed of their fate without consulting their wishes. But they were not so indifferent to the double discovery of finding themselves the subjects of a Dutch and a Protestant king. Without entering at large into any invidious discussion on the causes of the natural jealousy which they felt toward Holland, it may suffice to state that such did exist, and in no very moderate degree. The countries had hitherto had but very little community of interests with each other, and they formed elements so utterly discordant as to afford but slight hope that they would speedily coalesce. The lower classes of the Belgian population were ignorant as well as superstitious (not that these two qualities are to be considered as inseparable) and if they were averse to the Dutch, they were perhaps not more favorably disposed to the French and Austrians. The majority of the nobles may be said to have leaned more, at this period, to the latter than to either of the other two peoples. But the great majority of the industrious and better-informed portions of the middle orders felt different from the other two, because they had found tangible and positive advantages in their subjection to France which overpowered every sentiment of political degradation. On the whole, however, it is unquestionable that the Belgians would have preferred a restoration of the Catholic house of Austria, the historical heir of Burgundy and Flanders, to the union with Protestant Holland.

We thus see there was little sympathy between the members of the national family. The first glance at the geographical position of Holland and Belgium might lead to a belief that their interests were analogous. But we have traced the anomalies in government and religion in the two countries which led to totally different pursuits and feelings. Holland had sacrificed manufactures to commerce. The introduction, duty free, of grain from the northern parts of Europe, though checking the progress of agriculture, had not prevented it from flourishing marvelously, considering this obstacle to culture; and, faithful to their traditional notions, the Dutch saw the elements of well-being only in that liberty of importation which had made their harbors the marts and magazines of Europe.

Totally unaccustomed to the free principles of trade so cherished by the Dutch, the Belgians, on the other hand, had found, under the protection of the French custom-house laws, an internal commerce and agricultural advantages which composed their peculiar prosperity. They found a consumption for the produce of their well-cultivated lands, at high prices, in the neighboring provinces of France. The webs woven by the Belgian peasantry, and generally all the manufactures of the country, met no rivalry from those of England, which were strictly prohibited; and being commonly superior to those of France, the sale was sure and the profit considerable.

Belgium was as naturally desirous of this state of things as Holland was indifferent to it, but it could only have been accomplished by the destruction of free trade and the exclusive protection of internal manufactures. Under such discrepancies as we have thus traced in religion, character, and local interests the two countries were made one, and on the new monarch developed the hard and delicate task of reconciling each party in the ill-assorted match and inspiring them with sentiments of mutual moderation.

Under the title of governor-general of the Netherlands (for his intended elevation to the throne and the definitive junction of Holland and Belgium were still publicly unknown), the Prince of Orange repaired to his new state. He arrived at Brussels in the month of August, 1814, and his first effort was to gain the hearts and the confidence of the people, though he saw the nobles and the higher orders of the inferior classes (with the exception of the merchants) intriguing all around him for the reëstablishment of the Austrian power. Petitions on this subject were printed and distributed, and the models of those anti-national documents may still be referred to in a work published at the time.

As soon as the moment came for promulgating the decision of the sovereign powers as to the actual extent of the new kingdom—that is to say, in the month of February, 1815—the whole plan was made public, and a commission, consisting of twenty-seven members, Dutch and Belgian, was formed to consider the modifications necessary in the fundamental law of Holland in pursuance of the stipulation of the treaty of London. After due deliberation these modifications were formed, and the great political pact was completed for the final acceptance of the king and people.

As a document so important merits particular consideration in reference to the formation of the new monarchy, we shall briefly condense the reasonings of the most impartial and well-informed classes in the country on the constitution now about to be framed. Everyone agreed that some radical change in the whole form of government was necessary, and that its main improvement should be the strengthening of the executive power. That possessed by the former stadtholders of Holland was often found to be too much for the chief of a republic, too little for the head of a monarchy. The assembly of the states-general, as of old constructed. was defective in many points; in none so glaringly so as in that condition which required unanimity in questions of peace or war, and in the provision, from which they had no power to swerve, that all the taxes should be uniform. Both these stipulations were, of sheer necessity, continually disregarded, so that the government could be carried on at all only by repeated violations of the constitution. In order to excuse measures dictated by this necessity, each stadtholder was perpetually obliged to form partisans, and he thus became the hereditary head of a faction. His legitimate power was trifling, but his influence was capable of fearful increase, for the principle which allowed him to infringe the constitution, even on occasions of public good, might be easily warped into a pretext for encroachments that had no bounds but his own will.

Besides, the preponderance of the deputies from the commercial towns in the states-general caused the others to become mere ciphers in times of peace, only capable of clogging the march of affairs and of being, on occasions of civil dissensions, the mere tools of whatever party possessed the greatest tact in turning them to their purpose. Hence a wide field was open to corruption. Uncertainty embarrassed every operation of the government. The Hague became an arena for the conflicting intrigues of every court in Europe. Holland was dragged into almost every war, and thus gradually weakened from its rank among independent nations, it at length fell an easy prey to the French invaders.

To prevent the recurrence of such evils as these, and to establish a kingdom on the solid basis of a monarchy, unequivocal in its essence, yet restrained in its prerogative, the constitution we are now examining was established. According to the report of the commissioners who framed it, " it is founded on the manners and habits of the nation, on its public economy and its old institutions, with a disregard for the ephemeral constitutions of the age. It is not a mere abstraction, more or less ingenious, but a law adapted to the state of the country in the nineteenth century. It did not reconstruct what was worn out by time, but it revived all that was worth preserving. In such a system of laws and institutions well adapted to each other the members of the commission belonging to the Belgian provinces recognized the basis of their ancient charters and the principles of their former liberty. They found no difficulty in adapting this law so as to make it common to the two nations united by ties which had been broken only for their own misfortune and that of Europe, and which it was once more the interest of Europe to render indissoluble."

The news of the elevation of William I. to the throne was received in the Dutch provinces with great joy, in as far as it concerned him personally; but a joy considerably tempered by doubt and jealousy, as regarded their junction with a country sufficiently large to counterbalance Holland, oppose interests to interests, and people to people. National pride and oversanguine expectations prevented a calm judgment on the existing state of Europe, and on the impossibility of Holland, in its ancient limits, maintaining the influence which it was hoped it would acquire.

In Belgium the formation of the new monarchy excited the most lively sensation. The clergy and the nobility were considerably agitated and not slightly alarmed, the latter fearing the resentment of the king for their avowed predilection in favor of Austria, and perceiving the destruction of every hope of aristocratical domination. The more elevated of the middle classes also saw an end to their exclusive occupation of magisterial and municipal employments. The manufacturers, great and small, saw the ruin of monopoly staring them in the face. The whole people took fright at the weight of the Dutch debt, which was considerably greater than that of Belgium. No one seemed to look beyond the present moment. The advantage of colonial possessions seemed remote and questionable to those who possessed no maritime commerce, and the pride of national independence was foreign to the feelings of those who had never yet tasted its blessings.

It was in this state of public feeling that intelligence was received, in March, 1815, of the reappearance in France of the Emperor Napoleon. At the head of three hundred men he had taken the resolution, without parallel even among the grandest of his own powerful conceptions, of invading a country containing thirty millions of people, girded by the protecting armies of coalesced Europe, and imbued, beyond all doubt, with an almost general objection to the former despot who now put his foot on its shores, with imperial pretensions only founded on the memory of his bygone glory. His march to Paris was a miracle, and the vigor of his subsequent measures redeems the ambitious imbecility with which he had hurried on the catastrophe of his previous fall.

The flight of Louis XVIII. from Paris was the sure signal to the kingdom of the Netherlands, in which he took refuge, that it was about to become the scene of another contest for the life or death of despotism. Had the invasion of Belgium, which now took place, been led on by one of the Bourbon family, it is probable that the priesthood, the people, and even the nobility, would have given it not merely a negative support. But the name of Napoleon was a bugbear for every class, and the efforts of the king and government, which met with most enthusiastic support in the northern provinces, were seconded with zeal and courage by the rest of the kingdom.

The national force was soon in the field, under the command of the Prince of Orange, the king's eldest son and heir apparent to the throne for which he now prepared to fight. His brother, Prince Frederick, commanded a division under him. The English army, under the Duke of Wellington, occupied Brussels and the various cantonments in its neighborhood, and the Prussians, commanded by Marshal Blücher, were in readiness to coöperate with their allies on the first movement of the invaders.

Napoleon, hurrying from Paris to strike some rapid and decisive blow, passed the Sambre on June 15, at the head of the French army 150,000 strong, driving the Prussians before him beyond Charleroi and back on the plain of Fleurus with some loss. On the 16th was fought the bloody battle of Ligny, in which the Prussians sustained a decided defeat, but they retreated in good order on the little River Lys, followed by Marshal Grouchy with 30,000 men detached by Napoleon in their pursuit. On the same day the British advanced position at Quatre Bras and the *corps d'armée* commanded by the Prince of Orange were fiercely attacked by Marshal Ney, a battalion of Belgian infantry and a brigade of horse artillery having been engaged in a skirmish the preceding evening at Frasnes with the French advanced troops.

The affair of Quatre Bras was sustained with admirable firmness by the allied English and Netherland forces against an enemy infinitely superior in number and commanded by one of the best generals in France. The Prince of Orange, with only 9000 men, maintained his position till three o'clock in the afternoon, despite the continual attacks of Marshal Ney, who commanded the left of the French army, consisting of 43,000 men. But the interest of this combat and the details of the loss in killed and wounded are so merged in the succeeding battle, which took place on the 18th, that they form in most minds a combination of exploits which the interval of a day can scarcely be considered to have separated.

The 17th was occupied by a retrograde movement of the allied army, directed by the Duke of Wellington, for the purpose of taking its stand on the position he had previously fixed on for the pitched battle, the decisive nature of which his determined foresight had anticipated. Several affairs between the French and English cavalry took place during this movement, and it is pretty well established that the enemy, flushed with the victory over Blücher of the preceding day, were deceived by this short retreat of Wellington and formed a very mistaken notion of its real object, or of the desperate reception destined for the morrow's attack.

The battle of Waterloo has been over and over described and profoundly felt, until its records may be said to exist in the very hearts and memories of the nations.[2] The fiery valor of the assault and the unshakable firmness of the resistance are perhaps without parallel in the annals of war. The immense stake depending on the result, the grandeur of Napoleon's isolated efforts against the flower of the European forces, and the awful responsibility resting on the great leader of these latter, give to the conflict a romantic sublimity unshared by all the maneuvering of science in a hundred commonplace combats of other wars. It forms an epoch in the history of battles. It is to the full as memorable as an individual vent as it is for the consequences which followed it. It was fought by no rules, and gained by no tactics. It was a fair stand-up fight on level ground, where downright manly courage was alone to decide the issue. This derogates in nothing from the splendid talents and deep knowledge of the rival commanders. Their reputation for all the intricate qualities of generalship rests on the broad base of previous victories. This day was to be won by strength of nerve and steadiness of heart, and a moral grandeur is thrown over its result by the reflection that human skill had little to do where so much was left to Providence.

We abstain from entering on details of the battle. It is enough to state that throughout the day the troops of the Netherlands sustained the character for courage which so many centuries

---

[2] Perhaps the best account of the battle ever written will be found in Victor Hugo's "*Les Miserables.*"

had established. Various opinions have gone forth as to the conduct of the Belgian troops on this memorable occasion. Isolated instances were possibly found among a mass of several thousands of that nervous weakness which neither the noblest incitements nor the finest examples can conquer. Old associations and feelings not effaced might have slackened the efforts of a few, directed against former comrades or personal friends whom the stern necessity of politics had placed in opposing ranks. Raw troops might here and there have shrunk from attacks the most desperate on record, but that the great principle of public duty, on grounds purely national, pervaded the army, is to be found in the official reports of its loss—2068 men killed and 2084 wounded prove indelibly that the troops of the Netherlands had their full share in the honor of the day.[3] The victory was cemented by the blood of the Prince of Orange, who stood the brunt of the fight with his gallant soldiers. His conduct was conformable to the character of his whole race, and to his own reputation during a long series of service with the British army in the Spanish peninsula. He stood bravely at the head of his troops during the murderous conflict, or, like Wellington, in whose school he was formed and whose example was beside him, rode from rank to rank and column to column, inspiring his men by the proofs of his untiring courage.

Several anecdotes are related of the prince's conduct throughout the day. One is remarkable as affording an example of those pithy epigrams of the battlefield with which history abounds, accompanied by an act that speaks a fine knowledge of the soldier's heart. On occasion of one peculiarly desperate charge, the prince, hurried on by his ardor, was actually in the midst of the French, and was in the greatest danger, when a Belgian battalion rushed forward, and, after a fierce struggle, repulsed the enemy and disengaged the prince. In the impulse of his admiration and gratitude he tore from his breast one of those decorations gained by his own conduct on some preceding occasion, and flung it among the battalion, calling out, "Take it, take it, my lads! you have all earned it!" This decoration was immediately grappled for, and tied to the regimental standard, amid loud shouts of "Long live the prince!" and vows to defend the trophy, in the very utterance of which many a brave fellow received the stroke of death.

[3] The charges of cowardice made against the Belgian troops are refuted in Mr. Boulger's "Belgians at Waterloo."

A short time afterward, and just half an hour before that terrible charge of the whole line which decided the victory, the prince was struck by a musket-ball in the left shoulder. He was carried from the field and conveyed that evening to Brussels, in the same cart with one of his wounded aides-de-camp, supported by another, and displaying throughout as much indifference to pain as he had previously shown contempt of danger.

The battle of Waterloo consolidated the kingdom of the Netherlands. The wound of the Prince of Orange was perhaps one of the most fortunate that was ever received by an individual or sympathized in by a nation. To a warlike people, wavering in their allegiance, this evidence of the prince's valor acted like a talisman against disaffection. The organization of the kingdom was immediately proceeded on. The commission charged with the revision of the fundamental law and the modification required by the increase of territory presented its report on July 31. The inauguration of the king took place at Brussels on September 21, in presence of the states-general, and the ceremony received additional interest from the appearance of the sovereign supported by his two sons who had so valiantly fought for the rights he now swore to maintain, the heir to the crown yet bearing his wounded arm in a scarf, and showing in his countenance the marks of recent suffering.

Chapter XXIV

THE BELGIAN REVOLUTION. 1815-1832

THE statesmen who met at Vienna in 1814 to remake the map of Europe obliterated by the storms of the revolutionary wars showed in many ways their inability to appreciate the lessons of the last twenty-five years. Their work, based on the old principles of absolutism and balance of power, neglected to reckon with the tremendous growth of liberalism and national feeling which the vast upheaval of the French Revolution and the Napoleonic wars had first inspired, then provoked. This blindness to actual conditions was well shown in the union of Holland and Belgium into one state. The political map-makers of Vienna had thought only to create a strong minor state capable of maintaining itself by its own resources, to serve as a bulwark against any renewal of French aggression. They entirely forgot to consider the differences of race, speech, religion, and political development which made the union of Holland and Belgium an unnatural and precarious one.

The difficulties which King William I. had to face were indeed tremendous. He was called to rule impartially over two countries whose character and interests were in many cases vitally different. Holland was Protestant in religion, and her prosperity was based almost wholly on her commerce. The Belgic provinces were Catholic, had no commerce, and were just entering on a great industrial development which called for very different treatment from the commercial interests of the northern partner. The union made without consulting them had from the first been distasteful to many of the Belgians. This opposition soon crystallized in two parties very different in character and aims, but brought together in common dislike for the new state of things.

The Clericals, the same ultramontane party which had opposed the liberal reforms of Joseph II., saw with horror their submission to a Calvinist monarch, and opposed most bitterly those clauses in the new constitution which provided for complete religious liberty. The liberal party, on the other hand, an outgrowth of the French Revolution, were dissatisfied with the conservative character of the constitution, which, while providing for a legislature, really left to the king and his ministers the real power in the state, while the liberties of the people, apparently guaranteed, were in fact left at the mercy of the administration. Thus it happened that when, on August 18, 1815, the Fundamental Law, as the new constitution was called, was submitted to an assembly of Belgian notables, it was rejected by a large majority of 796 votes to 527.

King William received this first check with the greatest surprise and indignation. However, after a little hesitation, the king declared that the votes of those who had rejected the constitution for religious reasons should not be counted, while the 280 notables who had not voted might be regarded as favorable. Thus was declared adopted the Fundamental Law of the kingdom of the Netherlands.

The union thus inauspiciously begun might still have hoped for a peaceful future under a wise and tactful ruler. The mass of the Belgian people were well disposed to the ruling dynasty and quite content to accept the new constitution. But unfortunately King William, though not lacking ability or firmness of will, was by no means a wise or tactful man. He made no attempt to conceal his strong Dutch proclivities, or his lack of sympathy with his Belgian subjects. The king had begun his reign by several acts calculated to win the regard of his new subjects. The censorship of the press was abolished, certain obnoxious government monopolies were moved, the rigors of the French penal code in force in Belgium was softened, and the right of petition, a very dear one to the Belgians, was restored. But the ill-advised rejection of the constitution had greatly angered him, and the conduct of the Belgian clergy completed his alienation. The Catholic clergy had from the first opposed steadfastly those clauses in the Fundamental Law which guaranteed protection and freedom of worship to all sects alike. This they declared was subversion to the Catholic Church, and they demanded the restoration of all the rights and privileges which the church had enjoyed before 1789. The king's anger was particularly directed against Maurice de Broglie, the Prince-Bishop of Ghent, who had already suffered imprisonment in Napoleon's time for his fearless advocacy of the rights of the church.

De Broglie had been the leader among the opponents of the Fundamental Law, and, far from ceasing his opposition with its enforcement, he in company with other bishops issued a doctrinal judgment to the Belgian Catholics, forbidding the faithful to take the oath to uphold the constitution, whose articles granting free exercise of all religious faiths and freedom of the press were declared " opposed to the spirit and maxims of the Catholic religion." In consequence of this pastoral judgment the Bishop of Ghent was proceeded against before the courts and, on his retiring to Paris, was sentenced in contumacy to expulsion from the realm. The arrest and punishment of other less prominent clericals soon followed.

The religious question was, however, by no means the sole ground of difficulty between the two countries. From the first the Dutch treated Belgium as a conquered province, and were careful to secure for themselves the control of all branches of the public service. Though the population of Belgium was nearly three and a half millions, while that of Holland was but two millions, both states were equally represented in the popular branch of the states-general, which frequently rendered the decision of important measures extremely difficult when the question affected the two countries in different ways. On ordinary matters the government was usually able to detach enough Belgian votes to give it a working majority. In the upper chamber the right of nomination by the king gave the government an overwhelming majority. Still worse was the situation of the Belgians in the army and the official world, for, in spite of the provisions of the constitution for equal representation, almost all the chief officials were Hollanders. In the Ministry of the Interior in 1830 of 117 officials only 11 were Belgians; in the Ministry of War of 102 officials only 3 were natives of the southern provinces. Finally, out of the 1967 commissioned officers in the army, but 288 were of Belgian birth. All the public establishments, the national banks, the highest courts, the military schools, were in Holland. It seemed indeed as if the efforts of the government were directed toward assimilating the Belgians with the Dutch. Since 1819 all public officials were required to know the Dutch language, which was made the official language of the courts and bureaucracy, although French had hitherto been prevalent in the southern provinces. The government, too, endeavored in every way to suppress all expressions of discontent in Belgium. The obnoxious censorship laws were restored and recalcitrant journalists were summoned before the tribunals. Finally the economic policy of the state seemed wholly dictated by the interests of the northern provinces, for the commerce of Amsterdam and Rotterdam was favored by a low tariff system at the exense of the manufacturing interests of Brussels and Antwerp.

The Belgians had to share in the burden of the heavy Dutch debt and to pay new and unpopular taxes on land and food, which bore most heavily on the industrial and agricultural classes of the south. Yet in spite of the economic policy of the government the Belgian provinces prospered greatly during this period. The mineral wealth of the country was largely exploited. Iron manufactures sprang up at Liege and woolen manufactures at Verviers, while the cotton goods of Ghent rivaled those of Manchester. The reopening of the Scheldt, closed to the Belgians for 250 years, raised Antwerp again to a port of the first rank, while the foreign and colonial trade gave new markets for Belgian products. Nor were the northern provinces less prosperous. The restoration to the Netherlands in 1815 of her colonial empire in the East Indies had given impulse to the general revival of commercial activity which had been so long suspended. In general, the Netherlands were prospering more than they had for many years.

The internal prosperity of the kingdom had, however, little effect in allaying the growing hostility of the Belgians to their northern neighbors. While the Belgian liberals were demanding the repeal of the obnoxious press laws and reform of the taxes, the clerical party found new ground for complaint against the government in the education question. The public education in Belgium was almost wholly in the hands of religious orders whose members were often educated abroad and strongly suspected of being affiliated with the proscribed Jesuits. With a view of securing greater control over education, the government forbade any schools to be opened without its consent, and required that every priest, before his induction into orders, should spend at least two years at the new government college at Louvain, where many of the professors were Protestants. Moreover, it was decreed that no Belgian educated abroad could hold any office, civil or religious, in the state.

These acts of the government aroused the most intense opposition on the part of the Catholic party, and the Belgian liberals, who had at first supported the government consistently, soon made secret cause with the clericals. In 1828 a formal alliance of the two parties was made in the so-called constitutional association—the liberals demanding freedom of the press, the clericals freedom of education.

The year 1830 opened with the tension between the Belgians and the government strained to the uttermost. The banishment of the revolutionary leader of the liberals, Louis de Potter, the removal from office of many Belgians who had incurred the displeasure of the Dutch government, and other arbitrary acts had almost completed the breach between the two countries. In Brussels especially the discontent was most widespread. Brussels had become a city of refuge for the discontented of all Europe. A violent press teeming with libels and inflammatory statements kept the people in a constant state of political excitment. Only a spark was needed to set the city on fire, and this came with the sensational news of the revolution of July in France, which expelled the Bourbons from the throne.

Through the first weeks in August the city became more and more excited. So great was the unrest that the officials dared not allow the celebration of the king's birthday, August 24, for already ominous placards bearing the significant warning, " Monday, fireworks; Tuesday, illumination; Wednesday, revolution!" had appeared. On the 25th, just a month after the revolution in Paris, a play of inflammatory nature, called *" La Muette,"* was performed in the theater. At the close of the performance the excited people rushed into the street shouting "Let us imitate the Parisians." The streets were soon filled with the mob, which broke into the arsenal and the shops in search of weapons, destroyed *The National,* a pro-Dutch newspaper, and burned to the ground the house of Van Maanen, the hated Minister of Justice. The few troops in the city made no effective attempt to disperse the rioters and withdrew to the Place Royal. The mob proceeded to burn and pillage at will, till a burgher guard from the better classes succeeded, after some bloodshed, in restoring order. Once armed, however, the burghers determined not to relinquish their advantage till the government had made them some concessions.

A bill of rights demanding the removal of the obnoxious Van

Maanen, the strict observance of the constitution, and the withdrawal of the oppressive edicts, was drawn up and dispatched to the king, and a committee was appointed to take temporary charge of the movement. On the 28th 800 Dutch troops from Antwerp appeared before the city, but were refused entrance by the burgher guard on the ground that it would only renew the disorders. The Dutch generals hesitated where prompt action was necessary, and the city remained in the hands of the revolutionists.

The rising in Brussels was promptly imitated throughout the Belgian provinces. Liege hoisted her city colors and sent deputies to Brussels to demand the calling of the states-general. Her example was followed by the other cities of the south, until only Antwerp and Ghent remained true to the government. King William was now thoroughly alarmed at the extent of the movement. He accepted the resignation of the unpopular Van Maanen, and sent his sons, the Prince of Orange and Prince Frederick, to Brussels to negotiate with the people after order was restored. But the pretensions of the Belgians had already increased, and they now demanded an absolute separation of Belgium from Holland, with the king as the only link between the two countries. On September 13 the estates of the Netherlands met in extra session to consider the crisis. But a deadlock soon developed, for the Belgian deputies, in spite of a conciliatory speech on the part of the king, refused to consider any settlement until the withdrawal of all Dutch troops from Belgium.

Meantime the situation at Brussels grew more and more critical. The populace, recruited by crowds of artisans thrown out of work, and by additions from the surrounding country, grew impatient of the control of the burgher guard. On September 19 a new outbreak occurred. Crowds surrounded the town-hall, where the Committee of Public Safety sat, crying *" Vive la liberté!"* and demanding arms. On the refusal of the committee to grant their demands, the mob overpowered the burgher guard and seized the town-hall, where the arms were kept. The Committee of Safety was dissolved and a new provisional government, headed by Louis de Potter, took its place. On hearing the news of these fresh disorders, Prince Frederick, who commanded the Dutch troops at Antwerp, determined to advance on Brussels and suppress the revolution with one blow. At the report of the advance of the Dutch the best citizens retired in consternation to their houses, but the mass of the people, inspired by able leaders, determined to resist to the uttermost. Barricades were thrown up in the chief streets, and stones and all sorts of missiles collected on the housetops, which were lined with armed men. On September 23 the Dutch troops advanced in six columns against six of the city gates, which were soon cleared with cannon shot. But on penetrating the city the troops were met everywhere by barricades and exposed to a constant fire from the housetops. For two days a fierce conflict raged in the streets between the troops and the people, who were constantly reinforced by recruits who poured in from all sides. On the 27th Prince Frederick abandoned the attack and withdrew toward Antwerp.

The successful defense of Brussels, with its challenge of open war, produced the utmost excitement throughout Belgium, though the Dutch people still remained indifferent. It was in vain, now, that the states-general voted for a separation of the two countries and left it in the hands of the king to set up a new administration and secure the throne for his family. The recent fighting had determined the Belgian leaders to reject the house of Orange, and the provisional government declined to treat with the Prince of Orange, whom King William had appointed his deputy. Almost all Belgium was now in the hands of the revolutionists. At Liege the Dutch troops were allowed to march out unmolested, Ghent came over to the popular party October 18, and soon only the fortresses of Antwerp, Maastricht, and Luxemburg remained in the hands of the Dutch.

The provisional government, now headed by such eminent men as M. Van de Weyer, Gerlache, De Chokier and the Duke of Aerschot, apparently secure in power, took the final steps for the consolidation of the new state. New proposals from the Prince of Orange, who without his father's knowledge offered himself as head of the Belgians, were rejected. Luxemburg, though part of the German confederation, was declared to be united to Belgium. A national congress was called to draw up a constitution, and steps were taken to expel the royal troops from their remaining strongholds on Belgian soil. On October 25 the Belgians carried the suburbs of Antwerp after a severe struggle, and, aided by the citizens, took possession of the town while the Dutch garrison under General Chasse retired to the powerful citadel whose guns commanded the city. An armistice was arranged between the insurgents and the troops, but was soon broken by the former, who attempted to storm the arsenal. In reply to this act of treachery the citadel and the Dutch frigates in the river opened fire on the town with red-hot shot, and when Antwerp seemed threatened with total destruction the insurgents consented to withdraw from the town into the suburbs.

The successful rising of the Belgian provinces, following so closely on the heels of the revolution of July in France, came as a distinct shock to the legitimist governments of Europe, who saw the system so carefully established in 1815 already beginning to crumble. The Emperor Nicholas of Russia was particularly anxious to support Holland, and put 50,000 troops under arms, while a strong party at Berlin favored the suppression of the revolt by Prussian troops. On the other hand, the new French government of Louis Philippe was ready to support Belgium by all means in its power. In England conservative principles of legitimacy and the strong Protestant feeling were adverse to the Belgians. Coupled to these was a strong suspicion, scarce allayed by French assurances, that the French government would take advantage of the movement to renew its hold on the Belgian provinces and the great port of Antwerp.[1]

On the other hand the weak resistance offered to the revolution by the Dutch had made a bad impression, and the Duke of Wellington, then Premier, had in private declared the retreat of Prince Frederick from Brussels to be a "devilish bad affair." So, when in October King William applied to England for aid in restoring him to the throne guaranteed to him in 1815, the Tory ministry had declined and advised him to accept the mediation of the great powers, Austria, France, Russia, Prussia, and England. Such an offer could not be refused, and a conference for the settlement of the future of Belgium met at London on November 5.

Meantime the national convention called by the Belgian provisional government had assembled at Brussels. The republican party, led by De Potter, which had led the revolutionary movement, had by this time lost strength through its violence, and a conservative element, headed by Baron Nothomb, the most eminent Belgian statesman, who declared, "as a monarchy you will be a power, as a republic an anarchy," was in the ascendant. A constitution based

---

[1] The contemporary British Tory view of the revolt of Belgium is well shown in the essay of Mr. Alison, the eminent historian.

on that of France was drawn up, and the proposal to exclude the house of Nassau was carried by a great majority. The question of the disposal of the crown was, however, a more difficult one. The majority of the assembly favored the Duke of Leuchtenberg, son of Eugene Beauharnais, but both France and England declared that they would never recognize so near a relative of the great Napoleon. To these representations the Belgians yielded under protest. Next, as a compliment to France, the assembly elected as king the Duc de Nemours, younger son of Louis Philippe. But France, though prepared to fight for the integrity of Belgium, was not ready to support a French prince at Brussels in the face of the certain hostility of the rest of Europe. Louis Philippe, declaring that he would not play the part of a Louis XIV. or a Napoleon, refused to permit his son to accept the crown. The Belgians, twice rebuffed, now determined to proceed to an election without regard to foreign advice. The election resulted in the choice of Prince Leopold of Saxe-Coburg, who had only shortly before refused the crown of Greece. The choice was a happy one. Leopold, as widower of the Princess Charlotte of England, was closely connected with the English royal family, and being, moreover, a Protestant, his election secured for the new state the warm support of the English government. Born in 1790, Prince Leopold had served in the Russian army and taken part in the German War of Liberation in 1813. His military capacity was known, and the Belgians were to find that they had also selected a man of rare political ability and wisdom. Nevertheless for a time it seemed as if the Belgians would have to seek again for a ruler of the new state.

While the Belgians had been seeking a prince the London conference had pursued the task of settling the future of the new state. The result was wholly favorable to the cause of Belgium. At the time of the calling of the conference the only power at all well-disposed to the Belgians was France. But with the accession to power in England of a liberal Whig ministry, headed by Earl Grey, the Belgians gained a new ally. The Duke of Wellington had looked with disfavor on the Brussels revolutionists, but the new ministry, more sympathetic with the liberal movement in Europe, soon abandoned the cause of King William and joined France in supporting the partition of the Netherlands. Thus abandoned by the very power he had appealed to for aid, King William could find little support elsewhere. The Polish Revolution, which broke out in Warsaw November 29, occupied the whole attention of the Emperor Nicholas, the warmest supporter of the Dutch, while the German rulers, however well-disposed, were too busy stamping out the revolutionary ideas which had spread out from France, to afford much help to the cause of legitimacy in the Netherlands. The cause of Belgium, vigorously supported by France and England, prevailed. On December 20 the powers agreed to recognize the independence of Belgium, which was to consist of those territories which had been added to the Netherlands by the treaty of 1815, with the exception of Luxemburg. At the instance of Von Bülow, the Prussian envoy, the important principle of the neutralization of the new state was proclaimed. Belgium was to assume about one-half of the heavy national debt of the Netherlands.

King William had consented to the London conference in full confidence that his authority over the revolted provinces would be confirmed. But the sudden reversal of England's attitude, and the lack of active support elsewhere, soon opened his eyes to the true posture of affairs. Bowing to the inevitable, he declared his willingness to accept the terms proposed at London. Not so the newly elected king of the Belgians. Leopold had already refused the crown of Greece because its boundaries were too narrow. In the same spirit he now declined to accept the proposed treaty unless both Luxemburg and Limburg were included in the new state. This resolute stand was entirely successful. The London conference, at the instance of Leopold's warm supporters, England and France, consented to reopen the whole question, and a new protocol was drawn up assigning to Belgium both Luxemburg and Limburg, neither of which had ever been a part of the Belgian provinces. His point thus gained, Leopold accepted the crown, and, entering Belgium by way of Calais, proceeded amid the greatest enthusiasm to Brussels, where he was solemnly crowned July 21, 1831. Scarcely were the coronation festivities over when the new king found himself face to face with an attack which threatened the very existence of the state.

To King William the new convention of London seemed but a new breach of faith on the part of his quondam allies, and he resolutely refused to accept any but the old terms. The Dutch people, too, hitherto remarkably indifferent to the course of events, were aroused to intense irritation at the triumphal progress of

Leopold through the Belgian cities. On August 4 war was declared, and 70,000 Dutch troops under the Prince of Orange crossed the border. The utter weakness of the new state before any vigorous assault instantly became patent. Antwerp fell into Dutch hands without resistance. A Belgian force, which was characterized by one of its own leaders as nothing but an armed mob, was seized with a panic at Hasselt and fled without striking a blow. King Leopold himself was defeated in an engagement near Louvain, and the way to Brussels lay open to the Dutch army. But again England and France intervened on behalf of their protégé. A French army 50,000 strong crossed the frontier, and at the demand of the two powers the Dutch army was forced to withdraw into Holland. Belgium was saved, but, as its own historians confess, without honor. Leopold long after declared that the very thought of the campaign caused him the most intense pain.[2] The presence of the French army in Belgium seemed scarcely less of a threat to the new state than the Dutch invasion. Already while the French minister, Casimir Perier, was proclaiming the integrity of Belgium in the Chamber of Deputies, that prince of intriguers, Talleyrand, was proposing in London the partition of the provinces between France, Prussia, and Holland. But the English ministry took alarm, and at their demand the French troops withdrew from the country after King William's consent to an armistice had been obtained.

The campaign of the Dutch had not been wholly in vain. It had shown the powers the confusion and weakness of the Belgian state, and it secured correspondingly better terms for Holland. On October 15 the London conference drew up the third and last instrument for the separation of Holland and Belgium, and declared it to be irrevocable. This final adjustment provided for the neutralization of Belgium, the return to Holland of the great fortress of Maastricht and the German parts of Luxemburg and Limburg, the assumption by Belgium of half the debt of the extinct kingdom of the Netherlands, and the opening of the Scheldt to Belgian commerce. The Belgians, however discontented, were prompt to accept this final agreement. All that remained was to gain the adhesion of King William, and this he steadily refused to give. Whatever else they might concede, national pride and commercial interest combined to make the Dutch most unwilling to give up the control of the Scheldt, held by them since the great

[2] "*Leopold I. et Leopold II.*," Th. Juste, Brussels, 1879.

War of Independence. Antwerp was still in their hands, and King William steadily refused to command its evacuation.

In the face of this stubborn attitude the powers were slow to act. Russia, Prussia, and Austria, though they had guaranteed the treaty, refused to coerce the King of Holland, and at the same time declined to enter into diplomatic relations with the Belgian state. England and France moved but slowly, and not till King

Leopold, now become son-in-law of the French monarch, had declared his intention of renewing the war did they decide to force King William to terms. On November 4, 1832, two years after the declaration of Belgian independence, an Anglo-French fleet blockaded the coast of Holland and a French army of 56,000 men under Marshal Gerard advanced to expel the Dutch garrison of Antwerp. The citadel of Antwerp, rebuilt at the order of Napoleon when he had dreamed of making Antwerp the great est naval port in Europe, was still regarded as one of the strongest on the Continent, and was defended by the able General Chasse, with 5000 men. On November 30 the besieging army arrived before the fortress and demanded its surrender. Though Chasse had been assured that he could receive no aid from Holland, he determined to resist, and promptly refused the summons. By mutual agreement the town of Antwerp was declared neutral, and accordingly the French opened their trenches on the further side of the citadel. On December 4 the siege guns were in position, and a tremendous fire was opened on the fortress. Under the bombardment the walls crumbled away, but the garrison held out till December 23, when General Chasse, finding his bomb-proofs demolished, consented to surrender. During the siege the French had opened over nine miles of trenches and fired 63,000 cannon-balls. The siege of Antwerp, which closed the drama of the Belgian revolution, was certainly one of the most peculiar of modern times. Fought by troops of two countries which were not at war with each other, who had no national animosity toward each other, it was conducted with as much humanity and respect for the safety of non-combatants as possible. In fact, it was conducted as a purely professional piece of work with as little loss of life as was possible. Compared with such a siege as that of Sebastopol, twenty years later, it seems indeed a very mimicry of war and thoroughly characteristic of the reign of the peace-loving bourgeoise king of France. With the fall of Antwerp the final stage in the establishment of Belgium as an independent state was reached. King William, however, still refused to accept the terms of peace, and the Belgians were in no hurry to end the trouble with Holland, for not till the treaty was signed would Belgium have to take up her share in the heavy Netherlands debt. Thus it happened that seven years passed before the formalities of the separation of the Netherlands were finally settled. By that time Belgium had proved by its progress under a wise and able ruler an unchallengeable right to a place among independent Europe states.

Chapter XXV

BELGIUM AS AN INDEPENDENT KINGDOM. 1830—

THE history of Belgium since 1830 is bound up in the history of the reigns of her two remarkable sovereigns, Leopold I. and Leopold II. The period has been marked with little stirring event, and Belgium's victories in the last half-century have fortunately been those of peace and progress. Though her kings have won for themselves by strength of sheer ability a prominent place in European affairs, the true interest in the life of the new Belgium has lain in its complex internal development, economic, social, and political. Freed at last from participation in the politics of Europe, protected by its international neutrality, and no longer bearing the unenviable distinction of being the "battle-ground of Europe," Belgium has once more assumed much the same position that the counties of Flanders and Brabant held five hundred years ago. It is once again the busiest and most thickly populated part of Europe, and, thanks to its swarming population, its vast industries, its commercial and colonial enterprise, is to-day one of the wealthiest and most prosperous of states. In it the political, economic, and social movements of the era have been most quickly developed and their tendencies most clearly expressed. Situated, as Belgium is, between three of the leading nations of Europe, and facing a fourth across a narrow strip of sea, the little state has with truth been called the microcosm of Europe where the new problems of a new age are being worked out to their solution.

The Belgians had built even better than they knew in the choice of Leopold of Saxe-Coburg as king. The rare tact and wisdom with which he guided the state during the first troubled years of his reign won for him the love of his subjects and the respect of all men. Lacking, perhaps, the intellectual powers and wideness of vision of a great statesman, his tact and the uprightness of his character made him the trusted advisor of many European sovereigns. His close relationship with several ruling families, and his vast experience, for he was in correspondence with all the great men of his time, from Alexander I. of Russia to Napoleon III., gave him a peculiarly influential position in European affairs out of all proportion to the importance of the state which he governed. The trusted counselor and friend of his niece, Queen Victoria, England owes much of the glory of her reign to the wisdom and common sense of the Belgian king. In truth, Leopold's proud titles of the Nestor and the Peacemaker of Europe were no idle ones. Nor was his influence confined to Europe alone. The United States called on him to arbitrate in a dispute with Spain and sought his advice at the time of the Civil War. In 1863 Mr. Seward, the Secretary of State, wrote to the American minister at Brussels: "The king will see that it is not in the power of the slaveholders to dictate conditions, but it is to their interest to propose a compromise. I am authorized by the President to submit this idea to the King of the Belgians. In performing this duty I cannot omit adding that the king by his generous and disinterested attitude toward the United States has acquired the right to give advice to our government, and his advice has always been received with respectful affection and recognizance." Leopold was one of the first European sovereigns to fully appreciate the true position of a constitutional ruler—a delicate one at any time. As King of Belgium, whose independence he had been the first to make secure, he, with the aid of such worthy assistants as Gerlache, Nothomb, and Van der Werder, raised the little kingdom to the rank of a model state.

The first years of the king's reign were eventful only in the rapid strides toward prosperity which the new kingdom was making. In the face of the ever-threatening attitude of Holland, with whom no peace had yet been made, the country remained a unit, undisturbed by the factions of political parties. To be sure, a small Orangist faction still remained, but finally disappeared when the birth of an heir to the throne in 1835 consolidated the succession of the dynasty. In the rapid development of the commerce and industries of Belgium the state took a prominent part. The first railroad in Europe was opened in 1834 by King Leopold in person.

In 1839 the final act of the Belgian revolution was consummated. King William, of Holland, after seven years of obduracy, now announced his readiness to conclude peace with Belgium on the terms provided for by the London Conference.

Though the position of Belgium had for the past few years been a somewhat anomalous one, for some of the powers still declined to regard her as an independent state, nevertheless the Belgians viewed the conclusion of a general peace with little favor. To them it meant the surrender to Holland of the provinces of Luxemburg and Limburg, which now seemed to be integral parts of the state. So it happened that the demand for the surrender of these provinces provoked the greatest excitement and indignation. The legislature passed a vote urging the king to preserve the integrity of the country at all costs, and the army was placed on a war footing. Leopold himself was not averse to a new campaign which would consolidate the country and wipe out the still rankling disgrace of 1831. But in the face of the determined attitude of both France and England, who insisted on a rigid adherence to treaty obligations, he saw that resistance was hopeless, and reluctantly consented to the surrender of the disputed provinces to Holland. The Belgian revolution had owed much of its success to the coalition between the liberal and clerical elements of the population, which had remained hitherto unbroken. Now the signature of the treaty of peace removed the last threat to national independence, and the revival of political parties, Liberals and Clericals, inevitably began. It was, perhaps, fortunate for Belgium that a strong liberal government was in power at the time, when, in 1848, the storms of revolution again swept Europe. The rising of 1830 in France had provoked a similar one in Belgium. But the republican movement of 1848 met with but little sympathy in Belgium, where loyalty to the sovereign had become a most profound feeling. Almost alone in Europe, Belgium remained calm during the convulsions which shook the strongest thrones to their foundations. A few hundred adventurers, principally republicans from Paris, sought to raise the standard of revolt near Quivrain, but were soon surrounded by troops and bands of armed peasants and forced to surrender. This fiasco was only the signal for an outburst of loyalty to the king which was certainly a rare spectacle in Europe at that time.

The French Revolution of 1848 had one result, however, which threatened to have a vital influence in the future of Belgium. The dethroned house of Orleans had been the chief friend and support of the Belgian kingdom, and as long as Leopold's father-in-law, Louis Philippe, reigned Belgium had nothing to dread from French ambitions. With the establishment of a militant republic in France, and with the accession to power of Louis Napoleon, the nephew of the great conqueror, the situation was radically changed. Louis Napoleon had come to revive the old traditions of the first empire, of which Belgium had been a province, and he openly declared his lifework to be the restoration of France to her old preëminence in Europe. Such a political programme could not but seem a menace to Belgian independence, and for twenty years Belgian statesmen were haunted by the specter of a possible French invasion. The violent attacks on the French emperor in the virulent Brussels press, edited by political refugees and subject to little restraint, offered a convenient pretext for war. Indeed, Napoleon seems to have contemplated the conquest of Belgium as early as 1853, but abandoned the plan on being convinced that all Europe would resist such an outrage. King Leopold succeeded in establishing personally friendly relations with Napoleon, while on the other side, a meeting at Liege between the kings of Belgium and Holland, resulted in a healing of the wide breach between the two neighbors.

The Belgians were indirectly interested in the ill-fated Mexican expedition of Louis Napoleon, for the king's daughter, Charlotte, was the wife of the Archduke Maximilian, on whom the Mexican crown had been conferred by Napoleon. Knowledge of the tragic close of the enterprise, with the capture and execution of Maximilian by the Mexicans, and the subsequent insanity of his wife, was spared to King Leopold, who had feared its failure from the first. The king died in 1865, after a long and prosperous reign of thirty-four years. Few rulers have deserved as justly as he the title of the "Father of his People," affectionately conferred on him by the Belgians.

Leopold II., the next king of Belgium, ascended the throne at a time when a series of most dramatic events was impending, destined to change the map of Europe. The first five years of his reign witnessed the break-up of the old Germanic confederation, the establishment of two new European powers, the German empire and a united Italy, and the sudden destruction of the second French empire. The period was a most critical one for Belgium. Amid the startling events which were rapidly changing the face of Europe, the smaller continental states could not but tremble for their own existence.

The sudden and unexpected success of Prussia over Austria in 1866, and the consequent aggrandizement of the victors by the annexation of most of the small states of northern Germany, led Napoleon III. to demand some territorial compensation for France as a reward of his neutrality. But in Count Bismarck, the Prussian minister, who was fast becoming the dominant political figure in Europe, Napoleon met a man more than his match in the wiles of diplomacy. Bismarck had no intention of permitting the enlargement of the French empire, in which he saw the one great opponent to German unity; but he was willing for the time to amuse Napoleon with empty negotiations. At first the French emperor demanded the cession of the left bank of the Rhine as far as the city of Mainz, but this was met by the declaration that Prussia could not consent to the alienation of German ground. A new plan was now proposed. France and Prussia were to enter into a secret alliance, offensive as well as defensive. Prussia was to have a free hand in Germany, while France was to annex the little duchy of Luxemburg, and at the proper moment was to be permitted to seize upon the kingdom of Belgium itself. In the course of the discussion of this nefarious plan the French ambassadors fell blindly into a trap neatly set by Count Bismarck. At the Prussian minister's suggestion he was indiscreet enough to draw up in his own hand the terms of the proposed treaty, and to permit Bismarck to take possession of the paper. Armed with this damning bit of evidence as to French ambition, Bismarck saw no further advantage in continuing the negotiations. Secure in the support of Russia, which demanded nothing, Bismarck felt no further need of conciliating France, and the negotiations were brought to an abrupt close. But the evidence of French designs on a neutral and friendly state was retained by the Prussian minister, to be made effective use of at the proper moment.

Napoleon persevered, notwithstanding his rebuff from Prussia, and did not abandon his hopes of territorial expansion. Direct negotiations with Holland for the purchase of Luxemburg failed, thanks again to Prussian interference, and the emperor turned once more to his long-cherished scheme of the conquest of Belgium. An attempt to gain control for France of the Luxemburg railroad as an opening wedge also failed, through the vigilance of the Belgian government. But the proposed conquest of Belgium continued to be a subject of common talk in Parisian official circles, and Marshal

Niel, the French chief of engineers, had already made an official inspection of the frontiers. The outbreak of the Franco-Prussian war finally put an end to these threats against Belgian independence. On the eve of the war Napoleon, in a letter to King Leopold, declared his intention of respecting the neutrality of Belgium. A few days later the London *Times* published the text of the proposed treaty of 1866, which had been furnished by Prince Bismarck. This revelation, coming as sudden and unexpected as a bolt out of a clear sky, caused the most tremendous sensation, especially in England and Belgium. In Belgium the army was promptly placed on a war footing. In England the government demanded of Parliament a supplementary credit and an addition of 20,000 men to the forces. Nor was the British government content with these preparations. A treaty was drawn up, which was promptly signed by both France and Prussia, providing that Great Britain should declare war on the first of the belligerents who should violate Belgian territory. In Belgium the result of the disclosure was to throw public opinion to the side of Germany, though French sympathizers were numerous and active, especially in the journals.

As the tide of war rolled toward the Belgian frontier the anxiety became intense, and the whole Belgian army was drawn up on the frontier. But no serious results followed. After the fall of Sedan several thousand French troops fled across the frontier, but peacefully laid down their arms, according to convention, and remained interned in Belgium during the rest of the war.

Since the war of 1870 Belgium has been free from participation in European politics, and her history has been a quiet one. Internally the reign of Leopold II. has been signalized by steady progress in industry and wealth, and less happily by a marked development of a more and more bitter party spirit. The latter years of Leopold I. had seen the revival of the old Liberal and Clerical parties, the former recruited from the middle classes in the towns, the latter from the aristocracy and the Flemish peasantry. With the tremendous industrial development of the country, and the consequent rise of problems of capital and labor, a new party, the Socialist, made its appearance, drawing its strength from the mining regions of the east.

Hitherto the chief questions which had agitated the country had been ones of education and the relations of church to state.

But in 1886 the country was shocked with the news of a great Socialist rising in the mining regions on the anniversary of the establishment of the Commune in Paris. Troops were immediately dispatched to the scene of the disturbance, martial law proclaimed, and after sharp fighting the rising was put down. But the attention of the nation had been called to the state of the vast class of industrial workers, hitherto neglected, and a movement for better economic conditions and universal suffrage was set on foot. A long parliamentary struggle between the Radicals and Conservatives reached a crisis in 1893, when a universal suffrage bill passed the Chamber of Deputies, but was rejected in the upper house. In reply the labor party called for a political strike, and fifty thousand artisans left their work in the various cities. The situation was a critical one, and riots had already broken out when a compromise measure was passed, granting universal suffrage, with added votes for property qualifications. Since then the Socialist-Labor party has modified its views as it has grown in power, and has approached the more radical wing of the Liberal party in a common opposition to clericalism.

The elections of May 29, 1906, showed a decided increase in the Liberal vote, as a result of aroused public interest. The meeting of the Belgium and Dutch commissioners at Brussels, on March 12, 1907, was a long step forward in Belgium history, as it evidenced a tendency of the country to meet the Netherlands in an economical alliance. The Venezuelan question agitated Belgium, as it did a number of other countries interested there, until Belgium was notified on August 6, 1907, that claims of its creditors would be paid according to the decision of The Hague tribunal. However, the matter of most moment before the Belgium people during 1907 and part of 1908, was a betterment of the condition of the Congo Free State, and its annexation. Matters were set in motion on August 23, 1907, by the appointment by the Belgium government and the Congo Free State, of a committee to draw up a treaty for the annexation of the latter. After prolonged discussion a treaty was finally drawn up, which provided that King Leopold should retain his rights during his lifetime. Debating on this treaty began April 15, 1908, in the Belgium Parliament, and was continued until August 20, 1908, when it was passed by a vote of eighty-three to fifty-five. On August 27th, the Senate began its debating on it, finally passing it on September 9th, and endorsing the action of the

Chamber of Deputies with regard to it. Popular opinion was deferred to, when, on March 9, 1909, Lieutenant Arnold was sentenced to twelve years' imprisonment for his atrocities in the Congo. The International Conference of Maritime Law which convened at Brussels, passed some very admirable resolutions regarding matters relating to salvage and other maritime questions, during September, 1909; and at about the same time the International Peace Bureau of that city, suggested that a general fund be established upon which draft could be made in time of calamity. King Leopold, realizing his unpopularity in the Congo, sought to rehabilitate himself by promising, on October 28, 1909, to give a large sum of money to fight disease there. The high Belgium officials also felt the burden of the universal criticism of Belgium rule in the Congo, and on December 5th, registered their protest against such charges. The death of King Leopold on December 17, 1909, was followed by some confusion owing to the reports being circulated of a deathbed marriage of the late king, but on December 21st, Albert I. ascended the throne, his first official act being promising reform in the Congo. He showed no disposition to change his cabinet, requesting Premier Scollaert and the other ministers to retain their portfolios. The principal question before the Belgium government, in the early part of 1910, was the carrying out of the promises made by Albert I, upon his succession, with regard to the Congo, the mismanagement of which has so long been a blot upon Belgium history.

The present political conditions in Belgium are peculiarly interesting, for, as has been said, the country presents a picture of European problems on a small scale and at an advanced stage. The old Liberal party, which won the struggle for independence and long held the power in the state, has disintegrated before the rise of Socialism, and more extreme parties have taken its place. On the one hand is the conservative Clerical party, closely allied to the Vatican and largely recruited from the peasants, led to-day, as for centuries, by their parish priests. At the other end of the scale is the Radical or Socialist party, the champion of the vast army of industrial labor, which comprises almost half the population of the country. The future of Belgium seems to lie between these two parties, and the struggle between such extreme exemplifications of the tendencies of the day cannot fail to appeal to the interest of all thoughtful citizens.

Hist. Nat. XIII-21

The external relations of Belgium have of late centered about her commercial and colonial expansion, with the king himself as the leading figure. Leopold II. was essentially a business man of rare ability, who, if placed as a private citizen in America, would undoubtedly have ranked as one of its "captains of industry." The greatest traveler among the sovereigns of Europe, he had before his accession to the throne visited the countries of North Africa, as well as Syria and the Far East. His active spirit chafed against the narrow limits of his little state, and from the first he was an advocate of colonial expansion. The journeys of Livingstone and Stanley centered the king's interest in Africa, and he was quick to see the great commercial possibilities of the vast central regions of the Dark Continent. After an exhaustive study of conditions, the king called, in 1876, an international conference at Brussels, composed of geographers, travelers, and scientists. To this distinguished body Leopold proposed the establishment of an international state in the Congo valley for the purpose of scientific explorations, the suppression of the slave trade, and the opening of the region to the world's commerce. The plan met with ready approval, and the king was chosen president of the international committee which was to administer the new state. In 1884-1885 the Berlin Congress, which met to settle the partition of Africa among the powers, placed the Congo Free State under the complete control of King Leopold, though the powers and functions of the state were carefully defined, and Belgium reserved the right to annex the territory at some future time. Under the able direction of Leopold systematic explorations were carried on, the Congo River was opened by a line of steamboats, the Arab slave trade, the curse of Africa, was broken up, and an extensive trade established. But though the state has been commercially a success, serious accusations, apparently well founded, have of late been made against the Belgium administration. The reported establishment of a system of tribute and forced labor, which has reduced the natives to practical bondage, and the horrible atrocities committed by the native soldiery under white commanders, have settled a dark stain on the administration of the Congo Free State which has not yet been removed, although King Albert has promised extensive reforms.

Belgium has no reason to be ashamed of its position to-day in the ranks of nations. Possessed of the richest coal and iron mines in Europe, with the most thickly populated territory of any nation, with the possible exception of China, Belgium has unrivalled facilities for industrial enterprise, and has employed them well. Commercially the little state ranks sixth among the nations, with a foreign trade greater than that of the vast Russian empire. The port of Antwerp, once the busiest in Europe, has again, after the lapse of three centuries, resumed its importance, and ranks with Hamburg and Marseilles among the greatest in Europe. Nor has it been in material prosperity alone that Belgium has progressed. The rise of a new Belgian school of literature, with Verhaeren and Maeterlinck among its chief exponents, and the revival of Flemish as a national language, opposed to the prevailing French, tend to disprove the charge so often made that Belgium has no national individuality of its own. The growth of a spirit of patriotism, so carefully fostered by Leopold I., and the tendency toward the establishment of a distinct national identity, are among the most cheering signs for the future maintenance of Belgium as an independent state.

All through the year 1911 the subject of electoral reform was violently debated in the Belgian Chamber of Representatives. Proportional representation has been in force during the past ten years, but in communal elections the system of absolute majorities is still in force, as well as the system of plural votes. A Parliamentary Commission was appointed which brought out a measure to reform the communal and provincial elections and put them on the same basis as the Parliamentary elections.

While these measures were before Parliament the government introduced a bill to subsidize the clerical schools, placing them on the same financial basis as the public schools. This measure of the Clerical Party was bitterly opposed by the Liberal and Socialist Parties, resulting in a deadlock, during which time no budget was passed. The general elections were held in June, 1912, and resulted in a victory for the Clerical Party, who gained a majority of 16 over the opposition coalition. This clerical victory was immediately followed by rioting all over the country. Many persons were killed, and the militia were finally called out to restore order. The soldiers, however, in many instances, made common cause with the rioters. The leaders of the opposition claimed that the clerical victory was entirely due to fraud and the system of plural voting. Every citizen of Belgium, over twenty-five years, has one vote. Heads of families, who are over thirty-five years of age and pay a certain house tax, have an additional vote. Two supplementary votes can be gained by possessing certain scholastic qualifications. The Socialists claim that this greatly strengthens the Conservative or Clerical forces at the expense of the mass of the people.

Women voted in the last election in great numbers. In Brussels alone it is claimed that fully a third of the votes cast were by women. Even the opposition press stated that the new women electors have disarmed all critics.

Race discord in the Walloon provinces brought out many incipient conflicts. Here French is the common language, and many of the inhabitants would favor annexation to France. The Flemish minority, however, are loyal to the Belgian government.

The beginning of 1913 saw one of the greatest strikes in the history of the world. In April over a million workmen went on a strike as a protest against the refusal of the government to introduce a franchise bill embodying equal manhood suffrage. The Belgian workman is contented and comparatively well paid, and this strike was in no sense a labor demonstration but a political weapon used for a political purpose.

The strike was ended on April 24, 1913, by a compromise, the government agreeing to appoint a commission which should draft changes in the franchise law to do away with plural voting in both provincial and communal elections.

On May 29 the government passed the new revised bill regulating military service. By its terms compulsory service was made general. This service extends over fifteen months, and all male members of a family were compelled to join the colors instead of one son in each family. Under the new law the peace strength of the army was increased to 55,000 men, and the war strength to 340,000 men. The first cost of the addition to the nation's armed forces was estimated at $57,000,000. The annual increase of the army budget was $9,000,000, which will be paid by the institution of new taxes on the income from corporation securities and foreign bonds, automobiles, motion-picture films, and spirits.

One of the events of the year 1913 was the successful exhibition which opened in Ghent in April, 1913. In 1914 the election in May reduced the majority of the de Broqueville government from 16 to 12. The strength of the various parties being as follows: Catholics 99, Liberals 45, Socialists 40, and 2 Democrats.

When the Balkan crisis came to an open rupture between Austria, Germany, and Russia in July, 1914, the position of Belgium became critical. When mobilization of the troops of the great European nations became general in July, Great Britain instructed her ambassadors at Berlin and Paris to ascertain whether in the event of hostilities the Belgian neutrality could be respected. France replied at once that the French government were resolved to respect the neutrality of Belgium, and that only in the event of some other power first breaking that neutrality France for her own protection might be forced to act otherwise.

On August 2, 1914, Germany made overtures to Belgium to allow the passage of German troops through Belgian territory, claiming that Germany had reliable information that the French forces were about to march on the Meuse by way of Ghent and Namur and that thus Germany was subject to attack through Belgium.

The terms of the German demand upon Belgium were as follows:

1. Germany does not contemplate any act of hostility against Belgium. If Belgium consents in the war about to commence to take up an attitude of friendly neutrality toward Germany, the German government on its part undertakes on the declaration of peace to guarantee the kingdom and its possessions in their whole extent.

2. Germany undertakes under the condition laid down to evacuate Belgian territory as soon as peace is concluded.

3. If Belgium preserves a friendly attitude, Germany is prepared, in agreement with the authorities of the Belgian government, to buy against cash all that is required by her troops and to give indemnity for the damages caused in Belgium.

4. If Belgium behaves in a hostile manner toward the German troops and in particular raises difficulties against their advance by the opposition of the fortifications of the Meuse or by destroying roads, railways, tunnels, or other engineering works, Germany will be compelled to consider Belgium as an enemy.

The German government granted Belgium a time limit of twelve hours in which to accede to her demands. The Belgian government promptly refused the German demands, cited the treaties made with France and Germany which established the independence of Belgium and guaranteed her neutrality.

Germany at once, on August 4, 1914, invaded Belgian territory and thereby forced Belgium to become a participant in the great war. Germany's violation of Belgium's neutrality was based, so stated the German Chancellor, on considerations of national safety. Without doubt Germany considered it absolutely vital to throw her troops through Belgian territory with rapidity if she hoped to strike the first blow on her western front.

The German Foreign Secretary, Herr von Jagow, thus gives the justification of the German violation of Belgian neutrality. "Germany had consequently to disregard Belgian neutrality, it being for her a question of life or death to prevent French advances." Belgium at once appealed to Great Britain, France, and Russia, and began a stubborn defense, desperately fighting to stay the great German army of invasion.

Chapter XXVI

THE GERMAN INVASION OF BELGIUM. 1914.

THE German invasion of Belgium was destined to have far-reaching and long-lasting effects. It not only shocked the entire civilized world, but created almost universal distrust of German motives, and the subsequent horrors that followed occupation united the opinion of Christendom that a great wrong had been done by a course which the Kaiser's spokesmen vainly attempted to explain away.

The invasion of a weak state by a powerful empire violating a solemn pledge was not an act of self-defense but part of a plan to conquer France, a breach of international morality that found few to condone it outside of Germany and her allies. This act of violence was to handicap the Germans throughout the war, and remains an evil memory that will not be effaced for many years from the minds of men.

It was the first and most serious of the blunders made by Germany, which alienated the sympathy of the greater part of the civilized world, which united to censure a nation which, preaching a doctrine that force was the sole consideration, was recognized as a general danger. Furthermore, the British Empire, which might or might not enter the war as a member of the Triple Entente and an ally of France and Russia, had now the additional obligation of supporting the original treaty guaranteeing the neutrality of Belgium.

Did Belgium by halting the advance of the German armies save Europe? The claim has been made and merits consideration. The powerful opposition the invaders encountered disarranged their carefully laid plans, enabling the French to prepare, and the British Expeditionary Force to link up with her Ally. Weeks were to pass before the German armies could get within reach of the French forces, instead of the few days the German Military authorities had counted on. It has since been recognized that if the Germans had respected Belgian neutrality and invaded France their progress would have been more rapid, and they would have escaped the world-wide opprobrium that greeted their assault on a weak nation, and their plans might have succeeded.

Germany declared war on Belgium on August 4, 1914. The beginning of hostilities was followed by a hurried mobilization of Belgian forces. The first movement was the concentration of about 20,000 men along the River Dyle to cover an advance on Brussels and Antwerp. The immediate task before General Leman, commanding the Army of Liége, was to gain time. Until the northern forts were silenced, no progress could be made by rail to the Belgian plain.

The German Military command did not rank the Belgians at first as a formidable foe, and their striking force of three divisions was inadequately equipped with siege artillery, but they believed they were strong enough to break through the fortress barriers, occupy Liége and hold the railway running west.

Liége is built on both sides of the main stream of the Meuse and was without defenses itself. The approaches to the city were defended by a circle of six main forts of the pentagonal type, and six lesser forts triangular in shape. The average distance of each fort from the city was about four miles. Theoretically the forts formed a double line of defenses so that if one should be silenced the enemy could be held up by neighboring forts on the left and right. The greatest distance between any two forts was 7,000 yards, and the average something less than 4,000. The forts built by the distinguished engineer Henri Brialmont were largely underground structures presenting externally a low mound surrounded by a deep ditch. The walls and roof of the forts were of masonry and concrete covered with earth, broken at the top by circular pits in which the gun-turrets slid up and down. The interior of these forts was hollowed out into passages and rooms capable of sheltering garrisons of not more than a hundred men.

In the afternoon of August 4, 1914, Belgian scouts encountered advance guards of von Emmich's forces. The Germans moved down the Ourthe and the Vesdre attacking the forts of Boncelles, Embourg, Chaudfontaine and Fléron with field artillery, using high explosive shells. The German heavy siege guns had not arrived, but the lighter guns worked effectively, their shells exploding on the ramparts of the forts wrought considerable damage. The forts replied to this bombardment, but without much result, as owing to the broken country it was easy for the Germans to conceal gun positions. The artillery duel continued during the night and early in the morning German infantry in dense formation attacked, but after four hours' fighting were forced to retire.

Early on this date the fort of Fléron was silenced, German shells having smashed the machinery of the turrets. The loss of this stronghold was serious for the Belgians, as it gave the railway line to the invaders. The nearest forts of Evegnée and Chaudfontaine were at too great a distance from each other to protect the pass and the Belgians did not have the men to maintain a defensive line between the forts.

On August 6, 1914, the heavy German siege guns had been brought into the fighting zone and threw great shells, smashing the heavy concrete walls of the forts, some twelve feet thick, as readily as if made of glass. First Chaudfontaine, then Evegnée and Barchon fell, and German patrols entered the city of Liége. The ineffectiveness of the Belgian forts was a blow to the Allies.

General Leman hastened to withdraw his troops before the city was invested, believing that they could be more usefully employed with the army in the field. So hurried was the retreat of the Belgians that only one bridge was destroyed while twelve others were left intact. But the withdrawal was effected with small loss and the troops joined the Belgian concentration on the River Dyle. General Leman remained to await the progress of events in the northern forts which overlooked the plateau and commanded the railway lines to France. Both Germans and Belgians had lost heavily, but the casualties among the invaders were far the greater. The stout-hearted defenders of the little kingdom had fought against overwhelming odds and gained their main purpose, which was to delay the advance.

The first German infantry entered Liége on August 7, 1914. They numbered about 10,000, the bulk of von Emmich's forces having joined a larger concentration on the right bank of the Meuse above and below the city.

The capture of Liége and the silencing of forts Evegnée, Chaudfontaine and Barchon were operations of importance, but not of great strategic value. The northern forts still held out, and as long as they continued in fighting condition, the Germans could not advance. Belgian resistance during these days had served to convince the invaders that they had underestimated the fighting powers of their foe.

The Belgian army under General Selliers de Moranville, numbering about 100,000 men, was in position along the line of the River Dyle, detachments of cavalry being pushed forward to hamper the German advance.

On August 12, 1914, German cavalry encountered a Belgian Cavalry division and a mixed brigade of about 10,000 which had barricaded the river bridges at the village of Hallen. The Germans tried to rush the bridges, but were driven back and completely routed when the Belgian cavalry charged. A sharp fight followed among the cornfields, the Germans losing heavily. They succeeded in carrying off their wounded and were not pursued. On the same day a German column attempted to force the bridge over the Velpe at Cortenaecken, but the Belgians after a four hours' fight beat them off. Desultory fighting continued on the following day, the Belgians defeating an attack made by several thousand German cavalry on the town of Tirlemont. At Engheezee on the left German cavalry bivouacking in the village were surprised by a sortie of Belgian cavalry from Namur, and driven out of the place with the loss of machine guns, and leaving many dead on the field.

These small successes gave the Belgians overconfidence in their ability to conquer the invaders. They had no knowledge that the great armies of von Kluck and von Buelow were already on Belgian soil and sweeping on, an irresistible flood of field-grey fighting men, abundantly supplied with guns, and howitzers of 42 centimetres capable of reducing a twelve foot wall of concrete to powder.

The Germans began to shell the fortress of Embourg to the north of Liége on August 13, 1914. Boncelles refusing the summons to surrender was bombarded for twenty-four hours and only after the cupolas and concrete chambers were smashed and the structure a mass of smoking ruins was a white flag displayed. Fort Loncin was shattered in a like manner by the heavy guns, and finally the explosion of the magazine blew up what remained of the ruins. Few defenders were found alive within the broken walls. General Leman, the Belgian commander, was discovered unconscious under heavy fallen beams. But the stout resistance offered by the little garrison of Fort Loncin was not without results. The German advance had been held up for a week.

A few days later von Kluck's main force got in touch with the Belgian right at Wavre and attempted an enveloping movement which failed, and for the time the German advance here was checked. On the following day the German right and centre, making a hurried advance, overran Tirlemont and forced the inhabitants of the villages along the Gethe to flee towards Brussels. Nothing could stay the German drive now, and the Belgians defending the line of the Dyle were swept away, and a general retreat was made down the river to the shelter of the Antwerp forts, where King Albert's Government was already established.

At first there was some intention of defending Brussels, but wiser counsels prevailed, as it became certain that resistance would result in the destruction of that beautiful city. The Burgomaster, M. Max, having been empowered to arrange for a peaceful occupation, the Civic Guard was disarmed. Early in the afternoon of August 20, 1914, the German troops to the number of about 40,000, commanded by General Sixtus von Arnim, entered the city with flags flying and every regimental band playing German national airs. One of the first acts of the German commander was to impose on the city a war indemnity of $40,000,000.

The bulk of the German armies never came near the Belgian capital. A number of army corps moved along the north bank of the Meuse toward Namur, and south of the river through the woods of the Ardennes other great bodies of German troops were pushing toward the Allied front.

While the interest of the moment was centred on Brussels and Antwerp it was the fate of Namur on which the hopes of the Allies depended. To understand the situation and the importance of Namur it is necessary to describe the disposition of the French and British troops.

The British Army, consisting of two army corps and a cavalry division, commanded by Field Marshal Sir John French, did not get into position until the evening of August 21, 1914. General Joffre was in supreme command of the Allied forces. The French armies were disposed as follows, beginning at Verdun: The 3rd Army, under General Ruffey, stretched from Montmédy by Sedan to Rocroi, facing the advance of the German Crown Prince from Neufchateau. General de Langle de Cary and the 4th Army held the valley of the Central Meuse to the north. The 5th Army, under General Lanrezac, lay in the angle of the Sambre and crossed the river to a point near Charleroi. To the west were the British, forming the left wing of the Allied front. General Sordet commanded three cavalry corps in reserve back of Maubeuge, and at Arras were two Reserve divisions under General d'Amade.

This front involved a sharp salient, and was exposed to flank attacks. Namur was the key to the situation, for if Namur fell the French could not hold their position; they would be penned in an angle between the Sambre and the Meuse.

The city of Namur was surrounded by four forts and five fortins mounting 350 guns, at a distance of from two and a half to five miles. Namur was held by a Belgian army of 26,000 under General Michel.

The Germans began the bombardment of the forts on August 20, 1914. They were out of range of the Belgian guns and there was no means of replying. After whole regiments had been annihilated the Belgian infantry withdrew from the trenches and the Germans entered the ring of forts. In the meantime the forts of Marchovelette and Maizeret had fallen. Andoy, Dave and St. Heribert were silenced by August 21. The arrival of 5,000 French Turcos did not change the situation. General Michel, to save his forces for the field army, withdrew them by the western route, still open. In the angle of the river, French and Belgians met heavy defeat, escaping as best they could. The Germans entered Namur on August 23. The last stand of the Belgians was made in the trenches between Fort Suarlée and Emines. The hopeless resistance was maintained until August 25, when they retreated to the woods on the Sambre, where, being surrounded, they surrendered on August 26. The last of the forts had been blown up. Namur, deemed impregnable, had fallen, a terrible blow to the Allies.

Belgium was now at the mercy of the invaders, though still holding a portion of West Flanders, Antwerp, Ostend, and the coast. General de Moranville, whose defeated but unbroken army had found shelter under the forts of Antwerp, marched south on August 24, 1914, and drove the Germans out of Malines. The capture of the town was of considerable strategic importance for it commanded the shortest railway communication between Germany and West Flanders. At the time the German forces were active in northwestern Belgium and the coast. Von Boehm's Corps was marching on Bruges and Ghent with the purpose of later reinforcing the army of von Kluck. Belgian Civic Guards at Ostend had defeated an attack by Uhlans and the town was now occupied by British marines, who might be the advance guard of a new British army. The situation alarmed the German Command, fearing that the communications with their great armies would be broken. The effect of the Belgian offensive was the return eastward of von Boehm's corps, and von Kluck was thus deprived of reinforcements.

The Germans had reason to fear that their communications were in danger. In the three weeks following, the fighting in Belgium was almost continuous, principally in a triangle of territory of which Antwerp was the top and Termonde to Aerschot the base. Had the British been able to land two divisions at Ostend at this time the German occupation of Belgium would have been gravely menaced. As it was, the Belgians almost succeeded in cutting the communications of the German armies with Brussels. They captured Alost and then besieged Cortenberg on the railway between Louvain and the capital. Von Boehm's corps, hurriedly recalled, had been reinforced by a naval division and reserve regiments, bringing the German strength up to at least 250,000. The Belgians were outnumbered more than two to one, and the enemy had an overwhelming superiority in guns. A great battle was staged in the middle of September, 1914, and continued steadily for four days. The hardest fighting took place on the line of the Malines-Louvain railway, which the invaders finally carried. This broke the Belgian defense and a retreat was in order upon Antwerp.

The Belgians were defeated, but they had won imperishable fame by their valorous resistance in defending their native soil against the invaders—the most perfect military organization in Europe. The German armies of occupation while not less courageous in battle earned an unenviable renown for the reign of terror they established in many towns and cities. The outrages committed upon helpless civilians by the German troops are too firmly established by the evidence of neutral observers and by the Germans themselves to be passed over as common happenings incident to warfare even in a historical record of this character. It was a part of the German military plan, and approved by many of her principal military writers, that terrorizing the inhabitants of an invaded country would create in the hearts of the people a longing for speedy peace. The Germans in Belgium in too many instances followed this course, and even defended it.

Of individual outrages this is not the place to speak, but mention must be made of the vandalism which resulted in the destruction of beautiful Belgian cities. The fate of Louvain will not soon fade from the minds of men. Here was one of the chief university towns of the kingdom, its Gothic town hall ranking among the architectural glories of Europe. The library of Louvain was stored with rare books and manuscripts, many unique and irreplaceable. The Church of St. Peter contained art treasures of painting and carving of priceless value. There were many other splendid examples of Flemish Renaissance dating back to the fifteenth century.

Following German occupation and after the inhabitants, including the Civic Guard, had been disarmed there was an outburst of rifle fire in one section of the town and several Germans were struck. The Belgians asserted that a detachment of Germans retiring from Malines had, through error, fired upon their fellow soldiers. The German Command declared that it was the result of a plot instigated by the Belgian Government. The Belgian version is trustworthy because the population of the town had been disarmed and all rifles had been confiscated, while abundant proofs have been supplied that many of the German garrison were intoxicated. Major von Manteuffel, the German commander, then ordered the destruction of the city, and if the orders were not entirely consummated it was not because his soldiers showed any reluctance to perform the task. The troops all carried for such purposes small incendiary disks and fagots soaked in chemicals which were flung through broken windows of the houses after they had been systematically looted. Louvain was soon in flames. The university and the splendid library were among the first to be reduced to smoking ruins, and of St. Peter's church and other beautiful buildings only a few tottering walls were left standing.

The Belgians had driven the Germans out of Malines, but could not hold it, and the invaders wreaked vengeance on the splendid town by bombarding it after they had withdrawn. The Cathedral of St. Rombaut, an almost unique specimen of thirteenth century architecture, was riddled with shells, its tower shattered to pieces. On three successive occasions Malines was bombarded after the inhabitants had fled. The town was now aflame in a number of places and for days the fire raged, reducing many fine structures of Flemish architecture to blackened heaps of stone. Termonde, another town of historic importance, with its majestic Cathedral of Notre Dame, containing paintings by Van Dyck and Rubens, a Hotel de Ville of surpassing architectural beauty, was destroyed by the Germans because the fine levied was not at once forthcoming. Here the ruin was complete, the destructive work being carried out systematically. German soldiers with oil-carts and hose went through the streets spraying the houses, which were then set on fire.

Hundreds of small villages were also plundered and reduced to ashes. Their destruction served no military purpose save to inspire terror in the conquered, and make the invaders' task easier. Whether a town was bombarded or burned the Germans plundered with true Teutonic thoroughness, and what they could not carry away was generally destroyed, or flung into the streets.

The German idea, to which they clung throughout the war, that terrorizing civilians in occupied territory would hasten peace, had quite the contrary result in Belgium and elsewhere. When the Belgians heard from the lips of panic-stricken refugees of the tragic happenings in their towns and cities, at once the gulf that had long divided Walloon and Fleming, Catholic and Socialist, disappeared and all united in brotherhood of arms.

On September 28, 1914, the Germans, having crushed Belgian opposition, began to bombard the southern forts of Antwerp. Their big guns shattered the cupolas and concrete works as easily as those at Liége had been destroyed. Fort Wavre was silenced on the second day of the bombardment, when the magazine blew up. Shells broke the embankment of the great Antwerp reservoir and infantry trenches around the fort were flooded, driving out the troops and submerging the guns. All the southern forts were silenced or destroyed by October 1, 1914. Termonde was evacuated by the Belgians, who were forced across the Scheldt. It was necessary to abandon the ruined fortress and fall back to prepared entrenchments on the northern bank of the Nethe.

Antwerp was a doomed city. The Belgian Government and the Foreign Legations left for Ostend on October 3. Members of the French and British colonies and most of the wealthier citizens of Antwerp sailed for Holland and England on the same day. The arrival of three British naval brigades from Ostend brought brief hope to the Belgian soldiers and civilians. It was believed by the military authorities that these marines were the forerunners of at least an army corps.

The Belgians were holding a line north of the Nethe on which the Germans concentrated a steady fire of some 400 field-guns. Villages to the Belgian rear were destroyed and their inhabitants fled toward Antwerp. German troops who attempted to cross the river by pontoon bridges were destroyed by Belgian fire. Efforts made at other points on the stream were defeated by the British Marines, but the Germans were so much stronger in men and guns than their opponents that they could only be held back for a brief time. A strong German attack made on the Belgian centre followed, and in the night thousands of Germans swam the river and established themselves on the opposite shore. On October 6, the passage of the river had been won, and it only remained for the defenders to fall back on the inner circle of forts, which had no defensive value, their armament being obsolete.

All the district between the Nethe and the inner circle of forts was devastated, the villages in ruins. The inhabitants, on foot and in carts, streamed along the highways toward Antwerp or Holland.

Within the doomed city, the truth was at last realized—that the day was lost. Warnings of the forthcoming bombardment were posted on the walls. The great oil-tanks on the Scheldt were fired and a service of steamers was prepared for refugees. On October 7, Antwerp contained at least half a million people, but by evening on that day half of them had fled, and on the following day the city was almost deserted.

Many escaped to Holland, where they were received with the warmest hospitality. How many died from hunger and exposure during that panic flight may never be known.

After the Belgians had retired to the minor forts, several divisions were hurriedly despatched through Antwerp across the Scheldt toward the Ghent railway to hold the western road and block flank attacks.

The Germans continued to bring forward their heavy guns and the inner forts were heavily bombarded. Attempts were made to cut off the retreat of the Antwerp garrison crossing the river at Termonde and other points. The Belgian advance guards made a gallant stand and the invaders were held up for two days and unable to reach the railway—their objective.

The official bombardment of Antwerp began at midnight on October 7, and the suburb of Berchem was destroyed by fire. There was stiff fighting on the following day in the inner ring of forts as the British and Belgian troops were withdrawn across the River Scheldt. By night most of the garrison had fallen back across the river and several forts had fallen. The British battalions of the Naval Division, owing to faulty staff work, were so late in leaving that they found the pontoon bridge across the river destroyed, and were forced to cross on rafts. Some found their way to the Dutch frontier without knowing it, and were interned. Another party reached Niewerken, occupied by Germans, and were forced to surrender. Eighteen thousand Belgians were driven into Holland and the Germans made many prisoners.

The bombardment of Antwerp, which began on October 7, continued throughout the following day. The citizens who remained had taken to the cellars and only the hospitals were busy. The smoke from the burning oil-tanks shrouded the city in a black pall of smoke. As the street lamps were not burning, the only light came from the flashes of bursting shells, or when an incendiary bomb created a red chasm in the gloom.

The bombardment ceased on October 9, the inner forts having fallen, and the gates of the city were opened to the invader. German officers in motor cars were first to enter, about one o'clock in the afternoon. Antwerp was now a German city.

The army followed, but several divisions were left behind to cross the Scheldt and pursue the retreating Belgian forces. Antwerp was now a desert place, and there were no crowds, as in Brussels, to witness the passing of the German hosts. The inhabitants of the once brilliant city remained invisible. Not a flag was displayed, nor a face was seen at the windows as the victors tramped along, singing patriotic songs and displaying their admired Prussian parade step.

Chapter XXVII

BELGIUM UNDER THE GERMANS. 1914-1918

AFTER the fall of Antwerp the Belgian army retreated to the Yser, where by October 17 the Allies had formed a front which closed the way to the Channel ports between Arras and Nieuport. The Belgian army, to which a brigade of French marines was attached, was to hold the Yser from the sea to Zuidschoote. Till the end of the war, Belgian forces held a fragment of their country against the invaders.

The German aim was to break the Allies' front at chosen points and reach the shores of the Channel. At Arras, La Bassée, on the Yser and near Ypres the attacks were made. The heavier blows were launched on and along the Yser, and near Ypres, and to the Belgians and the British fell the honor of crushing the Germans' most formidable onslaught. The part assigned to the Belgians was to break the first shock of the enemy, hold him, and at all costs, prevent him from crossing the Yser before the arrival of reinforcements, then on the way. It was a hard task for an army which for two and a half months had been fighting continually. Though numbering from 70,000 to 80,000 men, the combatant effectives were not more than 48,000 bayonets.

The Germans far surpassed the Belgian army in numbers. The 4th Army, commanded by the Duke of Württemberg, advancing between the sea and the Lys, comprised some 140 battalions supported by over 500 guns. At the beginning of the Battle of the Yser 100,000 men and 350 guns attacked the Belgian positions.

The ground occupied by the defenders was a low-lying plain, the fields marked off by ditches full of water. Farms and small groups of houses around a church here and there formed the only cover in this district. There were many waterways only passable by footbridges. The Yser, about sixty feet wide, winds through the country north and south. A terrain that offered so little shelter made it easy for enemy aviators to make observations and to discover the position of batteries. As the course of the Yser presented salients and re-entrants that would assist hostile attacks the Belgians established solid bridgeheads at Nieuport and Dixmude to defend the weak points.

The struggle began on October 16 at the advanced positions of the Belgians in front of the Yser. On the following day strong German columns moved toward the stream in close formation. There were skirmishes at several points. Ratteville was bombarded and caught fire. Germans occupying St. Pierre Capelle were driven out by a detachment of Belgian cavalry.

South of the Yser front other German columns were marching on Zaren from Staden. To cover the right of the army against surprise, French cavalry divisions, turning by the north of the forest of Houthulst, drove out of this region the German advance guards. On their right the Belgians shelled enemy columns debouching from Staden, but when the German howitzers opened fire they were forced to retreat to the Forest of Houthulst.

The real battle of the Yser began on October 18, when violent attacks were made along the whole front except at Dixmude. At the height of the attack the Germans found themselves enfiladed by Hood's British monitor flotilla off the coast. Thrown into confusion by this unforseen attack, the Germans at Lombartzyde were forced back, but at other points they were more successful.

Belgian trenches dug in the Yser embankment now came under fire. St. Georges was bombarded, and the Belgian battery positions received special attention from enemy gunners.

The first day of the battle passed, and the Belgian line was unbroken. During the 19th the German assault was intensified along the whole front, and a great effort was made against the advanced positions at Nieuport and the defenses at Lombartzyde.

The Germans established batteries on the seashore, but the British vessels were out of range and the guns of the monitors destroyed many of the guns directed against them.

At Lombartzyde the Belgian 2nd Division held fast, though the Germans had brought up heavy guns, and shells fell thick and fast on the defenders, who repulsed three strong attacks. By way of reprisal the Germans bombarded Nieuport vigorously with their heavy artillery. Pont de l'Union and the trenches near, and St. Georges, were also the targets.

On the front of the Belgian Fourth Division the Germans made progress. The defenders of Beerst were driven out by heavy gun fire, and Keyem, which had been won in a counter-attack, was abandoned to the enemy.

A Belgian attack from Dixmude, assisted by French marines, was a success, Beerst was occupied, also Vladsloc, and at nightfall the enemy fell back. Gaining ground more and more to the north, the Belgians and French broke through the enemy elements opposing them and threatened the Germans' flank. But at this moment strong German columns debouched from Roulers and marched on Staden, threatening the flank of the Franco-Belgian offensive.

The Belgian 5th Division and the French marines were forced to retire by Dixmude to the left bank of the Yser under a rain of shells. In the night the Belgian 4th Division was compelled to fall back and yield Beerst and Keyem. The Germans were now master of all the Belgian front line advanced positions, except at the Dixmude bridgehead and in the Lombertzyde-Groote-Bamburgh farm sector.

On October 20 the enemy concentrated attacks on these two extremities of the front. The Groote-Bamburgh farm position was alternately won and lost, but remained at the close of the struggle in German hands. After thirteen hours' fighting the Germans occupied Lombertzyde, where they were held by the Belgian artillery.

Dixmude was now heavily shelled by the German guns, the inhabitants hurriedly fleeing across the Yser, where the bridge was still standing. On the morning of October 20, Colonel Meiser's 12th Line Regiment and six companies of the 11th occupied the Dixmude bridgehead. Reserves were at Caeskerke, and machine-gun sections blocked the approaches to the place. The German shells continued to fall in the town and suburbs. The heavy guns brought from Antwerp, howitzers, and field artillery united to crush the bridgehead under weight of iron. Covered by the bombardment the Germans advanced along all the roads on the north and east which converged on Dixmude. The 12th Line Regiment in half-demolished trenches received the brunt of the enemy attack. Reinforcements from Dixmude were dispersed by the German fire before they could leave the town. Only one company succeeded in advancing to the relief of the sorely pressed 12th Line Regiment. The Germans having wrecked the Belgian trenches and killed all the officers, the survivors retired to a little trench in the rear. The position of the Belgians was extremely perilous, for the adjoining defenses were threatened and Colonel Jacques had no more reserve. But while the Belgian and French guns held back the Germans, reinforcements unexpectedly arrived from Caeskerke and crossed the bridge to join the defenders at Dixmude. At dusk the north and northeast bridgehead positions were in Belgian hands.

On the morning of October 21 the German forces were echeloned as follows on the front: The 4th Reserve Division was opposite Nieuport; the 3rd Reserve Army Corps from Nieuport to Keyem; the 22nd Reserve Corps north of Dixmude, and the 23rd Reserve Corps opposite and south of the town. It was arranged with the French command that the Belgian defense line on the Yser should stop at the height of St. Jacques Cappelle. French troops held the line south to protect them against a turning movement.

King Albert's army held a front of twenty kilometers against which the Germans brought 4,000 guns, great and small, into action. On the 21st they prepared by cannonade to force the Yser. Shells fell on Dixmude and Belgian positions at the rate of twenty and thirty a minute. To the southeast of Dixmude the Belgians defeated seven attacks. Dixmude and Nieuport remained in their hands.

Early in the morning of October 23 the Germans captured a footbridge east of Tervaete and crossed to the left bank of the river.

After repeated efforts the Germans were thrust back across the stream, but by night the Belgians were exhausted. Tervaete was occupied and the 6th and 44th German Divisions had crossed the river and dug themselves in.

The Belgians' collapse was averted by the arrival of French reinforcements and they held on to all the positions along the Yser.

At the Tervaete bend in the Yser the Germans succeeded in throwing six bridges over the stream, and in the course of the day held it from St. Georges to Oud-Stuyvekenskerke. The Belgian defense was in peril at many points. On the 24th the Germans delivered no less than twenty-six attacks in the northern and southern sectors, until at last they, too, were compelled to break off from exhaustion.

On October 25 the Belgian High Command ordered the inundation of the area between the railway embankment and the dikes of the Yser. Several days were required to form on a front of six leagues a vast lagoon four or five kilometers in breadth, and four or five feet in depth.

On the 26th, on the left and centre of the Belgian front a retreat was made to the railway embankment. There they were commanded to hold fast at all costs. It was the last barrier on the road to Calais and Dunkirk.

The Germans' advance on Dixmude by the left bank was still barred by Belgian troops. Colonel Meiser's brigade and the marines held the trenches at the bridgehead. The Nieuport bridgehead also remained in Belgian hands.

On the 29th the Duke of Württemberg's army made an attack on the Belgian centre—and were twice repulsed. On the following day a more powerful assault was delivered against the entire Allied front from the sea to La Bassée.

Owing to the flooded area the railway was now the German objective. That won and held, they could force the defenders to yield the Dixmude and Nieuport bridgeheads. The German hosts advanced with a rush on the railway. The Belgians, overborne by weight of numbers, retired, their line was pierced, and the road to Furnes lay open. In the afternoon and evening the Belgians and French attacked Ramscapelle, which was occupied by the enemy, and in the face of terrific machine-gun fire and hand-to-hand fighting continued for hours. The village finally was won and also the railway from Dixmude to Nieuport. On November 1 the Germans began to retreat along the whole Belgian front. The Kaiser, who was present at the last assault of his troops, went to Ypres, where his armies met another reverse.

The Belgians had barred the coast-road to the German 4th Army and given the Allies time to make a barrier across the way to Calais. They had held and defeated three complete army corps reinforced by a third reserve division. The 11th and 12th Belgian Regiments lost a quarter of their men and half their officers before Dixmude. The infantry was reduced to 32,000 bayonets as against the 48,000 present when the fight began.

The Battle of the Yser must rank with the great battles of the war, for the fortunes of the Allied armies were at stake. Had the Belgians given way the French left wing would have been left in the air, the Germans would have driven them across the Lys—perhaps to the Somme. For eight days the exhausted Belgian army had fought off and defeated vastly superior forces.

The Belgian people now entered upon a period of economic

distress that was to last until, and beyond, the conclusion of the war. The little Kingdom had become in the course of recent years of development one of the great manufacturing countries of the world, but the German occupation closed workshops, factories, mills, and mines, except those which they managed themselves. Previous to the war Belgium had to import seventy-eight per cent of breadstuffs. The greater part of the harvest had been destroyed by the invading army. The Germans proceeded to commandeer grain, metals, and manufactured articles, and what the army of occupation could not use was despatched to Germany. Thousands of troops were quartered on Belgian families who had neither the means nor the food to adequately supply their own needs. In December, 1914, Governor von Bissing decreed that a war contribution of eight million dollars, to be paid monthly, was imposed on the population of Belgium. The German Governor held that this decree was based on Article 49 of the Hague Convention. Article 48 should be read in this connection and the German claim of legality is disproved. The $96,000,000 assessment a year was more than six times the amount which the Belgian government derived from direct taxation. The German administration collected the taxes in addition to the war assessment. Large sums were obtained also by a system of petty fines inflicted on the people for infractions of drastic laws and very few escaped being mulcted for some trifling offense.

A great part of the country had been pillaged by the invading soldiery and special fines were levied on towns and cities. Under such conditions the Belgian people faced starvation. Many relief societies were started, but they could do little to cope with the tremendous demands made upon them. The German authorities did nothing important to relieve the distress. At Brussels the American and Spanish ministers, Mr. Brand Whitlock and the Marquis of Villalobar, were active in the formation of a relief association known as the Central Relief Committee. Having obtained permission from the German authorities to import food for the starving people of the country, they were fortunate in securing the help of an American engineer, Herbert Clark Hoover.

Mr. Hoover formed an American committee under the patronage of the ministers of the United States and Spain, in London, Berlin, The Hague, and Brussels, and obtained permission from the British to transport foodstuffs by way of Rotterdam.

In Belgium there were four thousand **communal committees**

for the distribution of food. Contributions were sent from all parts of the world; the British and French Governments appropriated large sums every month for the help of the stricken people.

An outstanding and heroic figure in Belgium during the period of German occupation was Cardinal Mercier, Archbishop of Malines, who on New Year's day issued his famous pastoral:

"Belgium gave her word of honor to defend her independence. She has kept her word. The other powers had agreed to protect and to respect Belgium's neutrality. Germany has broken her word, England has been faithful to it. These are the facts. I consider it an obligation of my pastoral charge to define to you your conscientious duties toward the power which has invaded our soil, and which for the moment occupies the greater part of it. This power has no authority, and, therefore, in the depth of your heart, you should render it no esteem, nor attachment, nor respect. The only legitimate power in Belgium, is that which belongs to our King, to his government, to the representatives of the nation; that alone is authority for us; that alone has a right to our heart's affection and to our submission."

The Germans tried to suppress the Cardinal's pastoral; forcible seizures were made and people were searched, but it circulated everywhere despite their prohibition.

Unemployment became serious, and a plan for relief was drawn up by the National Committee. Large numbers were to be employed by communal organizations in ditching, draining, making roads, and in other public enterprises.

The relief work of the Central Relief Committee later extended to Northern France, where some two million people were within the zone of German occupation.

The deportation of Belgian workmen to Germany increased the bitterness of the people toward their conquerors, and this feeling was intensified when numbers of the deported were sent back ruined in health and bearing marks of ill-treatment.

At the beginning of 1917, the German Government took steps for splitting Belgium into two distinct states, dividing the French-speaking Walloons from the Dutch-speaking Flemish. The Germans divided the administration, making Brussels the headquarters of a "Flanders" which included the provinces of Antwerp, Limburg, East Flanders, and West Flanders, and the districts of Brussels and Louvain, and making Namur the headquarters of the provinces of Hainaut, Liége, Luxembourg, and Namur, and the district of Nivelles. They organized a Council of Flanders and got together 250 "trustworthy delegates," who announced on December 22 that they had unanimously resolved on the independence of Flanders. The "Council" offered itself for a new election, "to give the Flemish people the opportunity to proclaim its will concerning the declaration of independence." Sham elections were held in February. This was a new peril, and the Belgians devised countermeasures.

Early in February, 1918, a resolution was drawn up by Belgian Ministers of State, Senators and Deputies, requesting the Court of Appeals of Brussels to institute prosecutions against certain members of the "Council of Flanders." The Court of Appeals met and decided unanimously on the prosecution of the members specified. Two members of the so-called "Council," Borms and Tack, were arrested. The German Governor ordered their release and forbade criminal proceedings against them. At the same time three out of four Presidents of the Court of Appeals were arrested and taken to Germany, charged with acting under orders from the Belgian Government at Havre.

In the summer of 1918, the tide turned in favor of the Allies. In September, General Foch determined to make two great thrusts against the Germans in Belgium, one on the south between the Argonne and the Meuse, which resulted in the capture of Montfaucon and Varennes, and finally led to the destruction of the German control of the Paris-Chalons-Verdun railway, one of their most valued lines of communication. The Belgians, in conjunction with General Plumer's Second Army, attacked on a front extending from the Dixmude Canal to the Lys. The Germans were driven out of the entire Ypres salient. They retreated over the Passchendaele Ridge and down into the Flanders plain beyond the heights. On the Belgian coast, the British fleet bombarded the defenses.

The Belgian army, fighting under King Albert, took Roulers on September 30. The advance halted while the Allies consolidated their new positions; then, on October 14, British, Belgians and French made a drive on Ghent and Courtrai, capturing many towns and thousands of prisoners. The German retreat continued all along the front. The Belgians swept down the coast, driving the enemy before them. King Albert and Queen Elizabeth entered

Ostend on October 17. Zeebrugge, the last Belgian port in German hands, was taken on the 18th.

The reception of the King and Queen at Bruges foreshadowed the enthusiastic welcome they received throughout Belgium. They entered the capital, Brussels, on September 22, 1918.

At the Peace Conference, Belgium claimed that her reparations for damages wrought by Germany should be the first lien upon German assets, as she was first invaded and her neutrality violated. This claim was admitted by the Peace Conference.

Belgium's recovery was rapid. In spite of, or perhaps because of, the occupation by German troops, less damage had been done to industrial machinery in Belgium than in countries where warfare had continued. Cardinal Mercier, King Albert, the Queen and the Crown Prince all visited the United States in the autumn of 1919 and were received with enthusiasm.

Changes were made in the constitution to liberalize voting. Elections were held on November 16, 1919. No party had a majority; there were 73 of the Catholic Party, 70 Socialists and 34 Liberals, besides a few others.

Chapter XXVIII

PEACE AND RECONSTRUCTION IN BELGIUM. 1919-1935

AFTER his triumphal entry into Brussels, King Albert endeavored to perpetuate the unity that had characterized Belgium in the war. He appointed Leon Delacroix Premier, who made up a three-party Cabinet, with Catholic, Liberal and Socialist members. Each of these chief parties was really a *bloc* made of various minor political groups. A question at issue between the Catholics and the others since the Catholic Party came into power in 1884 had been that of government money for "free" schools, in which religion must be taught, on an equality with the communal schools. These free schools were established and the Catholic Party had maintained its control of the Government. The Socialist Party had demanded manhood suffrage since 1890. A compromise system had granted general voting, but permitted plural voting or extra votes to men who had certain property and educational qualifications, a system which gave the Catholic Party the advantage and hampered the Liberals, who nevertheless received some representation because of the system of proportional representation adopted. The first election after the war was conducted under universal male suffrage, which proved to give none of the three parties a majority and made a coalition government advisable if it could be effected.

The most important question for Belgian statesmen and diplomats is that of national security. Reparations and reconstruction were problems on which the parties did not differ materially. The Flemish question, on which the Germans had tried to separate the nation during the war, was revived with considerable bitterness. In 1921, the Flemings won a victory when a measure was passed, to go into effect in 1922, requiring the use of both French and Flemish as official languages not only in the Flemish provinces but among the Walloons as well. In 1923, the Nolf measure made the University of Ghent Flemish, but with some instruction in French as well.

Belgium was no longer a neutralized nation. She must maintain friendship with England and France and an equilibrium between the two.

In recognition of what she had suffered through violation of her neutrality and of her heroic defense of it, Belgium had been granted priority in receiving reparations. At the Conference of London in 1921, the amount of German reparations had been reduced to 132,000,000,000 gold marks, of which sum Belgium was to receive 10,560,000,000 gold marks, or 8 per cent of the whole.

In Europe, Belgium had received a small increase of territory —Eupen, Malmédy and St. Vith. These regions were organized in accordance with a liberal policy and in 1924 the Minister of the Interior announced that they were so thoroughly Belgicized that they might be considered an integral part of the country.

In Africa, about 19,000 square miles had been added to the Belgian Congo, including considerable portions of Urundi and Ruanda, formerly in the northwestern part of German East Africa, and some adjustments of the Congo-Uganda frontier, much of the new territory being in the important African lake region. The Belgian Congo is a very rich possession, producing copper, palm oil, cotton, gold, ivory, tin, radium, iron, cocoa, rice, copal and a great variety of other tropical products, and capable of almost indefinite development. Its present area is estimated at about 910,000 square miles. Money for governmental purposes is raised by taxes on imports and exports, a poll tax on native male adults, a tax on incomes of Europeans, a tax on ivory, and a government appropriation of part of the products of mines. Nevertheless, the responsibility for government, development and defense of a colony so large and so distant is considerable for a country no larger than Belgium. The native population is estimated at about 11,000,000 and the white population at 8,250.

A unique reservation in the Kivu region has been made for a gorilla sanctuary.

Belgium endeavored to obtain some adjustments of boundary with Holland and was disappointed at not securing control of one of the port channels fronting the port of Antwerp. The harbor of Antwerp was considerably improved and in December, 1924, it was announced that the largest liners no longer found it difficult to dock there.

A treaty with Luxemburg in 1922 established the customs frontier between the two countries, substituted Belgian for Luxemburg currency (the latter to be withdrawn), and Belgian consuls for Dutch to oversee duties.

The Delacroix coalition government fell in November, 1920. The next premier was Henri Carton de Wiart of the Catholic Party. He also endeavored to make up a three-party cabinet. The Socialists, who had polled more votes than either of the other parties, refused places in the cabinet and made up the opposition. A two-party cabinet was organized, composed of Catholics and Liberals. The Flemings won a victory in 1921, to go into effect in 1922, when a law was passed making it necessary to use both French and Flemish languages in the administration of all the provinces. The De Wiart Cabinet fell toward the close of 1921. With the same hope of unity, King Albert selected to head the new government a distinguished financier, Jasper Theunis, who did not identify himself with any of the three parties.

In April, 1922, women voted for the first time in the municipal elections. There was considerable agitation later on for granting women suffrage in provincial elections. The situation was somewhat strange, as the Catholic Party, supposed in principle to oppose suffrage and economic freedom for women, favored it; the Socialists and a considerable part of the Liberals, whose principles were supposed to include equal rights for women, were opposed, holding that further political training for women was needed and that the Theunis government had come into power on the understanding that it would concern itself only with finance and war reconstruction.

The Flemings won another victory in 1923 when the Nolf law made the University of Ghent a Flemish institution, though some courses might be conducted in French.

The question of German reparations concerned the Belgians very deeply, and on January 11, 1923, Belgium joined with France in occupation of the Ruhr. Belgium's economic evacuation of the Ruhr began in August, 1924, after acceptance of the Dawes plan. Belgian coal mines had experienced great prosperity during the occupation, and the fall in prices and wages due to the changed situation led to a serious miners' strike, which ended on October 11, 1924.

In December, 1924, a Belgian loan of $50,000,000 was floated in New York. By this time reconstruction was practically completed. Of 1,175 public buildings, including schools, churches and others destroyed, 1046 had been rebuilt and 135 were building. Of some 100,000 private buildings destroyed, about 60,000 had been rebuilt by private enterprise and 33,075 by government aid. Nearly 2,000 kilometers of road had been reconstructed.

With many cabinet changes, M. Theunis continued at the head of the government until after the elections of April 5, 1925. No party received a majority of the votes, Socialists leading in the Chamber and Catholics in the Senate. After the resignation of Theunis, one leader after another tried to form a Cabinet and failed. The long period without a government created no serious difficulty, for the questions pending were largely only disputes among the parties.

On June 17, 1925, M. Poullet was able to form a Coalition Cabinet, composed of five Catholics, five Socialists and three Liberals. Poullet retained the Ministry of Economic Affairs. Vandervelde, the famous Socialist, became Minister of Foreign Affairs. Vandervelde hoped to renew some of the Belgian interests in Russia, but stated that guarantees would be demanded.

The Belgian War Debt mission reached Washington on August 1, 1925. The Belgian Ambassador, Baron de Cartier de Marchienne, was considered its head and the group contained also ex-Premier Theunis. They found the United States Government willing to honor a pledge of Woodrow Wilson's that the Belgian debt should be given special treatment. An agreement was reached on August 18. The pre-Armistice debt of $171,780,000 bears no interest and is to be paid off in annual installments stretching over 62 years. The installments begin at $1,000,000 and increase to a maximum of $2,900,000 by 1932, the last payment being somewhat smaller. The post-Armistice debt with interest was placed at $246,000,000 in the summer of 1925. It is to be paid in 62 annual installments, fixed arbitrarily until the expiration of ten years, when the amount will be somewhat less than $10,000,000; that is, the maximum amount of a single annual installment for the two debts will be between $12,000,000 and $13,000,000. On returning to Belgium, it was announced that the settlement made it easy for Belgium to pay her debt, provided German reparations came to hand as expected.

A policy of rigid economy was decided upon by the Government on December 17, 1925, and the new policy was promptly put into effect in the Ministry of National Defense and in other departments, forcing a maximum of reductions in budgets for the coming year.

Cardinal Mercier, a national hero of Belgium for his valorous conduct in the World War period, died on January 23, 1926, mourned by the nation and by the world.

The ratification of the American loan of $150,000,000 was made on February 22, 1926. The Belgian franc continued to fall, reaching a level on March 15 where it was quoted at 4.04⅛ cents, and by March 26 it had still further fallen to 3.97 cents. The failure finally to secure the $150,000,000 American loan, although authorized by the Belgian Government, sent the value of the franc in May to new low records and resulted in the formation of a new ministry. This was completed by M. Henri Jaspar on May 18, 1926. He had formerly been Minister of Foreign Affairs. Besides himself as Premier, the leading cabinet members were Baron Maurice Houtart, Minister of Finance, Comte de Broqueville, Minister of National Defense, M. Emile Vandervelde, Minister of Foreign Affairs, and M. Henri L. Baels, Minister of Agriculture and of Public Works. The Premier announced that the chief aim of the Government would be to solve the financial problems that confronted the nation. On June 5, the Senate approved the budget of the new Government, which added 1,500,000,000 francs to the revenues, obtained principally by additional taxes on motor cars, theatres and incomes derived from real estate. The franc was still much depreciated, being 38.50 to the dollar on July 6. On July 14, the Senate and Chamber voted to confer upon the King full power to issue decrees to help stabilization of the franc. One of the first steps taken under the new order was the passage of a bill turning the state railroads over to private control and operation. Freight and passenger rates were immediately advanced 25 per cent. On August 11, it was announced that the telephone and telegraph service were also to be turned over to management similar to that controlling the railroads. On August 14, increased taxes were levied upon all foreigners. M. Francqui, Minister without Portfolio, was given almost complete charge of the finances, becoming practically Minister of Finance. In October, Belgium succeeded in putting her currency upon a gold basis. The basis of the new monetary system is to be the belga with a fixed gold value of .209211 grams. The belga, however, is merely a name signifying five francs. The value was, therefore, fixed on a gold basis, with exchange value, in dollars, of one to thirty-six.

In the elections held in October, 1926, the Catholic and Conservative parties made notable gains at the expense of the Socialists and Liberals. It was emphatically shown that the people had decided to support loyally the present Conservative dictatorship in its policies of financial reforms. The Crown Prince of Belgium, Prince Leopold, was married on November 4, 1926, to Princess Astrid of Sweden at Stockholm, and arrived at Antwerp November 9.

In December, 1926, the treaty revising the 1839 treaty between Belgium and The Netherlands was ratified. In February, 1927, plans were completed for mobilization of Belgium in the event of war, by a committee of Parliament. It was claimed that Belgium was less prepared now for war than she had been in 1914. A demand was made on March 15, 1927, by a Socialist Deputy, that a new plebiscite should be held upon Eupen and Malmédy, former German provinces transferred to Belgium by the Treaty of Versailles. Prime Minister Jaspar stated that the Government would not grant the measure, but on the other hand would take effectual means to end the pro-German propaganda in these provinces.

On June 21, 1927, Marquis Negrotto, the Italian ambassador to Belgium, was recalled as a protest against the extreme anti-Fascism of the Belgian Foreign Minister, Emile Vandervelde. The Foreign Minister's stand received the full support of the Belgian Chamber. On September 2, the Cabinet rejected the request of the German Government to appoint a bi-party commission to investigate certain accusations against Germany's procedures in the World War.

On October 16, Premier Jaspar stated that no reductions of army service would be considered before all measures of security were taken. This was in answer to a demand from the Socialists that the term of military service be reduced to six months. The Cabinet of Premier Jaspar, containing Catholics, Socialists and Liberals, who had joined forces to effect financial recovery, resigned on November 21, 1927, the military demands of the Socialists forcing the resignation. The Cabinet was succeeded on November 22 by a Cabinet again headed by Premier Jaspar and this time a coalition of the Catholic, Liberal and Christian Democratic parties. M. Paul Hymans succeeded M. Vandervelde as Foreign Minister.

In any summary of developments in Europe over twelve months, especially since the World War, there is disproportionate attention given to those countries in which there is strife and confusion. Current history has some of the qualities of news, and news is the reporting of dramatic and unusual happenings. Not all of Europe has been disturbed by conflict or given over to controversies. Side by side with contending nations are millions of people who go on year after year, sharing in some measure the general economic conditions of their neighbors, but not in their squabbles.

Even Belgium, affected by the war as disastrously as any of the participants, has been only slightly disturbed by the recent phases of the afterwar controversies and is enjoying a measure of prosperity. Under agreement with Germany, Belgium was to receive annuities of about $76,800,000. Belgium has also been reaping large financial benefits from the Belgian Congo, which has vast mineral and other resources, now being exploited to a greater extent than ever before. In the May election of 1929, Socialists and Liberals both made gains but the Catholic party was still the strongest numerically and Premier Henri Jaspar, representing that party, remained in office. At the close of the year, the Belgians were apparently far more interested in the forthcoming royal wedding of Princess Marie José to Prince Humbert of Italy than they were in politics. Both were of the Roman Catholic faith.

Belgium was less disturbed than most of her neighbors by the economic depression of 1930-1931. The outstanding political issue of 1930 developed over the old language controversy between the Walloons and the Flemings. Premier Jaspar offered his resignation to King Albert on November 11, 1930, but was asked to continue in office. Of larger significance was a campaign inaugurated by Emil Vandervelde, Socialist and former Minister of Foreign Affairs, to abrogate the military agreement between Belgium and France entered into in 1920. This, and the question of spending $80,000,000 for fortifications on the German border, led to considerable discussion in Belgium and France, where the breaking away of Belgium was regarded with concern. Early in December a deadly fog, hovering over the Meuse Valley, killed 75 persons and many cattle and created a state of panic that lasted for days.

A troublesome question, in view of the desire to forget the hatreds engendered by the World War had to do with the inscription for the balustrade of the Louvain Library, which had been rebuilt under the direction of an American architect, Whitney Warren, and with money supplied by Americans. A reference to "Teutonic fury" in the inscription was no longer approved by the Belgians, but was insisted on by the architect as part of his original and accepted design. A lower court had upheld his contention. The matter was in all probability finally settled when the Belgian Court of Appeals, on December 15, 1930, declared that the inscription need not be used on the balustrade.

In February, 1931, a report was made concerning the mysterious deadly vapor that had ended so many lives in December. The poisonous factor was said to be sulphurous anhydride from factories of the region. The gas is probably escaping as a usual thing and dissipating into the atmosphere without any serious results from its noxious qualities. An unusually heavy blanket of fog on the day in question was believed to have held the sulphurous anhydride close to the earth and caused the death of people who faced it.

The pact with France for mutual military aid was a matter of bitter discussion in the Belgian Chamber of Deputies in 1931. Many Belgians believed the nation should reduce its military expenditures. Paul Hymans, Foreign Minister and famous internationalist, defended the pact, declaring that its terms demanded military aid from Belgium to France only in the event of unprovoked aggression on the part of Germany.

Premier Jaspar was considered by the Liberals to be too mild in this matter and not to insist urgently enough on the necessity for national defense. He and his Cabinet resigned on May 21, 1931, partly because of the military pact dispute, partly because of frequent changes in his Ministry without other warrant than his own. He was succeeded as Premier by Jules Renkin, who headed a new Cabinet on June 5. He asked a vote of 210,000,000 francs for strengthening frontier fortifications.

The Belgian Congo was a source of some anxiety during the year, partly because of native revolts and partly because of dissatisfaction among the Belgian colonists there, who demanded better educational facilities for their sons and better opportunities for them in securing official positions in the colony.

Parliament ratified on July 16, 1931, the agreement of Oslo previously signed by Belgium, Sweden, Norway, Denmark and the Netherlands, whereby the tariff truce proposed in the Convention of Geneva was to be carried out. It had been strongly opposed by the Socialists and Liberals on the theory that it would weaken the bond between Belgium and France, and by others for fear of increased competition that would be occasioned with Denmark. When Minister of Foreign Affairs Hymans assured Parliament that tariffs could be increased if necessary, opposition was withdrawn.

The hundredth anniversary of the separation of Belgium and Holland and the inauguration of the first King of Belgium, King Leopold I, was celebrated on July 19 in Furnes, La Panne and Ostend. King Albert and the Queen attended the ceremonies.

A survey of the economic condition of Belgium, completed in September, 1931, showed that the country was making progress in spite of the world depression. It had been necessary in July, however, to impose new taxes to meet the deficit expected in the 1930-1931 budget. At the close of the fiscal year 1931-1932, the budget showed a large deficit as a result of deep inroads in the country's industries and consequent unemployment. Even the 10 per cent cuts in Government salaries and pensions and the 10 per cent taxes imposed in March, 1932, failed to balance the budget. On September 7 the Chamber authorized the Government to issue a long-term loan of $42,000,000, to issue Treasury bonds for $1,400,000, and to renew the Treasury bonds for $1,000,000 maturing October 1.

The language controversy, which had disrupted the country so long, became an important political issue early in 1932. On March 2 it neared settlement when the Chamber passed a bill dividing Belgium into three sections: Wallonia, where only French was to be the official language; Flanders, where Flemish would be official, and the Brussels district, which would be bilingual. The Senate passed the bill on July 18. A second language was required in the secondary schools and optional in primary grades.

Premier Renkin, having failed in his efforts to support the French-speaking advocates, resigned on May 18, but was urged by King Albert to form a new Cabinet. The municipal elections held in October showed opposition to his administration and he again resigned on October 18. Count Charles de Broqueville, formerly Premier of Belgium, formed a Coalition Cabinet of Catholics and Liberals on October 22. Parliament was dissolved three days later.

Belgium, Holland and Luxemburg signed an agreement in June, 1932, to form a tariff union in order to remove as rapidly as possible the economic barriers which were destroying their trade. Other countries were free to join the union.

The Parliamentary elections held on November 27, 1932, resulted in gains for both Catholic and Socialist parties. For the Senate, 74 Catholic, 63 Socialists and 21 Liberals were elected; for the Chamber, 79 Catholics, 73 Socialists, and 24 Liberals. Under normal conditions the Cabinet would have resigned after the elections, but it decided to delay this action until a vote had been taken on the payment of the $2,125,000 war debt installment due the United States on December 15.

On December 13, the Cabinet voted to refuse to pay the United States on the ground that, the reparations agreement at Lausanne having cut off her income from Germany, she was not able to continue these payments. Directly after this vote was taken the Cabinet resigned. De Broqueville quickly formed a new Cabinet, which was a coalition of Catholics and Liberals. The Socialists refused to join the Cabinet.

In order to balance the 1932-1933 budget, drastic cuts were made in Government expenses, which, it was estimated, would save $12,000,000. Unemployment relief and old-age pensions were reduced and the dole taken away from married women. This and the continued food taxes aroused the Socialists to public demonstrations. At Louviers 4,000 workers went on strike. A few days later 20,000 women staged a parade in Brussels, protesting against the decrease of unemployment relief and increase of the war budget. A more riotous demonstration broke out on May 11, when 6,000 Communists and unemployed attacked the Brussels police with furniture from cafés. The demonstration took place while the Chamber was voting plenary powers to the Cabinet for three months. The Cabinet was enabled through the bill adopted to make needed financial reforms in order to meet the threatened deficit of 600,000,000 francs in the budget, to contract loans, and to protect the interests of Belgium at the World Economic Conference.

Belgium defaulted on both her June 15, 1933, and December 15, 1933, debt installments, maintaining that she was not able to pay.

The policies of Chancellor Hitler stirred up anew in Belgium a distrust and fear of Germany and led to extensive plans for strengthening old fortifications and building new ones. The Government announced on September 2 that it would float a loan of 1,500,000,000 francs ($60,000,000 at current exchange) for the purpose of financing the fortifications on the German frontier. The Cabinet voted a credit of 750,000,000 francs on October 11 to be applied to the completion of the fortifications.

Not only Belgium but the entire world was shocked by the

death, on February 17, 1934, of the universally respected Belgian king, Albert I, killed by a fall while climbing a mountain peak alone at Marche les Dames. His eldest son, aged thirty-three, succeeded to the throne, on February 23, under the title of Leopold III. The young king was faced with extraordinary difficulties in the economic situation, including rising unemployment, lowered exports, and the strain of keeping to the gold standard. The unpopularity of measures designed to improve conditions had led to the resignation of the Cabinet of Count de Broqueville on November 13. King Albert had turned to Georges Theunis, a wealthy capitalist, to form a new government, committed also to support of the gold standard.

The early months of 1935 were characterized by increasing economic distress, and persistent threats of general strikes. Efforts to stem the tide of popular dissatisfaction were evident in the consideration of various New Deal measures, such as code supervision of industry, fixing of lower food prices, and salary cuts for public officials. Hope was aroused by the signing of a reciprocal trade treaty with the United States in February.

Finally, owing to the growing difficulty of adhering to the gold standard in spite of heroic efforts to do so, the Theunis Cabinet resigned on March 20. King Leopold requested Dr. Paul Van Zeeland, noted banker and economist, to form a new Cabinet.

After several days of rumors and counter-rumors, the new Premier announced the suspension of the gold standard. Going energetically to work on the economic situation, his Cabinet, known as the National Emergency Government, secured from the Chamber of Deputies a grant of extraordinary power for one year. Their "National Renovation" program included practical aids to industry and reduced taxation. A gesture of confidence was seen in the opening of a World's Fair in Brussels in April. In June, Belgium again defaulted on the war debt to the United States.

The general European reaction to Hitler's military program in the opening of 1935 was evidenced in Belgium also, by the recommendations of a special military commission for compulsory service and for an extension of the enlistment period from one year to eighteen months.

In July the recognition of the Soviet Union was arranged in Paris, through the Belgian and Soviet ambassadors to France. Plans were made for the establishment of diplomatic relations and for commercial agreements between the two countries.

A second tragedy plunged Belgium into grief on August 29, 1935, when the beloved Queen Astrid met her death in an automobile accident, while driving with the King near Lucerne, Switzerland.

Fearing complications in the Italo-Ethiopian conflict, since Belgian military advisers had been unofficially in the employ of Haile Selassie for some time, the Belgian government in September forbade the enlistment of Belgian officers in foreign armies and strongly urged private citizens to abide by the same rule.

Chapter XXIX

THE KINGDOM OF THE NETHERLANDS. 1840-1935

THE people of Holland had, on the whole, displayed extraordinary indifference to the Belgian revolution, and had accepted the dissolution of the kingdom of the Netherlands philosophically and with no great amount of reluctance. The union with Belgium had, in fact, been little to the taste of the bulk of the Dutch people. The differences which had developed in the two peoples since the final breach between them over two centuries before were too profound to be affected by so short a period of union as fifteen years, and though the manner in which the separation was effected was galling to Dutch pride, the fact itself was regarded by many as rather to the advantage of the nation than otherwise. So it happened that the Dutch people showed less interest in the severance of the ties with Belgium than in the brilliant conclusion of a long and expensive war in the East, which ended with the total subjection of the Island of Java by Dutch arms, and drew consolation for the loss of the southern provinces in the remarkable period of prosperity in the East Indies inaugurated by the able governor, Van der Bosch.

The conclusion of the final treaty with Belgium was generally welcomed in Holland, though the Dutch, jealous of the reviving prosperity of Antwerp, were still unwilling to grant the free navigation of the Scheldt to their southern neighbors, and the obnoxious tolls remained in force till 1863.

The signature of the treaty with Belgium was the last important event of the eventful reign of William I. Worn out by the disappointments of his reign, the king abdicated in 1840, to be succeeded by his son, William II., a remarkable personage with great force of character. A born soldier, the new king when Prince of Orange had served with distinction under the Duke of Wellington in the Peninsular campaign, and had been wounded while leading the Dutch troops at Waterloo. His soldierly conduct won the admiration and life-long friendship of the Iron Duke, and made him for a time a most popular figure in Belgium as well as in Holland. But William was utterly lacking in the instincts of a statesman. His secret negotiations with the Belgians and his practical recognition of their independence, which was immediately repudiated by his father, greatly incensed the Dutch people, and not even his brilliant campaign in 1831 could restore him to favor. It was openly proposed that the prince be excluded from the throne for treacherous communication with the enemy, and he was obliged to retire for a time from the country till this feeling was partially allayed. Thus the position of William II. on his accession to the throne was anything but a satisfactory one. Not only was the king personally unpopular, but the country itself was in a depressed condition, burdened with heavy taxation, confused finances, and, above all, with a cumbersome, illiberal constitution, which put far too much power in the hands of the king. Yet William was not politic enough to see the necessity of change, and his marriage with a Russian princess served to confirm him in his autocratic tendencies. The reform movement, ever growing more powerful and insistent, served to bring into the political arena the most striking figure in recent Dutch history. Jan Thorbecke, a statesman, the most eminent Holland has seen since the time of Heinsius, and pronounced by an English statesman to be "too great a man for so small a country," had been a professor in the University of Leyden till the question of constitutional revision called him to the leadership of the Liberal party. As early as 1844 Thorbecke had completed the draft of a new constitution; but it was not till three years later that the king, warned by popular outbreaks in various parts of Holland, and even in The Hague, was prepared to yield. A commission for revision headed by Thorbecke was appointed, and a new liberal constitution was drawn up. The revision had come just in time, for it probably saved the Netherlands from experiencing the full force of the revolutionary movement which swept over Europe in the year 1848. Its signature was the last official act of King William, who died March 19, 1849.

King William III., whose reign was to cover a longer period than that of any of his predecessors, was a very different character from his father. Of a quiet and convivial nature, he had no ambition to play at statescraft, and was not likely to endanger by his policy the national tranquillity of the Netherlands. Indeed, the foreign policy of the country was more influenced by the brilliant Queen Sophia than by her husband. From his Russian mother the king had inherited a strong taste for autocratic methods of government, which showed itself to especial disadvantage in his own family. His manners were frank, even to brutality, and his habits punctilious to excess. But he was essentially popular with the people, who felt under the harsh exterior the true goodness of heart which displayed itself in noble self-sacrifice during the disastrous floods of 1855 and 1861, and they readily forgave the king the domestic blunders which estranged him from his family and drove his son into voluntary exile. The king disliked his great minister, Thorbecke, as was perhaps natural, but recognized in him a man of superior mind, and generally yielded his own inclinations to the advice of the Liberal statesman. Thorbecke was indeed the dominant figure in Dutch politics to the day of his death. His career was given to the consolidation of the principles of the new constitution, which it had been his first great task to create. Among the achievements of the great minister were the establishment of a system of local self-government such as few states of Europe enjoyed, the reform of the East Indian possessions, the raising of state credit, and the introduction of a free-trade policy, which was effective in increasing the shipping interests of Holland to the utmost. For a time the work of Thorbecke was interrupted by a contest with the Catholic Church. The Pope, Pius IX., had decided to reëstablish the old bishoprics in Holland, after a lapse of over two centuries, and this untimely action revived the old anti-Catholic feeling among the people of Holland to a remarkable degree. Thorbecke, who had sought to maintain a moderate attitude, was violently assailed by the ultra-Protestant party, accused of treason, and finally was forced out of power for nearly nine years.

The year 1860 was marked by the commencement of a vast programme of state railway building, and by 1872 a network of state-owned roads covered the country, built, be it noted, by the profits of the exploited East Indian colonies, and hence unique as being absolutely free from debt. The second ministry of Thorbecke was marked by a renewal of his reform programme, successfully carried out in spite of a violent and sometimes personal opposition from the Conservative party, headed by the brilliant, though erratic, Van Heemskirk. A new educational system, the abolition of slavery in the West Indies, and vast internal works. canals, and railways, mark this progressive period.

Since the loss of Belgium the Netherlands had kept free of foreign complications, though the fact that the king, through his possession of Luxemburg and Limburg, was a member of the Germanic confederation was for a time a menace to the neutral attitude of Holland. But the rivalry between France and Prussia after 1866, and the aggressive designs of both powers, threatened at one time to involve the intermediate state of the Netherlands.

We have seen how Napoleon III. had sought to involve Prussia in a treaty for the conquest of Belgium, and how he had been outwitted by the diplomacy of Bismarck. Repulsed in his overtures to Prussia, the French emperor turned to Luxemburg, and opened negotiations with Holland for the purchase of the little duchy. Luxemburg, since the dissolution of the Germanic confederation an independent possession of the king of the Netherlands, though territorially insignificant, was, in view of its central position, a place of great strategic importance. Though no longer connected with Germany, a Prussian garrison still occupied the great fortress, famous throughout Europe, which overlooked the sleepy little capital of the duchy. In his negotiations for the possession of this coveted spot, the Emperor Napoleon found a firm ally in the talented Queen Sophia of Holland, by birth a Württemberg princess, of whom it was said that she knew the affairs of Europe better than most statesmen. From being a warm admirer of Bismarck, the queen had at this time become an active enemy, and to her influence the Iron Chancellor has ascribed in great part the hostile attitude of southern Germany to Prussia during the Austro-Prussian War of 1866. Queen Sophia was possessed of a continual fear of Prussian aggression in the direction of Holland, and Bismarck tells us in his memoirs that a sensational speech made by a French minister of state, declaring that France would never tolerate Prussian advance on the Zuyder Zee, was directly inspired by her. So the queen was by no means averse to the sale of Luxemburg to Napoleon, for whom she had a strong friendship, which outlasted the days of the emperor's prosperity. King William, though unwilling to offend Prussia, was finally persuaded to consent to the sale. But the news of the transaction had reached the Prussian chancellory, and Count Bismarck took care that it should be spread broadcast throughout Germany. The result was what he had anticipated—a storm of indignant protest was raised, for Luxemburg was still considered to be German ground, and the Prussian envoy at The Hague was instructed to declare that in view of the popular resentment Prussia would be forced to consider the cession of Luxemburg to be a *casus belli*. The effect of this declaration was decisive, for the Dutch government hastily withdrew its consent to the treaty of cession on the very eve of its signature. Foiled for a second time by his great opponent, Napoleon determined at least not to leave the field in possession of his rivals, and so demanded the withdrawal of the Prussian garrison from Luxemburg. The demand was promptly refused, on the ground that Prussia would not consent on any terms to the withdrawal of Luxemburg from German influence. But for once Bismarck was compelled to yield his ground. At the suggestion of Russia a conference was called at London to settle the question of Luxemburg, and by the treaty of May 11, 1867, Prussia was ordered to withdraw her garrison, while the contracting powers guaranteed the neutrality of the duchy under the crown of Holland.

The Luxemburg question formed but one of those diplomatic skirmishes which ushered in the Franco-Prussian War. Queen Sophia had clearly seen how events were trending, and had repeatedly, though vainly, warned Napoleon of the designs of Prussia against him. During the war Holland, like Belgium, stood in a precarious position between two great powers engaged in a mortal struggle, the more so as her court was notoriously favorable to the defeated party. But an able ministry succeeded in maintaining a strictly neutral attitude.

In 1872 the Netherlands lost her greatest figure in Thorbecke, who died after seeing such progress under the reforms he had instituted that he who had once been regarded as a revolutionist was now called a Tory. His death was at the time overshadowed by the brilliant festivities held throughout the country to celebrate the three hundredth anniversary of that greatest event in Dutch history, the capture of Brill by the Sea Beggars, which inaugurated the War of Independence. In 1877 the nation mourned another loss in the death of Queen Sophia. Her character has been eloquently described by Motley as " full of charity, constantly occupied by thoughts of others, forgetful of self, and deeply interested in all great subjects which occupy the more elevated intellects." [1] The death of Queen Sophia was most disastrious to the harmony of the royal family. With the removal of her restraining influence open quarrels broke out between the king and the Prince of

---

[1] The memoirs of two noted Englishmen, Lord Malmesbury and Henry Reeves, contain much that is of interest about this notable queen.

Orange, who after some violent scenes retired to Paris, where he died in 1879. A man of unusual ability, and very popular, the prince had promised to rank among the great ones of his race. With his death the direct line of the house of Orange seemed threatened with extinction, and the possible claims of a Prussian prince renewed the fears of German aggression and added to the general alarm. But all these fears were dispelled by the marriage of the king to Princess Emma of Waldeck, and the birth, in 1880, of an heiress to the house of Orange, the present Queen Wilhelmina. King William died in 1890, after a prosperous reign of forty years, and Queen Emma was appointed regent for the young queen, while Luxemburg, following the Salic law, now became separated from Holland and passed to the Duke of Nassau.

Since 1870 the relations of Holland with her neighbors have been peaceful and in the main uneventful. The war between the Boers and the English in 1881 aroused the Dutch to a remembrance of the fact that these sturdy South African farmers were their descendants and kinsmen. Moved by popular feeling, the government was induced to offer to mediate in the struggle, but found that the British premier, Gladstone, had already decided to grant the Transvaal its independence. The Jameson Raid in 1896, and the second Boer War, concluded in 1902, again awakened intense interest, and in the wonderful fight of the little South African republics against the greatest empire of the world the Dutch people saw a replica of their ancestors' heroic struggle against Spanish rule. Popular feeling ran high against England, but the attitude of the government was strictly neutral, though offers of mediation were made, and it is on record that the Dutch ministry had advised President Krüger against a declaration of war. The young Queen Wilhelmina reached her majority in 1898, and was solemnly enthroned in the new church at Amsterdam, taking the oath of fidelity with the customary ceremonies in the presence of the states-general. Her marriage, three years later, to Duke Henry of Mecklenburg was generally popular, though some saw renewed the bugbear of a German invasion. However, the conferring on the duke of the title of Prince Henry of the Netherlands, happily reviving the memory of a popular brother of William III., created great satisfaction.

But perhaps the event in the recent history of the Netherlands which created the most general interest was the meeting at The Hague of the International Peace Conference in 1899. In the fall of the preceding year the Emperor Nicholas of Russia issued his famous rescript, inviting the states of the civilized world to attend a conference in the interests of international peace and arbitration. Holland, as a small and neutral state, the birthplace of Grotius, the father of international law, and always foremost advocate of arbitration, was fittingly selected as the seat of the conference. The queen placed the royal palace near The Hague, known as The House in the Wood, at the disposal of the congress. Here on May 18, 1899, in the historic Orange Hall, erected by the widow of the stadtholder, Prince Frederick Henry, and decorated by the leading Dutch artists of the seventeenth century, was assembled a distinguished company of delegates from almost all the leading nations of the earth, men noted as diplomats, lawyers, and soldiers. Space forbids us more than a mere sketch of the discussions and conclusions of this assembly, which, whatever its immediate results may be, was certainly epoch-making in its general significance. In brief, the objects of the conference were twofold—the reduction of military armaments, with restrictions in the methods of modern warfare, and the construction of some definite scheme for international arbitration. The projects of a general disarmament failed completely, chiefly through the declaration, in a remarkable speech by the German military delegate, Von Schwartzhoff, that his country neither needed nor desired any such action. Of more especial interest to Americans, who are not afflicted with the crushing military burdens that constitute the armed peace of Europe, was the successful establishment of a permanent court of arbitration, to sit at The Hague and apply the code of international law to disputes between nations. Though this court has not as yet fulfilled the hopes of success it first inspired, it should be a matter of pride for Americans that their country was the first to refer a dispute to the arbitration of The Hague tribunal.[2]

Internally the history of the Netherlands has been marked in the last generation by a marvelous increase in commerce and industry, bringing inevitably in its course new and difficult social and political problems. Perhaps the most striking indication of the spirit of the age has been the rise of a Socialist or Labor party in a country noted for centuries as the typical home of the middle class merchant and shopkeeper.

[2] In the dispute with Mexico over the Pious Fund. The best account of the Peace Conference will be found in a book by the late Federick Holls, secretary to the American delegation.

The chief political parties in the Netherlands have been the Liberal, drawn mostly from the middle classes of the cities; the Conservative-Protestant, recruited from the ranks of the aristocracy and the Calvinist peasantry; and the Catholic party, strong in the southern provinces of Brabant and Limburg. The rise of the Social-Labor movement dates from the days of the famous International Society of Workingmen, whose dreaded power was at its height in the sixties of the last century. Little noted for some years, the Socialists took advantage, in 1886, of a general economic crisis to spread their propaganda among the working classes. The ill-advised repressive measures of the government, alarmed perhaps by the Communist rising in Belgium in the same year, led to riots in Amsterdam and much bloodshed. Excluded from political power by a restricted suffrage, the Socialist party advocated at first, in violent phrases, the suppression of private property by force. Later came a split in the party, and the moderate element adopted the more sensible and effective means of advancing its views by purely political agitation. A later interesting phase of the labor question in Holland was furnished by the great strike in 1903 on the state-owned railroads, and the passage by the states-general of a bill forbidding, under heavy penalty, any more strikes on public works.

Prince Henry, the royal consort, took advantage of an opportunity to establish himself in the hearts of the people of the Netherlands, when on February 21, 1907, the "Berlin" went ashore off the Hook of Holland, and many lives were lost. He personally aided in the rescue, and his bravery will not be forgotten. The Dutch were very much agitated over the lack of an heir to the throne, always fearing German succession, which fortunately has been definitely settled. During 1907, the whole country looked forward to the meeting of the Hague tribunal, and on February 22nd, the government announced that on or about June 1st, delegates would be received. The session at Brussels of the Belgium and Dutch commissioners marked a new epoch in the relations between the two countries, arrangements being effected for a more economical alliance between them. The convening of the second Peace Conference, on June 15, 1907, filled the Dutch city with delegates from all over the world, and for the following few months, matters that had disturbed the various nations, were peacefully discussed and settled by their various representatives at The

KINGDOM OF NETHERLANDS

Hague. The Queen received the various delegates on July 1st, charming them all with her sweet dignity and royal bearing. The Netherlands have always been thrifty as a people and a government, and the bill introduced in parliament, in November, 1907, for the redemption of 40,000 acres of land from the Zuyder Zee, at a cost of $1,200,000, was in line with its general policy.

The Netherlands took a decided stand with regard to Venezuelan affairs. When their colonists appealed to them on July 5, 1908, they did not hesitate to promise sufficient protection, and they instantly resented the expulsion of their minister, M. de Rue, on July 25th, from Venezuela, sending a government cruiser after him. The Gelderland, a war ship, was sent from Willemstad for Venezuela, on July 27th, and on July 29th, the Dutch residents of the former port, started a boycott against Venezuela schooners. The battleships were ordered on July 30th, to be made ready for instant sailing to the Caribbean sea. The Venezuelan government, on July 31st, sent a note to the Netherlands, endeavoring to excuse their action, by setting forth the insults to which they claimed they had been subject, and on August 1st, President Castro followed this by the demand for an apology from Holland. The Gelderland sent on August 2nd, a report to the home government, that the authorities refused to allow them to send any communications sent ashore. The trouble between the two countries attracted the attention of the whole world, and on August 18th, the United States outlined her policy by notifying Holland that any action, save that of an endeavor to gain territory, would be satisfactory to her. Holland showed her intentions fully and openly in issuing an order on August 19th, that the warships be cleared for action. Matters were in this condition for several weeks, Castro further involving himself by refusing to allow shipment of goods to Dutch ports from Venezuela. This high-handed action resulted in revocation of the treaty of 1894, between Holland and Venezuela. This was followed by the seizing by the Gelderland of several of the Venezuelan vessels, but after the fleeing of Castro, the Gelderland was recalled, although, on January 18, 1909, Holland issued her intention of keeping her warships near Venezuela until the pending questions were definitely decided.

In the midst of the grave questions of war and statesmanship, the country was delighted over the birth of the Princess Juliana, on April 30, 1909, which gave Holland the long desired heir. The christening of this little princess was celebrated with great pomp, June 4th, and she is now, in April, 1910, a year old, and the idol of the people she may one day rule over.

This sketch of the present conditions in the Netherlands would be incomplete without a glance at the vast colonial empire which the enterprise of Holland's sturdy seamen and thrifty merchants built up for her in the East Indian seas. The Netherlands' colonial empire to-day includes the richest and most populous islands of the East Indies, Java, Sumatra, Celebes, the Spice Islands, and vast regions in Borneo and New Guinea. This vast empire over seas is sixty times the size of the mother country, with a population over six times as great. The gradual development of the Dutch colonial empire has been traced incidentally in these pages from the time when Houtman made his daring voyage into the Portuguese main in 1595, through the long and eventful period of struggle with the Spaniards and Portuguese, which ended in a complete triumph for the Dutch and the commercial monopoly of the great spice trade by the East India Company. By the middle of the eighteenth century Holland's colonial empire had reached its height. The Dutch controlled Java, Sumatra, the Spice Islands, Ceylon, and the Cape of Good Hope, and had important trading stations in India, China, and in Japan, where they were the only Europeans to be tolerated. The disastrous wars of the latter part of the century, culminating in the French Revolution, delivered the Dutch colonies for the time into the hands of their greatest rivals, the English. The rule of the great East India Company ceased in 1798, when the stadtholder, William V., a fugitive from his native land, placed the Netherlands' colonies under British protection. Dutch governors continued for a time to administer the East Indies regardless of changes in the mother country, until 1811, when on the annexation of Holland to the French empire the islands were annexed to the British empire. Four years passed, and after the fall of Napoleon most of the colonies were restored to Holland, though Ceylon and the Cape Colony had permanently passed into British hands. Many succeeding years were spent by the Dutch in a practical reconquest of their former ground. Sumatra, Celebes, and the Moluccas had to be subdued by force, and a long and bloody war, in which thousands of Europeans perished, was necessary before the whole of Java submitted to the brilliant genius of General Koch. Only in the northern part of Sumatra have the Dutch failed as yet to completely establish their authority. The little mountainous state of Atchin bravely resisted all attempts at subjugation, and a final war for its conquest, begun in 1870, has continued sporadically to the present time with little real advantage and no glory to the Dutch arms.

The monopolistic rule of the East India Company ceased, as has been said, in 1798. On their recession to Holland the colonies were directly administered by the Dutch government with little or no regard for the welfare of the natives and solely for the benefit of the mother country. A system of forced labor, called the culture system, was universally introduced, and the home treasury was swelled by the huge profits of the state-owned plantations. A new era for the Indies began, however, with the revision of the constitution in 1848, by which the supervision of the colonial administration was placed more nearly in the hands of the representatives of the Dutch people. A new conception of a government of the colonies for the benefit of the natives began to gain ground, and this humanitarian movement was given new impulse in 1860 by the publication of an epoch-making novel, "Max Havelaar," by a former colonial official, Eduard Douwes Dekker, in which the abuses of the culture system were painted in startling colors. The Liberal party found it necessary to adopt a different policy. The culture system of forced labor was gradually abolished or alleviated, and the revenues of the Indies were no longer poured into the Dutch treasury, but retained for the local benefit. The result has been a marvelous increase in the wealth and prosperity of the colonies. Under the able administration of such men as Frans Van der Putte the population has more than doubled in less than fifty years, and, though the natives have as yet little share in the government, affairs have been administered in general greatly to their benefit. In fact, the Dutch Indies present to-day one of the too few successful examples of prosperous colonial government, and form an interesting object lesson worthy of careful study by those nations whose career of colonial expansion has just begun.

Though the Netherlands no longer occupy the great place among nations which was theirs two centuries ago, the little state lives by no means merely in the memories of a glorious past. The Dutch people govern one of the greatest colonial empires in the world; despite the slender natural resources of their land, wrested by centuries of painful labor from the sea, they rival the greatest nations in works of peace and enterprises of activity. With a commerce which has increased fivefold in the last half century, Holland stands to-day as the fifth commercial power of the world, with a trade extending to every sea, infinitely greater than she enjoyed in the days of her former greatness. Her internal advancement has kept pace with her commercial prosperity. Great ship canals have opened such interior cities as Rotterdam and Amsterdam to the world's commerce, and placed them among the leading ports of Europe; and the gigantic project of draining the shallow Zuyder Zee and reclaiming a vast area to agriculture has lately been seriously agitated.

The Dutch people have retained all the enterprise and the capacity for painful, determined labor in the face of obstacles which distinguished their ancestors and gave the nation its proudest boast: *"Deus mare, Batavus litora fecit."*[3] In an age when the future existence of small independent states seems everywhere to be menaced, this people will yet have nothing to fear if they have also retained their forefather's love of liberty and of country, and if, mindful of the lessons of a glorious past, they remember and adhere faithfully to the motto of their greatest leader, *"Je maintiendrai."*

In 1912 the political questions which were most pronounced were the Tariff Reform and Coast Defence Bills. The first of these bills met such strong opposition that the government was forced to withdraw some of the proposed duties. The Coast Defence Bill was also materially modified and the amount of appropriation reduced. The Queen in opening the States-General on September 17, 1912, said in the Speech from the Throne that the Tariff Reform Bill was necessary for the permanent interest of revenue. A new copyright bill was passed in 1912 after Holland had joined the Convention of Bern. In the budget statement the Finance Minister announced that the revenue deficit of 1913 would be met by a tax on tobacco, and a revised tax on income and capital.

During the year 1913 the Dutch people celebrated the centenary of the establishment of the monarchy after the collapse of the Napoleonic régime of 1813. Exhibitions were held in many cities, all of which proved successful. In February the government brought in proposals for the revision of the Constitution which gave the franchise to heads of families of twenty-five years of age.

[3] God made the sea, the Batavi made the shore.

The legislature was also given power to class as heads of families certain other persons.

In March, 1913, a bill was introduced adopting a system of compulsory old-age insurance for workmen. In June the general elections resulted in a decided reaction against Clerical politics. The Clerical majority was displaced by one of Liberals and Socialists. The Clerical government was forced to resign, and Dr. Bos, Liberal Democrat, was first asked to form a ministry. On his failing to secure proper support M. Cort van der Linden was entrusted by the Queen to form a cabinet. The budget presented in September showed a decided deficit and forced the serious consideration of the increase of taxes on incomes.

In December, 1913, the Queen and Prince Consort attended a centenary pageant at Scheveningen. Here the Prince of Holland landed in 1813 after the Netherlands had regained its independence. In December, 1913, too, the old age Pension Act came into operation and over 80,000 persons of seventy years and over received the first weekly payment of about 85 cents.

The year 1914 saw considerable discussion of the plan to enclose and partially drain the Zuyder Zee. This would result in bringing to cultivation a vast area of land, and would greatly increase the opportunities for agricultural labor. The opponents of the scheme, of course, were the small army of fishermen who annually make nearly $1,000,000 from the fishing in the Zuyder Zee. But the gain for the value of the redeemed land and the resulting crops would greatly outweigh any loss sustained by the fishing interests. The plan is to dyke in four separate areas, one around the island of Wieringen, one to the south of the town of Hoarn, one near the river Eem, and the fourth at the south coast of Friesland. These redeemed areas would contain over 500,000 acres. A fresh-water lake is to be formed in the center of the areas to furnish water to the surrounding districts.

With the rapid progress of events during the summer of 1914 following the Balkan crisis, the position of the Netherlands became one of great danger. Placed near the boundary of the two great nations, Germany and France, which were certain to clash once hostilities were started by their allies, the Netherlands bid fair to be overrun by the contending armies.

On August 2 the Netherlands together with the three Scandinavian countries announced her intention to hold herself to a strict neutrality. At once the army was mobilized and her frontiers strengthened with every force at hand to repel any invasion of her territory. By August 4, 1914, when general hostilities began, the Netherlands was practically an armed camp in her heroic endeavor to maintain her independence and protect her borders from invasion.

Too much cannot be said in praise of Holland for the generous hospitality afforded the Belgian refugees, who fled before the German hosts from their ravaged country in the first weeks of the war to find peace with the Dutch people.

The Netherlands Government acted promptly, and spent money lavishly in providing for the stricken people. Comfortable, sanitary camps were established as soon as possible, scattered families were brought together under one roof, and for a considerable time Holland paid the expenses out of her own treasury. If Holland leaned toward the German Empire when the war broke out, her sentiments changed materially after Belgian refugees had poured over her borders, with first-hand accounts of the devastation of Belgium.

Holland was in a difficult position on the edge of the warzone, but she was far from helpless. With a fine army of 400,000 men, she stood ready to repel any German attack by striking at Aix-la-Chapelle. She held a sword at the back of Germany and could give a good account of herself if attempts were made to violate her neutrality.

Holland suffered principally from economic causes. On the one hand the Allies were anxious to prevent her sending supplies to Germany, and could deprive her of goods she needed, as they controlled the sea. Germany used the same threat of withholding supplies, unless Holland furnished a certain amount of food-stuffs. Throughout the war this struggle went on, Holland being the victim of threats now from the Allies and now from Germany.

If Holland had entered the war, it would not have been of her own will, but because she had been forced into it under pressure of conditions that could not be avoided. Had she become an Ally of the Germans, her splendid troops would have proved an added strength to their armies on the Western Front, but by this act she would have opened the way to the Allies to deliver a blow to a vital part of Germany, Westphalia. If, on the other hand, Holland took sides with the Allies, they could have cut the communications of the German army in Flanders, and dealt perhaps a decisive blow at the German forces on the Western Front.

KINGDOM OF NETHERLANDS

Holland never seriously contemplated abandoning her neutrality, though she maintained her position at a heavy cost. She had the expense of a mobilized army that did not fight. Her trade was crippled and she was burdened with the care of thousands of destitute refugees.

Holland was notified on March 14, 1918, that the United States and British Governments intended to take over all the Dutch ships in their ports, to be compensated for and returned after the war. Holland had delayed for seven months the acceptance of a proposal from the two governments, by which that country was to be supplied with food and fuel, provided the ships lying idle were leased to the United States and Great Britain. The United States then decided to exercise the sovereign rights of a belligerent under the international law of "angary," and place the Dutch ships under American jurisdiction.

The seizure of the Dutch ships was accomplished without friction, the Dutch crews being replaced by Americans. The public press of Holland bitterly denounced the action as unwarranted, but this was perhaps for the effect it would have on German public opinion.

On November 10, 1918, the day before the Armistice went into effect, a train of automobiles arrived at Eysden, on the Dutch frontier. German officers stepped out and demanded that the guard accord passage to the German Kaiser, declaring that everything had been arranged with the Dutch Government, and that the distinguished guest was expected. The guard permitted the Kaiser and his party to enter Holland. After many vexations a refuge was found for him in the home of Count Bentinck, at Amerongen. He was joined soon after his arrival in Holland by the Empress. Here he remained until the fall of 1919, when he bought an estate of his own at Doorn where he has since resided. The Crown Prince was interned on the island of Wieringen, but returned to Germany, November 10, 1923.

In the Summer of 1919, the Government bill for a 45-hour week was passed by the Legislative or Second Chamber of the States General, by a vote of 69 to 3.

As a result of the Peace Treaty with Germany it had become necessary to reconstruct the Treaty of 1839 which regulated the relations between Holland and Belgium. Certain claims which were put forward by Belgium as a basis for this reconstruction involved the cession of the Dutch Province of Limburg and of that part of Zealand south of the Scheldt, or else the right of way over the Ghent-Terneuzen Canal. These claims were vigorously opposed by Holland and relations between Holland and Belgium for a considerable period of the year 1919 were strained.

Late in 1919 the Government of Holland displayed considerable anxiety regarding the spread of radical ideas. Dutch Consuls in all foreign countries were instructed to be especially careful in regard to the visé of passports. On December 5, 1919, the Dutch-German frontier was closed temporarily, almost 10,000 persons being held up on that day at the little frontier town of Heerenberg.

Holland took quick advantage of the conditions following the close of the war and established commercial relations with Germany. A group of Dutch bankers, in October, 1919, granted a credit of over 23 million dollars for the purchase of raw material for German industry, especially cotton.

Holland is called a Protestant country, but the largest single political party is usually the Roman Catholic. A Catholic premier, Mr. Ruys de Beerenbrouck, was appointed September 9, 1918, his Cabinet being Calvinist-Catholic. Woman's suffrage was in full effect by the elections of 1921.

As in England, after-effects of the war took in Holland the form of unemployment, especially during the French and Belgian occupation of the Ruhr, when Holland's usual sources of supply of coal and iron were under French and Belgian control. In the first half of 1925, unemployment had considerably lessened. When economy was a pressing question for the government, Mr. H. Coljin, a former Minister of War and ex-Director of the Royal Dutch Petroleum Company, became Minister of Finance. Reduction of state salaries was one method of retrenchment employed. This necessity for economy was used as an argument against the Army and Navy bills of 1924, which were then defeated and which are coming up again with changes in 1925. Socialists, who make up the chief opposition, urge disarmament. The Navy question is considered important by the government because of Holland's great possessions in the East Indies, neutrality of which must be defended in war. The plan of the British to construct a huge naval base at Singapore, almost in the midst of Dutch possessions, caused some anxiety.

KINGDOM OF NETHERLANDS

1925-1926

Negotiations between Holland and Belgium concerning the mouth of the Scheldt and the Ghent-Terneuzen Canal, broken off in 1920, were renewed in 1925. The Dutch and Belgian Foreign Ministers signed an agreement on April 3, 1925. A joint commission will supervise the canal and the mouth of the Scheldt. In peace, the Scheldt will be open to all vessels; in war, it will be closed to war vessels only. No agreement was reached on the Weilingen channel.

A project for reclaiming land from Zuyder Zee was begun in 1924. Two great dams are to be constructed, one from the west shore of the Zuyder Zee to the Island of Wieringen, one and a half miles long; the other will extend from the Island of Wieringen to the east shore of the Zuyder Zee and be seventeen and a half miles long. More than thirteen hundred square miles are to be reclaimed, adding a tenth to the kingdom.

In January, 1925, an arrangement was made to arbitrate the ownership of the Island of Palmas, near the Philippines, with the United States.

Elections held on July 1, 1925, resulted in a strengthening of the Social Democrats in the Second Chamber and considerably weakened the Right Coalition, made up of the Roman Catholic Party and two Calvinist parties, the Calvinist Anti-Revolutionary and the Christian Historical. Queen Wilhelmina selected M. Coljin to form a new government.

Another cabinet crisis occurred in November, 1925, over an amendment to the budget bill, by which the legation of the Netherlands to the Vatican was abolished by a vote of 52 to 42. At once, the four Catholic members of the Cabinet resigned, and in a few days Premier Coljin handed his resignation to Queen Wilhelmina. Before its overthrow, the Coljin Government passed a bill to establish a Government censorship of moving picture films. The abolishing of the visa between the Netherlands and Germany allowed the former Crown Prince Frederick William of Germany to visit his father, the former Kaiser William II, at Doorn, on February 1, 1926. The prolonged cabinet crisis, which had lasted since November 14, 1925, ended on March 4, 1926, with the formation of a Ministry by former Finance Minister D. J. de Geer, who accepted the invitation of Queen Wilhelmina to make a cabinet without regard to the situation in Parliament. Dr. de Geer also assumed the Ministry of Finance, and H. A. van Karnebeek retained his post as Foreign Minister.

Development in the general trade conditions in Holland and her colonies showed increasing profits, which were reflected generally in bank deposits. Imports for the first five months of 1926 increased, but exports for the same period were slightly less than for the year previous. The new Governor-General of the Dutch East Indies, Dr. A. C. D. de Graeff, assumed his duties in September, 1926. In November, 1925, internal troubles agitated the Dutch East Indies, Communist outbreaks occurring in both East and West Java. They were suppressed by vigorous measures taken by the Dutch authorities. Again in January, 1927, new rebellious outbreaks occurred in Sumatra, similar to those which had taken place in Java. Armed attacks were made upon the Dutch forces, but the casualties were not great. The uprisings were promptly suppressed.

Reduction in the number of working hours in Dutch factories brought about in 1926 and early in 1927 resulted in decided increase of production. Workmen's living conditions and general health improved.

In March, 1927, Mr. J. H. van Royen was appointed Minister from the Netherlands to the United States.

The new economic treaty between Holland and Belgium, which passed the Second Chamber in November, 1926, was defeated in the First Chamber on March 24, 1927, by a vote of 33 to 17. This treaty had chiefly to do with the regulation of navigation on the Scheldt and the Rhine at points where the interests of the two countries coincide.

In July, 1927, Mr. Van Lear Black, an American newspaper proprietor of Baltimore, flew in a Dutch commercial airplane with two Dutch pilots from Amsterdam to Java, making a 39-day trip.

On September 20, 1927, the Dutch Parliament was opened and the Queen's speech featured the difficulties of the financial situation and heavy taxation. Improvement marked the closing months of 1927 and the budget for 1928 was lightened.

The Netherlands had an election in the summer of 1929, when, under the compulsory voting law, 3,380,217 persons went to the polls, but without changing materially the alignments in the Chamber of the States-General. Nevertheless, a new government was formed in August, headed by C. J. M. van Beerenbrouck.

An important event of 1930 was the opening of the Ymuiden Lock of the North Sea Canal, largest canal lock in the world.

Some communistic disorders in Java occurred in 1931.

KINGDOM OF NETHERLANDS 322i
1931-1933

The First Chamber on October 24, 1931, ratified the Oslo Treaty, whereby Holland, Belgium, Norway, Sweden and Denmark agreed to carry out the tariff truce proposed in the Convention of Geneva. On June 20, 1932, Holland, Belgium and Luxemburg signed a customs union pact, in which the countries bound themselves gradually to reduce tariffs affecting the signatories, and agreed not to impose new tariffs.

The seventeen-and-one-half mile dam extending from the Island of Wieringen to the east shore of the Zuyder Zee was completed on May 28, 1932, transforming the Zuyder Zee into an inland lake. About three-quarters of the lake is to be drained in order to acquire approximately 500,000 acres for farm land. The remaining lake will be named Ijsselmeer.

A mutiny in the Dutch navy broke out in Surabaya, Netherlands India in January, 1933, as a result of resentment over a cut in the seamen's pay. On February 5, four hundred of the crew of the battleship *De Zeven Provincien* mutinied at Kotaraja, Northern Sumatra, seizing the ship while most of the officers were ashore and sailing out to the Indian Ocean. The Government dispatched seaplanes, submarines, destroyers and a cruiser to capture the ship. The mutineers sent a wireless message offering to surrender if given immunity and if the wage cut were restored. The Government, however, demanded unconditional surrender, and when this was not forthcoming aerial bombs were dropped from the seaplanes. Several of the mutineers, including most of the leaders, were killed and more wounded. The mutiny had lasted five days. The Communists, who were accused of spreading propaganda leading to the mutiny, supported the mutineers of the battleship. The Socialists refrained from actual support, but did protest against the wage cut.

At the elections for the Lower Chamber, held on April 26, important gains were made by the anti-revolutionary parties. The Socialists and Catholics lost many seats and no Fascist was elected.

Continued Nazi activity in the province of Limburg led to the deportation in July of Herr Tyfler, leader of the Nazi propaganda in that section. Early in August, two other Nazis accused of spreading propaganda in the Heerlen mining district were expelled.

Though the Government had saved approximately $225,000,000 by salary reductions from 1921 to 1933, in October, 1933, a still further salary reduction averaging 5 per cent was announced. This brought the total average cut since 1921 to 26 per cent. On October

17, the Government offered a 200,000,000 guilder (approximately $118,500,000 at current exchange) public works issue at 4 per cent. This was over-subscribed. The Upper Chamber, on October 25, passed a turnover tax bill which was expected to yield approximately $51,850,000. It had been passed previously by the Lower Chamber.

The Government continued to withstand the severe drains of her gold stocks resulting from Japan's departure from the gold standard, the closing of the banks in the United States in March, 1933, and the falling off of revenues from her trade, and remained on the gold standard. The deficit of the 1934 budget was estimated at $124,000,000.

The Netherlands suffered severely from the economic depression in 1934. Foreign trade fell to the lowest level in many years and home industry also declined. The Government, adopting a deflationary policy, made drastic cuts in public expenditures, including a reduction in unemployment benefits. The latter led to rioting in Amsterdam for five days, in July, in which several were killed, and to disturbances in Rotterdam and other cities.

The death of the Prince-Consort, Henry of Mecklenburg-Schwerin, occurred on July 3.

In October, the word "Dutch" was officially banned, in favor of "Netherland," in reference to anything connected with Holland.

The fear of decreased revenues for the fiscal year found the government forced to consider rigid economies in the spring of 1935, taxation having reached its limit. Many of the contemplated measures were opposed by the Socialists. A special emergency fund was set aside for the benefit of agriculture. In the face of Belgium's suspension of the gold standard in March, however, the Netherlands held firm.

HISTORY OF SWITZERLAND

PART I

EARLY SWITZERLAND AND THE RISE OF THE CONFEDERATION.   -1516 A. D.

PART I

EARLY SWITZERLAND AND THE RISE OF THE CONFEDERATION. —1516 A.D.

HISTORY OF SWITZERLAND

Chapter I

THE ANCIENT RACES AND THEIR CIVILIZATION
1000 B. C.—750 A. D.

WE have no information, nor even any tradition, to tell us when and how Switzerland was first peopled. But monuments and remains of hoary antiquity teach us that it was inhabited at the earliest time when mankind appears at all in Europe. Here, as in France and Belgium, human implements made of flint, together with the bones of mammalia long since extinct, such as the mammoth, reindeer, and cave bear, have been found in caves in many places, notably at Thäyngen, in Canton Schaffhausen. The nature of the country and the climate must in those days have been rude and inhospitable, as they now are in the extreme north, and men lived like the savages of to-day, dwelling probably mostly in caves ("Cave-Dwellers" or "Troglodytes"). But their origin, their fate, and their disappearance are wrapped in obscurity.

Many centuries, possibly hundreds of thousands of years, must have elapsed after this before nature assumed her present form. The first settlements, of the period when men took to fixed dwellings and began to seek a higher civilization, were the lake (or pile) dwellings, of which the first discoveries of importance were made at Overmeilen, on the Lake of Zurich, during the winter of 1853-1854. Their existence is traced to the first thousand years before Christ. These dwellings were made of wicker-work, clay, and straw, and stood upon a row of piles driven firmly into the bed of the lake, and joined together by wooden planks. It is not quite clear whether these remarkable habitations were chosen by the inhabitants for the sake of fishing, or from the necessity of defending themselves against wild beasts and savage tribes. But a distinct picture of the mode of life of the inhabitants is handed down to us by the numberless utensils, implements, and animal and vegetable remains which have been found on the sites of such lake-dwellings deeply embedded under layers of peat or in the beds of lakes. Judging by these articles, the pile-builders had already taken the first step toward a higher civilization; they were no longer in the primitive condition of mere hunters and fishers, but already engaged in cattle-farming and agriculture; they kept oxen, sheep, goats, and pigs; they planted barley, wheat, and flax, and were at least acquainted with fruit trees, if they did not cultivate them. For these purposes they used implements skillfully fashioned out of stone, bone, wood, and horn, such as knives, hatchets, chisels, awls, and needles. When they later, probably by means of barter, became acquainted with the metals, bronze and iron, they employed these more pliable and more durable materials, and could then make their implements much more perfect. By the pile-dwellings of the lakes of Neuchâtel and Bienne we find that this progress was first made in western Switzerland, which lay nearer to the advanced civilization of the Rhone district. In very early times, too, the lake-dwellers knew how to make excellent thread and cord, cloth and clothing out of flax and linen, and could mold cooking utensils, plates, and dishes out of clay. Time perfected their skill; their household utensils became more numerous and more artistic, and soon ornaments and trinkets, such as rings and bracelets, brooches, and hairpins, came into use, which show that the necessaries of life and its customs were growing gradually more refined. Little by little men forsook these lake-dwellings, few of which seem to have been preserved even as late as the time of the Romans, and settled themselves on the mainland in the vicinity. Most of the pile-buildings were destroyed by fire, and many were forsaken in very early times, even before the discovery of metals.

We speak of the Celtic tribes, but in reality we know no more of the name and descent of the population than we do of the period of the lake-dwellings. It seems to have belonged to the Indo-European race; and as the objects that have been found belonging to the epoch of the lake-dwellers bear a close resemblance to those discovered on the mainland in the tombs and ruins of a later period, which are undoubtedly Celtic (Gallic) in origin, it is thought that those older settlements may also be ascribed to that race. The Celts originally inhabited almost the whole of Middle and Western Europe, and also Switzerland, before they were driven out by the Romans and the Teutonic tribes; but the first certain information we have of those in Switzerland comes to us through Romans and

Greeks of the last two centuries before Christ. A number of different tribes then occupied this land, by nature so varied in aspect: the Allobroges around Geneva, the Sequani around the lakes of Neuchâtel and Bienne, chiefly beyond the Jura, the Raurici around Basle, the Rhætians, a mingled race of Celts and Etruscans, throughout the Alpine district of the southeast, as far as the Lake of Zug, the upper Lake of Zurich and the Lake of Constance, the Veragri and Seduin in Valais.

The most noteworthy are the Helvetians, who originally occupied southern Germany as far as the Main, besides central Switzerland, and whose power surpassed that of any other Celtic tribe. They were divided into almost independent tribes or counties (*Gaue*), such as those of the Tigorini, Verbigeni, etc., the county assemblies managing common affairs. In the possession of many elements of a higher civilization, such as gold coinage and the Greek alphabet, they were also, as Cæsar, later their conqueror, says, "the bravest people of the Gauls." At the commencement of the great German migration, with the invasion of the Cimbri and Teutons, they followed the general course toward the sunny south, and in the year 107 B.C., under their youthful leader, Divico, totally defeated the Romans at Aginnum (now Agen) on the Garonne, and forced them to pass under the yoke. But failing to follow up their victory, they were forced to retreat, after the greater part of them had been defeated (101 B. C.), together with the Cimbri, by Marius in the plains of Lombardy.

The Celts did not remain independent much longer after this: the brilliant victory obtained by the Romans over the Cimbri and Teutons, and the gradual advance of the Roman eagles across the Alps, menaced their freedom; divided, scattered, and incapable of founding any durable state, they became an easy prey to the warlike conquerors of the world. The Romans had already found a footing at Geneva by conquering the country of the Allobroges, when the Helvetians, remembering the sunny lands of southern Gaul, wishing to avoid the continual aggressions made upon them by Teutonic hordes from the north, and also incited by their ambitious chief, Orgetorix, migrated afresh, under the leadership of Divico, on March 28, 58 B. C., after having set fire to all their twelve towns and four hundred villages. Notwithstanding their valiant resistance, they were defeated by Cæsar, then engaged in the conquest of Gaul, at **Bibracte** (Mount Beuvrais, west of

Autun). The survivors were sent back home by him, as Roman subjects, to defend the Rhine frontier against the Teutons. In the following year Valais was brought into subjection by one of Cæsar's generals, and about forty years later, in 15 B.C., the wild Rhætian tribes, who had frequently ravaged the valley of the Po, succumbed to the might of the Roman legions, and the persistence of Drusus and Tiberius, the stepsons of the Emperor Augustus.

The Celts of the land were thus subjected to the Romans, and their own national development was entirely arrested. They have left a durable heritage behind them, inasmuch as a number of places, which have now grown into flourishing towns, owe their origin to them, as for instance, Geneva, Lausanne, Avenches, Soleure, Zurich, Basle, and Coire; many mountains and rivers also received their present names from them, as the Jura, Albis, Kamor, and Sentis; the Rhine, Töss, Thur, Rhone, and Reuss.

The Celts did not attain to any high or lasting degree of civilization; the neighboring tribes of the Helvetians in especial eked out a miserable and unquiet existence, the Rhætians and Allobroges led a wild life of war and pillage; moreover, the country was as yet only partially cultivated, the valley of the Rhine toward the Lake of Constance still consisting of wild and impenetrable forest and marsh land.

The Romans brought with them a more refined civilization, the product of southern soil. In the course of the conquest the political and military organizations were formed as follows: The territory conquered by Cæsar and before his time formed a part of Gaul, while the country of the Allobroges was united to the province of Narbonne (Provence), that of the Sequani, Raurici, and Helvetians to Belgian Gaul; the southeast, however, formed a part of the province of Rhætia, including what are now Bavaria and the Tyrol; the "Valais" (meaning "valley") was at first considered part of Rhætia, but afterward formed a separate province on account of its isolated position. Every several territory had its own provincial governor; various subordinate officials came into the country to collect taxes and tolls and to command the garrisons. Custom-houses were established at all places of commercial importance on the frontiers, at Zurich (Turicum), St. Maurice, and other places. The conquered people were not, on the whole, oppressed, and the Romans did their utmost to accommodate their arrangements to existing conditions. The Helvetians, for instance, still, as hitherto, formed a separate community, as did the Allobroges and others, and the division into counties was preserved. Aventicum (Avenches) and Augusta Rauricorum (Basel-augst) both became towns after the Italian style; they had their own mayor and their municipal council; both were, like Nyon (Noviodunum), colonies with Roman rights; Octodurum (Martigny) had a purely civic constitution. Aventicum was still the chief town of the Helvetians, and its senate formed the central Helvetic authority.

The Helvetians soon took an active part in the development of the empire, but amid the disorders of the civil war after Nero's death in 68-69 A.D. they drew upon themselves a total defeat by embracing the cause of Galba: Alienus Cäcina, lieutenant-general of Galba's rival Vitellius, routed them at the Bözerg (near Baden), took Aventicum the capital, and put Julius Alpinus,[1] the leader of the revolt, to death; further chastisement was only averted by the persuasive eloquence of Cossus, the Helvetic envoy. With this exception the vanquished peoples of the land seem to have enjoyed a peaceful quietude. The Romans were more concerned about military precautions toward the north than about the enjoyment of their supremacy. To this end a line of fortresses was constructed along the course of the Rhine (Arbon, Stein, Zurzach, Basel-augst, and others). The military center was at Windisch (Vindonissa), which, situated at the junction of the Aar and the Reuss in the vicinity of the Rhine, formed a natural defense and an excellent strategic center. Out of the three legions which served to protect the frontier of the Upper Rhine of Gaul against the Teutons, one had their camp at Windisch. Military roads were made for military communication. Two of these led from Italy northward, one over the great St. Bernard through Lower Valais, by Aventicum and Soleure to Basel-augst; the other over the passes of the Grisons to Coire, and through the Rheintal along the Lake of Constance to Bregenz. They were united in the north by a road leading from Basel-augst through Windisch, over Winterthur (Vitudurum), Pfin (Ad fines) to Arbon and Bregenz. The garrisons and fortresses were mostly occupied by foreign troops.

This military organization soon underwent a change, as in the time of the Emperor Domitian or Trajan, about 100 A.D.,

---

[1] The story of Julia Alpinula, his supposed daughter, rests upon a gross falsification of an inscription.

when the adjacent territory beyond the Rhine nearly as far as the Danube was united to the Roman empire, and the frontier troops were also pushed forward. The land of the Helvetians was now free from troops for 150 years, and seems to have remained undisturbed by any war, a condition of things particularly favorable to the development of Roman civilization.

To meet the military requirements, workshops, inns, and towns were established. The veterans, who were discharged soldiers, built themselves many villas or country houses after the Roman style, with splendid mosaics and frescoes, baths, and like luxuries and adornments. In Baden or Aquæ (Canton Aargau) public baths were established of great size and magnificence, and became much frequented. Romans betook themselves thither in numbers. The miserable conditions of the Celtic period vanished by degrees before Roman civilization; roads were made across the Alps, over the Julier, Splügen, Septimer, and St. Bernard; even across the wild forest and marshland of the Rheintal and around the Lake of Constance a passable and broad road was constructed by the energy of Rome. Commerce developed rapidly; various products found their way from the north of France and Germany through Switzerland to Italy, and the products of the country most esteemed by the Romans, such as cheese, wax, honey, pinewood, and resin, were likewise exported. The wares of the south were in return brought into the country, such as oil, oysters, and wine; and vineyards were planted around the Lake of Geneva and in the Pays de Vaud. With Roman civilization their pompous state religion was also introduced, and the rude rites of the Celtic worship almost disappeared. Roman culture exercised a salutary influence even over the dispositions and habits of the people: the Allobroges now exchanged the sword for the plow, the predatory Rhætians adopted gentler habits, and conducted the traveler and his sumpter mule, whom formerly they would have robbed, peaceably across the mountains, or employed themselves in agriculture and Alpine farming. In the larger towns, such as Aventicum and Augusta, the Celts learned divers arts and crafts from their Roman masters.

Thus was the foundation laid of an entirely new development. Roman civilization took much deeper and more lasting root in what is now western Switzerland than it did further eastward. The former lying in close proximity to the southern part of Gaul, which had become altogether Roman, Roman colonies sprang up, forming centers of culture. Here the manners of Rome were adopted, as also her arts and learning. Aventicum, about ten times as large as the modern Avenches, surrounded by walls, protected by between eighty and ninety towers, had an amphitheater for gladiatorial contests, a theater, a temple, a triumphal arch, a public gymnasium, trade guilds, and even an academy with Roman professors. The magnificent capitals of columns, friezes, and ornaments which have been found there prove that they had attained to great perfection in Italian art. The Celtic language and customs, which the few colonists in eastern Switzerland were insufficient to expel, vanished in the west before those of Rome, and the Latin tongue took such firm root that it withstood the storms of migration, and is still preserved, though in a modified form, in western Switzerland and Lower Valais, while the Roman culture of the eastern parts being but little disseminated and little developed, crumbled like a rotten edifice under the blows of the German conquerors.

But the golden age of Roman civilization lasted barely a century and a half in Switzerland. As early as the third century the Roman empire began to totter before the advance of the hardy Teuton. Amid the universal ruin under Gallienus, about 260 A.D., the Alamanni, a Teutonic tribe, overran Switzerland and burned beautiful Aventicum to the ground, to lie thenceforth almost in ashes. The Romans were forced to cede the frontier of the Danube, and to withdraw behind the Rhine, and the old fortresses along the Rhine from Basel-augst to Arbon became once more Roman points of defense. Repeatedly destroyed, they were always rebuilt and fortified afresh, as were Oberwinterthur and Stein under Diocletian and Maximian, about 300 A. D.; several emperors (Constantine Chlorus, Julian, Valentinian I., and Gratian) achieved passing successes in their advances through northern Switzerland; public buildings, bridges, and roads were from time to time repaired, and in 374 Basle, the " royal city," arose at the great bend of the Rhine. But no imperial hand could long protect the empire from the youthful daring of the Alamanni; the latter had already established themselves in Alsace and on the Lake of Constance, and were striving for the possession of Switzerland; the inhabitants fled in terror from their property, buried their most treasured possessions, hoping to enjoy them again in better days, or migrated to the south; the empire, meanwhile, divided and enfeebled, was sinking fast.

This period of the decline of the Roman empire was not without beneficent effects in other ways. As early as the second century Christianity, with its world-regenerating moral and religious principles, began to develop into the religion of the world; amid the universal decay, when all things seemed to totter, it became the anchor of hope to which thousands joyfully clung. By the many roads made by the Romans the trade of Gaul and Italy reached Swiss territory, beginning in 200-300 A.D. at Geneva, Valais, and Rhætia; an official Christian inscription has been found in Valais dating from the year 377. From these districts Christianity penetrated into the interior, being chiefly propagated by legionaries, by whose instrumentality it probably reached Zurich from Italy by way of Rhætia. Bishoprics were soon established in the larger Roman towns, Geneva, Aventicum, Basel-augst, Windisch (afterward Constance), Octodurum (Martigny), and Coire. But Christianity only gained the victory after many hardships and struggles, the natural clinging to an ancient faith and the power and might of the religion of the Romans forming obstacles hard to overcome. The Roman emperors necessarily looked upon Christianity as hostile to the state; their governors were enjoined to hinder its progress, and in the third century violent persecutions began. The most severe and extensive—under Diocletian, 303-304 A. D.—seems to have extended to what is now Switzerland, for Christian tradition tells of several martyrs of that time, mostly Christian legionaries, such as the "Thebans" St. Maurice and his fellows at St. Maurice, Ursus and Victor at Soleure, Felix and Regula at Zurich, all of whom firmly refused to sacrifice to idols, and were put to death amid excruciating tortures. The fame of these Christian martyrs surrounded the Christian churches of these places with a halo of sanctity, and gave a great impetus to the Christian church; without the luster shed by the honored martyrs the ideal seeds of religious life sown by Christianity would hardly have survived the wild storms of this and the following periods.

In the beginning of the fifth century the obstinate struggle between the Roman and the Teuton was finally decided entirely in favor of the latter. In order to defend the heart of the distressed empire, garrisons were withdrawn from the Rhine to Italy, and the Rhine frontier was thus left exposed. Consequently, when the great migration of tribes set in at the end of 406 A.D., pouring from Germany toward the southwest, the Alamanni crossed the Rhine on the night of New Year's Eve, as is said, and the wild storm of devastation ruthlessly swept away the last vestiges of Roman culture. In the succeeding years the Alamanni advanced nearly to the Rhætian Alps (Grisons), and by the middle of the century Roman supremacy was at an end in the northeast of Switzerland. Besides this territory, the Alamanni, like the Helvetians of former times, held the country between the Rhine and the Main, as also Alsace. Roman manners and the Roman tongue continued only in the rocky districts of Rhætia and in the southwest of Switzerland, being protected in the former by the mountains, and having taken deep root in the latter. But in neither of these parts was the Roman speech preserved in its purity; for while in Rhætia it mingled with the Celtic (Rhætian) tongue, in the southwest a Teutonic element was introduced by the Burgundians. These latter had followed in the wake of the Alamanni; in vain they had sought a new home on the banks of the Rhine, around Worms: their realm was laid waste by the Romans and the Huns; they subsequently pushed southward, and in 443 A.D. received "Sabaudia" from the hands of Ætius the Roman, *i. e.*, Savoy as far as the Lake of Geneva, Lower Valais and the southeastern part of Vaud; they extended their territory considerably to the west and south, embracing Provence, Besançon, and Langres; the Saane probably formed their eastern boundary. The Burgundians drove the Alamanni out of west Switzerland eastward. The kingdom flourished under King Gundobad, who in the year 500 thrust out his brother and ruled alone, and who sought by wise laws to civilize his people and to amalgamate them with the Romans.

The Alamanni and Burgundians met with very different conditions in their new land, and established themselves in quite different ways. During their fierce struggles of almost two centuries the Alamanni had conceived a deep hatred of the Romans. At the time of their conquest the population was thin and civilization at a low ebb; thus they were free from all Roman influence, and might settle down in their own fashion. They therefore took possession of the already Christianized land as pagans, sword in hand, effaced almost every trace of Roman civilization which still existed, and killed or enslaved the former inhabitants. They thus fully established a purely German mode of life, which has con-

Hist. Nat. XIII-25

tinued to this day. Their settlements were made altogether in old German style: relatives, families, and individuals settled wherever they pleased, attracted by some spring, field, or forest. They scorned to live like Romans, in towns and attached houses, preferring open villages and hamlets, or, better still, scattered farmsteads, where each man surrounded his dwelling with a courtyard and a hedge, then called an *"etter,"* such as may yet be seen in Appenzell and Toggenburg. The name of the first founder of the farmstead was afterward transferred to the place itself, hence the many place-names derived from the names of persons or families ending in *wiler, wil, hofen, hausen,* etc., from *weiler,* a hamlet, *hof,* a farm, and *haus,* a house: e. g., Bärentswil (from *Beroltes-wilare*), i. e., "Berolt's hamlet," and Irgenhusen (from *Iringes-husa*) i. e., "at the house of Iring."

With the Burgundians it was quite different. These latter stood in more friendly relations to the Romans than did the Alamanni; they obtained their land by a formal treaty, and shared it also peaceably with a number of Romans, the Burgundians receiving two-thirds of every house or farm, and of all arable lands and servants. In west Switzerland they were confronted by a far more fully developed civilization, respected and esteemed Roman ways, lived together in Roman fashion in enclosed towns or boroughs, and were soon merged into one nation with the Romans, as had been the case with the Franks, thus forming the basis of the Romance or French character.

But in spite of these important differences, the two races had certain political and social principles and institutions in common, such as the systematical division of "districts" and "hundreds" (*centenæ*), the legal constitution (*Wergeld*),[2] popular assemblies, and the divisions of rank, viz., freemen, subdivided into nobles (*primi*), landowners (*medii*), and freemen without land (*minoflidi*); freedmen (*liti*), and serfs or bondmen; as well as affairs relating to the community in general, the Almend,[3] Mark,[4] and the Markgenossenschaft.[5]

[2] i. e., the fine which a murderer was obliged to pay to the kindred of his victim. This was regulated according to the rank of the person injured; a higher "*Wergeld*" was set upon freemen than upon serfs, and the clergy and nobles were more highly valued than ordinary freemen.

[3] Undivided land surrounding a settlement.

[4] The boundary between two settlements.

[5] The "Association of the Mark."

The development of this new state was by no means free and unrestrained; the Teutonic peoples soon turned their arms against one another, and another Teutonic race, the Franks, succeeded, by their own energy and by a skillful use of their opportunities in gaining the supremacy over the others. The Alamanni were first overthrown by Clovis, in 496 A. D., in a battle on the Upper Rhine,

Internal dissensions soon brought about the fall of the Burgundians. Notwithstanding the zealous efforts of the Roman Catholic clergy, the Burgundians obstinately adhered to their Arian faith, Gundobad declaring emphatically that he " would not have two gods," because according to Catholic teaching Christ was a Divine Being, who had existed from everlasting, equal with God the Father, while according to Arianism he was dependent upon God the Father and subject unto Him. The dispute became keener, when after the conversion of the Frankish king Clovis to Catholic Christianity, after the battle against the Alamanni, the Roman Catholics fixed their hopes upon this enterprising prince; and Gundobad's own son Sigismund went over to the Catholics. Clovis made encroachments even in Gundobad's time, and after the death of the latter in 516 the confusion increased, and in 532 the sons of Clovis completely routed the Burgundians in the battle of Autun. Some years later, in 536, Coire-Rhætia was ceded to the Franks by the Ostrogoths, to whose empire it had belonged, and the Merovingians now reigned supreme throughout Switzerland.

The Franks encouraged the continuance of native institutions. Coire-Rhætia remained, as before, subject to a *präses* chosen by the people as chief magistrate and administrator, and from the end of the sixth century for a period of almost two hundred years this office remained hereditary in the hands of the family of the so-called Victorides, who even acquired the bishopric of Coire, and the customs of Coire-Rhætia remained undisturbed. Burgundy, too, had its own organization and administration. The Alamanni likewise retained their dukes and their national rights; these were, however, renewed and extended, in accordance with Christianity, at the beginning of the eighth century under Clotaire IV., king of the Franks, and were greatly expanded in favor of the church. The Franks also introduced the county system and royalties.

At this period of the supremacy of the Franks the propagation of Christian culture divides itself naturally among the three races. In this respect western Switzerland once more had the advantage over the eastern parts, as had been the case in the time of the Celts and Romans. For by its position Burgundy was naturally the first to feel the impulse given to Catholic Christianity in Gaul. Soon after St. Martin had introduced a great revival into the monastic life of Gaul, about the year 500, the two brothers Romanus and Lupicinus arrived in the wooded mountains of the Jura, and led there a life full of strict self-denial and earnest meditation. Romanus probably gave rise to the foundation of the famous monastery of Romainmotier (Canton Vaud). The sister foundation of Condat in the French Jura (St. Claude) was a nursery of cultured life; from it, "as from a beehive," says the biographer of Romanus, "sped hosts of missionaries and teachers in all direction," who brought the land under cultivation, founded monasteries and schools, and encouraged learning. Beside Condat and Romainmotier there flourished the monastery of St. Maurice in the Valais, founded by a bishop in honor of the "Thebans," and enlarged in 515 by the Burgundian King Sigismund. Octodurum (Martigny) and Aventicum had hitherto formed the center of church life; when, however, Aventicum fell into decay, the seat of the bishopric was removed to beautiful Lausanne (about 580), and that of Martigny to Sion. Bishop Marius, who conferred this favor upon Lausanne, encouraged Roman education, and found time in the midst of other labors to write a chronicle; it was he, too, who laid the foundation of the town of Payerne.

The Frankish kings and their clergy did their utmost to spread Christianity among the Alamanni. According to a somewhat doubtful tradition, St. Fridolin is said to have gone as a missionary to Alamannia, under the protection of Clovis himself; he founded Säckingen, and the Tal Glarua, which was soon united to Säckingen, honors him as its patron saint. The greatest influence over the Alamanni was exercised by Irish monks, who devoted themselves to their missionary labors with youthful enthusiasm and heroic self-sacrifice. Columban with his fellows, driven out of Gaul, came to the Lake of Zurich about 610. With fervent zeal he disturbed the pagans at Tuggen in the midst of their sacrifice, barely escaped being stoned to death, and proceeded to Arbon and Bregenz, Roman stations on the Lake of Constance, where he found Christians already, and a Christian minister in the midst of the heathen. Here, too, excess of zeal against pagan rites brought him and his companions into great peril; Columban escaped into Italy; Gallus, one of his disciples, remained behind on account of sickness, built himself a cell, in 614, on the wilds of Steinach, regardless of danger, gathered disciples and thus formed an oasis in the desert. Afterward, in 720, Othmar founded on the spot the Benedictine monastery of St. Gall, destined to become a beacon of Christian culture illuminating the land. The activity of Columban and his companions had a far-reaching effect, extending as far as western Switzerland and Rhætia; disciples and followers from both those parts founded the monasteries of Granval in the Bernese Jura, St. Ursanne on the Doubs, and Dissentis in the valley of the Upper Rhine. Pirminius, a native of the Grisons mountains, founded Pfäffers in 720 and also Reichenau. Such foundations were everywhere followed by cultivation of land, clearing of forests, and encouragement of learning. The ecclesiastical organization of Alamannia had also by this time become more settled. After the decay of Vindonissa, Constance became the ecclesiastical center of northeastern and central Switzerland. And the more Christianity was favored by those in authority, so much the more the ground gave way under the feet of paganism.

Chapter II

UNION UNDER CARLOVINGIAN AND GERMAN RULE
750-1057

THE Merovingians soon proved unequal to the great task of governing their realm; they were mostly incapable weaklings, and the kingdom fell to pieces. The German family of Carlovingians, which originally held only the rank of mayors of the palace, thereupon rose more and more into power, and in 751 dispossessed the Merovingians. The new dynasty abolished the dukedom of Alamannia and took the country under their immediate control. The same alteration took place with regard to Burgundy and Coire-Rhætia, and thus, about 800, the whole land became a province and an integral part of the empire of Charlemange.

The uniform organization which was now introduced into every one of the different parts furthered a general development and cohesion. The whole land was still divided into counties according to older local institutions. The most important counties were: Thurgau (comprising northeastern Switzerland), Zürichgau, Aargau, Augstgau, Vaud, Valais, Coire, and Geneva. The counts were royal governors, who administered justice and mustered troops in the king's name. The feudal system also now came into existence. In Rhætia, too, bishops and counts gathered around themselves a following of liegemen, to whom they granted lands, privileges, and offices, and who in their turn had their own servants and vassals. Charles alone was able to avert the fatal results of this system. It is chiefly after his time that the influential position of the church becomes noticeable. The clergy gradually acquired great temporal riches by donations and enfeoffments. Charles assigned them tithes as a source of regular income. He specially favored bishops; the bishops of Coire and Basle were befriended by him; by the help of Charles the Bishop of Constance was enabled to maintain his claims against the monastery of St. Gall, which had been obliged to resist the pretensions of the bishops even in the time of Pepin: St. Gall was now forced to pay a yearly tribute to Constance in token of dependence. Charles also encouraged the clergy in their custom of living together (canons); the management of the Institute of Canons (*Chorherrenstift*) of Zurich seems to have been settled by his orders, and the canons of the Grossmünster always thenceforth honored him as their patron, and even, erroneously, as their founder. Zurich tradition, however, rightly reveres him as the first founder of the cathedral school or *Carolinum,* and has kept his unbounded administrative activity in well-deserved remembrance. Tradition speaks of a house called the " House of the Hole " ("*Zum Loch*") where a snake begged for his aid against a toad, and to this day the statue of the incomparable emperor adorns the *Grossmünster,* with the sword of justice on his knees, like a patron protecting the town. His grandson, Louis the German, afterward, in 853, founded the abbey in Zurich called the *Fraumünster,* and bestowed upon it his estates in the little canton of Uri, and many other possessions.

At Charles' instigation a life of learning was roused into activity in the religious houses and everywhere among the clergy. Bishop Hatto, of Basle, issued orders commanding priests to collect books; the monastery of Reichenau had already a considerable library, and was in a very flourishing condition. At this time agriculture, trade, and commerce also made great progress under the splendid legislation and excellent administration of the emperor. The position of freemen was protected, and the nobility were kept in check.

Thus Switzerland also benefited by the many-sided creative and organizing activity of the emperor. But after his death in 814 the uniform administration collapsed, and manifold differences arose.

The county system was dissolved. The counties became hereditary fiefs in the hands of powerful families; numerous episcopal and monastic churches received "immunity" or freedom from the jurisdiction of courts, and established their own courts of justice, as St. Gall, Pfäffers, the *Fraumünster* of Zurich and Coire. A reaction against enforced uniformity also set in on the part of the various races and divisions of the empire. The immediate result of this reaction was the division of the empire by the **Treaty of Verdun in 843; the present German or Alamannian**

Switzerland, with Coire-Rhætia, went to Louis the German and his empire of the East Franks; western Switzerland and Valais to Lothaire and his " Middle Empire," and afterward to the empire of the West Franks. Thus Burgundy and Alamannia remained for a long time separate, and soon formed themselves into separate states. In the confusion caused by the fall of the Carlovingian dynasty, Burgundian Switzerland came into the Guelph family, and Rudolf I. succeeded in establishing himself as an almost independent prince in the country between the Jura, the Lake of Geneva, and the Alps. In January, 888, he was made king at St. Maurice of a realm extending as far as Basle. Fierce struggles in Alamannia were followed by a like result. Count Burkhard of Rhætia, aspiring to become a duke, was prevented by two ambitious officers of the Thurgau exchequer, Erchanger and Berchtold, and by Salomon III., the crafty Bishop of Constance and Abbot of St. Gall, and was slain at a diet in 911. His young son of the same name profited by a dispute between the bishop and the officers of the exchequer to make a faction for himself, and finally obtained the ducal rank in 917, the officers having been overthrown by the bishop. Thus arose the dukedom of Alamannia or Suabia, which lasted till the thirteenth century.

The people suffered much at this time. Not only did the neighboring predatory peoples of the Hungarians, and the Saracens from the south of France, begin to make raids upon the land, to penetrate into towns, villages, and monasteries, to devastate the fields and interrupt traffic, but among themselves feuds and civil wars raged. The haughty nobles strove one against another, and the peasants were unprotected. The condition of the freemen became worse and worse; they either yielded themselves as vassals or copyhold tenants to some temporal or spiritual lord or else became bondmen and freedmen of the nobility. A powerful aristocracy was gradually developed.

During this dissolution of political conditions, about the end of the ninth and the beginning of the tenth century, ecclesiastical learning developed greatly. The more wealthy monasteries of Reichenau, Rheinau, St. Gall, and Zurich, which had become independent domains, cultivated the intellectual life which had been awakened in the time of Charles the Great. The monastery of St. Gall specially distinguished itself. It set itself free from all dependence upon the bishops of Constance, and the monastery itself was rebuilt in magnificent style. It included about forty buildings, for besides the actual monastic accommodation it contained wide-stretching domestic buildings, bakehouses, breweries, mills, and various workshops, and so formed a small town in itself. From thence the abbots zealously cultivated intellectual life. There were two schools, an inner school for monks and an outer for the laity. The discipline is said to have been so exemplary that when King Conrad I. visited the monastery and tempted the young scholars during their exercises with gold pieces and apples they would not even glance at them. Eminent teachers, such as the famous singer and composer, Notker the Stammerer or the Saint, Ratbert of Zurich, the historian of the monastery, and Tutilo, the great master-sculptor, labored here. The ancient classics were read; boys learned to make extempore Latin hexameters and pentameters, and were taught to play stringed instruments. All the arts and sciences were taught and cultivated; here the study of the German language received a powerful stimulus, and here the first German celestial globe was finished. St. Gall was also the school of music and song of that age; it produced numerous compositions for the service of the mass, and a contemporary historian writes that St. Gall had filled the church of God with brightness and joy, not only in Alamannia, but in all lands from one sea to another, by his hymns, songs, and melodies. Writing and painting became high arts at St. Gall. These arts were cultivated quite like manufactures—some made parchment, others drew lines; some wrote, while others again illuminated and painted the titles and initial letters with magnificent ornament; others bound the books in covers, which were often adorned with beautiful carved work in ivory, silver, and gold. Such perfection was attained nowhere else in all these arts and sciences, and the influence of St. Gall in this respect extended to the monasteries of Rheinau, Reichenau, and Pfäffers.

In striking contrast to Alamannia, Burgundy remained for centuries later intellectually dead; the rude and warlike nobility reduced the kingdom to a state of confusion, which has enveloped the history of that land in a profound obscurity. Alamannia and the German element, therefore, took the lead in the development of the land. The influence of this German element was considerably increased by the rule of the German emperors, which now also united Burgundy with Alamannia and Coire-Rhætia.

From the time when Henry I. united the German races into

one permanent empire, in 919, the whole of the present Switzerland and Burgundy, as also Alamannia and Rhætia, became closely united to Germany; and at the same time the several parts were more firmly attached to one another. Burkhard I. of Alamannia, Count of Zurich and of Coire-Rhætia, was the first to yield voluntarily to the success in arms of Henry I. in 920; he surrendered himself and his land to the German monarch; Henry, however, contented himself with the position of chief feudal lord, and allowed Burkhard to keep his dukedom. From that time the dukedom of Suabia became an integral part of the German empire. The Emperor Otto I. afterward in 948 made his son Liudolf Duke of Alamannia and Count of Coire-Rhætia. Liudolf's successor, Burkhard II., was related to Otto, and that emperor often visited the present Swiss territories. The succeeding dukes remained in close friendship or relationship with the imperial house, and the emperor in return often stayed in German Switzerland, especially in Zurich. Henry II. held imperial diets at Zurich in 1004 and 1018, and tradition, probably with truth, attributes the foundation of the cathedal of Basle and the golden altar-piece to the liberality of Henry II. and his consort Kunigunde.

Burgundy, too, came under German influence. Rudolf II. pressed his conquests beyond the Lake of Zurich, but was there encountered by Burkhard I., and defeated at Winterthur in 919. They made terms of peace, however, and Burkhard's daughter Bertha gave her hand to King Rudolf. This marriage formed a bond of union between east and west Switzerland; with Bertha the German territory in upper Aargau was annexed to Burgundy. The alliance must have become still more effective when Burgundy shortly afterward came under the dominion of Germany. For Conrad, the young and feeble son of Rudolf II., was placed in 940 by the nobles of Burgundy under the protection and guardianship of Otto I.; and ten years later Otto married Conrad's sister, the beautiful and famous Adelaide, Bertha's daughter, Queen of Italy. These two women, Adelaide and Bertha, are held in lasting remembrance in Burgundy; the former strove to restore the Peace of Burgundy, disturbed by intestine troubles, and Bertha was the "Guardian Angel" of the people at a time when internal feuds were raging, and the enemies already alluded to were making predatory inroads; she is said to have founded the religious house at Payerne in 962. Tradition represents her as spinning like the goddess Freya, and all that was beautiful and good in antiquity is ascribed to her, the honored mother of her country, the promoter of good works and holiness. Later generations lamented bitterly "the times are no more when Bertha spun." Succeeding kings of Burgundy undertook nothing without the advice and consent of the German emperor.

It now only remained to incorporate Alamannia and Burgundy entirely into the German empire. Rudolf III. of Burgundy (993-1032) was a feeble, bigoted prince, who relied upon the church for support against the encroachments of the nobles, and bestowed lands and privileges upon it with so liberal a hand that he was forced at last to look to the alms of the bishops for his own maintenance. Being more and more oppressed by the nobles, who wished to depose him, the government became a burden to him, and he took refuge with his sister's son, the German emperor Henry II., who already had designs upon Burgundy, and appointed him as his heir and successor. Henry, however, could only establish his authority by force of arms; what he was unable himself to achieve was completed by his successor, Conrad II. ("*der Salier*," or the "Salic"), who advanced with his victorious army as far as Morat and Neuchâtel, had himself made king and crowned at Payerne in 1033 after the death of Rudolf III., and received general recognition in the cathedral at Geneva. In 1038, at Soleure, he conferred Burgundy upon his son Henry amid the rejoicings of the people. In the same year he also ceded to this son Alamannia and Rhætia, and thus almost the whole of the present Switzerland came under German rule. Henry III. (1039-1056) managed his affairs personally as far as possible; he visited Basle and Zurich, staying in the latter town at six different times; he took these opportunities to hold diets, and to settle important national matters. By provisions made at diets held at Soleure, he subdued Burgundy with a strong hand, where, owing to the avarice and arrogance of the nobles, club law (*Faustrecht*) had prevailed.

The attention which the German emperor paid to this country was of no little benefit to the religious foundations, which became centers of intellectual life. At this time the land possessed a number of master minds, and was in the forefront of learning among German lands. St. Gall formed an educational school for the whole of Germany. Ekkehard I. (*ob.* 973), from Toggenburg, the head of the inner monastic school, cultivated German poetry

(*Walthari-Lied*) under the patronage of Otto I. Ekkehard II., his nephew (*ob.* 990), was the most renowned scholar of his time; he instructed Hedwig, Duchess of Alamannia, in the classics at the castle of Hohentwiel, and Otto appointed him as tutor to his son. Notker III. (*Labeo* or the "Thick-lipped," *ob.* 1022) distinguished himself in almost every branch of learning, especially in the knowledge of languages and philosophy; he interested himself in German, wrote both poetry and prose in that language, and translated the most notable works of classic literature and portions of the Bible into German. His pupil, Ekkehard IV. (*ob.* 1056), at one time the head of the school of St. Gall, then of the cathedral school in Mayence, and the historian of St. Gall, was likewise master of all the knowledge of his time, and was held in high honor by the imperial court; the emperor's sister-in-law was once so charmed with his song that she placed her own ring upon his finger. St. Gall, however, did not long continue the only educational center; it was eagerly followed by Reichenau and Constance, and more notably by the monastery of Einsiedeln, which, built in the tenth century upon the spot hallowed by the sufferings of St. Meinrad, and raised to eminence by the favor of the ducal family of Alamannia and of the German imperial court, cultivated the arts and sciences in its famous school.

An important event of this period was the advance of the German population. From the eleventh century we find Germans in great numbers in Romance territory; the Rhætian aristocracy, the ruling class, was chiefly formed of Germans (German names of castles and German records have been found even in completely Romance valleys of the Rhine district). In like manner the German population advanced to the southwest; the Bernese Oberland and Engelberg were now eagerly colonized from Alamannia, and later on Upper Valais was also peopled and settled by those of the Bernese Oberland; Germans advanced even to the valley of the Saane. According to tradition, Romance shepherds, passing up the river through the woods with their flocks, met with shepherds of another tongue, which was German. Thus the predominant character of Switzerland became gradually German.

Chapter III

TERRITORIAL DIVISIONS. 1057-1218

AFTER the death of Henry III. the feeble Empress Agnes in 1057 bestowed the dukedom of Alamannia upon her favorite, Rudolf of Rheinfeld. Rudolf had likewise great possessions in Burgundy, between the Saane, the great St. Bernard, Geneva, and the Jura. Thus the Swiss territories were again united and came under the rule of a native prince. Rudolf, in whom the empress had hoped to find a supporter of the court, soon ranged himself on the side of the opposition against the youthful Henry IV., and when the latter was excommunicated by the Pope he caused himself to be made a rival king by the princes in 1077, chiefly by the help of Duke Guelph of Bavaria and Berchthold of Zäringen. But in Switzerland Rudolf met with an energetic resistance at Constance, St. Gall, and Zurich; the bishops of Lausanne and Basle raised an army and devastated his estates. After Rudolf's death in 1080 the Zäringen and Guelph faction took up the cause; but there arose against them the Staufen faction, with Frederick of Staufen, to whom Henry IV. had ceded Alamannia, at their head. A devastating war broke out, and many monasteries, towns, castles, and churches were destroyed.

The struggle was also carried on with spiritual weapons; the monks of Cluny, eager for the revival of ecclesiastical discipline and for the development of the papal power, disseminated the idea of the independence and omnipotence of the church. Romainmotier and Payerne had become dependent upon Cluny as early as the tenth century, and now other Cluniac foundations were erected as at Rougemont and Rüeggisberg. The example of Cluny was followed by the monasteries of Einsiedeln, Muri, Allerheiligen (Schaffhausen), and Rheinau; the monks, in concert with the Zäringen-Guelph party, preached war to the death against the excommunicated emperor and his followers. The Zäringens meanwhile had taken the place of the house of Rheinfeld; when the last of the Rheinfelds died in 1090, Berchthold II. of Zäringen inherited all the estates of that house, and was made Duke of

Suabia in opposition to Frederick of Staufen. It was one continual party strife, until by the peace of 1097 Berchthold II. of Zäringen renounced the dukedom of Alamannia, and received in its stead the imperial bailiwick of Zurich with the title of duke. In the decay of all authority under the Staufens and Zäringens, and the division of the dukedom of Alamannia, the first step was made toward the independent development of Switzerland.

Through the acquisition of Zurich by the peace of 1097 the Zäringens became the largest landowners of Switzerland; since the

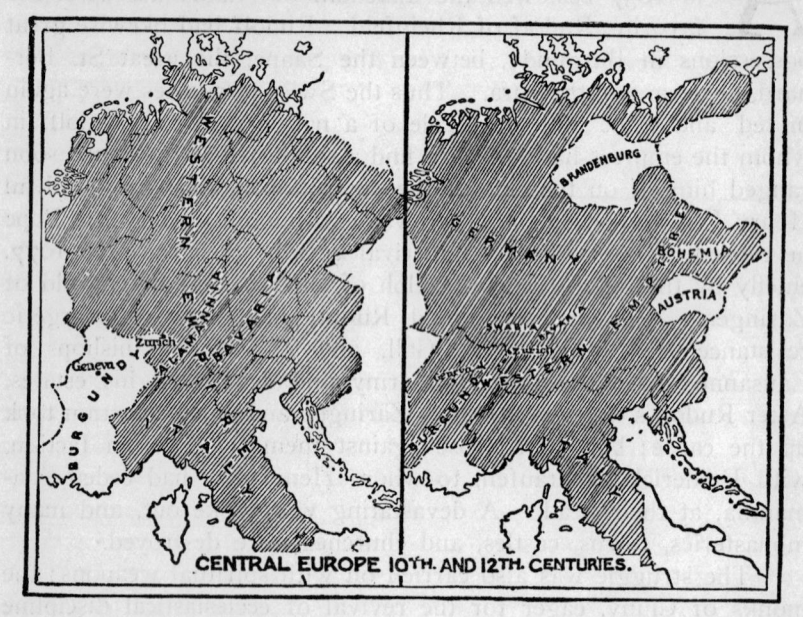

CENTRAL EUROPE 10TH. AND 12TH. CENTURIES.

tenth century they had possessed the county of Thurgau; from the house of Rheinfeld they received an extensive property between the Reuss and the Aar. Zurich itself was so flourishing in the twelfth century that a German writer calls it the chief town of Suabia; an inscription over the gate of the town [1]—" Zurich the noble with abundance of many things "—is supposed to have denoted its wealth and prosperity. Supported by these possessions the Zäringens might well conceive the idea of occupying once more the position of Henry III. and Rudolf of Rheinfeld. The powers and rights inherited by them from the house of Rheinfeld were, however, called in question by the counts of Upper Burgundy, till in 1127 William IV. of Upper Burgundy was killed, and

[1] "Das edle Zürich mit Uberfluss an vielen Dingen."

Conrad III. of Zäringen, a relative of William, was declared
"Rector" (*Reichsvicar*), and make Duke of Burgundy by the
Emperor Lothaire, in opposition to a Burgundian kinsman. But
the Burgundian lords of Geneva, Ottingen, Grandson, and Gruyeres, and the bishops, in all of whom the dislike to German
supremacy was once more aroused, rose against the Zäringens as
one man, and a succession of passionate struggles and terrible
feuds raged as long as the Zäringens lived. The latter sought to
find in the towns and boroughs a counterbalance against the
haughty nobles. They erected castles and fortresses, around which
larger places gradually arose, or they fortified the settlements already standing, manned them with forces capable of resistance, and
bestowed upon them estates (*Burglehen*) [2] and privileges. Thus
Berchthold IV., about 1177, founded the fortress of Fribourg.
To him or to his son Berchthold V. the fortifications and first
municipal laws of Burgdorf, Moudon, Yverdon, Laupen, Gümminen, and Thun, also owe their origin. Berchthold V. had to
maintain a hard struggle. The whole nobility of Burgundy conspired against him. Berchthold, however, defeated some at
Avenches, others in the valley of Grindelwald, and afterward, in
1191, established the town of Berne [3] on an island in the
Aar, which was imperial soil, as a strong bulwark, whence he
could easily dominate the surrounding country as from a castle.
But all these efforts had no lasting result. The Burgundians and
the house of Savoy revolted afresh, and Berchthold V., driven back
from the Vaud and Valais, was obliged in his last days to look upon
the wreck of all his plans; his race died with him in 1218, having
attained celebrity by the foundation of many towns.

The German empire, under whose rule Switzerland had come
in the eleventh century, and to whom it practically belonged until
the end of the fifteenth century, was advancing from the twelfth
century toward an internal dissolution. The strong and uniform
imperial authority which Otto I. and the "Salic" rulers had established was gradually relaxed. The authority of the empire became

[2] *i. e.*, the tenure of a feudal castle and the land attached to it.

[3] This name, sometimes said to be derived from *Bären* (bears) in allusion
to the figures on the armorial bearings of the city, has on the contrary nothing
whatever to do with "bears." Verona, which was in possession of the Zäringens,
was in German called Bern. The fact that Berne was founded upon imperial
soil constitutes an essential difference between that town and Fribourg, it had
therefore afterward the character of an imperial town.

more and more limited, partly by the ambition of powerful and bold vassals and nobles, partly by the heavy blows which were inflicted on the empire by the Popes and the church. The imperial estates were wasted; the representatives of the empire, the emperors themselves, undermined their own power by the remission of royalties (coinage, customs, rights of hunting and fishing, and feudal sovereignty), and by the granting of numerous privileges and liberties, being forced thereto by political circumstances; and under either feeble rulers or despots who wasted their time and strength upon the foundation of a dominion in Italy numberless petty states were formed which rendered useless the empire and the imperial authority.

The all-absorbing feudal system formed an important factor in this process of disorganization. Not only were estates and lands bestowed in fee, but even offices and rights of lordship, and when in the eleventh century fiefs became generally hereditary, the bond between vassals and their lords became lax; the former became more independent, and finally cared nothing for their feudal lords. Thus dukedoms and earldoms became the hereditary property of powerful families. But the division went further. These great lords or crown-vassals, forming the high nobility, also distributed fiefs, and bestowed portions of their principalities, smaller counties, or the dominion over separate villages, upon vassals, dependents of the lower nobility, who in their turn contrived to make themselves more free. Thus the county system, which had formed the solid basis of imperial government under the Franks, was dissolved.

This dissolution of the county system and the development of the feudal system were essentially furthered by the "Immunity," or the right of exemption from the county jurisdiction, which was first granted to monastic houses and bishops, and later to royal vassals also. The foundation was thereby laid for the formation of smaller states within each county. The bishops and abbots, not being allowed to exercise criminal jurisdiction themselves, appointed either for themselves or by the king a deputy or advocate to administer for them, called a bailiff or governor (*Vogt*), who entirely managed their temporal and agricultural affairs (*Kastvogtei*). Even the office of governor was afterward converted into a hereditary possession, and temporal lords also appointed similar governors.

1218

This localization of authority was very closely connected with a change of another kind. From the eighth century families of the nobility had increasingly succeeded, either by purchase or by craft and force, favored by the growing need and impoverishment of the small peasants, in uniting enormous landed possessions in their own hands. Thus large estates became the rule everywhere, and the small holding of the freeman an ever rarer exception. Part of these estates was bestowed upon vassals (*ministeriales,* or retainers) under obligation of military or knight's service; and part upon dependents, bondmen, or free peasants, as copyhold tenants. These great landed proprietors in counties or villages sought to acquire political power, and abrogated to themselves everywhere rights of dominion and jurisdiction. They received a manorial jurisdiction, that is, the right of punishing offenses in wood and field, and the control over affairs of the soil. Many lords of manors then contrived to obtain the office of under-governor or bailiff, that is, the jurisdiction over smaller misdemeanors not punishable by death. The office of the higher bailiff, or criminal jurisdiction, was quite separate, being the right of punishing more serious offenses, such as theft, robbery, arson, and murder, but even this might chance to come to the hands of the lower jurisdiction or lord of the manor. These feudal relations were altogether different in different places, and were but little regulated by law and rule. On the other hand, the rights of the different lords and those of their subjects were everywhere definitely limited and fixed. Handed down at first from generation to generation by oral tradition, they were fixed in writing in the fourteenth and fifteenth centuries by publication (*Offnungen*) of legal sentences and rules of court. Every time that the lords held their courts, in spring and autumn, these rights and customs were read aloud before the people as a continual reminder. These spring and autumn courts, at which all those who were under any sort of obligation to the lord had to appear, were either held by the lord himself or by his manorial officers, the steward or cellarer (*Keller*), who received rents and made inspection. The constitution of these courts tended more than anything else to dispossess the old uniform constitution, which had rested upon the county system.

The political conditions of the people were very various, according to their rank. All power was in the hands of the higher and lower nobility, who lived upon their freeholds or their feudal estates. The officers of house bailiff, or imperial bailiff, etc., had their dwellings in strong towers and castles, dressed in handsome armor, and found their pleasure in hunting, in feuds and tournaments, and also here and there practiced minstrelsy (*Minnegesang*). The worst position was that of the bondmen (*Leibeigenen*), who, being far removed from their lord, and not attached to the estate, could be sold at any time, and in their miserable wooden huts had scarcely means of subsistence. The freedmen (*Hörigen*) were in rather better circumstances, and could only be exchanged with the estate upon which they lived. Freedmen and bondmen had other feudal obligations to discharge, besides their rents and feudal duties, such as death-dues or "*Besthaupt*" which probably corresponded to the Anglo-Saxon *Wergild*, and socage. The dependents of a religious house or of a church (*Gotteshausleute*) enjoyed special advantages over these servile folk; they were not under any hereditary lordship, and could claim the immunity above alluded to. Outside the nobility, the best position, at least in social respects, was that of the freemen, who possessed either freehold or copyhold estates; but even they found but a very scanty livelihood. For a copyhold tenement a ground-rent had to be paid in kind to the lord of the manor. These customary free tenants, however, lived in continual danger of being robbed of their freedom, for the lords sought perpetually to extend and complete their own authority, to efface the rights of the various classes, and to depress all into a similar subjection. On the other hand, the lower classes in their despair struggled upward more and more, and strove to obtain a better position either by force or by attaining to the freedom of the empire.

Under such forms the conditions of mediæval government progressed. The spiritual territories were first formed by means of the Immunity, and by the grants to bishops of royalties and county rights, which became very frequent after the tenth century. Thus the bishops of Lausanne, Sion, Basle, Constance, and Coire, the abbots of St. Gall, Einsiedeln, Muri, and Engelberg, the abbess of the Fraumünsterstift, became powerful manorial lords and possessors of princely rights. Among the most notable of the secular lords were the counts of Savoy, of Geneva, Gruyères, and Neuchâtel in west Switzerland, the counts of Lenzburg, Kiburg, Hapsburg, Rapperswil, and Toggenburg, the barons of Regensberg, and others in east Switzerland. The Hapsburgs were the most fortunate in the extension of their territory; in addition to their hereditary estates in Alsace and Aargau, they inherited in 1172 and 1173 the possessions of the Lenzburgs in Aargau and in the Forest States; and later, in the thirteenth century, those of the families of Rapperswil and Kiburg. They seemed to have taken the place of the houses of Rheinfeld and Zäringen.

A counterbalance to the overweening power of the nobility was formed by the communes. A large number of houses and farmsteads lying near together formed sooner or later a domestic and political society, called a "commune" (*Gemeinde*) or peasantry (*Pursame*). Such a fellowship related especially to the possession of a common portion of wood and pasture, undivided and enjoyed by the whole community, called the "Mark" or Almend. This *Markgenossenschaft,* or association of the Mark, also looked after other agricultural concerns, and fixed the time for vintage, harvest, and the like. Some communes succeeded in extending these rights, and in obtaining their freedom by increasing limitations of the rights of their lords, by purchase or by force, and in the formation of these free communes we find the germ of Swiss liberty.

The communes in towns were of special importance. They were formed in places surrounded by walls, with houses adjoining one another. This method of colonization, once so detested by the Alamanni, came more and more into favor as an excellent means of defense during the time of the Hungarian inroads and intestine feuds. Such walled towns gradually received considerable privileges beyond those of the villages: the right of holding fairs, privileges of jurisdiction and tolls, rights of coinage, and the right to elect municipal officers, etc. The development of these towns differed according to their origin. Some—and those by far the greater part—rose around some religious institution, or around the court of a spiritual lord, such as the episcopal towns of Geneva, Lausanne, Basle, Coire, and Sion, or towns dependent upon monasteries and religious foundations, such as Soleure, St. Gall, Lucerne, etc. These from their commencement enjoyed the privilege of Immunity, and had the earliest municipal councils. But with the decline of ecclesiastical power in the thirteenth century these towns were enfranchised little by little and acquired the right of electing their own town councils. Moreover, being under no hereditary rule, and the bailiffs being nominated by the empire, most of them preserved a certain connection with the empire, and managed to raise themselves to the rank of imperial towns and to withdraw from the spiritual control. Other towns were founded by temporal lords for military purposes or in the interests of trade, such as Fribourg, Berne, and others built by the house of Zäringen; Winterthur, Diessenhofen, and Frauenfeld by that of Kiburg. Some of these, such as the towns of the Zäringens, enjoyed special privileges from the first; others acquired them when their lords were in difficulties and required their service; they, too, gradually succeeded in obtaining their freedom. Lastly, there were towns toward whose foundation and development various circumstances had contributed, such as Zurich, which was partly a royal town, and partly ecclesiastical.

All the towns, however, rose to distinction in the twelfth and thirteenth centuries chiefly by their trade and manufactures, and in this way they became the seats of a new civilization. The population within the walls was a very mixed one in point of rank: side by side with the freedmen and bondmen of the lords of the town dwelt the vassals or officers of the crown and numerous freemen; the former lived by their handicrafts, the latter by knight's service, agriculture, and commerce. Only knights and freemen originally took part in the civic administration, and the bondmen or handicraftsmen first obtained political rights in the fourteenth century. Thus the towns became of the greatest importance in social and political development. A free political spirit ruled within them. Bondmen and freedmen who settled in a town became free if they were not fetched back by their lords within a year. ("The air of towns sets one free.") So the class of freemen whose very existence had been so seriously threatened by the feudal system gradually increased.

The valley communes developed like the towns. The people in the mountain valleys of Uri, Schwyz, Unterwalden, Glarus, Hasle, etc., followed the example of the towns. They were protected by their mountains, as were the towns by their walls. The freemen everywhere formed a nucleus to which the bondmen attached themselves in order to avail themselves of favorable circumstances for their emancipation; for the dwellers in the valleys were mostly united (as in Uri and Schwyz) by the possession of a common or Almend. Uri was first settled by subjects of the empire; then in 853 it came under the mild ecclesiastical rule of the *Fraumünster* of Zurich, and acquired the right of Immunity. The higher administration of justice was exercised by the bailiffs of the convent, and in the twelfth century and the beginning of the thirteenth by the Zäringens. But the *Gotteshausleute* of Uri [4] gradually acquired many precious liberties. There was in Schwyz a whole commune of freemen, over whom the counts of the district exercised sovereignty. Hence Schwyz also early became unusually powerful and independent. It had a quarrel with the monastery of Einsiedeln about the wood and pasture land on its borders; and although Henry V., in 1114, and Conrad III., in 1144, decided in favor of Einsiedeln, and in spite of the spiritual weapon of excommunication directed against them, they adhered immovably to their claims. Compared to the two valleys already named, Unterwalden was politically backward. It is true that here, too, there existed a fair number of freemen in and about Sarnen and Stanz; but they were scattered, and the land was divided among divers spiritual and temporal lords. But in the thirteenth century they also were struggling for freedom with other valley communities.

Since the ninth and tenth centuries the power of the church had increased mightily. She amassed enormous riches by gifts, donations, festivals, masses, etc. The bishops and higher clergy supported the imperial government, and received royalties and princely powers. The popes, the highest bishops, acquired an ever-increasing ascendency, and made successful use of the religious agitations of the eleventh and twelfth centuries to their own advantage and that of the church. They interfered in all ecclesiastical concerns, organized crusades, and deposed emperors and kings.

Ecclesiastical institutions and orders multiplied incredibly. The oldest order was that of the Benedictines, to which belonged numbers of the famous monasteries of the land—St. Gall, Einsiedeln, Dissentis, Pfäffers, Rheinau, Muri, and Engelberg. In the tenth century, when this order languished somewhat, that of Cluny arose to a fresh struggle in the cause of the papacy, the church, and asceticism. When the strength of this order also began to flag (about 1100) the Cistercian, Premonstratensian, and Carthusian orders were founded. To the first of these orders belonged Lützel near Soleure, Hauterêt in Vaud, Hauterive near Fribourg,

---

[4] "People of God's house," a name applied to certain inhabitants of Uri in partial subjection to the abbey of Zurich.

St. Urban, Kappel, Wettingen, and others. The second included Bellelay, Rüti in canton Zurich, and others; the third, La Lance, Ittingen, and others likewise. Together with asceticism, these orders attached great importance to manual labor and solitude as the principal methods of strict discipline. The new monasteries carried on the cultivation of the land, cleared the forests, drained marshes, and planted vineyards. But in the thirteenth century, when it became needful to prevent the downfall of the church, and to reassert the principle of renunciation of the world, the monasteries of mendicant friars arose in every town: the Dominicans or preaching friars, and the Franciscans or barefooted friars. A number of nunneries were likewise founded, and the religious orders of knights also established themselves in Switzerland. By means of these orders and ecclesiastical societies the church became a stupendous power, to which magnificent cathedrals and minsters, beautiful churches and splendid ecclesiastical monuments still testify.[5] But the more wealth the church amassed, and the more she mingled in worldly concerns, so much the more her inner life waned. She neglected her holy calling and the cultivation of intellectual life. Monasteries which had formerly been distinguished by their literary and artistic performances were remarkable in the thirteenth century for their ignorance. Opposition to the church grew apace, sectarian tendencies increased, and in all parts recourse was had to the authorities of the state to restrain the power of the church.

[5] Of ancient churches in the Romanesque (or round-arch) style, we may name Payerne, the *Grossmünster* in Zurich, Neuchâtel, Ufenau, Coire, Katzis, Dissentis, and Sion. Later ones in the Gothic (or pointed-arch) style: Geneva, Lausanne, Berne, Kappel, and the churches of the mendicant friars everywhere.

Chapter IV

FORMATION OF THE LEAGUES 1218-1315

THE death of Berchthold V. and the extinction of the house of Zäringen preserved Switzerland from the fate of many other parts of the empire, that of becoming permanently a royal possession. The estates of the Zäringens in west Switzerland (such as Herzogenbuchsee, Thun, Burgdorf, and Fribourg) fell, it is true, to the house of Kiburg; the rectorate of Burgundy, however, reverted to the emperor and became extinct; the dynasties, which had been dependent upon the rector as such, and the towns which had been conferred upon the Zäringens as imperial estates, likewise reverted to the empire, and so obtained a sort of independence or freedom of the empire (*Reichsfreiheit*). This was the case with the counts of Buchegg, Neuchâtel, and others, and the towns of Zurich, Berne, Soleure, Laupen, Gümminen, and Morat. By these means their free development was greatly advanced, but could not make much progress without hard struggles.

The house of Kiburg united powerful possessions in eastern Switzerland, the county of Thurgau and Baden, to the hereditary estates of the house of Zäringen in west Switzerland, and thus, like that house, conceived the idea of forming a united principality in Switzerland. In the southwest, in Valais and Geneva, a menacing attitude was adopted by the house of Savoy; the bitterest enemy of which house being removed by the extinction of the Zäringens, it was now at liberty to attack the northern territories of western Switzerland. The house of Hapsburg had at last obtained a firm footing in central Switzerland and in the east; it occupied the left bank of the Reuss in Aargau, the counties of Zurich and Aargau, and extensive though scattered possessions in Zug, Schwyz, Unterwalden, and Lucerne. Thus the free communes were straitened and threatened on all sides.

These antagonists first came into collision with the outbreak of the struggle between the papacy and the empire in the time of

Frederick II. The towns and free communes of Switzerland then openly espoused the cause of the emperor, looking to him to protect them against the overwhelming power of the aristocracy; only by his help could they hope to save their imperial freedom. The counts and lords, however, like the Guelphs and Zäringens of former days, inclined rather to the side of the papacy.

The Forest States commenced the attack. The jurisdiction of the Zäringens over Uri had been transferred to Count Rudolf the Old of Hapsburg [1] in 1218 as an imperial fee. The imperial bailiwicks and fees being at this time gradually converted into hereditary sovereignties and provinces, the people of Uri began to fear they would come under the dominion of the house of Hapsburg and lose their Immunity. They therefore had recourse to King Henry, the son of Frederick, who managed the affairs of the empire in his father's absence, and who granted them a charter on May 26, 1231, placing them under the protection and sovereignty of the empire. The bailiwick seems to have been acquired by the Hapsburgs by purchase. Uri had thus lawfully secured her freedom, and from that time the valley takes its place as a free and independent commune. In 1243 it had its own seal, like the towns. The freemen of Schwyz were not less hampered by the Hapsburgs; here also the authority of the counts seems to have been converted into a hereditary sovereignty, as was the case with the imperial bailiwick in Uri. When in 1232 the power of the house of Hapsburg was shattered by its division between the younger (or Laufenburg) [2] and the elder line, the people of Schwyz also determined to avail themselves of the help of the emperor in order to obtain the freedom of the empire like their neighbors. In 1240 they sent delegates to Frederick II., when the latter, then under papal excommunication, was besieging Faenza in Italy; and the emperor,

---

[1] The following genealogical table will serve as explanation.

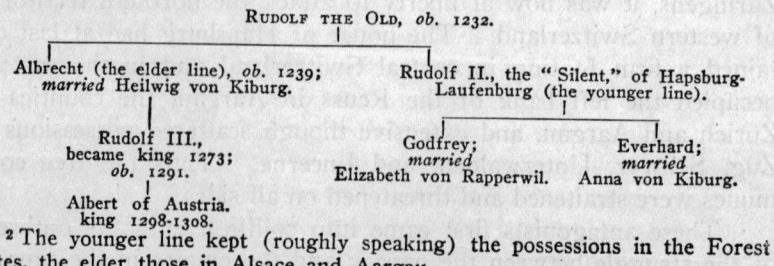

RUDOLF THE OLD, *ob.* 1232.

Albrecht (the elder line), *ob.* 1239; *married* Heilwig von Kiburg.

Rudolf III., became king 1273; *ob.* 1291.

Albert of Austria. king 1298-1308.

Rudolf II., the "Silent," of Hapsburg-Laufenburg (the younger line).

Godfrey; *married* Elizabeth von Rapperwil.

Everhard; *married* Anna von Kiburg.

[2] The younger line kept (roughly speaking) the possessions in the Forest States, the elder those in Alsace and Aargau.

in December, 1240, probably out of gratitude for help rendered, acknowledged the people of Schwyz as subjects of the empire by a charter under his own hand.

Hitherto circumstances had been extremely favorable to these progressive movements, but the situation was completely altered when Frederick II. was excommunicated in 1245 at the Council of Lyons by Pope Innocent IV., the adherents of the church increased in number, and the wars of the time of Henry IV. were renewed. All towns and states which adhered to the emperor were threatened with excommunication, and Zurich, which had most zealously taken Frederick's part, was laid under an interdict. The whole empire was divided into two hostile camps, those of the Ghibellines and the Guelphs, and a tempest raged throughout the land, the effects of which extended even to the remote Alpine valleys. The free communes, however, nothing daunted, took energetic measures to secure their liberties. Zurich expelled the Dominican monks from her walls for inciting against Frederick, and also the clergy who refused to hold divine service; Lucerne revolted against the rule of the Abbot of Murbach and the Count of Hapsburg, as did also the Forest States.

In order to advance more safely upon the beaten track both town and country communes followed the example of the Lombardic and a few North German towns, and entered into alliances with one another for the maintenance of peace and for the protection of traffic in troublous times. Thus in 1243 Berne concluded an offensive and defensive alliance with Fribourg to secure herself against the attacks of the Kiburgs; for the same cause Fribourg and Morat combined, as did also Berne and Lucerne. Following the example of the towns, Schwyz also made a league with Unterwalden and Uri, and about 1245-1247 they entered into an alliance with Lucerne and Zurich. This was the first mutual alliance of town and country communes, a prelude to the founding of the Confederation! The Forest States then took up arms bravely, and the Count of Hapsburg was obliged to form an advantageous military outpost by building the castle of New Hapsburg on the lake. Strife arose around the lake of the Four Cantons. Then at last were the hostile officials of the haughty retainers of the Hapsburg nobility expelled and their strongholds destroyed. In vain did Rudolf II. of Hapsburg implore the aid of Pope Innocent IV.; the latter threatened Schwyz, Sarnen, and Lucerne with an interdict, but the struggle went on for many years, and only came to an end when the commencement of the "Interregnum" in 1256 effaced all party strife.

The people of Uri, whose liberty rested on a firm foundation, remained free, but Schwyz and Unterwalden appear to have been forced to submit once more to the Hapsburgs. About 1250 began that troublous time without an emperor, that period of confusion, when unbridled passion made all parts unsafe, and "club-law" prevailed. The encroachments of the nobility upon the towns recommenced everywhere. In western Switzerland Hartmann von Kiburg tried to extend his rights, and to possess himself of the estates of the empire; but the imperial states of Berne, Morat, and Basle found an able protector in his chief opponent, the bold Count of Savoy, Peter II. This powerful champion of the house of Savoy had exchanged his spiritual calling for the sword, and now (1230-1260) extended his dominion by inheritance, purchase, and conquest over the greater part of the Romance territory; little by little he gained the whole of the Pays de Vaud and repulsed the encroachments of the Kiburgs. He endeavored to attach the Vaud to himself by securing the constitution. His laws and statutes made him famous and he was styled "The second Charlemagne." In eastern Switzerland also feuds raged. Zurich was attacked by the barons of Regensberg and other nobles of the neighborhood, but afterward joined Rudolf III. of Hapsburg, the opponent of the Regensbergs,[3] and destroyed many of the enemy's castles. The towns enjoying the freedom of the empire were now practically free, since the empire had no generally recognized head. The imperial castles of Lindenhof in Zurich and Nidegg in Berne were either left to decay or destroyed. Other towns, too, were struggling for freedom; Winterthur destroyed the citadel of the Counts of Kiburg, Lucerne broke into a castle belonging to its ecclesiastical lord of Murbach, and Zug withstood the surrounding nobility.

In those times of the surging of party strife the towns formed a quiet refuge for the cultivation of intellectual life. Chivalrous poetry flourished in the castles of the knights of Thurgau, Aargau, and Zurich (Klingenberg, Toggenburg, Wart, Teufen, Regensberg, Sax, and Montfort), and within the walls of the town of

---

[3] The Regensbergs laid claim to the county of Kiburg, which Rudolf had inherited in 1264.

Zurich the sweet notes of the minnesingers resounded in love songs collected by a knight of Zurich, the "*Manessische Liedersammlung,*" or "Songs of Manegg." In Zurich we find, side by side with the poet John Hadlaub, the famous poet, singer, and writer, Conrad von Mure.

At the very moment when the house of Hapsburg seemed to tremble a man placed himself at its head who devoted his whole life to strengthen and consolidate its power; this was Count Rudolf III. of Hapsburg, one of the elder line. By a clever use of various opportunities, by the support of divers boroughs, including Zurich, Basle, and Winterthur, and also by force, he gradually attained on this side of the Rhine to such power as approached that of the Zäringens.

When in 1263 and 1264 the male representatives of the house of Kiburg expired with Hartmann the Younger and his uncle Hartmann the Elder,[4] Rudolf, not content with the portion of the Kiburg inheritance which he inherited in his mother's right, laid claim to the whole of the possessions of that house in eastern and western Switzerland; disregarding the equally legitimate claims of the house of Savoy, for the wife of the last of the Kiburgs was Margaret of Savoy, sister of Peter II., he defeated Peter II., and in 1267 acquired the dominions of the Kiburgs by the peace of Morat. He next made war upon the Bishop of Basle, in consequence of some territorial disputes in Alsace, and in 1273 he obtained the estates of the younger Hapsburg-Laufenburg line in the Forest States for a very trifling sum. His election as King of Germany followed speedily in the same year. He availed himself of his royal dignity to restore and extend the power of his house; he secured for it the duchy of Austria, and now openly strove to tread in the footsteps of the Zäringens, and to reëstablish the kingdom of Burgundy. He pushed his way over the Aar by force of arms and besieged Berne, which opposed his schemes, in concert with Savoy and the Burgundian dynasties (1288). The Bernese withstood him manfully, and Rudolf was obliged to raise the siege. It was not until the spring of 1289 that a band of Bernese was defeated by an ambuscade of Rudolf's troops at Schoosshalde. By purchase and intrigue Rudolf gradually acquired Fribourg, Neu-

[4] Anna, the daughter of the younger Count Hartmann of Kiburg, afterward (1273) married Count Eberhard of Hapsburg-Laufenburg, and thence sprang the new house of Kilburg.

châtel, Lenzburg, Einsiedeln, Pfäffers, Säckingen, the stewardship of Glarus, and the bailiwick of Urseren; even the monastery of St. Gall, whose rich landed possessions he coveted, was frequently threatened and driven to great straits. By these acquisitions Rudolf made enemies of many towns, and harassed them, moreover, by heavy taxes. He recognized, it is true, the imperial freedom of Uri, but his double powers as king and claimant of the title of landgrave must have filled them with alarm. The people of Schwyz fared the worst. He strenuously asserted the rights of his house, appointing vassals of the Hapsburgs as judges in the valleys, and shortly before his death he obtained Lucerne by purchase from the Abbey of Murbach.

The whole of Switzerland seemed to be caught in the net of the powerful Hapsburgs; little was wanting to make the whole land between the Alps, the Rhine, and the Jura one united principality under that house. But Rudolf died suddenly on July 15, 1291, and it may well be imagined that on this side of the Rhine all breathed more freely—towns, communes, and dynasties feeling relieved from oppression. Hopes of freedom revived once more, and the formerly free communes now boldly pursued the course they had taken under Frederick II. and during the Interregnum, until arrested by Rudolf. While in eastern and western Switzerland leagues were formed directed against the Hapsburgs, in the east under the Bishop of Constance and in the west under the house of Savoy, the three states of Uri, Schwyz, and Unterwalden met together a fortnight after Rudolf's death, on August 1, 1291, and swore to adhere forever to their old alliance made in the time of the struggle between Fredrick II. and the Pope. They pledged themselves to faithful aid in every need and danger against all aggression, to acknowledge none but natives of the soil as judges in the valleys, to punish impartially all disturbers of the peace, and thus to preserve the peace of the country; in all other respects everyone should serve his lord dutifully as hitherto.[5] Disputes among the Confederates themselves were to be peaceably settled by the "Wise men."

This first Perpetual League became the historical basis of the Confederation. Like the earlier and contemporary alliances of towns, it was not directed against the emperor or his realm, the

---

[5] Schiller has represented this last point absolutely accurately in "William Tell" (Act II. Scene II., toward the end: the proceedings on the Rütli).

Confederates having but one aim—that of providing for themselves by their own united strength the protection which the imperial power could not offer them. But in this case the allies were not wealthy towns, such as those of Italy and Germany, but simple, homely country-folk, who, with a full perception of the political situation, had the courage to strike out a path for themselves. The league was to be "forever," and it has endured without interruption. While the leagues of the towns died out in the course of time, the Swiss Federation developed, steeled by necessity in the after days into an irresistible power, before which the house of Hapsburg in Switzerland, and finally the nobility itself, sank even as stars vanish before the rising sun.

For further support the Forest States of Uri and Schwyz shortly after the formation of the Perpetual League attached themselves to Zurich, and joined the alliance formed in eastern Switzerland against the Hapsburgs. The house of Austria, descended from the Hapsburgs, was at that time represented by Rudolf's son Albert, who entertained hopes of the crown. When Adolf of Nassau, his rival, was elected King of Germany, every enemy of the house of Hapsburg took his part, and war broke out. But the men of Zurich, who had marched against the Austrian town of Winterthur, were defeated there in April, 1292, with much slaughter; Albert thereupon advanced swiftly upon Zurich. "He was unable to swallow it," according to the tradition,[6] but induced the town to make peace in August, and to promise military service. Thus the league formed against the Hapsburgs was broken, and even the Forest States and Lucerne were finally obliged to give up the struggle. King Adolf secured imperial freedom to Uri and Schwyz in 1297.

In the west the cause of Austria underwent a defeat in 1298 by the victory of the Bernese at the battle of Dornbühl. Albert, however, being made king by the electors in opposition to Adolf, and remaining sole monarch after the fall of his adversary, refused to acknowledge the liberties of the Forest States and Berne, and did all he could to place the Austrian power on a firm basis in the whole of eastern and central Switzerland, and to extend the Austro-Hapsburg patrimony, first established by Rudolf. Once more, as under Rudolf, the desires of the Forest States for free-

[6] The *Sage von den Frauen*, or, "Tradition of the Women," the text of which is given in full in Dr. Dändliker's larger history.—ED.

dom seemed about to be stifled in subjection to the Hapsburgs, when suddenly, in May, 1308, Albert was murdered at Brugg by his own nephew, John of Austria, whose claims to Bohemia he had refused to recognize, and some discontented knights, Rudolf von Wart, Walter von Eschenbach, Conrad von Tegerfeld, and Rudolf von Balm.

The Forest States took the opportunity to wring fresh charters from the new king, Henry VII. of Luxemburg. At that time Werner von Attinghausen took the lead in Uri and one of the Stauffach family in Schwyz; Unterwalden also was now for the first time admitted to the imperial freedom (1309), and so stood on an equal footing with the other Forest States. Henry by his deed formed the Forest States into a separate jurisdiction, and appointed one of his knights, Werner von Homberg, imperial bailiff there. The Dukes of Austria vainly tried to reëstablish their rights, and proceeded to take vengeance on the regicides. In 1313, shortly after Henry VII. had become reconciled to them, and had effected a treaty of arbitration, settling the rights of the Hapsburgs and those of the empire in the Forest States, he was snatched away by death in Italy.

In 1314 a disputed election to the throne between Louis the Bavarian and Frederick of Austria gave fresh occasion to the Forest States to array themselves against Austria; the people of Schwyz even went so far as to attack the monastery of Einsiedeln, then under the protection of Austria and with which they had been for two centuries at strife, and to possess themselves of the Austrian town of Art. Frederic then determined to subdue the Forest States by force of arms, and commissioned his brother Leopold to carry out his project. On November 14, 1315, the latter assembled his contingent in Zug in order to attack Schwyz; another portion of his army was to advance over the Brunig pass against Obwalden; and lastly the men of Lucerne were to engage Nidwalden and Uri by the lake. But as soon as the inhabitants of Schwyz grasped the intention of the main army, they occupied the heights and the narrow pass of Morgarten, the natural defense of the land on the northwest, and as it were the gate of the little state of Schwyz. On the morning of November 15 the cavalry advanced along the Lake of Egeri, the infantry following, full of thoughtless gayety. Suddenly, from the heights, the men of Schwyz rolled down trunks of trees and blocks of stone, and wrought terrible confusion among their enemies;[7] then, swift and sure-footed as the chamois, they rushed boldly and fearlessly from their hiding-places, and Leopold's army fell under the battle-axes of Swiss peasants like a flock led to the slaughter. Many were drowned in the adjacent lake. Half dead with terror and excitement, Leopold's hasty flight brought him to Winterthur, and the Austrian power seemed shattered at a blow by a handful of peasants. The troops which had crossed the Brunig pass turned back upon the news of Leopold's defeat.

This first great victory had decisive results. It not only freed the three states from the dominion of Austria, but it also tightened the old alliance. United more firmly by a common danger, the three states renewed the league of 1291 at Brunnen on December 9, 1315. The unity of the allied states was declared yet more emphatically; no single state was to accept any lord or to conclude any negotiations or treaties without the knowledge and consent of the others; whoever should either assail or betray any one of the states should be hated and outlawed by all. In the following year Louis ratified the charter of the Forest States; Austria, however, concluded a truce with them in 1318, by which the enjoyment of the rents and revenues of estates was confirmed to Austria, but the sovereign rights of the counts were declared void.

The memory of these glorious events in the struggle for freedom long remained in the minds of the people, and since there was at first no chronicler found, it was handed down by word of mouth from generation to generation. The father told the son, the latter the grandson, the grandson the great-grandson, with fervor and enthusiasm, of the joys and sorrows of the Confederates, of actors and scenes in the past. It was inevitable that here and there the coloring became rather vivid, and that occasionally a fresh and fragrant flower sprang of itself out of the ever-fresh gardens of tradition. Many things were obliterated from the minds of later generations; others became unduly prominent; others, again, became confused in the various narratives, as always happens when the popular imagination transmits and elaborates history. In this way events were misplaced, and the whole course of develop-

[7] In Justinger's Bernese Chronicle, 1420, tradition ascribes this deed to some exiles, who endeavored in this way to win their pardon. John of Winterthur (about 1330), who describes the battle in more detail from the accounts of eye-witnesses, says nothing of such exiles, and on the whole it is more probable that the feat was accomplished by the army of Schwyz itself.

ment was gradually quite differently conceived, rather as it was imagined to have been, than as things had actually occurred. Little by little people forgot that Swiss liberty first arose on the basis of the original legal conditions of the population, by slow birth and growth, in the same way and at the same time that the towns were attaining their rights and liberties step by step. The different revolts against the Hapsburgs (1245-1273 and 1291-1315) became confused in the minds of the people, and were combined into one single and sudden revolution. In order to justify the latter, the condition of imperial freedom, to which states had in reality attained gradually, was erroneously referred to the most ancient times, that the dispute might assume the character of a struggle for ancient and holy rights against impious oppression. In the fifteenth and sixteenth centuries popular and learned authors did their part toward the formation of more decided opinions, by adding personal conjectures, their own combinations and arrangements, and sometimes even their own errors as historical truth. At the beginning of the fifteenth century the Bernese chronicler Conrad Justinger (about 1420) knew with certainty from records that Schwyz and Unterwalden had been under the Hapsburgs, but that Uri had maintained an exceptional position as belonging to the Fraumünster of Zurich. He likewise knew that the Austrian Hapsburgs had purchased their rights in the Forest States of the earlier or younger line of Hapsburg, and that two rebellions had taken place, against the Hapsburgs and the Austrian Hapsburgs. According to tales, which he probably gathered from the people, he then proceeds to relate that the bailiffs and officials of the Hapsburgs had indulged in wicked actions against "pious folk."

Twenty or thirty years later we meet with isolated episodes out of these traditions. Hämmerlin, canon of Zurich, in a lampoon upon the people of Schwyz, in 1450, relates that a bailiff of Schwyz, appointed by the Hapsburgs, was murdered by two of the inhabitants at the castle of Lowerz because he had insulted their sister. When the Count of Hapsburg would have interfered with punishment, these men of Schwyz were said to have joined with others, and finally all combined, and to have destroyed the said castle. When the people of Unterwalden, neighbors of Schwyz, heard it, they had possessed themselves of the castle of Sarnen and destroyed it while their lord, a noble of Landenberg, was at mass on Christmas Day, and had afterward allied themselves with the men of Schwyz.

The whole wealth of the rich cycle of tradition of the liberation of the Forest States is first produced in the *"Chronik des weissen Buches"* or "Chronicle of the White Book," about 1470, now in the archives of Sarnen. After Rudolf's time, so runs this record, the bailiffs and the officers of the house of Hapsburg proceeded with great arrogance in the Forest States; one Gesler in Uri and Schwyz, and one Landenberg in Unterwalden. Secure in their castles, they greatly oppressed the surrounding people. Landenberg caused the oxen of a peasant in Melchi, near Sarnen, to be taken from the plow by one of his men, and when the peasant's son, in self-defense, injured one of the serving-man's fingers, Landenberg, finding himself unable to catch the culprit, had the father brought to Sarnen, where his eyes were put out. In Altsellen the lord became attached to the wife of an honest man, went to the house when the husband was away, and had a bath prepared. Meanwhile, however, arrived the husband, went in, and killed the bailiff in his bath with his ax. About the same time one Staupacher of Schwyz, who had built himself a handsome stone house, was harassed by Gesler's demanding the name of the owner. His wife asked the cause of his trouble, and gave him no peace till he told her. She then urged him to go to Uri, and to join with others of like mind, reminding him specially of the families called "Fürst" and "Zur Frauen," and urging him to make inquiries in Unterwalden. Staupacher accordingly allied himself with one of the Fürsts of Uri, and with the son of the poor man of Melchi, who had fled thither. Other people joined them secretly, and they took an oath of mutual fidelity and help to defend themselves against the lords. And whenever they held their discussions they betook themselves by night by the Mythenstein to a place there called the Rütli. Now it happened once that Gesler came to Uri, caused a hat to be stuck upon a pole there, and bade everyone bow to the hat as though it were the lord. One of Staupacher's fellow-conspirators, and his comrade, an honest man of the name of Tall (or Tell), would not do this, and complaint was made of him to the lord. The lord sentenced him to shoot an apple from the head of one of his children. Tell yielded to necessity, put one arrow in his bosom, and another on his bow, asked God's help, and shot the apple off the child's head. But Gesler wanted to know why he had taken the second arrow in his bosom. Tell tried to excuse himself, and only confessed upon Gesler's promising him his life, that had his first shot failed the second arrow was destined for the lord. Thereupon the latter caused Tell to be bound, in order to carry him to a place where he would see neither sun nor moon, and rowed with him and his serving-men along the lake of Uri as far as the Axen. There a terrible storm came on, and they thought they would be drowned. Gesler's men urged him to loosen Tell's bonds and make him row, for he was a strong man. This was done. Tell, however, kept his eye on his bow and arrows, which were in the stern of the boat, and when he came to Tell's rock (*Tellenplatte*) he called to the others to pull hard; if they reached that rock all danger would be over. While they obeyed his orders, he swung the little boat against the slab of rock, seized his bow and arrows, and sprang out, pushing the boat from the bank as he did so, then ran swiftly over the mountains to the "Hohle Gasse" in Küssnach, and there awaited the lord, lurking behind bushes. When the governor passed by with his train Tell drew his bow and shot him, then, taking his way over the mountains, went home to Uri. After this Staupacher and his fellows began to storm the castles of the lords, first in Uri, where fell Twing-Uri, then Schwanau, then on to Schwyz and Stanz. The fortress on the Rotzberg was won by a maiden. In Sarnen people came on Christmas Day to the castle to bring presents while the lord was at church. And when there were enough of them within the castle they made a sign to others who had hidden themselves among the alders behind the mill, and who now came up, took the castle, and destroyed it. The bailiff fled with his retainers. Thus the three states made a league together to resist the lords.

Thus far the drift of the copious work of the first chronicler; he probably drew from some older Swiss chronicle and from living tradition, but evidently did not omit to heighten the effect of his narrative with his own bright coloring till he had completed his picture. It was therefore inevitable that when this composition was used by Petermann Etterlin in his "Lucerne Chronicle" of 1507, and was reproduced in print with very little alteration, it became at once the common property of historian and people.[8]

Yet the manner in which these things were depicted in the "White Book" was not the only form in which they were imagined and related. There were essential differences in the "Traditions

[8] Etterlin, however, always calls the bailiff Gesler "Grissler."

PRAYER OF THE SWISS BEFORE THE BATTLE OF SEMPACH
Painting by P. Janssen

—page 381

of Uri." According to the "Lay of Tell," of about 1470, Staupacher is not the central figure, but Tell: his appearance and conduct form the center of the whole transaction, the occasion of the league, and of the revolt against the lords, and Uri is the land whence sprang the league. The play of Uri of " William Tell," dating from the beginning of the sixteenth century, about 1512, which erroneously places the rising in the year 1296, went still further, and made Tell one of the three Confederates, representing him as treating with the people, inciting them to rebellion, and winning them over to the secret league. So the chronicle of Melchior Russ of Lucerne (1482), who derived his information from Uri, where he had relatives and acquaintances, and whose version, moreover, deviating from the " White Book " and being more in accordance with the actual circumstances, relates that the bailiff wanted to take Tell to Schwyz to the "castle on the lake," *i. e.*, to Lowerz, and not to Küssnach, and that Tell shot the bailiff immediately upon springing from the boat. Diebold Schilling, of Lucerne (about 1510), represents Tell as compelled by a count or lord of Seedorf to shoot the apple, and that on the 13th of the "haymonth" (July), 1334 (!). Stumpf in his Swiss chronicle (1548) also follows the Uri version by admitting Tell among the three Confederates. Instead of the fugitive from Unterwalden, he places the man of Altsellen among the three founders of the league and shifts these events to the year 1314. Thus the traditions down to the beginning of the sixteenth century were uncertain, and to some extent contradictory.

The great chronicler Giles Tschudi of Glarus (1570) put an end to this uncertainty. Full of a lively patriotism, he desired to glorify the fame of the Confederation by a brilliant and thrilling description, and therefore treated the history of the foundation of the Swiss league with great freedom, like a romance. He set to work like a painter, who is required to paint a historical picture, but who is left perfectly free to choose his own figures and so to arrange them as to produce the desired impression. He followed the description in the " White Book," but amplified and embellished it partly by verbal traditions of the country and partly by using a poet's license. Then he supported the whole by a firm, but purely arbitrary, chronological framework, which even assigned exact dates to all the various incidents. Following the " White Book," which had misplaced the rising in the time after Rudolf, and a casual assertion in the "Klingenberg Chronicle" of the fifteenth century, that the league was founded in 1306, he erroneously placed the chief events in Albert's time, and even in his last years (1307 and 1308), where they seemed to him to fit in best, and from that point he divided the preceding events back to 1304, when Albert was supposed to have sent the foreign bailiffs. Albert himself, contrary to authentic history, is briefly portrayed as a tyrant of the deepest dye. Tschudi also gives the persons more exact designations than did the earlier writers. It is he who first names the man of Altsellen (probably according to popular tradition) "Conrad Baumgarten." To Fürst, of Uri, he gives the Christian name of Walter, to Staupacher that of Werner, and to Gessler that of Hermann, because he found these names in records of the time. The surnames of Anderhalden and Wolfenschiess are also first met with in his writings.

In this way Tschudi impressed upon these traditions the stamp of completeness and of absolute certainty, and obtained such credit for them as remained unshaken through many generations. His version dominated all works of history in after days, and became the common property of the civilized world through Joh. von Müller's history of Switzerland (1780) and Schiller's magnificent drama of "William Tell" (1804).

Yet criticism was soon aroused. About 1600 Franz Guillimann of Fribourg ventured to doubt the story of William Tell, on the ground of the contradictions and diversities in the accounts. In the eighteenth century it began to be noticed that in the folk-lore of Denmark and Iceland, much older traditions than those of Switzerland, there were tales of a skillful marksman (Toko, Eigil), who was forced to shoot an apple from the head of his favorite little son, and who drew out a second or third arrow in order to kill the cruel tyrant in case of failure. The first to notice this important circumstance were J. C. Iselin and Uriel Freudenberger, the latter in his pamphlet entitled *"Guillaume Tell, fable danoise"* (1760). Tell's advocates exerted themselves so much the more, and even resorted to forgery, in order to furnish documentary evidence for Tell's history. In the journal of Schattorf the name "*Trullo*" was altered to "*de Tello*"; in the parish register of Attinghausen "*Näll*" became "*Täll*." A story was also invented of a decision of the *Landsgemeinde* of Uri in 1387, by which a pilgrimage to Stein was revived, and it was also ordained that in Bürglen, where stood the house of William Tell, the "first restorer of freedom," a sermon should be preached; and of testimony given by 114 persons in Uri in 1388 to the *Landsgemeinde* that they had known Tell: as if it would have been necessary, supposing Tell to have been a historical personage, to refute doubts about him only seventy or eighty years after his existence!

Through the labors of Joseph Eutych Kopp, who from 1832 to 1835 sifted and published all the records bearing upon the origin of the Confederation, criticism gained a complete victory. It was then shown that the inhabitants of the Forest States were originally mostly serfs and dependents, and that they only obtained the freedom of the empire gradually, step by step, in the course of the thirteenth century, in close connection with the events of the history of the German empire. It became evident that the Perpetual League was concluded in 1291, and not in 1308; that it is barely conceivable that there were bailiffs in Uri appointed by the Hapsburgs after 1231, and that the Geslers were never lords of Küssnach, etc. It is, indeed, shown that the traditions concerning the storming of the castles and the founders of the league on the Rütli [9] rests upon historical foundation, yet they can by no means lay claim to acceptance as absolutely authentic history in detail. The worth and charm of the old folk-lore, as such, was all the more recognized, at least in its earliest form, before the time of Tschudi, in the chronicle of the "White Book." In these traditions we learn to treasure the principles, ideas, and customs of the primitive Swiss as the truthful and worthy product of the Swiss mind. Often have they inspired Swiss hearts to patriotic deeds, and even now no Swiss youth grows to manhood without imbibing something of the heroism and the enthusiasm for freedom ascribed to the first Confederates.

[9] The Rütli may have been the historical site of the first alliance between the years 1245 and 1250. Various ruins witness to the destruction of castles, and narratives such as those of Sarnen, Lowerz, and Rotzloch may rest upon a historical foundation. The characters of Staupacher and Fürst are also historical in the main.

Chapter V

GROWTH OF THE CONFEDERATION. 1315-1400

NOTWITHSTANDING the violent shock which the battle of Morgarten had given to the Austrian power, the latter could not resist the temptation to form her territory into one compact principality, by striving to obtain complete possession of the Forest States. Shortly before this, in 1313, she had brought the Kiburgs and their landgraviate of Burgundy into subjection, and she now sought in the west to obtain forces and aid for a fresh struggle. But the Burgundian towns of Fribourg, Berne, Soleure, Morat, and Bienne formed an alliance against the duke in 1318. Leopold endeavored to reduce them by force, and in 1318 besieged Soleure; the inhabitants, however, held out bravely for ten weeks, and are said to have generously rescued their foes when the bridge over the Aar broke down beneath their weight. The plan formed against the Forest States was thus frustrated; and as the house of Austria was for very many years following occupied with disturbances and misfortunes elsewhere in the empire against Louis the Bavarian, the Forest States found a favorable opportunity to ally themselves with others like-minded and to enlarge their field of action. With this end in view, they entered into alliance in 1323 with the Burgundian towns, notably with Berne and Thun, to whom they were drawn by a common danger; and they then proceeded to endeavor to win to their side the very neighbor whose hostile policy had chiefly troubled them in the past, and whose friendship was now become an urgent necessity, namely, Lucerne.

As long ago as the time of the first revolt against the Hapsburgs in 1250 Lucerne had formed an alliance with the Forest States. The frequency of intercourse by means of the lake and the requirements of trade gave rise to constant friendly relations between that town and the three Forest States. This alliance was cemented when Lucerne also rebelled against the Austrian dominion. For since this town had passed from the mild ecclesiastical rule of the monastery of Murbach to that of the Austrian house of Hapsburg, she had come under secular dominion, and into a condition of strict dependence. The perpetual demands of the inhabitants for an extension of their municipal liberties found no hearing. One party, therefore, urged an alliance with the Forest States. The breach between the town and its rulers was widened, when a few burgesses, and soon afterward the whole community, bound themselves by a general resolution and a solemn oath to repel all encroachments in those unquiet times. The Austrian bailiff at Rotenburg, to whose jurisdiction Lucerne belonged, considered these proceedings of the burgesses dangerous to his rule, and seriously threatened the town. Thereupon the federal party took the upper hand, and on November 7, 1332, Lucerne concluded a Perpetual League with the three Forest States. This gave rise to fierce and devastating struggles of many years' duration between Lucerne, the Forest States, and the Austrian party. The bailiff of Rotenburg fell upon the men of Lucerne at Buonas, and compelled them to obedience, but it does not appear that the league with the Forest States was dissolved (June, 1336). The town was also visited by a conflagration, during which the people of Nidwalden lent their aid as faithful Confederates, notwithstanding a quarrel then existing between them and Lucerne. Meanwhile the Federal League had a severe test to undergo: on St. James's Day, 1343, the adherents of Austria formed a conspiracy against it and raised a tumult. Their evil designs were, however, betrayed, and the conspirators were banished, though the event probably gave rise to the later development of the tradition of the massacre of Lucerne. This league of the four Forest States formed the first introduction of towns into the Confederation. Thus the latter passed beyond its mountain limits and gained a footing in the plain, the Burgundian towns having previously espoused its cause. The struggle was now resumed on all sides; in the present western Switzerland, as in the east, burgher and peasant alike flung down the gauntlet to their sworn enemy, the noble.

The citizens of Berne immediately began to gain ground in the west by taking advantage of the financial and internal ruin of the nobility of Kiburg. In the dispute about the partition of the Kiburg inheritance Hartmann von Kiburg had been murdered by his younger brother Eberhard in the castle of Thun in 1322. The murderer now had to fear the revenge of the Austrian government, which had been favorable to Hartmann. He therefore sought the protection of Berne, invested that town with the feudal lordship of Thun, and raised expectations with regard to Burgdorf. The Bernese enticed King Louis into the alliance against Austria, and in 1323 the Forest States also, and began the struggle. In 1324 they acquired Laupen by purchase, destroyed some castles in the Jura, and joined Eberhard in attacking the counts of Neuchâtel. In 1330, however, Louis became reconciled to Austria, and Count Eberhard found his dependence upon Berne so irksome as time went on that he finally joined the opponents of that town. The Bernese now stood almost alone, and their thirst for action was thoroughly aroused: they destroyed the castle of Gümminen, belonging to Fribourg, in 1332, took the field against Eberhard, attacked the lords of Weissenburg and overthrew them completely, destroyed Strättlingen and other castles, and finally, in 1334, won the valley of Hasle from the lords of Weissenburg.

These daring enterprises on the part of Berne exasperated the entire nobility to the utmost, and the latter soon found a favorable opportunity for making their hatred felt by that town. The Emperor Louis, being at this time under the papal ban, was not acknowledged by Berne, and therefore declared war against the latter. The nobles of Burgundy now readily entered into an alliance with one another and with Louis against Berne, particularly the Counts of Kiburg, Nidau, Aarburg, Strassburg, Neuchâtel, and Gruyère, together with the Dukes of Austria; the town of Fribourg also joined them, moved by jealousy against Berne. These opponents all assembled one day at Nidau and renewed their ancient demands and claims, and upon Berne refusing to comply with all their desires, determined to destroy the town; all peaceable overtures were scornfully rejected, and when any of the nobles met a citizen of Berne they would mock him with the words: "If thou art from Berne, bow down and let us pass!"[1] In the spring of 1339 they marched upon Laupen more than 15,000 men strong; the place was bravely defended by John von Bubenberg, the younger, till the Bernese hastened to the rescue under the skillful leadership of Rudolf von Erlach. They brought with them auxiliaries from Soleure, the Forest States, and the valleys of Hasle and Simmen, gathered under the banner of the White Cross—only 5000 men in all. But the enemy was forced to give way to the violent and simultaneous attacks of the Bernese and the Forest States; the infantry first yielded, and after about an hour and a

[1] "*Bist von Bern, so duck' dich und lass übergahn!*"

half the cavalry also. This brilliant victory of Laupen, which took place on June 21, 1339, the eve of the Ten Thousand Knights' Day, again turned the scale completely in favor of the Bernese. They destroyed the castle of the knight, Jordan von Gurgistein (who had vented his malicious joy in biting sarcasm at the distress of Berne), and richly retaliated upon the nobility for all feuds; advanced upon Fribourg, completely routed the forces of that town, and set fire to its environs. Berne was everywhere victorious; that town seemed to gain ground on all sides, and men said in amazement that God Himself had become a citizen of Berne, and was fighting for her. But both Berne and her foes soon longed for peace, which was concluded in 1340 through the intervention of Queen Agnes with Austria, and was shortly afterward followed by a ten years' league, the Bernese engaging to furnish auxiliary troops when needed. The town also renewed her league with the Forest States, which was in no wise forbidden by the Austrian alliance; the help rendered by those states at Laupen and their common danger had linked the two parties very closely together. Berne formed as it were the western bulwark of the league of the Forest States, and the embarrassments of Austria in eastern Switzerland renewing the struggle, Berne became a permanent member of the Confederation.

Zurich formed the center of operations in the east, as did Berne in the west; but, unlike Berne, Zurich first tried to gain the ascendency by a union with Austria. Ever since 1292 Austria had exerted a growing influence in eastern Switzerland, until internal affairs caused a breach between the imperial town and its rulers.

Here, as in other German towns, the handicraftsmen had long been endeavoring to form guilds and to obtain equal rights with the aristocracy. The government was fiercely attacked by the citizens and accused of divers offenses. Rudolf Brun took an opportunity to possess himself of the management of the town. This clever, able, and ambitious statesman in 1336 wrought a change in the constitution, which conceded certain political rights to the artisans in common with the aristocracy (for the constitution of guilds), and conferred upon himself the office of burgomaster for life. The old councilors were for the most part removed and some of them banished. Brun now sought the support of Austria, and the latter brought about a reconciliation between the town and the exiled councilors. But these last, brooding secretly over their wrongs, obtained the assistance of Count Hans von Rapperswil, and sought the ruin of the burgomaster and his faction. Brun was on the alert, however, and sufficiently informed of their designs to take precautions. On the very night that he was to be assassinated, the night of the Zurich massacre, February 23, 1350, he caused the alarm-bell to be rung, and many conspirators to be themselves put to death; only a remnant of these escaped. He then advanced upon Rapperswil and administered the oath of allegiance to the inhabitants. He endeavored to come to an understanding with Austria, and even to form an alliance with that power, but this came to nothing. A party in Zurich hostile to Brun gained the upper hand, and speedily destroyed both old and new Rapperswil (September, 1350). By this means Zurich drew upon itself the enmity of the nobility, and even of Austria, its former friend, and Brun lost his essential support, and was driven to form a league with the peasants of the mountains; for Zurich, like Berne in the Laupen war, turned to the Forest States, with whom it had been occasionally connected for a century past. Brun sought to gain what advantage he might from so undesirable a connection. Thus on May 1, 1351, the imperial free town of Zurich entered the Perpetual League of the Confederates, and by this means the Federation was firmly established in the plains.

It was, however, impossible that Austria should look on in silence while the Confederation increased step by step at her expense. Duke Albert, therefore, renewed the attempt (in which his brother had failed at the battle of Morgarten) to destroy the Confederation. In September, 1351, with 16,000 men, he laid siege to Zurich, which was defended by a federal garrison. The Confederates inclined to peace, but the demands of Austria were so exorbitant that negotiations were abandoned and the war was continued. In December, 1351, troops from Zurich, after devastating the baths at Baden, were surprised at Tätwil on their return journey by Austrians, and had some difficulty in making their escape. In this second struggle Zurich and the Forest States conquered Glarus. This latter territory, which belonged to Austria, having been long at variance with its rulers, and having entered into alliance with the Forest States as early at 1323, welcomed the Confederates as deliverers. The inhabitants repulsed the Austrian bailiff at Rautifeld near Näfels, and on June 4, 1352, joyfully entered the Perpetual League of the Confederates. Zug also, forsaken by Duke Albert, now yielded to the Confederates, and joined the league June 27, 1352. Upon this, Duke Albert resolved to retrieve his losses at one blow. All his adherents supplied him with troops, and Berne too was obliged to send a contingent, in accordance with the former alliance. On June 21, 1352, he advanced upon Zurich, as in the previous year, that being the nearest important outpost of the Confederates, but encountered such valiant resistance on the part of the men of Zurich and their allies that in three weeks' time he raised the siege, internal dissensions arising among his own troops. But under Brun's management Zurich had assumed a sort of intermediate position between Austria and the Confederation, and felt itself rather a free imperial town than a member of the Federal League, and consequently the peace which was now concluded in September, 1352, called from its negotiator the Peace of Brandenburg, was somewhat unfavorable to the Confederates. Glarus and Zug were to be once more in subjection to Austria, even Schwyz and Unterwalden were again forced to pay tribute and taxes to that power, and all the Confederates bound themselves to form no further alliances with other towns or lands belonging to the duke.

In return, the league was increased by the accession of the town of Berne. The Bernese had been obliged to furnish Austria with auxiliaries against Zurich, but they had not the slightest intention of quarreling with the Forest States, who had befriended them at the time of the campaign of Laupen. Immediately upon the reconciliation between Austria and the Forest States by the Peace of Brandenburg, Berne concluded a Perpetual League with the Confederates on March 6, 1353; this could be done without coming into direct hostility with Austria, since the Austrian League permitted the renewal of former amities. Thus a second imperial town joined the Confederation, a town whose position and authority dominated the whole of what is now western Switzerland. Berne formed a powerful bulwark toward the southwest, as did Zurich toward the northeast. Hence the entrance of both these towns into the Federal League not only assured the continuance of the Confederation, but also secured for it a certain amount of political power in the German empire.

Some conditions of the Peace of Brandenburg remaining unfulfilled, Duke Albert of Austria accused the Confederates of breaking the peace, carrying his complaint to the Emperor Charles IV., then at the head of the empire. The latter, after many attempts had been made to come to terms, declared war against the Confederation in the name of the empire in June, 1354. He appeared before Zurich at the head of a considerable imperial army, and was joined by Duke Albert and his adherents. Zurich now for the fourth time (since 1292) saw Austrian troops before her gates—with as little result as before, however, for the Confederates defied the enemy, though the numbers of the latter were ten times as great as their own. Owing to delay, dissensions arose in the camp of the imperial army; many of the nobility were offended by the haughty Duke of Austria; the imperial towns feared to injure their own position and to give the princes an advantage by attacking the imperial town of Zurich, and the Emperor Charles IV. was himself inclined to peace. Brun was not slow to avail himself of this disposition. He caused the imperial flag to be hoisted on the walls of Zurich, in order to call to mind the loyalty of Zurich to the empire. The feud with Zurich being thus made to appear a merely Austrian undertaking, the imperial towns withdrew their allegiance. Charles IV. therefore raised the siege, and himself offered to act as mediator; which offer Zurich, wearied by the protracted struggle with Albert, finally accepted. Terms were settled on July 24, 1355, by the Peace of Regensburg. The latter was almost identical with the Peace of Brandenburg; Zurich again negotiated quite as a free imperial town, and undertook to induce the Confederates to accept the peace; and the oath was taken. Brun even succeeded in persuading Zurich to enter into alliance with Austria. This equivocal demeanor on the part of Zurich only ended with the death of Brun in 1360, and the Confederates then once more advanced against Austria with one accord. Schwyz took possession of the town and territory of Zug, and Austria was forced to give her consent to this step, in 1368, by the Peace of Thorberg; Zug was now once more a member of the league.

A long period of peace next followed, during which both parties recruited their strength, and even joined hands in friendship, being unexpectedly united by the presence of a common foe. Baron Ingelram von Coucy, grandson of Leopold I. of Austria, and son-in-law of Edward III. of England, required the dukes of Austria to give up Aargau, which he claimed in his mother's right; and not obtaining it, he invaded Switzerland in 1375 with a numerous army of French and English mercenaries.[2] Terror and dismay were universal at the devastation wrought by these undisciplined troops. Wherever they went crops were destroyed, men and cattle butchered, and villages, churches, and monasteries set on fire. In this emergency Austria sought reconciliation with the Confederates, and renewed the Peace of Thorberg. She also concluded an offensive and defensive alliance with the towns, from which, however, the country districts held aloof out of hatred to Austria.

The Confederates advanced immediately against the "Guglers"; in December, 1375, a few troops from Lucerne, Entlebuch, and Unterwalden repulsed one division of mercenaries at Buttisholz in the district of Sursee; troops from Berne and Fribourg attacked another division at Ins (or Jens), and the Bernese alone finally gained a brilliant victory over the main army near the monastery of Fraubrunnen. The rest of the invaders, partly owing to these defeats and partly to the want of provisions and the severity of the winter, were compelled to withdraw without attaining their object. The love of war and enterprise was no little aroused in the Confederates, and notably in Berne, by these events; and the first Swiss war songs celebrated the victories of Berne over France and England. The common danger had, however, confirmed the peace with Austria.

The second half of the fourteenth century, the period of the greatest and most rapid growth of the Confederation, was very favorable to the development of civic communities. In both France and Germany the towns fearlessly opposed the nobility and princes, and even seemed to aim at the government of the empire. Beyond the Rhine the town of Berne was especially disposed to wage a war of extermination against the nobility. Before this town there lay a field ripe already to harvest, for the Burgundian nobility either died out or became increasingly impoverished by the then growing want of money. The Counts of Kiburg, too, were much reduced, and obliged to sell or mortgage one estate after another. Count Rudolf still tried to obtain money and spoil by violent attacks upon the towns; and in 1382 he endeavored to surprise the town of Soleure under cover of night and fog (Massacre of Soleure). But the plot was discovered, it is said, by Hans Roth

---

[2] These troops received the nickname of "*Gugler*" on account of their headgear resembling a cowl (Swiss-German, "*Gugel*").

of Rumisberg, a peasant. Soleure and Berne called upon the Confederates for aid, and a protracted war was commenced against the house of Kiburg, which ended to the advantage of the towns, in spite of a futile siege of Burgdorf. Berne, with the help of the Confederates, destroyed the fortresses and castles of the nobility of Kiburg, and acquired the towns of Burgdorf and Thun, which were retained till 1384; and the house of Kiburg was forced to promise to commence no future war without the consent of Berne and Soleure. By this means Berne became lord of the upper and middle districts of the Aar.

But this again led to friction with Austria, since during the war with the house of Kiburg, Austria, notwithstanding promises to the contrary, had secretly supported that house and seemed disposed to avenge its destruction. The Confederates also no longer hesitated to support the enemies of Austria. In order to be able successfully to oppose the princes and nobles of South Germany, the southern towns of Germany had formed themselves into a great alliance, and thus had come into conflict with Leopold III., Duke of Austria. In February, 1385, Zurich, Berne, Soleure, Lucerne, and Zug made common cause with the allied towns in opposition to Leopold; the three Forest States held aloof, probably fearing the ascendency of the towns. Leopold thought to avail himself of this division of interests among the Confederates, and endeavored by all manner of favors to win the rural communes to his cause while venting his wrath upon the towns. Notwithstanding many urgent entreaties, he denied to Lucerne the abolition of the burdensome toll of Rothenburg. At the same time he sought to keep the peace as long as possible. The Confederates, however, who had formerly waited to be attacked, now themselves urged on the war, although the peace with Austria—renewed for eleven years in 1376—was not yet expired. War was declared by them on all sides: Zurich attacked Rapperswil; Zug the Austrian fortress of Saint-André on the Lake of Zug; Lucerne on Christmas Day destroyed Rothenburg, admitted Entlebuch, then hard pressed by the lord of Thorberg, the Austrian bailiff, into a civil alliance, and finally did the same for Sempach, which was striving to free itself from the Austrian dominion (January, 1386).

After such gross violations of the treaty Austria could hesitate no longer. The imperial towns, it is true, sought even yet to adjust matters peaceably; but these attempts at reconciliation merely caused delay, and the towns, being just then threatened by Bavaria, made terms with Austria and forsook the Confederates. The valiant Duke Leopold now resolved to strike a decisive blow at the Confederation. The universal dislike and animosity felt by the nobility toward both townsmen and peasants favored his desires, and a numerous body of knights joined him from the Austrian territories of Thurgau and Aargau, and from Suabia, Burgundy, and Alsace. In order probably to separate the forces of the Confederates, Leopold sent a portion of his army against Zurich, while he himself, with the main body of his troops—6000 men in all—advanced, in the beginning of July, 1386, against Sempach, Rothenburg, and Lucerne. The Confederates left the inhabitants of Zurich to defend their own territory, and marched against Leopold with a force of only about 1500 men.

On July 9 the two armies met unexpectedly at Sempach, and a battle ensued. The nobles prepared for the attack by alighting from their horses, the ground being unsuitable for the use of horses. The Austrians formed a close column, with their spears pointed against the Confederates, who were chiefly furnished with short weapons, and were drawn up in the form of a wedge. The Austrians, moreover, stood on higher ground, and hence the Confederates suffered severely at the commencement of the action, and Leopold imagined the victory secure. But then (according to later but authentic accounts) one of the Confederates, the brave Arnold Winkelried, is said to have pressed forward careless of his own life, and opened a breach in the hostile ranks. Encouraged by this heroic example, the Confederates, their wedge shape broken, dashed forward upon the Austrians, over the corpse of the slain man, and dealt such blows with their halbeards and clubs upon the enemy that the latter, suffering greatly at the same time from the weight of their armor in the sultry heat of July, could not long hold out. In vain did Duke Leopold dash into the thick of the fight to arrest the flight of his men; his life was sacrificed with those of the bravest of his knights. Part of the Austrian army—mostly pages with the horses—had already taken to flight. Between 700 and 1500 Austrians had fallen, among them 600 of the highest nobility, while the Confederates lost only about 120. This brilliant and encouraging victory of the Confederates made a deep and far-reaching impression. In it the fate of the Austrian power in Switzerland was determined. The Bernese, who had hitherto held aloof from the struggle because the Peace of Thorberg was not yet expired, now also took up arms, and possessed themselves of the dominions of Fribourg and Austria in the Bernese Oberland (Obersimmenthal, Unterseen, and Oberhofen) and in Seeland. The remainder of the Confederates joined Glarus, their ancient ally, took possession of the Austrian town of Wesen in August, 1386, and placed a garrison there. Glarus drove out the Austrian bailiffs, and in 1387 was annexed to the Confederation as an independent and free community.

Meanwhile Duke Albert, Leopold's brother, unwilling to surrender his dominions so easily, turned his force against Glarus. Wesen was first recovered by treachery and cruelty. Austrian soldiers were smuggled into the town by the help of some of the townsmen, and put the Federal garrison to death (Massacre of Wesen, February 22, 1388). The Austrians—6000 strong—next advanced against Glarus, and were encountered on April 9, 1388, by 500 men of Glarus and a handful from Schwyz at Näfels. The men of Glarus posted themselves behind the "Letzi" (a rampart) which enclosed the entrance to the valley, but were forced to yield to superior numbers. While the Austrians dashed blindly up the valley in search of plunder the men of Glarus assembled themselves at the side of the valley on a hillock on the slope of the Rautiberg. The Austrians turned hastily in that direction, but were received with a shower of stones and thrown into confusion. The men of Glarus, under Mathias Ambühl, dashed impetuously down, threw themselves upon the enemy, and drove them in a protracted struggle down the valley toward the "Letzi," and over it as far as Wesen: 1700 of the enemy are said to have perished; many were drowned in the Linth. Wesen was taken by the men of Glarus and given to the flames. After many castles had been destroyed, in April, 1389, the imperial towns effected a truce of seven years between Austria and the Confederates, which secured their conquests to the latter.

Austria afterward sought to retrieve her losses by entering into alliance with Schöno, the burgomaster, and the small council of Zurich, who were still well disposed toward Austria, as they had been in 1356. But the citizens, most of whom were loyal to the Confederation, destroyed the treaty and expelled the traitorous faction in 1393. An alteration in the constitution strengthened the democratic element in Zurich, and the new union of the Confederates found worthy expression in the Convention of Sempach. An amicable settlement was made with Austria, and on July 16, 1394, the seven years' peace was lengthened to twenty years. Glarus, like Zug, now formed a free member of the Confederation. The war of liberation, which had lasted almost a century, was brought

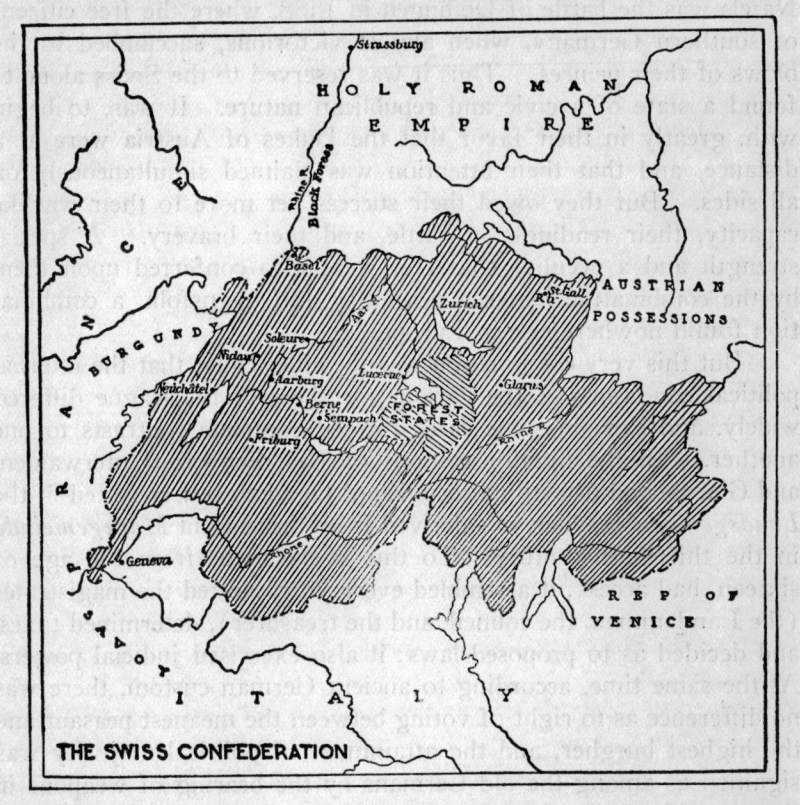

THE SWISS CONFEDERATION

to a conclusion in May, 1412, by a further extension of the peace for fifty years.

After so many struggles and hostilities the position of the Confederation was at length assured for a long time to come. Austria surrendered her claims to the dominion of Schwyz and Unterwalden, her rights over Lucerne, Zug, and Glarus for as long as the peace should last. The power of the nobility in the Confederation was shattered.

The wars of freedom of the Swiss peasants and townsfolk, which form but a link in the great chain of the struggles of those times between aristocracy and democracy, acquired a more general significance from the fact that similar democratical efforts had been suppressed in other lands. The rising of the peasants in England and the revolt of French citizens, which took place about the same time, failed; and contemporary with the victories of Sempach and Näfels was the battle of Döffingen in 1388, where the free citizens of southern Germany, when almost victorious, succumbed to the blows of their princes. Thus it was reserved to the Swiss alone to found a state of a civic and republican nature. It was, to begin with, greatly in their favor that the Dukes of Austria were at a distance, and that their attention was claimed simultaneously on all sides. But they owed their success yet more to their warlike capacity, their readiness in battle, and their bravery. A special strength and a peculiar character were also conferred upon them by the combination between peasantry and townsfolk, a combination found nowhere else in Europe.

But this very combination was the chief cause that the internal political conditions of the various members of the league differed widely, and even in some cases formed complete contrasts to one another. In the interior cantons of Uri, Schwyz, Unterwalden, and Glarus, and partially also in Zug,[3] the chief power rested in the *Landsgemeinde,* which was derived from the ancient *Markgemeinde* in the thirteenth century. To this every man, from the age of sixteen, had access; it assembled every year, elected the magistrates (the Landamman, the council, and the treasurer), determined taxes, and decided as to proposed laws; it also exercised judicial powers. At the same time, according to ancient German custom, there was no difference as to right of voting between the meanest peasant and the highest burgher, and the attainment of political majority was signified as among the old Germans by the bearing of weapons in the assembly.

The towns had a more aristocratic constitution. But even among them there were again great differences, especially between Zurich and Berne. In Zurich since Rudolf Brun's time the guilds formed of tradesmen and artisans had a share in the government, and much resembled the old free and knightly families or patricians, who alone had formerly been entitled to vote. The wardens, *i. e.,* the masters of the thirteen guilds, with the thirteen councilors, the

---

[3] Zug had indeed a civic constitution of its own, but formed a *Landsgemeinde* canton collectively with Menzingen, Aegeri and Baar (the "Amt")

representatives of the *Constafel* (the society of noble citizens of ancient descent), together formed the council. By the side of the existing "small council" an enlarged "great council" (of the 200) gradually developed in course of time, privileged to represent the communes. But whereas Brun had endowed the office of a burgomaster with almost monarchical powers, divers events, especially the treachery of Schöno in 1393, led to a restriction of that office and a strengthening of the great council, as also of the college of wardens. In contrast to those of Zurich, the artisans of Berne acquired no influence whatever; the guilds could take no active part in political matters, and the government was carried on exclusively by the council, composed of members of distinguished families of the nobility. There were also great differences as to the position in the league which the various states occupied, as well as in their internal constitutional conditions. The three Forest States formed a group by themselves, and became the nucleus around which the other members gathered. All the remaining states, which had concluded no special league among themselves, allied themselves to them, and they were united by the closest bond of fellowship among themselves. The provisions of the league were the same for all three. They mutually bound themselves to render constant and prompt aid to one another; none of the three might enter into foreign negotiations without the knowledge and advice of the others; the punishment of offenses in matters concerning the league appertained to all in common. Being thus bound by a species of community of rights dating from the Perpetual League of 1315, they already represented a league in the modern sense of the word. The other states, on the contrary, were by no means so closely united among themselves. The Confederation was formed gradually by the accession of new members, till at last a many-sided whole was produced. The treaties of alliance were in every case regulated according to the special needs of the moment and local conditions. Thus the League of Lucerne differs essentially from others. The rendering of aid is made conditional upon the distressed state affirming itself upon oath to be in the right, and upon formal notice given. No member may interfere with the internal affairs of another, and no party to the League may conclude an alliance without the consent of all the Confederates.

The League of Zurich is the first to describe a Federal circle within which aid should be rendered—Grimsel, Aare, Rhine, Thur,

Ringgenberg near Truns, Platifer near Faido, Doisel near Lax in Upper Valais—and the stipulations with regard to such aid are fixed more definitely. Internal dissensions are to be settled by arbitration, each party to elect two judges, and they to deliberate at Einsiedeln. Should there be no majority, an arbitrator is elected, whose decision shall be final. Further, every party retains the right of forming alliances, and Zurich moreover asserts her right to demand immediate assistance of the Forest States should her guilds or her burgomaster be in danger. Finally, all ancient rights and customs are guaranteed at the outset. Every ten years both old and young shall swear to this alliance. In contrast to Zurich, Glarus is treated with scant respect in her league, and almost like a dependency, while Zug enters into the rights enjoyed by the Forest States in the Treaty of Zurich. Berne maintained a favorable position, including freedom of alliance and a guarantee for her existing territory. Thus the Confederation was by no means a political structure. It was but loosely held together; Zurich, Berne, and Lucerne, for example, were not directly allied to one another at all, but only through the medium of the Forest States.

Yet, notwithstanding this slight formation, the league was durable. While the leagues of the German and Italian towns, and even of the Hans towns, fell to pieces, the Swiss Federation, after centuries of duration, is the only example of a state which had its origin in free alliances. Notwithstanding local differences, we find even in these early times essential points in common between the political aims and views of the Confederates. For instance, from the earliest times the various states would suffer no exceptional advantages to be given to the clergy, and in spite of violent protest regularly assessed the monasteries within their territory (*e. g.*, Uri laid taxes upon Wettingen, Schwyz upon Einsiedeln), and the towns likewise subjected their religious houses to the authority of the state.

Twice (in 1248 and 1338) Zurich expelled the insubordinate clergy, drew taxes from their estates in spite of the prohibition of the Bishop of Constance, and kept a watchful eye upon their conduct and management. The rural communities vied with the well-to-do towns in the abolition of ground-rents and feudal rights, which they owed to divers spiritual and temporal lords, and in the course of the fourteenth century they gradually freed themselves by purchase from the greater part of these burdens, as for example

Uri from Wettingen and Fraumünster, Schwyz from Einsiedeln, Kappel and Engleberg, Glarus from Säckingen. Both the towns and the rural communities were exceedingly anxious to induce the emperor to release them from their obligations to the empire and from its jurisdiction, and desired to obtain dominion and sovereign rights, such as county courts, penal judicature, and the rights of coinage over their adjacent territory, and to annex the latter. The efforts of Uri, Schwyz, Lucerne, Berne, and Zurich were successful, and the latter as early as the beginning of the fifteenth century had little by little acquired dominion over the greater part of the present canton, and had by strenuous efforts obtained her emancipation from imperial bailiffs, tolls, and taxes.[4]

The course of events soon obliged the Confederates to establish federal principles which should be generally binding, and to enact federal laws. When Bruno Brun, Provost of the *Grossmünster* in Zurich, and his brother, Herdegen Brun, the two sons of the burgomaster, having taken part in an attack upon Peter von Gundoldingen, Mayor of Lucerne, refused, as ecclesiastics, to appear before the secular court, it was ordained by the "Priests' Charter" (*Pfaffenbrief*) of October 7, 1370, by the majority of the Confederates (six states), that ecclesiastics should be under the authority of the state and should occupy no exceptional position; that all feuds and assaults should be forbidden and all roads protected. On July 10, 1393, all the eight states united with Soleure in the formation of a common military ordinance, called the Convention of Sempach (*Sempacherbrief*). The voluntary enterprises of individuals, unauthorized pillage, and the ill-treatment of sacred spots and of defenseless women were prohibited by this ordinance. This is the only example in those days of fierce and warlike passions of any statutory settlement of military discipline in the interests of order and humanity, and it testifies amply to the high purpose of the Federal League, and also to earnest endeavor toward a firmer alliance.

From all these circumstances it is evident that the Confederates

[4] The most important acquisitions of Zurich (mostly obtained by purchase) were: 1358, Zollikon; 1384, Küssnach and Goldbach, Höngg; 1385, Thalwil; 1400, Erlenbach; 1402, Greifensee; 1405, Männedorf; 1406, Maschwanden, Horgen, Rüschlikon; 1408, Grüningen, Stäfa, Hombrechtikon, Mönchaltorf; 1409, Regensberg and Bülach; 1410, Meilen; 1415, Freiamt (by conquest); 1424, Rümlang; 1424 and 1452, the county of Kiburg (Tösstal, lower Glattal, the "Wine Land"); 1484, Stein on the Rhine; 1496, Eglisau, etc.

had no definite preconceived idea in view, nor did they advance in full consciousness of a task to be achieved, but only sought to realize step by step whatever was attainable and possible under existing conditions. In contrast to the unbridled revolutionary attempts of the lower classes in France, England, and other parts, which occurred about this time, the Confederation, by their moderate measures, averted any strong reaction, and rendered steady progress possible.

Chapter VI

SWITZERLAND AT THE HEIGHT OF HER POWER
1400-1516

HAD the Federal League of eight states remained unmolested after the victorious issue of the war of independence, and unnoticed by surrounding neighbors, it would hardly have expanded of itself. But it had set an example which began to kindle the surrounding countries and aroused such desires after freedom that the Confederates could not remain inactive. Hence the league began to spread on all sides, and the Confederation soon stood, as it were, surrounded by a strong rampart of free communities, the largest and most important of which were Appenzell, Valais, and the Grisons.

The right of dominion over Appenzell and over the towns of St. Gall had gradually devolved to a great extent upon the Abbot of St. Gall. But while the abbots were endeavoring to maintain, and even to extend their rights, the inhabitants of Appenzell, St. Gall, and other dependencies were striving for greater freedom in face of the various struggles for independence going on around them. As early as 1377 Abbot George von Wildenstein was unable to hinder the people of Appenzell, Hundwil, Gais, and Teufen from allying themselves with southern German towns around the Lake of Constance, and from appointing a common administration freely elected by themselves. The election of this administration gradually led to the regular establishment of the so-called *Landsgemeinde*. Insubordination quickly made its appearance on all sides. The town of St. Gall, which possessed an imperial charter dating from the thirteenth century, and had for many years had its own corporation, had previously entered the league of the towns. An insurrection broke out in Wil. Abbot George's successor, however, Cuno von Stoffeln, who became abbot in 1379, seemed to have mastered the movement by skillful policy and rigid discipline. He even entered into alliance with the imperial towns, and by their help forced the inhabitants of Appenzell to do him homage, and to pay tributes, rents, and tithes; double taxes were laid upon the malcontents.

This was the signal for an open and general rising. The people of Appenzell, in desperation, leagued themselves in 1401 with the town of St. Gall and advancing upon the castle of Clanx, which belonged to the abbot, they took it. By the efforts of the imperial towns, however—the abbot himself having become a burgher of Lindau—St. Gall was once more reconciled to the abbot. But the people of Appenzell persisted in their rebellion, allied themselves in 1402 with Schwyz, which sent them aid, and prepared for war, destroying many castles and carrying their ravages almost to St. Gall itself. Meanwhile the troops of the imperial towns, summoned by Cuno, had arrived at that town. On May 15, 1403, these troops, together with the abbot's retainers and the men of St. Gall—5000 men in all—advanced toward the heights of Vögelinseck on the "Letzi"[1] (near Speicher), where 200 men from Appenzell, with 300 from Schwyz and 200 from Glarus, awaited them. After a brief engagement the enemy was forced to yield; 250 of them remained dead upon the field. The imperial towns then concluded a peace with the inhabitants of Appenzell, leaving the abbot to continue the struggle (1404). The latter sought help from Austria, and Duke Frederick reluctantly consented to interpose. Upon this the inhabitants of St. Gall again attached themselves to those of Appenzell, and the latter were also supported by Count Rudolf von Werdenberg, who had been, through his own fault, dispossessed of his estates by Austria.

The Austrians advanced in two divisions, one encamped before St. Gall and the other prepared to attack Altstätten. While the former, under Duke Frederick, devastated the neighborhood of St. Gall, the latter advanced from Altstätten toward the frontier at the Stoss.[2] The Austrians crossed the "Letzi" successfully; but the men of Appenzell and Schwyz dashed suddenly down upon them from the heights, hurling down stones and trunks of trees; the Austrians could scarcely keep their feet upon the slippery ground and were soon put to flight, from four to five hundred being slain. The division under the duke retired to St. Gall. This was on June 17, 1405.

The duke, discouraged, withdrew from the war, whereupon the men of Appenzell, giving rein to their youthful prowess, speedily

---

[1] A redoubt or rampart. [2] The name of a mountain-spur.

achieved unexpected successes. They renewed their league with St. Gall, and in the course of their victorious march conquered the whole of the Rheintal, liberated the towns of Werdenberg, Sargans, Feldkirch, and Bludenz, and concluded with them the "League above the Lake"[3]; the province of Toggenburg also entered this alliance. This league formed as it were a second Confederation side by side with that of the Swiss, held its own diets, and acted as an independent power toward foreign countries. In the flush of victory, and in revenge for old scores, the men of Appenzell devastated the territories of neighboring lords and hostile towns; they proclaimed liberty to the peasant everywhere, and in a brief space of time destroyed over fifty castles. Thurgau and Vorarlberg were overrun; the county of Kiburg and the whole of Suabia were thrown into alarm and excitement by the unbridled fury of the invincible mountain folk. Every effort was therefore made to oppose them. In the first instance the burgesses of Constance and the nobility of Suabia joined, fell upon the men of Appenzell suddenly, in January, 1408, before Bregenz, the lake being frozen, and put them to flight.

In consequence of this defeat the "League above the Lake" was dissolved, and the pride of the inhabitants of Appenzell was crushed; they now desisted from further interference with neighboring districts. But now they were again threatened on their own territory, the emperor endeavoring to force them into subjection to the abbot. The Confederates, on the other hand, supported them, and on November 24, 1411, they were received by the seven states, all the eight states except Berne, as a subordinate member of the league, and taken under protection by a treaty of perpetual citizenship.[4] Liberty was secured to Appenzell by its accession to the Swiss League.

In the next year the town of St. Gall followed its example, after having compelled the new abbot to acknowledge its freedom and independence. In vain did the abbots endeavor to recover their sovereign rights; they were obliged to content themselves with certain rents and taxes, which, moreover, were gradually remitted. The alliance of Appenzell and St. Gall with the Confederates was renewed after the Zurich War, in which they had served as a support against Austria, and was confirmed for all time.

The inhabitants of Valais, like those of Appenzell, turned to

---

[3] "Bund ob dem See."   [4] "Ein ewiges Burg- und Landrecht."

the Confederates for help in obtaining their freedom. Here, too, there had existed since very early times a tolerable number of free folk, confronted by a powerful nobility. The land was divided politically into two districts. Upper Valais, which was chiefly German, was under the Bishop of Sion; Lower Valais, with a Romance (French) population, under the Count of Savoy. The former gradually acquired a position of freedom, like the inhabitants of Appenzell under their abbot, and like so many provinces under ecclesiastical dominion; several communities called *Zehnten* acquired certain liberties which in 1354 were ratified by the Emperor Charles IV. Every *Zehnte* had its own jurisdiction, and all stood alike under one council and one governor general.

The bishop had often formerly sought to defend himself against such efforts for freedom by a league with the counts of Savoy; the latter, however, thought to avail themselves of this alliance to extend their own rights in the Valais. With this view, Count Amadeus VII. of Savoy interfered in a dispute between the nobility and the people. A devastating war broke out, in which, in 1388, soon after the victory of the Confederates at Näfels, Amadeus and the nobility were defeated at Visp by the Valaisans. Upper Valais was by this means secured against Savoy.

But a new danger threatened from the direction of the mighty Baron von Raron. The family of Raron was at that time the most powerful in the Valais, and united the offices of a bishop and a governor general; it was also strongly supported by Berne, in which town the family enjoyed civic rights, and by the dukes of Milan. The barons therefore expected to be easily able to subjugate the land. But in 1414, the Confederates being expelled by them in concert with Savoy from Eschental, which had been taken from Milan, the Valaisans rose in revolt; the *Landsturm*[5] was called out, the *mazza*[6] was raised, and all flocked to their country's flag. Beauregard, the ancestral castle of the Rarons, was destroyed and the family driven out in 1415. The Raron family then seeking the help of the Duke of Savoy, the people of Upper Valais concluded in 1416 a ten years' treaty of citizenship with Uri, Unterwalden, and Lucerne, with whom they had long been on terms of friendly alliance for purposes of trade. The Bernese, however, supported the

---

[5] A general levy of the people.
[6] A club upon which was carved a human face in agony, which was carried from village to village as a symbol of revolt.

Raron family as their fellow-citizens. War broke out afresh, and a furious struggle ensued. Now the Bernese and Witschard von Raron invaded Valais, robbing and plundering; now the men of Valais made incursions into Bernese territory. The Bernese and their allies advanced against Upper Valais in 1419 with a powerful force. Devastation followed in their train and a fearful panic ensued. Then a gallant patriot, Thomas Riedi by name, assembled a few hundred adherents, fell upon the enemy at Ulrich, and compelled them to retreat. Valais once more was saved.

In 1420 the Confederates negotiated a peace, which, owing to the machinations of Berne and Savoy, proved unfavorable to the inhabitants of the Valais, and the latter was allotted to Berne and the Raron family as indemnification. On the other hand, the Valaisans had achieved an enduring success. The position of governor general was thenceforth always occupied by a native of the district agreeable to the people. A new constitution gave the people a greater share in the government, such as the choice of officers, judges, sergeants, and members of council; and the bishop might not nominate his officials without the consent of the country. The Rarons left the land.

Hardly any other district had undergone so many territorial divisions as ancient Rhætia. Upon the heights which encircle the valleys of the Rhine and its tributaries there stood, and as romantic ruins still remain, numerous castles then in the possession of powerful nobles, as those of Razuns, Montfort, Werdenberg, Belmont, Triens, Aspermont, Montsax (Misox), and Vaz. The bishops of Coire owned a specially extensive territory; almost the whole land was under their rule, with the exception of the valleys of the Upper Rhine, Prätigau, and Davos, and not a few noble families were their feudal vassals. But at the same time many free communes existed there, similar to the *Zehnten* in Valais; these were called Jurisdictions (*Gerichte*), and were the champions of freedom. Their gradual emancipation was favored by the circumstance that their many lords either held one another in check or made common cause with the people, in order to restrict the power of the bishops' ecclesiastical dominion. For this reason the people of those parts mostly lived on unusually friendly terms with the nobility.

Here, as elsewhere, liberty was acquired by means of alliances, the earliest of which originated in the bishops' territory. Bishop

Peter, neglecting the administration of his community and entering the service of Austria, his subjects, in 1367, concluded the "League of God's House" (*Gotteshausbund*). Later we find adherents of this league taking an active part in all important matters; they held formal diets, superintended the administration, and only tolerated the bishops at their will.

Soon after the "League of God's House," which embraced the central and southern parts (Engadine) of the present Grisons, there appeared in 1395 a similar league of lords and communes in the west, in the valley of the Upper Rhine, on the territory of the monastery of Dissentis, which was afterward designated the "Upper" or "Gray" League. This league, to which the various feuds of the lords had chiefly given rise, provided a standing court of arbitration, and was also allied to the Forest States and Glarus. In 1424 it was solemnly renewed under the maple at Trons; all participators, both high and low, enjoyed equal rights.

To these two leagues a third was afterward added. The ten jurisdictions in the eastern part of Rhætia (Prätigau, Schanfigg, and Davos), which were under the Counts of Toggenburg, joined in a league in 1436, on the death of the last Toggenburg, in order to avoid dispersion. By about the middle of the century these three leagues had little by little formed themselves into one united league, which, however, left all possible liberty to the separate leagues and to the high jurisdictions. After this the united leagues held common diets, and in 1486 they jointly conquered the districts of Cleves, the Valtelline, and Worms, which afterward became subject-lands of the three leagues in common; and Puschlav, which fell to the bishopric of Coire.

The threatening encroachments of Austria led them to form an alliance with the Confederation. Sigismund, Duke of Austria, in 1477 acquired the greater part of the Ten Jurisdictions, and Maximilian tried to obtain the whole of the Münsterthal, the jurisdiction of which he shared with the bishop, in order to enjoy safe communication with Milan. For this reason the Upper League concluded a perpetual league with the Confederates in 1497, and the "League of God's House" in 1498; only the Ten Jurisdictions were kept aloof by Austria. The struggle known as the Suabian War, which was thus brought about, established the alliance of the Grisons with the Confederation for all time.

The original cantons had early cultivated friendly relations with the district on the southern slope of the St. Gotthard. The traffic carried on by means of this—the latest of the great Alpine passes—brought about an ever-increasing commerce between the Forest States and Milan in Italy. Interruptions occurring in this commerce caused Uri to turn her attention to the possession of the higher district of the Tessin, the territory of Livinen (Val Leventina). In the year 1331 it had already been found necessary to secure the Upper Tessin by a warlike campaign. Then, in 1402, certain officials of the Viscounts of Milan having deprived the people of the Forest States of cattle, which they were taking to market at Varese, on account of their refusal to pay the appointed toll, troops from Uri and Obwalden marched over the St. Gotthard and conquered Livinen; this valley was the first possession held by the Confederates in common. After this, in 1410, some lords from Eschental, adherents of the Government of Milan, having robbed some people from Faido, who were subjects of Uri and Odwalden, of their cattle upon one of the Alps, and let fall some mocking words against the men of Uri, all the Confederates advanced over the St. Gotthard and across the pass of Giacomo into the Eschental as far as Domo d'Ossola, and conquered the whole territory, which thus became the second common possession. Meanwhile the enemies of the Confederates in Valais, the lords of Raron and dukes of Savoy, looked on in displeasure, and in 1414 an army from Savoy, aided by the Rarons, invaded the Eschental and drove out the Confederates. The latter, however, would not yield, and after several expeditions recovered the province in 1417. Uri and Obwalden in the following year purchased in addition the dominion of Bellinzona of the family of Sax.

Milan now exerted her powers to the utmost. The duke prepared to strike a decisive blow, and attacked Bellinzona. The Confederates immediately marched out; but at variance among themselves, and in scattered bands, they were defeated at many places in crossing the Alps. So it came to pass that the vanguard of the Confederates from Uri, Lucerne, Zug, and Unterwalden, occupying a disadvantageous position near Arbedo, above Bellinzona, was surprised by the Milanese on June 30, 1422, and suffered a sanguinary defeat in spite of heroic resistance (*die Koline von Zug*) The Confederates were all obliged to retire and lost all their possessions south of the St. Gotthard. In 1425 volunteers under Peter Rissi once more ventured over the Alps, and by a bold stroke captured Domo d'Ossola, but were afterward surrounded and hard pressed by Milanese troops. All the Confederates, even the Bernese, promptly came to their aid, but were unable to do more than rescue their distressed comrades. It was not until 1440 that Uri contrived to repossess herself of Livinen, which territory remained thenceforth a subject-land of Uri.

For the continuance and the untrammeled development of the Swiss Federation it was not sufficient merely to check the claims of Austria, for this seemed to have been already achieved by the peace of 1412. The Confederates were still surrounded on all sides and separated from one another by Austrian territory, and therefore it was soon felt to be absolutely necessary to enlarge their borders.

The first occasion of war came from without. A great Council had assembled in 1414 in the imperial town of Constance, under the auspices of King Sigismund, to discuss the subjects of schism and church reform. There were at that time three rival Popes, of whom John XXIII. possessed seemingly strong claims to the pontificate, but was the worst of the three as regarded character and morals. He hoped to support his position, but finding it impossible, simulated repentance and announced his resignation. Immediately regretting this step, however, in order to embarrass the Council he formed an alliance with Frederick, Duke of Austria, a rival of Sigismund, and by his connivance, disguised as a post-boy, fled to Schaffhausen, whence he fulminated anathemas against the Council. The assembly of the church, however, took energetic measures against both Pope and duke. The latter was put under the ban, and at the command of Sigismund an imperial war was forthwith commenced against Frederick in 1415. Sigismund made a special appeal to the Confederates. The latter could with difficulty bring themselves to violate the peace of 1412; and it was only after repeated and urgent warnings from Sigismund and the Council and also after many and ample privileges and liberties had been conceded, that they silenced their conscience and undertook an expedition against Aargau. The Bernese were the first to march out, and Zofingen, Aarburg, Aarau, Lenzburg, Brugg, and Hapsburg in quick succession flocked to the imperial standard. Zurich next followed and conquered a portion of the Free Bailiwick (the bailiwick of Knonau). Soon there was no canton which held aloof. Troops from Lucerne took Sursee, Vilmergen, and Beromünster, and the six cantons took Mellingen and Bremgarten. Finally, the seven cantons, together with Berne, took Baden by storm on May 18, destroying the castle by fire (the *Stein*).

All these conquests, having been achieved by the Confederates as subjects of the German empire, were bestowed upon them by Sigismund as imperial estates for a money payment, and in 1418 Frederick was forced to resign all claim to them. The partition was so made that the west fell to Berne, the bailiwick of Knonau to Zurich, and the south to Lucerne; but that conquest in which all had taken part (Baden and the Free Bailiwicks) became the common property of the six, and later of the seven, cantons. Thus did the Confederates acquire their first enduring "common domain." Frederick's kindred, however, refused to recognize his renunciation, and therefore saw with pleasure the dispute which soon afterward arose about the inheritance of the last Count of Toggenburg, and did their utmost to widen the breach between the Confederates and to break up the detested league.

For a long time past there had been antagonisms between the towns and rural districts, which had arisen out of divers causes and occurrences, and specially between Zurich and Schwyz, when the two latter states were brought into conflict with one another during their efforts at expansion, after the extinction of the line of Toggenburg.

Among all the families of the higher nobility in the territory of the Confederates the Counts of Toggenburg had not only been able to hold their own, but had even succeeded in extending their power considerably. Frederick VII. of Toggenburg (1400-1436), besides the original possessions of his house (Toggenburg, Utznach, and the Upper March) and the inheritance of the Vaz family in Rhætia, which had fallen to the Toggenburgs in the fourteenth century (Prätigau, Schanfigg, Davos, Churwalden, Maienfeld, and Malans), had also obtained the mortgage of the intervening lands of Sargans, Gaster, Wesen, and Windegg, the Rheintal and Vorarlberg. During the strife between Austria and the Confederates he cunningly contrived to keep in with both parties, and also succeeded in defending his own territories against the efforts after liberty of the people of Appenzell, now by menaces, now by friendship. He earnestly sought the friendship of the Confederates. At the commencement of his rule he concluded a civil alliance with Zurich for eighteen years, placing himself, his country, and his people under the protection of Zurich; in 1405 he renewed this treaty for a similar period, and ten years later, in 1416, it was once more renewed, to endure till five years after the death of Frederick. In 1417 he concluded a treaty with Schwyz, but only for ten years; upon its expiration he renewed it, to endure till five years after his death.

The people of both Zurich and Schwyz exerted themselves to be of service to him, that they might by his means preserve their own lands and estates. Zurich in particular spared no trouble or sacrifice, and the count was greatly indebted to that town, Zurich endeavoring to obtain from the count in return the domains of Wesen, Windegg, and Gaster. Schwyz entertained hopes of acquiring the Mark. The count being childless, and the direct line likely to die with him, the question of succession gradually became more urgent. But Frederick left his numerous kinsmen and the Confederates quite in the dark on the subject. Being repeatedly urged by Zurich to nominate a successor, he evaded the question, and when they became importunate about Wesen and Gaster he showed more favor to Schwyz. On April 30, 1436, he died suddenly, leaving no will.

A vehement agitation now arose; the widowed countess claimed the inheritance, and was stoutly supported by Zurich. The count's kinsmen, however, Von Mätsch, Von Montfort, Von Brandis, Von Aarburg, Von Raron, and Von Razüns, maintained the will of the count to have been that the countess should have her dower and a pension, but that his lands should descend to his kinsmen. Schwyz took their part. The affairs of that state were then managed by the clever, able, and sagacious Landamman Ital Reding, the elder, who was resolved not only to hinder the extension of the power of Zurich, but to gain for his people a territory which would secure them a passage from the upper lake of Zurich to Rhætia, and to make Schwyz the dominating power in the whole of the northeast of the present Switzerland. In opposition to Reding were the ambitious, passionate, and self-opinionated burgomaster, Rudolf Stüssi, and the clever town clerk, Michael Graf, a Suabian. Each party endeavored to overreach the other. Wesen, Windegg, and Gaster being taken back by Austria, Zurich succeeded in obtaining Utznach from the countess; Schwyz took the Mark, concluded a treaty with the inhabitants of Gaster, the little town of Sargans, Utznach, and Toggenburg; Zurich was only able to effect an alliance with Wallenstadt and the province of Sargans.

After lengthy negotiations the dispute about the inheritance was decided in 1437 in favor of the count's kinsmen, and the latter immediately hastened to form a perpetual alliance with Schwyz and Glarus, and to sell Utznach to Schwyz. In 1438 Austria also mortgaged Wesen, Windegg, and Gaster to Schwyz and Glarus. Thus Schwyz saw her highest hopes fulfilled, while Zurich came off empty-handed. The latter being unable to obtain anything from the Confederates, endeavored to coerce Schwyz by cutting them off from all means of subsistence, but without success. Schwyz proposed to Zurich to abide by the Federal decree of 1351, but Zurich pleaded that as an imperial town it was not binding upon her, and that she could only acknowledge a decree in which the empire had taken part. Their differences were irreconcilable, and both parties became so incensed that in May, 1439, they flew to arms. The people of Zurich were at variance among themselves, one faction adhering to the Confederates, and they were easily defeated on the Etzel. A truce gave opportunity for fresh preparations, and in the autumn of 1440 they faced one another once more on the Etzel, above Pfäffikon. Stüssi had hoped that the other Forest States and the Confederates would either decide in favor of Zurich or else remain neutral; hence the sudden appearance of troops from Unterwalden and Uri, in aid of Schwyz and Glarus, so dismayed the men of Zurich that they left their breakfast on the tables and retreated in haste. The result of this was that the whole of the left bank of the lake, together with the bailiwick of Knonau, fell into the hands of the enemy; Zurich was moreover obliged to reopen traffic, to surrender the territory of Sargans to Schwyz and Glarus; and Pfäffikon, Wallerau, Hurden, and Ufenau ("the upper farmsteads") to Schwyz. It was a bitter humiliation.

This was in the year 1441. Thenceforth Stüssi and Graf thought of nought else but how to avenge their shame upon the Confederates, and to wrest the spoil again from Schwyz. A league with Austria seemed the most available means. Like Brun in 1356, and Schöno in 1393, so Stüssi and his faction did not scruple to depend entirely upon Austria. Under her influence (chiefly indeed through the agency of the foreign town clerk), the burgesses of Zurich, in June, 1442, concluded a formal defensive alliance with Austria (the Emperor Frederick III. and his brother Albert), in spite of the opposition of the Federal faction (led by Meiss, Trinkler, and Bluntschli), and even promised to surrender to Austria the greater part of the county of Kiburg.[7] Frederick on his part undertook to secure Toggenburg and Utznach to Zurich, and it was further intended to found a new Austrian Confederation with Zurich at its head. Frederick III. ratified the agreement by a personal visit which he paid to Zurich, which town received him joyfully with the insignia of Austria, peacocks' feathers and red crosses. The town then received Austrian governors, Thüring von Hallwil and William von Hochberg. The righteous wrath of the whole Confederation was directed against the recreant member. Zurich protested her right of free alliance, reserved to her indeed by the terms of the Zurich League of 1351, but limited by the interests of the Federal leagues: in the eyes of the Confederates it was justly regarded as an offense against the spirit of the league, against old friends and inherited principles. The conduct of Zurich gave to the hereditary enemy of the Confederates an opportunity once more to assert his authority in the midst of the Confederation. The whole German empire regarded this feud merely as an Austrian enterprise and refused their help, in spite of all Frederick's efforts.

Zurich refusing to give up the Austrian alliance, the Forest States on May 20, 1443, declared war against that town and Austria. The forces of Zurich, after an unfortunate engagement on the frontier near Freienbach, retreated as far as the "Letzi" on the heights of Hirzel. But here also they met with no success for want of unity among themselves, their main force being on the heights of the Albis. Thus for the second time the left bank of the lake and the Free Bailiwick fell into the hands of the Confederates.

Berne also now took part against Zurich, and all the Confederates took possession of the whole of her territory. They then withdrew to attend to their own affairs, and after a month's rest a second expedition was set on foot, intended to advance straight upon Zurich through the Free Bailiwick. The inhabitants of Zurich, contrary to the advice of their Austrian commanders, advanced across the Sihl to meet them, and on July 22, 1443, they engaged in a battle near the Sihl at St. Jakob, in which, without order and without discipline, they were overcome, and soon completely routed. Stüssi himself fell while endeavoring to arrest the flight with a few faithful followers by a valiant defense of the bridge over the

---

[7] The county of Kiburg had been mortgaged to Zurich by Austria in 1424. Only the New Bailiwick, the district on the left side of the Glatt, now remained to Zurich.

Sihl. The enemy was with difficulty prevented from entering the town itself. Graf, the town clerk, was stabbed by a fellow-countryman. Through the agency of the Bishop of Constance a peace was brought about, which was so little observed by either side that it obtained the name of the *böse* or "bad" peace. But in the spring of 1444, when a definite peace was about to be arranged, party strife broke out once more, and the Austrians incited their partisans in Zurich to the utmost against the leaders of the Federal party, branding them as traitors. A rising of the people ensued; Brunner, Meiss, Zörnli, Effinger, Bluntschli, and other adherents of the Confederates were arrested as enemies of the "Fatherland," and several of them were executed in April.

After the expiration of the truce the Confederates took the field once more with a large force in April, 1444, and overran the territory of Zurich for the third time, devastating the whole district; they then sat down before the stronghold of Greifensee, which was bravely defended under Wildhans von Breitenlandenberg for almost four weeks. Finally the garrison was obliged to yield, and out of sixty-two men all but ten were mercilessly beheaded at the end of May in a meadow at Nänikon. Soon afterward, in June, Zurich itself was surrounded and besieged. The town, however, suffered little, being defended with the utmost vigilance; a party of adventurous youths of Zurich (afterward called the *Böcke* or "Valiant") did considerable damage among the Confederates by surprises and pillage, but could not induce them to raise the siege.

In order to bring matters to some decisive issue, Austria began to look for outside help, and incited Charles VII. of France to an enterprise against the Swiss. Meanwhile, and until these auxiliaries should come to their relief, the Austrians endeavored to divert the Confederates from Zurich. In July Thomas von Falkenstein, on behalf of the Austrians, surprised the little Bernese town of Brugg, but was obliged to retire with his forces to the Farnsburg. Thereupon the Bernese, with some auxiliary troops of the Confederates, besieged that fortress.

At length, on August 23, the dauphin advanced upon Basle with 30,000 predatory mercenaries, called Armagnacs,[8] to the relief of the Farnsburg and Zurich, and to enable the Austrians to conquer the Confederation. A little band of about 1300 Confederates hastened to meet him from the Farnsburg and Zurich, but with injunctions not to be drawn into an engagement. After obtaining

[8] Because one of their former leaders had been a Count of Armagnac.

insignificant victories over the advanced guards at Pratteln and Muttenz (August 26), however, the moment they came in sight of the hostile forces on the Birs they threw themselves upon them, and, notwithstanding the prohibition of the authorities, dashed across the river with reckless confidence toward the mighty army. But being soon hard pressed by the enemy's cavalry, they established themselves behind the garden wall of the Hospital of St. Jakob an der Birs and fought with the courage of lions. The Armagnacs flagged and desired peace. The Austrian knight, Burkhard Münch, went to the garden wall to come to terms with the Confederates; but, letting fall some scornful words, a Swiss flung a stone at him, causing a wound of which he soon afterward died. The strife endured till the last of the Confederates had fallen. In death they were victorious, for the loss of the dauphin was so great (2000 men) that he abandoned the enterprise, made peace in October, and withdrew. The Confederates before Zurich also retired, and a desultory war was carried on until, after the lapse of two years, the Confederates having won a brilliant victory over the Austrians at Ragatz, in March, 1446, general exhaustion caused both parties to desire peace.

Zurich still obstinately continued to insist upon her rights as a free imperial town in regard to the Austrian League, and thus protracted the negotiations (1446-1450). At length, by the decision of Heinrich von Bubenberg, of Berne, appointed as arbitrator in the name of the imperial towns, it was finally settled that Zurich must abandon the Austrian alliance in the interests of the Confederation. Thenceforth the Swiss League was no longer to be regarded merely as a loose alliance of individual states, but as a political union, to be forever binding upon every member. The Confederates gave back to Zurich all the lands they had conquered with the exception of the "upper farmsteads" on the Lake of Zurich. In Zurich itself Federal principles once more obtained entirely; and thus it came to pass that during the celebration of Shrove Tuesday in Zurich, in 1454, Hämmerlin, the canon, was surprised by a number of Confederates and taken a prisoner to Gottlieben, because in his writings about the nobility he had ridiculed the men of Schwyz as "effeminate cows' mouths" (*weibische Kuhmäuler*), and had represented them as a mob of detestable and depraved peasants. The spirit of the league seemed to have revived; Zurich and the Confederates held once more firmly together and rejoiced in their newly acquired independence of Austria. But the destructive effects and consequences of the war might long be traced in agricultural damages and a serious retrogression in the habits of the people.

After the old Zurich War the Federal leagues were extended. As early as 1450 Glarus had obtained a new league, placing her on an equality with the other states. In the years 1451 and 1454 Zurich, Lucerne, Schwyz, and Glarus took first the abbot and then the town of St. Gall into a perpetual civil alliance. In 1452 the seven states (the eight with the exception of Berne) took Appenzell again into the league as an allied state. As soon as the Confederates were once more united among themselves they felt their strength, and let no opportunity pass of exhibiting their military prowess and extending their territory. The period now began during which they neglected the occupations of peace for the profession of arms, in which they had already so often been put to the test; the period when an overweening and almost ungovernable passion for war animated every Swiss and drew him from one war into another. Young companions in arms, eager for adventure, advanced now into Hegau, now into Thurgau, to punish their neighbors for mere teasing and pestering. In this mood they were not likely to spare their old enemy, Austria. Upon the return of an expedition against Constance in 1458 (*Plappartkrieg*), forces from the Forest States offered their aid to the Federal faction in Rapperswil, where complaints were being made of the Austrian Government, and conquered that town. Even earlier, in 1454, the Austrian town of Schaffhausen had also concluded a league for twenty-five years with the Confederates; Stein on the Rhine now followed suit, and in 1459 formed an alliance with the states of Zurich and Schaffhausen.

Duke Sigmund, of Austria, a son of Frederick, considered these proceedings a fresh breach of the peace and prepared for war; a truce was, however, made. Soon afterward the Confederates were incited against the duke by his foes, the detested barons of Gradner, and were finally actually urged to war by Pope Pius II., who nad quarreled with the duke. In the midst of the peace youths from the Forest States, Zurich, and Glarus marched into Thurgau. The main army followed, and in September, 1460, rapidly conquered the greater part of that district; Diessenhofen, too, was obliged to yield, and Winterthur only maintained a successful resistance. Appenzell simultaneously wrested from Austria the Rheintal, claimed by that power. Duke Sigmund, by a peace concluded in 1461 for fifteen years, was forced to acquiesce in the cession of all conquests to the Confederates. Austria thus lost the Rhine; a triumphant song of that time rejoices that Sigmund will now be able to throw no more bridges over the Rhine.

Austria soon afterward lost Mülhausen, another post on the Middle Rhine. Harassed by the nobility of Alsace, this town, in 1466, concluded a defensive alliance for twenty-five years with Berne and Soleure, and when the nobility, detesting the Swiss, inflicted all sorts of injuries on this "Swiss cowshed," the allies placed a garrison in the town. The Austrian governor thereupon wanted to take the town by force, but his attempt only resulted in all the states advancing before the town and occupying Sundgau in 1468. Schaffhausen, the outpost of the Swiss toward the north, being also continually harassed by the surrounding nobles, and it being fruitless to complain to Austria, the Confederates openly declared war against Duke Sigmund, and in July, 1468, on their return from Sundgau, besieged the strong fortress of Waldshut.

The people of southern Germany were now so favorably disposed toward the Confederates, and so disaffected toward Austria and the nobility, that it seemed almost as if the whole district of the Black Forest might attach themselves to the former. But the garrison of Waldshut exhibited unexpected bravery, so that the Confederates achieved nothing, and peaceable terms were arranged. By the Peace of Waldshut, of August, 1468, Sigmund promised satisfaction to the town of Mülhausen and Schaffhausen, and to the Confederates the sum of 10,000 florins toward the expenses of the war; Waldshut and the Black Forest were appointed pledges. Thus the struggles with the Confederates resulted in ever fresh debts and losses of territory on the part of Austria. The duke having been compelled a year previously, in 1467, to sell Winterthur to Zurich (upon the wish of the burgesses of the former), all the possessions of Austria beyond the Rhine, with the exception of Frickthal, were now alienated. Austria conceived an inveterate hatred of the Confederates, and the two parties were only to be reconciled by extraordinary events menacing both the Confederates and Austria.

From the time of the battle of St. Jakob an der Birs the Confederates, having measured their strength so successfully with one of the most powerful military forces of Europe, enjoyed the respect of the Continent. The Swiss were held to be without rivals in the arts of war, and that nation was considered fortunate which could obtain their services. Experienced men and adventurous youths betook themselves in troops to foreign princes and towns and rendered their services in war. The much-harassed kingdom of France sought the friendship of the Confederates, and afterward their arms, with the utmost eagerness. This was a great advantage to them, for whereas from the time of the battle of St. Jakob an der Birs the Confederates had had cause to fear the menacing danger of an alliance between France and Austria, they might now hope to find in France a support against Austria. In 1452, therefore, they willingly concluded a treaty of amity with Charles VII., which was renewed in 1463 with his son Louis XI., who had made their acquaintance at St. Jakob. But Louis XI. was not the man to further the interests of the Swiss from disinterested motives; he rather desired to obtain the favor of Austria and the Confederates in order, by their help, to overthrow his mightiest vassal and mortal foe, Charles the Bold of Burgundy. The Confederates also cultivated friendly relations with Burgundy; the towns of Berne, Fribourg, Soleure, and Zurich had concluded a treaty of neutrality in 1467 with Philip the Good, the father of Charles, and with the latter himself.

Matters stood thus when Austria, in 1469 (after the Peace of Waldshut had been revoked by the Emperor Frederick III., cousin of Duke Sigmund), sought in the west financial support and help in case of need in a war against the Confederates. Meeting with a refusal from Louis XI., Duke Sigmund turned to Burgundy. Charles the Bold, who thereupon began to build great hopes for an extension of his power eastward toward Germany, seized the opportunity with avidity, entered into an alliance with Sigmund in May, 1469, paid the latter 50,000 florins, and received in exchange Alsace, Waldshut, and the Black Forest. For this the Swiss received 10,000 florins indemnity. But at the same time Charles was obliged to undertake to reconcile Austria with the Confederates, and in the case of hostilities on the part of the Swiss, or a war between Switzerland and Austria, to take part with and defend the latter. This completely contradicted the treaty of neutrality of 1467; Charles wantonly violated that treaty and by that means gave great umbrage to the Confederates.

In addition to this, the new Burgundian bailiff in the mortgaged lands of Alsace, Peter von Hagenbach, offended the Confederates, provoked them by all manner of intrigues, and especially endeavored to annul the alliance of 1466 between the Bernese and Mülhausen. Upon the Confederates complaining to Duke Charles, the latter gave harsh and equivocal answers or did nothing toward their satisfaction. The intended reconciliation between the Confederates and Austria not being achieved, the breach was widened between the two parties, as also that between the Confederates and Burgundy. Berne was naturally the leading state in these matters and watched with increasing exasperation the growing arrogance of Charles and Hagenbach. The more Burgundy repulsed the Confederates so much more the Swiss inclined toward France and Louis XI. The Lords of Diesbach earnestly advocated French interests in Berne, and in the then state of affairs they easily overcame Adrian von Bubenberg, the friend of Charles the Bold, and his faction. Louis hoped in time to induce the Swiss to enter into an offensive and defensive alliance against Burgundy, to ally Austria with Switzerland, and to take the field against Burgundy. His efforts were extraordinarily facilitated by the further course of events.

For meanwhile a breach and division had taken place between Austria and Burgundy. One day in the autumn of 1473, when Charles the Bold was awaiting at Tréves the betrothal of Max, son of the emperor, with his daughter Maria, his own elevation to the rank of king, and investment with German imperial lands, the Emperor Frederick III. suddenly left him in the lurch and withdrew, in order to rid himself of burdensome obligations. Duke Sigmund at the same time quarreled with Charles because the latter had not fulfilled his expectations, and was no longer willing to surrender Alsace. Sigmund and Frederick next allied themselves with Louis XI., and the latter exerted himself to the utmost to effect a permanent reconciliation between the Confederates and Austria. This was achieved by the "Perpetual Peace" of March, 1474. Austria renounced everything she had lost to the Confederates, receiving in return the latter's promise of help in war and assistance in the recovery of the lands mortgaged to Burgundy. The Confederates likewise joined the "Lower Union," the alliance of the Alsatian towns.

Matters quickly came to a crisis. The people of Alsace revolted against their cruel and oppressive bailiff, and on May 9 Hagenbach was put to death with the coöperation of the Swiss. While Charles, detained by a quarrel with Cologne and the siege of Neuss, was preparing to avenge the removal of his bailiff, Louis XI. succeeded in the autumn in forming an alliance with the Confederates for the purpose of a united struggle against Burgundy, and also summoned Frederick III., all subjects of the German empire, and more particularly the Swiss, to the war against Burgundy.

On October 25 war was declared by Berne. Barely two days afterward the Bernese and their allies advanced from Fribourg, Soleure, and Bienne into Franche Comté, and together with the rest of the Confederates (8000 in number) and the army of the Upper Rhine (18,000 men in all), besieged Héricourt, which is southwest of Belfort, and there on November 13 defeated an army of 10,000 Burgundians and took the town. Thinking that they had thus fulfilled their duty to the empire, they then returned and declined to take part in the relief of Neuss at the request of Frederick III., desiring to protect "their fatherland and the territories of Upper Germany."

Louis XI. congratulated them and distributed liberal pensions; this was the first time that the Swiss reaped such alluring and dangerous fruits of their labors. In January, 1475, Savoy formed a league with Burgundy, and from that time Berne and the western towns were constantly threatened from the side of the Pays de Vaud and the Jura, and in the spring there followed a succession of expeditions made by Berne and her allies into the territories of Savoy. On April 2, 1475, the troops of Berne, Soleure, and Lucerne took Pontarlier. The Bernese already conceived the idea of the extension of the Confederation as far as the Jura, her natural boundary on the west; they conquered Grandson and Orbe, belonging to vassals of Savoy, and in the autumn of 1475 recovered one by one the places taken in the Pays de Vaud by Peter of Savoy. Geneva preserved herself from attack by a promise of money. A Savoyan army, which advanced as far as Sion, was repulsed by troops from Upper Valais and Berne; Lower Valais yielded to Upper Valais. The power of Savoy seemed to be suddenly banished beyond the frontier of Switzerland.

Meanwhile, however, Charles had conquered Lorraine with its capital, Nancy; and, moreover, Louis and the emperor were faithless enough to come to terms with him, and shamelessly to desert the Confederates. Charles now found himself in a position to advance in great force against the Confederates. He marched rapidly through the Vaud to Grandson, and owing to the dilatoriness of the

Confederates was enabled to take the little town, and finally the castle as well. The garrison, which had been promised protection in case of surrender, was cruelly put to death. At length the Confederates and their allies, 18,000 men strong, advanced toward the army of the Burgundians, at least twice as numerous as their own, and the battle of Grandson was fought on March 2, 1476. A band of men from Schwyz, Berne, Lucerne, and Soleure, who had separated themselves from the main army, took up a position on the heights northeast of Grandson, among the vines, and valiantly engaged in battle, without waiting for the rest of the army. In order to entice them down into the plain and there to overwhelm them, Charles, finding the efforts of his artillery and archers unavailing, commanded a retreat from Grandson toward the plain; the rear took this for a flight, fell into confusion and gave way. At that moment the weapons and armor of the advancing Swiss force glittered on the heights; loud blew the horns of Uri and Lucerne, spreading terror and dismay among the Burgundians. Charles tried in vain to arrest the flight of his men: attacked in the van, the rear, and the flank, the Burgundians fled impetuously, and their camp, with all stores, valuables, and jewels, fell into the hands of the Confederates. Charles' fine and well-disciplined army was totally defeated by the peasant-folk he had so greatly despised; the confident hope of the Alsatian nobility, that the Swiss would be overthrown, was dashed to the ground! This victory was one of the richest in spoil ever gained by any people.

Far from being daunted by this unprecedented defeat, Charles, with all haste, made his preparations at Lausanne for a fresh campaign, while Berne and Fribourg occupied the important outpost of Morat, or Murten. As early as June 9 the duke appeared before that place. The Bernese commander, Adrian von Bubenberg, held it with only 15,000 men, but who resolved to spend their last drop of blood rather than yield. By a most prudent defense, by a constant renewal of the bulwarks, by excellent discipline, and lastly by bold sallies, Bubenberg succeeded in holding the duke at bay till the forces of the Confederates—after long tarrying and many irresolute delays—advanced to the number of about 24,000 men. Charles, however, was at the head of about 35,000 men. On June 22, the Ten Thousand Knights' Day, and but one day after the anniversary of Laupen, following the example of the knights, the Confederates marched from the forest of Morat to the plateau northeast of the town, near Salvenach and Münchenwiler. There the advanced guard of the Confederates encountered that of the Burgundians and were forced to retreat to the forest after a short resistance. The main body of the Burgundian army pursued them amid torrents of rain, and, fortified by their artillery, posted themselves behind quickset hedges. The main army of the Confederates arriving, led by Hans Waldmann, a violent struggle ensued. The Swiss van (under Hans von Hallvil) succeeded in breaking through the hedges, and the spirited and heavy advance of the Confederates compelled the Burgundians after a few hours to retire into the plain, where the terrible slaughter inflicted by the Confederates sealed their defeat. On the Burgundian side from 8000 to 10,000 men are said to have fallen, while the Swiss lost only 500! The whole of Switzerland was filled with rejoicing, and bells were rung throughout the land.

The immediate result of this victory of the Confederates was a peace concluded with them by Savoy, by which the latter surrendered to Berne and Fribourg their conquered territories of Morat, Echallens, Illens, Orbe, and Grandson, released Fribourg, which had fallen to Savoy in 1452, and ceded Lower Valais to Upper Valais. No peace was as yet effected with Burgundy. Charles intended to try his fortune once more against the Confederates, but was deterred by a revolt in Lorraine. René, Duke of Lorraine, exiled by Charles, sought help from the Confederates, at whose side he had fought at Grandson; at the Diet of Lucerne he with tears implored help in holding Nancy, his capital, against Charles. No Federal aid was granted to him, but he was allowed to levy men at will; and about 8000 Swiss mercenaries, under Hans Waldmann, fought with him at Nancy, where the haughty Duke of Burgundy fell in the rout like a common soldier. This was the death-blow to the Burgundian power (January 5, 1477).

The next question was the partition of the conquests and of the possessions of the fallen duke. The duchy of Burgundy fell to France. The Netherlands devolved upon Maximilian of Austria, who married Maria of Burgundy, daughter of Charles the Bold. Louis XI. and Maximilian contended for Upper Burgundy or Franche Comté, and both courted the favor of the Confederates, in whose hands lay that territory. A number of Federal states, however, and Berne in particular, were specially desirous of keeping High Burgundy for themselves, and extending the Confederation toward the west. But the states were soon divided, some, notably

Zurich, considering the country too remote; and it was finally agreed to sell High Burgundy, and thus to choose France as a neighbor rather than the Austrian Hapsburgs. France obtained Franche Comté for 150,000 florins, but shortly afterward it fell during a war to the Hapsburgs, in whose hands it remained till the seventeenth century. Meanwhile the Confederates had by this war assured their position toward the west; the barricade of Savoy was broken down by the conquest of strong places in the Vaud and in Lower Valais. Fribourg and Soleure now joined the Confederates entirely; and Neuchâtel, whose count had rendered help to the Bernese, also entered into alliance with them. Thus the western frontier of the Swiss Federation gradually approached the Jura. The Confederation had now taken its stand as a European power, and the fame of the Swiss was in every mouth as of the finest warriors in Europe.

The Burgundian wars had stirred the spirit of the people to its utmost depths, avarice and love of adventure were aroused, and the bands of discipline and order became lax. Divers causes of friction likewise arose: the states were divided as to their future political attitude, towns and rural districts filled with mutual mistrust. The towns had developed considerable power in these wars, and had assumed the position of leaders of the Confederation, and when the two towns of Fribourg and Soleure, which had fought faithfully at the side of the others during the Burgundian War, afterward desired admission to the league, the position and influence of the towns seemed to be growing in a way that the rural states felt keenly. The latter passionately resisted this tendency, especially as the towns tried to put a stop to the liberty of foreign service, while the rural states were in favor of it. The people, too, became mistrustful of the despotic government of their lords, and in the spring of 1477 popular riots broke out in various states. In Art and Weggis particularly the malcontents assembled on Shrove Tuesday and lamented the policy of the towns and the new rule (*Herrentum*). It was decided to fetch from Geneva the ransom money yet unpaid and to divide it among themselves. With a wild desire for war and booty, and taking a club and a sow for the design of their banner, they formed themselves into the "Band of the Mad Life," marched through Lucerne, Berne, and Fribourg, extorting entertainment wherever they went. But the diet and government of Savoy succeeded in inducing the rioters to retreat before they had

AT HEIGHT OF POWER

attained their goal. The authorities in the rural states having favored this undertaking, the towns in anger resolved upon the formation of a separate league (*Sonderbund*); and on May 23, 1477, the five towns of Zurich, Berne, Lucerne, Fribourg, and Soleure united in a perpetual treaty (*Burgrecht*). They agreed to protect one another against such attacks as that of the "March of the Sow-banner," and to insist upon the admission into the league of Fribourg and Soleure. A great breach was occasioned in the Confederation; the rural states were embittered to the utmost and tried to destroy this treaty. They specially attacked the town of Lucerne, which had no right, according to the tenor of the league, to make any alliance without the consent of the other Forest States. The people of Obwalden avenged themselves by inciting the subjects of Lucerne in Entlebuch to revolt. Peter Amstalden, the governor of the district, an innkeeper of Schüpfheim in Entlebuch, headed the rebels. Lucerne, hearing of the affair, enticed Amstalden into the town, had him arrested and hastily executed, in November, 1478, without regular trial. Great excitement followed. The situation was so critical that the dissolution of the Confederation was feared. Fruitless efforts were made during many diets to effect a reconciliation. At this critical moment Lucerne and the rural states turned to Nicholas von der Flüe of Einsiedeln, a man who led a godly life on the brink of a lake near Sachseln, deeply respected throughout the whole of Switzerland, and even far beyond its borders, who gave loving counsel to all, and was revered among the people as a worker of miracles. Many times were messengers sent to him to ask his advice. By the end of November, 1481, things had gone so far that a scheme was drawn up for a new league, by which, in the interest of the towns, all anarchical movements were to be suppressed, and a league was also projected with Fribourg and Soleure, in which the only restriction laid upon those two towns was that they might enter into no alliance without the consent of the eight states. These agreements needed only to be ratified by instructions from the authorities.

Assembling once more in Stans on December 18, 1481, the old dispute was renewed with redoubled violence as to the admission of the two towns into the league, and after wrangling for three days the deputies separated on December 22 in great irritation. In this extremity the pious pastor Heinrich Imgrund of Stans hastened to "Brother Klaus" for advice. He came back bathed in perspiration, fetched the deputies from their various inns, and in the name of the monk of Einsiedeln prevailed upon them to assemble once more. He then brought forward the proposals of his venerable friend, and within an hour a reconciliation was effected. The towns yielded and relinquished their separate league, and the rural states on their part consented to the admission of Fribourg and Soleure into the Perpetual League, although under the further restriction that they should be subordinate to the eight states in war. In order to avoid similar disputes in future, and to strengthen and invigorate the league, the already projected covenant of Stans was definitely accepted. What the towns had wanted to obtain by their separate league became now the concern of the whole Federal League; for every town engaged to refrain from instigating the subjects of the others to rebellion (as had been the case in the revolt of Entlebuch), and from injuring the territory of the others. Dangerous or unusual societies and assemblies, which might do harm to anyone (as, for instance, the assembly of Art, which gave rise to the "mad life"), were forbidden, and the states pledged themselves to mutual support against such attacks and insurrections. Finally, that both old and young might the more firmly bear the leagues in mind, every five years the Convention of Sempach and this Covenant of Stans were to be renewed and confirmed by oath.

This concord formed an important advance in the life of the league, and to a certain extent strengthened its power; thereby legitimate bounds were set to all tumultuary attempts, and all arbitrary dealings, to the freebooting and licentiousness, so abundantly manifest in the Middle Ages. It is true that in later times these provisions, though directed against any actually violent breach of the peace, were abused, in that the governments, by their support, suppressed mere popular assemblies, and claimed Federal aid to repudiate the just demands of the people. This strengthening of the central power corresponded to the tendency then simultaneously manifesting itself in Spain, France, Germany, and England toward the foundation of the modern state.

But the internal disquiets of the Confederation were not yet allayed by the Covenant of Stans. By the acquisition of subject-lands on the part of individual states, and by the increase of the number of towns in the league, the Confederation had gradually assumed quite an altered character. There was no longer, as at the time of the battles of Morgarten and Sempach, one people of almost equal rights, but a separation was already introduced between lords and subjects. In the towns, especially in Berne and Zurich, the idea of a united executive power, exercised from one center (as already in use in great monarchies), was gaining ground; a sense of sovereignty was beginning to make itself felt among the governments of the towns. A tendency arose to establish an absolute rule of the towns over the country. In addition to this an effort was being made within the towns themselves to strengthen the power of the burgomaster and wardens [9] among the artisan class.

This new idea was pursued in Berne by Peter Kistler. He had risen by his own efforts from the rank of a butcher to that of a standard-bearer, and in 1470 was elected mayor. Thereupon the nobler burgesses who possessed manorial estates in the country over which they exercised a despotic authority (*Twingherrschaften*), the families of Erlach, Diesbach, and Bubenberg left the town in a body. Kistler endeavored to humiliate them, to limit their jurisdiction, and to subject them to sumptuary laws. But the country folk, feeling oppressed by the town, took part with their manorial lords, and a revolution was only averted by the mediation of the Confederates. The nobles acknowledged the sovereignty of the town of Berne, but were released from the sumptuary laws in 1471. The manorial lords returned amid the rejoicings of the burghers.

A similar tendency shortly afterward found place in Zurich under Hans Waldmann. Born at Blickensdorf, in the canton of Zug, settled in Zurich, and there enfranchised, Waldmann early distinguished himself during mercenary and other military expeditions in the sixth and seventh decades of the century. He rose rapidly by his extraordinary talents, his activity and untiring energy, by his fortune and family alliances. He established his fame during the Burgundian wars, and ranked among the foremost as a leader in war and as a politician. Through the influence of the guilds he was chosen a member of council, became a landlord, chief warden, and finally burgomaster in 1483, upon the removal of the aristocratic Heinrich Göldli. Toward the aristocracy, who despised him, he bore an inveterate hatred, and he now turned old clauses of the constitution to account somewhat unfairly, in

[9] The heads or masters of the trade guilds.

order to humble the *Constafel*,[10] and to establish the supremacy of the guilds. He reduced the number of aristocrats in the council from twelve to six; he offended the Göldli family to the utmost. At the same time he kept discipline and order among the clergy and did much toward the adornment and improvement of Zurich. In the management of the state he endeavored to establish greater uniformity and equality in place of the glaring inequalities of mediæval times. He held the country folk in strict subordination, as had long been the custom, bound them remorselessly by statutes old and new relating to manners, clothing, agriculture, handicrafts, and forestry, and thereby aroused much bitter feeling. In Federal matters he obtained for Zurich an almost absolute supremacy, endeavored to suppress foreign service, and by so doing exasperated Lucerne and the rural states, and came into violent conflict with the leader of mercenaries, Frischhans Teiling, of Lucerne. Their antagonism dated from an expedition to Milan in 1478.

The Sforzas, who succeeded to Milan upon the extinction of the Visconti family in 1447, concluded a capitulation or treaty with the Confederates in 1467, but did not keep the promises therein made, such as the renunciation of the Val Leventina (the *Livinen*), freedom from tolls, etc. Negotiations having failed of their aim, Uri prepared for war; and in December, 1478, under the conduct of Hans Waldmann, 10,000 to 14,000 Confederates advanced as far as Bellinzona (*Bellenz*), and besieged it. But owing to dissensions and the cold of the winter, the Confederates were obliged to retreat, leaving only a small garrison in Giornico. Thereupon the Milanese advanced, 10,000 strong, but were opposed by the garrison, aided by 350 of the inhabitants of the Val Leventina, under the leadership of Frischhans Teiling, of Lucerne. By stopping the mountain streams, whose waters immediately froze, they had secured their position; and as the enemy advanced they rolled down stones and rocks, fell upon their opponents, and put them to flight. It was a glorious act of heroism, and Frischhans Teiling was thenceforth honored as a hero of war. Teiling arrogantly ridiculed the banner of Zurich as a "beggar's wallet," and the Zurich folk as "perjured wretches." Later, in 1487, when

---

[10] There were in Zurich two great electoral bodies; the first, or aristocratic class, was styled the "*Constafel*," and consisted of knights, nobles, and the more well-to-do burghers. The second class consisted of the artisans forming the thirteen guilds.

Waldman defeated an expedition into the Eschenthal, an attempt being nevertheless made to force a passage, 800 men were slain, he abused the burgomaster of Zurich as a "villain, a murderer, and a traitor." For these things Teiling, going to mass at Zurich in the autumn of 1487, was arrested and mercilessly put to death. A cry of indignation rang through the heart of Switzerland, and the animosity against Waldmann reached its height, as an inexorable advocate of the supremacy of the towns, the chief representative of the system of pensions, and the suppressor of foreign service.

In the spring of 1489 disturbances broke out in the rural disticts of Zurich, because Waldmann had been betrayed into setting proceedings on foot against the large and dangerous dogs of the peasants. The peasants held meetings on the banks of the Lake of Zurich, at Meilen and Küssnach, and in March advanced upon the town. Having allowed themselves to be appeased, and then finding that the town would not keep the treaty, they marched out in April for the second time. Meanwhile within the town the Göldli family and their adherents were exasperating and inciting the townsfolk against Waldmann, and the council hall was besieged by a tumultuous mob. Federal deputies hastened to intervene, but, instead of allaying the tumult, they yielded to the urgency of the people, delivered up Waldmann and his friends, and led them to the Wellenberg.[11] In a tumultuous assembly of the burgesses fresh councilors were elected, and Waldmann's opponents took the helm. General accusations against Waldmann were spread abroad, and after summary proceedings he was finally condemned to death. The hero of Morat went to his death with manly courage on April 6, 1489.

The new council slaked its thirst for revenge by a succession of further condemnations and executions, and by its harshness and cruelty earned the name of the "Horny Council." By the intervention of Federal deputies a reconciliation was effected between the town and the rural districts. Ancient liberties and rights were confirmed to the various domains and districts by charters containing the decrees of Waldmann, by which also a number of innovations were abolished, and freedom of trade, commerce, and manufacture was assured. The greatest concessions were made to the dwellers around the lake, especially the right of making their wants and wishes known to the government. Lastly, the munici-

[11] The state prison of Zurich.

pal constitution was legally settled for the time to come, and, in so far as concerned the position of the aristocracy and wardens in the council, essentially in accordance with Waldmann's ideas.

The fall of Waldmann produced a general excitement throughout the Confederation and occasioned similar agitations in several places against despotism and against the drawing of pensions. A like storm broke out against the Government of Lucerne, and the council was forced to bind itself to levy no taxes, form no alliances, and commence no war without the consent of the community. In 1489 the town of St. Gall, the League of God's House, and the people of Appenzell revolted against the harsh Abbot Ulrich Rösch, reputed a friend of Waldmann, and destroyed the buildings of a new monastery commenced by the abbot at Rorschach. Burgomaster Farnbühler had already planned a great Confederation in the east, with the addition of Thurgau, to be under the direction of the town of St. Gall. With the help of the Federal protection, however, the abbot quelled the insurrection; Farnbühler was forced to fly, and the insurgents were heavily fined (1490). Meanwhile Federal affairs were likewise in a state of fermentation. At the Diet of Lucerne a prohibition of pensions and service-money was mooted, "it being seen how much harm Waldmann had caused by pensions," and Schwyz suggested the idea of assembling the communities in all parts, even in the town cantons, in order to discuss these matters. But the towns, with Berne at their head, opposed this, and through their influence it was finally decided to abide by the Covenant of Stans, as published in 1481. The abolition of such pressing grievances as foreign service, the system of pensions, and the laxity of the league was deferred.

After Switzerland had by her own strength overthrown one of the powers of Europe in the Burgundian wars, the bonds uniting her to the German empire were gradually slackened. Hitherto no Swiss had dreamed of such a thing as separation from the empire; they all unreservedly considered themselves members of the empire, just as the Bavarians, Franks, or Saxons. Their privileges were ratified by the emperor; they took part in imperial diets and imperial wars, and even in the Burgundian war they had professed to be obliged to fight, and to wish to do so, as members of the empire. But these relations had gradually become mere formalities. As a matter of fact, Switzerland had long been alienated from the empire, because she no longer needed its protection. The

THE FLIGHT OF CHARLES THE BOLD AFTER THE BATTLE OF NANCY
Painting by E. Burnand

feeling of connection was the more readily lost that the German empire was wanting in any firm union which could hold the different parts together. For more than two centuries past a total dissolution had been gradually approaching. There was no generally recognized imperial authority; the princes and towns forming the individual members were almost independent. Thus the Swiss, too, were able to strike out an independent course; often enough in later times they had shirked their duties toward the empire, and gone unpunished.

Moreover, powers had gained the ascendent in Germany, which were by their very nature incompatible with Switzerland. At one time the haughty nobles of Suabia caused continual friction; the biting scorn which they poured forth upon the peasants and cowherds across the Rhine not only gave rise to reciprocal mockings, but even caused the Confederates to take to arms. Then from the year 1438 the Austrian house of Hapsburg had filled the German throne, and that house could never forget that the Confederation had become great at her expense. The long reign of Frederick III. (1440-1493) specially alienated Switzerland from the empire; for it was he who, in the first Zurich War, under pretext of imperial interests, had endeavored to destroy the Federal League. The fresh demands made by Maximilian, Frederick's son, in the name of the empire, brought matters to a crisis. The first prince of his age to take any real interest in the affairs of the empire, he wanted to subject Switzerland, as a regular member of the empire, to the newly established regulations for the public peace, to the Imperial Chamber and to imperial taxes (1496); and St. Gall, an allied state of the Confederates, refusing to submit to a sentence of the Imperial Chamber, was outlawed. The Confederates did not scruple to repudiate such demands. They had no need of the special precautions of Germany for the preservation of the public peace, for they were sufficiently defended by their leagues. Moreover, at the new Imperial Diet the towns and burghers were but feebly represented, the peasants not at all; and Switzerland, like North America nearly three hundred years later, could not recognize any obligations to a parliamentary body from which they were, so to speak, excluded. " The way is open to find a master for you, and I will accomplish it by the pen in my hand," cried the Imperial Chancellor. But a Confederate replied: " Others formerly failed in what you now threaten, though they attempted it with halberds, which are more to be feared than goose-quills!" With yet greater indignation the Confederates rejected the suggestion that they should join the Suabian League, then under the influence of Austria and the nobility of southern Germany. The nobility now desired nothing more earnestly than the overthrow of Switzerland; north of the Rhine one vied with another in scornful ridicule and base accusations against the Swiss, and protracted, fruitless trials and processes drove them from exasperation to the thirst for war.

A trivial cause finally led to the outbreak of war. Maximilian's advisers, who were urgent for war, caused the Münsterthal (the jurisdiction of which was shared by Austria and the Bishop of Coire) to be seized in the king's absence, because the Gray League and the League of God's House had joined the Confederates in opposition to Austria; even the Suabian League was applied to for help. The Grisons sought and obtained the help of the Confederates in January, 1490, and soon the armed forces of both parties confronted one another along the banks of the Rhine from Basle to Maienfeld. The Suabian troops acquired Maienfeld by treachery and occupied Luziensteig; but on February 9, 1499, the Confederates forded the Rhine at Triesen and repulsed the enemy. Meanwhile the Royalists had assembled at Bregenz. The Confederates attacked them at Hard or Fussach, and rushing upon the enemy, as at Grandson, with desperate courage under a heavy fire, they won a signal victory.

One month later, on March 22, Suabians from Sundgau and the Black Forest, attacking Soleure and retiring hastily, were totally defeated at Bruderholz on the rising ground south of Basle. Once more the Suabian League took courage; its troops took up their position at Constance, and thence attacked Ermatingen in Thurgau. The Suabians were, however, again surprised by the Confederates, and defeated on April 11 at Schwaderloo, south of Constance. The Swiss arms were shortly afterward victorious in the Oberland. Austrians from the Tyrol and Wallgau assembled at Frastenz (east of Feldkirch) behind an intrenchment. The Confederates determined to make a decisive attack upon them, and on April 20, by a skillfully planned maneuver, executed by Heinrich Wolleb of Uri, they remained masters of the field after a hot struggle. The brave Wolleb himself was the first victim, falling when in the act of giving the signal for advance against the guns of the enemy, dealing out death and destruction. Three thousand of the enemy were slain.

Meanwhile Maximilian had returned and resolved to take the war in hand in good earnest. But there appeared small inclination for it in the empire, the war being regarded merely as an Austrian feud. Maximilian assembled his troops on the frontier between the Tyrol and the Grisons, and specially fortified the outlet of the Münsterthal into the Tyrol, in the neighborhood of the lower Rambach. At the gorge of the latter stream (the "*Calven*") a battle took place. Only 6300 Grisons rushed upon 15,000 Imperialists, intrenched behind fortifications. Glorious deeds of heroism were done. Benedict Fontana, one of the leaders of the League of God's House, hastening at the head of his men to the attack on the intrenchment, was wounded by a bullet, but still shouted words of encouragement to his followers. The Grisons pressed forward from all sides, and the Imperialists were forced to give way on March 22.

While the emperor attempted another attack from Constance, Austrian troops from Sundgau advanced toward Soleure, but being surprised while feasting and bathing at Dorneck (Dornach), they were put to the rout. Both sides were now weary of the war, for in the course of eight months 20,000 soldiers had been slain, nearly 2000 places burned, and the land devastated far and wide; and the people were terribly oppressed by want of money, scarcity, and famine. All therefore longed for peace, which was concluded on September 22, 1499, at Basle. The emperor suspended all proceedings and decrees of the Imperial Chamber against the Swiss; he ceded to the Confederates the rural jurisdiction of Thurgau, and by that means foreign jurisdiction was entirely banished from their territory. The Ten Jurisdictions (Prätigau, Schanfigg, and Davos) were obliged to do homage to the emperor as their sovereign, but remained in alliance with the Confederates, as did the other leagues of the Grisons. Nothing was indeed definitely settled as to the general position of Switzerland with regard to the German empire; but as a matter of fact imperial regulations had no real force among the Swiss, and fresh orders being issued a hundred and fifty years later, in 1648, led to the formal separation of Switzerland from the German empire forever. After the Suabian War, Basle and Schaffhausen, which had been most exposed to danger during the war, joined the Perpetual League of the Confederates, on June 8 and August 10, 1501, and so completed the Federal territory toward the north.

The French kings who succeeded Louis XI. sought, as that monarch had done, to avail themselves of the warlike powers of the Swiss. In 1484 Charles VIII. renewed his father's alliance, and ten years later conquered Naples chiefly by Swiss mercenaries. His successor, Louis XII., in 1499 concluded a treaty for ten years, and thought by the help of the Confederates to conquer Milan (to which he laid just claim in right of his grandmother), and to drive out the Sforzas. In that same year, at the head of Swiss mercenaries, he expelled Louis Sforza, surnamed the Moor. But the latter had made an alliance with certain Federal States, and in February, 1500, succeeded in recovering Milan. Then arrived an army of 24,000 French. Louis the Moor held Novara, but suffered greatly from want. His Swiss followers shrank from fighting against their brother Confederates, and capitulated behind his back. They promised, however, to take him with them on their retreat. But by the treachery of a Swiss soldier in the French army Louis the Moor was delivered up to the French, and ended his life ten years later in a French prison. In this way Milan once more became French. Louis XII. renewed the capitulation of Milan, and engaged to restore Bellinzona, which he had conquered, to the Forest States. But the Confederates were at length obliged to wrest it from him in 1503 by a special campaign.

Now, however, the powerful position which France had acquired in Italy by the possession of Milan threatened the balance of power among the nations of Europe, and offended the patriotic pride of the Italians. Hence fresh wars broke out, in which almost all the noted rulers of that time were concerned in which the Confederates played a specially important part. Just as in the Burgundian wars they had been led by France and the emperor to take the field against Burgundy, so in the Italian struggle they were urged by the other interested powers against France. At the same time, however, the Confederates had once more their own interests to maintain, so that they were not merely the puppets of the powers. It was to their interest to secure their possession of the territory of Ticino (Tessin), and to show France that they would not be used as a mere tool. Louis XII., following the faithless and cunning policy of Louis XI., did not keep his promises, and offended the Confederates by a haughty and despotic course of action. The alliance with France coming to an end in 1510, the Swiss thought it well to show Louis that "money is only useful to him who owns iron too," and they lent their ear to the enemies of France, and particularly to Pope Julius II., whose highest aim was the expulsion of the French from Italy.

By order of the Pope, Matthew Schinner, Bishop of Sion, an able, intelligent and eloquent man, addressed himself to the Confederates, and induced them in 1510 to conclude a treaty with the papal throne for five years, by which they engaged to furnish troops to the papacy, to the exclusion of all others. Having further allied himself with Spain, the emperor, Venice and England (the "Holy League"), Julius opened the war against France.

Two Alpine expeditions of the Confederates failed—the campaign of Chiasso in 1510, and the "cold winter campaign" of 1511. On April 11, 1512, the French defeated the army of the league at Ravenna. Julius II. now rested his hopes solely upon the Swiss, and was not disappointed. A Swiss army of 18,000 men marched across the Alps, made a successful expedition through Lombardy in concert with the Venetians, and conquered Pavia and the whole duchy of Milan. This expedition, which took place in July, 1512, and was called the "great expedition of Pavia," met with brilliant success. For themselves the Confederates obtained Domo d'Ossola, the territory of the present canton of Ticino, Locarno, Lugano, Mendrisio, and Maiental, the Grison Leagues acquiring the Valtelline, Chiavenna, and Bormio. The whole range from Monte Rosa to the Wormser Joch was now brought into permanent connection with the Confederation. In Italy, however, the Confederates were greeted with rejoicings as deliverers from the yoke of France, and they were highly honored and richly rewarded by the Pope. They even decided the important question as to the possession of Milan; and Schmid, burgomaster of Zurich, delivered the key of the city to Maximilian Sforza, the son of the unfortunate Louis the Moor. They at the same time concluded a treaty with Sforza, and engaged to protect Milan. Louis XII. next attempting to recover Milan by force of arms, the Confederates were again obliged to take the field. On June 4, 1513, the French bombarded Novara, which was garrisoned by Swiss troops under Sforza. The French hoped events would turn out as twelve years previously, but the garrison maintained a firm resistance until the main army of the Confederates came up. On June 6 a sanguinary battle took place outside the gates of the town, in which the Confederates, inspired by the heroic courage of their forefathers, defied the artillery and cavalry of the enemy, killed 8000 Frenchmen, and put the rest to flight. This was a red-letter day for the Confederation.

The Confederates had about this time undertaken an invasion of Burgundy, known as the "Campaign of Dijon," in concert with an imperial army, but allowed themselves to be put off with idle promises. Milan fell for the second time into the hands of the Swiss, and the French were by them a second time driven out of Italy. The Swiss, with haughty self-confidence, compared themselves already to the Romans; and one of the cleverest Italians of that day, Machiavelli the historian, prophesied that they would become the rulers of the whole of Italy. But this was not to be. Francis I., the valiant successor of Louis XII., appeared upon the scene with a fresh and powerful army, and the Swiss encountered him at Marignano. In spite of the warnings of the majority of their leaders, one division imprudently and impetuously commenced the attack on the evening of September 13, 1515, and fought with lion-like courage and partial success till night put an end to the slaughter. On the following day the struggle was renewed. Once more the Confederates precipitated themselves upon an army of double their number, but they were terribly cut to pieces by the artillery and cavalry of the enemy, and were moreover menaced in the rear by a Venetian army. That they might not undergo the fate of St. Jakob, they took the wounded on their shoulders, the artillery in their midst, and withdrew toward Milan in perfect order, "bruised rather than defeated." Twelve thousand corpses—the majority of them those of Confederates—covered the field of battle.

This—the first defeat that the Confederates met with—which laid the foundations of the reputation of Francis I. and of the supremacy of France, gave a new direction to the course of Swiss affairs. Among the Confederates it began to be generally recognized that the position of power to which they had so rapidly and unexpectedly attained could not long be tenable, nor the many evils wrought by endless wars be endured; and consequently, on November 29, 1516, a perpetual peace was concluded between Switzerland and France, which united those two powers more closely than ever. Hostilities were to cease forever on both sides, full freedom of trade and peaceful relations to connect the two nations, and neither party should support the enemies of the other.

Thenceforth the independent part played by Switzerland in European politics was at an end, and she maintained a neutral position in European disputes. The only lasting advantage gained was the conquest of the territories of Ticino, the Valtelline, and Cleves (*Cläven*), the possession of which was guaranteed by France to the Confederates in the perpetual peace. The two last-named districts fell to the Grisons, the former became the common property of the Confederates, and from 1803 onward formed the present canton of Ticino; and thus the Federal territory received its southern boundary.

The fifteenth century, that time of glorious wars abroad and the dawn of intellectual progress at home, also brought important political changes; and the lax league developed gradually into a firm and well-ordered state.

In the first instance, as regarded the mutual relations of the states, the Forest States in the fourteenth century had formed as it were the only bond of union of the league. But in the fifteenth century, states not hitherto allied concluded perpetual leagues among themselves, as for instance Berne and Lucerne in 1421, Zurich and Berne in 1423. And the five new states which joined later, Fribourg (1481), Soleure (1481), Basle (1501), Schaffhausen (1501), and Appenzell (1513), entered into agreements not only with the Forest States, but also with all the eight. At the same time they were in many ways restricted and slighted in comparison to the older states. At the accession of Fribourg and Soleure the eight states restricted the circle of Federal aid; the two new states might enter into no foreign alliance without the consent of the rest, and were to submit themselves to the majority of the eight states in cases of peace and war. The latter stipulation was also made with Basle, Schaffhausen, and Appenzell. These three states were, moreover, obliged to promise to remain neutral during any disputes among the others.

Together with these thirteen fully qualified members of the Confederation, there were also some "allied" (or "friendly") states (*Zugewandte Orte*), that is, such as were mostly only in alliance with individual members of the Confederation, and either took no part in the transactions of the Diet, or had an inferior representation (only one instead of two delegates), and moreover had their places apart. Such were the Abbot of St. Gall, who in 1451 had become allied to the four states of Zurich, Lucerne,

Schywz, and Glarus; the town of St. Gall; Bienne, allied only with Berne, Soleure, and Fribourg; the Grisons, Valais, the counts of Neuchâtel, allied in 1406 with the same states as Bienne; Mülhausen (1515) and Rotwil (1519), allied with all the thirteen states. All the above-named held quite different positions. All were, however, shut out from any share in the common domains.

The Confederation of the fifteenth century differs from that of the fourteenth century by the acquisition of domain lands. This also distinguished the Swiss League from other leagues in the empire which were like it in origin, and it was this which specially contributed to convert the Confederation into a compact state. At that time the liberal principle, that acquired territories should be placed on an equal footing with other states, was quite unknown; no one ever thought of such a thing. The Confederates, therefore, thought nothing of gaining as many subject lands as they could, and thus making their own position more assured. So in 1415 they had acquired the domains of Aargau, Baden, and the Free Bailiwicks, in 1460 Thurgau, 1483 Sargans, 1490 Rheintal, and in 1512 the territories of Ticino, viz., Lugano, Locarno, Mendrisio, and Maggiatal. All, or a large majority, of the Federal states took part in the government of these territories. Every one of the participating states in turn sent a bailiff to the various subject lands to maintain the sovereign authority. The latter, however, did not extend very far; in some domains, as in Thurgau and Rheintal, the Confederates had only the execution of the higher jurisdiction (the criminal court), the control of the communal administration and commercial affairs; while the lower jurisdiction was vested in the nobility, bishops, and so on; or they granted no small liberties (a council of their own election, and their own jurisdiction) to various towns, such as Baden, Bremgarten, Mellingen, Frauenfeld, Diessenhofen, and Pugano, to engage them in their interests. The bailiffs collected the revenue from taxes, tolls, feudal rents, and fines, in time of war took the lead of the men fit for service, and executed justice in the case of crimes worthy of death, with a court of justice appointed by the Confederation. The bailiffs were obliged to give account to the Diet every year for revenue received, and any surplus over the costs of administration of the district was divided among the participating states; in doubtful cases the bailiffs were referred to the Diet.

The great development which had taken place in the political life of the Confederates, partly through their common territories, and partly by their taking part in the contests of Europe, may be seen by the increased activity and authority of the Diet. This was still, as formerly, merely a meeting of delegates or "messengers" (*Boten*) from the governments of the states, who possessed no actual power of passing legal measures. On the contrary, the delegates, convened by the capital for the time being (from the end of the fifteenth century Zurich was usually the capital), had to get their instructions as to their votes from their home governments. After every session the votes were given to the deputies in writing on their departure,[12] that they might lay them before their governments or "take them home." The decision was then made by the majority of the states, not of the delegates. In other ways, too, the assembly was not formally constituted. It was not bound to any particular time or place; an assembly was held regularly at least once a year at Baden, to which the yearly accounts of the bailiffs of common territories were brought. But besides this many extraordinary sessions were held at divers places, Zurich, Soleure, Lucerne, and Schwyz, and the sphere of business of the Diet gradually became almost as extensive as that of an established Federal government.

Its appointments and arrangements related in the first instance to foreign affairs; it lay in its power to send embassies and dispatches to the Pope and the emperor, to princes and cities, to conclude treaties, as well as to appoint frontier forces and defenses in time of danger. The debates of the Diet next dealt with matters relating to trade and to public morals and public health in the widest sense; orders were issued against vagrants, beggars, thieves, and tinkers; and also about the isolation of persons suffering from infectious diseases, and the stoppage of traffic during prevalent epidemics; prohibitions were issued against swearing and indecent clothing; improvements and repairs of the main roads throughout the territory of the Confederation were often ordered; and the consent of the Diet was necessary for the introduction of new tolls, or the raising of old ones. By it arrangements were frequently made as to the coinage. Even church matters were dealt with as common Federal affairs. Finally, the Diet also interposed in

---

[12] These writings were called "*Abschiede*," and were of the nature of **reports** of the proceedings of the Diet.

disputes between different states or between individuals.[13] Thus the Diet was an assembly in which prominent men from the various states gained knowledge and experience in affairs of state; and the very fact that it was incumbent upon them to care for the domains common to all exercised a beneficial influence upon many branches of the administration which might otherwise have been neglected.

It is true that the decisions of the Diet were often not carried out in all the states; they had mostly to be repeated again and again, being rather of the nature of suggestions or friendly advice to the various states, and were only binding upon those which agreed to them. In 1515 it was first enacted that in matters concerning the honor and well-being of the Confederation the minority should yield to the majority; but this resolution fared like many others which existed only on paper. In contrast, however, to the succeeding centuries, with all their internal dissensions and frequent friction between the towns and the rural states, the necessity of arriving at a common resolution and carrying out united measures always prevailed. The events of war naturally produced a reaction in the conditions of the Confederation both at home and abroad.

The heroic days of Grandson, Morat, and Novara made the name of the Confederates famous. Their military prowess had stood the test gloriously, and was acknowledged even by their enemies. While at that time cavalry usually played the chief part in war, with the Swiss the infantry formed the main part. They drew up in closely compact lines in perfect order, the foremost provided with long pikes—the chief weapon of the Confederates—and standing as firm as a wall. The various divisions were so arranged as not to get in one another's way during maneuvers, and that the flight of any one portion might not cause that of the rest, as had been the case at Morat on the Burgundian side. The enemy always admired in the Swiss the excellent order, in which they were themselves wanting, and the heroic courage of their men, which was never stained by cowardice. Cavalry could do nothing against the impenetrable forest of bristling pikes of their close lines; and when the van had by this means broken the enemy's order of battle, the halberds, clubs, battle-axes, and heavy swords of the rear proved murderous weapons. Artillery alone could be of any use against this order; but firing was very slow work in those days, and the Confederates having escaped the effects of the

[13] This was called Federal Intervention or Mediation.

first fire by stooping low, dashed immediately upon the batteries and took them from the enemy. Thus, says a contemporary, they revived the fame of the bravery of foot-soldiers, and became the first warriors of the world.

This military superiority gave the Confederation great political importance abroad. Milan, Savoy, Austria, France, the Popes, and even the remote Matthew Corvin of Hungary, sought their favor. The chief views of foreign powers in so doing was to obtain Swiss mercenary troops; and those who gained their help usually played a winning game in the struggle. Hence, after the middle of the fifteenth century, the fate of European wars was decided by the Swiss, and their sword often turned the scale of European policy. They themselves, indeed, had no extensive or high aim in view by these foreign connections and relations; they aimed only at easily-earned material advantages, either the drawing of annuities or pensions for the benefit of the community in general, or advantages of trade and commerce, such as freedom of customs and reduction of duties; from France they desired free entry into the University of Paris, as also in their treaties with Milan and the Pope.

By their military and political position and their relations with the outer world, the inner life of Switzerland was benefited in many ways. We owe a large number of beautiful war-songs to the spirit of patriotism aroused to consciousness among the Swiss by their brilliant victories. Enthusiasm for the freedom and fame of the fatherland inspired many a poet among peasants and handicraftsmen, as Hans Auer, of Lucerne, about 1430, Hans Viol, and afterward Veit Weber and Matthias Zoller, both about the time of the Burgundian wars. These had mostly earned their fame by the sword; after dangers undergone they turned homeward, and extolled the heroic days in sweet songs, which speedily went the round among the people, and were sung in quiet cottages as well as on public holidays. Arising entirely from the sphere of thought of the people, these poems gave a powerful popular impulse to German literature.

Side by side with the song writers we find historians, who, impelled alike by their own share in the struggles and by the triumphant fame of their nation, narrated events in a naïve and popular style. Such were Konrad Justinger in Berne (1420), Johannes Fründ in Schwyz (1450), Melchior Russ, Petermann Etterlin and Diebold Schilling in Lucerne, Diebold Schilling in Berne, before or after the wars of Burgundy, and Gerold Edlibach, the stepson of Hans Waldmann, in Zurich.

Simultaneously with this movement of the popular mind, a corresponding stir of higher scientific activity was brought about by contact with foreign parts. The enthusiasm for the study of the classics of Greece and Rome (*Humanismus*), which emanated from Italy, took firm root in France and Germany, and produced an entirely new culture, soon spread to Switzerland also. The first traces appear, though yet very imperfectly, with Felix Hemmerli, a canon of Zurich in 1440, who had tasted the classics at their source in Italy, and was one of the most learned men of his time. The famous dean of the monastery of Einsiedeln, Albert von Bonstetten (*cir.* 1470), also brought the new learning into Switzerland from foreign schools. Among the Confederates it was looked upon as most important that the Swiss should study in foreign schools, and therefore in all treaties with foreign powers as to the pay of mercenaries, a stipulation was always made for the free admission of a certain number of Swiss scholars into their universities.

Basle was a great center of learning in Switzerland, and there, by the coöperation of Pope Pius II., a university was founded, which soon gained renown in Europe. Theology, law, medicine, and the "seven free arts,"[14] were taught here; the most distinguished families of all the Swiss cantons sent their sons hither. The names of learned Swiss who labored here, such as Thomas Wittenbach and Glarean (Heinrich Loriti, of Glarus), were held in repute also in other lands; and learned Germans of high fame, like Erasmus and Reuchlin, lived and labored successfully in Basle. As early as 1460 the art of printing had established itself in Basle, its first seat in Switzerland, and this town became a chief seat of the book trade. We find it a little later in Beromünster, Burgdorf, and Geneva.

Both material and artistic culture flourished rapidly after the time of the wars of freedom. What had been denied to their land by the niggardly hand of Nature was supplied by the energy of its people. Foreign relations gave rise to brisk commercial intercourse, and gave an impulse to home industries. The silk industry early established itself in Zurich, and the linen industry in St. Gall; and Basle, Berne, Fribourg, and Zurzach became famous for trade

[14] Grammar, dialectics, rhetoric, arithmetic, geometry, astronomy, and music.

and industries; they had all extensive relations with the great adjacent lands on the north, west, and south; as, for instance, the cloth goods of Fribourg attained great repute in Germany, France, and Italy. By this means no less than by the great annuities which were received according to agreements for the pay of mercenaries, and the magnificent spoils carried off from the great wars, the wealth of the burgesses increased greatly. Hence, in Switzerland, too, both in town and country, men began to beautify existence by art. Household utensils, tables, chairs, beds, cupboards, and wainscots were manufactured of beautiful wood, freely ornamented with carving; windows with beautifully painted panes, armorial bearings, stoves with allegorical and historical pictures, and even the outsides of houses were often adorned with frescoes. Council and guildhouses were endowed even more richly than private dwellings with delicate carving, pictures, and painted glass; and from the end of the fifteenth century onward Switzerland produced much that was pleasing and really great in those arts most closely connected with actual life.

Gothic ecclesiastical architecture was yet in its second bloom: the church of St. Nicholas in Fribourg, the minster at Berne, the church of St. Oswald in Zug, the *Wasserkirche* in Zurich, date from this period. But the Gothic no longer reigned alone. A preference for the beautiful forms of the Greeks and Romans gradually obtained, the so-called Renaissance style, which was for the arts what the study of the ancient classics was for learning. The new birth of art, especially as regarded painting, found an early place in Switzerland, owing to its close relations to Italy, and also owing to the skillful artists who labored there, as Holbein in Basle, Urs Graf in Soleure, Nicholas Manuel in Berne, as is attested by the designs for the colored glass in the Council Hall of date 1520 and the Holbein frescoes on the Hertenstein's house in Lucerne, which were executed a little earlier.

All these circumstances also produced a reaction in social life. Foreign customs and splendid luxury were introduced, and clothing became more costly. The desire for intellectual enjoyment found vent in the introduction of the drama and the theater, as in Lucerne in 1470; the genial sociability of the fatherland found expression in national Federal festivals, such as public shooting matches, a very large one being held in Zurich in 1504. But this desire did not degenerate into a mere pursuit of pleasure; the affairs of the fatherland were eagerly discussed, and the common people talked politics daily, even at weddings and in the parlors of inns and taverns.

Yet the splendor and the progress thus developing in every walk of life brought lamentable drawbacks in their train. Above all, the pensions paid to the Swiss by foreign powers, notably by France, had a most fatal influence on the public spirit; for besides the various states influential individuals also secretly drew such pensions for themselves, often from many princes simultaneously. The statesman Waldmann drew 400 florins from the Austrian dominions, besides an additional 4000 florins for distribution, and from René, of Lorraine, 100 florins. From such practices it seems probable that the leaders of the state were not seldom influenced in their decisions and endeavors by money.

Further, foreign influence and increased wealth fostered a laxity of morals that was most injurious. Former simplicity was despised, and men began to array themselves in silk, velvet, costly furs, silver and gold embroideries set with jewels; and Spanish and French fashions came into vogue. The mercenaries on their return home usually brought with them a habit of gossip, and much vexatious slander prevailed. The governments soon found themselves forced to issue prohibitions against unseemly and improper clothing, as also against immoderate drinking and swearing, and to punish mercenaries for insolence. Many mercenaries no longer cared to work at home and became idlers and vagabonds, who squandered their pay and then lived by robbery and plunder. In the year 1480 about 1500 thieves and vagabonds had to be executed in the course of a few months, most of whom were discharged mercenaries. In regard to this prevailing wantonness, and the corruption wrought by pensions and by foreign hire, a great task of reform lay before the sixteenth century.

Chapter VII

THE ERA OF THE REFORMATION. 1516-1600

THE great changes which came about in every department of life in all the great states of Europe about the end of the fifteenth and beginning of the sixteenth centuries soon made themselves felt in Switzerland also. The Confederates, everywhere victorious, overflowed with exuberant vitality; their national life grew more active and more varied on the stage of European politics, while private life became richer in comforts, and the arts and sciences permeated a wider circle of society. The church alone, whose guidance lay in other hands, followed the beaten track, and blemishes became apparent in social and moral life in startling contrast to the new culture and new views of life.

In Switzerland, the condition was on a par with that in Germany. In Switzerland, too, the life of the church had become torpid. Men inclined more and more to a mechanical following of outward ordinances, and leaned to the conception of religion as a matter of externals. Even flourishing monasteries with a glorious past behind them, such as St. Gall, degenerated and allowed the treasures of knowledge to decay. An ordinance of Bishop Hugo of Constance gives us a gloomy picture of the times; the chief pastor complains that so many ecclesiastics and priests pay no attention to discipline and morality, sit with the laity in taverns, gamble, quarrel, get drunk, enter into unlawful contracts, and the like.

Many noble-minded men watched this mental and moral decay of the church and clergy with grief and indignation. As early as the time of the old Zurich War, Felix Hemmerli, the broad-minded canon of Zurich, openly condemned this negligence, frivolity, and licentiousness. In Berne the painter and poet Nicholas Manuel denounced the worldliness of the clergy in his "Dance of Death," painted in the monastery of the Preaching Friars, as also in his "Carnival plays" (*Fastnachtspielen*), which were performed in public, and represented Christ with the crown of thorns, followed by the poor and the sick, in contrast to the Pope riding on a splendid steed, with his richly adorned retinue.

Meanwhile the " humanities " (*Humanismus*), reviving the spirit of antiquity, were leading men of culture to a wider conception of faith. Famous professors at Basle, such as Thomas Wittenback, were moved to attack existing institutions. Their untrammeled efforts rapidly kindled a spark among the youth of the schools and universities; a new generation grew up, freer in thought than the former, and determined to turn conviction into action. The authorities had already set to work in Switzerland to remedy individual abuses, although ecclesiastical affairs did not come under the authority of the state.

The Diet, however, had long since included ecclesiastical as well as political matters in the sphere of its debates and in 1479 sent a serious warning to the Abbot of Pfäffers and threatened to take the monastery into their own hands. In Zurich attempts had already been made under Waldmann to restrict the claims of the clergy, and to compel them to discipline by the coercion of the state. The Council of Zurich laid its prohibitions on the monks, and deprived Abbot Trinkler of his office. In Berne the government adopted a like policy.

Other abuses, chiefly of a social nature, such as the oppression of the peasantry, began to make themselves felt. Switzerland was less affected in this way than the rest of Germany, but on the other hand Switzerland suffered from a peculiar political canker. From the time of the Burgundian wars she had formed the center and aim of European policy, whence all the powers of Europe borrowed their forces for war; she was, as it were, " a great human market, where wholesale merchants sought to outbid one another." Even little Glarus was traversed by envoys from the Pope, the emperor, from Milan, Venice, Savoy, and France. Not only did foreign service often lead the Confederates against one another in war, but it also drained the land of its best resources, introduced evil habits, and destroyed the spirit of patriotism; the Swiss became dependent upon foreign powers, and only too often their policy was determined by money.

The native sense of the people, it is true, early realized the uncertainty and danger of this state of things, notably at the time of Waldmann's downfall, when the selfish ends of the leaders of the mercenary bands, who were the chief gainers by the system, became apparent. In their exasperation against the dominant class which had sprung up by means of foreign pay and pensions, the people tried to obtain a prohibition of all annuities, salaries, and donations; somewhat later, at the time of the battles of Novara (1513) and Marignano (1515) organized rebellions [1] took place in Berne, Soleure, and Lucern against the French faction. Different classes of people at various times proposed a general prohibition of pensions, but the majority was always against it. Popular risings were everywhere suppressed; the dominant class remained and aroused dissatisfaction among the country people, whose instincts were those of freeborn Swiss. A general revolution was therefore only to be desired. But a reorganization must necessarily meet with so much the more opposition, since not only the ecclesiastics as well as the ignorant ranged themselves against it, but all the advocates of the foreign hire and pension system and of the old Federal conditions did likewise.

The founder of this Swiss Reformation was Ulrich Zwingli, the first among a great number of men like-minded who dared openly and effectually to resist existing conditions. Born at Wildhaus, in Toggenburg, in 1484, son of the chief magistrate of the commune, his religious instincts were early aroused in his own home; his parents, probably through the influence of two uncles who were priests, destined him for the ecclesiastical profession. One of these uncles, Bartholomew Zwingli, dean of Wesen, a most humane and enlightened man, took charge of the talented boy and sent him in his tenth year to a good school at Basle, and afterward to Berne, where Zwingli enjoyed the instruction of Wölflin (Lupulus), one of the most famous humanists; and he finally attended the University of Vienna from 1500 to 1502. Animated by a keen thirst for knowledge, he became, under the teaching of Lupulus, specially enamored of the beauties and the brilliant world of thought of the Greek and Roman classics. Classical studies took such complete possession of his mind that we find him for a time practicing as a teacher of Latin at Basle. There he found in Thomas Wittenbach a teacher in whom were united deep religious convictions with a liberal turn of mind, one who had already cast off the fetters of the scholastic methods which had hitherto pre-

---

[1] These were styled risings against the "crown eaters" (*Kronenfresser*), i. e., against those in the Council who were suspected of taking bribes in French money—crowns.

vailed. Zwingli was strangely moved and determined to devote himself to this new creed.

In 1506 he became a parish priest in Glarus, and besides the duties of his office he spent all his leisure time in study. He steeped himself in the philosophy of the ancients, specially that of Plato and Seneca, whose ideas he so esteemed that he says they had drunk of "the heavenly spring," even though they were not Christians. In addition, he read the New Testament in the original, and doubts arose within him as to the authenticity of the teaching of the Fathers of the Church and the papacy. He had an opportunity, moreover, of discovering political abuses as field-chaplain in the Italian campaigns; he rejoiced, like a true patriot, it is true, in the great expedition to Pavia in 1512, at the prowess and bravery of his countrymen; but in the expedition of Marignano, in 1515, his inmost soul was roused to indignation by the moral corruption and profligacy of his country.

He left Glarus, where his opponents of the French faction were triumphant, and in 1516 was appointed preacher to Einsiedeln, the famous place of pilgrimage. As yet, however, he made no open attack upon the teaching of the church. It was only after Luther had ventured the first bold step in Germany, and when he himself in December, 1518, was called as a secular priest to Zurich, where a great number of the enlightened citizens already shared his views, that he resolved upon any decisive breach with established tradition. Without troubling himself about church usage, he began at once, on New Year's Day, 1519, by preaching and expounding the Gospel, and his hearers testified that they had never heard the like.

Zwingli, the humanist, had never been so much attached to the old ecclesiastical system as Luther, the monk, therefore it cost him less to tear himself from it. It was not with him, as with Luther, the anxiety of an oppressed spirit which could find no rest that led him to the Reformation, but, before all things, the reasonable love of truth which he had imbibed from the classics. Zwingli was a Republican withal, took a lively interest in political affairs, which he brought within the range of his practical efforts, and thus aimed at Reformation not in creed only, but in every department of life. Just as he attacked the clergy, so he condemned secular abuses, the system of pensions and foreign hire, and foreign alliances; and himself now, in 1520, formally and openly resigned the pension which the Pope had sent him for some years in succession as a supporter of his political interests.

He speedily met with considerable sympathy in Zurich, and in the very first year could reckon upon more than two thousand who shared his views. The Diet assembled in Zurich also denounced Bernhardin Samson, the shameless hawker of indulgences, and succeeded in keeping him out of the town. At Zwingli's instigation, and with the full consent of the *Landsgemeinden,* who had to give in their votes in due form, the Council rejected the alliance with France concluded by the twelve states in May, 1521. The adherents of the old régime, however, now began to bestir themselves; in spite of all Zwingli's efforts, the advocates of foreign service induced Zurich to provide the Pope with mercenary troops for the expedition to Piacenza in 1521. Meanwhile Zwingli's preaching began to take effect. The reformer having declared that fasting was not obligatory, certain of the inhabitants of Zurich in 1522 disregarded a mandate of the bishop enjoining a fast, for which they were punished.

Zwingli therefore wished to establish the truth of his views, and to convince everyone of the hollowness of all reasoning to the contrary, by open discussion with his opponents. Hence, on January 29, 1523, the first disputation was held at Zurich. Faber— the episcopal vicar-general of Constance, a learned man who had formerly himself had some leanings toward the Reformation, but who had changed his attitude in order to obtain preferment—entered the lists as Zwingli's chief opponent, but he was completely worsted by the latter.

Henceforth began the actual Reformation. The council decided that Zwingli should continue as heretofore; and he immediately set to work to remodel the monasteries, especially the Institute of Canons in the town of Zurich. For the first time an ecclesiastic, Wilhelm Röubli, of Wytikon, now ventured to be publicly married (April, 1523); soon a number of other eminent ecclesiastics followed his example: and in the following year Zwingli himself married the excellent Anna Reinhart, the widow of a nobleman of Zurich, with whom he led the happiest family life. Thenceforth marriage became the rule among the clergy of the Reformation.

Zwingli's friends, however, being guilty of many rash proceedings and seeking to get rid of pictures and church furniture by force, violent opposition soon arose, until the second disputation at Zurich in October, 1523, established Zwingli's points more clearly and put a stop to all violent dealings. Konrad Schmied, a friend of Zwingli's and the distinguished head of the monastery of the Order of St. John, in Küssnacht, on the Lake of Zurich, urged that the weaker brethren should not be harassed, but treated with indulgence. The greater council—chiefly composed of Zwingli's adherents—pursued their efforts in the cause of the Reformation with fresh courage. But just as he had established it within the city by instruction, not by violence, so in the country he secured the consent of the people. Zwingli and his friends went among the various communities, and by their influence opinions were formed which were vehemently expressed in favor of the Reformation. Consequently, almost without opposition or tumult, pictures were abolished in 1524, then the monasteries were dissolved, and in 1525 the mass was discontinued. Under Zwingli's guidance Zurich was completely changed. The temporal possessions and rights of the canons of the *Grossmünster,* which, like a kind of small principality, had hitherto formed a state within a state, he transferred to the state. Out of the revenues he erected a school for theologians and humanists (the *Carolinum*), and invited such eminent men as Pelligan, Ceporin, Myconius, and Collin to be its teachers. Zurich was raised into a nursery of the higher culture. The religious houses, both in the city and in the country districts, were converted into hospitals, almshouses, and schools, and regulations were issued for the poor and the sick, and also concerning marriage, for the whole state.

Among the many whom these changes failed to satisfy the sect known as Anabaptists were conspicuous. That the latter should reject infant baptism and insist upon the baptism of adults was a deviation of little importance; but they were very zealous for the strictest application of the Gospel and the conditions of primitive Christianity, and equally so against the prevailing social system, the difference between rich and poor, and against the oppressive feudal taxes (tithes and ground rents), and thus once more aroused the efforts of the oppressed peasants. To these demands, which were to some extent reasonable, they united fanatical and extravagant ideas about the coming of the kingdom of God, thought they had received revelations, imagined themselves the "chosen of the Lord," and wanted to purge the church of the "impure," or to form a church of the pure and holy. These Anabaptists appeared in Switzerland (in Zurich and St. Gall, for example) about the same time as in Germany. Their most zealous leaders were Konrad Grebel and Felix Manz, both of Zurich, learned men of spirit and understanding, but full of passionate zeal. The excesses of the Anabaptists were naturally regarded as dangerously inimical to the Reformation. The state itself saw its very existence threatened by them, all the disputations having hitherto availed nothing for their instruction. Authoritative measures were taken against them, and severe punishments were inflicted upon them, as was the spirit of the age; some were drowned, and among them Felix Manz.

The peasants next began to grow restless. When in 1525 the collective peasantry of southern Germany rose in revolt, and in twelve articles demanded the abolition of tithes, of villainage, of hunting monopolies, the diminution of taxes and compulsory service, these ideas spread to their neighbors of Basle, Zurich, and Schaffhausen. In many places, at Eglisau, Grüningen, Rütli, and Greifensee, the peasants declared that God had created water, the woods, fields, birds, wild game, and fish freely for every man without distinction, and that it was but righteous and just that every man in the country districts should pursue his craft or trade as in the city, and that everyone in the country should have free access to and intercourse with the city. They complained bitterly of the oppressive innovations which had been introduced in Waldmann's time. Popular riots ensued; the monasteries of Rütli and Bubikon were attacked and plundered, and on June 5 a popular assembly was brought about at Töss. The authorities and Zwingli, however, allayed the storm. The gentle and conciliatory works of Rudolf Lavater, the bailiff of Kiburg in Töss, and the liberal hospitality practiced by the town of Winterthur, succeeded in appeasing the vehemently excited minds of the populace. At Zwingli's instigation the Council abolished villainage, as far as lay in their power,[2] the tithes were lessened, and a prospect held out of their partial remission. The Council of Basle made similar grants, and Zurich added that from all time the city and the lake communes had been one, and that the latter should be regarded as burgesses of the town. Schaffhausen resorted to force. The

[2] Namely, only for the bondmen who belonged to the state of Zurich, and not to outside owners.

unfavorable issue of the Peasants' War in Germany afterward materially contributed to intimidate the peasants in Switzerland.

The Forest States became more and more adverse and hostile in their attitude toward the commenced work of the Reformation. From the outset they clung more to the glorious inheritance received from their forefathers. In their simple conditions they saw less of the abuses of the system, and a liberal education was unknown among them; even social abuses were not so severely felt by them as by the other states. Moreover, they saw their most important source of gain threatened by Zwingli's zeal against mercenary service and foreign alliances; and on this point the other states were at one with them, particularly Lucerne, which was strongly influenced by French money, and was striving to obtain a position of power similar to that of Zurich. Hence, when Zwingli abolished the mass and purged the churches, the Forest States prevailed upon the Diet held at Lucerne in 1524 to decide to hold fast to the old faith, and if necessary to resort to punishments. Zurich was admonished to reëstablish the old religion, and as this produced no effect, the Forest States withdrew their Federal friendship; some people even suggested publishing the Federal charters to the state so desirous of innovation.

The first conflict broke out in the common dominion of Thurgau. The Thurgau, as common subject-land, was obliged on all occasions to have recourse to Zurich as the seat of government, and through her intercourse with that town the Reformation speedily took root throughout the districts of the territory of Thurgau. But the bailiffs of the Forest towns hindered it, and availed themselves of every slightest occasion to take violent measures against the new doctrine; they specially turned their attention to Stammheim and Stein, dependencies of Zurich, which were under the high jurisdiction of the Thurgau. Both these places readily accepted the Reformation with Zurich, but when they began to abolish images, Amberg, the bailiff from Schwyz, interfered and caused Pastor Öchslin to be imprisoned in the castle of Stein. Thereupon a popular tumult broke out, and the Carthusian monastery of Ittingen, a stronghold of the old faith, was burned to the ground in July, 1524. The under-bailiffs, Wirth and Rüttimann, of Stammheim and Nussbaumen, were falsely accused of instigating the riot, together with the pastors there, sons of Wirth, and were thrown into prison. Zurich could effect nothing by her intercession, but was obliged to submit to the majority of the governing states; three of the innocent prisoners were condemned at Baden and mercilessly executed. Thus fell the first victims to religious hatred, and a war very nearly broke out; but the severe defeat which the Swiss mercenaries had sustained in February, 1525, with the French at Pavia at the hands of the imperialists had damped the warlike zeal of the five Catholic states—Uri, Schwyz, Unterwalden, Lucerne, and Zug.

Meanwhile, however, in spite of bitter opposition, the Reformation had already forced its way into a great part of the Confederation. As early as the second disputation delegates from Schaffhausen and St. Gall had taken its part. In Schaffhausen, where the ecclesiastical movement was closely connected with a political one, the victory of the guilds over the nobility, there labored friends of Zwingli, such as Sebastian Wagner (*Hofmeister*). In St. Gall the celebrated city-physician and humanist, Joachim von Watt (Vadian), afterward burgomaster, labored for the Gospel, as did John Kessler, writer and saddler, who had studied with Luther and Melanchthon at Wittenberg. In Glarus the Reformation was advanced by divers liberal-minded pastors, disciples of Zwingli, notably Valentine Tschudin.

Basle soon cast off the episcopal dominion; several learned men at the university, especially Zwingli's friend, Ökolampadius, " the light of the house," were there active on behalf of the new doctrine. Berne found a reformer in Zwingli's friend, Berthold Haller. Young priests, disciples of Zwingli, carried the new ideas even into the little state of Appenzell; the more enlightened population of the lowland portion (the present Outer Rhodes) in 1524 obtained a decision of the *Landsgemeinde* in favor of religious liberty, whereupon a number of communes accepted the Reformation. Friends of Zwingli and clergy from Zurich carried the seed of the Reformation even to the remote Grisons, where its cause was essentially advanced by an antagonism of long standing to the episcopal rule. Liberty of faith having been established at a disputation at Ilanz in 1526, the bishop and clergy were afterward excluded from the Federal Diet, and from appointments to secular offices; by this means the Grisons also took an important step toward independence. Thus little by little the Reformation gained the ascendent in the whole of the northeast of Switzerland. In 1525 the neutral states of Basle, Schaffhausen, and Appenzell separated themselves from the other Catholic states; and also Soleure, Berne, and Glarus assumed either a neutral position or one favorable to the Reformation, and disapproved of the very severe decisions of the Diet against Zurich.

Meanwhile the remaining six Catholic states hoped to succeed in gaining the victory for their religion in the same way as Zwingli had in Zurich, by arranging a disputation at Baden in May, 1526. Their plan seemed to meet with brilliant success, for Zurich held aloof, because impartial management was not to be expected, and also fears were entertained for Zwingli's life, for in 1523, at the instigation of Lucerne, a Diet had decided that he should be arrested wherever found on Federal soil. On the Catholic side there appeared Dr. Eck, the most able controversialist of Germany, and other learned men of mark, such as Faber, the vicar-general, and Murner, the Franciscan monk, who defended the ancient church with such assurance and such ability that the Catholics might well triumph in their victory. The reformers disputed the victory with their opponents, and complained of fraud in the report drawn up by the other faction.

The places which had hitherto remained neutral (with the exception of Soleure) now took up a much more decided position of hostility toward the strict Catholics and aided Zurich. Berne in especial now took part openly with the Reformation, having quarreled with the Forest States, who refused to publish the acts of Baden. A reëlection of the Council (1527) turned completely in favor of the partisans of the Reformation, and the government arranged a disputation in January, 1528, in order to bring the wavering to a decision. On the papal side only very insignificant speakers attended; Zwingli, on the other hand, distinguished himself by his perspicuity and depth of thought. When at the close of the disputation he preached in the minster, a priest who was just preparing for the mass was so overcome by the force of his words that he threw aside his vestments, and cried: "If it be so with the mass, then will I neither to-day nor ever henceforth hold mass!" Berne joined Zurich in carrying out the Reformation, and also concurred in insisting upon the abolition of the pension system and such-like Federal matters. The secession of this powerful and important city with her vast territory secured the continuance of the new doctrine in the whole of Switzerland, for the step taken by Berne also led to the complete establishment of the Reformation in Basle, Schaffhausen, and St. Gall. Most of the professors at Basle left the university, and the bishop removed to Porrentruy (*Pruntrut*), in the Jura.

With the increasing spread of evangelical teaching, the antagonism between the Catholic and the Reformed states was heightened. The immense progress of the Reformation in the common domains, in particular, led to constant disputes. In addition to the Thurgau, evangelical doctrines had won the day in the Rheintal, belonging to the eight original states (1527), then in Sargans and Gaster, and in the common domains of Baden and the Free Bailiwicks it had likewise gained ground. Hitherto the principle had indeed been maintained that in the common dominions all things should be decided by the majority; Zurich and Berne, however, would not allow that principle to hold good in religious matters, and insisted that every commune should enjoy unconditional religious liberty. The reforming of these territories resulted in a constant decrease there of the influence of the Catholic states. Zurich meanwhile had extended her power by other measures. As early as 1527 she concluded an " Evangelical Alliance " with the reformed town of Constance, thus forming a separate league; this was joined by Berne, St. Gall, Mülhausen, and Bienne, after the triumph of the new doctrine in each of those states respectively. Zwingli, who by his paramount influence in Zurich held sway even in political matters, and was practically to a certain extent burgomaster, town clerk, and council all in one, proceeded in consequence with even more energy. In order to make their opponents feel their supremacy, the inhabitants of Zurich punished most severely every offense against their creed, and now tried to procure the triumph of their opinions in the territory of their adversaries by force. Thus Max Wehrli, the bailiff's officer (*Landweibel*) in the Thurgau, was put to death for alleged aspersions upon Zurich, and thus a cruel revenge was taken for the sanguinary decree of Ittingen.

Zurich specially exasperated her enemies by supporting the subjects of the Abbot of St. Gall, who sided with the Reformation and applied to Zurich as one of the protecting states of the abbey.[3] When the evangelicals attacked the church in Toggenburg in 1528, denounced the monastery of St. John, and drove out its abbot, Zurich

[3] The Abbey of St. Gall was under the protection of Zurich, Lucerne, Glarus, and Schwyz.

encouraged the Toggenburg folk to refuse homage to the Abbot of St. Gall; a similar course was pursued in the "Old Territory," where the town of St. Gall, Rorschach, and several communes abolished Catholic worship and refused obedience to the abbot. The other states protecting the abbey, especially Schwyz, embraced contrary measures, and mutual preparations for war speedily ensued. During these disputes Murner, the Franciscan, hurled such bitter satires and invectives at Zurich and Berne that these states demanded satisfaction at the Diet; Lucerne, however, took Murner under her protection.

A separate league entered into by the Catholic states accelerated the rupture. In order to be able to depend upon the support of their coreligionists, these states resolved upon the fatal step taken by Zurich a hundred years earlier, namely, an offensive and defensive alliance with Austria, concluded in April, 1529 ("the Christian Alliance," or the "Treaty of Ferdinand"). This union gave a greater shock to the Federal Leagues than even the union of Zurich with Constance. At this crisis the Reformed pastor, Jakob Kaiser, of Schwerzenbach, being taken prisoner by the men of Schwyz and burned to death for promulgating the new doctrine upon their territory, and Murner pouring forth fresh invectives, a civil war broke out.

Zwingli was resolved upon war; he hoped by its means to advance the cause of religion, and induced Zurich to take arms so much the more eagerly, that he believed it necessary to oppose the power of the emperor and of Ferdinand in the name of the Reformation. Zurich forestalled the enemy, speedily took possession of the Free Bailiwicks, and stationed her main army at Kappel in June, 1529. The Bernese, although not so eager for war, also marched out. But the people had not lost all sense of Federal brotherhood; sentries and advanced guards encountered one another in friendly fashion; when for instance a number of boon companions from the Forest States had got possession of a large vessel full of milk, but had no bread, they placed it on the frontier and called to the men of Zurich; the latter brought bread, and they shared milk porridge amid merry jests. Jakob Sturm, Mayor (*Stadtmeister*) of Strassburg, said of them: "You Confederates are a wonderful people; even in discord you are at one, and never forget your old friendship!" This frame of mind at that time still prevailed, and most shrank from civil war. Neither were the Catholics very eager for war, since the Reformers were better armed and had a more powerful force in the field. The Landammann Aebli of Glarus therefore succeeded in effecting a truce, and through the intervention of the neutral states on June 25, 1529, the first Peace of Kappel was concluded, seemingly against Zwingli's wish. By it mutual liberty of faith was secured, the right of decision in religious matters in the common domains was yielded to the communes on the principle of majority, and the Austrian alliance was broken off.

Still further encouraged by the concessions of their adversaries, Zwingli and his adherents endeavored to completely subjugate the five states. Without any reference to the other protecting states (Lucerne and Schwyz), the two states of Zurich and Glarus, challenged by their opponents, declared that the Abbot of St. Gall, who had fled, had forfeited his domain, disposed absolutely of the goods of the monasteries, and gave a free constitution to the Toggenburg, the home of the Reformation. The evangelicals next concluded a league with Philip of Hesse. Zwingli, whose plan of operations extended far beyond Switzerland, had long seen with anxiety the growing power of Charles V. and his hostile intentions toward the Reformation. He wanted to effect a league to oppose him, and therefore endeavored at the religious conference at Marburg, in October, 1529, to form an agreement and an alliance with the German Protestants. This failing, he immediately attacked his opponents in Switzerland. It was his intention to dominate the Forest States, whom he regarded as incapable, to deprive them of all right to the common domains, and to degrade them into vassals of Zurich and Berne. These two cities, which surpassed all the other states put together in extent of territory and in population, and which had formed the starting-point of the Reformation, he considered as the basis of the Confederation. It was his aim to establish a uniform Federal Government, in which the larger states should be paramount, to carry reform throughout the Confederation, and to sweep away the system of pensions and mercenary service. He once more allowed himself to be torn from these lofty aims to seek a decision at the sword's point. In the emperor and in his brother Ferdinand of Austria, with whom the five states cultivated friendly relations, he not only saw the bitterest foes of the German Reformation, but also credited them with an intention of exterminating the Reformed party in Switzerland, in concert with the five states. He therefore entered into negotiations with Francis I. of France, the chief enemy of Charles V., and with Venice, and when in Germany also, to his joy, the party prepared for the struggle at Schmalcalden, he thought the moment had come for open warfare.

Various causes combined to give him his opportunity. Jacob of Medici, lord of the Castle of Musso, on the Lake of Como, apparently in collusion with Austria, attacked and surprised the Valtelline, a subject-land of the Grisons. The Grisons called in the help of the Confederates, but only the Protestant states marched out (April, 1531), while the five states refused their aid. This aroused the suspicion that they were in conspiracy with the enemy, and Zurich accused them of breaking the league. Then came all manner of spiteful invectives and accusations on the part of the five states. The war with Musso now taking a favorable turn, the Confederation prepared for a second religious war. Zurich considered that peace was no longer possible, and hoped to obtain more favorable conditions by the decision of war. She was with difficulty persuaded, at the desire of the allied towns, in May, 1531, to coerce the five states by a blockade of provisions only. This measure had the opposite effect: instead of submission, the Catholics offered a most daring resistance, and on October 9 they declared war.

Zurich had not expected this; she had neither secured the aid of her coreligionists nor made due preparations herself. Paralyzed by dissensions within her own territories, and not less by the coolness and alienation of Berne, Zurich tardily sent 1200 men to Kappel on October 10, under Captain George Göldli, who was inimical to Zwingli, with injunctions not to let himself be drawn into a battle until the main army should come up. Instead of obeying, Göldli, on October 11, allowed himself, though occupying a most unfavorable position, to be drawn into a battle with the powerful army of the five states, numbering about 8000 men; and when about midday on the same day a reinforcement of 1500 men appeared under Rudolf Lavater, accompanied by Zwingli himself, the conflict was already almost decided. The manly courage displayed by the men of Zurich was all in vain: by a flank movement the five states rendered the position of the Zurich troops untenable. Zwingli himself fell beneath a tree. Recognized by the light of the torches, the dying man received his death-blow from a captain of mercenaries from Unterwalden; but Pastor Schönbrunner, of Zug, exclaimed as he looked at the corpse: "Whatever thou hast been as to thy faith, I know thou hast been a good Confederate!" Over 500 of the men of Zurich, many of them of the foremost of the city, remained dead on the field. In vain did the Bernese and others of the Reformed religion advance to the help of the Zurich troops; they were altogether wanting in unity and confidence; and the victory of the Catholics was completed by an attack made on the night of October 24 on the Gubel, near Zug, upon the men of Zurich and their allies.

The five states were at first resolved to pursue their advantage to the utmost against Zurich; but Golder, the chief magistrate of Lucerne, urged them to treat the men of Zurich as brothers and fellow-Confederates, and to be lenient with them, and his advice at length prevailed. So the second Peace of Kappel (November 20) assured the free exercise of religion to every state, and religious liberty even to the common domains; but a Protestant majority was not to be allowed to compel a Catholic minority to change their religion, and all separate leagues were abolished.

The Reformed party was terribly disheartened by the result of the second war of Kappel. The adherents of the older faith became more arrogant in their bearing; not only was the scheme for the further spread of the Reformation shattered, but with it that of the political reform of the Confederation, and Zwingli's cherished hope of establishing the supremacy of Berne and Zurich was dashed to the ground. The territories of those two cities were in a state of violent fermentation, and general dissatisfaction with the arbitrary proceedings of the authorities reigned. In order to avoid an insurrection, Zurich was forced, in December, 1531, to promise by the "Charter of Kappel" to consult the rural districts on all matters of importance, and particularly to commence no war without their consent. Berne was obliged to concede the same to her country-folk, to grant free trade, and to lighten the tithes. Zwingli's place as chief pastor (*Antist*) of the church of Zurich was taken by Henry Bullinger, of Bremgarten, who, supported by Leo Jud, carried on Zwingli's eccelesiastical work with fidelity and discretion, but relinquished his political schemes and undertakings.

In consequence, however, of the preëminence of the five states after the battle of Kappel, a Catholic reaction rapidly ensued. In certain communes in Glarus Catholic worship was reëstablished, as also in Rapperswil, in the Free Bailiwicks, in Utznach, Wesen, and Gaster. The Abbot of St. Gall returned to the protection of the five states, completely reëstablished the sway of the monastery over the "Old Territory" and Toggenburg, and partially restored Catholicism. The five states were specially successful in Soleure, where the Catholics sought to crush the Reformation completely. In October, 1532, the two factions were already in arms against one another, when Nicholas Wengi, the Catholic mayor, rushing in front of the guns of his faction, exclaimed: "If the blood of my fellow-citizens must flow, then let mine be the first!" The combatants yielded in astonishment, and civil war was averted. The Reformed party, however, were so alarmed that many left the town, and others joined the Catholics, so that the counter-reformation prevailed.

As a result of this reaction the religious conditions of Switzerland took definite shape; the five states, with Valais, the Free Bailiwicks, Rapperswil, Utznach, and Gaster forming one united Catholic Federal territory, and acting as a bulwark to Fribourg and Soleure on the west, and to Inner Rhodes in Appenzell and St. Gall on the east. Separated from one another on all sides, and to a certain extent encircled by arms of the Catholic territory, or by "districts of parity"[4] (Baden, the Thurgau, Toggenburg, Rheintal, and Glarus), the Reformed territories of Berne, Basle, Zurich, Schaffhausen, Outer Rhodes in Appenzell, Werdenberg, and the Grisons were more isolated. On this account the Reformed party labored under a disadvantage, but an opportunity soon arose for a considerable extension of their power in the territories of western Switzerland.

Owing to the immense strides taken by the house of Savoy during the thirteenth century, the bond between the present western Switzerland and eastern Switzerland had grown lax, until during the Burgundian War Berne conceived the great design of restoring the old kingdom of Burgundy, and in concert with Fribourg conquered the domain of Morat, and Orbe, Grandson, and Echallens in the Pays de Vaud. The attempts of Charles III., Duke of Savoy, to bring completely under his sway the episcopal towns of Geneva and Lausanne (then making strenuous efforts after liberty), where his house possessed certain rights of dominion conjointly with the bishops and the civic communes, next induced

[4] *I. e.,* recognizing equality of political rights between the two confessions.

ERA OF REFORMATION

Lausanne in 1525 and Geneva in 1526 to conclude alliances with Fribourg and Berne for the protection of their liberties and rights. Since the beginning of the sixteenth century two opposite factions had existed in Geneva: the Savoyards (or "Mamelukes") and the "children of Geneva," the latter under the leadership of the high-minded Philibert Berthelier. Charles III. endeavored to crush his opponents, and in 1519 caused Berthelier to be put to death. But in Bezanson Hugues the party of Berthelier found another able leader, and the civil alliance with Berne and Fribourg was the result of his initiative.

The nobles of Savoy made a fierce attack upon the town (*Löffelbund*), and Bonivard, the Genevese historian, was arrested in the Vaud and thrown into a dungeon of the Castle of Chillon. Geneva now tried to obtain complete freedom, and in 1530 succeeded, by the help of the Confederates; the duke was forced to promise to respect the liberties of Geneva. By this, the Peace of St. Julien, if the peace were not observed, the Pays de Vaud was to be surrendered.

The aim of the efforts of Berne was to drive the house of Savoy completely out of the Pays de Vaud and to annex the latter themselves, for which the Reformation afforded them a welcome expedient. Under the direction of Berne there came to the Vaud William Farel, an ardent preacher, who had been exiled from his home in the south of France. He traversed the country with unflagging zeal, preaching in Aigle (1526), Morat, Neuchâtel, Grandson, and Orbe with great success. The most violent opposition did not discourage him; often surprised, beaten, and imprisoned, he always returned undaunted to the struggle, and shrank from no danger. Thus in 1532 he came to Geneva and there found a favorable soil, because the citizens were then striving to throw off all dependence upon the bishops, and had been won over to the Reformation, after the treaty of 1526, by the efforts of Berne. But while the Reformed party relied upon Berne, the sympathies of their opponents were with Savoy and the bishop. Many hostile encounters took place, and victory long hung in the balance, until Berne threatened to dissolve the league and the bishop tried to take the town by surprise.

The Reformers gained the victory in a disputation; an ecclesiastical storm followed, but in 1535 the Reformation was established. Duke Charles thereupon besieging the town, the Bernese declared war upon him, advanced into the Vaud in January, 1536, with 6000 men under the conduct of Franz Nägeli, conquered the whole country almost without striking a blow, as also Gex, Genevois, and Chablais, and drove out the troops of Savoy. In a second expedition they happily succeeded in releasing Bonivard from Chillon. The duke was obliged to yield the territories just named to Berne.

The town of Geneva, however, owing her deliverance to the Bernese, bound herself to enter into no alliance without the consent of Berne, so that the latter exercised a species of protective right. Thus was the foundation laid of an enduring political and intellectual alliance between those French territories and the German Confederation. With the regulations introduced into the acquired territory by Berne, the constitution of the Vaud was gradually swept away, bailiffs were sent into the country, and the laws of Berne introduced, though with reservation of the communal liberties; the reformed teaching was disseminated throughout by force, and Catholicism interdicted. But the greatest services rendered by Berne to the Vaud were the erection of schools, the establishment of a poor fund, and the founding of the University of Lausanne, where the famous theologian, Peter Viret, of Orbe, a colleague of Farel, and Theodore Beza, a later disciple of Calvin in Geneva, taught. While the Pays de Vaud was being thus linked to Switzerland an important change was taking place in Geneva. The old order of things was indeed demolished, but everything was still in a state of ferment, and Farel, who was wanting in talent for organization, was painfully perplexed until he finally found a powerful supporter in Calvin.

John Calvin, born at Noyon, in Picardy, in 1509, and very strictly brought up, at first studied for the law, which left a lasting impression upon him in a certain austerity and consistency. The Reformed doctrines reached him in the midst of his studies, and won the day after fierce inward struggles; the classics, to which he had for some time devoted himself, were soon driven out by the Bible and the early Fathers. But when he openly proclaimed his faith he found himself endangered, and was forced to fly. At Basle in 1535 he wrote his famous confession of faith, the "*Institutio Religionis Christianæ,*" in which he—a deep thinker—put aside all the imperfections and contradictions of the Lutheran teaching, and laid down a rigid system of Christian doctrine (predestination, foreordaining, or election). One evening he arrived, weary, at Geneva, intending to pass through it; Farel came to him and begged him to remain. Calvin refusing, Farel menaced him with the wrath of God until Calvin, much moved, promised to remain (1536). He was at once appointed chief preacher.

He gave great offense, however, by his violent and aribitrary proceedings, by favoring the French, and by departing too much from the doctrines and usages of German-Swiss Protestantism, which Berne had introduced into the Vaud and had joyfully extended to Geneva. When in 1538 he and Farel refused to administer the Lord's Supper to the "godless" population, they were both forced to leave the town. Farel went to Neuchâtel, Calvin to Strassburg. But after a short time Calvin's following strengthened; and the tumults increasing and the encroachments of Berne becoming dangerous, a strong, guiding hand was urgently desired, and in 1541 Calvin was recalled. Amid the violent struggles of his opponents, the "Libertines," he founded a new church.

Geneva, which ever afterward formed a refuge for French Protestantism, assumed an entirely new character under Calvin's direction. At the head of his ecclesiastical system there stood two lay "Elders" or "Presbyters" chosen from the council, who, together with the clergy of the town, formed a moral tribunal called the "Consistorium." This exercised the strictest supervision over the conduct of the whole community, both in public and in private; every slightest offense, every careless speech, even jests, were reported and punished. Every luxury, all amusements (dancing, card-playing, singing, and the theater), were strictly forbidden. The whole state was to be ruled by the church, as the body by the soul; anyone who did not conform, or who ventured to gainsay, might expect to be severely punished by the council, or even put to death. Between 1541 and 1546 from 800 to 900 persons were imprisoned, fifty-eight put to death, and Servet, the Spaniard, who denied the doctrine of the Trinity, was burned. Even distinguished and eminent persons were not exempt. By such severities a system of church polity was erected which was most exemplary in externals, and which was imitated in France, Scotland, the Netherlands, and several German states (the Palatinate). Geneva, where Calvin, in 1559, founded the famous university, became the "Protestant Rome" to which numerous strangers from France found their way.

These proceedings, however, produced an estrangement between Geneva and Berne, for the latter would fain have kept Geneva in subjection. But while the political alliance between Geneva and Switzerland was being loosened a friendly union was springing up between the Calvinistic and the Zwinglian churches. In 1549 Calvin and Farel went to Zurich, and in consultation with the theologians of Zurich, notably Bullinger, drew up the "Compromise of Zurich" (*Consensus Tigurinus*)—a union of the two confessions of faith. But most of the reformed towns opposed this amalgamation of differing doctrines; and it was not till after Calvin's death (which took place in 1564) that the "Helvetic Confession," composed by Bullinger, and freed from Calvin's crudities, was accepted by the states of Zurich, Berne, Schaffhausen, St. Gall, the Grisons, Bienne, Mülhausen, and Basle.

After the peace of 1516 the Confederation as such assumed the position of a neutral state; it was no longer necessary, as it had been in the fifteenth century, to take the field almost every year for the protection of their own hearths and homes, and they no longer took any direct part in the proceedings of other powers. Liberty was achieved, their territory assured and its limits defined, and the passion for war had cooled to a great extent. They therefore betook themselves rather to the occupations of peace, although indeed a portion of the population still took part in foreign wars.

This development was essentially furthered by the Reformation, which sought to permeate every department of life with an austere moral earnestness as with leaven. Scorning all pretenses, the clergy in their sermons taught the means and the way to a truly pure and honorable life; the authorities themselves from time to time published so-called "moral mandates" (*Sittenmandate*), laid severe penalties upon all excess and vice, intemperance, luxury, gambling, cursing, and swearing, and kept a watchful eye upon the manners of the community. Zurich, for instance, appointed a commission for the inspection and punishment of all disorderly and extravagant households. Thus there were far fewer riotous outbreaks among the people after the Reformation than before; many hitherto customary excesses were discontinued; clothing became more decent; women and girls sought to distinguish themselves by domestic virtues. It is evident that men were thoroughly in earnest in their endeavors to improve their manner of life, for the slightest transgression was punished severely and even harshly, and the most trivial faults and offenses of the clergy, censured by the synods, were visited with dismissal and heavy penalties. Many a man who had formerly led a rollicking life as a mercenary in foreign lands hung his sword on the wall and devoted himself to business—tannery, the linen industry, trade, the silk industry, or labors of a similar sort.

The industries particularly flourished in the cantons of Zurich, St. Gall, and Appenzell, where manufactures were carried on of flax, hemp, and cotton. The linen trade now sprang up in Appenzell, and later manufactures of woolen and muslin fabrics. In Zurich the silk industry, which had fallen completely into decay, was revived by refugees from Locarno; the immigrant families of Muralt and Orelli were the founders of this flourishing industry. Frequent intercourse with Italy and southern Germany furnished an ample market for home manufactures, and these peaceable industries increased the general prosperity in astonishing fashion; on festive occasions almost every family, even of the middle class, could display silver vessels, embroidered cloths, gold chains, etc. The outward appearance of the Swiss towns of that time bears particularly certain evidence of the affluence then prevalent. Montaigne, the Frenchman, considers them finer than French towns; he praises their wide streets, their squares adorned with fountains, the fronts of the houses ornamented with frescoes; the painted glass, handsome stoves, polished floors, and beautiful wrought iron within the houses.

A higher tone of thought and the pursuit of nobler ideals among the middle classes were also among the best fruits of the Reformation. Everywhere the sense of hospitality and benevolence was awakening. In various districts, as in Basle, Geneva, and Zurich, French refugees and English Protestants found a kind asylum, and the English Protestants in particular looked back with touching gratitude upon the kindly care which they had enjoyed in Zurich. Zurich showed the same spirit toward the exiles from Locarno, whom she received and provided with all necessaries, notwithstanding a prevalent scarcity. Public spirit had now found a broader and a nobler field of action, and money that was formerly spent upon masses, and in providing images of saints and ornaments for churches and chapels, was now bestowed upon benevolent institutions, almshouses, and hospitals, which were founded or enriched by legacies.

The reorganizing and creative force, which, emanating from the Reformation, permeated the whole of political and social life, was perhaps most strongly evident in the sphere of popular education and the cultivation of the arts and sciences. The more peaceable disposition which had taken possession of the popular mind, and the increase of prosperity, must in themselves have assisted the advance of mental culture. Moreover, the Reformation fought chiefly with spiritual weapons, and therefore first awakened the desire for universal education. Hence the clergy, particularly Bullinger in Zurich, made it their duty to give instruction in reading, writing, and Christian doctrine. Equal attention was paid to the training of qualified teachers and capable ministers; and this was furthered by the enthusiasm for the revival of the literature and culture of antiquity. A great impulse was given to learning by this Humanist movement.

Formerly the youth of Switzerland had been almost always sent to the schools of other lands for every higher branch of education; there, as Thomas Platter relates of himself, they were forced to gain a scanty subsistence by begging, to endure hunger and thirst, to undergo almost intolerable hardships, and often enough they fell into bad company, so that they not infrequently came very near to being miserably ruined. Now, however, schools for higher education sprang up on all sides in Switzerland itself. Zwingli took the lead in Zurich by the foundation of the " Carolinum "; and soon Schaffhausen, Berne, Basle (in addition to the university), Lausanne, and Geneva erected schools for the study of the ancient classics and languages, called " gymnasiums," or " schools of the humanities." Even small towns, such as Brugg and Stein-on-the-Rhine, did much in this respect. Poor and talented youths were supported by scholarships, mostly derived from former ecclesiastical institutions and donations. At the same time large libraries were established in Zurich, St. Gall, and Berne.

But these efforts for universal education and the spread of learning still met with manifold hindrances; many a famous teacher of those days was forced to ply some trade in addition to his learning, as, for example, Thomas Platter, who worked as a ropemaker by day and gave lessons in the evening, and was so poorly clothed that any stranger visiting the school would certainly not have taken him for the professor. Notwithstanding such miserable conditions, the thirst and craving for knowledge were indescribably great; all difficulties and pains counted for nought in the effort to obtain the treasure of learning; even an old man of eighty learned Hebrew with Platter. Many used all imaginable means to curtail their rest in order to satisfy their thirst for knowledge.

As regards individual studies, the Reformation in the first instance gave a special impulse to theology. In Zurich the Bible was translated into German by Leo Jud and Collin, and a French translation appeared in Neuchâtel. Everywhere were found men ready to expound and interpret the various books of the Bible with affection, enthusiasm, and thorough knowledge of the subject. The theological writings of Bullinger enjoyed the highest esteem, not only in Switzerland, but even in England and the Netherlands; the foremost men in England, Germany, and France, even princes and statesmen, kept up a lively correspondence with him, and embraced his theological views. Theology in those days was not a mere matter for clergy and men of learning, but also for statesmen and even for ordinary men.

Next to the study of theology that of the Greek and Roman classics was most cultivated. These were translated and explained, and numerous copies printed in Zurich and Basle. Excellent editions of the classics were produced by Glarean, Ceporin, Vadian, Konrad Gessner, Rellikan, and others. By its very novelty the resuscitation of antiquity possessed such a wonderful charm for the world of those days, and the delight in it went so far, that Latin and Greek began once more to be spoken in the classical form as the ancients spoke them; and even theatrical representations were given in the Greek or Latin tongue. For instance, at the New Year's festival of 1531, a comedy of Aristophanes, the Attic comedian, to which Collin had composed a prologue and Zwingli a musical accompaniment, was performed in the Greek language at the new school in Zurich by twelve men and youths— some of them noted men of learning and professors.

The study of antiquity also bore fruit in other branches of learning. From the ancient classics men imbibed a sense of beauty and a taste for thorough scientific research; the profound thought and observation of the old philosophers and writers aroused fresh independent thought. This was specially noticeable in historical writings. The hitherto existing chronicles were already found too inartistic and too narrow; all that distinguished the historians of antiquity was wanting in them—their broader manner of viewing things, their systematic arrangement of the whole, and their knowledge of manners and customs. Hence, a number of more widely comprehensive histories and descriptions of Switzerland were produced after their pattern. In 1547 Johannes Stumpf published his "Swiss Chronicle," a history, geography, and topography of Switzerland, which became a favorite book with the people, and was even circulated in other lands. With similar industry and zeal for research, Bullinger in his chronicle wrote a history of Switzerland with special reference to Zurich. His work, however, was for centuries long only circulated in manuscript; as was also the case with the Helvetic chronicle of Giles Tschudi, of Glarus, who by the help of numerous records wrote the history of Switzerland from the year 1000 to 1470, and who, full of patriotic enthusiasm, succeeded in delineating it so gracefully and so brilliantly that when his chronicle appeared in print in 1734 it supplanted all other descriptions.

While Stumpf, Bullinger, and Tschudi occupied themselves in narrating the various historical facts and notable events as they followed in course of time, Josias Simmler of Zurich, on the other hand, in his book, *Vom Regiment der löblichen Eidgenossenschaft*," 1576, endeavored to represent the internal development of Switzerland in respect to its constitutional and political conditions; even in the sixteenth century his book was translated into many languages, and passed through quite a number of editions. This development of the art of history gives unmistakable evidence of the awakening of patriotic enthusiasm and national feeling, which also manifests itself in the fine paintings on glass, wood carvings, and tiled stoves of this period, for which by preference scenes from the history of the fatherland were selected, such as the battles of Morgarten and Sempach, and the story of William Tell.

From this time geography and the physical sciences were cultivated almost like entirely new sciences. The ancient classics had also aroused sense and interest for the contemplation and observation of Nature. Men like Rellikan, Vadian, and Konrad Gessner began to scale the heights of the Lower Alps, to admire and extol their beauties, and to describe the vegetable and animal species found there. Simmler devotes a separate volume to a description of Valais, while Stumpf gives the preference in his chronicle to the customs of the Alpine folk. Men saw at length the inadequateness of the methods hitherto pursued in the interpretation of Nature, according to which absolute reliance had been placed on traditional opinions, and now new paths were opened by independent research. Thus Paracelsus of Einsiedeln, about 1530, zealously opposed the prescriptions and theory of medicine handed down by tradition, and would learn only in the great school of Nature.

The greatest celebrity as a naturalist, however, was attained by Konrad Gessner, of Zurich (*ob.* 1565). In spite of poverty and ill-health, he raised himself by incredible exertions to the rank of one of the most learned men of his time. But it was after studying and comparing all earlier works on natural science that he first really noticed the great gaps in the then existing knowledge, and extended his own attainments by travel, and by getting his friends in other lands of Europe to send him pictures and descriptions of plants and animals he was the first to try to classify them from a scientific standpoint. Famous men from every part of Europe hastened to visit him, but he remained unshaken in his modesty and simplicity.

Of the arts, special progress was made during the latter part of the century in painting on glass, in which Swiss artists earned a reputation which stretched far beyond their own borders. Their work excelled in power, lucidity, and warmth of color, in delicate and fine execution. Equally delicate and masterly are other works of Swiss artists in sculpture and wood carving, as well as the stoves of this period. And in architecture the Renaissance style now attained to brilliant development, as the Town Hall at Lucerne and the house in Berne in the *Kirchgasse,* bore witness.

Great, however, as were the changes which were taking place in every sphere of life, a total transformation could not so rapidly be effected; contrasting with the light many shadows were visible, unlovely heirlooms of an earlier barbarism, forming so many obstacles to progress. Thus the Reformation could not put an end to the general and widespread superstition, or at once do away with the prevalent barbarity of the age. Even educated people believed in ghosts and all sorts of witchcraft; the authorities actually caused numberless persons in Zurich, Lucerne, and Berne, accused of witchcraft or of repudiating the faith of the church, to be tortured in most horrible fashion, such as having their tongues slit or being tormented with hot irons, and many were put to death, quartered, racked, burned, or drowned. Whippings, the rack, tortures, and inhuman executions were among the customary sentences.

Such barbarity and superstition hindered moral and political progress, education, and humanity quite as much as the mercenary system and foreign service, which still continued in the Catholic, and in several of the Reformed cantons.

The Catholic reaction, which in Switzerland followed the battle of Kappel, was, as it were, a prelude to the European counter-reformation which occupied the latter half of the sixteenth century. It seemed as though a new generation had arisen; the noble and conciliatory spirits of such men as Aebli, Golder, Wengi, and others had vanished, and mutual intolerance increased into the utmost violence.

Berne was the first to adopt the principle—" To whom the territory belongs, let theirs be the religion" (*wessen die Gegend, dessen die Religion*)—by depriving the harmless folk of the newly conquered valley of the Saane of their Catholic religion, and even of their pleasures and popular festivals, in 1555. A companion picture was formed in the same year by events in the Italian bailiwicks. The seed of the Reformation had been carried to Locarno by Reformed bailiffs from Zurich and Glarus, and had there found fruitful soil; and Beccaria, a zealous preacher, soon stood at the head of a considerable congregation. The five states, however, would not suffer this, and passed a resolution at the Diet which left no alternative to the Protestants of those parts but a return to Catholicism or banishment. The perplexed people steadfastly refused to recant, willing to sacrifice their all for their faith; accordingly in midwinter more than one hundred persons crossed the snow-clad Alps, and found a welcome in hospitable Zurich, and a new home there and in Basle (March, 1555). Great services were afterward rendered by the families of Muralt and Orelli.

On this occasion the Papal Legate and the Roman Inquisition were already active; thenceforth the Catholic states became more and more closely connected with the papal policy. Thus they took part in the reform of Catholicism carried out by the Pope and the Jesuits at the Council of Trent (1545 to 1563), which widened the breach between Catholicism and Protestantism. Moreover, without regard to their fellow-confederates, they associated themselves with the most intolerant of the Catholic powers. In 1565 they allied themselves to Pope Pius IV., who promised them aid in matters of faith, made like connections with Spain and Savoy, and took counsel as to ways and means of exterminating the new faith

ERA OF REFORMATION

by force. The foreigners increased their zeal by secret agitation and by granting them great privileges.

Carlo Borromeo in particular, the Archbishop of Milan, who had carried on a counter-reformation in his own territory with rigor, selected Switzerland as the chief field of his activity. He introduced the counter-reformation into Misocco, tried to win over the Catholic states by his efforts for the erection of a Catholic theological seminary, and hoped in return to introduce the Inquisition and the Jesuits into Switzerland. His restless endeavors, however, went too far even for the Catholics, and the clergy complained of the innovations and encroachments of Carlo Borromeo. The states next requested the Pope to send his nuncio to set in order the affairs of the church. In 1580, therefore, Buonhomo, the first papal nuncio, appeared in Switzerland, and established himself in Lucerne. Borromeo, however, pursued his aim with untiring energy. He started upon his journey, traversed Ticino, the Val Blegno, the valley of the Upper Rhine, and the inner states; he was everywhere received by the people with enthusiasm, and everywhere encouraged them for the coming religious struggle, while everywhere vigorously combating all moral and ecclesiastical abuses. The nuncio was equally active; upon his tour he was not only attacked by the Reformed states and accused of inciting others against them, but even from several of the Catholic states, Fribourg and Valais, obtained no recognition, as they feared any encroachments upon their liberties. The clergy petitioned against such a foreign visitation, finding that he punished all faults and omissions with severity, and at length it became necessary to recall him. Meanwhile, however, through the influence of Borromeo and the leaders of the Catholic party, among them Melchior Lussi of Stans, and Ludwig Pfyffer of Lucerne, formidable religious combatants were introduced into Switzerland. These were the Jesuits, who arrived in Lucerne in 1574 and in Fribourg in 1581, and the Capuchins, who established themselves in Altdorf in 1581, Stans in 1582, and Appenzell in 1588. While the Jesuits were working systematically in schools and in the houses of the upper classes, the barefooted Capuchins, with their coarse cowls, became the darlings of the populace, laboring in the hovels of the common people.

Thus did the breach between the two parties grow ever wider. In 1579 the Catholic states concluded a league with the Bishop of Basle, who was eagerly carrying on the counter-reformation. This annoyed the Reformed party, who were just then zealously supporting the town of Geneva in a struggle against Savoy, and were assisting Henry of Navarre and the Huguenot party in France, while the Catholic states took the part of Savoy and of the French Catholics. Men's minds were still further inflamed by the dispute about the calendar, which began in 1582. A religious civil war had very nearly broken out. On October 5, 1586, the Catholic states of Uri, Schwyz, Unterwalden, Lucerne, Zug, Fribourg, and Soleure entered into a separate offensive and defensive alliance, known as the Borromean or Golden League,[5] for the defense and maintenance of the Catholic religion. This was a skillfully laid scheme of Ludwig Pfyffer's. The states at the same time concluded an alliance with the new Pope, Sixtus V., and in 1587 also with Philip II., of Spain, the great foe of heresy.

Thus from the time of the Council of Trent the Catholic states had become more and more estranged from their fellow-confederates. By this means the Confederation had been split into two camps, from whom it was useless to expect any united and concerted action; on the contrary, the states constantly opposed one another, either openly or in secret. This is already evident in the period between the Council of Trent and the Borromean League; not only did the Catholic states attempt a counter-reformation in all directions, but they specially resisted the accession of new members to the league who professed the principles of the Reformation.

Supported by the Catholic states, the Bishop of Basle, who had been forced to fly to Porrentruy, endeavored to obtain his restoration, and reintroduced Catholic worship in Laufen by force. In Valais, where as early as 1551 the Reformed party had grown so strong that universal tolerance and equality of rights had been decreed, the Catholic states effected the revocation of this decision, and a partial restoration of Catholic worship; and when about the end of the century the Jesuits made their appearance here too, the Protestants were openly persecuted and driven into exile.

With the help of the Catholic states, Philibert Emmanuel, Duke of Savoy, in 1564 obtained the restitution of the districts of Chablais, Genevois, and Gex, conquered by Berne in 1536, and gradually converted to the principles of the Reformation, where he caused the Catholic worship to be restored by the Jesuit Francis de Sales.

[5] So called in memory of Borromeo, who died in 1584, and because the initial letters of the treaty were illuminated in gold.

Attempts were also made to alienate the Vaud from the Bernese, but the latter succeeded in retaining it; they engaged to maintain all the liberties of the Vaud, and the peace thereupon concluded was guaranteed by France in 1565. In return, Charles Emmanuel of Savoy (from 1580) several times attempted to repossess himself of Geneva, and to establish the episcopal authority there, in which attempts he had the Catholic states, the Pope, and Spain on his side. The solicitations of Geneva to be received into the Swiss League were frustrated by the dissensions between the Federal States themselves. In 1602, after several unsuccessful attempts upon Geneva, the duke resolved to carry it by surprise, and placed an army before the town by night. A number of soldiers had already mounted the walls unnoticed by means of blackened ladders, when a shot awakened the citizens, and the Savoyards were once more repulsed. This was the so-called "Escalade" of December 21 and 22. Charles Emmanuel was once more forced to acknowledge the independence of Geneva.

The efforts of the Catholics in the Grisons were equally far from attaining their object. The religious factions here also partook of a political nature, for France and Austria alternately solicited their alliance. Under the Plantas, the Austrian party, which was laboring by command of the Pope for the restoration of Catholicism, suffered its first defeat in 1565 at the hands of the French faction under the Salis. From that time for centuries long the two parties opposed one another with the utmost ferocity and cruelty; whichever party was victorious would pass judgment for the banishment and persecution of its opponents. This could only occur in a country where, as in Rhætia, the judisdiction was under the management of the communes (*Hochgerichte*). The Catholic states sympathizing with the Catholic factions, the request of the influential Protestant League of the Ten Jurisdictions,[6] in 1567, to be received into the Confederation was denied.

Strassburg was also among the places which desired to be received into the Federal League. But the Catholic members refused this, upon which the Reformed states concluded a separate league with that town in 1588, after a number of young men from

---

[6] The Grisons (or *Graubünden*) comprised three leagues, the Gray League (*Grauerbund* or *Ligue Grise*), the League of God's House (*Gotteshausbund, Ligue de la Maison Dieu* or *Caddea*), and the League of the Ten Jurisdictions (*Zehngerichtenbund* or *Ligue des dix Droitures*).

Zurich had given proof that Strassburg did not lie too far from the Confederation, by one day taking a boat down the Limmat, the Aar, and the Rhine containing an enormous kettle full of hot lentils, which was still warm when they reached Strassburg (*Hirsbreifahrt*).

But not only were no new members received into the league on account of the breach in the Confederation, for even old members were abandoned. As early as 1548 Constance was taken by storm by the Austrians in the war of Schmalcalden, and thus cut off not only from the Federal League, but even from the Reformation itself. And in 1586 the Catholic states even ejected Protestant Mülhausen from the league.

At length the secession of the canton of Appenzell followed as an evil effect of this party system. The majority in Outer Rhodes had inclined to the Reformation, while Inner Rhodes remained true to the old faith, and adhered to the seven states. On various occasions, such as the dispute about the calendar, the introduction of the Capuchins, and the conclusion of the Spanish alliance, violent conflicts arose; and in order to avoid a civil war the Diet at last found themselves forced to arrange a separation in 1597. The Protestants of Inner Rhodes were driven into Outer Rhodes, and vice versa, and the land held in common was divided. But in Federal affairs the two halves of the canton were reckoned as having each only half a vote. In the year 1600 Inner Rhodes joined the Spanish and Borromean Leagues.

Thus during the period succeeding the Council of Trent the attitude of the Confederation toward the outer world was that of a double state with conflicting halves, and moreover the Catholic states at the instigation of Lucerne and of Ludwig Pfyffer, her great politician (the "Swiss King"), rendered effectual aid to France in her wars against the Huguenots. Whole hosts of soldiers poured from the inner cantons into France, and helped to gain the victories of Dreux in 1562, St. Denis, Jarnac, etc.; and as the Protestants supported the Huguenots a civil war had almost ensued among the Swiss in France. The situation was only altered by the accession of Henry IV. One part of the Catholics then fought for Spain, another part inclined to Henry, who was allied to the Protestants; when in 1593 Henry formally embraced Catholicism at St. Denis he was joined by the once hostile Catholic states, and peace was for a time secured within the Confederation.

Chapter VIII

RELIGIOUS WARS AND THE ARISTOCRATIC CONSTITUTIONS. 1600-1712

AFTER the division of the Confederation into two camps, and more especially after the year 1526, the periodical confirmation of the old leagues by oath—prescribed in the Federal charters—was totally neglected, and special Diets were frequently held by both Catholic and Reformed states to advise upon their affairs, while general Diets became more and more rare, and lost all significance. At the same time the relations between the factions continued to be very strained—a condition of things which was purposely aggravated by the Jesuits, the Capuchins, and the Catholic powers. Disputes were rife about the common domains and the subject-lands which belonged to both Catholic and Reformed states alike, as, for instance, between Glarus and Schwyz about Utznach, Berne and Fribourg about the Vaud, Zurich and the five states about the Thurgau. Meanwhile the antagonism between France on the one hand and the Austrian Hapsburgs together with Spain on the other hand had a decisive influence upon the internal and external relations of Switzerland. In the struggle for European supremacy these powers contended with one another for the favor of Switzerland. France triumphed at first. In 1602 Henry IV. concluded an alliance with the twelve states, which was also joined by Zurich in 1614, Zwingli's principles being abandoned. The opponents of France now did their utmost. The Count of Fuentes, the Spanish governor of Milan, distributed money with a free hand, and effected a renewal of the alliance with the Catholic states in 1604. At the entrance to the Valtelline he built the gigantic fortress which bore his name ("Fort Fuentes") and endeavored to attach the leagues of the Grisons to himself. But the Alpine passes forming a passage from Milan through the Valtelline to the Tyrol were only opened to the enemies of France by the death of Henry IV. in 1610. The Spanish and Austrian party in Rhætia, under the leadership of Rudolf Planta, triumphed over their opponents, the adherents of France and Venice. A revolt against the Plantas next broke out, headed by George Jenatsch, a minister of the Reformed church, and by a decree of 1618 the Planta family and their adherents were banished to Thusis. A tumultuous reign of terror ensued, during which the Planta faction was supported by the Catholic, and their opponents by the Reformed states of the Confederation.

So matters stood when the Thirty Years' War broke out in Germany. The religious schism in the empire fostered afresh the factions in Switzerland. The Reformed states, it is true, notably Zurich, resolved to take no active part in the struggle, nor even to support their fellow-Protestants, in order that they might not exasperate the Catholic states and possibly kindle a civil war, for which reason they also declined to make any league with the German Protestant Union. The Catholic states shared their desire of not meddling with that fatal war, and in order to preserve Switzerland from forming a battlefield for the combatants, merely wished to defend the frontiers. Hence the system of neutrality was for the first time adopted as a principle, though it had practically been in operation since 1516, inasmuch as the Confederation had not since then interfered in any foreign war as an independent party. From the commencement, however, these good intentions were only half carried out; for it would frequently happen that sometimes one party, sometimes the other, would favor the powers and the troops holding their own views, especially as the central position of the Confederation made each of the belligerent powers anxious to engage its interest, and to claim the advantages of free passage and levies of mercenaries.

These circumstances so paralyzed Switzerland that she was unable to fulfill her duties to her own fellow-confederates or to preserve her neutrality as was fitting. This is specially evident in the affairs of the Grisons, that state becoming in a most lamentable way the puppet of the combatants. During the passionate struggles between the two religious and political factions, after the decree of Thusis, a terrible reaction set in against the arbitrary rule of the Reformers, which had its origin in the Valtelline, the subject-land of the Grisons Leagues. A relative of the Plantas, named Robustelli, who was in collusion with the Catholic powers, fell upon this valley with bands of the lowest assassins, and in the massacre of the Valtelline, July, 1620, slaughtered five hundred

Protestant Grisons. The Valtelline, Bormio, and the Münsterthal were now acquired by the Spaniards and Austrians with but little trouble. In spite of the attempts of the Catholic states to block their passage, Zurich and Berne sent troops to the help of the Grisons, but they were defeated at Tirano. Mercenaries from the five states, under Beroldingen of Uri, marched to the help of their coreligionists. Now ensued the most frightful party struggle, accompanied by outbreaks of blind fury, rapine, fire, and sword. Pompey Planta, the brother of Rudolf, was attacked and slain in 1621 by the Protestants in the Engadine, under the conduct of Pastor George Jenatsch. The troops of the five states and of the Spaniards were repulsed. But the very same year the tide turned: the Spaniards and Austrians made a fresh invasion; Jenatsch was obliged to fly, and now became a soldier. Once more the Austrians were driven out, and once more they returned; and in 1629, the year when the power of the emperor was at its height, an imperial army marched upon Coire (*Chur*) and conquered the leagues for the third time, while the Confederates left that land completely in the lurch.

France next endeavored to interpose and to undermine the Austrian power in the Grisons. By the command of Richelieu, the Duc de Rohan, the former leader of the Huguenots, appeared with an army, and in 1635, with the help of Jenatsch, who had returned and taken the command, defeated the Austrians and Spaniards. But when France refused to accede to the requests of the leagues, that their subject-lands should be preserved to them unimpaired as formerly, the mood of the Grisons changed; Jenatsch deserted the French and went over to the Spanish party, raised a revolt against the French, and in 1637 drove them completely out of the country.

The strife of parties raged for some years longer. Rudolf Planta, a son of the murdered Pompey, next arrived in the land in 1639 and attacked and killed George Jenatsch at a festival, with the assistance of disguised accomplices. Tranquillity was gradually restored, and in 1639 a perpetual peace was concluded with Spain. The Valtelline was restored to the leagues, but on terms favorable to the Catholic religion; and Spain might now send bodies of troops unhindered over the passes of the Grisons. Austria, with whom peace was likewise concluded, consented to sell her rights over the Ten Jurisdictions and the Lower Engadine. It was, however, primarily due to the divisions among the Confederates that the three leagues thus became the puppets of foreign powers.

The northern frontiers fared hardly any better as regarded protection than those of the southeast. While the five states granted frequent passage to Spanish troops, Zurich favored those of Sweden, and this opposition often led to unpleasant collisions. On one occasion Bernese troops hastening to the relief of their fellow-confederates of Mülhausen, then hard pressed, were overtaken in the Klus, near Balsthal, by peasants of Soleure, and many of them slain (1632). A civil war was nearly breaking out in Switzerland. When in the following year the Swedish General Horn marched past Stein (Canton Zurich), and through the Thurgau to Constance, the five states took Kilian Kesselring, the Protestant governor of the Thurgau, prisoner, thinking that he had summoned the Swedes into the country, and that Zurich, of which Kesselring was a citizen, was in collusion with Horn. Kesselring was long kept a prisoner, and it was not until the Protestants threatened to prepare for war that he was released for a high ransom. The five states also renewed their league with Spain, which caused Berne and Zurich to consider the advisability of a formal alliance with Sweden, whose ruin they considered would be their own.

Basle occupied a specially difficult position, being most exposed to the enemy, and was only able to preserve her neutrality with great difficulty, since she was totally forsaken by the other states; her frontiers were violated in 1624 by Tilly's troops, and in 1636 Bernhard of Weimar crossed the territory of Basle into the Fricktal. Schaffhausen and Mülhausen were in similar situations, so that they likewise were often in great danger; and finally, in 1632, Rotwil, one of the allied states, was totally abandoned by the Protestants because it had taken part with Austria, and assisted the five states.

Thus the weakness of the Confederation became everywhere apparent, and yet this war might so well have led them to greater unity; for in moments of most serious danger (as for instance in 1636, when Basle and Soleure were threatened by Bernhard, Duke of Weimar, and in 1647 when Wrangel and Turenne approached the Swiss frontier) they recognized that unity alone could save them, and that they must for their own security make common cause to keep all foreign armies at a distance from Swiss soil.

Hence in the course of the war a scheme was several times devised for a joint military system of land defense (*Defensionale*), which was at length formally drawn up in 1647. But in 1648 the much-desired peace was concluded in Münster and Osnabrück.

When the question arose as to the representation of the Confederation at Münster, and the maintenance of Swiss interests, their lack of unity seemed likely to ruin everything. Notwithstanding the Peace of Basle of 1499, in the latter times inhabitants of Mülhausen and Basle had repeatedly been harassed and sued by the court of the Imperial Chamber; Basle therefore endeavored to induce the rest of the states to send a joint Federal deputation to Münster, which should procure the unconditional release of all Confederate citizens from the jurisdiction of the Imperial Chamber. But the Catholic states would take no part, and it was only at the instigation of the Reformed states that Rudolf Wettstein, the gallant burgomaster of Basle, conducted the negotiations at the Peace Congress. By his ability and the activity of his single-minded patriotism, and no less by the efforts of other eminent Confederates with foreign powers, of whom Major General Hans Ludwig von Erlach, Zwier von Evibach, Landammann of Uri, may be noted, and by the coöperation of the imperial ambassador, it came to pass that in the "Peace of Westphalia" the formal declaration of the total separation of Switzerland from the German empire was published.

In the fourteenth and fifteenth centuries, when the Confederate States were forming their leagues, the inhabitants of every town or of every state enjoyed, generally speaking, equal rights. The freedom of a city might be acquired without payment, or for a small sum, and the road to office and dignity was open to all. In the seventeenth century it was quite otherwise. In all parts there arose a small class within each community who gradually succeeded in obtaining exclusive possession of the rights of government, and becoming the sole bearers of political power. As early as the sixteenth century this phase had commenced. It had its origin in the fact that as the population increased, both in the towns and in the several villages, the original citizens and residents held more and more aloof from the mere tenants or copyholders, fixed a certain sum for the purchase of citizenship (formerly gratuitously bestowed), raised this sum increasingly, and tried in every way to hinder the admission of strangers. At the same time in many places the distribution of pensions paid to the citizens of individual states by foreign powers contributed greatly to limit the number of the "citizens," of participators. In this way the influence of individual families who had attained riches and eminence by means of trade and manufactures, or by pensions and mercenary service, made itself increasingly felt, and such families by various means converted their offices into hereditary successions, and possessed themselves exclusively of the government.

The right of the governing body to make up their number themselves served them as an effectual means to this end. Both the small and great councils in the cities had the right of completing their number themselves, or of mutually electing one another. Hence it tacitly became the rule that appointments to positions in the councils should be held for life, or even hereditary; in Lucerne, for instance, the son succeeded the father, and the brother the brother. But when the end could not be attained lawfully, unlawful means, such as bribery, were brought to bear. Thus the burghers separated themselves into a distinct caste, with the sole and hereditary right of governing the whole state. The road to any government appointment was totally barred to all who were not by birth freemen of the city. Members of the government took the title of "Esquire" (*Junker*), placed the attribute "*von*" before their surnames, and adopted arms and crests.

Meanwhile an important difference became evident in the various states. In the democratic cantons the *Landsgemeinden* at first formed an effectual barrier against the formation of a system of government by powerful families; they passed severe laws against the fraudulent acquisition and the inheriting of offices. Similarly in the guild cities of Zurich, Basle, and Schaffhausen the guilds prevented individual families from obtaining exclusive sway, so that here the government could never be completely monopolized by a limited number who should exclude others by law. In the cities of what was formerly Burgundian Switzerland, on the other hand, where the guilds never attained any political significance, as in Berne, Fribourg, and Soleure, and also in Lucerne, a purely aristocratic system was gradually formed, or as it was called, after a life system of ancient Rome, a "Patriciate." In Fribourg, for instance, it was determined in 1627 to exclude all families who were not at that time within the pale of the council from holding any public offices; a "secret chamber" of twenty-four members elected the great and small councils and all government officials, and completed itself; thus the political rights were limited to only seventy-one families.

No city, however, guarded the rights of aristocratic families more strictly than Berne, where in 1640 Frischherz, the treasurer, was executed for attacking prevalent abuses, and in 1646 Müsslin, the former bailiff, was sentenced to a heavy fine, a humble apology and banishment for making use of invectives.

The formation of these aristocracies in Switzerland was quite in keeping with the general tendency of European policy at that time, for in all parts in other countries of Europe efforts were being made to extend and strengthen the powers of government. The Reformation itself had contributed to this, for in the Reformed states the power of the church had been by law transferred to the governments, while in the Catholic states the government lent her arm to the church, to defend and expand it. This union of ecclesiastical and political interests tended, both in republics and in monarchical states, to the revival of despotism; hence every Swiss state now began to look anxiously to the preservation of her sovereign rights. The chief aim of the various states was to increase their power in all directions, and to suffer no encroachments from without. They cut themselves totally adrift from one another, as from alien states.

Great as were the differences between the internal conditions of the aristocracies in the towns, they all held a like position with regard to the rural population, whom they endeavored to reduce to the condition of subjects with no voice in the government. These endeavors had become very evident by the latter half of the fifteenth century; then, however, the country folk made an energetic resistance, as in the time of Waldmann. The position of the several territories was usually settled by covenants; from the first the various districts in the common domains had enjoyed peculiar liberties, which were guaranteed to them by the Confederates when they took possession; such was also the case with the territories acquired by the various cities. If at any time these were curtailed or disregarded, the peasants would obtain from their lords fresh charters of recognition, such as the Charters of Waldmann (*Waldmannischen Spruchbriefe*) in Zurich (1489), and the "Treaties of Kappel" there (1531), and likewise in Berne by the latter treaties.

Warned by the refractoriness and vigilance of the people, the governments for a time adopted another course, and tried to establish more friendly relations with their subjects. Hence from the end of the fifteenth century it became the rule in Zurich and Berne to consult the peasantry and advise with them upon all important acts of government, such as the declaration of war, the conclusion of peace, alliances, taxes, etc. During the course of the sixteenth century, however, the idea gradually obtained that the authorities wielded the sword of protection and punishment in God's name, and that the divine law required obedience from subjects in all cases. The example of the monarchs of that time, who displayed their sovereign magnificence as " gracious lords ruling in God's stead," and who required unconditional obedience from their subjects, was imitated by the authorities in the republics. Just as the former sought to set aside the authority of parliaments and states, so the latter tried to destroy the influence of the people, more especially after an exclusive ruling faction had arisen within the cities themselves. Berne appealed to the rural district in 1589 for the last time, Zurich in 1620 and 1640; divers individuals in Zurich were of opinion that it was contrary to the liberties of the town to render any account to purchased subjects.

Every effort was made to deprive the people of the rights and liberties formerly conferred and increased, or to bury them in oblivion; thus Zurich withdrew the charters of Waldmann and of Kappel unnoticed, and Berne simply caused the charters of Kappel and the liberties of the Vaud to be effaced. The authorities next tried to abolish the many diverse customs and legal conditions, and to reduce the inhabitants of all parts of the land into a similar condition of subjection. The towns, moreover, were anxious to secure financial advantages for themselves by fresh claims and privileges. That which Waldmann had already attempted was now carried into execution; the towns appropriated numerous monopolies (such as the sale of salt and powder and the practice of industries), and restricted trade in general—the sale of cattle by a duty called *Trattengeld*,[1] the sale of wine by another called *Ungeld* or *Ohmgeld*. The taxes caused even more bitterness than these institutions. The levying of taxes from time to time had commenced indeed at the end of the fifteenth century; the subject-

---

[1] The expression comes from *traite;* in their wrath the peasants called it scornfully *Krottengeld*.

lands, however, were unaccustomed to it, and regarded it as an unlawful innovation.

The peasants of Switzerland prided themselves upon being, in many respects, better situated than those of other lands; after the Reformation a very small proportion of them were bondmen, the greater number being free landowners, who rejoiced in their prosperity and in the consciousness of a great past and Republican liberties. They therefore watched the temper of the authorities very carefully, and were quick to resent any encroachments upon their traditional liberties, more especially in the matter of fresh impositions. Thus in 1570 the peasantry of Lucerne marched upon the town on account of some such innovation; in 1594 Basle with difficulty succeeded in quelling an armed revolt of the peasants against the town (*Rappenkrieg,* or " War of Farthings "); in 1599 the peasantry around the lake of Zurich and in the bailiwick of Grüningen rose in revolt about a war tax. The peasants refused to admit the excuse of the towns, that the Thirty Years' War had entailed extraordinary outlay for fortifications. When in 1641 Berne levied a property tax without reference to the country district, a rising took place in the neighborhood of Thun and in the Emmental, and a civil war must have ensued had not the Reformed states interposed. Some years later Kiburg, Wädenswil, and Knonau refused to pay a tax levied by Zurich, relying upon the charters of Waldmann and Kappel; they demanded greater rights and liberties equal to those of the citizens, and when these were denied they flew to arms. Zurich, however, succeeded in effecting a reconciliation with the county of Kiburg, took possession of Wädenswil in 1646 by an armed force, and represented to the inhabitants that they deserved to be cut down to a man without quarter. Four ringleaders were executed, others condemned to pay fines; the men of Wädenswil were compelled—" to the sorrow of many honorable patriots," as writes Waser, the noble burgomaster of Zurich—to implore upon their knees that their charters of liberties should be confiscated! In other bailiwicks and districts these were withdrawn by the bailiffs; but one remained, and that in Küssnach, on the Lake of Zurich.

Finding that isolated risings were easily suppressed, the peasantry took the earliest opportunity of combining for a united effort. In almost every country of Europe the lower classes were at that time in a violent ferment; efforts were being everywhere made to shake off the yoke of despotism. In England the Parliament and people were successful in their rebellion against absolute monarchy in the revolution, usually styled the Great Rebellion; in France people and nobles combined against ministerial despotism (the Fronde); in Catalonia and Naples the people rose against the oppressive taxes and arbitrary rule of Spain. Might not the free peasants of Switzerland also hope for success, if they could only make common cause? An occasion offered itself immediately after the close of the Thirty Years' War.

During the Thirty Years' War numberless fugitives established themselves in Switzerland with their fortunes, that country being but little if at all disturbed by the war, and consequently the prices of houses, land, and provisions rose. The peasants of Switzerland made splendid sales, and enjoyed a period of luxury; the mercenaries, too, had ample opportunity of making money in foreign service. After the close of the war, however, the fugitives withdrew, the value and price of provisions, and consequently of land also, dropped with every year and every month, and the occasion for foreign service was also at an end. Want of money and discontent everywhere ensued.

In addition to all this, peculiar innovations were now made in the coinage, which greatly embarrassed the peasantry. During the war, in order to raise money, the authorities had issued a base coinage. Now, in 1652, they suddenly once more debased the small coin, and even called in some. In Berne one batz [2] became worth half a batz, in Fribourg and Soleure three-quarters. This was a sensible loss to the peasants, and moreover sufficient time was not allowed them for exchange. The people of Entlebuch were the first to rise. Often enough already they had joined issue with the authorities of Lucerne, when the latter had indulged in any encroachments upon their liberties and rights. They sent delegates to the government on January 8, 1653, to implore help in this financial perplexity, and the abolition of the latest restrictions on trade, manufactures, and commerce. They found small hearing, however; a member of the committee of the Council encountered them angrily, called them troublesome, pig-headed fellows, who must be brought to order by severity and rigor; they would never be quiet till four or five hundred French-Swiss, sword-proof and sure-footed, should be sent to bring them to reason! At a second discussion, when the people of Entlebuch further demanded

[2] A Swiss coin = four kreutzers.

the abolition of prosecutions for debt and a reduction of rents, the magistrate confronted them with the rights of the powers ordained of God. But a sturdy fellow of Entlebuch exclaimed: "Yes, yes! you are of God, if you rule righteously, but of the devil if you rule unrighteously!" Negotiations availing nothing, the men of Entlebuch proceeded to arm themselves with clubs and battle-axes. At the same time they endeavored to form a combination and union with the other bailiwicks, and prevailed upon a large majority to join them; on February 26, 1653, the people of ten bailiwicks assembled at a *Landsgemeinde* at Wolhusen in Entlebuch, and solemnly pledged themselves to mutual assistance for the redress of their grievances. Certain Bernese peasants assisted at this league, and by their means the revolt spread into Bernese territory, particularly into the neighboring Emmental, where young Nicholas Leuenberger incited the peasants to revolt. On March 14 peasants from Berne and Lucerne held a joint assembly at Langnau in the Emmental, declared their grievances and encouraged the Bernese Aargau to join them also, whereupon the peasants in the Aargau and in the territory of Soleure and Basle likewise rose. Then first came into use the party epithets of the "Soft ones" (*Linden*) or adherents of the government, and the "Hard ones" (*Harten*) or opponents of the government.

These early movements, however, were quickly suppressed; Lucerne, like Zurich in 1489, requested Federal mediation, and assembled troops from the territories which had remained true to her when the peasants advanced upon the town. The rebellious peasants, powerless against the fortified town, were forced to agree to a truce on March 18, declaring the League of Wolhusen null and void. In the Aargau the peasants subsided after preventing Aarau from being garrisoned by Federal troops; the governments of Basle, Berne, and Soleure came to terms with the insurgents, by which certain imposts were abated.

The Diet, however, exasperated them afresh by calling their grievances "the futile excuses of bankrupts," and by resolving to lend ready aid to the authorities of every state against insurrections of the peasantry, without reference to the justice or injustice of the revolt. The lords based this decision upon the provisions of the Covenant of Stans, that the Federal states should render one another aid against rebellious subjects. This demeanor on the part of the Diet soon fanned the still glowing embers into flame. The peasants everywhere regretted that they had allowed themselves to be so easily appeased; in Entlebuch the discontent was fanned by Christian Schibi, of Escholzmatt, a hoary warrior of powerful physique; the inhabitants of the Emmental once more ranged themselves under Leuenberger, and fresh ferments arose in the territories of Soleure and Basle. In opposition to the "League of the Lords" arose the idea of a great "League of the People" (or subjects). Hence, on April 23, 1653, a Federal *Landsgemeinde* was assembled at Sumiswald, composed of delegates from the peasantry of Lucerne, Berne, Soleure, and Basle, and made a compact, by which they engaged to defend one another with their property and their lives, to act in concert and to compel the authorities to abolish the new impositions; Nicholas Leuenberger himself was elected president, much against his will. At a fresh *Landsgemeinde* at Hutwil on April 30, which 5000 peasants attended, the people solemnly ratified this compact. The peasants vowed body and soul, life and property, for mutual defense. Conscious of a righteous cause, and full of indignation at the injustice of the new system of government, they rose above all the religious differences which had sundered the Confederation for centuries past; Catholics and Protestants realized that they were members of the same stock, one united people, as had once been the case with the Confederates at the sealing of the first leagues during the danger menaced by the Hapsburgs. The tradition of the oath on the Rütli was vividly present in their minds: three men of Entlebuch represented the "Three Tells" at an official assembly at Schüpfheim, and many a man looked back upon the "time of William Tell" as a sort of "Paradise Lost." The demands of the peasants were not exorbitant; the majority only wanted the abolition of the new imposts and restrictions, the restoration of their former better legal status, and the establishment of greater confidence between the people and their rulers. Yet even this was not to be conceded.

At the end of April and the beginning of May the Diet decreed that the rising should be suppressed by force of arms, whereupon the several states summoned their contingents. The peasants meanwhile had won the Free Bailiwicks over to their cause, and displayed the greatest activity in all directions; they assembled in crowds, and guarded all the roads and passes. Nicholas Leuenberger, their leader, at first enjoyed unqualified respect, and exercised dictatorial authority, to which a ready obedience was yielded.

It was originally intended to take Berne by surprise; Leuenberger, however, confined himself to threats, and a hollow peace was concluded on May 24, in which Berne made many fair promises. This "Peace of Murifeld" was broken by both parties. Leuenberger undermined his own position by this course, and had no longer sufficient authority to restrain his followers from acts of violence, and from invading the territories of Lucerne and Aargau. Berne also now broke the terms of the peace, and summoned auxiliaries from the Vaud and Fribourg. Meanwhile an army from Zurich and from the eastern states, being ignorant of the peace of Murifeld, advanced toward Mellingen, under the conduct of General Conrad Werdmüller, who had occupied Wädenswil in 1646. Thereupon the Bernese peasants combined afresh, took up arms once more under Leuenberger, and hastened to the help of the army of the rebels then in Aargau, commanded by Schibi. But Werdmüller's troops, though few in number, were better armed and better trained; they had, moreover, acquired an exact knowledge of the peasants' plan of action through a citizen of Zurich. A heated combat at Wohlenswil, on June 3, therefore terminated in a defeat of the peasantry. Two days later, on June 5, General Zwier of Uri attacked the peasants of Lucerne at the bridge of Gislikon, but was forced to retreat, and on June 8 Sigmund von Erlach, the Bernese general, gained a victory at Herzogenbuchsee over the troops which Leuenberger had again assembled for the struggle. The peasants of Basle also yielded. The last act of the tragedy ended, where it began, in Entlebuch. When the government required the oath of allegiance, the "Three Tells" raised a revolt; but this ended when, in September, 1653, the leaders died.

The victorious rulers were merciless in their sentences; Leuenberger and Schibi were tortured and beheaded, and a number of prisoners were fearfully tormented, mutilated, and put to death. Thus the cause of the peasants, which had made such a brilliant start, was completely shattered by dissensions, imprudence, and treachery, and remained in abeyance for almost a hundred and fifty years. The struggles for liberty in Switzerland, therefore, shared the fate of those in other continental lands, all of which were obliged to succumb; and here, as in Spain and France, only afforded a fair field for despotism to strike its roots the deeper and more firmly.

The aristocratic development reached its perfection in the

latter half of the century. In Berne, Soleure, and Fribourg admission to the rights of citizenship was totally suspended from 1680 to 1690, in Soleure with the express condition: Until the number of reigning families be reduced to twenty-five! In Berne the governing families or "patricians" disputed among themselves for rank and title. Three distinct classes began to be recognized; the first and most honored was entitled the "highly-respected nobility" (*wohledelfeste*), the second the "respected nobility" (*edelfeste*), and the third the "nobility" (*feste*) only. Violations of these formalities were considered punishable offenses. The most powerful families were those of Steiger, Wattenwyl, Stürler, Graffenried, etc., by whom most of the appointments were occupied. Efforts were also made in the guild cities to establish a similar rule of powerful families, and these towns also suspended the admission of citizens. In Zurich, the most conspicuous of the guild towns, the guilds and city companies lost their original significance. The great council was no longer elected by the guilds, but only by a committee of them, who formed at the same time a portion of the council. In Schaffhausen and Basle the council, which was renewed by itself from a few families, was all powerful; at Basle, in 1666, all the more important positions in the council were in the hands of the single family of Burckhardt. Moreover, it frequently happened that individual families resorted to all sorts of intrigues and corruption in order to attain to power; and these often became so bad that it was found necessary to introduce the ballot at elections, as was the case in Schaffhausen in 1689, and in Berne in 1710.

There was no longer any talk of communicating with the rural population about political matters; the country people were even excluded from all public appointments. All upper bailiffs and country bailiffs, officers, captains, parish clerks, and ministers were citizens, and the habit of command imbued the citizens with an idea of higher rank, as though they were of better blood than the country folk, whom they had nevertheless, a hundred and fifty years earlier, declared to be equal members of the state and dear kinsmen. In the civic cantons, moreover, the whole of the public burdens pressed upon the poor country districts; the inhabitants of the town and capitalists did not contribute a farthing; for instance, while the property of citizens might be inherited with freedom, a legacy duty had to be paid for the very smallest inheritance in the country. The rulers, bailiffs, officials, clerks, beneficiaries, and such-like grew rich upon tithes, Lenten offerings, and feudal rents, but needed to pay nothing themselves. Even men holding offices and dignities ventured publicly to attack and censure this aristocratic system with its abuses, as for example Pastor (*Antistes*) Werenfels in Basle, and Pastor (*Antistes*) Breitinger in Zurich. In certain states public dissatisfaction found vent from time to time in revolutions and rebellions, such as occurred in Schaffhausen in 1688, Basle in 1691, and Zurich in 1713; but these efforts for the most part met with small success, or were suppressed and rendered abortive.

The Peasants' War had called attention to many failings in the Federal laws and their administration. Remedies were devised, and in May, 1655, a proposition was made at the Diet to draw up a common uniform Federal charter. As the Confederation in the main merely represented a number of heterogeneous alliances between individual states, and therefore certain states holding unequal positions were somewhat estranged from one another, a wholesome national unity might well have been introduced had this decision been carried into execution. Waser, Burgomaster of Zurich, and Colonel Sigmund von Erlach, of Berne (nephew of the major general), drew up a Federal charter embodying the several previous alliances in one comprehensive whole. But when the time for its acceptance arrived, the older and more privileged states could not make up their minds to sacrifice their advantages in favor of a common league; moreover, men feared the supremacy of Zurich and Berne, which had once formed Zwingli's ideal, and refused to give up the separate leagues. The proposed alteration therefore fell to the ground, and as if in defiance the Catholic states renewed the Borromean League in 1655, and made a fresh alliance with France, contrary to a former prohibition of the Diet. Even the Reformed states now contemplated a separate league, and entered into negotiations with Holland and England. So the two parties once more confronted one another in hostile fashion, almost as they had done just before the wars of Kappel. How differently had the despised peasants, the "heretics and rebels," stood the test, when in spite of all religious differences they had revived the Federal sense of brotherhood by a common league! The breach between the two religious camps was so great that an event in itself insignificant led to a civil war.

Thirty-eight Protestants of Art, who had formed a secret

Reformed commune, and endeavored to spread their religious tenets, fled from persecution to Zurich, and, supported by that town, demanded the restoration of their property. Schwyz, however, not only refused this, but also punished the kindred of the fugitives most cruelly and demanded the surrender of the fugitives from Zurich; presuming upon its cantonal sovereignty, it would hear nothing of Federal judicial proceedings. Finding it hopeless to attempt an amicable settlement, Zurich impetuously took the law into her own hands, and declared war on January 6, 1656, in the name of all the Reformed states, accusing Schwyz of violating the peace of 1531. Kappel was at once garrisoned, the Aargau and Thurgau protected. General Rudolf Werdmüller (a cousin of Conrad) advanced upon Rapperswil with 10,000 men; but while he was aimlessly and hopelessly besieging that little town, he left the Bernese, who had marched slowly toward Aargau, completely exposed to the main army of the enemy. The Bernese on their part, heedless and undisciplined, next occupied Vilmergen, but were surprised and defeated on January 23 by troops from Lucerne. Through the mediation of the neutral states and of foreign powers a truce was effected, and by the exertions of Wettstein, Burgomaster of Basle, peace was concluded at Baden on March 7. In this peace the views of the Catholic states were adopted, as of the victorious party, and hence for centuries Federal interests were sacrificed to the separatist spirit of those states or to cantonal sovereignty. The sovereign rights of every state were to remain forever undisputed; and above all, every state was to be at liberty to use her own discretion in matters concerning the migration of those holding different religious views. Just as in 1648 the sovereign independence of the members of the German empire had been assured, so it was now with the members of the Swiss League; with the result that the political system of Switzerland also presented a like picture of a maimed body and a powerless organism.

While in the internal governments of the individual states interested motives and selfishness appear as the prevalent evils of the time, an incredible inconsistency is apparent in their dealings with foreign powers, as in this respect also every state acted according to her own will and pleasure; the Swiss were never more shamelessly sold to the highest bidder than at this time. Thus France used Switzerland completely to her own advantage. The alliance of 1602 expiring in 1651, the Court of Paris was anxious for its renewal. De la Barde, the envoy, by threats, promises, and various artifices enlisted first the Catholic and then the Reformed states in his cause. Disregarding the urgent warnings of Wettstein, the patriotic Burgomaster of Basle, the thirteen states renewed the old alliance with France at Soleure on September 24, 1663. In return for certain advantages of trade and commerce, for an annuity of 3000 francs for every canton, and the pay of the troops, the Confederation engaged to allow France to levy from 6000 to 16,000 men. On November 18 this alliance was confirmed by oath in Notre Dame, in Paris; the Swiss, however, were grievously mortified, and Louis XIV. did not abide by the terms of the alliance. There could be no talk of the payment of arrears (30 millions), for Moulier, the crafty French ambassador, had easily succeeded in bribing the states by gifts and false promises.

For the rest, the Confederation took up a neutral position during the great wars of Louis XIV., as in the Thirty Years' War. But the task of preserving an armed neutrality was again left unfulfilled, and any uniform measures which they adopted proved but transitory.

In the first war of Louis, that in the Netherlands (1666-1668), the Confederation should have protected Franche Comté, which, according to ancient treaties, had been included in the Swiss neutrality. When, in January, 1668, it was attacked by a French army, in whose ranks were even some Swiss troops, the states actually united in a decision that the mercenaries should be withdrawn and all French levies prohibited. The Reformed states at the same time revived the notion of the *Defensionale,* adopted during the Thirty Years' War; the danger brought the Catholics to their side, so that a common military system now took a definite form. A council of war, consisting of delegates from every canton or state, and a war exchequer, supplied by subsidies from the several states, were established; every state was to contribute a certain contingent of troops to the Federal army, which was affixed at 40,000 men. This course of action, if continued, might in time have proved the means of an important advance in the Federal constitution, the first step toward national unity; but France soon knew how to draw the states back to her side and to shake their good resolutions. Moulier the ambassador began by negotiating with each state separately, and the prohibition of levies immediately fell to the ground: both the Catholic and the Reformed states once more sent mercenaries to Louis. By the Peace of Aix-la-Chapelle the latter was obliged to restore Franche Comté.

During the second war, that against Holland (1672-1678), Louis XIV. violated the treaties outrageously by leading Swiss mercenaries to take the field against Protestant and republican Holland. Erlach's Bernese regiment at first refused to cross the Rhine, and Captain Rahn of Zurich returned home. Louis was quietly allowed to take permanent possession of Franche Comté. The *Defensionale* was powerless to effect any practical union of the states, and remained a well-meant project. The Catholic cantons, encouraged by the Pope, labored to oppose it as a "work of heresy"; Schwyz complained that the younger states might command the older ones, and therefore withdrew from it, and was soon followed by the rest of the Catholic cantons (1676-1680).

Strassburg, the old ally of the Confederates, fell to Louis, like Franche Comté, in 1681. He even threatened the Swiss by erecting the great fortress of Hüningen opposite Basle. The Huguenots, whom he expelled in 1685, found refuge in the Reformed states. Mercenaries flocked to France in crowds during the later wars of Louis. In the war in the Palatinate (1688-1697) about 35,000 fought at his side with a courage and heroism worthy of a better cause. Louis owed his brilliant victories in this war chiefly to the bravery of the Swiss mercenaries. How many of them shed their blood in the cause of the foreign despot is shown by the expressions of Stuppa, the chief mercenary leader, who, when Louvois spoke reproachfully of the amount of gold which France had bestowed upon the Swiss, saying that a military road might be paved with *thalers* from Paris to Basle, answered quickly: "That is possible; but a canal from Basle to Paris might be filled with the blood shed by the Swiss in your service!"

It was therefore vain to hope for the preservation of neutrality at home; in the moment of need unity of action was always wanting. The Reformed states gradually inclined more and more to the side of the Protestant powers of the north, Holland, England, and Prussia, and especially in the war of the Spanish succession (1700-1713), when they combined in opposition to France. Hence they also favored the interests of the allies with regard to the principality of Neuchâtel. Here the reigning dynasty expired in 1707, and Louis XIV. was anxious to confer the principality upon a French prince. Neuchâtel hastily renewed her civil alliance with the Swiss towns, and favored the hereditary claims of the Prussian king, which were likewise supported by Switzerland. On November 3, 1707, the estates of Neuchâtel elected King Frederick of Prussia as their prince, and this transfer of Neuchâtel to Prussia was subsequently ratified by the European Peace of Utrecht in 1713. From this time forward military service in Holland was specially popular in Switzerland; the Protestant Swiss felt themselves more akin to the Dutch in faith, in political views, and in simplicity of life than to the Catholic, monarchical, and aristocratic French. Meanwhile Austrian, French, and English gold still exercised its force of attraction among them, and Switzerland became a recruiting ground for all nations.

Amid the confusion of foreign wars the states were constantly at variance among themselves about their ecclesiastical and political rights, chiefly in regard to the common domains, where their rights of dominion came into collision. Trivial occurrences often alarmed both Protestants and Catholics, so that many times civil war seemed imminent, as in 1664, when an attempt was made to interfere with Protestant worship in the neighborhood of Wigoldingen (in the Thurgau), and in 1694, when a similar effort was made to introduce Catholic worship side by side with the Protestant at Wartau, in the Rhine valley. The Spanish war of succession accentuated religious differences, and finally troubles in the Toggenburg led to a fresh resort to arms. The religious and political liberties of this district were constantly threatened by the abbots of St. Gall and their tyrannical officials. Supported by Schwyz and Lucerne, the abbots were perpetually extending their princely power and endeavoring to secure the supremacy of the Catholic religion, to the exclusion of the influence of Zurich, which was allied to Toggenburg.

Abbot Leodegar Bürgisser now forced the inhabitants of Toggenburg, in the interests of the Catholic states, to construct a great road through the "Hummelwald," in order to facilitate communication between the five states and the territories of St. Gall, while separating Zurich, Glarus, and the Grisons. Opposition arising, however, and Zurich inciting the Toggenburg folk to revolt, with his usual equivocal policy—the saying went that he "sometimes put on Suabian breeches, sometimes Swiss"—he concluded, in 1702, an alliance with the emperor, who had raised him to the rank of a prince of the empire. By this he made enemies of the states of Schwyz and Glarus, and so defeated his own ends. Nothing daunted, however, he ingratiated himself with Zurich and Berne as easily as with the emperor, alarmed the Catholic states by this alliance, and forced them to conform to his will. Schwyz engaged to render help to the abbot, and required Toggenburg to separate from Zurich and Berne, to whom she had applied in the cause of religious liberty. But the Toggenburg folk considered their liberty in danger, took up arms, and called Zurich and Berne to their aid. The latter immediately took up their cause. Troops from Zurich occupied the old district of St. Gall, took Wil (May 22), the monastery of St. Gall, and the Rheintal. The Bernese occupied the Free Bailiwicks and took Mellingen, Bremgarten, and also Baden, where they demolished the fortress. The Catholic states were divided and when some suggested a peace, the exasperated Catholic populace arose, and 4000 armed men precipitated themselves upon the Free Bailiwicks. Once again, as in 1656, a battle was fought at Vilmergen on July 25, 1712, but this time the Protestants were victorious, although the Catholics were only induced to yield by the advance of the Zurich troops upon Rapperswil, Schwyz, and Zug, and by fresh expeditions on the part of the Bernese. By the Peace of Aarau, on August 11, the five states were excluded from any share in the government of the county of Baden and the lower part of the Free Bailiwicks, while Berne was admitted to the share in the government of the Thurgau, the Rheintal, and the upper and lower Free Bailiwicks. Zurich, with Berne and Glarus, took Rapperswil and Hurden under her protection, and thus obtained a strong point of support against Catholic Schwyz. Peace was not effected between Toggenburg and the abbot till 1718; the political and religious liberties of the district were secured, and in return it submitted to the abbot.

This event destroyed the supremacy of the Catholic states established by the first war of Vilmergen. Henceforward success and power lay on the side of the Reformed party, and Zwingli's plan of making Zurich and Berne sovereign states seemed about to be realized. But the Catholic states felt the sting deeply, and therefore mutual aversion afterward grew into an actual division and breach, so that thenceforth there were literally two Confederations in existence side by side.

Outwardly considered, the aristocracy developed a certain splendor and opulence, and presented an appearance of no inconsiderable prosperity, especially in the administration. The general conditions and necessities of the time led to many useful institutions. France, in particular, under Richelieu and Louis XIV., presented an example of an ostentatious political administration, which was eagerly imitated both by princes and by Republican governments. In Berne, Zurich, Zug, Basle, and even in Soleure, Lucerne, and Stans, public almshouses, hospitals, orphan asylums, improved houses of correction, and prisons, were established. The governments of Zurich, Berne, Basle, and Zug made more extensive provision than formerly for scholastic institutions, scientific collections and libraries, for commerce and industry. In Berne and Zurich the government bought up large stores of fruit to aid the country districts in times of need and scarcity; about the middle of the century a postal system, imitating that of other lands, was adopted in those states; and in 1690 Berne also introduced manufactures at the expense of the state. A number of splendid public buildings of that period, in the late Renaissance style, still adorn the principal towns of Switzerland, as for example the *Rathaüser* in Zurich and Lucerne. Berne drained the Kander, raised Morges into a place of considerable trade, and endeavored to connect the lakes of Neuchâtel and Geneva.

Soleure, the seat of the French ambassador, and Berne, the haughty patrician city, attained the greatest magnificence. The former state amassed considerable treasure, so that it was able to lend vast sums to the French Government, and to erect many handsome buildings, such as the arsenal, the embassy, the town hall, water supply (*Brunnenleitung*), and the bridge of Olten; while Berne made all the arrangements of a great state. The government managed the several branches of the administration by means of separate chambers—the chambers of war, of salt, of corn, of trade, and of appeal; Berne was also able to lend to all the banks of Europe, and her public treasure excited the envy and covetousness of other nations. The authorities of the various states vied with one another in their efforts to further the material welfare of their subjects in "fatherly" fashion, to support them in times of misfortune, of bad harvests, of famine, etc., and to check beggary, pauperism, and the like by numerous mandates. Viewed externally, many parts of Switzerland presented a more cheering appearance than the numerous provinces of other lands, mostly depopulated and devastated by war.

Together with the administration, the aristocracy paid special attention to science and art. Beautiful private houses, some of them absolute palaces, arose, as in Berne, Frauenfeld, and Schaffhausen, and the Fruler palace in Näfels. The apartments of wealthy burghers and of officials and all public buildings were beautifully decorated and furnished. Paintings on glass and artistic stoves formed the chief decoration, representing historical scenes, studies from nature and from daily life with wonderful delicacy and refinement, and bearing witty verses and merry proverbs.

Manifold progress was made in the higher studies. A society in Zurich established in 1630 the public library for citizens, the town library at the *Wasserkirche,* and this about thirty years later already numbered 6000 volumes; in 1636 the town library of Schaffhausen was founded, while the libraries of Berne and Basle were considerably increased and extended. From the ranks of the aristocracy, especially in Zurich, arose notable men of learning, who cultivated theology, and in close connection with that the study of languages and history. Johann Heinrich Hottinger, of Zurich (1620-1667), was one of the most celebrated masters of Oriental languages, and wrote a copious universal church history; his son, Johann Jakob, wrote a history of the church in Switzerland. Johann Heinrich Heidegger acquired European fame by his theological writings, as did Kaspar Schweizer by his knowledge of Greek. A like celebrity was attained by professors of languages and theology in western Switzerland, among them Turretin and Tonchin. In natural sciences, J. J. Scheuchzer, of Zurich, and the Bernoullis in Basle specially distinguished themselves; as chroniclers, J. H. Rahn of Zurich and Michael Stettler of Berne; as topographer, Mathias Merian of Basle.

Once more for every ray of light there was also a shadow; narrow-mindedness and bigotry reigned supreme, in a way which it is now hardly possible to conceive. As regarded intellectual life, much was written by learned men, almost without exception members of the aristocracy, of the dominating families. These authors wrote in Latin, and therefore only for their peers and not for the people. The subjects of their writings were likewise suited almost entirely to learned men and their colleagues; the sciences were confined to the study and the lecture hall, and did not come in contact with life. Higher schools were, indeed, provided, but on the other hand hardly anything was done toward educating the people. The teachers in the popular schools were ignorant artisans, discharged soldiers, or uneducated youths; the education consisted merely in learning mechanically by rote and without understanding religious matter out of the catechism and various devotional books. By this means ignorance was systematically cultivated, and the minds of the people were stifled rather than awakened. Intellectual life was entirely under the control of the authorities, secular and religious, who feared that a liberal education might create restlessness among the people. Writings which displeased the authorities, even innocent poems and popular songs, were unhesitatingly suppressed; everything had to undergo the censorship of severe masters. The teaching of Copernicus, the tenets of the new philosophers, Spinoza, Descartes, etc., were prohibited under pain of the most severe punishments. Rahn of Zurich was not allowed to print a large Federal history, because it contained much that was offensive to the authorities; political history was in itself considered so dangerous that it was in many states not admitted among the professorships.

Theology presented still greater difficulties, for the clergy wielded the sword of the executioner as well as the government. It was not enough to declare the very letter of the Bible and of the church prayers holy and infallible; everything was condemned which did not absolutely agree with those letters. (Consensus formula of 1675.) Scheuchzer and Bernoulli suffered many attacks on this account on the part of the clergy; even the expression of Scheuchzer: "God is everywhere present!" was reckoned as heresy, because the words of the Lord's Prayer say "in heaven." Thus a religious coercion was practiced which almost equaled the Inquisition: a Jew was put to death for saying that Christ was the son of a Jew; General Rudolf Werdmüller, a remarkable man, one who rose far above the superstitions of the age, but indulged in rough jests about the church and the clergy, suspected of heresy, of witchcraft, and of forming a league with the devil, was condemned, after a trial of six years' duration, and forced to quit his country. Michael Zingg, a kindly minister and professor of mathematics in Zurich, was called to account in 1661 for rejecting the decisions of the synod of Dortrecht (1618), which sanctioned strictly Calvinistic views; they threatened to behead him, and even to immure him; he was compelled to fly, and to gain a scanty subsistence as an exile.

All other symptoms of life among the people were as carefully watched as their opinions and confessions of faith. The restraints which had been put upon industrial activity were even increased; foreign imports were prohibited, as also free competition. Raw material might not be procured from without, but must be bought in the town; and the peasant was not allowed to sell his agricultural produce where he would, but had to take it to the market in the town. In the municipal cantons trade and manufactures might only be carried on at all in the towns; if anyone wished to transact business elsewhere, he was obliged to get permission from the guild concerned, and any opposition was severely punished.

No less heavy were the fetters which lay upon social and civic life. The authorities forbade showy and fashionable dress; they prescribed the exact form and color of garments; dancing, card-playing, skittles, etc., were punished by fines and imprisonment; smoking and snuff were forbidden. The evil moral consequences of misgovernment were not wanting. Johann Kaspar Escher, the philanthropic Bailiff of Kiburg, about 1720, lays great stress upon this in his account of the time of his administration. Such prohibitions, he says, gave rise to secret revels; the younger generation lost all heart and love for and all delight in their fatherland, thinking that in other lands there was more liberty; and even the country folk were embittered by the townsmen being in all things preferred before them, which was most unjust, and by the rich being free to indulge in such pleasures openly on payment of money. But the voice of Escher died away, like that of many a nobler-minded man, and no attempt was made to check the source of these abuses.

PART II
MODERN SWITZERLAND. 1712-1935

PART II
MODERN SWITZERLAND, 1291–1956

Chapter IX

POLITICAL DISUNION OF THE EIGHTEENTH CENTURY
1712-1798

THE political conditions of the Confederation in the eighteenth century were somewhat miserable. After the Toggenburg war, the one constant thought and aim of the Catholic states was to recover what they had lost in that war. They pursued their efforts for this restitution for about eighty years without intermission. In 1715 they concluded with France the *Trücklibund,* so called because the document was preserved in a closed box, and thus sought the help of that power to coerce Zurich and Berne. But on the part of the Protestants also, who indulged in a malicious triumph after the war of Toggenburg, there reigned only hatred against all holding other views than their own. Both sides regarded their fellow-confederates of the other faith not as brothers in league, but as heretics and heathen, from whom they must keep as far aloof as possible. The antagonism rose to such a height that in Zurich and Berne the most severe punishments were laid by order of the state upon marriages contracted with Catholics.

In consequence of this want of unity, the neutrality of Switzerland could with difficulty be preserved during the foreign wars which affected her in any way, such as the Polish and Austrian war of succession, and the Seven Years' War. Only once during this century was any united action taken toward a foreign land, and that was in August, 1777, when the French alliance of 1663 was renewed by all the thirteen cantons at Soleure. But this was only a patched-up agreement due to foreign influence, for the French had resorted to every possible art of bribery and corruption in order to reconcile all the states of that league; the Confederates had not united of themselves, and a hopeless want of union prevailed after as before. "Every man for himself!" was their motto, according to a contemporary. Individuals only felt themselves to be citizens of their state or adherents of the Catholic or Protestant party, but never Swiss. Every state had its own coinage, its own law; if a

Swiss wanted to settle in another canton, he was there accounted almost as a foreigner. The *Defensionale* remained forgotten, the Diet was a ponderous machine; the execution of any uniform arrangements in coinage, or the police, the military, or the legal systems was always frustrated by the want of unity and the selfishness of the states. The most important affairs were thus protracted for years and years, either not settled at all, or only after many years; and in the common domains the most urgent reforms were neglected.

Thus in the eighteenth century the Confederation resembled a weather-beaten ruin, ready to fall. But just as "out of ruins there springs forth a new young world of fresh verdure," so even in this apparently hopeless period "bright visions began to appear, prophetically foretelling the new and regenerate Switzerland of the nineteenth century."

Although in political matters dissensions prevailed, yet in intellectual and scientific life a sense of the unity of the fatherland was beginning to arise, notably in the Reformed towns, where intellectual life had made great strides since the success of the war of Toggenburg. Men began to study their own position, learned to know the individuality of Switzerland, and drew thence the hope of a brighter future. The pioneers of the movement were Scheuchzer of Zurich, and Haller of Berne. J. J. Scheuchzer (1672-1733), physician and naturalist, made himself famous by various journeys into the Swiss Alps, wrote the first natural history of Switzerland, and also completed a large map of Switzerland, by which labors he put new life into patriotism. Albrecht von Haller (*ob.* 1777), the great poet and naturalist, by unrivaled industry acquired an extensive and learned education; he also possessed a strong poetic vein, and a warm and patriotic heart. Among his poems which appeared in 1732, "*Die Alpen*" ("The Alps") made a great impression by its poetic depth and the novelty of its ideas. Full of indignation at the depravity of the time, and yearning for natural and unspoiled conditions, he there depicts with vigorous touches the life of nature and of men in the Alps, the simple beautiful customs of the Alpine folk, with a patriotic warmth and enthusiasm before unknown. In another poem, "*Der Mann der Welt*" ("The Man of the World"), he laments the degeneration of his fatherland; in a third, "*Die verdorbenen Sitten*" ("Demoralization"), in contradistinction to the good old times, he apostrophizes the decay of his own day, exclaiming, "O Helvetia! once the land of heroes, how is it possible that the men whom we now behold could have descended from thy former inhabitants?"[1] By his poems and his researches in natural science Haller became so famous in other lands that he received a number of honorable calls, but declined them all, as he wanted to devote his powers to his beloved country, and from 1753 until his end he served her as a government official with affectionate devotion and self-sacrifice.

In addition to these motions on the part of the Swiss themselves we find the influence of other lands, England, France, and Germany, in whose newly awakened intellectual life the learned men of Switzerland took a lively interest. The writings of Montesquieu and Rousseau, and of all those men, burning with love of liberty and of their fellow-men, who in England and France were fighting against the intellectual bondage and political oppression under which the people lay, were eagerly read; Rousseau himself, a chief supporter of the new political and social ideas as to the welfare of the people and popular government, was a citizen of Geneva; hence his writings made a great sensation in western Switzerland. On the lovely shores of the lake of Geneva eminent writers from both France and England spent much time together —Voltaire at Lausanne and Ferney, and Gibbon, the historian of the Roman empire, at Lausanne—and disseminated their views; and intellectual societies, such as were in vogue in France, here also invited both natives and foreigners to enjoyments of a high order.

Switzerland took no less interest in the development of German literature. At that time a close connection was formed between German and Swiss literature, and Johann Bodmer and Johann Breitinger, both of Zurich, incited by English authors, opened a contest with Gottsched and his school, in 1740, in order to establish the principles of the art of genuine, true, and pure poetry, and thus prepared the way for the great classical poets of Germany—Klopstock, Herder, and Goethe. Following the example of England and Germany, Bodmer also brought about the formation of learned societies, which facilitated a more lively exchange of thought among Swiss men of letters. Thus Zurich became the center of an active and eminently productive intellectual life, and

---

[1] *Sag an, Helvetien, du Heldenvaterland,*
Wie ist dein altes Volk dem jetzigen verwandt?
(Translation by Mrs. Howorth, 1794.)

here, too, German writers, such as Klopstock, Wieland, Kleist, Goethe, and Fichte, loved to sojourn.

All these stirring influences gradually led to the intellectual regeneration of the whole Swiss people. Day began to dawn on all sides. Existing conditions were measured by the requirements of the new ideas, actual facts aroused numerous complaints, and from theories men proceeded to practical suggestions for the improvement of matters in the state, the church, and in social and intellectual life.

Bodmer was already working zealously in this direction, and gave a great impulse to all efforts aiming at the public good and the improvement of the conditions of the people. In Basle Isaak Iselin, philanthropist, labored, both by his words and writings, for the improvement of social conditions. Then, in 1758, Franz Urs Balthasar of Lucerne published his work, "*Patriotische Träume eines Eidgenossen von einem Mittel, die veraltete Eidgenossenschaft wieder zu verjüngen,*" [2] in which he recommends the erection of a national Swiss institute of education, where youthful aristocrats should be trained to become useful citizens and politicians, and might be taught the history and politics of Switzerland and military science. Only by such means could love and unity, long torpid, be reawakened, and Switzerland preserved from threatened ruin. Salomon Gessner, poet of Zurich, wrote at this same time his widely read " Idylls," in which he extolled the simple, contented rural and shepherd life as compared with the pleasure-seeking, luxurious life of the rich and great. A definite example in illustration of this was given by his friend, Dr. Hans Kaspar Hirzel, the famous physician of Zurich, a noble and genial philanthropist, in his story of the so-called Farmer Kleinjogg. Kleinjogg, really Jacob Gujer, was a farmer at Wermatsweil (in the commune of Uster), distinguished by his penetration, his wit, and also by his diligence, who by his thrift and his admirably sensible agricultural management converted the worst farm of the neighborhood into a flourishing model farm. " He made use of every blade of straw, every twig of pine-wood, every moment." By his representation and description of the activity of this remarkable peasant Hirzel sought to influence a wider circle, and to put before " the selfish, idle aristocracy a faithful picture of Swiss manhood and ability,

---

[2] "The patriotic dreams of a Confederate of a way to rejuvenate the ancient Confederation."

such as was still to be found among the people." Such words and hints quickly kindled all noble spirits, and soon the scattered voices of the friends of reform were joined in one chorus "to make hearts tremble with the thunder of patriotic enthusiasm."

In the year 1762 a circle of zealous patriots, incited by Balthasar's work, was formed at Schinznach, called the "Helvetic Society," and including Gessner, Hirzel, and Iselin. As time went on this society united all the most famous men both of French and German Switzerland in annual meetings, whose aim was the enthusiastic awakening of the consciousness of Swiss interdependence. While, broadly speaking, religious differences still divided the Confederation into two hostile camps, in this society Reformed and Catholic Swiss lived together on terms of cordiality; in familiar intercourse they learned mutual respect, and in pure love of their country they felt themselves at one. From that time they returned home from their gatherings encouraged, and, disseminating their public spirit throughout the states, the scattered seed slowly sprang up. Under the auspices of the society the young Johann Caspar Lavater, of Zurich, composed the popular "*Schweizerlieder*," condemning dissensions, and extolling unity as the chief source of national prosperity:

> "What is it alone can save us
> When all power and wealth do fail?
> Union only, brothers, union!
> Pray for this, and thus prevail!
> Steadfast in the midst of danger,
> Conquering ever in the fight,
> Never missed the Swiss their purpose
> By the force of union's might." [3]

These songs became "Songs of the People" in a very real sense, and were sung almost throughout Switzerland by men and women, old and young. The Helvetic Society, however, went still further, and sometimes included within the sphere of its labors criticisms upon the degradation in public matters, the improvement

[3] "*Wer ist's, der uns schützt und rettet,*
Wenn es Macht und Gold nicht kann?
Eintracht! Eintracht! Brüder, betet,
Fleht Gott nur um Eintracht an.
Unbeweglich in Gefahren,
Unbesiegbar in dem Streit,
Alles, was sie wollten, waren
Schweizer stets durch Einigkeit."

of morals, and the removal of prejudices; within it were focused all efforts at reform in the domains of intellect and of public utility, partly because it prompted such efforts itself, and partly because it was joined by most of the advocates of reform.

Iselin of Basle, one of the founders of the society, who had imbibed enlightened principles from French authors, ventured early, though indeed diffidently, to attack the privileges of the governing class and the inequalities of rank. The energetic younger generation, however, threw itself cheerfully and unhesitatingly into the new movement, and adopted his views in thorough earnest. Some young men of Zurich—Lavater, Schinz, Füssli, Escher, and Pestalozzi—formed a league, in order to initiate immediate reforms in the territory of Zurich; they prosecuted all instances of oppression and injustice on the part of bailiffs and municipal officers, and attacked worthless ministers, while seeking to support the poor and lowly in their demands to extend the rights of the people. When Grebel, the aristocratic bailiff in Grüningen, like some of his colleagues, practiced extortion and corruption, and the complainants could get no redress, Lavater, then a youth of twenty-one, burning with a noble indignation, wrote his work, " The Unjust Bailiff, or the Complaint of a Patriot," and would not rest till Grebel was put upon his trial. This bold course of action created a great sensation throughout Switzerland. Individual leaders of the Helvetic Society went still further in their demands. Canon Gugger of Soleure (1773), as president of the society, vigorously opposed place-hunting and office-seeking, and also all ideas of subjection, and maintained Rousseau's principle—that the highest authority lies with the people. Stockar of Schaffhausen lamented bitterly in 1777 that the noble ideal of a common fatherland was as yet unrealized, and desired national representation; he expressed the daring wish, which as yet had escaped the lips of no man, that the divers free states of Switzerland might be merged into one single state, whose burghers should all have equal rights, and be under equal obligations. Others denounced foreign military service, and were eager for an increase of the Swiss military force and a uniform military system. Such manifestations seemed dangerous to the alarmed authorities, who trembled for their privileges; Berne, Soleure, and Fribourg therefore issued formal prohibitions against the society. The latter, however, defied all persecution, and remained the steadfast refuge of all efforts of high purpose. Besides the improvement of public conditions, its chief aim was the advancement of education and the system of schools; the ideas of Bodmer and Balthasar were discussed, and Iselin, in particular, was urgent for an improvement in education. The society encouraged various practical attempts at a new method of education and instruction, and within its ranks the notion of a common Federal university, and of the introduction of better popular schools, found many adherents and supporters.

The chief effect on private life of this tendency toward a general reorganization was an increase of industrial activity. In Zurich, in addition to the silk industry, a remarkable impulse was given to cotton and woolen manufactures, in Basle to the weaving of silk ribbons; while St. Gall became one of the most flourishing towns through its linen trade, cotton manufactures, and embroidery. Muslin embroidery was brought to great perfection in Appenzell, Outer Rhodes. The industrial spirit even spread to the mountainous districts of Switzerland, hitherto quite shut off. In the highlying district of La Chaux de Fonds manufactures of watches and jewelry were commenced, as also in Geneva; in Glarus cotton spinning formed the most considerable branch of industry; in the canton of Berne the fabrication of velvets, silks, and cloths was commenced; even in the remote valleys of Emmen and Engelberg weaving and spinning were established, and about the middle of the century Schwyz and Gersau also applied themselves to these industries. Switzerland adopted the use of machinery at an early period. This peaceable industrial activity soon led to the decline of mercenary service; the French cabinet expressed its regret that the inhabitants of the Swiss cantons had become merchants rather than soldiers, and that the Swiss were retiring more and more from military service, and working peacefully in factories.

The advancement of industry was followed by that of agriculture. The agricultural societies in Berne, Zurich, and Basle labored specially to this end; through their exertions the cultivation of new products, such as clover, lucerne, esparcet, and potatoes, was introduced, in addition to the artificial irrigation of meadows, stall-feeding, the breaking up of fallow ground and other innovations, now long since become general. The authorities and societies further labored zealously to facilitate traffic by improving the roads. Good roads were become so much the more necessary since in other lands men were beginning to appreciate the beauties of the Swiss

Alps and glaciers, and to travel frequently in Switzerland. There were certainly great difficulties to be overcome—chasms must be filled in, rocks and boulders blasted, and costly bridges built; but skill and perseverance overcame them. The states of Berne, Zurich, the Grisons, Basle, and Glarus distinguished themselves by their good roads; over the Passwang, the Gemmi, the Hauenstein, highways were constructed. The brothers Grubenmann, of Appenzell, were among the most accomplished builders of bridges of that day: the bridge over the Rhine at Schaffhausen, that over the Limmat at Wettingen, and many of the bridges in Glarus were constructed in the years from 1750 to 1760. In the course of the century, moreover, and especially in the latter half, numerous benevolent institutions and public buildings were erected, such as orphanages, infirmaries, magazines, loan offices, and savings banks.

Hand in hand with such material progress we find an improvement in social life. In individual cantons smaller societies were laboring, like the Helvetic Society throughout Switzerland, toward intellectual and economical progress, and were inculcating a love for the arts and sciences, enlightenment and public utility. In 1779, at the instigation of the Helvetic Society, a Swiss military association was started, aiming at a fundamental improvement of the Swiss military system with a view to greater uniformity. In Zurich, Basle, Berne, Geneva, and Lausanne reading clubs were formed, and societies of all kinds—naturalist, agricultural, beneficent, musical, etc., and in Zurich a society of artists; while even smaller places, such as Rolle and Yverdon in the Vaud, and Wädenswil, Stäfa, Winterthur, etc., in the canton of Zurich, had their reading and musical societies, and realized the necessity of intellectual education. Printing offices increased in number, and were kept fully occupied in satisfying this intellectual craving. Thus an exceedingly abundant and enlightened literature was produced, which permeated all classes, and produced an essential alteration in the views of that time. The different societies themselves started periodicals (*Museen, Bibliotheken*) for the instruction of the people by means of reliable treatises on historical, philosophical, and public subjects. Fäsi and Füssli produced excellent Swiss political and physical geographies; Saussure, the great naturalist of Geneva, graphic descriptions of travels; Ebel, a German, wrote the first Swiss guide book; the æsthetic Sulzer, of Winterthur, propagated new ideas on art, and Lavater on religion, philosophy, and physiognomy. But the chief distinction was attained by the Swiss historian, Johann von Müller of Schaffhausen in 1780, who made the first attempt at a popular history that could be enjoyed by all classes. Müller embraced the history of the Confederation as a great whole, and for the invigorating and strengthening of patriotic feeling, wrote it in the lofty, fine, and thrilling style of the ancient classics. His contemporaries felt its elevating influence, and " once more believed in their fatherland." [4]

A splendid impulse was given to art as well as to literature. A number of very remarkable churches in the baroque and old-fashioned [5] or antique style date from that period in Schwyz, St. Gall, Berne, and Soleure. There are also handsome secular buildings in the antique style which are even yet worthy of note, such as the houses in Zurich called the " Crown " and the " Titmouse," the white and blue house in Basle, and houses in Soleure and Frauenfeld. Landscape and portrait painting were greatly developed, as also the art of copperplate engraving. Men talked and wrote about art and the history of art. Churches and schools, too, were fain to fall in with the new modes of thought. A more liberal spirit sprang up in them, and orthodoxy was confronted by rationalism. Little by little men threw off the restraints of church and creed, little by little modern tolerance forced its way. In the Catholic church a storm broke out against the Jesuits, which led to the suppression of the order in 1773. The improvement of the scholastic and educational system was zealously pursued. A brilliant commencement was made by Dr. Planta, a Grison, who founded an educational institution at Haldenstein in 1761, in which the way was paved for instruction by object-lessons according to the principles of philanthropists, and special preference was given to the sciences most useful in daily life; while at the same time the sense of a common humanity, patriotic virtues, and religious toleration were strengthened and nourished. The Helvetic Society encouraged this establishment, which seemed to realize Balthasar's dream, and a number of distinguished men, who labored in succession for the reformation of their country, were trained at this fine institution. Other institutions besides Haldenstein soon sprang into existence, and the various states, such as Zurich and Berne, also improved their schools, both the higher town schools and the lower rural schools,

[4] An expression used by Mülinen, then studying in foreign lands.
[5] Somewhat similar to the contemporaneous Georgian style in England.

and special attention was paid to the education and development of girls.

For the better advancement of their plans and ideas, the Helvetic Society offered prizes for the best suggestions for the improvement of the educational system. This had a specially stirring influence upon the man who, more than any other, devoted his whole life to the task of educating the people. This man was Johann Heinrich Pestalozzi of Zurich. The ignorance of the schoolteachers, the unkind treatment of the children, and the stultifying, arbitrary methods of instruction filled him with indignation. The hitherto existing institutions for popular education seemed to him to be merely " artful machines for suffocation." When he put his own hand to the work, he resolved to begin where the need was greatest—with the lowest and most abandoned classes of the population, and in 1776 gathered poor children around him on his country estate of " Neuhof" near Hapsburg in the Aargau, and endeavored to arouse and develop their physical, mental, and moral powers by manual labor, mental and verbal exercises, mental arithmetic, reading, and writing. But not being sufficiently supported by the authorities, this fine undertaking fell through in 1780 for want of means for its maintenance. He now tried to spread his views by his words and writings, and among other things in 1781, wrote his famous and popular book, " *Lienhard und Gertrud,*" in which he draws, in the portrait of Hummel the bailiff, a thrilling picture of the degeneracy of the governmental system, while on the other hand in Gertrud and her household he represents the beneficial effects of a loving and religious moral training.

But in spite of all efforts Pestalozzi was unable to achieve any new practical results, and was still forced to build all his hopes of support upon the future. It was useless to think of any Federal measures being taken so long as the old and rotten political fabric existed. And this remained absolutely untouched, in spite of the urgent wishes and entreaties which were from time to time expressed in the Helvetic Society. No attempt was ventured to strengthen the central authority, and to give the people a share in the government. It is true that in 1778 certain patricians of Berne made the suggestion that the subject-lands should at least be put upon an equal footing with the allied states, but the matter ended in good intentions. Men preached to deaf ears; the majority of the governing body were unwilling to deprive themselves of their privileges, and did their utmost toward the preservation of existing conditions. Thus there remained to the oppressed no means of acquiring their rights but those of violence.

In the course of the eighteenth century the aristocracy became only more bigoted, willfully closing its eyes to the evil results of the system of government. In Berne the circle of families entitled to a share in the government became ever narrower; in 1776 there were only eighteen families represented in the Council of the Two Hundred, among whom were six of the family of Erlach, eight of Diesbach, eleven of Tscharner, twelve of Stürler, thirteen of Wattenwyl, of Graffenried, etc. Under pain of imprisonment artisans and other persons were forbidden to carry any wares under the arcades (arbors or walks), that the patricians and their wives might be able to walk in comfort; and they always first of all chose the finest and best at the daily vegetable market, while other citizens were not admitted until eleven o'clock, and were obliged to content themselves with what was left. Hunting was permitted to patricians only, and they alone might give balls as often as they pleased; exception after exception was made in their favor in the sumptuary laws, and if a patrician offended against the laws of the state, he was treated far more leniently than other people; in severe cases at the utmost he was banished to his country estate, or secretly ordered to absent himself from his home. In Lucerne, too, the patricians mutually blinked at one another's offenses and defalcations. The arrogant bearing of the citizens of Zurich toward the country folk likewise increased, and they even grudged to the town of Winterthur the development of her industry, and prevented the introduction of silk manufactures there; the citizens of Zurich claimed a monopoly of the latter, and whoever infringed their privilege was severely punished.

During the course of the eighteenth century a spirit of opposition, which became more and more pronounced, was aroused against such narrow-mindedness. The sense of injustice, the ever-increasing enlightenment, the new views concerning the welfare and sovereign rights of the people, which had found their way from England and France by means of numerous pamphlets and were eagerly welcomed—all combined to arouse the bitterest hatred among the people, and to drive them at length to action.

The first impulse to violent revolt against the aristocracy was given by Geneva, which state was, in fact, only connected with the Confederation at all through Zurich and Berne, and had hitherto had little influence upon the course of Federal affairs. The power of the Genevese aristocracy was vested in the smaller council, which filled any vacancies in the great council and almost all other offices, while the *conseil général* itself, or the community of the burghers, had lost the right of legislation. The small council consisted of twenty-five members, who were appointed from the few governing families. Meanwhile a democratic and antagonistic element had sprung up gradually among the many French settlers who had found a new home in Geneva. Quite at the beginning of the century, in 1707, a committee of the council, at whose head was Pierre Fatio the lawyer, under pressure from the people, required the abolition of the one-sided system of government by families, the regular assembling of the *conseil général,* and free initiative. The movement, however, was suppressed by military interference, imprisonment and executions, Fatio himself being thrown into prison. Afterward, when the government caused costly fortifications to be erected in a despotical manner, the democratic party arose, and in 1737 were victorious in the struggle, and extorted a recognition of the principle that the highest authority, the choice of officers, the right of making war and peace, and the right of legislation and taxation should rest with the burghers (*Bürgergemeinde*).

This victory of the popular faction in Geneva soon had its effect upon Berne. From the year 1710 attack after attack, lampoon after lampoon, had followed one another in quick succession, directed against the aristocracy; special exception was taken to the claim made by the patricians of the sole right over official appointments. The patricians mockingly observed that the citizens must be stripped of their feathers, that they might not want to fly. New petitions were, however, presented, and in 1744 a proclamation was issued, calling upon the burghers to help themselves as the Genevese had done. Those concerned were punished by banishment, among them Samuel Henzi, a cultivated and enlightened citizen, famous as a clever French poet and author. The latter being pardoned before the expiration of his term, thought of entering the Modenese service as a means of earning a livelihood, but being prevented, and so remaining in Berne, was entangled in fresh political agitations in 1749. He showed some disposition to take part in fresh efforts at petitions; but the leaders, Wernier and

Fueter, spoke of a conspiracy, the overthrow of the government, burning of the town, etc. Everything was betrayed, and the name of Samuel Henzi was specially coupled with those of Wernier and Fueter as one of the chief ringleaders. The government, filled with terror and dismay, took stringent measures, and all those already named paid the penalty with their lives upon the scaffold. But such severity did not avail to restore respect for the patricians, and thenceforward the government was never safe from conspiracies.

Violent storms shook the patriciate of Lucerne. The citizens there had long complained that the authorities purchased domains, concluded alliances, appropriated French annuities, etc., without consulting them. An ecclesiastical dispute added fuel to the fire of dissension. A patrician of Lucerne had in 1768 published a work on the rights of the state as opposed to those of the church, and showed how the Swiss should guard against the encroachments of Rome; another work demanded the abolition of the religious orders and restrictions upon monasteries. A family quarrel was added to these agitations, for at the head of the patricians at that time stood the family of Meyer, which was attacked with great violence by the family of Schuhmacher. Placidus Schuhmacher, whose father had been ruined by one of the Meyers, sought help from the burgesses during the despotism of Valentine Meyer by adopting their cause and seeking to defend their rights; he was, however, executed in 1764 on the plea of his having concocted a secret plot. The Schuhmacher family next tried to get at their mortal enemies from another point. Valentine Meyer being held to be the author of the work against the monasteries, they availed themselves of the agitation stirred up by the clergy for the overthrow of their foes. There was nothing to be gained for the popular rights from these disputes, and they were forgotten: it was even forbidden to talk over the sentences and mandates of the authorities.

The government of Soleure pursued a similar course, upon some citizens censuring prevalent abuses; and Zurich too was not behind the rest in severity. When in 1777 the authorities violated the right of the community legally established in 1713 of being consulted 'in alliances, by concluding the French alliance, disturbances arose among the citizens, in which the old Pastor Waser played a leading part. The latter had been previously unjustly deprived of his office, and threw himself with zeal and success into all researches in natural history, history, agriculture, and statistics. In revenge he wrote articles in the journal of statistics of Professor Schlözer in Göttingen, touching upon divers abuses in the political system of Zurich, and revealing political conditions hitherto kept secret. For this he was brought to trial, found guilty of high treason, and condemned to death in 1780.

Opposition against the aristocracy and the governing class was about this time aroused among the burghers of Fribourg, and once more broke out in Geneva. In the year 1762 the government of Geneva caused Rousseau's "*Contrat Social*," setting forth the democratic principles of liberty and equality as the right of all men, to be burned. The popular faction thereupon rose, and in 1768 forced the government to restore to the *conseil général* the right of electing councilors. But this provision was made only with respect to the citizens of long standing, and the new citizens (or "natives"),[6] hitherto slighted in every way, now rose and demanded at least a share in these rights, while Voltaire from his seat in Ferney added fuel to the flame. A rebellion broke out; the government summoned troops from Berne, Savoy, and France for its suppression. These struggles in the little republic formed as it were a prelude to the great French Revolution, and all the rest of Switzerland took great interest in them. The people considered the cause of the opposition their own; for instance, while the population of Zurich had willingly marched out in the Peasants' War for the suppression of the populace in other cantons, they refused to do so when summoned against Geneva, and Berne had reason to fear that the disaffection would spread to the Vaud.

In the rural cantons, too, struggles were rife like those of the town cantons, in which the adherents of the oligarchical government styled themselves the *Linden* and their opponents the *Harten*, as in the time of the Peasants' War. In Outer Rhodes of Appenzell and in Zug a dispute about various portions of land was interwoven with this party strife. In the first-named little canton the *Harten* accused the government of neglecting to consult their *Landsgemeinde* at the Peace of Toggenburg, and they gained a victory in 1732. They had taken up their position by preference in the portion west of the Sitter, the *Linden* in that east of the Sitter. For some time the defeated faction adhered to their sep-

---

[6] *Natifs* or *habitans*, old inhabitants of Geneva, excluded by birth from taking part in public affairs.

arate government under violent persecution from the *Harten,* till both parties were exhausted.

In Zug the *Harten* (who found their chief support in the bailiwicks in opposition to the town) overthrew the family of Zurlauben, who were in receipt of French pensions; but they having introduced a " reign of terror " under Joseph Anton Schuhmacher, the *Linden* once more gained the upper hand, and in 1735 Schuhmacher was sent to the galleys. Owing to the changed conditions of French service, the *Harten* were victorious in 1764 in a tumultuous popular assembly; the *Landsgemeinden* of Zug demanded an equal division of pensions among the people, and established an extraordinary tribunal which settled matters peaceably. Meanwhile in Schwyz, too, the battle raged between *Linden* and *Harten,* the latter being victorious, and the dominion of the Reding family was for a time severely shaken. In Inner Rhodes of Appenzell the popular party gained the upper hand under Anton Joseph Suter, who became bailiff of the Rheintal, and in 1762 Swiss magistrate in opposition to a candidate of the aristocratic faction. But Suter incurring blame for certain blunders, the *Linden* stirred up an agitation against him and effected his overthrow. Suter was forced to leave the country, but was afterward treacherously captured by his foes, brought to trial, and executed in 1784.

Not only were the aristocrats attacked by their slighted fellow-citizens, but for a long time past those from whom they had most to fear, their oppressed subjects, had been clamoring at the doors. These also endeavored to secure and extend their rights by revolts and demonstrations, and did not scruple to proceed to extremities. For instance, the community of Wilchingen in Schaffhausen (1717-1729), the towns of Winterthur and Stein on the Rhine (1783), the two latter being subjects of Zurich, in conflict with their rulers even turned to the emperor for help. The risings, however, were mostly put down by force of arms.

The inhabitants of Werdenberg complained that they were deprived by Glarus of their charter of liberties, but they found no hearing, and Glarus discovering a plot in 1721, caused the whole district to be occupied by the military and the conspirators to be severely punished. Major Daniel Abraham Davel, of the Pays de Vaud, an enthusiastic but good-natured and harmless advocate of liberty, availed himself of the opportunity of a muster to call upon his countrymen to emancipate themselves, and endeavored to raise the Vaud into an independent canton, but was taken prisoner by subtlety and beheaded in 1723. The inhabitants of Livinen had in 1713 extorted certain liberties, and in 1755, deeming these infringed by Uri, they rose in resolute resistance. The government of Uri, however, sent an armed force and disarmed the men of Livinen; the latter were forced once more to render homage on their knees, and to watch the execution of their leaders, and the district was deprived of all its liberties.

Although, however, the people had not obtained their rights, they were at least aroused; they learned that the proceedings of their lords and rulers were no longer to be deemed infallible; while the latter had in many parts sown the seeds of hatred and bitterness. In the Vaud especially the fuel of discontent was heaped high; in the Italian bailiwicks, well-nigh devastated by the negligence of the Diet and the harshness of the bailiffs, it was only with the deepest resentment that the population bore the yoke of the Federal bailiffs, against whom elsewhere also many a man chafed in secret. Only the kindling spark was wanting to set the whole political fabric in flames.

Chapter X

REVOLUTION AND ATTEMPTS AT REORGANIZATION
1798-1830

THE rosy dawn of a new era rose over mankind as the French Revolution sounded the call to liberty and equality, to the shaking off of every tyranny and the destruction of feudal rights. The reforming efforts of enlightened men had prepared the soil in Switzerland, too, so that from the beginning the Revolution found warm sympathy among many cultured men of high position in Switzerland. Meyer von Schauensee, an aristocrat of Lucerne, pointed out in a thrilling speech before the Helvetic Society the wholesome effects of that society upon the civic and political equality of all classes. Revolutionary ideas were specially warmly welcomed and upheld by three advocates, bound by the closest ties of fellowship: Dr. Albrecht Rengger of Brugg, Konrad Escher ("von der Linth"), and Paul Usteri of Zurich. These not only gave energetic and enthusiastic expression in the Helvetic Society to their conviction of the wholesomeness of the aim of the Revolution, but also sought by their writings to overthrow existing prejudices. Escher expressed his desire that Switzerland might enjoy more than the mere shade of the French tree of liberty! Revolutionary notions were disseminated among the people, particularly in 1791 and 1792, during the occupation of the frontier in the time of the war of the coalition. For here, in the immediate vicinity of the great events, the Swiss soldiers, too, were seized by the fiery zeal of the neighboring people; the cry of victory: "*Liberté, egalité,*" the trees of liberty, the language of democratic clubs, kindled the warmest emotions in every liberal-minded Swiss. There was soon no Swiss town where there might not be found some who had a fellow-feeling for the French, and soon the watch-words "liberty and equality" were in the mouth of almost every Swiss. On the other hand the new ideas gave a great shock to the governing class, and many of them not only feared the overthrow of existing conditions, but apprehended danger from the west to the freedom of their country.

The first attempt toward the realization of these ideas in Switzerland originated in the Swiss Club at Paris. This was a society chiefly composed of men from the Pays de Vaud and Fribourg, who, long dissatisfied with things at home and specially with their subject condition, wanted to extend the revolution to their native land. For this purpose they entered into correspondence with those like-minded at home, as also with the leading statesmen of France, and sent French speeches to Switzerland, which awakened lively sympathy, particularly in the western and Romance districts. The earliest results were seen in the French Lower Valais. This district ever since the Burgundian wars had been under the rule of German Upper Valais, and was harassed and fleeced by harsh bailiffs. Hence it needed only the slightest encouragement from Paris to cause the population of Monthey and St. Maurice to revolt (September, 1790), to plant trees of liberty, and to drive out the bailiffs. Soon afterward, under similar instigation, the people of Porrentruy rebelled against their harsh ruler, the Bishop of Basle. The revolt of the Valais folk was, however, suppressed with the help of Berne; Porrentruy indeed proclaimed itself free under the title of the " Rauracian Republic," but in order to avoid total anarchy, was obliged to annex itself to France in 1793 as the department Mont Terrible. Revolutionary movements sprang up simultaneously in Geneva and in the Pays de Vaud. In Geneva the " natives " once more revolted; the example of France was here faithfully imitated both for good and evil, and among the perilous waves of party strife many endeavored to form connections with France.

The determining influence chiefly at work in the Vaud was that of Frederick Cæsar Laharpe of Rolle. Filled even as a boy with burning indignation against all injustice, at the seminary at Haldenstein Laharpe imbibed enthusiasm for a united Helvetic Republic through the influence of historical studies and liberal-minded teachers. As a lawyer in Berne he gained a fuller knowledge of the narrow-minded and selfish aristocratic government, and he himself relates the deep impression made upon him by the harsh reply he received from one of the noblest patricians in speaking of the spirit of innovation: " Remember that you are our subjects!" Deeply affronted, he left his home, and through the recommendation of an acquaintance was received at the Russian court, where the Empress Catherine appointed him tutor to her grandsons. But like a stout republican, he did not renounce his liberty even at the foot of the throne, and labored unceasingly by his writings for the good of his countrymen, who first declared their sympathy with the events in France by banquets. He at length returned in 1796, poor and without means of subsistence, to liberate his ardently loved country by the power of his words and of his arm. But the watchful policy of Berne was before him, and refused him entrance to his fatherland as a rebel. Often he would sit and rest upon a boundary-stone on the Swiss frontier, and cast longing glances over into the Vaud; he heard how his friends and relatives were condemned and banished; finally he felt no longer safe on the frontier, and fled to Paris, where, having resolved upon a life-and-death struggle with Berne and the aristocracy, he labored indefatigably for the emancipation of the Vaud.

The movements which took place in the territory of Zurich were far more serious and proved more enduring than all those of western Switzerland. On their return from the occupation of the frontiers many of the men of Zurich were filled with enthusiasm for the French, notably those dwelling around the lake, who, as formerly in the days of Waldmann, of the wars of Kappel, and of the Thirty Years' War, were once more the most zealous for the liberty of their country. They took an intense interest in the proceedings in France, and frequently assembled to talk over political affairs. The more zealous among them founded a reading society at Stäfa, where they discussed historical and political subjects, and read the pamphlets and speeches of the leaders of the French Revolution. In 1794 they presented a memorial to the government setting forth their chief grievances, insisting that the town and the rural district should be placed upon an equality in one common constitution, and demanding freedom of trade, liberty to study, relief from feudal burdens, and the admission of country people into the body of officials. They called attention to their ancient charters of liberty of 1489 and 1531, of which they had been deprived by the government. The government, however, thought it necessary to encounter the rapidly spreading spirit of revolution with severity, and caused those chiefly implicated—Pfenninger of Stäfa, Stapfer of Horgen, and Neeracher, a potter of Stäfa, the author of the memorial—to be arrested, fined, and banished. But these methods of intimidation had quite a contrary effect to what was intended; a yet more eager search was made for the ancient charters, and these being actually found among the archives at Küssnach,[1] were rapidly disseminated by means of copies, and once more the government was required to abide by these charters (1795). By way of reply, preparations were made to suppress the new "rebellion" by force of arms, whereupon the community of Stäfa resolved to stand by one another "all for each, and each for all." The government, fearing the consequences of this demeanor, immediately dispatched a body of troops 1700 strong; the community of Stäfa was disarmed, a sword was brandished over the head of Bodmer, the treasurer, as one of the chief leaders; he was condemned to imprisonment for life, and about 250 citizens in all were punished. "Rulers must command, people obey without question," proclaimed the unyielding authorities.

The country folk of St. Gall found more indulgence from their lord, the princely Abbot Beda of St. Gall. Provoked by the useless extravagance of the latter, and incited by John Künzle, a letter-carrier, an enlightened and eloquent man, they revolted against their superior lord. Beda was good-natured and patriotic enough to yield, but in so doing neglected to consult the chapter, or assembly of monks of the monastery, who were hostile to him (1795). They therefore protested against his action, and Pancraz Forster, the new abbot who succeeded, who was one of Beda's chief opponents, would not hold to the terms made by Beda with the people. The states protecting the monastery, however, seeking to mediate, finally ranged themselves on the side of the people, the latter giving vent to their excitement in menaces and imprecations. The people obtained the right of electing a rural council, of which Künzle himself became president in 1797, and peace was restored. This might well have formed an example for other governments, showing how they might come to an understanding with the people in peaceable fashion, and make their rule more popular. But the latter remained inexorable. They did not even seem to notice the dangers threatening from without; mistrust and dissension reigned everywhere. So much the easier was it for the French to spread their net further and further over Switzerland. Just as they had before taken rebellious Porrentruy, so now in the Italian wars of 1797, under their General Napoleon Bonaparte, they liberated the lands subject to the Grisons, the Valtelline, Bormio, and Chiavenna,

[1] On the Lake of Zurich.

which had revolted against their harsh rulers, and annexed them to the kindred states of the Cisalpine Republic. In the same way in April, 1798, Geneva became the prey of the French. The latter very nearly took possession of the Vaud; but the governments had no suspicion of this, and lulled themselves in comfortable security till the thunder of French cannon in Switzerland roused them roughly enough from their slumber.

The fugitive democrats of the Pays de Vaud, notably Laharpe, continually labored while in France to influence public opinion in the "homeland." Laharpe published a treatise on the situation of the Pays de Vaud, and demanded its restoration from Berne. His hopes and those of his colleagues, of obtaining their liberty by the help of France, were much raised when, by the *coup d'état* of 18 Fructidor (September 5), 1797, the war party took the helm in France. Reubel, an Alsatian, and a member of the Directory, who as a barrister had once lost a suit in the courts of Berne, and therefore cordially hated the Bernese, specially urged a war against Switzerland, and the Directory soon issued menacing notes to the Confederation concerning favors alleged to have been shown to the allies and emigrants. The exiles from the Vaud encouraged this action, and desired not only an intervention in their favor, but also violent interference on the part of the French in Swiss affairs. In their name Laharpe requested the Directory to intervene, with a not very apt allusion to the treaty of 1564. It was undoubtedly Laharpe's honest conviction that France would aid the people in gaining liberty, not in order to abuse it, but simply for their benefit. The Directory, however, was induced to invade Switzerland by no such ideal and unselfish motives, but by certain private and mostly selfish interests. For it was above all things important to the warlike operations of France to be able to hold Switzerland in a state of dependence, and at her disposal; and the Directory, in need of money, specially coveted the rich treasure of Berne, the value of which was greatly exaggerated by common report. It actually consisted of about seven millions in money and twelve millions in bonds.

The designs and aims of France took more definite form, and became more evident, after the Congress of Rastadt, where the affairs of Europe were to be arranged after the splendid conquests of Bonaparte in Italy. The Confederation desired from the Congress a guarantee of their territorial position and of their constitution. They were not, however, permitted to send a representative; on the contrary, their fate was arbitrarily settled in Paris, and that chiefly by the influence of Napoleon Bonaparte and Peter Ochs of Basle, who drew up their plans during the Congress. Bonaparte being privy to the designs of the Directory, purposely took his journey to Rastadt by way of Switzerland in November, 1797, in order to discover the disposition of the people and to make a preliminary survey of the land. He was everywhere received with enthusiasm as an honored hero; in the Vaud, in Liestal and Basle he was openly welcomed as their "Deliverer," or "Liberator," which seemed to him to promise a favorable issue for the French. He had also confidential interviews with eminent malcontents, particularly with Peter Ochs, the chief guildmaster of Basle, who, like Laharpe and many other Swiss, had become convinced that the difference between citizens and subjects must be abolished at all costs, even though it were by the help of foreigners. Ochs soon afterward went to Paris as envoy from Basle on secret affairs touching the surrender of Fricktal to Basle; there he was also drawn into the interests of the Directory, and became thenceforth a devoted servant of France. Hence, directly after the return of Bonaparte the schemes against Switzerland were finally settled. Ochs, as leader of the "Patriots," discussed the reorganization of Switzerland with Napoleon and the Director Reubel. The Directory had been hitherto undecided whether to make of Switzerland one united state or to divide it. The "Patriots" now urged their project of a united state, the threads of which might be easily kept in hand by France, and which would make Switzerland a strong bulwark of France. Finally, on December 28, 1797, the Directory issued a notice to Switzerland concerning the Vaud, and resolved upon the complete annexation of the Val de Moutier, which was immediately put under military occupation. By this means Swiss neutrality was violated, and practically war was declared against the Confederation.

Notwithstanding these menacing dangers, Switzerland remained incomprehensibly quiet and inactive, totally crippled by the old want of unity. Warnings and admonitions were certainly not lacking. Johann von Müller, the historian, in eloquent words exhorted them to a unity which should ignore all boundaries between cantons, all walls between towns and rural districts. Doctor Ebel, too, the author of the first Swiss guide-book, who, though a

German by birth, entertained a warm feeling for Switzerland, exhorted men to come forward to support the ancient Confederation in the face of the growing danger, and to give up the old system of government of their own accord—but all in vain! The nearer the danger came, the greater was the blindness, the more helpless the attitude. In alarm, an assurance was given to France that her wishes should be followed; at length, on December 27, a general Diet was assembled at Aarau. This, however, instead of negotiating, instead of generously striving after a free constitution, and throwing aside all mutual mistrust and all exaggerated fears, determined upon a renewal of the ancient Federal charters, which had not been confirmed since 1526. The Federal oath was taken with great solemnity on January 25. The Diet hoped thus "to show the foreigner how united and happy Switzerland was under her existing constitution." But what availed a renewal of the letter of the old leagues, when Federal feeling and spirit were long since dead? As an actual fact the boasted unity seemed very doubtful; among the democracies there prevailed a deep mistrust of the policy of the aristocracies; Appenzell, Glarus, and other democratic states opposed the renewal of the Federal oath; Basle formally abstained from taking part in it; and while the lords of the Diet were drinking toasts to the existing constitution at the taking of the oath, the friends of Ochs in Basle were drinking to the democratic reorganization of Switzerland. Moreover, the governments of the various states were no less divided, the adherents of the old and the new standing in sharp opposition to one another. The people, too, remained quite unconcerned by the act of the Diet, since their wishes were not regarded; in the Federal oath they only saw the union of lords against subjects, for indeed the league had long since ceased to be a really popular alliance.

Therefore, since nothing was achieved by peaceful methods, a violent revolution became necessary. In January and February, 1798, the subjects rose on all sides, encouraged by the conduct of France; while Mengaud, the crafty French ambassador, openly fanned the flame and labored for the revolution. Basle was the first place to come to terms with its subjects, by proclaiming equality of rights on January 20. Once more disturbances broke out along the Lake of Zurich, and the government was forced to release the prisoners arrested in 1795; the people of Schaffhausen next rebelled, and compelled their government to resign; while the ancient territory of St. Gall and Toggenburg emancipated itself, besides Thurgau, Rheintal, Sargans, and the bailiwicks of Ticino, and constituted themselves independent communities. Glarus was obliged for herself to give up Werdenberg, and in concert with Schwyz to surrender Gaster and Utznach. The patrician government of Lucerne, terrified by a movement which was spreading like wild-fire, resigned to make room for one more modern and more liberal-minded.

Thus the whole fabric was suddenly on fire, the flames raging most wildly in the Vaud. Here committees were formed in every town to circulate and obtain signatures to petitions requiring the restoration of ancient rights; and when Berne hesitated and assembled troops, the populace arose in many parts to carry the revolution by force. On January 25 the arms and portraits of the governing families were demolished in almost every place, trees of liberty planted, and the green colors of the Vaud hoisted in the place of the colors of Berne; the Vaud was now to form a separate state, independent of Berne, under the title of the " *République du Léman.*" The committees entered into correspondence with the French troops then in the Pays de Gex under the command of Menard, and on January 28 Menard entered the Vaud with 15,000 men, Berne being unable to take any effectual step to oppose him, all appeals for help to her fellow-Confederates having remained unanswered. It now became impossible to continue the Diet; revolutions breaking out on all sides, and the French, whom no one ventured to oppose, commencing hostilities, the ground gave way beneath its feet, so that on the last day of January, 1798, it was dissolved. Hardly had the Federal delegates departed when Aarau, at the instigation of Mengaud, planted the tree of liberty, which had already been held in readiness for some days. The last hour of the Confederation was drawing near!

Berne—thrown upon her own resources by the Diet—stood almost alone against the foe, and the eyes of the adherents of the old régime were now fixed upon that state as upon the stronghold of Switzerland. Meanwhile, Berne herself was undecided how to meet the French; the latter, however, desired not peace, but war, and prepared for an overwhelming assault. In February Menard was replaced in the Vaud by Brune, under whom was General Schauenburg, who advanced with a division of troops from the Jura. Both together were to coerce by force of arms those governments which would not voluntarily accept democracy, and to convert the whole of Switzerland into a united republic. By craft and duplicity Brune maintained a truce with Berne, and issued an ultimatum containing specific demands; then, when the latter were only partially fulfilled, he broke the truce and set his troops in motion.

Soleure and Fribourg capitulated at once in the beginning of March; but Berne, where there were two opposing parties in the councils (the peace party under Von Frisching, the treasurer, and the war party under Von Steiger, the mayor), hesitated whether to make a vigorous resistance or to adopt a shameful policy of *laissez-faire;* and it was only the brave conduct of General Ludwig von Erlach which succeeded in bringing his native town to the honorable decision to take up arms for their liberties. Of the other states, Zurich, Uri, Schwyz, Glarus, Appenzell, and the town of St. Gall alone sent any auxiliary troops; the rest had no desire to protect the aristocracy of Berne. But Berne could not even rely upon her own troops, for these were not only very few in number and widely scattered, but were also torn by dissensions and ready to mutiny: many of the soldiers would not obey their leaders, and fostered mistrust of them and of the government; even the life of Erlach himself was threatened! The issue, therefore, could not be doubtful. Notwithstanding their weakness and paucity, the Bernese troops yet bore themselves bravely in the battle itself. At Neueneck, southwest of Berne, to which a division of Brune's army had advanced, they gave battle under Johannes Weber, adjutant general of Colonel von Graffenried, with truly heroic courage, and put the enemy to flight March 5. On the north side of the town, however, against which Schauenburg's troops had advanced, all was lost: Erlach's outposts yielded at Fraubrunnen; in the little wood of Grauholz, two hours' march from Berne, Erlach, after a brief but valiant resistance, was obliged to retire before a flank movement of the French, who were four times as strong as himself. At Breitfeld he assembled his men once more; but in the town all resistance had already been abandoned, and on March 5 a capitulation ensued. Unfortunate as was the end of the struggle, the Bernese did at least save the honor of ancient Switzerland; but in their fall the Bernese aristocracy carried with them the whole of the Switzerland of old days. The other states immediately gave up all opposition.

Hist. Nat. xiii-36

While Brune and Schauenburg were occupying Switzerland, zealous attempts were being made in Paris to settle the details of the new order of things in Swiss affairs. From the pen of Ochs, the cultured and clever politician, came a scheme of a united Helvetic Constitution, abolishing cantonal differences and establishing a uniform government. The Directory and Bonaparte assented to the scheme with very slight alterations. It was drawn up after the pattern of the constitution of the French Directory. Switzerland was to form a state "one and indivisible," with a central government. All citizens of the former states or cantons were to be Swiss citizens without distinction or difference. All conditions of dependence were abolished; subjects and allied states received equal rights with the hitherto governing states, and the political power of sovereignty was vested in the hands of all the citizens. As in France, the form of government was a representative democracy with two chambers. The legislative power was to be exercised by a Senate and a greater council, the executive by a Directory of five members, assisted by four ministers; while the judicial power was vested in a high court of justice. Lucerne was made the capital.

For purposes of administration, jurisdiction, and election the whole of Switzerland was divided into twenty-two cantons or jurisdictions defined by geographical boundaries; to the thirteen states were added Leman (Vaud), Aargau, Thurgau, Bellinzona, Lugano, Sargans with Rheintal, St. Gall, Valais, and Rhætia. The cantons were further divided into districts. At the head of every canton there was a governor appointed by the Directory, and an administrative chamber. The constitution was submitted to the general vote of the citizens; universal suffrage was established for the election of district and communal officials: in the communes there were primary assemblies, in the jurisdictions electoral assemblies of delegates elected by the people. The personal rights of the citizens were exactly like those in France. Privileges, prerogatives of the nobility, titles, and such-like were abolished. Anyone might be admitted to office; restrictions were taken off trade and manufactures, and feudal burdens were swept away. To every citizen were guaranteed liberty of conscience and of religion, freedom of the press, and the right of petition as inalienable rights.

The lofty aim of the whole constitution was to further the welfare, the ennobling, and the enlightenment of the people, and to induce every individual without distinction to take an active part in political life. But the French themselves discredited their work and procured enemies to the constitution by at once treating Switzerland as conquered territory, seizing the hoarded treasures, levying contributions, and harassing the population. From the cantons of Berne, Fribourg, Soleure, Lucerne, and Zurich alone they extorted a war tax of fifteen millions; the public chests and arsenals were robbed right and left; in Berne (according to a computation of 1815) in all over seventeen million francs were stolen. Laharpe himself was appalled at the faithless and shameful course of action adopted by the deliverers of his country.

This circumstance more than anything else strengthened the opposition already existing in Switzerland against the united constitution; the "deliverance" seemed more like subjugation. When therefore the French commissary invited all the cantons to send their delegates to Aarau on April 12 to accept the constitution, only the ten cantons of Zurich, Berne, Lucerne, Soleure, Fribourg, Basle, Schaffhausen, Aargau, Oberland, and the Vaud complied, the interior and eastern cantons holding aloof. This assembly in Aarau elected the new officials, the Directory, and the ministers. Admonished by the Directory, the states of eastern Switzerland next embraced the constitution; only the original cantons, Uri, Schwyz, and Unterwalden, where the sense of independence had been strong for centuries, resisted with an obstinacy born of an affronted sense of honor and liberty; but they lost the historical and lawful precedence which they had maintained for centuries! In these cantons, too, the priests had great influence, and certain of the Catholic church pointed out unfavorable clauses of the constitution, such as the confiscation of the monastic treasures and the licensing of mixed marriages, to arouse opposition among the people. A separate Diet at Schwyz protested against the Helvetic Constitution; and Schauenburg adopting violent measures, Schwyz actually fixed upon the bold plan of restoring the old Confederation and making head against the victorious nation. A violent patriotic and religious enthusiasm took possession of all classes; young and old, women and children, took up arms, and ecclesiastics, like Marianus Herzog of Einsiedeln and the Capuchin Paul Styger, placed themselves at their head. A commencement was made by invading the neighboring territories of Zug, Rapperswil, and Lucerne, in order to wrench the country piece by piece from the Helvetic Republic. Schauenburg on the other hand now conceived the plan of an attack to be made on all sides, and the men of Schwyz were forced to give way. Part of the French troops advanced from Zurich along the lake, took Wollerau and Pfäffikon by storm on April 30, 1798, and marched against the Etzel and the Schindellegi. Pastor Marianus Herzog was the first to treacherously desert his post, and thus to open the way to Einsiedeln to the enemy; hence the remaining forces of Schwyz, under Alois Reding, after defending themselves most valiantly and successfully, to avoid being surrounded were forced to retire upon Rothenthurm and Morgarten, where meanwhile another division of the French had been successfully encountered; and, almost frantic with enthusiasm, on May 2 they again defeated the united hosts of the enemy. The French forces, however, far outnumbered those of Schwyz, and the latter were moreover cut off from their fellows. When, therefore, after a truce, it became necessary for the *Landsgemeinde* of Schwyz to come to a decision, they arranged an honorable peace (May 4).

The time soon came when the whole of Switzerland was required to swear to the Helvetic Constitution, and then the resentment broke out afresh in Schwyz, and also in Nidwalden. The latter, incited by the clergy, flew to arms; Schauenburg, however, invaded the little territory with from 9000 to 10,000 men, and conquered it on September 9, after a short struggle, though it is true, with much difficulty; for, mindful of the deeds of their ancestors, the descendants of the heroes of Morgarten, Sempach, and Murten did not yield till they could carry the fame of incomparable bravery with them to the grave. Terrible indeed was the fate of the country: wherever the French bayonets appeared the ground was dyed with streams of blood; dwellings were burned down, and misery knew no bounds in "the days of terror of Nidwalden." Thus was the Helvetic Constitution imposed upon them only by force.

Meanwhile the Directory and its ministers applied themselves vigorously to the performance of their task. Specially serviceable were the efforts of the two ministers, Dr. Albrecht Rengger and Albrecht Stapfer, both natives of the little (formerly Bernese) town of Brugg. While Rengger, as minister of the interior, busied himself with the introduction of new regulations in the communes, Stapfer, minister of the arts and sciences, was untiring in his endeavors to improve the educational system. A clause of the Helvetic Constitution defines enlightenment as the chief foundation of public welfare, speaking of it as preferable to all outward prosperity. It was in this spirit that Stapfer embarked upon his task, and the intense activity which was now displayed in the sphere of education is one of the finest points of the Helvetic system; the ideas which then sprang into existence were as the first tokens of the spring of modern times, and have to some extent been only quite lately carried into execution. Stapfer caused all the cantons to send him reports of the condition of their system of schools and education, together with ideas and suggestions for their improvement. Federal regulations for schools were drawn up, which embraced all scientific and pedagogic institutions, and produced a very great advance as compared with conditions existing prior to 1798. In the chief town of every canton a council of education was established consisting of seven members; a commissioner or inspector of public instruction chosen by the council of education watched over every district, to see that the communal schools were provided with capable teachers; and in every canton a seminary was to be erected for the training of good teachers. Pestalozzi now gained his opportunity of laboring effectually for the renovation of the method of teaching by publishing a popular paper at the request of Stapfer. Stapfer specially directed his efforts toward curing the evils wrought by the war; with this aim he erected a house of education at Stans for poor orphan children, which was intrusted to the direction of Pestalozzi; here the latter labored night and day, full of love and devotion for the little ones. Stapfer was also anxious to effectually promote higher education, the arts and sciences. He provided for the erection of "gymnasiums," or grammar-schools, and even suggested the establishment of a Swiss university or academy; he endeavored also to establish in all parts literary societies for the promotion of public spirit, enlightenment, and culture. Besides all this, he made arrangements for the foundation of a Swiss society of arts, and directed his energy toward preserving and throwing open the monastic libraries and collections (National Museum). The number of daily papers increased, and Federal newspapers sprang into existence, such as the *Schweizerischer Republikaner,* of Escher and Usteri, and the *Journal von und für Helvetien.*

These praiseworthy efforts, however, did not always meet with a favorable reception. The means were not adequate to the plans; the finances of the central government were altogether insufficient for the carrying out of the proposed institutions, and moreover much prejudice against all innovations still prevailed among the people; even Pestalozzi, notwithstanding his self-sacrificing activity, was so combated and hampered in the original cantons of Uri, Schwyz, and Unterwalden that he was almost in despair. But the new seed suffered most from the boundless misery left everywhere by the French invasion. Many districts were deprived of all means of subsistence; gardens and fields were laid waste, and disease and famine followed like dismal specters in the wake of the French armies.

The efforts of the Directory to help by contributions of produce and money were as a drop in the ocean; the contributions required by the French for transport, provisions, and fortifications swallowed up all, and increased from day to day. For Switzerland having in August, 1798, abandoned her neutrality and concluded an alliance with France, had become the battlefield of the second European war of coalition, which fearfully harassed the land, and although in the main quite foreign to her interests, yet had a distinct effect upon the course of political events in Switzerland.

At the commencement of the war of 1799 the Austrians were at first victorious; the Archduke Charles crossed the Rhine and forced his way through the territories of Schaffhausen, Thurgau, and Zurich, driving the French before him; while from the Grisons in the southeast a division advanced under Hotze (a native of Richterswil) and drove back the enemy from the districts of the interior. After a fierce encounter near Zurich on June 4, 1799, Massena was obliged to retire before Charles and Hotze behind the Limmat. A reaction ensued in the east of Switzerland; the opponents of the Helvetic Constitution and of the French received the Austrians with rejoicings and bore themselves triumphantly; Abbot Pancraz Forster revoked his former concessions to the people and once more established his dominion; in Thurgau, the numerous lords of manors and squires again possessed themselves of their privileges; the canton or district of St. Gall was abolished, and the constitution of Appenzell restored by the help of the Austrians, while the trees of liberty were destroyed.

But the joy of the reactionary party was not of long duration. For scarcely had the Archduke Charles been recalled from Switzerland, and marched away along the Rhine to Germany, when Massena successfully assumed the offensive, and defeated the Russians under Korsakow on September 26, in the scond battle near Zurich, whereupon Zurich and the whole of the northeast of Switzerland fell into his hands. Suvarov, the Russian general, endeavoring to lead his own troops and the Austrian auxiliaries from Italy over the St. Gothard, found his way blocked at the Lake of the Four Cantons, and it was only after indescribable difficulties and by a desperate march across the Alps, over the Kinzigkulm, Pragel, and the pass of Panix, that he succeeded in striking out a circuitous route toward the east. By this means Switzerland once more falling completely into the hands of the French, the Helvetic Republic was again established in its entirety. But the unhappy land had yet to suffer grievously for having become the battlefield of foreign armies. Great excesses were committed by the soldiers of both sides, and the demands for the maintenance of the army became more and more oppressive. In the short time from September to December Thurgau alone was forced to disburse almost a million and a half of florins for the French army; while the town of Arbon had to pay 75,000 francs, and Zurich and Basle as much as 800,000 francs! All this was not calculated to reconcile the people to the new order of things; every evil was ascribed chiefly to the new constitution. Hence, after the close of the war of the coalition there arose a conflict between the factions in Switzerland itself, which at length brought about the downfall of the Helvetic Constitution.

After the introduction of the united Helvetic Constitution two parties bitterly opposed one another throughout the whole of Switzerland: the Unionists or Centralists, adherents of the uniform system, and the Federalists, or adherents of the old Federal Constitution and of the Confederation. This schism was specially troublesome in the councils and in the government; while at the same time the friends of the new order of things were split up into various smaller divisions, perpetually at strife among themselves, and alternately seeking to obtain a leading influence in the government, and to alter the constitution to suit their own views. Four *coups d'état* succeeded one another in five years, and four changes of the constitution.

At first the government was entirely central, but after changing several of the persons composing it, the leading members themselves—Ochs and Laharpe—were expelled; the Directory then dissolved, and in its stead, on January 8, 1800, an executive committee of seven members (mostly "Moderates") was established by the legislative councils. This came about by the help of Napoleon Bonaparte, who had likewise abolished the Directory in France, and had raised himself to the position of First Consul. But the Centralists in the legislative councils becoming once more active, the Moderate party went further, and by the help of French troops compassed the dissolution of the councils, whereupon, on August 7, 1800, a council of legislation of fifty members was set up. With the attempt to establish a new constitution, however, the bitterest party strife broke out, and the influence of France became very active. The First Consul was gradually adopting the views of the Federalists, and at length, by a new constitution of May 29, 1801, styled the "Scheme of Malmaison," he almost entirely restored the sovereignty of the cantons and the Diet. This constitution, however, did not last; the Centralists, under Usteri, succeeded at the Diet called together to receive the constitution in remodeling it according to their own ideas. A counter-stroke on the part of the Federalists (Reding, Reinhard, etc.) quickly followed; they drove out the Helvetic officials, established a senate of their own party, and drew up a constitution, which was really still more Federal than the scheme of Napoleon (November, 1801, to February, 1802). But in the spring of 1802 the Centralists again rallied, and once more obtained a united constitution.

This exasperated the Federalists, and they braced themselves for a desperate struggle. The withdrawal of the French troops, which took place in consequence of the Peace of Amiens, in the summer of 1802, gave the signal for the outbreak. Under the name of a "Swiss Brotherhood" a conspiracy was formed against the Centralists and the Helvetic Government, the two states of Berne and Zurich supporting the democratic cantons. Twelve cantons assembled at a Diet at Schwyz, Zurich, as the capital, taking the lead. The Helvetic Government found itself confronted by an open revolt, which it endeavored to quell by force of arms; but the troops were defeated by those of Unterwalden at the Rengg August 27-28, upon which it called upon the French to intervene.

It was in vain that Zurich was besieged in September, 1802, by the Helvetic General Andermatt. No longer safe even in Berne, the government was forced to fly to the Vaud, where, however, the troops under General Bachmann were likewise defeated at Morat and Avenches by the troops of the "Swiss Brotherhood" under Rudolf von Erlach.[2] The Centralists now began to give way, and the Helvetic Government, no longer safe in Lausanne, was about to take refuge in Savoy, when General Rapp, Napoleon's plenipotentiary, suddenly arrived, and in the name of the First Consul, who offered himself as a mediator between the parties, commanded a halt. The revolted districts were occupied by a French army, the leaders of the revolt beheaded, and the Helvetic Government reëntered Berne in October, 1802, under the protection of French troops.

The First Consul had now got the exhausted Switzerland completely into his power. With a view to the reorganization of Swiss affairs he summoned delegates of both parties to a consultation at Paris to advise with him as to guiding principles, which might, if possible, satisfy both Federalists and Centralists. The late struggles had convinced him that the united Helvetic Constitution could not be maintained, since it endeavored too rapidly to efface with one stroke all the conditions which had become historical, and offended too many interests and views; he was even of opinion that the very diversity of nature in Switzerland was opposed to a uniform system. Above all, he considered the constitution of the democratic *Landsgemeinde* a fine and historically noteworthy peculiarity, of which Switzerland ought not to be deprived. But just as little did he desire the mere restoration of the old order of things; the fundamental idea of the French Revolution was the benefit of humanity, and the promotion of liberty, equality, and the welfare of the people; and he could not suffer a system to be adopted in Switzerland which was favored by Austria and in direct opposition to France, or in which adherents of the enemies of France took the lead. He therefore adopted a middle course, in which proceeding he was constantly encouraged by his conferences and discussions with the members of the " Consulta." He paid no heed to any opposition, and with rare sagacity succeeded in silencing or overawing his opponents. After mature consideration, on February 19, 1803, he submitted to the committee of consultation an Act of Mediation compiled by himself, which he desired should be deemed unalterable without any inquiry into the will of the nation itself. At the same time he did not fail to remind the delegates that only in this way could Switzerland be saved from shipwreck,

[2] This war is commonly called the "*Stecklikrieg*," or "*Guerre aux Batons*," from the insurgents having armed themselves with sticks (*stöcke*) and clubs.

and find in him a happy refuge. In the constitution itself everything tended inevitably to make Switzerland dependent upon France.

As regarded the settlement of details, six new cantons were added to the thirteen old ones, formed out of former common domains, subject-lands, or allied states, namely, St. Gall, Thurgau, the Grisons, Ticino, the Vaud, and Aargau (to which was added the Fricktal, the last Austrian possession in Switzerland). Then the Diet was reëstablished, in which the people as such were not represented at all, the delegates being bound by the instructions of the governments of the cantons. Yet the Federal power was strengthened by penalties laid upon all rebellion against the decisions of the Diet, and unity found expression in the person of a "Landammann." There were to be six seats of government, each for one year—Fribourg, Berne, Soleure, Basle, Zurich, and Lucerne. The burgomaster, or mayor of the capital, was the Landammann for the time being. The subject-lands and all privileges of nobility, birth, or family were swept away. On the other hand, very few popular rights were preserved: there was no mention of the right of petition or of liberty of the press, nor even of the sovereignty of the people. The constitutions of the cantons reverted to old historical conditions (*Landsgemeinde,* the guilds, and patricians), while the constitutions of the new cantons were more liberal, the purchase of tithes and ground-rent was rendered difficult, and the suffrage was confined to those paying a certain amount of taxes.

In consequence of its combination and fusion of the old with the new, the "Mediation" was a characterless middle course, and, as was inevitable, many traces of former conditions soon came once more to the fore, such as titles, torture, the obligation imposed upon artisans to join a guild, the public censorship, etc. Violent irritation was also aroused by the curtailing of popular privileges with regard to tithes and suffrage. In the canton of Zurich the population along the left bank of the lake showed signs of insubordination, especially those of Horgen under one Willi, a shoemaker. The military advanced against them and took possession of Horgen, but were obliged to retire before Willi and his troops to the heights of Bocken in April, 1804. The country folk now became alarmed; Willi could get no reinforcements, and the troops succeeded on their second march in completely disarming the insurgents. The leaders were taken, brought before an extraordinary court-martial, and put to death without mercy. The spirit of 1795 seemed about to return. With the exception of this rising, Switzerland, after the reception of the constitution, enjoyed eleven years of peace and of salutary development, and was happily enabled to recover gradually from the wounds inflicted upon her.

Under the protection of the peace, an increased intellectual advancement became evident in every respect during the time of the "Mediation." The new ideas propagated by the patriots of the eighteenth century silently permeated life, and gradually transformed the old historical conditions. Now again, as in the eighteenth century, progress was chiefly brought about by individual societies. The Helvetic Society, their jubilant songs and merry clinking of glasses drowned in the thunder of the cannon of Neueneck and Grauholz, had had no time to assemble during the party strife of the Helvetic Constitution, but they now met once more, and endeavored to effect a reconciliation of all parties upon a national basis. For the improvement of regulations concerning the relief of the poor, education and industrial life the Swiss Society for Public Benefit sprang into existence; the Swiss society of artists, founded by Martin Usteri, aimed at giving a national direction to Swiss art; a society for historical research and a society of Swiss teachers were also started. As a distraction from the dreary political outlook, men immersed themselves in the life of the people, the natural beauties of their land and its glorious past, and a patriotic spirit dominated the arts and sciences. The lofty peaks of the Alps were scaled, measured, and described. General Pfyffer and Müller, an engineer of Engelberg, completed high-relief maps of the greater part of Switzerland; Swiss atlases appeared (such as that of Rudolf Meier), Swiss maps (of Heinrich Keller), descriptions of Swiss plants (of Hegetschweiler), and delicate, finely engraved pictures of Swiss towns, Swiss costumes, and the festivals of the *Alpenrosen* and *helvetischer Almanach*. As a historian, Johann von Müller led the van; full of an intense love of his country, he labored at this time upon the flourishing period of the fourteenth and fifteenth centuries, as if to lay a wreath upon the tomb of the old Confederation. This period is characterized by the special attention paid to Swiss history; popular histories of Switzerland and histories for the young (of Zschokke, Schuler, etc.), were written and eagerly read. Pastor Stalder of Escholzmatt laid the foundation of a Swiss *Idiotikon* or dictionary of dialects; a separate Swiss poetry sprang into existence in the popular dialect, specially through the amiable poet and artist Martin Usteri of Zurich, who wrote "*De Herr Heiri*" and "*De Vikari.*" With the popular poetry there arose also a nobler order of popular songs, of which the composer, Hans Georg Nägeli of Wetzikon (canton Zurich), is still honored as the founder. "His melodies ring out in merry companies, at excursions on our lakes, from boys in the streets, and the low and worthless songs which had formerly been sung could never have been extirpated by any prohibition as they were by the 'Nägeli-Lieder' (songs of Nägeli)." His melodies were even appreciated in other lands; in Switzerland itself Nägeli became the founder of choral societies, and a great favorite with the people, who called him "Father Nägeli."

The beneficent and educational efforts of this period proved a lasting blessing to the whole life of the people. In 1810 the Swiss Society for Public Benefit was founded; it numbered members from every canton, who now pledged themselves to labor, each in his own sphere, for the relief of the poor, the starving, and the wretched, and to promote the establishment of almshouses, orphanges, poor-funds, storehouses, etc. Savings banks came into existence, the first at Zurich in 1805, and insurance offices also. Moreover, in the domain of material culture progress was made in various ways common to the period; forestry and agriculture underwent a rational improvement, the latter particularly through the exertions of the Bernese Emanuel von Fellenberg, who erected an agricultural school and model-institute with all the best agricultural appliances on his estate of Hofwil, the monasteries of Kreuzlingen in the Thurgau and Altenryf in Fribourg following his example. Machines were introduced for cotton manufactures in Zurich and St. Gall. But the greatest undertaking of this time was the Linth canal, which was achieved (1804-1822) through the untiring and philanthropic exertions of the self-sacrificing Hans Konrad Escher of Zurich, hence styled "von der Linth," and which forever rescued the population of that district from the depths of misery.[3]

In educational and scholastic matters the activity of Pestalozzi, first in Burgdorf, and afterward in Yverdon, attracted more and more attention; with him labored also his pupils Fellenberg and Wehrli. His method of object-teaching, training the mind to

---

[3] This canal connects the Lake of Zurich with the Lake of Wallenstadt.

think and find out for itself, was recognized as the best by the greatest thinkers and schoolmen of the day, and soon called forth imitation, both in Switzerland and other lands. But he was himself wanting in the necessary practical ability for the management of an educational institute for the poor. In this his friend Emanuel von Fellenberg succeeded better, who during his agricultural exertions had noted with the deepest pain the impoverishment and neglect of the lower classes, and founded a charitable institution upon his already-mentioned estate. From 1810 he intrusted the management of the latter to Wehrli, the able and gifted friend of the poor, and of whom Pestalozzi joyfully asserted that he had realized his idea of a school for the poor. In addition to this, Eellenberg also founded an institute for boys of the upper classes, which was greatly sought after, and held courses of instruction for training teachers for popular schools. It was reserved to the canton of Aargau to erect, in 1810, the first training college for teachers in Switzerland. Noteworthy improvements were also effected in the system of higher instruction. Cantonal schools arose in Coire and Aarau, grammar-schools (*Gymnasien*) in the Vaud and other parts, an institute for higher education in St. Gall, a political institute in Zurich for lawyers and statesmen; Berne also introduced new and excellent regulations for schools.

While as regarded internal matters Switzerland managed her own affairs, toward the outer world she took up rather the position of a province of France, to which country she was bound by a defensive alliance and a military capitulation. She had come under the yoke of her powerful mediator, Napoleon, who had risen to the rank of emperor in 1804, and now shared the fortunes of the Napoleonic Empire. Swiss trade suffered severely under the continental blockade: Napoleon suddenly and most despotically placed a military occupation in Ticino, under pretense of hindering English contraband trade. Swiss territory seemed to exist only to serve the interests of France: Neuchâtel became a subject principality of France, and in 1810 the great emperor arbitrarily annexed Valais to his empire as the "Département du Simplon," in order to hold unconditional sway over the road which he had constructed across the Simplon. Switzerland was also the market where the French found their soldiers. Federal troops, always from 12,000 to 16,000 in number, were forced to fight for the glory and aggrandizement of France in Spain, Austria, and lastly in Russia, where they displayed heroic courage and unrivaled valor in 1812, but finally shared the miserable fate of the great army, out of 12,000 only 2200 remaining! Any powerful or independent action on the part of Switzerland was impossible; "neutrality" was to Napoleon a "word without meaning"; Switzerland must be guided by France alone. The emperor, therefore, purposely hindered the formation of a strong Federal military force. His agents maintained a strict supervision over the Swiss press and all freedom of speech, and the policy of Swiss statesmen was determined by his will.

From the time of the overthrow of the "great army" upon the snowfields of Russia, the power of the "Emperor of the Universe" was on the wane. Prussia, Austria, and England rose to assist Russia, and after the "Battle of the Nations" at Leipsic October 16-18, 1813, the allies advanced toward the Rhine in order to penetrate into France. Napoleon's plans were thus frustrated, and the question was raised in Switzerland, too, whether the constitution imposed by Napoleon should or should not be any longer preserved. An inclination in its favor, however, prevailed; it had procured peace to the country, preserved certain liberal principles, and given life and existence to six new cantons. Fresh storms and troubles were feared. The Diet, therefore, declined to join the allies, and decided to observe their neutrality and to raise an army.

But the adherents of the old conditions, previous to 1798, in Zurich, Berne, etc., desired an invasion on the part of the allies, by whose help they hoped to gain their end. They formed the "Society of Restoration," a secret committee of which negotiated with the allies at Waldshut. The Swiss army was destined to guard the Rhine frontier from Basle to Schaffhausen and the Grisons. But the military force of Switzerland had been crippled by Napoleon, and from motives of economy Landammann Reinhard put insufficient troops in the field. Swiss statesmen, too, allowed themselves to be deceived by the allies into thinking that there was no question of any invasion of Switzerland. Hence they were lamentably taken by surprise and overcome.

When the allies announced their intention of invading the country, General von Wattenwil, who, considering the disproportionate inequality of his force of 12,500 against 160,000 men, deemed any resistance not only futile, but dangerous, ordered a retreat from the frontier on December 20, when not a shot had been fired for the preservation of neutrality. The allies passed quietly along the Rhine from Basle to Schaffhausen, and poured into Swiss territory without finding any opposition. The immediate result of this was the downfall of the constitution of "Mediation." Metternich, the Austrian minister, was specially active toward its abolition, in spite of promises made to Switzerland that her internal concerns should not be interfered with. Under repeated pressure from the Austrian ambassador and from an insolent emissary of Metternich, the Count of Senft-Pilsach, the "Mediation" government in Berne resigned on December 23, and its downfall was followed by that of the governments of Soleure, Fribourg, and Lucerne. At the end of December an extraordinary Diet assembled in Zurich, and formally declared the Constitution of Mediation extinct.

But when it came to the establishment of a new order of things, opinions were widely divided. Berne wanted totally to ignore all that had passed since the Revolution, desired to get back her former subject-lands of the Vaud and Aargau, and demanded the restoration of the old Confederation of Thirteen Cantons, in which she was supported by the patrician states and the formerly privileged democratic cantons. The liberal towns on the other hand adopted a middle course, while the new cantons wished if possible to maintain existing conditions. In opposition to the liberal Diet in Zurich a reactionary one was soon assembled in Lucerne on March 20, and only the menaces of the powers, declaring themselves in favor of a Confederation of nineteen cantons, succeeded in effecting an outward reconciliation of the two Diets, in the beginning of April, 1814. Internal dissensions, however, continued, Berne and the cantons of similar opinions persisting in their claims upon the subject-lands. The cantons of Aargau and Vaud, finding their very existence thus threatened, prepared for an armed resistance. The claims of Schwyz and Glarus gave rise to tumults in Utznach and Sargans, parts of the new canton of St. Gall; as did those of Uri in Livinen (Val Leventina), belonging to the canton of Ticino. The canton of Ticino threatened to separate itself; the Grisons sought to repossess themselves of their former domains in the Valtelline, Cleves, and Worms; Bienne and the former bishopric of Basle endeavored to obtain a union with Switzerland, as did Neuchâtel, Valais, and Geneva.

The Diet, earnestly endeavoring to quell the disturbances, was for a long time prevented from completing the scheme of the new constitution, and the representatives of Prussia, Austria, and Russia were forced repeatedly to urge dispatch. It seemed impossible in Switzerland to settle conflicting claims, and to agree upon territorial changes. At length the Congress of Vienna, which had been sitting since the autumn of 1814, interposed, in order to re-

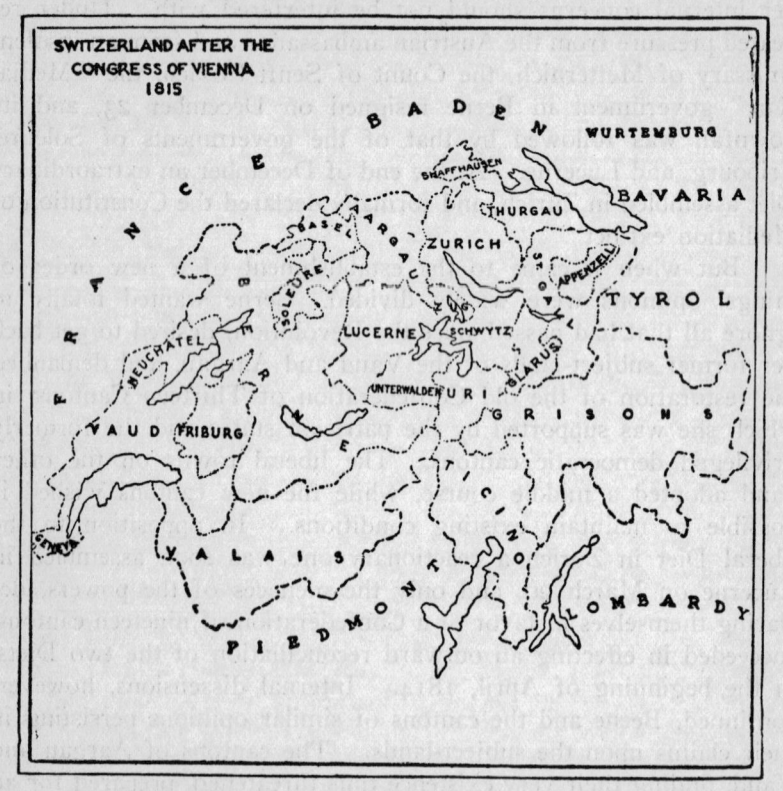

move the chief causes of dispute. Switzerland had sent delegates to Vienna, but even they could not agree among themselves, and actually opposed one another's measures, which caused great delay in Swiss affairs.

Meanwhile Napoleon had been deposed and banished to Elba. Suddenly, however, he returned, and in March, 1815, attempted to reinstate his empire. The powers quickly combined, and Switzerland, too, occupied her western frontier, under General

Bachmann. On March 20, 1815, Swiss matters were adjusted by the congress. The powers started from the assumption that Switzerland needed strengthening that she might act as a buffer against France. Valais, Neuchâtel, and Geneva were, therefore, added as new cantons to the nineteen already existing, and thus the foundation was laid once for all of the Confederation of twenty-two states. On the other hand, the Valtelline, Chiavenna, and Worms had to be surrendered to Austria, and the Grisons were forced to content themselves with the hitherto Austrian domain of Räzüns. In regard to internal affairs, all claims upon the formerly subject-lands were declared null and void. Berne was indemnified for the loss of hers by receiving the greater part of the bishopric of Basle, together with Bienne; the remainder of the bishopric fell to Basle. The indemnities of the remaining cantons were discharged in money.

Under foreign pressure, Switzerland in the summer of 1815 forsook her policy of neutrality, and took part in the struggle against Napoleon by invading Upper Burgundy, and also by her coöperation in besieging and taking Hüningen.[4] Thus fully satisfied, the powers appointed fixed limits to the territory of Geneva, and forced France to pay an indemnity for her depredations in 1798; moreover they, on November 20, 1815, took the territorial position of Switzerland under their protection, and acknowledged her perpetual neutrality, in which the two provinces of northern Savoy, Faucigny, and Chablais, conquered by Berne in the sixteen century, were included.

During these events the "Long Diet" at Zurich was evolving a new Federal constitution, the so-called "Federal Pact," which, approved by the Congress of Vienna, was signed and accepted in August, 1815. During the deliberations many voices had been raised in favor of maintaining a strong Federal authority, but the majority of the members of the Diet were enthusiastically attached to the system of petty states which had prevailed before 1798; the cantons hankered after their old sovereign rights, and the aristocracy after their privileges. Thus the broad basis of the Federal State was totally abandoned, and Switzerland was transformed into a loose Confederation, in which all the twenty-two cantons enjoyed the full right of self-government, and only acted in concert in mat-

[4] This fortress, erected by Louis XIV. (1679-1681), had always been a thorn in the side to the Swiss.

ters of foreign policy, and for the maintenance of peace and order in the interior. The system of rendering assistance and levying troops was much the same as in the time of the old Confederation, before 1798, as was also the mode of settling internal disputes. There was no distinct and unmistakable prohibition of the privileges of certain states and of birth, no mention of the people being at liberty to choose their place of residence, or of free trade, nor were the rights of Swiss citizenship established. It is true that the holding of lands in subjection was forbidden, but in the enjoyment of political privileges exclusiveness alone was prohibited.

The Diet returned to the old and cumbersome system of "Instructions," and the interchange of commerce between certain leading states. Zurich, Berne, and Lucerne were to become capitals in rotation, changing every two years. The continuance of the religious houses was guaranteed, so far as depended upon the cantonal governments; but a very wide latitude was given to mercenary service, by the fact that the settlement of military capitulations was left to the option of the states. The constitution of the cantons was left to the discretion of the various states themselves, and in them very few concessions were made to the less privileged classes. Four cantons almost entirely restored the old patrician constitution (Berne, Fribourg, Soleure, and Lucerne), and the new cantons also approached more nearly to the aristocratic system than during the period of the "Mediation." Among the civic cantons the chief cities once more obtained the ascendency. In Soleure the town had 68 representatives, the rural district only 33; in Zurich the city had 130 representatives, the country 82; in Fribourg the town had 108, the country only 36; in Berne the city 200, the country only 99. The franchise, as also the right to be elected, was still more restricted, according to the amount of property (*Census*), and thus the dominion of the higher classes and of the rich was once more established, though slightly enfeebled.

There was no more talk of popular liberties. The elections were excessively indirect, and the freedom of the communes was almost extinct. The obligation of belonging to a guild was once more enforced, and torture also reappeared.

This reaction corresponded to the alarm at all radical innovations, and the universal lassitude and stagnation which prevailed everywhere after the great revolution. At this time the Bernese professor, Karl L. von Haller, successfully advocated opposition to all liberal institutions, and the "Restoration of the Middle Ages." Liberal teachers were persecuted. Professor Troxler, of Lucerne, who in his book "*Fürst und Volk*"[5] propagated democratic opinions, was, in 1821, deprived of his appointment. This reaction was chiefly owing to the influence of the "Holy Alliance," which Switzerland had joined in 1817. Liberal agitations becoming rife in the surrounding countries, the governments interposed with persecutions, and numberless fugitives gathered in Switzerland. Liberal pamphlets indulged freely in criticism of the "Restoration" policy of other lands, and the fugitives also, safe on Swiss soil, incited to rebellion against their home governments. At last Switzerland, long threatened by the powers, by a decision of the Diet (*Konklusum*), in 1823, published strict regulations for the press, and laid restrictions upon the liberty of harboring refugees. Switzerland lay for years under the ban of the surrounding countries.

The church, too, helped the reaction. In 1818 the Jesuits established themselves in Fribourg, as they had formerly done in Valais. Father Girard, a noble Franciscan, and a friend of Pestalozzi, who had improved and renovated the instruction in the schools of Fribourg, was by them persecuted, and finally in 1823 expelled. Similar attacks were made, chiefly at the instigation of the papal nuncio in Lucerne, upon Baron von Wessenberg, vicar-general of the Bishop of Constance, who was laboring to further the culture and enlightenment of the clergy, and to establish a more popular form of divine service, having the sermon and the mass in the mother-tongue, hymns, and exposition of the gospels. In order to withdraw his influence from Switzerland, he was removed from the bishopric of Constance in 1815 by a papal decree, and placed under an apostolical vicar, Göldlin, provost of Beromünster. After the death of Göldlin, in 1819, the Catholics of the east of Switzerland came under the direction of the Bishop of Coire; in 1828, however, a number of cantons (Berne, Soleure, Lucerne, Zug, Aargau, Thurgau, and Basle) revived the bishopric of Basle, and placed its seat in Soleure. From this time the papal system struck its roots deeper and deeper in Catholic Switzerland, and "Ultramontanism"[6] prevailed, while the relations between Catholic and Prot-

[5] "Prince and People."
[6] From *ultra montes,* "beyond the mountains," meaning the papal seat south of the Alps.

estants were almost as strained as they were in the seventeenth century.

Thus beneath the weight of the policy of restoration it seemed as though all free development must be stifled: yet the spirit of the people could not remain forever fettered, and even during the time of oppression it was gathering strength in order the sooner to gain a free field. Patriotic enthusiasm, which had shown itself in many ways during the time of the " Mediation," was still at work; for instance, creative art still gave the preference to patriotic subjects —witness the painters Vogel in Zurich and Disteli in Olten. The poets, too, chose subjects which kindled the people: Abraham Emanuel Fröhlich, of Aargau, in his fables lashed the abuses of the time, and the Bernese J. Rudolf Wyss the younger gave Switzerland her thrilling national anthem in the song "*Rufst du, mein Vaterland.*"[7] Men turned once more to seek their country, and finding its very conception lost to all appearance, they lived upon the memory of their splendid past, erecting monuments to patriotic heroes, such as the obelisk at Morat, the Mengistein, and the monument at St. Jakob an der Birs. The younger generation was imbued with a spirit of exertion and creation, " free progress " was written on their banners, and a number of newly founded societies grew into workshops where the times were remodeled. From 1815 the Society for Natural Research had united the learned forces of Switzerland; the Association of Zofingen, founded in 1819, united all the students of Switzerland upon the basis of scientific effort and patriotic enthusiasm. Patriotic feeling was strengthened by the Society of Sempach, and by the shooting matches which were held regularly after 1824, when the first gathering of the Rifle Association took place in Aarau. A similar effect was everywhere produced by gymnastic and choral societies.

None of these societies, however, took up so determined and aggressive an attitude as did the Helvetic Society. Since its reassembling at Schinznach in 1819, when the noise of war had ceased, the policy of a merely hesitating and cautious opposition against existing conditions was abandoned, all aristocratic tendencies were shaken off, and it was formally converted into a political association, its chief aim being to combat the abuses of the " Restoration." Thaddäus Müller, a minister of the town of Lucerne, as president of the society, in 1821 attacked the intrigues

[7] "Callest thou, O my fatherland."

of the hierarchy, while Troxler combated the condition of intellectual tutelage. Johann Kaspar Orelli, the philologist of Zurich, before a large assembly of friends, drew a lively picture of the policy of "Restoration" as a whole, its intellectual darkness, the censure of the press, mercenary service, the spirit of persecution, etc., urging his hearers to exert themselves for the revival of mental culture, and comforting the more enlightened with the assurance that truth had always proved victorious in spite of scorn and opposition.

The Federal Pact of 1815 became in 1829 the subject of a cutting criticism by Zschokke, who lauded national unity, which he considered better expressed in the Act of Mediation than in the pact, and placed before the society the noble aim of laboring for such national unity. In May, 1830, Dr. Schinz, the chief justice of Zurich, proclaimed the absolute necessity of a general alteration, and would have all governments recognize that they "exist only from the people, by the people, and for the people." Thus was expressed the principle of the new revolution, the establishment of a representative democracy.

The press chiefly contributed to this revolution, having acquired considerable influence over the public life since the French Revolution. Liberal movements found advocates in the *Neue Zürche Zeitung* of Paul Usteri, in Zschokke's *Schweizerbote,* and in the *Appenzelle Zeitung,* established in Trogen in 1828. The latter became the organ of all the Swiss radicals; they criticised the abuses which were coming to light on all sides, and that in no measured terms.

But before the reform was introduced into Federal territory, several states had attempted to remodel the cantons; these were specially Lucerne, Appenzell, the Vaud, and Ticino. The new aristocracy in Lucerne was overthrown in 1829 by the efforts of the brothers Kasimir and Eduard Pfyffer, and a division of power was undertaken; the small council lost the right of recruiting itself, and the title of "Town and Republic" was abolished. In Inner Rhodes of Appenzell a revision was pushed through in 1829, extending the rights of the *Landsgemeinde.* Through the influence of the dauntless Paul Usteri the censure was abolished in Zurich, upon which, in 1829, the Diet also abandoned the *Konklusum,* while the authority of the great council was strengthened. In the

Vaud the demand for reform became more and more urgent, especially after it had been proposed by Laharpe in May, 1829. But in Ticino the most fundamental alterations were necessary, for here the old abuses which had existed before 1798, such as corruption, waste, and nepotism, had been brought back. Under the direction of the teacher and editor Franscini a total revision in a democratic spirit was drawn up, which in June, 1830, was accepted by the people.

Chapter XI

INTERNAL REORGANIZATION. 1830-1848

IN Switzerland as elsewhere the "Revolution of July" in France gave a great impulse to the movements which were already in agitation, and lent them great force. They were welcomed with joy by the reform party, and the current soon spread through every rank of society. Demands for revision increased daily; the press revived with redoubled vigor: the sovereignty of the people, equality of rights, separation of the powers, publicity of discussion, and the freedom of the press became watchwords. Tumultuous movements now followed one another in quick succession in the hitherto quiet cantons. In Aargau an assembly of Liberals at Lenzburg directed a petition to the government on September 12, 1830, desiring that a revision might be taken in hand; and the government receiving it coldly and with hesitation, a popular assembly at Wohlenswil on November 7 emphatically demanded a thorough change of constitution. In Thurgau Pastor Bornhauser, of Matzingen, proclaimed the rosy dawn of a new day with enthusiasm, and appealed to his hearers to better the constitution. The first popular assembly in Weinfelden, on October 22, voted for a total revision, and a second at the same place, on November 18, required direct popular elections of new officials and publicity of discussions. The council of Burgdorf, headed by the brothers Ludwig Schnell, town clerk, and Karl Schnell, barrister, demanded of the Bernese Government a reform of the constitution, in October; and in Porrentruy violent tumults took place, purporting to effect their separation from Berne. In Basle, too, the country district, led by Liestal, demanded full equality of rights with the town, and an assembly of delegates from the communes in Bubendorfer-Bade, on November 18, required a revision of the constitution. A similar demand was made by an assembly at Olten, in Soleure. In Lucerne the exiled Professor Troxler fanned the flame by spreading broadcast through the land a pamphlet requiring full restoration of popular rights. A popular assembly at Sursee on November 21 espoused the same cause with one consent.

These efforts for the most part failed to reach the goal at once; the aristocracies clung fast to existing conditions. The governments of Lucerne and Thurgau hesitated, the councils of Soleure and Basle resisted, and Berne actually made preparations to suppress all by the help of the military; and being the seat of government, even exhorted the members of the Federation by a public appeal to take measures against the movement. In this danger Zurich placed herself at the head of Swiss liberalism, rejected the suggestions of Berne, and aided the victory of freedom. Not altogether in vain had such men as Paul Usteri, Escher von der Linth, Hirzel the magistrate, Hottinger, and Professor Johann Kaspar Orelli been laboring for Liberal reform ever since about 1820. Even had the attempt been vain to improve the common system of schools they had at least succeeded in abolishing the censure and arousing political thought.

There was still great uncertainty as to how to adjust the relative positions of the towns and the country districts; an assembly of councilors from the rural district held at Uster in October formulated very moderate demands as to the revision of constitution required by them, and still yielded precedence to the town in the matter of representation. It was reserved to a fugitive stranger from Nassau, Dr. Ludwig Snell, to give the movement a wider aim. As a German professor he had taken part in the patriotic struggles for liberty of the years 1817-1820; but when these were frustrated he was driven out by the prevailing spirit of persecution, and finally banished to Switzerland, where he allied himself to the zealous partisans of reform, fought for the liberty of the press, and endeavored specially to influence Zurich, which he looked upon as the intellectual head of the Confederation. At the time of the revolution in Paris he met with some of the most influential citizens of Zurich upon the Rigi; their narrow-minded views of the reforms to be undertaken induced him to try to convert Zurich to the principles of equality of rights for the citizens of every canton, the sovereignty of the people, and popular education. He wanted to establish "Constitutional Councils" (*Verfassungsräte*), and was the first to use this expression. Enlightened as to the general condition of things in the canton of Zurich by his interview with some of her citizens, he was made more intimately acquainted with the discontent and desires of the population around the Lake of Zurich by his friend Dr. Streuli in Küssnach, and when pressed by Dr. Streuli to formulate their wishes publicly in a definite form, he drew up the "Memorial of Küssnach" in concert with the communal association of Küssnach, setting forth the programme of reform. According to this memorial, which produced a great effect, the country district was to elect by universal suffrage two-thirds of the 212 representatives in the great council, who should thus form the representatives of the sovereign people; the division of powers, publicity of administration, the abolition of the "*Census,*" or limited suffrage, the right of petition and liberty of the press were further required. In order to work upon the government by a popular public demonstration, an assembly in Stäfa summoned a popular assembly. At the latter, which took place on November 22, 1830, at Uster, 12,000 burghers were present. Jakob Gujer, of Bauma, opened the assembly, asserting its purpose to be to remodel the hitherto imperfect and insufficient constitution according to the needs of the people and the spirit of the time. Hegetschweiler, of Stäfa, recalled the words of Schiller:

"Ye may dread the slave when his fetters break,
But in face of the Freeman never shake!"

Steffan von Wädenswil spoke in favor of material alleviations and educational reforms. The assembly bore itself with gravity and dignity, and unanimously declared itself in favor of the wishes expressed, which were subsequently embodied in a new form as the "Memorial of Uster," and laid before the great council. This "Day of Uster" made a decisive impression; the government did not dare to defy the power of public opinion, and therefore, to meet the requirements of the assembly of Uster, ordered the immediate election of a new great council. Snell's scheme was taken as the basis of the deliberations upon the new constitution, and with this regeneration or transformation of public conditions a new era in the history of Zurich was introduced.

These events in Zurich made a powerful impression upon the rest of Switzerland, and turned the scale in favor of the Liberal cause. Fresh agitations immediately commenced in the other cantons. Morat, the active and Protestant German town in the canton of Fribourg, was the first to raise its voice against the existing constitution on November 25, and the great council hesitating, the exasperated populace rushed in arms upon the capital and extorted a revision, while in December the *Landsturm* of the cantons of Aargau and Vaud forced the towns to yield. The excitement of the factions so wrought upon the governments of St. Gall and Lucerne that they could no longer remain passive. In St. Gall the revision was mooted by Jakob Baumgartner, the chancellor (*Staatsschreiber*), and the government hesitating (especially the Landammann Müller-Friedberg), various popular assemblies in Wattwil, Altstätten (December 5), and St. Gallenkappel, demanded radical reforms, and the government yielded. The Government of Lucerne, too, after fresh menaces, complied with the demands of the people by summoning a constitutional council on December 10. On December 22 a popular assembly at Balsthal, in Soleure, where Joseph Munzinger proclaimed the sovereignty of the people in impassioned words, declared itself in favor of revision, and the *Landsturm* also bringing its threats to bear, the great council ceded the request.

The greatest opposition to all Liberal efforts still continued at Berne, which was prepared to suppress the movement, and continued to encourage the other cantons to withstand the revision. The Bernese Government had recourse to an extraordinary Diet, which assembled on December 23, in order to consult upon the military measures to be taken on account of the menacing danger of a war in France and Germany; and the government endeavored to further the cause of reaction by requiring the Diet to interpose in favor of former conditions. Zurich, however, the head of Liberalism, entered an energetic protest against the placing of any hindrance in the way of the efforts of the cantons for the improvement of their constitutions, alleging that only the speedy and unhindered completion of the work could secure peace at home, and that combined warlike measures were out of place except in the case of attacks from without. This view was upheld by those cantons where the revolution was either completed or already in train; and hence, to the great dissatisfaction of the foreign powers, the Diet decided to preserve unanimously with life and property a strict neutrality toward the storm and strife of other lands, but not to interfere in any way with the constitutional reforms of the cantons. This served as a distinct warning for Berne, and while the revolutionary movement was encouraged, the Bernese Government realized that its power was shattered. A popular assembly conducted by the brothers Schnell at Münsingen on January 10, 1831, threatened violent action if a constitutional council were not summoned and the sovereignty of the people acknowledged, and at length the great council yielded.

Thus hopes were everywhere aroused that the reform might be peaceably accomplished; but in Basle it was less successful. Here the great council obstinately maintained the precedence of the town; the country-folk, however, adhered with equal firmness to their radical demands. On January 4, 1831, a popular assembly at Liestal protested, and determined to establish a separate government, which actually came to pass. The town, exasperated, made military preparations, and a battle ensued. The townspeople got the start of the country-folk, and gained the victory; the insurgents were dispersed, Liestal received a military occupation, and the rural district was completely subjugated (January 13-15, 1831). A Federal deputation established a hollow peace in the town's favor, making the representation of the latter almost equal to that of the rural district, the country seventy-nine, and the town seventy-five. This defeat of the country-folk of Basle, however, appealed to all the Liberals of Switzerland to throw themselves into the struggle, and a plan was formed for a great popular expedition of riflemen against Basle; but this, happily, was not carried into execution.

In the course of the year 1831 constitutional councils met almost everywhere, and in the first half of the year the constitutions of Soleure, Aargau, Zurich, St. Gall, Thurgau, the Vaud, Schaffhausen, and Berne (partially) were successively accepted by a splendid majority of the people. So much the less could the country people in the canton of Basle now be pacified. The town refused to grant an unconditional amnesty; the civil war broke out afresh, and the two districts actually confronted one another as two states with separate governments. The town of Basle, however, refusing all concessions, the calm was but temporary. After repeated excesses had been committed by the country-folk in August, 1831, the town undertook a second expedition, which, however, failed, and led to a complete separation in February, 1832. Only after a third encounter, which took place at Gelterkinden on April 6 and 7, and again proved disastrous for the town, and after the failure of repeated efforts at mediation, did the Diet at length resolve, on September 14, 1832, upon a division of the canton into two parts—the town with the twenty-one communes which still adhered to it, and the rural district with forty-six communes,[1] while in twelve other communes the separation had still to be put to the vote. Similar disturbances agitated the canton of Schwyz. Here also a separation took place, but it proved only temporary. In April, 1832, the "outer districts," that is to say, the purchased or conquered portions, which were in many ways at a disadvantage compared to the old original communes of Schwyz, and enjoyed fewer privileges, separated themselves, and became the "outer country," consisting of the districts of March, Einsiedeln, Pfäffikon, and (later) Küssnach, under the direction of Lachen, and received the assent of the Diet.

As in the case of the town and rural districts of Basle, and the inner and outer lands of Schwyz, so Upper and Lower Valais threatened to separate, the former still refusing to abandon all supremacy over the latter. But the attempt at separation made by the Lower Valais was frustrated by Federal troops.

A violent conflict took place in monarchical Neuchâtel. A republican faction there desired to be separated from Prussia, and in September, 1831, endeavored to accomplish their end by force, but without success. A second outbreak in December resulted in the defeat of the Republicans; the Prussian faction gained the upper hand, and in 1832 urged a separation from Switzerland.

During these disturbances in Basle, Schwyz, and Neuchâtel the revision of the cantonal constitutions was brought to a conclusion. The cantons of Geneva, the Grisons, Unterwalden, Uri, and Zug remained comparatively undisturbed, and made no changes in their constitutions; some, like Geneva and the Grisons, because no pressing grievances presented themselves; others, because a powerful and predominant faction, chiefly clerical, nipped every innovation in the bud. But wherever new constitutions were introduced, the sovereignty of the people and equality of rights were accepted as first principles.

In all parts great stress was now laid upon the political representation of the people, which was no longer regulated by the government, but on the contrary exercised a species of control over that body. Baselland and St. Gall even introduced the veto. All the constitutions alike established publicity of administration, the publication of the debates of the great council and of judicial

---

[1] These two halves, forming one canton, are known as Baselstadt (the town of Basle), and Baselland (the rural district of Basle).

affairs, and a proportionate division of the public burdens, and endeavored to institute more liberal communal regulations. Liberty of the press and of assembly, the right of petition, liberty of trade, and free choice of residence were guaranteed. Finally, a fundamental improvement of the educational system was projected.

But the constitutions of all the different cantons did not carry these principles into execution with equal thoroughness. Many towns, such as Lucerne, Zurich, Schaffhausen, Soleure, and St. Gall, still possessed certain privileges in the way of representation, and in most cantons the system of direct election was not immediately introduced, but a mixed system, and in Fribourg and Berne the elections were indirect only. In like manner the three powers were not at first equally sharply defined in all the cantons, nor religious liberty fully established; for instance, in Lucerne the franchise was only extended to Catholics, and in Fribourg the suffrage was withdrawn from those undergoing ecclesiastical penance. Thus in most of the cantons only a stage of transition had been reached, in which preparations could be made for the gradual expansion of the constitution with progressive experience, for all the constitutions provided for a future revision, and that at no very distant date in many cases.

From the very beginning of these cantonal reforms efforts had been made to carry reform into the sphere of the Federal constitution. All noble spirits were once more inspired by the beautiful dream of those Swiss patriots of the middle of the previous century. That which had been exaggerated by the Helvetic Constitution and lightly discarded by the Restoration, seemed now capable of realization: national unity, the creation of a united and strong political system in Switzerland. Under the Restoration, Zschokke had specially urged the necessity of strengthening the Federal authority, which was also advocated by Paul Usteri in Zurich during the tumults of 1830. Then, in January, 1831, when the Diet removed to Lucerne, Dr. Kasimir Pfyffer in eloquent words encouraged his native town to move the revision of the Confederation, complained that the people were not represented in the Confederation, and required that the lax political league should be converted into a firm Federal state with national institutions. The idea was eagerly discussed first of all in the Helvetic Society, of which Pfyffer was president; Dr. Ludwig Keller in Zurich, Landammann Sidler in Zug, and Joseph Munzinger in Soleure allied themselves with

Pfyffer for the purpose of preparing the soil for a revision of the Confederation.

On May 25, 1831, the Government of Thurgau gave official expression to this demand by moving a revision of the Federal Pact of 1815 in an address to the capital. The Diet, indeed, received the suggestion coldly, but it was loudly echoed by public opinion. In September, 1831, a Swiss Rifle Association was started throughout the country with a view to paving the way for Federal revision. Almost immediately afterward, on March 17, 1832, the seven Liberal cantons of Lucerne, Zurich, Berne, Soleure, St. Gall, Aargau, and Thurgau formed an alliance for the mutual security of their new constitutions, and for the carrying out of Federal reform (*Siebnerkonkordat*). This was done in self-defense, but it had very bad results. An address in favor of revision, with almost 10,000 votes attached, was forwarded to the Diet. The latter finally yielded by passing a resolution in favor of revision on July 17, 1832, and appointing a commission to draw up a scheme. After wearisome discussions, the commission acquitted itself of its task by the following December. Its work was essentially the product of the predominating faction in the commission, the so-called *juste-milieu* party, the advocates of a middle course, who only desired a partial improvement of existing conditions; hence it was but a patchwork of half-measures, which satisfied no one.

Many among the Liberals were against the scheme, because it did not go far enough (especially in the matter of popular representation); the more so as the propositions of the commission were afterward still further curtailed at the conference of the Diet. Among the adherents of the old régime, on the other hand, the efforts of centralization aroused the alarm of their old bugbear, the united Helvetic State, and at last most of the cantons absolutely declined to cede in the interests of the whole community any of the rights and privileges which they had hitherto enjoyed.

Unfortunately, too, foreign influence was brought to bear upon the matter. After the leading powers, Prussia and Austria, had introduced the most complete reaction into Germany, and suppressed the revolutionary movements, they turned their attention to the efforts for reform which were being made in Switzerland, and used all their influence in favor of the maintenance of the Federal Pact of 1815. Thus encouraged, the delegates of the six states of Basle, Uri, Schwyz, Unterwalden, Valais, and

Neuchâtel assembled at Sarnen on November 14, and at once announced their opposition to the division of Basle, and to the admission to the Diet of delegates from the rural district of Basle and from Outer Schwyz, such divisions being a breach of the league. They hoped thus to bring the whole matter of Federal revision to the ground at once; then, relying upon foreign powers, they sedulously opposed the scheme at the Federal Diet, and poured their scorn upon the *Ochsenbüchlein,* or " Little Book of Ochs," and upon the *Kasimirfütterung,*[2] or "cashmere lining" of the Federal shepherd's shirt.

Finally, they assembled a special Diet at Schwyz, and there formed a formal *Sonderbund,* or separate league. The Diet of Zurich held its ground, and in April decreed also the division of Schwyz. But in July, 1833, there being no enthusiasm in any party in favor of the Federal constitution, it was rejected by popular vote. This gave the signal for a fresh reaction. Disregarding the decision of the Diet concerning the separation of Schwyz, Colonel Abyberg, one of the chief leaders of the leaguers of Sarnen, summoned by the distressed Conservatives, advanced with troops from Schwyz upon Küssnach, and occupied it on July 31, 1833. This open defiance of the Federal authority aroused an immense sensation, and had the effect of an evil example upon the already strained relations between the half-cantons of Basle. Under pressure from the Conservatives, Colonel Vischer advanced upon Liestal with troops and artillery, in order to protect the adherents of the town in the country, but was repulsed on August 3 in a sanguinary battle on the heights of Pratteln. The Diet thereupon declared both proceedings to be a breach of the Federal League, and sent military forces and commissioners into both cantons: the members of the League of Sarnen evacuated Schwyz, and the Diet, maintaining its position with energy, decreed the dissolution of the League of Sarnen; whereupon most of the emissaries forming the conference of Sarnen resumed their places in the Diet.

The disturbances in Basle and Schwyz, and also in Neuchâtel, were happily settled for the moment. In Schwyz a reunion of the two parts was effected; in Basle a fresh partition was made, by which Baselstadt kept only the three communes of Riehen, Bettingen, and Klein-Hüningen. Federal revision, however, was

[2] The first an allusion to the Helvetic Constitution drawn up by Ochs in 1798, the second to the appeal of Dr. Kasimir Pfyffer.

frustrated for a long time to come. Zurich made one more effort in its favor, and urged the establishment of a Swiss constitutional council; the Swiss National Society was also formed from within the circle of the already-existing Rifle Association, for the purpose of founding a united national state; the whole was, however, frustrated by the obstinate resistance of the inner cantons, the absolutely antagonistic views of the others, and above all by the serious conflicts and complications with other countries concerning the matter of fugitives such as Mazzini, Snell, Conseil, and Louis Napoleon.

Meanwhile some compensation was afforded for the frustration of the Federal revision by the manifold reorganization in the internal conditions of individual cantons—the best preparation for the future progress of the whole. In 1834 Outer Rhodes of Appenzell accepted the very constitutional revision which had been rejected a year previously; Schaffhausen extended the franchise in the country district; subsequently in 1837 and 1838 Zurich swept away the last barrier between town and country, and established absolutely equal popular representation; in 1836 the principle of perfect equality of rights and the separation of powers was realized by the revision of Glarus, where the educational system was improved in most exemplary fashion. Thurgau abolished the institution of a separate ecclesiastical jurisdiction. Encouraging reforms also met with success in other spheres, specially in the educational system, in which the time had come for a fundamental and universal reorganization. All ranks were affected by it, from the highest to the lowest, and in many states the authorities, people, and professors alike were seized with a veritable enthusiasm for the improvement of the methods of instruction.

A beginning was made by the foundation of seminaries for the training of efficient teachers. In Zurich at Küssnach in 1832, under the direction of Dr. Thomas Scherr, in Thurgau, at Kreuzlingen in 1833, under Wehrli, in Berne, at Münchenbuchsee in 1833, in Soleure, and the Vaud, such institutions were established. The inspection of schools was made obligatory, scholastic institutions were carefully classified and comprised in one organic whole; while new subjects, especially the exact and historical sciences, were taken up, new methods of teaching were invented, and the modern principles of education of Pestalozzi and Fellenberg were introduced. In Zurich the Director of the Seminary, Dr. Thomas

Scherr, who was chosen for this high office by the Liberal leaders, Melchior Hirzel the burgomaster and Dr. Keller, was the soul of every effort connected with popular education; he also organized a system of popular schools, which became the model for other cantons, and likewise introduced the modern appliances for teaching in popular schools. On the other hand the noble-spirited Professor Orelli devoted all his powers to the erection of the cantonal school and the formation of a university in 1832. This example was followed by Berne, where a cantonal school and a university were established in 1833.

In ecclesiastical matters the Liberal tendency was evinced in the Catholic cantons. In Rapperswil two liberal-minded ecclesiastics, Alois Fuchs and Christopher Fuchs, labored zealously, and through the exertions of the Pfyffer family Lucerne became the starting-point of a Liberal-Catholic propaganda. A conference of delegates from Lucerne, Berne, Soleure, Baselland, St. Gall, Aargau, and Thurgau was held at Baden in 1834, and emphatically declared itself in opposition to the claims of the papal court, and in favor of the erection of a Swiss archbishopric, and passed a resolution to resist the interference of the nuncio within the episcopal jurisdiction, to exercise political control over all ecclesiastical arrangements, and in general to place restrictions upon the spiritual jurisdiction. It was next desired to deprive the religious houses of the right of self-government, to place them under episcopal jurisdiction, and compel them to pay taxes. A diminution in the number of *fête* days was likewise decided upon, and a desire expressed for the abolition of the nunciature. The papal court resisted these radical proceedings, and in the Bernese Jura a tumult was raised by the Ultramontanists or advocates of the papal rights, and the foreign powers also interposed in favor of the hierarchy, so that the resolutions could not be carried into effect, although the movement was not without traceable result. In Aargau the religious houses were placed under state supervision and in St. Gall the monastery of Pfäffers was abolished.

Traffic was also included in the universal reform, a fine network of roads being constructed; the commercial system was improved, and the whole range of intellectual and material culture entered upon a stage of brilliant development.

United as the Liberal party had been in 1829 and 1830 in favor of progress, in the course of events the Radical branch broke loose from them, desiring to carry innovations much further. In opposition to both stood the Conservative or reactionary party, which, though defeated, was by no means annihilated; on the contrary, the more eagerly the Radicals advanced, the more impetuous, reckless, and violent their proceedings, the more they rode rough-shod over the will of the people, so much the more ground did the Conservatives gain in public opinion. By these proceedings of the extreme factions the tension was brought to a crisis, while at the same time questions of an ecclesiastical nature came to the fore and inflamed men's minds.

The Conservatives regained their ascendency first in Schwyz. In 1834 their leader and chief, Abyberg, became Landammann, and in 1836 the Jesuits were summoned to Schwyz by his direction. The Liberal party under old Landammann Reding opposed this proceeding; a dispute about the partition and appropriations of the estates of the "Allmend" still further embittered both parties (the "*Klauenmänner*" and "*Hornmänner*"),[3] and at the *Landsgemeinde* at Rothenthurm in 1838 a riot took place, in consequence of which the country district was disarmed by order of Lucerne, the capital. But the matter being left in suspense, the predominant "Horn" party gained the day, and Abyberg remained Landammann.

Far more attention was aroused by the victory of reaction in Zurich. Here Liberalism seemed to have taken deeper root than anywhere else; yet it exhibited distinctly Radical tendencies, and filled not only the adherents of the old régime, but even the moderate party, with fears which were only too well grounded. In a very short space of time an entirely new and exemplary system of education had been brought into being; the criminal jurisdiction, military system, and divers other branches of the administration completely reorganized. But these reforms being often harshly and inconsiderately carried out, a silent discontent began gradually to prevail on all sides. The older generation followed the rapid advance of the younger most unwillingly, while many interests were injured and many wishes left unfulfilled. As early as 1832 a reaction was threatened, and the anniversary of the "Day of

---

[3] The party of the "Horn-men," so called because they drove horned cattle to pasture, consisted of the rich aristocracy; while the "Claw-men," who could only drive small cattle, such as sheep and goats, to graze on the "Allmend," consisted of poor country-folk.

Uster" was disturbed by exasperated artisans setting fire to a large factory (*Usterbrand*). The greatest offense was given by the open endeavors of leading statesmen to sever the school from the influence of the church and to annihilate orthodoxy. Actual insurrections took place when the "*Lehrmeister*" (a religious educational work), the catechism and the testament were abolished from the day schools and the educational appliances prepared by Scherr in accordance with modern Liberal ideas were introduced. Many considered the old faith of the church to be thereby seriously threatened, and the discontent was fanned by both laity and clergy belonging to the aristocratic families in Zurich, who hoped thus to bring the Radical government to the ground.

The government, however, and the Board of Education in particular, consisting of intellectually gifted advocates of progress, such as Melchior Hirzel, Ludwig Keller, Professor von Orelli, Scherr, the director of the seminary, etc., rather carelessly neglected this opposition; and the chair of theology at the university becoming vacant, they hastily seized the opportunity to introduce the most extreme Liberal tendencies in theology into the highest institution in the state. They therefore summoned Dr. David Strauss, who in his "*Leben Jesu*" had applied the sharp knife of criticism to the narratives of the New Testament, had called many of them legends, and endeavored to divest the person of Christ of its supernatural character. This abrupt act was naturally deemed a fresh outrage upon the church and Christianity; there was a simultaneous outcry throughout the land, and the majority of the clergy urged resistance. Addresses and petitions poured in against Strauss, against the Board of Education, the free-thinking seminary, and against the government; "Committees of Faith" were formed under the direction of Hürlimann-Landis, a manufacturer of Richterswil, who was on friendly terms with the aristocracy of the town, and open rebellion already threatened. The government next sought to allay the storm by pensioning off Strauss before he had so much as seen Zurich.

It soon became evident, however, that in many circles there were other motives in close connection with the movement against Strauss, and what was really aimed at was the overthrow of the one-sided Radical system. Hürlimann-Landis, Dr. Rahn-Escher, and Spöndli the advocate, the leaders of the "Central Committee," had pressed their demands still further touching religious instruction, the seminary and the university, and their desires having been only partially satisfied by the government, a popular agitation was set in motion on September 2 at the popular assembly at Kloten. The government still failing to comply, resistance was openly urged. The idle rumor, probably willfully spread, that the government had summoned foreign troops, was all that was wanting to heighten the excitement to the utmost. In the night of September 5 to 6 Pastor Bernhard Hirzel, a learned but somewhat impulsive and ambitious man, had the alarm bell rung at Pfäffikon; the neighboring communes immediately followed suit, and before dawn from the whole *Oberland* numberless armed hosts poured upon the town, while at the same time the storm broke out in other parts of the canton. This blow proved decisive; a small skirmish which took place on the cathedral square between the *Landsturm* and the troops of the government ended, indeed, in favor of the latter, but the government, timid and divided, resigned, and made room for a new Conservative party, formed of youthful members of the aristocracy, with Dr. Bluntschli at their head; a new, and, as it was popularly styled, "faithful" Board of Education was appointed, Scherr was forced to leave the seminary, and the Liberals had to bear the consequences of their indiscreet and premature proceedings for many a year. Zurich withdrew from the League of the Seven Cantons (*Siebnerkonkordat*).

These proceedings on the part of Zurich, the place which had hitherto led the van in the Liberal movement, gave rise to a succession of tumults, particularly as Zurich was at that time the capital. The first symptoms appeared in Valais. The Diet had previously expressly established the unity of this canton under a Liberal constitution: Upper Valais, however, offered resistance, and accomplished a fresh separation. The Diet remaining inactive, war broke out. In March, 1840, the troops of Lower Valais subdued Upper Valais, dispersed the old government, and forced the state to acknowledge the Liberal constitution. Struggles in Ticino and Soleure led to similar victories on the side of the Liberals. In May, 1839, the Conservatives in Ticino regained the upper hand, and drove out the Radicals. The latter (Franscini, Luvini), strong in numbers in Lugano and Mendrisio, the southern portions of the canton, made their preparations, and the government showing unfair partiality, they marched with an armed force upon Bellinzona and Locarno, on December 6, and set up a distinctly

Liberal government. In Soleure, as in Zurich, the Conservatives formed committees on the occasion of the revision, arranged popular assemblies in 1840 in Mümliswil and Mariastein, and endeavored to overturn the government. The latter, however, took most energetic steps, frustrated a rising, and enforced a Liberal constitution.

So much the greater, therefore, was the triumph of the victorious reaction in Lucerne. Two men here took the lead as champions of the Ultramontanists: Joseph Leu of Ebersol, a councilor, a well-to-do farmer, but illiterate and a strong partisan of the church, and Konstantin Siegwart-Müller, the chancellor (*Staatsschreiber*), who had formerly been a most zealous Radical in his political and religious views, but having taken fright at the triumph of the " faithful " in Zurich, changed his colors: with them was associated Bernhard Meyer, the *Staatsschreiber*. They conceived the prevailing system to be one which would undermine the Catholic faith, and demanded the repeal of the resolutions of Baden, the recall of the Jesuits, and a new democratic constitution. Rejected at first in November, 1839, the Conservatives here, too, formed a committee known as the Committee of Russwil, and when, in January, votes were taken upon constitutional revision they were to a large extent successful; a new constitution favorable to the clergy was accepted, by which means Lucerne cut itself adrift both from Baden and from the League of the Seven Cantons, in order to accept the dominion of a strictly ecclesiastical spirit.

After the riots in Zurich ("*Züriputsch*") the reactionary party in Aargau began to bestir itself. The revision of the constitution coming under discussion, the Conservatives established the Committee of Buntzen, and in the popular assemblies of 1840 all sorts of ecclesiastical and democratic wishes were brought forward. The government party, however, succeeded in effecting the adoption of a Liberal constitution on January 5, 1841. The Committee of Buntzen protested, whereupon the government proceeded to arrest some of them. This aroused an uproar in the Free Bailiwick; at the instigation of the monasteries, notably Muri, the *Landsturm* broke out, but was defeated on January 11 by the troops of the government. The Free Bailiwick was occupied. The energetic government then took a step which must have been regarded as a throwing down of the gauntlet to all Swiss Conservatives, for, at the suggestion of the passionately excited director of the seminary,

Augustin Keller, the fatal resolution was adopted of the dissolution of the religious houses. A cry of indignation at this act of violence rang through the ranks of the Conservatives in Switzerland. The advocates of the monastic system protested, and appealed to the article concerning religious houses in the Federal Pact. The Diet, too, in April and July, denounced the decision of the government of Aargau as incompatible with the Federal constitution. Thus Aargau was forced to partially yield, and to reëstablish some of the religious houses.

In the meantime a strong agitation was spreading throughout Switzerland. Demonstrations in favor of the government of Aargau were organized in all parts by the Radicals. In Zurich the situation was peculiarly altered. The Radical leaders and newspapers and the Liberal professors opposed the reaction with all their might, and succeeded in reawakening the memory of the great day of Uster. In contrast to the " September government," a popular assembly at Schwamendingen, at which 20,000 men took part, voted for the hearty support of the government of Aargau (August, 1841); other cantons also followed suit, and the canton of Aargau having reinstated part of the religious houses, the majority of the states in August, 1843, declared themselves satisfied. But the cantons of Lucerne, Uri, Schwyz, Unterwalden, Zug, Fribourg, and Valais, which were greatly under the influence of the clergy, entered a protest, held a special conference in 1843, and " for the defense of the outraged rights of Catholic Switzerland " concluded a *Sonderbund,* or Separate League, the second since 1832: it was almost entirely composed of the very same states which had concluded the Borromean League of former days. The remaining cantons made an attempt at intimidation by threatening a formal separation. Men's minds were not as yet, however, so far inflamed as not to shrink mutually from civil war, had not a second urgent matter been added to the monastic question, which drove the factions to war—this was the question of the Jesuits.

The Jesuits everywhere strenuously opposed the Liberal policy, and it was to their influence that the Liberals ascribed the fact that in one canton, viz., Valais, which had at first held a little aloof, a sanguinary strife afterward ensued, and finally it definitely joined the *Sonderbund.* The inhabitants of Upper Valais yearned for satisfaction for the blow dealt them in 1840. Two associations confronted one another, the so-called ".Young Switzerland" or

Liberals, and "Old Switzerland" or Conservatives, and did their utmost to exasperate one another. Finally in May, 1844, through the fault of Lucerne, the capital, and its representative, Bernhard Meyer, who favored the cause of Upper Valais, a pitched battle ensued at Trientbach, in which the Liberals were defeated with much slaughter, and a military occupation was established in Lower Valais.

Soon afterward the prolonged efforts of Leu's party to obtain the recall of the Jesuits were at last successful. The Liberals who endeavored to avert this step were suppressed. The tide having now turned so completely in favor of Ultramontanism and reaction, the Swiss Liberal party rose to the occasion with energy. Fellenberg demanded that measures should be taken to emancipate Valais from the Jesuits, and Augustin Keller at the Diet painted in glowing colors the dangerous nature of that order, whose principles and influence threatened to stifle all free republican feeling.

The Diet, however, would venture no step at this juncture, and on October 24, 1844, the Jesuits were summoned to undertake the management of higher education in Zurich. Exasperated beyond endurance, the Liberals of Lucerne conceived the unfortunate idea of pushing their cause by force of arms, in conjunction with those of like views in the neighboring cantons. A first attempt made on December 8, 1844, by insurrectionary troops from Aargau and Lucerne, to take the city by surprise and drive out the Jesuits, failed. Numerous popular assemblies, specially those of the cantons of Berne and Zurich, next proffered a unanimous request to the Diet that the Jesuits might be expelled and Federal revision once more taken in hand. A profound impression was made by a proclamation issued January 26, 1845, by an assembly of 20,000 men at Unterstrass, near Zurich. The existing government in the Vaud was overturned by the *Landsturm,* and its place taken by Radicals. Thereupon Berne, Zurich, the Vaud, and Aargau unanimously voted for the expulsion of the Jesuits, but it was still opposed by the majority of the states.

In Lucerne, however, the victorious Ultramontanists exercised an absolute reign of terror. Many of their opponents were forced to fly for refuge to the surrounding cantons. Every injunction of the Diet recommending moderation proving futile, revolutionary troops once more assembled, particularly from the cantons of Aargau, Baselland, Soleure, and Berne, under the conduct of Colonels Ochsenbein of Nidau and Rothpletz of Aarau, in order to take possession of the town by the help of the fugitives from Lucerne; unity and discipline were, however, wanting, and time was wasted, so that the second insurrectionary expedition failed like the first, March 31, 1845. Lucerne, on the other hand, took the opportunity to proceed to still greater extremities. Dr. Steiger, the chief of the Liberals, was condemned to death, but succeeded in escaping to Zurich, and a considerable number were forced to undergo penal servitude. Subsequently, on July 20, 1845, Joseph Leu was treacherously shot by a depraved wretch, who imagined himself to be thus rendering a service to the Liberals; this was the occasion of fresh executions, and hundreds of persons were imprisoned, among them Dr. Kasimir Pfyffer. In consequence of the victory over the insurrectionary troops, the other cantons which were in alliance with Lucerne were also much emboldened. In the summer of 1845 the *Sonderbund* having assumed a more definite form, the allies resolved to take unanimous measures against all attacks upon their sovereign and territorial rights, and established a council of war. This step was brought about by Siegwart-Müller, and was unquestionably a gross violation of the Confederation.

During the triumph of reaction, the strength of the Liberal cause was silently increasing. The Liberal party in Zurich had completely regained their ascendency, the leaders of the "September system" (notably Bluntschli) had been forced to resign, and Dr. Furrer, a strong advocate of reform, was now at the head of the state. In Berne, where many Radicals had been elected in the great council, the government could no longer resist the demands of the people for the extension of the franchise and increase of their rights, and in July, 1846, a new constitution was granted. At the head of the Liberal government, side by side with Ochsenbein, the insurrectionary leader, stood Niggeler and Stämpfli. Berne and Zurich were now become the mainstay of the Liberals in Switzerland.

In the summer of 1846, however, when the attitude of the *Sonderbund* was discussed at the Diet, the votes of two states were wanting to procure a majority against that league and against the Jesuits, and it was not until the Radical party had prevailed in Geneva through the efforts of James Fazy, and until Baumgartner, who since 1839 had attached himself to the Conservatives, had been removed from St. Gall and a Liberal majority formed in that government, and thus those two states won over to the progressive party, that the latter lawfully obtained the ascendency.

At the Diet held at Berne on July 5, 1847, President Ochsenbein, the leader of the insurrectionary troops, once again spoke with great eloquence upon the question of progress versus stability, whereupon the Diet decreed the dissolution of the *Sonderbund.* This decision was received with great rejoicing by the crowds surrounding the building where the Diet was assembled, and also by all the Liberals throughout Switzerland. National life had gained a great accession of strength even in the Diet, which next summoned up courage to issue a decree against the Jesuits, and appointed a commission to draw up a scheme of Federal revision based upon the former decree of July, 1832.

The *Sonderbund,* however, still remained defiant, and, relying upon the sympathy of foreign powers, with whom it had entered into negotiations, prepared for war. After futile attempts at a peaceable accommodation, the Diet decided to put their decree into execution by force of arms, and after adjourning for some time in order to complete their instructions, they assembled for a final general session on October 18 amid the clash of arms. Even yet the delegates of the *Sonderbund* stubbornly persisted in their demands for the repeal of the decrees already issued, and the reëstablishment of the religious houses, laying great stress upon what they considered their lawful rights and their just cause, and finally on October 29 they left the hall in violent excitement, led by Bernhard Meyer. The Diet completed the preparations already commenced, and chose Heinrich Dufour of Geneva for their general. They urged upon the Confederation the necessity of unity in the struggle against that faction which "had already in 1813 opened the doors to foreign armies, had refused to guarantee the Liberal constitutions of 1831, had been indefatigable in their machinations in the cause of reaction, stirred up revolts in the Jura and other parts of Switzerland, raised an Ultramontane sedition in Aargau, and recalled the Jesuits to Valais, Fribourg, Schwyz, and Lucerne; and by whose triumph the country would gradually lose all those institutions upon which depended its true freedom, its intellectual development, its power, and its honor."

The adherents of the *Sonderbund* placed their forces under the command of a Grison, General von Salis-Soglio, a man whose gifts were far inferior to those of General Dufour, a soldier trained in the school of the first Napoleon. The Liberals were also stronger in numbers than the Leaguers,[4] and the latter were at variance among themselves. Dufour, with admirable speed and discretion, immediately reduced Fribourg by a double attack, and on November 14 that state announced its secession from the separate league. He next ordered an attack upon Lucerne. The Leaguers had already achieved some small successes in Ticino and the Free Bailiwick. Dufour advanced swiftly upon Aargau in order to give battle to the main army of the *Sonderbund,* then stationed near Gislikon and the Rooter Berg. Zug, being now completely surrounded, capitulated on November 21. On the 23d the main attack took place. The Leaguers had an excellent and almost impregnable position. Honau was taken after a violent struggle. At Gislikon the first attack proved unsuccessful; certain battalions were forced to give way, and it was only by the courageous personal interposition and advance of Colonels Egloff and Ziegler that the enemy was repulsed from the western side of the Rooter Berg. The Leaguers were simultaneously driven back from the eastern side at Meyerskappel after a short struggle, the issue of which was at first doubtful. Lucerne was besieged on all sides. The leaders of the *Sonderbund* fled, the town capitulated, and on November 24 the main body of the Federal army entered. The remaining cantons yielded and complied with the demands of the victors, Valais being the last to do so. The Jesuits were expelled, Liberal governments established, and the constitutions of the various cantons altered accordingly. Thus that for which men had been striving in the cantons ever since 1830 was now first fully attained.

After the defeat of the *Sonderbund* and the revolution in the inner cantons, the one hindrance in the way of the long-desired Federal revision lay in the unfavorable disposition of the majority of the foreign powers, without whose consent the Federal Pact of 1815 could hardly be altered. Austria and France had already attempted to interpose in favor of the Leaguers during the war of the *Sonderbund,* and on the part of England alone had any support been bestowed upon the Liberals: a menacing note received from

---

[4] Dufour's army numbered (without the *Landsturm*) about 98,000 men, that of the Leaguers 37,000, but the latter were joined by the *Landsturm* to the number of 47,000 men.

the powers was delayed by England (Palmerston) until the issue had been decided against the *Sonderbund*. Even after the close of the war, in January, 1848, France, Prussia, and Austria interposed as advocates of the cantonal sovereignty in favor of the defeated states.

Now, however, it was not only too late, but also the needful vigor was wanting to give force to their advocacy, for in the course of the very next month of February the revolution ensued in Paris, which spread like wild-fire to the surrounding countries, overturned existing governments, and laid the foundations of modern political conditions. While this movement frustrated the intervention of the foreigner, it essentially assisted the already commenced work of the reformation of the Swiss Federation, and gave a powerful impulse to the Liberal cause, particularly in Neuchâtel, where the Republicans, encouraged by the events in Paris, possessed themselves on March 1 of the capital and the castle, and introduced a new and Republican constitution; all of which Prussia was powerless to prevent.

The commission appointed for Federal revision now labored zealously at the scheme. No one any longer doubted that the Swiss people, as such, must be duly represented in the Confederation, as had for years past been required and been manifestly needful. But opinions were divided as to the desirability of uniform national representation, and as to how far centralization should be put in practice. Finally a compromise was agreed upon midway between the national and cantonal principles, or between the two systems of unity and federation, such as had already been expressed in the constitution of " Mediation "; and for this purpose the constitution of the United States of America, with its system of two chambers, was taken as a model, as had already been recommended by Dr. Troxler and others between 1830 and 1840, and was now advocated by James Fazy and Munzinger of Soleure.

The work of the commission was brought to a close in April in accordance with these leading points of view. The following were the chief stipulations: Cantonal sovereignty was guaranteed, but restricted by a strong Federal authority. The Federation no longer merely aimed at maintaining the independence of their country toward the outer world, and preserving peace and order in the interior, but also endeavored to support the liberties and rights of the Confederates, and to further their common welfare. Accordingly, the Federation alone has the right to declare war and make peace, to conclude alliances and political treaties, especially those relating to customs and commerce, with other countries. Particular alliances and treaties of a political nature between the several cantons are prohibited; official intercourse between the cantons and foreign countries is also placed under the supervision of the Federation, and in the case of violent disturbances in the cantons the Federation exercises the right of intervention. The following are guaranteed as inalienable rights of the Swiss people: the equality of all men in the eye of the law, freedom of domicile, liberty of the press, religious liberty, and the rights of association and of petition. Federal affairs further include the customs, coinage, and postal system, the settlement of weights and measures, and the disposal of the Federal army, formed out of contingents from the cantons. Finally, the Federation also received the right to erect a university and a polytechnic, and in general to establish or cause to be established any public works in the interest of the Confederation, or of the greater part of it. Thus a formidable barrier was set up against all efforts at separation and individualism, and the foundation laid of a necessary unification of the powers.

The executive of the Federal authority was so organized that the legislative power was placed in the hands of two councils: the National Council (*Nationalrat*) as representing the Swiss people, and the Council of the States (*Ständerat*) as representing the cantons. In the former each representative is chosen by 20,000 Swiss citizens, in the latter each canton elects two representatives, every half-canton electing one. The decisions of both councils are determined by the majority of votes, but the agreement of the two councils is requisite to render their decisions valid. The highest executive and directing authority is that of the Federal Council, consisting of seven members elected by the Federal Assembly,[5] presided over by the President of the Confederation. For the administration of the law, so far as it falls within the province of the Confederation, a Federal tribunal was established. Thus the people were now represented in the Confederation, and had at the same time acquired their essential rights, assured by the Federation: the foundation was laid of a universal Swiss citizenship, though still hampered by many limitations. The guarantee of free movement in the interior was of the greatest importance for the advance-

[5] The National Council and the Council of the States combined.

ment of industry and manufactures, giving facilities for settlement, greater freedom of buying and selling, the abolition of inland customs, and free entry, exit, and transit from one canton to another, though still encumbered by slight restrictions.

It is true that when the time came for this Federal constitution to be accepted, many were dissatisfied with what had been attained. While the inner cantons still cherished the idea of the old Confederation, the Radicals wanted absolutely uniform national representation, and a greater advance in the direction of centralization. They were of opinion that the Helvetic united government, universally detested as it had been under the circumstances then prevailing, had yet projected and initiated much that was good, and that in order to inculcate true Federal principles, not only must the restrictions yet remaining upon free intercourse and popular rights be removed, but also such matters as the educational, legal, and military systems must be completely in the hands of the Federation. In general, however, the idea prevailed that it was better not to go too far, lest through any rashness everything should once more be called in question. Even the advocates of uniformity consoled themselves by the consideration of what had been already attained, which they regarded as a transition stage leading to further progress.

Therefore, on September 12, 1848, the constitution was accepted by the majority of the cantons and of the voters from among the people.[6] The firing of cannon proclaimed the splendid result, and beacon fires blazed upon the mountains. The Swiss people entered upon an entirely new epoch, the most important since the founding of the Confederation. The league, formerly so lax, instituted in times of danger for purposes of defense, and chiefly useful in time of war, had forever given place to a permanent political system organized upon modern principles, having for its aim the advance of civilization in every respect, its strength and value depending solely upon the education and capacity for work of its people and upon the cultivation of humanity.

[6] Fifteen and one-half cantons accepted, six and one-half rejected it (including those of the *Sonderbund,* with the exception of Fribourg). The people took a very feeble part in the voting, almost half absenting themselves. The result was 169,743 ayes to 71,899 noes.

Chapter XII

THE CONSOLIDATION OF THE FEDERAL STATES
1848-1874

EUROPE looked on in wonderment at this transformation. Switzerland had remained exempt from the cruel agitations and terrible convulsions of other states, and, thanks to Dufour's judicious conduct in the war and the dissolution of the *Sonderbund,* had passed the crisis speedily and safely, and without, or rather notwithstanding, foreign interference, had procured for herself a popular constitution. Equally speedily and safely there now followed the introduction of the new constitution. On September 22, 1848, the Diet finally resigned, giving place to the new Federal Assembly. The latter then nominated Berne, the mediator between French and German Switzerland, to be the permanent Federal capital. The highest Federal offices were filled entirely by men who had renderd good service in the dissolution of the *Sonderbund* and the establishment of the constitution; Jonas Furrer of Winterthur was elected President of the Confederation, and his portrait even yet preserves in many a home the memory of the joyful transformation of the fatherland; while the Federal councilors were Druey of the Vaud, Munzinger of Soleure, Franscini of Ticino, Ochsenbein of Berne, Frei-Herosé of Aargau, and Näff of St. Gall.

The next question was to find a suitable form by which to enforce the details of the Federal constitution, and specially those branches of the administration which had come into the hands of the Confederation. The establishment of a uniform postal system was a very simple matter; Switzerland was divided into postal districts, and taxes and tariffs were fixed in due proportion. " Brightly colored stamps began to adorn the letters, while along all the high roads and over the cold heights of the Alpine passes rolled the large and roomy postal vans of the Confederation." The newly established telegraph system was next transferred to the Confederation in 1851, and electric wires passed from Berne throughout the whole of Switzerland.

Some disputes with regard to the railway system were terminated in 1852 by a decision in favor of leaving the construction of railways in private hands, and it was not until 1873 that the Confederation assumed the licensing and control of the railways.

The abolition of all restrictions upon commerce in the interior proceeded with some rapidity, and in some cantons there only remained the so-called *Ohmgelder,* duties paid upon the importation of wine, brandy, etc.

The establishment of a uniform system of coinage presented greater difficulties. All the various sorts of Swiss money, the *doublon,* the *bock,* the *batz,* the *schilling,* the *angster,* etc., had to be called in and carefully exchanged; and after long discussion it was decided that the new Swiss coinage should follow the French decimal system, which predominated in the commercial world; and thenceforth all Swiss money, copper, nickel, and silver, bore the Swiss arms with a wreath of oak leaves, or Helvetia enthroned, pointing to the mountains: gold coinage there was none, it being only introduced into Switzerland quite lately.

With the framing of the article about the rights of domicile it became necessary to establish some legal protection for mixed marriages, hitherto interdicted. It was now thought to be a violent infringement of the liberty of mankind that religious creed should remain any hindrance to marriage. A Radical party therefore arose among the Federal authorities, which insisted upon the abolition of this restriction, and passing beyond the letter of the Federal Constitution, obtained in 1850 a Federal law for the protection of mixed marriages.

The article as to a Federal educational institution was at length carried into at least partial execution. It is true that the project of a Federal university was rejected by the Council of States, but on the other hand the proposition of a Federal polytechnic was accepted by the majority. Zurich was fixed upon as its seat, for this city not having been made the seat of the Federal Government, it was thought to make amends by giving it the Federal academy. The institution was opened in 1855, and in 1864 took possession of the spacious edifice built by Zurich in the style of the Acropolis.

Such satisfactory developments gained more and more friends to the new order of things; the evil consequences predicted by the opposition party did not ensue, and many opponents were themselves forced to acknowledge the advantages of greater unity and freer motion. No sort of attempt was made to return to the old standpoint previous to 1848; on the contrary, the former opponents of Federal reform, as "Conservatives" or "Moderates," clung with all their might to the new constitution for protection against further innovations. The Radicals, on the other hand, to whom the new Confederation actually owed its existence, soon made a further forward movement, partly in order to obtain demands which had been put forward earlier but suppressed, and partly to open the way for further progress.

The Conservative governments of other countries resented the rapid and fundamental changes in Switzerland; and when, during the revolutionary storms in the neighboring countries in 1848 and 1849, fugitives once more involved Switzerland in difficulties, they made their irritation distinctly felt. Switzerland, however, preserved her neutrality as far as possible, and about 1855 it seemed as though the storm-clouds had quite passed away, when suddenly a formidable embarrassment was presented by the affair of Neuchâtel, such as had not been experienced since the wars of liberty and the invasion of the French. This territory, which had formerly (from 1406) been an allied state, had fallen to Prussia by inheritance in 1707, and in 1815 became a canton of Switzerland, with sovereign rights reserved to Prussia. Between 1830 and 1840 a republican party came to the fore, and the principality was convulsed by numerous revolutionary attempts. Shortly after the outbreak of the February revolution in Paris, however, by a revolution of March 1 the Republicans declared the rights of Prussia to be extinct. When, therefore, the Confederation was reorganized, Neuchâtel was inserted among the states of the modern Confederation, without any formal reservation of the rights of Prussia.

For a long time the King of Prussia was hindered from paying any attention to Neuchâtel by the revolutions in his own country and the constitutional struggles in Germany; but afterward, having in 1852 induced the powers to guarantee his rights in Neuchâtel, he encouraged the royalist party, which was in the minority, to resistance, and on September 3, 1856, the Royalists took possession of the castle, just as the Republicans had done in 1848. The Republicans of the mountain district immediately broke out, besieged the castle, and took it. Most of the royalist leaders were taken prisoners.

Judicial proceedings were at once instituted by the Confederation against the instigators of the rebellion, and the canton was occupied by Federal troops. Prussia protested, and was supported by the great powers. The French emperor, Napoleon III., endeavored to induce Switzerland to liberate the prisoners, and to give up all judicial proceedings, promising in return to prevail upon Prussia to abandon Neuchâtel. Switzerland, however, was anxious before all things to save her honor, and required first the renunciation of the Prussian king. To this Napoleon would not agree, and Prussia prepared for war, appointing January 2 as the final date when the negotiations should terminate; should Switzerland by that time not have yielded, war would ensue. In Switzerland itself the entire population with unanimous enthusiasm proclaimed itself in favor of the Republicans of Neuchâtel, and awaited the war with heroic composure and an almost religious calm. All the cantons prepared without hesitation to assist the one in need, as though the cause had been their own. In December the Federal Assembly ordered military preparations, and in a short time the whole of Switzerland was one great camp. Old and young hastened to the standards; members of the Polytechnic, students and gymnasts, practiced drilling daily at the barracks; high and low vied with one another in willing self-surrender to their country; even the school-children, with touching enthusiasm, brought money, clothing, and linen. By the beginning of January 30,000 men were already stationed on the northern frontier; the whole army under the command of Dufour numbered over 100,000 men. Meanwhile Prussia had been forced to defer putting her threats into execution; the states of southern Germany had, it is true, consented to give passage to the troops, but Austria kept Prussia at bay, and threw all sorts of obstacles in the way. Then on January 8, 1857, at a conference held between the Swiss envoys (Barmann and Dr. Kern) and Napoleon III., a treaty was effected, by which Switzerland engaged to liberate the prisoners, but the latter were to remain in exile until the affair of Neuchâtel should be settled. The authorities accepted these proposals; this acceptance gave great umbrage to many of the people, but it was the only right thing to do. At a conference held in Paris, which lasted till April 20, the powers succeeded in inducing Prussia to renounce all rights of sovereignty in

Hist. Nat. XIII-39

Neuchâtel in return for certain small concessions. Under the old Confederation such vigorous action would never have been possible, and thus the new Confederation stood its first test successfully.

It was again put to the proof, and came out no less brilliantly, throughout the course of the foreign relations during the ten years next ensuing. Switzerland now enjoyed a happy period of peace, which was particularly favorable to internal development. Whereas formerly, as a Confederation of states, she had completely followed in the wake of foreign powers, she now began with energy to evolve an independent national policy, and all parties united in maintaining Swiss independence.

Foreign military service was next abolished as unworthy of a free republican state. The Federal Constitution of 1848 had only prohibited the conclusion of any fresh engagements; in 1849, however, Naples having levied Swiss troops for the suppression of revolts in Lower Italy, the Radical party extorted a prohibition of levies; and in 1859, on the occasion of the Italian War, a formal prohibition was issued against the enlisting of Swiss soldiers in foreign mercenary armies, and thus the "traffic in Swiss blood," pursued for four centuries, was legally abolished.

Switzerland next found herself involved in troublesome disputes with France, but, thanks to the moderate and energetic attitude of the Federal Council, these were peaceably adjusted. These disputes arose as follows: Soon after the settlement of the question of Neuchâtel Napoleon III. engaged in some vexatious intrigues against Switzerland, because the latter, in consequence of the right of asylum conceded, had become a rallying-point for French refugees; he accused Switzerland of encouraging these disturbers of the peace, and punished her by restricting the freedom of traffic on the frontier (1858). Against this, however, the Federal Council warmly protested, and even succeeded in effecting a partial modification of the passport regulations. But in 1859 war broke out between Italy and Austria concerning Lombardy, and Napoleon engaged to help King Victor Emmanuel, receiving in return a promise of the surrender of Savoy. Switzerland was in the highest degree interested in this transaction, for by the Congress of Vienna the two provinces of northern Savoy, Faucigny and Chablais, which had been conquered by Berne in 1536, but had afterward to be given back, were included in the Swiss neutrality, and to Switzerland had been granted the right of placing a military occupation in these territories in case of war. The Federal authorities therefore immediately instituted military measures for the protection of the southern frontier of the Confederation, and once more appointed Dufour as general; their precautions in favor of northern Savoy were to all appearances favorably received by Napoleon, but were practically quite disregarded. This gave rise to great indignation in Switzerland; various widespread organizations, such as the "Helvetia" and "Grütli" societies, and numerous popular assemblies, openly advocated armed interference, and that with a view to the conquest of North Savoy. In the Federal council Dr. Stämpfli also advocated war. But in the Federal assembly the opinion prevailed that Switzerland had no right to the occupation of North Savoy, and that it would be sheer foolhardiness to provoke a war on that account. Napoleon caused the matter to be put to the vote in Savoy, and brought the influence of French agents to bear, and in June, 1860, he took possession of Savoy. The rest of the powers not daring to take any action against France, the situation remained unchanged, France undertaking to come to terms with Switzerland.

A simultaneous dispute with France about the Dappental terminated more successfully for Switzerland. This territory had been annexed by France during the time of the "Mediation," but restored to Switzerland by the Congress of Vienna. France, however, had never vacated it, but still kept a military occupation there, and otherwise infringed the territorial rights of the Swiss. Switzerland therefore demanded definite satisfaction, and finally in 1862 effected a peaceable division of the territory, France being at the same time forced to promise to erect no fortress there and levy no customs.

Switzerland remained thenceforth unmolested, and when danger threatened was able to set it aside by a determined and forcible attitude, and to make her position honored and respected by the outer world. In earlier times, since the Reformation, neutrality had been a necessity on account of internal dissensions and instability; now, however, it was consciously embraced as the noblest attitude, and the one most worthy of a popular republic: and whereas it had been formerly either carelessly preserved or not maintained at all, now all parties united to defend it, and Switzerland moreover possessed an efficient military force for the purpose. This was shown during the wars between Prussia and Austria in

1866, and between Germany and France in 1870-1871. During the former their chief concern was to cover the southeast frontier; the Münstertal in the Grisons was occupied by Federal troops, and preparations were made for a levy of the whole Federal army; but the speedy termination put to the war by Prussia made further proceedings unnecessary. During the Franco-German war Switzerland was still more exposed, for it was easily possible for either of the two powers to use her as a bridge, and she had reason to fear a fate similar to that of the coalition period.

The whole of Switzerland, therefore, as well as the foreign powers, heard with rejoicing the proclamation of the Federal Council that an armed neutrality would be strictly preserved under all circumstances. Colonel Herzog of Aargau was appointed general by the Federal Assembly, and with the greatest rapidity a body of about 50,000 men was placed on the western and northern frontiers, to repel any attack which might be made upon Switzerland. Only the fugitive army of Bourbaki, of 80,000 men, passed the frontier in February, 1871, and was disarmed, that it might be sheltered in the country; Switzerland exercised her right of hospitality in friendly fashion, and was indefatigable in rendering aid and nursing the wounded. The storm which shook the neighboring lands to their foundations was once more happily averted by Switzerland. Meanwhile, in both these perils of war of 1866 and 1870-1871, Switzerland recognized the serious defects of her somewhat neglected military system, and saw that it was only by keeping pace with foreign powers in the improvement of arms and tactics, and only by the possession of an army which should be as far as possible uniform in discipline, that she could feel secure against all attempts from without.

No party any longer maintained that Switzerland should play an independent part in foreign wars, as she had done in the fifteenth century. Rather is it characteristic that all should have united in recognizing that the one and only task for Switzerland should be to secure the blessings of peace to herself, and to labor also in the cause of peace for other lands.

A succession of treaties and transactions between Switzerland and other countries from 1860 to 1880 testify to the carrying out of this idea. Thus in 1864 the "Convention of Geneva" was called into existence by Switzerland, by which the powers bound themselves to improve the condition of the soldiers wounded in war, the "Red Cross League." In 1865 Switzerland formed the center of a European telegraph treaty, with the seat of the international bureau at Berne.

In 1872 she came once more to the fore, in order to settle by arbitration a dispute which had arisen between England and the United States about the steam vessel *Alabama*, constructed in England for the Southern States, which did great damage to the Federal Government during the Civil War. The *Alabama* arbitration tribunal met in Gevena, where Dr. Stämpfli represented Switzerland.

This attitude of Switzerland, this her task of becoming the promoter and the center of the interests of international civilization, finds its noblest and most distinct expression in the undertaking of the St. Gotthard railway, which, initiated by Switzerland, was rendered possible by the assistance of Italy and Germany in 1869 and 1871, the direction of the work being intrusted to Switzerland. The Federal Council took up a position far above all cantonal interests, which were in favor of other lines, and decreed in subsidies the sum of twenty million francs for this highly important international work.

After the introduction of the new Federation it became specially necessary for the several cantons to guard their Liberal institutions, since Switzerland also suffered from the influence of the general European reaction which set in after 1848, and threatened manifold injury to the fine achievements of the past. In Berne the Radical government, with Stämpfli at its head, was forced to make room for the Conservatives in 1850; the latter attacked the training school for teachers in Münchenbuchsee, which was managed on principles too liberal for the people, and expelled its director, Grunholzer of Zurich, thus imitating the proceedings of the September government in Zurich. In St. Gall the Ultramontanists violently opposed every constitutional revision, and specially directed their attacks against the cantonal school founded in 1856. The Liberal government of Fribourg, which had been appointed by the Federation in 1847, could find no firm footing. During the years 1848 to 1853 no fewer than four Ultramontane riots ("*Putsche*") followed one another in quick succession, under Carrard, Wuilleret, and Perrier, which finally, in 1857, led to the victory of reaction; in consequence of which the religious houses and the educational system favorable to the Jesuits were again restored, and more privileges were bestowed upon the bishops and clergy.

In the face of these events the Liberals of Switzerland roused themselves to make a desperate effort; the need of closer union began to be realized, and hence in October, 1858, the men's society, called "Helvetia," was formed in Langenthal, which took for its object a war of progress against Ultramontanism and reaction, for the elevation of Swiss intellectual and social life, and which for a time exhibited great activity. Meanwhile the general tendency of the public mind was moving forward, and by about 1860 much progress had already been made in cantonal affairs. Thus fundamental changes, both internal and external, were brought about in Geneva by the great popular leader, James Fazy. In Soleure the popular party under Landammann Wilhelm Vigier extended the rights of the people and promoted education and culture. Almost all the cantons revised their constitutions with a view to the increase and improvement of popular rights. In St. Gall, too, the Liberals now prevailed, and in 1861 inserted in their constitution the election of the great council according to political instead of communal divisions, the direction of the educational system by the state, mutual independence of the creeds in ecclesiastical affairs, an improved veto, and the like. In 1863 the numerous Jews in Aargau received the rights of citizenship.

The years 1860-1880 brought fundamental changes in political life. The Liberal governments, which had given a violent impetus to trade and industry, seemed to concern themselves rather with the interests of the higher classes, and to trouble themselves less about the wishes and interests of the people. Moreover, they consistently held fast to the principles of representative constitutions, and opposed all demands for an extension of the part taken by the people in legislation in the form of the Veto, the Referendum, and the Initiative.

Moreover fresh needs began to arise, both agricultural and social. The peasantry and artisan class being seen to be starving and in want, improvements in the material conditions of the people were demanded, such as the alleviation of military duty, the abolition of school fees, the reduction of the price of salt, equal division of taxes, the establishment of cantonal banks, the enlargement of the popular schools, the erection of technical and secondary schools, etc.

A Democratic party was thus formed almost everywhere, which endeavored to thrust aside the representative system, and to comply with these popular requirements. A succession of great constitutional changes ensued. Baselland took the lead in 1863; here the Democratic party gained the day, under Christoph Rolle, and carried the compulsory Referendum, the Initiative, the election of the government by the people, etc. Zurich next followed. After making many futile attacks upon the so-called "system" then existing under the auspices of Alfred Escher, the people were at length aroused in 1867. The leaders, Bleuler, Zangger, and others, determined to organize four great *Landsgemeinden* in Zurich, Uster, Winterthur, and Bülach on December 15. Between 26,000 and 27,000 signatures were given in favor of revision. The people accepted it by 50,000 votes against 7300, and in 1869 a Constitutional Council drew up a new constitution, with the Referendum, Initiative, free education, a cantonal bank, free military outfits, and abolition of the holding of offices for life.

In the same year revisions were adopted in the canton of Thurgau, where the influence of Fürsprech Häberlin was undermined, and a popular union under the direction of Sulzberger, Deucher, Anderwert, and others had set the revision in motion, as well as in the cantons of Berne, Soleure, and Lucerne, and the following year in Aargau.

After the Federal revision of 1874 a number of cantons, being forced to alter their constitutions, proceeded to introduce the Initiative or Referendum, or both together—Baselstadt in 1875, Schaffhausen in 1876, Geneva in 1881, Neuchâtel in 1882, and Ticino in 1883. Counting the *Landsgemeinde* cantons,[1] there are in all twenty-four cantons which allow the people a share in the legislation in one form or another; one canton only—that of Fribourg—still adheres to the representative system. This introduction of the popular state and popular government forms a distinctive feature of the home policy of this country.

As had been the case between 1830 and 1840, so again now progress in the cantons was followed by further efforts for Federal reorganization. It was not only required that the Federation should be made more uniform, and greater centralization effected in those departments where experience had proved it to be neces-

---

[1] Uri, Unterwalden (Obwalden and Nidwalden), Appenzell (Innerrhoden and Ausserrhoden) and Glarus.

sary, but a desire was also expressed that the democratic principles already established in several cantons (the Veto, Referendum, and Initiative) should be adopted by the Federation. A first and partial attempt was made in 1866, when, on the occasion of a commercial treaty with France, it was desired to expand the articles on the subjects of domicile and trade. But at the voting all the proposals contained in nine articles were rejected, with the exception of one which concerned the commercial treaty, namely, the one guaranteeing to the Jews rights of domicile equal to those of Christians.

Soon, however, further needs made themselves felt, notably at the time of the Franco-German war, when the modern German empire came into existence, and the absolute necessity of a uniform organization in the arms and in the legal system became evident. From the year 1869 onward various circumstances had conspired to smooth the way for a fundamental reformation, and hence in 1872 a total revision was effected. The deliberations of the Federal authorities resulted in the drawing up of an entirely new Federal Constitution, which in every way fulfilled the wishes of the Progressive, Centralist, and Democratic party: there was to be but one army and one law, and the Referendum and Initiative in the Federation itself were to be guaranteed to the people. But just on account of its extreme tendency the scheme met with violent opposition, and was rejected when put to the vote.

This, however, by no means brought matters to a standstill. On the contrary, almost half the voters (about 250,000) having agreed to this new scheme, men took courage and redoubled their exertions. Societies uniting the Swiss of all parts had already often carried the day in progressive questions; similar methods were now once more adopted, and at a popular assembly held at Soleure on June 15, 1873, at which Augustin Keller spoke, a *Volksverein* or Popular Association was founded, which, being taken up with enthusiasm, united the Swiss of all parties and of every tongue under the banner of revision, and cleared the way boldly in all directions.

The struggle against the ascendency of the church in the state (the so-called *Kulturkampf*), which exerted no small influence upon the cause of revision, broke out simultaneously in Germany and in Switzerland. The Catholic Church was making violent efforts to reassert her power. By the publication of the papal

"Syllabus" (the condemnation of all modern institutions), and of the dogma of the infallibility of the Pope (1870), the Ultramontane party exasperated the Liberals throughout the country. The governments hastily resolved not to acknowledge the new doctrine, involving as it did a certain amount of danger to the existing state; and even among the Catholics themselves it met with some opposition: communities were formed of "Old Catholics," who adhered to the old position, before the publication of the papal infallibility, and these were protected by the state as communities of Christian Catholics, under Bishop Herzog.

This question was taken up with special earnestness by the Catholics of Switzerland. With great rigor, here and there even with harshness, the authorities defended their rights against all intended encroachments. Mermillod, a priest, venturing to style himself "Bishop of Geneva" (although the bishopric of Geneva had been previously abolished by the Pope "forever"), was banished from the country by the Federation; the states belonging to the bishopric of Basle deposed Bishop Lachat in Soleure, because he had deprived certain ecclesiastics who refused to acknowledge the doctrine of infallibility. Berne, which carried on the struggle between church and state with much excitement and great vehemence, deprived more than sixty clergy in the district of the Jura for protesting against the authority of the state; and in 1873 the Federal authorities went so far as to expel the papal nuncio from Switzerland, because the Pope condemned these proceedings in strong terms.

All these events led men to hold more firmly together, and to recognize the necessity for closer union; and the more the Catholic clergy declaimed against the government, so much the more did the Volksverein and revision gain ground. In the struggle against the common foe, the progressive parties, Liberals and Radicals, Federalists and Centralists, French and German Swiss, stretched out a helping hand to one another, and in a new scheme for the Federal Constitution, drawn up in 1873, a work of reconciliation was effected, combining definite progress with discreet moderation. On Sunday, April 19, 1874, this constitution was accepted by an overwhelming majority of the Swiss people (about 340,000 votes against 198,000), and of the cantons (fourteen and a half against seven and a half); and the joyful event was celebrated on the first lovely day of spring, April 20, by beacon fires, the thunder of cannon, and patriotic songs which resounded from mountain to mountain and from valley to valley.

The principles contained in the newly accepted constitution established before all things greater centralization in the legal and military systems. Laws relating to bonds, commerce, and exchange were taken over by the Federal Government, as also the entire military system, including the training, equipment, and legislation of the whole army. The Confederation received more authority in ecclesiastical matters: liberty of faith and of conscience was more warmly embraced, and sacred and secular affairs were more sharply defined, especially by the establishment of the "civil estate" (*Civilstand*). The prohibition of the Jesuits was emphasized, the establishment of new religious houses was forbidden, and the erection of fresh bishoprics was made to depend upon the consent of the Federal Council.

More extensive powers were also conferred upon the Federal Government in matters of political economy, relating to railways, the system of banknotes, water-works, and forest regulations in the Alps, hunting and fishing, the factory system, and the condition of artisans. The jurisdiction of the Federation was extended in regard to intellectual culture, including the supervision of the system of primary schools, and the right of founding a Federal university and other institutions for higher education, or of supporting those already existing.

The rights of the people were also extended, as, for example, those of settlement and liberty of marriage, and the optional Referendum was introduced by the stipulation that Federal laws must be submitted to the popular vote, if required by 30,000 Swiss citizens entitled to vote, or by eight cantons. Finally, the Federal tribunal, with powers materially augmented, was made into a permanent court of justice, holding its sessions in Lausanne.

tures against Federal laws and of raising an opposition. Bills which have passed both houses of the Federal Assembly may be said to be on probation for ninety days, for if within that time a sufficiently numerous body of citizens—30,000 active citizens or the governments of eight cantons—demand a popular vote upon the bill, the vote must be ordered by the Federal Council, and the acceptance or rejection is finally decided by that. Certain measures are regarded as outside the sphere of the Referendum. These are resolutions not of general application, treaties with foreign states or financial matters, as the annual budget, estimates and appropriations for the purpose of acquiring war material, and Federal resolutions granting subsidies for the diking of rivers and the construction of roads. The first law to be submitted to popular vote since the introduction of the Federal Referendum was the law on marriage and the civil rite of December 24, 1874. This law placed the performance of the civil rite and the custody of the registers which refer to it in the hands of the civil authorities of the Confederation, forbade the imposing of conditions in restraint of marriage founded on differences of creed or the poverty of one or the other of the parties, and declared that a religious ceremony of marriage should not take place until after the legal celebration by a civil official. Divorce proceedings were further committed to the jurisdiction of Federal courts and the grounds sufficient for a divorce enumerated. In effect the act inaugurated a policy of centralization and secularization, and therefore met with much opposition. Catholics and Conservative Protestants to the number of 106,560 signed a demand for a Referendum. At the vote which followed the law was accepted by a small majority.[1]

The extension of Federal authority in the constitution of 1874 to cover labor legislation led to the passage of several acts for the protection of laborers, with the result that the Confederation has gone a long way toward establishing a uniform labor law. The law of July 1, 1875, made railroad and steamboat companies responsible for accidents to their employees. Another act of March 23, 1877, extended the same principle to the factories of Switzerland. The Constitution of 1874 gives the Federal Government the right to " enact uniform regulations upon the work of children in factories, upon the duration of the work of adults therein, and for the protection which should be accorded to workpeople employed in unhealthy and dangerous industries." Acting within authority

[1] 213,199 to 205,069

Chapter XIII

CENTRALIZATION AND SOCIALISM. 1874-1914

THE great political changes in the cantons, and still more the remodeling of the Confederation, were the results of a decided advance in public spirt. The struggles after 1840, the Federal reforms after 1850, the effects, so inspiring to patriotism, of the so-called " Prussian War," and the agitation for Federal reforms from 1869-1874, taught the people to interest themselves in national questions, and to think and feel like Confederates in a manner hitherto almost unknown. A lively interest in politics began to show itself in all parts among the great mass of the people, and everywhere men began eagerly to concern themselves about the weal and woe of the whole community. The press did its utmost to keep alive and to increase this interest; the many political clubs and great national associations for singing, and shooting, and gymnastics, with their regularly recurring national festivals, formed a no less important political school for the people.

The increased interest in politics has been kept at flood through the frequent opportunities for the discussion of national questions by the Referendum. No political institution of modern times has served so well to develop a true national life. The exercise of the Referendum is a periodic practical lesson in politics of inestimable value to the people at large. Party machinery and organization outside the legislature is almost entirely lacking in Switzerland. According to a distinguished publicist, " there are in the Confederation no national committees, no elaborate system of primary caucuses and general conventions, no men who make a business of arranging nominations and managing campaigns. The Clericals and Radicals do occasionally hold congresses, but these are simply intended to prevent disruption by discussing the questions of the day; they take no part in the nomination of candidates." In one way only do parties play an important rôle: they secure demand for the Referendum and draft Initiative petitions. A group of professional politicians, the *neinsager,* make a business of collecting signa-

the Federal Assembly enacted that all workrooms and machinery must be kept in such a state as shall not be injurious to the life or health of the laborers; that light and ventilation must be ample; that the legal liability of the owner in regard to accidents extends to all injuries sustained by employees which have been caused to the latter in the discharge of their duties, or by the default of the managers, overseers, or other representative officials, unless it can be proved that the accident was due to unpreventable causes or to negligence on the part of the victim. The law furthermore fixes the normal day at eleven hours, shortened to ten hours on Saturdays and the days preceding holidays. Women are specially protected by the law, and children under fourteen years of age may not legally be employed in factories. The factory act was submitted to popular vote by the Referendum on October 21, 1877, and was accepted by the people in spite of opposition in the industrial centers.

The act of 1877 is the basis of the factory laws of Switzerland. It has reduced the evils of child labor to small proportions and greatly improved the status of adult employees in the factories. The administration of the law has been improved year by year, and its benefits widely extended. The principal defect consists in its limitations. It does not go far enough to satisfy the social reformers or the cantonal legislatures. It entirely ignores the home industries where over a hundred thousand persons—men, women, and children—are employed. Such industries are beyond the jurisdiction of the Federal law, and therefore Federal inspection both regarding hours of work and the healthfulness of the places of work. Various attempts have been made by the cantonal legislatures to make up for these shortcomings, but the Federal Government has been unable to deal with the matter, largely because of the inherent difficulties in such legislation. Again, the factory act fails to control the trades and smaller industries. An attempt was made in 1894 to amend the Constitution so as to give the central authorities power to legislate for these. The amendment, however, was so broad in its terms that it gave the Confederation the right to legislate on labor organizations and even to compel workmen to join in trade-unions. As a decided reaction against socialistic and centralizing legislation had set in, the law was very unpopular. Either tendency would probably have been sufficient to defeat it at the polls, and therefore it was rejected at a Referendum by a decisive majority, though only about forty-three per cent. of the electors went to the polls. Several lesser acts of recent years have regulated the size, ventilation, and sanitary condition of workrooms so that to-day laborers are assured comfortable and healthful quarters in all larger factories. The best of evidence for the efficacy of the legislation upon factory and home sanitation lies in the fact that the rate of mortality is at the very low figure of 19 in 1000. Again, it has been pointed out that only three per cent. of the total number of deaths are from accidents to laborers in the course of their employment.

In the matter of regulating and improving the sanitary condition of the lodgings of the poor, Switzerland is well to the front among European countries. Several of the large cities have introduced excellent reforms in this respect. In Basle an elaborate law went into effect in 1895 which provides that every house must have at least one fireproof stairway, regulates the height of dwellings, and requires that there shall be no living or sleeping-rooms in cellars. As early as 1894 the city of Berne owned 66 buildings, which it rented to workingmen at a profit of from three to four per cent. Since then Berne has more than doubled the number of edifices for this purpose. Neuchâtel has 23 houses containing 210 rooms. Zurich has made a beginning. Lausanne bought ground for a similar experiment in 1898. And more recently Geneva has gone into the construction of a series of workingmen's houses whose combined cost is to be 2,024,000 francs. Swiss cities, in general, are building little cottages of two apartments each, with a garden attached, though Geneva is constructing four-story tenements.

Among the efforts which Switzerland has recently taken to alleviate the misery of its poorer classes insurance occupies an important place. Legislation of this character has gone farthest in the cantons. As early as 1855 the canton of Basle had an assistance fund to which contributions from journeymen workmen were obligatory. The canton of St. Gall began an experiment in 1885 with compulsory insurance for all residents. Other cantons have introduced similar experiments. In 1890 the people and cantons of Switzerland accepted the following amendment to the Federal Constitution: " The Confederation shall introduce, by means of legislation, a system of insurance against sickness and accidents, taking into account the existing friendly societies. It can declare that all persons shall compulsorily insure themselves or may confine it to certain classes of citizens." A Federal commission then reported in favor of compulsory insurance in case of sickness and accident. In 1893 the Federal Council, encouraged by the financial success of the alcohol monopoly, proposed a tobacco monopoly to provide means for a scheme of government insurance against accidents and sickness, a scheme which had met with approval in 1890. Nothing came of this particular project, but it emphasized the demand for some system of compulsory workingmen's insurance, and after many years of discussion on October 5, 1899, a law passed both houses of the Federal Assembly without a dissenting vote. The act was known as the "Law of Insurance against Sickness and Accident and of Military Insurance." It provided for the compulsory insurance of all persons above fourteen years of age, working for others, with certain exceptions. The insured were divided into ten classes, according to the amount of their daily earnings. All persons without an independent means of livelihood were to take out insurance against sickness and accident. Great care was taken to conciliate mutual benefit societies and the highly paid artisan class. The expense of the administration of the system and one-fifth of the premiums were charged to the Confederation. The law met with much opposition on account of the tendency to favor the careless and the drunkard rather than the conscientious hard worker, and because of the army of parasitic bureaucrats necessary to administer its intricacies. Moreover, the measure was complicated with restrictions and exceptions. Many believed that the plan was practically impossible of execution. The rural population disliked it; the industrial workers were indifferent. The opposition called for the Referendum, with the result that the law was rejected, May 20, 1900, with the very decisive majority of 337,000 to 146,000. It was estimated that the law would have cost the state annually eight million francs. Nevertheless, the idea of compulsory insurance administered by the Federal Government is highly favored by an increasing number of Swiss, so that it may be said that the rejection of the law of 1899 has simply postponed the matter for further discussion and study.

Another consideration of the highest importance in recent Swiss history has been the development of a system of railroads and the final nationalization of these. Since 1840 great zeal has been exhibited in the construction of carriage roads and highroads, and of good passes over the Alps. The fame which Berne and the

Grisons had enjoyed in this respect during the eighteenth century has been gradually extended to a great number of the cantons, and the Federation has expended great sums upon the making of mountain roads. Artistic bridges of stone and iron of wonderful construction have replaced the old wooden bridges.

Since 1830, too, traffic has been facilitated by the use of steam. The appearance of the lakes has been enlivened by steamboats, and the land has been intersected by numberless railroads. The first independent national railway of Switzerland was the line between Zurich and Baden, opened in 1847. Joint-stock companies were formed in all parts, and between 1854 and 1859 the main lines of the great network of Swiss railways came into existence, the Central and Northeastern, the United Swiss lines, the Western lines, etc. By and by a veritable "railway fever" raged, and the network of railways rapidly spread throughout the mountain defiles.

The mountain railways of Switzerland are very remarkable, and a world-wide reputation attaches to the international railroad through the St. Gotthard. The plans for this undertaking having been matured, chiefly through the efforts of Dr. Alfred Escher, and their execution having been rendered possible by the treaty of Italy and Germany with Switzerland, the Gotthard Company was formed, and stock and bonds were issued. The actual work of tunnel construction was begun in the summer of 1872, under the engineer Favre of Geneva. But many difficulties had yet to be overcome; the work of excavation was much harder, and the cost of the whole amounted to much more than had been expected. In 1878 and 1879 supplementary subsidies had to be added, eight millions by Switzerland, and ten millions by Germany and Italy. The "Gotthard crisis" was successfully passed through the patriotism of the Swiss people, and on February 29, 1880, the piercing of the St. Gotthard tunnel was achieved. Favre, however, did not live to see his work completed, having died of heart disease a short time previously in the tunnel itself. The first passenger train passed through November 1, 1881, and the whole stretch of 15,000 meters was formally opened for traffic in 1882. The marvelous structure of this Alpine railway, its windings above and beneath the earth, its imposing bridges, its tunnels, of which about fifty smaller ones may be counted—and no less its significance for the traffic of the whole world—all combine to elevate this into one of the most magnificent engineering undertakings of modern times, and Switzerland enjoys the honor of having accomplished the greater part of the work of its construction.

The question of state ownership of railroads in Switzerland dates back to the beginning of railroad building. A plan proposed by the Federal Council for the construction of a state system was rejected in 1852 in favor of construction by private companies under charters issued by the cantons with the approval of the Confederation. All the concessions which were made contained provisions looking to the ultimate purchase of the railroads. The charters gave opportunity for state purchase every fifteen years upon five years' previous notice. The first of these periods came in 1883 and the question of nationalization was raised in the Federal Council, but owing to the bad financial condition of the railroads nothing was done. As the next opportunity for the purchase of the railroads would not come until 1898, the friends of the movement agitated for voluntary purchases. In December, 1887, an agreement was nearly concluded for the purchase of the Northeast Railroad. The plan proposed in this case was for the Northeast Railroad Company to cede to the Confederation all its movable and immovable property and receive in return at their nominal value Swiss bonds bearing three and a half per cent. interest at the rate of 600 francs for each preferred share and 500 francs for every common share. However, the Federal Council became solicitous about securing a majority vote in the Federal Assembly and withdrew from the negotiations.

During 1890 and 1891 the Federal Council made an attempt to secure an influence over the policy of the Jura-Simplon railroad by the purchase of a large share of the preferred stock. The Confederation bought 77,090 shares at 120, paying three per cent. bonds quoted at 90, but no further purchases were attempted after 1891. This action simply made the government the controlling stockholder and the financial manager, but the control of this great railroad was an important step toward Federal ownership. In June, 1891, the Federal Assembly authorized the Federal Council to purchase the Central Railroad at the price of 1000 francs for every share of 500 francs, payable in three per cent. bonds quoted at par. These terms were, however, so unfavorable to the Confederation that a Referendum was resorted to, and the agreement was rejected by a large majority. As a result of a thorough investigation the Federal authorities reached the conclusion that nationalization was desirable, and set about systematically to accomplish that. The first step to prepare the way for such a measure was the Accounting law of 1895. This prescribed in detail the method of keeping accounts which railways were compelled to follow. The railway companies were required to lay printed copies of their reports before the Federal Council, and their accounts were regulated by the Department of Posts and Railways in much the same way that national banks are controlled in the United States. The principal object of the law was to secure publicity of accounts from which a more accurate determination of the "net annual revenue" and the "value of the plant" might be made. The law met with considerable opposition, especially in the Italian and French cantons of Switzerland. It was asserted to be an insidious attempt to commit the people to state ownership of railways. The excitement nearly resulted in a race conflict between Romance Switzerland and German Switzerland. The Referendum was called for, and the act was accepted by the people only after an exciting campaign. The result was a victory for the cause of nationalization. The Federal Council then proceeded to draft a law for the purchase and operation of the railroads, and laid this before the Federal Assembly, March 25, 1897. As most of the concessions granted by the Federal Government to the private companies expired on May 1, 1898, that date was regarded by many as a suitable time for the state to take over the railways. Inasmuch as five years' notice to the companies was necessary, the question of state ownership had to be settled promptly if the state was to take advantage of the next periodic opportunity. The project contemplated the purchase and the subsequent operation of the five principal Swiss railway systems—the Jura-Simplon, the Central, the Northeastern, the Swiss Union, and the St. Gotthard—with an aggregate length of 2374 miles built at an original cost of 1,210,931,534 francs—equivalent to $230,076,991.46.[2]

The Federal law for the acquisition and operation of the railways passed the Federal Assembly on October 15, 1897. The majority of the opponents of purchase was composed of the Clerical party and the Conservative Liberals, both of whom opposed the law on motives of principle. It was in a large degree a question of increasing centralization or preserving cantonal independence. The Socialist party supported the measure, though it did not fully come up to their demands. The Radical party, the one controlling large

[2] The statement is for cost to January 1, 1898.

majorities in both chambers, was the sponsor for the bill, and its members were almost unanimous in its support. At the Referendum February 20, 1898, a large vote was polled, and the measure was accepted by the overwhelming majority of 386,634 to 182,718, or by more than two to one. By this vote the Swiss people went on record in favor of placing railroads as a public service in line with the post office and telegraph.

The cost to the state to nationalize almost the entire railway system was already fixed by the charters of the roads, and was the net income multiplied by twenty-five. The income was measured by the average earnings of the last ten years. The investment, heavy as it naturally was, has secured a system in excellent condition, ready to pay from the beginning more than the interest on the loan. The purchase act provided that the funds necessary should be raised by the emission of obligations or coupon bonds to be canceled within sixty years. One article prescribed the complete separation of the accounts of the railways from those of the Confederation, so that it would always be impossible to operate the Federal railway for political purposes. The railroads must serve exclusively the general interests of traffic, that is, to reduce the cost of travel and transportation. For the administration of the Federal railways a distinct administrative department was created, decentralizing as far as possible their management. The state is divided into five circuits, each with its circuit directory in charge of the current business of the circuit. Over all is a general directory of five or seven members with its seat at Berne. In addition to these bodies in direct management, there is a circuit directory meeting quarterly to render opinions on all questions concerning railway affairs, especially time-tables and rates, in the circuit. An administrative council of fifty-five members supervises the entire administration, draws up the annual budget, examines the annual accounts, fixes the principles of rates, of classification of freight, of train schedules, ratifies contracts with other railways, domestic and foreign, fixes the remuneration of officials, and renders opinions on proposed changes in the laws and ordinances relating to railways. The acquisition of the railroads by the Confederation was completed in 1902 and the railroad bonds were converted into three and a half per cent. Federal bonds. Only a few secondary lines of normal gauge and narrow-gauge mountain railroads remained in the hands of private companies, and the Federal Council is authorized, with the consent of the Federal Assembly, to purchase these lines The purchase of the railroads was a decided triumph of centralization and socialism, and increased greatly the power and patronage of the Federal Government. It should be said that people believed in the promises of the Radicals to furnish them with a better service at less cost. The men employed on the railroads supported the step because they believed that they would fare better in the hands of the state than under private ownership. Above all there was a strong prejudice against corporations and foreign bondholders in Switzerland, and the Swiss people desired to be free from these influences. Again, the measure appealed to a patriotic feeling and was very popular. It is yet too early to speak of the results, but the Swiss claim that it has had effect already in an improvement of the service and a reduction of fares. "New and much-improved cars are being built; they are being attached to the fastest trains, and the fares are greatly reduced. Public ownership has not limited enterprise. The lines are being constantly improved, and new branches are being built." The Simplon Tunnel, the longest in the world ($12\frac{1}{4}$ miles), was actually pierced on February 24, 1905, and a medal was struck to commemorate the acomplishment of this world-famous engineering feat. Electric traction has been adopted, and the Simplon line will give Switzerland another most valuable transcontinental system.

The monopoly of telegraphs was established by Federal law in 1851. In like manner as soon as it was demonstrated that telephones were useful they were taken over by the Federal Government without any special opposition and made an integral part of the postal-telegraphic system. The Confederation has the right to erect lines of either telegraph or telephone through any state, but only after consultation with the authorities of the canton or commune through whose territories it is proposed to pass. Switzerland has more telephone instruments and telegraph offices in proportion to the population than any other country, the estimate for the latter reaching in 1904 a total of 5,590 miles of line and about five times that length of wire.

Everywhere in a cool matter-of-fact way government agencies have assumed control of industrial operations until Switzerland has become the political laboratory of the world. In order to check the spread of drunkenness the trade in alcohol was made a state monopoly in 1887. Peculiar conditions prevailed. Spirits were so cheap that the working class preferred spirits to beer and wine, and the consumption of spirits was increasing in an alarming degree. The Swiss set out deliberately to make alcohol harder to buy. Two methods presented themselves, either by a higher duty on imported spirits and a tax on domestic distillers or by a government monopoly. The latter appealed to the social and economic instinct of the people and was hence adopted. The former would have interfered with cantonal taxation and been obliged to face the unpopularity of all centralizing measures.

The enactment of the law required a tedious process, and that it succeeded in passing all the necessary stages is evidence of its popularity. In the first place it was necessary to take a Referendum upon the question whether the Constitution should be so altered as to give the Federal Government the power to create a monopoly of the wholesale trade in distilled alcohol. The proposed revision carried by a large majority on October 25, 1885. The Monopoly Act was then passed in the last days of December, 1886. The larger distillers followed up their opposition by an agitation for a Referendum, which was taken on May 15, 1887, with the result of an increased majority over the vote of 1885 for the law. By this act of 1887 the importation of alcohol and the distillation of potatoes, cereals, and foreign fruit passed into the hands of the Confederation. An exception to this monopoly in spirits was made in the case of the distillation of fruits and roots, which is free to anyone. This was done to encourage agriculture. Spirits used for technical and household purposes must be sold at cost of manufacture and must be rendered unfit for drinking by the addition of wood-spirits or other mixtures. The Federal Government may import spirits or make contracts with private persons for distilling. It is mandatory upon it to allot contracts with Swiss distillers for at least one-fourth part of the required amount for home consumption. This is a concession to private industry. The government only supplies liquors in quantities of 150 liters or more, so that its transactions are in wholesale. The small retail business is left entirely to private persons, and the licensing and regulating of this business is left wholly to the cantons. The net income from sales, taxes, and customs received by the Confederation must be handed over to the cantonal governments, divided among them in proportion to their population at the last census. Distillers were compensated for their losses in the diminished value of buildings and plants, but not for any losses in profits. The task of compensation to distillers was met with remarkable ease and success. Up to 1890 claims including costs of arbitration amounting to 4,037,950 francs ($767,210.50), were paid, or about forty-five per cent. of what the distillers asked. As an offset to the loss by depreciation in property according to the claims of the distillers of fifty-five per cent., it should be remembered that before 1888 only one-fourth of the alcohol consumed in Switzerland was of domestic manufacture, and still under the monopoly the government is pledged to have one-fourth of the alcohol produced by Swiss distillers using raw materials of home production. The monopoly is protected by high duties on imported liquors. In fact, so much higher are the prices of the Swiss products than those of neighboring countries, particularly Austria, that the Confederation practically pays a large annual bounty to its own distillers for the domestic product. The administration of the alcohol monopoly is committed to the Department of Finance and Customs. With the going into effect of the act the cantonal licenses to sell spirits expired. The Federal Government began the sale of spirits under its monopoly on January 1, 1888. The law seems to have been a success in two respects. The financial results have been remarkable, and the consumption of alcohol per head has been largely reduced. The cantons are obliged to spend one-tenth of their shares of the surplus in some way calculated to counteract the evil effects of alcohol. This tithe has been variously spent in recent years, as it is wholly within the power of each canton to determine what is "combating alcoholism." Such objects as "institutes for the cure of drunkards," "industrial institutes and reformatories," "lunatic asylums," "care of the sick, hospitals, etc.," "instruction in cookery and domestic economy, and food depots," "support of poor travelers," "temperance societies" and "reading rooms and good literature" are listed in the several cantonal reports. One canton, Valais, was allowed to use its tithe in erecting a training college for elementary teachers!

The manufacture and sale of gunpowder is exclusively a Federal monopoly, secured by the Constitution of 1874. In 1891 the Federal Government assumed the monopoly in the issue of banknotes. Of recent years there has been a demand for an increase in the number of industrial operations managed by the central authorities. A law of 1895 defeated at a Referendum made the manufacture and sale of matches a Federal monopoly. Paternalism once begun has seemed in the case of Switzerland to have no end. The triumphs of the Socialists have led them into more pretentious designs. In 1894 a constitutional amendment was proposed by which the hours of work in various industries were to be reduced, with the aim of giving employment to a greater number of laborers; workmen were to be provided gratuitously with work, and insured against the consequences of loss of work. The laborers have on numerous occasions attempted to secure state physicians and pharmacists who should give their services free to laborers, and they have tried to bring about a state monopoly in the sale of tobacco and cereals. In the cantons and in the cities the same socialistic tendency appears. In eighteen cantons the government has taken the place of private fire insurance companies, receiving premiums and paying losses. Government banks are maintained in a large majority of the cantons. The sale of salt is a government monopoly in every canton in the Confederation, though the mining or manufacture is in all cases undertaken by private companies under state charters or concessions. The city of Basle has assumed the monopoly of retail in high grades of alcoholic beverages. Various cantons and communes have in recent years assumed the burden of burying the dead. They give to all, rich and poor, the same sort of a burial, which is simple and inexpensive. Government burial is not usually made compulsory, but where it has been adopted it becomes practically universal. Geneva owns its lighting plant, and has utilized the power of the Rhone River, making it pump the city water and distribute power to the various industries of the city.

A matter of more than passing moment in the history of Switzerland has been the line of demarcation between the functions of the canton and of the Confederation. Such is the "Ticino Question," which began as early as 1876 with a constitutional conflict over representation and citizenship. The cantonal constitution prescribed that representation should be by districts without regard to population. This conflicted with a clause in the Federal Constitution. Again the "Ticino" law allowed citizens removing from its bounds to retain a domicile and return to vote. Federal decrees and decisions from 1876 to 1888 endeavored with varying success to stop this double citizenship. The Federal authorities interfered in local insurrections during 1889 and 1890 and maintained their right to preserve order in cantons without waiting for a summons from the latter. However, at other times the Swiss have shown an attachment to cantonal independence. Capital punishment, which had been formerly a matter of cantonal right, was abolished by Article 65 of the Federal Constitution of 1874. Many asserted that the abolition of capital punishment caused a fresh outbreak of crime, and started a popular agitation for its restoration. The Federal Assembly yielded to the popular outcry and passed an amendment in 1879 which was ratified in a Referendum by a good majority. The cantons are now free to reëstablish the death penalty for crimes at common law. Eight have done so, but none of them have exacted the penalty of the law.

The period since 1874 has been marked by a growing confidence in central government and a decline in cantonal separation. From time to time, after some violent party strife, a closer union, and a reconciled coöperation to solve national problems have been observable. Was the country at any time attacked or injured, was it a question of making some sacrifice for a patriotic purpose, such as the purchase of the Rutli in 1861, the erection of the Winkelried monument at Stans, the collection for the Winkelried fund; were oppressed fellow-Confederates in need of help and support, as after the conflagration in Glarus in 1861, the landslip of Elm in 1881, the destruction of the quay in Zug in 1887, in such cases a devoted and self-sacrificing sympathy has been shown by all sections of the population. The Swiss will inevitably feel, ever more and more deeply, the truth of the words:

> "*Ans Vaterland, ans theure, schliess' dich an,*
> *Dort sind die Wurzeln deiner Kraft!*"[3]

> "*Die angebornen Bande knüpfe fest,*
> *Ans Vaterland, ans theure, schliess' dich an,*
> *Das hälte fest mit deinem ganzen Herzen,*
> *Hier sind die stärken Wurzeln deiner Kraft.*"

Thus are gradually vanishing those antagonisms of the cantons, of creeds, and of party opinion which have in the past wrought such havoc among the Swiss people.

[3] "Knit fast the ties which form your heritage
And cleave to your beloved fatherland;
Hold to it firm with all your heart and soul;
Here are the hardy roots of all your power."
—"William Tell." Translated by Major-General Patrick Maxwell.

From time to time, too, a warm interest was manifested in educational questions. Mindful of the truth of Zschokke's expression: "Popular education is popular emancipation"—"*Volksbildung ist Volksbefreiung*"—the statesmen of 1830-1840 caused the requirements of the schools to be laid before them *en masse*, which might well serve as an example for all future time. Frequently between 1850 and 1870, various cantons made great efforts and many sacrifices for the improvement of the education of children, the enlargement of the popular schools, and the promoting of scientific and artistic culture. Great scientific establishments and institutes arose: the cantonal universities and academies, the Federal polytechnic, the cantonal and Federal collections of every kind, of natural science, archæology, and the history of art. From various centers of intellectual life brilliant results were produced. During 1889-1891 the famous international Catholic university was established at Fribourg. Time and again educational matters have been the subject of serious conflicts. In 1882 the Federal authorities raised a complaint against the sectarian teaching which prevailed in nearly all the elementary schools. By Article 27 of the Constitution, "The cantons shall make provision for elementary education, which must be adequate and placed exclusively under the direction of the civil authority. Such instruction shall be obligatory, and in the public schools free of charge. The public schools must be so organized that they may be frequented by those belonging to all denominations without prejudice to their freedom of belief or of conscience. The Confederation shall take such measures as may seem necessary against cantons who do not fulfill their obligations in this matter." The aim of the Radicals was to secure a new law by which education would be secular—the teachers laymen, the subjects secular, the methods secular, the school-houses secular—even in the purely Catholic communes. The attack was construed to be an attack on religion, and religious people of all sects united to oppose the Radicals. As a result the law was rejected by the people by one of the largest votes which a Referendum has ever brought out.[4] Though, indeed, there still remains much for which to wish and to strive, though there are yet considerable gaps to be filled and failings to be mended, though great progress is often checked by the indolence of individual cantons, of the flagging of the spirit of the age, yet the educational system of Switzerland has often met with due recognition.

[4] The vote was 318,139 to 172,010.

In certain sciences and branches of literature excellent results have been achieved. Since the year 1830 Switzerland has produced a succession of learned men and poets whose fame has spread far beyond the borders of their own land, such as the theologians, Alexander Schweizer, J. C. Biedermann, and K. Hagenbach; the learned chaplain, P. Gall Morell; the natural historians, Merian, Studer, Escher, Desor, and Oswald Heer; the philologist, Orelli; the professor of constitutional law, J. C. Bluntschli; the antiquarian, Ferd. Keller; the poets, Jeremiah Gotthelf, Konrad Ferd. Meyer, and Gottfried Keller. For the cultivation and extension of learning numerous clubs, reading societies, scientific, popular, and juvenile, were formed. The library movement was active, and by 1868 the number of public libraries had risen to nearly 3000.

This intellectual transformation called into existence a corresponding improvement in the comforts of life and in material culture. The towns underwent a change in accordance with modern tastes and requirements. From about the year 1830 the fortifications, mediæval walls, towers, and gates were gradually abolished, and old quarters pulled down and newly built. There arose everywhere fine broad streets, bordered by tasteful buildings; handsome schoolhouses, churches, town halls, and museums were erected; magnificent hotels, fitted with every comfort, fine promenades and quays, monuments and statues became the ornaments of modern towns.

A feature of Swiss political history since 1874 has been the extension of the principle of direct rule of the people. Switzerland has probably advanced farther in the direction of those democratic institutions designed to insure order and liberty and to prevent shameful despotism in government than any other country. The purely representative system has been almost wholly abolished. The fundamental principle in recent political experiments in Switzerland is that the people shall exercise a direct and effective control. Up to the present time the Swiss seem to have discovered about the only political tools enabling the people successfully to maintain an actual check on the politician. The two unique and distinguishing features of the Swiss Government are the absence of the party system and the direct intervention of the people in law-making by means of the Referendum and the Initiative. The formula, " the people exercise the law-making power with the assistance of the state legislature," expresses the Swiss practice, which is the reverse of the order elsewhere.

The Federal Council, a sort of an irresponsible cabinet chosen by the chambers, is made up of persons of different political views. It is not uncommon for members to oppose one another openly in the Federal Assembly. Representatives of the several parties find places in the executive department, though usually the Radicals and Liberal-Conservatives dominate. The Federal Council is in no sense a responsible cabinet, obliged to stand before the country for a distinct policy, and expected to resign collectively if that policy meets with defeat. Whatever the politics of a member of the Federal Council each one is elected to carry out within his own department the will of the Federal Assembly. Another important result of the non-party character of the Federal executive is for its membership to become permanent. Only twice since 1848 have Councilors willing to serve failed of reëlection. In a similar manner there is a lack of any strong party spirit in the elections of members to the Federal Assembly. No great agitation precedes elections, as in the United States. In 1887 only forty per cent. of the seats were contested. In the elections of 1896, out of the 160 members in the National Council there were only 25 new ones, and in the Council of States only 8 new ones. Between 1888 and 1896 the National Council has only lost 20 of its members by non-reëlection, while 62 retired voluntarily. M. Borgeaud has expressed the motives which influence the average Swiss elector in the following manner: " If the candidate is obliging and affable, and if he is a neighbor and decent fellow generally, and if he belongs to the party from which the elector has been in a habit of choosing, then the elector argues thus: Would it not be an undeserved reproach to turn X out? His opinions may be different from my own; well! what of that? If he does it again, one can always say, No." The legislator whose bill is rejected by the people is not discredited. He is simply in the position of a deputy whose bill has not passed. His employer is of a different opinion and sends it back to be altered.

The Referendum when introduced into the Federal Constitution in 1874 was most strenuously supported by the Radicals and equally strongly opposed by the Conservatives, who regarded it as the triumph of revolutionary principles. Curiously enough in the thirty years' practice it has shown itself adverse to centralization, to strong Federal power, and to heavy outlays—that is, hostile to a radical policy—and has played directly into the hands of the Conservatives. It is a strange fact that the same constituency which persistently elects Radical members to the Federal Assembly as persistently rejects all that they propose. It is an excellent sign that from sixty-six to eighty-eight per cent. of the population take advantage of their right to vote upon the appeal by the Referendum. A few radical measures, like the factory act, the alcohol monopoly, and the amendment on the compulsory insurance of workmen, have been approved by the people, but more so-called socialistic proposals, as the law on epidemics, on education, on the state bank, amendments for legislation on trades and for a match monopoly, have been defeated at the polls. The fact is the people are more conservative than their representatives. Swiss experience indicates that a law to be approved must not be too general or complicated, and that if it is prodigal of national money it will be rejected. The Swiss are economical in government and illiberal in salaries to their public servants. Prejudice plays a large part in determining whether a law will be accepted or rejected. If a measure is centralizing in its effect it will meet with opposition. If foreign journals recommend a measure it will be almost sure to be lost. The conservative results of the Referendum have been variously attributed. Doubtless the opponents of a law go to the polls in much greater numbers than the supporters. Two facts may be noted in examing the results of the Referendum. The first is the attachment of the cantons to their independence, which they regard as an historical right; and the second is a dislike for all expenses for which the people do not see the immediate utility. "The Referendum has made the people conservative," one writer says, "and it has often made laws fail which are very strongly supported and very cleverly defended. It is sufficient on these occasions for the different minorities to unite at the polls in order to obtain a compact and decisive majority." Stüssi sums up in his monograph on the Referendum in Zürich from 1869 to 1885 the results of cantonal experience as follows: "All the laws useful to the cantons have been accepted, even those which demanded considerable money sacrifices from the people. No law which would have really advanced either moral or material progress has been definitely laid aside. In those rare causes which seem to contradict this conclusion the Referendum has simply displayed its inherent ultra-conservative character, and delayed an advance which would seem to most too rapid." It is apparent that the tendency to reject measures that are in any way radical is more noticeable in the cantons than in the Confederation.

An event of great importance in the development of direct democratic government in Switzerland was that of July 5, 1891, when the people adopted a constitutional amendment establishing the popular Initiative in legislation on constitutional subjects. The idea was not new, having prevailed in several of the cantons. By the act of 1891 if 50,000 citizens request the amendment of the constitution in a particular manner, the Federal Assembly must act upon the subject. The petition may present the proposal in general terms or in the form of a bill already drafted. In the former case an Assembly in sympathy will draw up a bill incorporating the proposed change and submit it to the people by Referendum; an Assembly hostile to the amendment petitioned will merely submit the question as to whether the constitution shall be revised, and, if adopted by the people, work out the amendment afterward. In the other case where the formulated article is presented in the petition the Assembly may submit it as it stands or may submit along with it a modified draft or a counter measure to a popular Referendum. The legislature must act within one year from the receipt of the petition. In case the Assembly does not act within that period, the Federal Council must submit the amendment petitioned. The Initiative in Federal matters applies only to constitutional amendments, and not to statute law, as it does in the cantons.

Since 1891 several attempts have been made to amend the constitution in this way, but the Slaughter Act of 1893 has been the only successful one. The Society for the Prevention of Cruelty to Animals started an agitation in favor of prohibiting the Jewish manner of slaughtering animals for food by bleeding them before they are dead. The diets of several cantons responded with laws forbiding this form of slaughter. The question came into Federal politics through the appeal of the Jews for protection in their religious liberties. Race prejudices were easily aroused. The society having secured the necessary number of signatures for the Initiative, petitioned for a constitutional amendment prohibiting the Talmudic rules for butchering. The amendment to the constitution was carried at a Referendum August 20, 1893, by a vote of 191,527 to 127,000.

Recent efforts to further popularize the government of Switzerland received a striking setback at the hands of the people through the Referendum. Two amendments to the constitution passed the Chambers, one for the election of members of the Federal Council by the people at large in place of the present choice by the Legislature, and another for proportionate representation in the National Council, to be rejected by a Referendum, November 4, 1900, by large majorities, the former by a vote of 266,637 to 141,851, and the latter by 242,448 to 166,065. The defeat was the more striking because of the united support given them by Liberals, Radicals, and Socialists, and the extended agitation in their behalf, reaching back ten years. Proportionate representation already exists, however, in the local legislatures in five of the cantons and two of the large cities of Switzerland. The Swiss believe that representative democracy is a form of government which is doomed to disappear. It is their theory that the people should no longer delegate their sovereignty to elected representatives, but exercise it directly themselves. The *Landsgemeinde* most nearly realizes their ideal. This is folk-mote government. The *Landsgemeinde* is a mass meeting of all the male citizens of a district assembled to choose the permanent officials of the district and to make its laws. The powers of the *Landsgemeinde* usually cover the following subjects: partial as well as total revision of the Constitution, enactment of laws, imposition of direct taxes, incurrence of state debts, alienation of public domain, the granting of public privileges, admission of foreigners into state citizenship, establishing of new offices and the regulation of salaries, and election of cantonal executive and judicial offices. It is in form and function the tribal council of Tacitus resurrected. This type of government exists in six cantons, but is entirely unsuited to a large district or state. The Referendum is, on the other hand, practicable in a large city or state. But because a political institution works well in Switzerland is no evidence that the same institution would work in other states. Switzerland does not have, for example, several of the most serious problems which the United States must face. It does not have the problem of poverty. It has no very rich, the capitalists, nor any very poor, the paupers. It does not have the continual influx of foreigners difficult to assimilate. There are no great undeveloped regions to be opened—fields which arouse to the highest pitch all the gambling instincts of the people. It has not the discouraging problem of the great city. According to the census of 1904 the population of each of the four large cities of Switzerland was as follows: Zurich, 169,410; Basle, 120,897; Geneva, 110,954; Berne, 68,958.

Beginning with the sixteenth century, Switzerland has pursued a policy of neutrality. Geographical isolation has largely determined this course. The Congress of Vienna joined in 1815 in protecting this voluntarily assumed status by a convention for the neutralization of Switzerland. Switzerland has not, on the other hand, left its own neutrality to be dependent on the good will of other nations. An elaborate system of military defense has been constructed. Heavy fortifications stand at the strategic points of the frontier, and a thoroughly organized, well-trained militia is always ready for service. The Confederation possesses no large standing army in time of peace, and yet it might put more than 500,000 men into the field at a moment's notice.

Since 1871 Switzerland has had no occasion to assert its neutrality by armed force, but the right of asylum has been the cause of repeated friction with other powers. The Swiss regard the right to offer asylum to the oppressed of other lands as one of their most precious privileges. A beautiful humanitarian stand taken by the Swiss is this "Right of Asylum," comparable only to the long period of unrestricted immigration which the United States has so hospitably allowed. Unfortunately at times Swiss hospitality has been sadly abused. Within recent years refractory foreign elements have endangered the neutrality, even the very independence of the state. After the murder of Czar Alexander II. at St. Petersburg in 1881 earnest efforts were made by the Russian Government to induce Switzerland to curtail the right of asylum which it had extended to Russian Nihilists, many of whom resided in Geneva, Zurich, and Basle. Foreign representations that the plot had originated in Switzerland, supplemented by pressure from the Swiss people, who had no sympathy with the criminal outrages of the Nihilists, led the Federal Council to enter upon a restrictive policy. There was a genuine fear that the independence of Switzerland was endangered through the socialistic attitude of the radical elements. An attempt of the Socialists of Europe to hold a great congress at Zurich on September 2, 1881, was suppressed by the cantonal authorities. The Russian agitator Kuropatkin was sent from the country. During the summer of 1884 several more anarchists seeking asylum in Switzerland were arrested for spreading revolutionary literature, some imprisoned for a short period, most of them acquitted, and three of them, an Austrian and two Germans, were expelled from the country. More expulsions followed in 1885. One authority estimated that there were 1500 foreign anarchists in Switzerland in that year. Vigorous efforts were made by the Federal Council to rid the Confederation of these foreign revolutionists. The German Government during the same period brought pressure to bear on Switzerland to secure the suppression of the German Socialists, refugees in that land, and finally in 1888 a political police was provided to prevent the abuse of the right of asylum. Councilor Droz said in defense of the bill that "the majority of the Swiss people are determined that our house shall be respected by all who dwell in it. The air we breath is the air of healthy liberty. We will not allow it to be vitiated by the miasma of anarchism. Neither shall our house be a refuge whence assaults can be directed with impunity against the repose of other countries." Nevertheless, Germany became involved in a conflict with Switzerland, owing to the practice of the German authorities of maintaining a special police in Switzerland to watch the revolutionary Socialists. Wohlgemuth, a German police officer, was sent into Switzerland during the summer of 1889 to stir up the anarchists resident there to open deeds of violence, to the end that the latter might be detected and arrested. The Swiss promptly imprisoned Wohlgemuth on the charge of inciting to a breach of peace, and later politely conducted him to the frontier. Germany, still under the iron hand of Bismarck, protested and demanded that no hindrances should be placed in the way of the German secret agents. Russia and Austria joined with Germany in representing that unless Switzerland furnished the necessary safeguards against those threatening the peace of Europe, they would regard the neutrality guarantee as no longer in their interests. This threat drew out from Switzerland positive refusal to consider the subject of its internal order by diplomatic discussion, but at the same time the Swiss police system was strengthened to meet the need of a guard against foreign agitators. The question at issue with Germany was finally settled in 1890, but the ill-will between Germany and Switzerland excited during the heated newspaper war has not been entirely destroyed as yet.

The geographical situation and the permanent neutrality of Switzerland has especially marked it out to take an important rôle in international relations. It has become the natural agent of the other powers. Its capital, Berne, has become in a measure the capital of United Europe. Since the Geneva convention of 1864 Switzerland has been the meeting-ground for international congresses and the home of several important permanent bureaus, great central bureaus destined to be great links to bind Europe and the world into one harmonious world-state.

The oldest of these bureaus is that relating to telegraphs, which was established in 1865. The bureau coördinates and publishes information of every kind relating to international telegraphy, acts as a sort of intelligence department for the telegraph systems of the world, and executes the working agreement between forty-six countries in the matter of international telegraph rates. At a great international postal congress held at Berne in 1874 an international board was created, with a permanent seat in that city. By the convention agreed to at this session the international postal bureau must be supported by contributions graduated roughly from the postal traffic and rank of the states which are members of the union; the total expenses must not exceed 3000*l*. a year ($15,000). This bureau serves as a clearing-house between the several state postal administrations; it settles disputed questions which arise and acts as an arbitral judge in litigations between the various countries in the Postal Union. A third bureau developed from a convention in which sixteen states united to protect trade-marks and patents, in 1885. A supplementary protocol of 1886 extended the convention to copyrights. Switzerland assumed responsibility for the management of the central administration, and the joint bureau on industrial and literary property was located with the others at Berne. The last of these great organizations was the International Railway Bureau, established in 1893. Ten states of Central Europe are parties to the convention which gave origin to the railway bureau. It deals only with freight traffic, though Russia has recently proposed that the passenger traffic be also placed under its jurisdiction. The international railway convention unites all the railroads belonging to it in one network under a common tariff as regards international transportation. The bureau serves as an international arbitration court for disputes in international railroad traffic, and in common with the other bureaus as a bureau of information and publication upon the affairs of its own peculiar province.

Besides these permanent organizations of an international

character and based on conventions between great powers, two societies, with more or less temporary objects have located their central offices on Swiss soil. In August, 1891, the Peace Congress, working in behalf of permanent international peace, held its meetings at Berne, and established a bureau. The following year, from from August 29 to August 31, 1892, a session of the Inter-Parliamentary Conference sat at Berne. The conference met to consider methods of promoting peace by arbitration, and ended its session by establishing an International Arbitration Court as a sort of an executive body for the conference, with a permanent seat at Berne, where its records shall be kept. Swiss laborers initiated an International Congress in 1897 for the protection of labor. A total of 375 delegates met at Zurich in debate over labor questions—the number of hours, the status of women working in large industries, and the protection of labor. The congress requested the governments of Europe to establish an international office of labor. More and more European states are finding it convenient to hold great international gatherings on Swiss soil, and Switzerland by virtue of its neutralization, of its central location, of the cosmopolitan character of its people, and the high intelligence of its leaders, has become a most fitting agent for the numerous international undertakings where uniformity of administration is highly important.

The Swiss deserve this international preëminence and its domestic quiet and prosperity. Better than any other people they have observed the civilizing law of work. Switzerland is all activity. Thrift marks every home. The tranquillity which Switzerland has enjoyed since 1848, the free institutions in the interior, the diligence and enterprise of the people, have acted as powerful levers upon industrial life. Certain branches of activity, such as the cotton and silk industry, the art of watchmaking, the making of machinery, straw-plaiting, and wood-carving, have attained international importance, and grown to be chief sources of the national wealth. Industry has increased and spread even into the mountainous regions as far as the highest villages in the Alps, where often in the heart of the mountains one may catch sight of a factory worked by water-power, or see looms in motion. The water-power of Switzerland which is already available is estimated at more than 500,000 horse-power. Throughout the country the rivers are being made to turn great dynamos to light the cities and distribute power to thriving industries. The Swiss people no longer consist merely of shepherds, peasants, and a very small number of tradespeople, but are becoming more and more an industrial people, willing to enter into competition with other lands. At the great international exhibitions in London, Paris, and St. Louis Switzerland has obtained high recognition. The two national expositions, that of Zurich in 1883 and that of Geneva in 1896, have shown more thoroughly the industrial resources of the country. The Swiss have sought and found purchasers for the products of their industry in all lands, even in the most remote parts beyond the seas. Commercial treaties have been concluded with all important civilized states, not only of Europe, but also of other continents, America, Australia, the East Indies, and even with China and Japan (1868).

If a distinct falling off is at times observable in certain spheres of industry, it may serve to remind her people with what difficulties Switzerland has to contend in competition with her powerful neighbors, and to incite them to redoubled zeal. Switzerland, small and by nature sparingly endowed, surrounded by large and wealthy states by which she is almost stifled, can only keep that which she has already acquired, and only attain to that which remains to be achieved in her institutions, her culture, and her military system, by all her members and all her citizens being equally imbued with a sense of the high and holy responsibilities laid upon them by their fatherland and its history.

The triennial elections of the Nationalrath of the Swiss Parliament took place in the autumn of 1911 and resulted in an overwhelming majority for the Radicals.

The most striking feature of the census of 1910, however, is the great increase in the number of non-Swiss residents in Switzerland. This number was 565,200 or about 15 per cent. of the total population. This increase was caused by immigration from Italy, Germany and France, principally workmen who sought better wages and the freedom from military service.

One of the most important events in the recent history of Switzerland was the acceptance by popular vote of the Federal law establishing insurance against sickness and accidents.

A number of new railroads have recently been opened in the Alps. These include lines leading to the summit of the peaks Niesen, the Monte Mattarone and Monte Bre. Some lines have been completed over mountain passes such as the Bernina Pass and the Jaufen Pass.

The yearly election for President held in December, 1912, resulted in the election of Edward Muller of Bern with Arthur Hoffman as Vice-President. Both are Radicals in politics.

The year 1913 saw the ratification of the St. Gothard Convention. This convention, which was ratified by Germany in 1910 and by Italy in June, 1912, gives to Germany and Italy the most-favored-nation treatment over the entire Swiss Federal railroad system. They had already been given these privileges over the St. Gothard line because in the construction of the line the two nations had been the largest subscribers.

In 1914 Colonel Dr. Arthur Hoffman was elected President of the Republic, and Giuseppe Motta was elected Vice-President.

The year 1914 saw some decline in trade owing to the general restless state of Europe. The imports for the past year amounted to $385,000,000, while the exports were about $275,000,000. Switzerland together with all the nations of Europe was greatly affected by the ever-growing troubles in the Balkans. Her geographical position bordering Germany, Austria, Italy, and France made her feel the great unrest in each state. While her neutrality was guaranteed by the Treaty of Vienna in 1815 and her position as a neutral was indispensable to the general interests of Europe, yet with the breaking out of the war in August there was felt great uneasiness. When it was seen that neutrality treaties of nations could be as easily broken as made, the unrest greatly increased.

On July 31, 1914, Switzerland bravely announced her stand for neutrality, and on the same date mobilized her troops. "Let every railroad bridge and every mountain pass be guarded" were her orders as she saw herself hemmed in by three nations, Germany, Austria, and France, already in the field and having massed troops along her very borders.

Chapter XIV

SWITZERLAND A NEUTRAL NATION. HOME OF THE LEAGUE OF NATIONS. 1914-1935

SWITZERLAND has always been a haven for political refugees from every State in Europe, but in the first weeks of the war she was called upon to shelter thousands of all sorts and conditions of men. Italians thrown out of work in Germany and Austria streamed over her borders, and most of them were destitute. Every town of size organized relief associations and the refugees were clothed, and fed and sent on their way happy to their own country. Then the Russians came, many amply supplied with ruble notes which no one would accept, and they too were relieved. Even German-Switzerland was generous to the poor wanderers, though here and there a discordant note was sounded, especially in the case of the Belgian refugees. It was suggested that Switzerland was prejudicing her neutrality by harboring Belgians, that it was a demonstration against Germany, etc. But such voices were few. The Swiss treated all the destitute refugees with the same open-handed hospitality.

The position of Switzerland, "a small neutral state surrounded by war," was perhaps more difficult than that of Holland. French-Switzerland sympathized unofficially with France and German-Switzerland with Germany and after the mobilization of the Swiss army the French-speaking Swiss were called to defend the German border, and the German-speaking the French border. The Swiss Government had taken complete measures to protect her neutrality —every foot of her frontiers was armed, mined and barbed-wired.

The Swiss Army is small but efficient and of the highest physical quality, largely made up of hardy mountaineers who are all fine shots. The Kaiser, who witnessed the manœuvres of the Swiss army a few years before the outbreak of the war, was much impressed by the fine showing they made, and it probably influenced his decision not to invade Switzerland. The Swiss have always ranked in history as among the best fighters in Europe. The majority of the people of the country, whether of German,

French or Italian extraction, while they may have sympathized with the war-aims of the country from which they derived, were first and last pro-Swiss, and would have fought whole-heartedly against any nation, or group of nations which attempted to destroy their neutrality.

The mobilization of the army cost the Swiss $100,000 a day, a large sum for such a small nation to pay, while it was necessary to raise large amounts to help the destitute and to exercise supervision over the agents of the warring nations who were constantly plotting acts which, if successful, would constitute a breach of Swiss neutrality.

Switzerland has long been dependent on tourists and summer visitors for a large part of her national income, but in the first period of the war the famous resorts were deserted. Later the great hotels became rest homes for the wounded, but the income derived from such sources was small compared to what it would have been in times of peace. Like Holland, Switzerland suffered from economic pressure of the warring nations. She was between the hammer and the anvil of the Allies and the Central Powers.

On December 17, 1914, the National Assembly elected G. Motta, a Catholic Conservative, then holding the office of Vice-President, to the office of President for the year 1915. M. Camille DeCoppet, an anti-clerical Liberal, was elected Vice-President at the same time.

The necessity of keeping the Swiss army mobilized, other extraordinary expenditures caused by the need to maintain Switzerland's neutrality, and the economic disturbances resulting from the war, made the financial condition of Switzerland a very serious problem. Even as early as January, 1915, the President of Switzerland announced that the war had so far cost his country $22,000,000. A special referendum held June, 1915, provided for special war taxes and for three successive war loans totaling $36,000,000, in order to defray these special expenditures. At the end of the year the cost of the war to Switzerland had risen to $51,000,000.

One of the most important services which Switzerland was able to render to the various belligerents was its ability to act as a clearing house for the exchange of disabled prisoners. Thousands of these were sent from the various prison camps to be interned in Switzerland for varying periods of time, after which they were in most cases repatriated.

A NEUTRAL NATION

The maintenance of Swiss neutrality became more and more difficult as the war progressed. The country was overrun with spies and propagandists from all of the belligerent countries who did not always maintain the scrupulous regard for Swiss neutrality which Swiss hospitality ought to have made obligatory to them. A number of arrests were made and some of those arrested were tried. All of these trials stirred up considerable attention, although no serious developments resulted.

On December 15, 1915, Vice-President C. DeCoppet was elected President for 1916 and Edmund Schulthess Vice-President.

On March 15, 1916, the National Council voted to continue the extraordinary powers which had been conferred upon the Council of State. In June another war loan of 100,000,000 francs was issued which was oversubscribed by more than 50 per cent. In September, 1916, the Federal Council decreed a special war profits tax of 25 per cent, which was to be retroactive from January 1, 1915.

On December 14, 1916, Edmund Schulthess was elected President of Switzerland for 1917 and Felix Calonder Vice-President.

Early in 1917 rumors that Germany contemplated an invasion of Switzerland resulted in an increase of the mobilized forces of the country. Similar rumors that France contemplated such a step were promptly met by the French Government in the form of official assurances that France would continue to respect the neutrality of Switzerland. At various times during the year demonstrations took place against the high cost of living, especially in the larger centres of population. Although in some instances they resulted in disorder and in slight destruction of property, the local officials in every case succeeded in eventually maintaining order. On December 14, 1916, M. Felix Calonder, then Vice-President, was elected to the office of President for 1918.

In June, 1918, a new commercial agreement between Switzerland and Germany was concluded which was to last nine months. The commercial treaty between the United States and Switzerland expired in October, 1918, and negotiations to renew it were immediately put under way. On December 11, 1918, M. Gustave Ador, formerly president of the International Committee of the Red Cross, was elected President for 1919, and M. Molta Vice-President.

The desire of the former Austrian Crown Land Vorarlberg,

expressed by means of a plebiscite, to join Switzerland, found no very enthusiastic response in that country.

In the elections of 1919, the system of proportional representation applied, being afterward adopted by most of the cantons. Switzerland appreciated the fact of the location of the League of Nations at Geneva, yet there was some discussion as to the desirability of membership. On May 16, 1920, the matter was settled by popular vote in favor of the League.

Like many other nations, Switzerland suffered from unemployment following the war. This was at its height at the beginning of 1923, when some 100,000 were said to be out of work. The government, as one remedy, aided unemployed workmen to emigrate to Canada.

An unusual crime, in 1923, was the murder of V. V. Vorovsky, who represented the Russian Soviet Government at the Lausanne Conference. His assassin, one Maurice Conradi, was arrested and frankly admitted that he killed Vorovsky in revenge for cruelties suffered from the Soviet government. He implicated M. Polunin as an accessory. The trial was a strange one, in which stress was laid on Soviet atrocities to such purpose that both Vorovsky and Polunin were acquitted.

The Savoy Free Zones are duty free zones close to the boundary of Switzerland, established more than a hundred years ago in order that the French customs boundary might not approach so close to Geneva as the national boundary. Article 435 of the Treaty of Versailles arranged for a change here to be effected by France and Switzerland themselves. An agreement signed in 1921 was ratified by the Swiss legislature, but defeated in a popular referendum. The French prepared to advance their customs boundary in accordance with the agreement. After some international dispute, it was decided to refer the interpretation of the Treaty of Versailles to the International Court in November, 1924. France and Switzerland also agreed on a new treaty of conciliation and arbitration.

In spite of the attractions of licensed gambling for tourists, a popular vote in 1925 declared for discontinuing it. The matter was transferred to the National Council, in which the vote was even until the President gave the deciding vote for suppression.

Electrification of railways, possible because of Switzerland's great water power, has continued to progress since the war. The railways, under government control, were operating at a profit in

1925, though operation by electricity was found to be more expensive than the use of steam.

The total length of electrified lines in 1919 was only 107 kilometers, which was increased to over 1,000 kilometers by the end of 1926. More than 250 electric locomotives were operating regularly in 1926. By 1929, it was estimated that the electrified lines would extend for more than 1,500 kilometers.

In December, 1925, Henri Haeberlin was elected President of the Confederation of Switzerland for 1926.

Another Alpine railroad was completed in 1926. This is a 27-mile line extending from Brigue, in the Rhone Valley, over the Furka Pass to Andermatt, and thence to Disentis in the valley of the Rhine.

At the end of 1926, Dr. Guiseppe Motta was elected President for the year 1927. He had already served twice as President, in 1915 and in 1920.

Switzerland's differences with Soviet Russia over the Vorovsky assassination of 1923 and the acquittal of its perpetrators in the Swiss courts were finally adjusted on April 15, 1927, when the Swiss government sent a note to Russia expressing regret for the incident and promising financial compensation to Vorovsky's family. A renewal of diplomatic relations ensued and Soviet Russia was represented at the international economic and armament conferences held in Switzerland later in the year, her delegates taking an active initiative that was sometimes troublesome to other members.

In June, 1927, extensive harbor improvements were completed and new docks constructed to take care of the increasing business of freight sent up the Rhine from the Atlantic seaboard. Along this 545-mile course, the Rhine has been dredged and deepened. Coal from the Ruhr district and grain from the United States are transferred at Rotterdam to Swiss barges and drawn by Swiss tugs and imports are brought direct to docks at Basel. Owing to Basel's geographical position and its population of more than 150,000, this city now plays an important part in international commerce.

There has been a decided movement of population from the higher valleys within the last few years, and it is estimated that few farms will be cultivated above the 5,000-foot level. The lower farms, by means of modern agricultural machinery, have far outstripped the upper farm lands, where such machinery cannot be used. The development of factories in the lowlands has also put home industries of the uplands practically out of business.

The Swiss Parliament, in July, 1927, passed a bill regulating salaries of public officials. The new scale reduced the higher salaries and increased the lower, affecting in all some 65,000 office-holders. New tariffs on automobiles were imposed by the Swiss Council on November 1, 1927. The new rates seriously affected American manufacturers, which had been supplying fully 40 per cent of all motor cars sold in Switzerland.

Although the Swiss Army is merely a national militia, in December there was a strong anti-militarist attack on the part of the Swiss radicals, Socialists and Communists.

At the end of the year, Edmund Schultess, born in 1868, was elected President of the Confederation of Switzerland for 1928. In the ordinary course of events, each member of the Federal Council receives this honor once in seven years.

As a Franco-German tariff agreement had proved of some disadvantage to Switzerland, a Franco-Swiss arrangement tending to rectify this was signed on January 22, 1928. An interesting announcement of this year that concerned Swiss progress was to the effect that Switzerland had so far developed her enormous potential hydroelectric power as to be independent of other nations for fuel. The year 1928 was notable for some serious Communist demonstrations. It also saw the death of Gustav Ador, President of the International Committee of the Red Cross and distinguished in both Swiss and international affairs.

Among the events of 1929 was the defeat of an attempt to authorize local option in the sale of alcoholic liquors, the defeat of the measure being by a general referendum. Jean Marie Musy of Fribourg was President for 1930.

The long-discussed question of the rights of the Swiss in the "free zones" of Upper Savoy and Gex was partially settled by a decision of the Permanent Court of International Justice on December 6, 1930, which recognized the rights of the Swiss, but also declared that the borders could be policed by France, which too had some rights in laying duties. The countries were to negotiate in 1931.

The new United States tariff was held to considerably reduce Swiss exports in 1931. A treaty of arbitration and conciliation was signed between Switzerland and the United States in January of that year, and ratified at Washington in June. The membership of the National Council was reduced to 187 and the term of office made four years. The President for 1931 was Dr. H. Haeberlin of Thurgau.

At the Parliamentary elections held on October 25, 1931, there were elected to the National Council 52 Radicals, 49 Social Democrats, 44 Catholic Conservatives, 30 Agrarians, 6 Liberal Conservaties, 3 Communists, and 3 from other parties. The number of representatives in the National Council, in accordance with a law passed in August, 1930, had been cut from 198 to 187. There was a 5½ per cent increase in the popular vote, of which approximately 3¼ per cent was gained by the Social Democrats.

The world depression cut down the exports of Switzerland, upon which she is so dependent, over one-half from 1929 to 1932. This threw many out of work and over the same period the number of unemployed approximately quadrupled. Though the country had had a 2,000,000 franc surplus in its 1931 budget, it had a large deficit in its 1932 budget and expected a still larger one in 1933.

Giuseppe Motta was elected President for 1932. This was the fourth time he served as President.

On June 7, 1932, the World Court handed down its decision on the dispute between Switzerland and France over the free zone of Upper Savoy and the District of Gex. The decision held that the free zones should be maintained and that France must withdraw her customs line in conformity with the provisions of 116 years ago. The withdrawal was to be effected by January 1, 1934.

On November 9, 1932, Government troops became involved in a clash in Geneva with Socialists who had attempted to prevent the holding of an anti-Socialist meeting. The troops fired machine guns into the crowds, and eleven civilians and one soldier were killed and forty-five civilians wounded. Martial law was declared in Geneva and meetings in Geneva and Lausanne were forbidden. The trade unions called a 24-hour strike while the victims of the troop firing were being buried. Larger troops were called out to safeguard the city and there were no further disturbances.

Edmund Schultess, who had been President of the Swiss Confederation in 1917, 1921 and 1928, was again elected President on December 15 for the usual one-year term.

The Federal Council voted on April 25, 1933, that Switzerland should keep to the gold standard, maintaining that the Swiss franc was not affected by the action of the United States in withdrawing from the gold standard.

Continued Nazi parades and demonstrations on the Swiss border, and rumors of a German invasion in the autumn of 1933 alarmed the Government. The National Council in October voted an appropriation of 20,000,000 francs ($4,940,000 at current exchange) to build up the arms and military equipment of the country.

On December 14, 1933, Dr. Marcel Pilet-Golaz was elected President, and War Minister Rudolf Minger, Vice-President, for 1934.

There was little amelioration in the economic situation in 1934. The tourist trade continued to suffer from the general depression and the rise in living costs in the country itself.

When the Federal Council, in an effort to stem the growing menace of Socialist propaganda on the one hand and Fascism on the other, passed a bill to strengthen Government powers, it was defeated by a popular referendum, the extreme right joining with the Socialists in voting against it.

Rudolf Minger succeeded to the presidency on December 14.

Early in 1935, alarmed doubtless by the increasingly militaristic spirit of both Germany and Italy, the Government lengthened the period of compulsory military training, in spite of popular opposition.

Although the economic situation showed no signs of improvement, proposals to amend the Constitution, so as to permit extraordinary legislation for economic recovery and the abandoning of the gold standard, were voted down in a referendum.

BIBLIOGRAPHY

BIBLIOGRAPHY

Monuments and antiquities, which in the early periods are often the main resource of the historian, have only a secondary interest for the general reader. Chronicles and similar early written records make a hardly greater appeal. Accordingly the bibliographies appended are purposely limited to the chief modern literature concerning each country, and of this, for the most part, only the easily accessible books are itemized. Brief memoranda are given in most cases, sufficient to indicate the character or special value of the work considered.

HOLLAND AND BELGIUM

Amicis, Edmond d'.—"Holland." 2 vols. London, 1883.
    This work by the well-known Italian writer of travels will be found among the best of its class, recording true and vivid impressions of the country and people.

Bernard, F.—"*La Hollande, Geographique, Ethnologique, etc.*" Paris, 1900.
    A comprehensive, generally descriptive work.

Blok, P. J.—"History of the People of the Netherlands." English translation. First 4 vols. New York, 1898-1900.
    This work is one of the most thorough and scholarly histories of the Netherlands. The fourth volume brings the account up to 1648.

Bonaparte, Louis.—"Historical Documents and Reflections in the Government of Holland." 3 vols. London, 1820.
    Interesting to the student.

Boulger, Demetrius C.—"The History of Belgium." Pt. I. London, 1902.

Butler, Chas.—"Life of Hugo Grotius." London, 1826.
    This biography of the celebrated Dutch jurist of the seventeenth century, the founder of the science of international law, affords a closer view of the times and conditions of which he was a part.

Davies, C. M.—"History of Holland and the Dutch Nation." 3 vols. London, 1851.
    As a continuous history this still ranks among the most important works on Holland, though not of the highest intrinsic value.

Gachard (ed.).—"*Correspondance de Guillaume d'Orange.*" 6 vols. Brussels, 1847-1866.

——"*Correspondance de Marguerite d'Autriche et Philippe II.*" 3 vols. Brussels, 1867-1881.
    Letters of personages so important give splendid material to the historian or historical student. Unfortunately each of these collections is accessible only in the French as yet.

Gerlache, E. C. de.—"*Histoire du royaume des Pays Bas, 1814-1839.*" 3 vols. Brussels, 1859.

Griffis, William E.—"Brave Little Holland." Boston, 1903.
    One of the most universally acceptable little books, characterized by sympathetic treatment and calculated to inspire enthusiasm for the Dutch in history. It is distinctly "popular" in style.

Hare, A. J. C.—"Sketches in Holland and Scandinavia." London, 1885.
    Descriptive in style and very readable.

Harrison, Frederick.—"William the Silent." London, 1897.
    Another biography with important historic bearing.

Havard, H.—"In the Heart of Holland." London, 1880.
    English translation of a delightfully descriptive book.

Henne, Alexander.—"*Histoire du regne de Charles V. en Belgique.*" 10 vols. Brussels, 1858.
    Accessible only in French. Chiefly valuable for reference, as the work is obviously too voluminous for the purposes of the average reader.

Hough, P. M.—"Dutch Life in Town and Country." New York, 1901.
    Like all of the volumes in the unique "Town and Country" series, this volume is valuable as well as entertaining in its descriptions.

Juste, Théodore.—"*Leopold I. et Leopold II.*" Brussels, 1879.
    Important for its side-lights on the history of the Belgians.

Markham, Sir Clement.—"The Fighting Veres." Boston, 1888.
    Lives of two English generals in the Netherlands during the war with Spain.

Maxwell, Sir William Stirling.—"Don John of Austria." 2 vols. London, 1883.
    Passages from the history of the sixteenth century.

Mets, J. A.—"Naval Heroes of Holland." New York, 1902.
    A worthy treatment of an inspiring theme.

Motley, John Lothrop.—"Rise of the Dutch Republic." 3 vols. New York, 1856.
    Famous as literature as well as history. A splendid picture of a dramatic period,—though admittedly one-sided in its enthusiasm. Prescott's "Philip II." offers excellent comparison from the Spanish point of view.

——"History of the United Netherlands." 4 vols. New York, 1861-1868.
    More controversial in treatment and less dramatic in subject than Motley's previous work. Distinctly anti-Catholic in sympathy.

——"Life of John of Barneveld." 2 vols. New York, 1875.
    Deals with the period of the Twelve Years' Truce. Graphic and interesting, but noticeably less brilliant than the earlier works.

——"Correspondence." Edited by George William Curtis. 2 vols. New York, 1889.
    In Motley's letters will be found much bearing on the later political history of Holland.

Pirenne, Henri.—"*Histoire de Belgique.*" Vols. I and II. Brussels, 1902-1903.
    Recently published and still to be read only in the French.

Pontalis, Antonin.—"John de Witte." Translated from the French by S. E. and A. Stephenson. 2 vols. London, 1885.
    Another valuable biography.

Putnam, Ruth.—"William the Silent, Prince of Orange." 2 vols. New York, 1895.
    This life of the founder of the Republic of the United Netherlands will hardly be overlooked even by the general reader.

Rogers, J. E. T.—"Holland" ("Story of the Nations" series). London, 1886.
    A good, readable, one volume account.

...ler, Johann Christoph Friedrich von.—"The Revolt of the Netherlands." New York, 1885.
  Possesses a classic as well as historic interest.
...eignobos, C.—"Political History of Europe." London, 1900.
  This always valuable work will be found worth consulting.
Strada, Famian.—"The History of the Low Countrey Warres." London, 1667.
  An English translation of the first part of this famous old work.
Temple, Sir William.—"Letters." London, 1699.
  Letters from Sir William while ambassador at The Hague.
Traill, Henry Duff.—"William III." New York, 1888.
Trevor, Arthur.—"Life of William III." 2 vols. London, 1835.
Van Meteren, Emanuel.—"*Historien der Nederlanden.*" Amsterdam, 1663.
Wenzelhuger, K. T.—"*Geschichte der Niederlande.*" 2 vols. Gotha, 1879-1886.
Young, Alexander.—"History of the Netherlands." Boston, 1887.
  Deals chiefly with the sixteenth and seventeenth centuries; popular in style

SWITZERLAND

Adams, Sir F. O., and Cunningham, C. D.—"The Swiss Confederation." 1889.
  Important to consult on the government of Switzerland. Not a detailed history, but covers the seven phases of the Confederation from its origin in 1291 to the constitutions of 1848 and 1874.
Baker, Grenfell.—"The Model Republic." London, 1895.
  As its sub-title indicates, this is a consecutive narrative history of the rise and progress of the Swiss people.
Conway, Sir W. M.—"The Alps from End to End." London, 1895.
  Switzerland is not so rich in historical as in descriptive literature, of which this attractive volume furnishes a type.
Dawson, W. S.—"Social Switzerland." London, 1897.
  Affords an economic study.
Dent, C. T.—"Mountaineering." London, 1892.
  Another descriptive volume.
Forbes, J. D.—"Travels through the Alps." New edition. London, 1900.
  Descriptive and equally helpful to the traveler or interesting to the fireside reader.
Gribble, F.—"Lake Geneva and its Literary Landmarks." London, 1901.
  A pleasing style and attractive literary subject combine to make this volume an unusually companionable one for bookish readers.
Heir, J. C.—"*Die Schweiz.*" (In "Land and Lute" series.) Bielfield and Leipzig, 1902.
  A valuable recent work.
James, E. J.—"The Federal Constitution of Switzerland." Philadelphia, 1890.
MacCrachan, W. D.—"The Rise of the Swiss Republic." London, 1892.
——"Romance and Teutonic Switzerland." 2 vols. Boston.
Müller, Monnard and Vulliemin.—"*Histoire de la Suisse.*" 19 vols. Paris, 1837-1851.
  As a reference work this is indispensable to the serious student, although manifestly too elaborate for the general reader.
Read, Meredith.—"Historic Studies in Vaud, Berne and Savoy." 2 vols. London, 1897.
  A collection of valuable sketches.

Richman, I. B.—" Pure Democracy and Pastoral Life in Inner-Rhoden." London, 1895.
   A unique and valuable economic discussion.
Sowerby, J.—" The Forest Cantons of Switzerland." London, 1892.
   An interesting study.
Stead, R., and Hug, L.—" Switzerland." (" Story of the Nations " series.) London, 1890.
   A popular narrative history in brief compass.
Stephen, Leslie.—" The Playground of Europe." New York, 1894.
   A pleasing subject by an author with a distinctive and engaging style.
Story, A. T.—" Swiss Life in Town and Country." London, 1902.
   This little book will be found extremely entertaining, besides offering much actual information.
Umlauft, F.—" The Alps." Translated by L. Brough. London, 1889.
Winchester.—" The Swiss Republic." Philadelphia, 1891.
   A good discussion of Swiss government and an authority to be consulted on this significant phase of the Swiss people.
Whymper, E.—" Scrambles amongst the Alps, 1860-1869." London, 1893.
——" Chamounix and the Range of Mount Blanc." London, 1905.
——" Zermatt and the Matterhorn." London, 1905.
   All descriptive works of exceeding interest and substantial value.

RECENT BOOKS ON HOLLAND, BELGIUM AND SWITZERLAND

Bowen, Marjorie.—" Holland." New York, 1929.
   A general survey of the Netherlands.
Brooks, Robert C.—" Civic Training in Switzerland." Chicago, 1931.
   A study of Swiss politics and a survey of Swiss life in general.
Clough, Shepard Bancroft.—" History of the Flemish Movement in Belgium." New York, 1930.
De Beer, Gavin Rylands.—" Alps and Men." New York, 1932.
   Switzerland, 1750-1850, as seen in tourists' diaries.
Dechesne, Laurent.—*"Histoire économique et sociale de la Belgique depuis les origines jusqu'en 1914."* Paris, 1932.
   A general survey to the outbreak of the World War.
De Leeuw, Adele.—" Flavor of Holland." New York, 1928.
   Travel account of cities and villages in Holland.
Gade, John Allyne.—" Life of Cardinal Mercier." New York, 1934.
   Appreciative study of Belgium's heroic Cardinal as teacher, philosopher, and patriot.
Lichtervelde, Louis de.—" Leopold First, Founder of Modern Belgium." Tr. by Thomas H. Reed. New York, 1930.
——" Leopold of the Belgians." Tr. by Thomas H. Reed. New York, 1929.
Renier, Gustaaf Johannes.—" William of Orange." London, 1932.
   A brief and popular life of William III.
Scheffler, Karl.—" Holland." Tr. by Caroline Frederick. New York, 1932.
   A volume which deals with different phases of Dutch life.
Trevelyan, Mary Caroline.—" William the Third, and the Defence of Holland." New York, 1931.
   A history of the conquest of the Dutch Republic.